Natural Resource Conservation

NATURAL

RESOURCE CONSERVATION

Fifth Edition

An Ecological Approach

OLIVER S. OWEN
UNIVERSITY OF WISCONSIN, EAU CLAIRE

DANIEL D. CHIRAS
ADJUNCT PROFESSOR, UNIVERSITY OF COLORADO, DENVER

MACMILLAN PUBLISHING COMPANY
New York
COLLIER MACMILLAN PUBLISHERS
London

Editor: Bob Rogers
Production Supervisor: Dora Rizzuto
Text and Cover Designer: Sheree Goodman
Cover photograph: Comstock

This book was set in 10/12 Else by 20 pi, printed and bound by Von Hoffmann.
The cover was printed by Von Hoffmann.

Macmillan Publishing Company
866 Third Avenue, New York, New York 10022

Collier Macmillan Canada, Inc.

Library of Congress Cataloging-in-Publication Data
Owen, Oliver S. (date)
    Natural resource conservation : an ecological approach / Oliver S.
Owen, Daniel D. Chiras.—5th ed.
        p.   cm.
    ISBN 0-02-390111-X
    1. Conservation of natural resources. 2. Ecology.
3. Environmental protection.   4. Conservation of natural resources—
United States.   5. Ecology—United States.   6. Environmental
protection—United States.   I. Chiras, Daniel D.   II. Title.
S938.O87   1990
333.7'2'0973—dc20   89-12616
                                                      CIP

Printing: 1 2 3 4 5 6 7 8   Year: 0 1 2 3 4 5 6 7 8 9

To my loving wife, Carol,
and our children, Tom, Tim, and Stephanie.

May they never be denied the privilege of
hiking through a forest wilderness,
stalking a deer, or listening to the dusk-
chant of a whippoorwill.

O.S.O.

To my wife, Kathleen, and my son, Skyler,
with love and affection.

D.D.C.

Preface

Natural Resource Conservation is written for the introductory resource conservation course. The first edition of this book was published a year after the first Earth Day in 1970. To many observers, Earth Day marked the beginning of the formal environmental movement in the United States. Since that time, impressive gains have been made in air and water pollution control and species protection.

Despite this progress, many environmental problems still remain. Many others have actually grown worse. In 1970, for instance, the world population hovered around 3 billion. Today, it is over 5 billion and growing by nearly 90 million people a year. Hunger and starvation have become a way of life in the Third World nations. An estimated 42 million people die each year of starvation or of disease worsened by hunger and malnutrition.

Species extinction continues as well. Today, one species of vertebrate becomes extinct every nine months. Add the plants, insects, and microorganisms to the list and the rate of extinction climbs to one species a day.

In the United States and abroad, soil erosion and rangeland deterioration continue. One third of America's topsoil has been washed away in the past 100 years and a large proportion of our public and private rangelands are in poor or only fair condition.

Added to the list of growing problems are a whole host of new ones that have cropped up along the way, such as groundwater pollution, ozone depletion, global warming, and growing mountains of urban trash. Solving these many problems will not be easy.

We think there is good reason for hope. But to address these problems in meaningful ways, dramatic changes are needed in the way we live and work. Many observers argue the need to create a new and sustainable relationship with the environment. This new relationship will require us to practice conservation and to recycle virtually everything we can. It will mean a shift to the use of renewable resources such as solar energy and wind. And, more than anything, it will mean stabilizing world population. Conservation, recycling, renewable resources, and population control are the operating principles of a sustainable society. They could ensure an enduring relationship with nature.

These operating principles, however, must be complemented by a change in our attitudes. We can no longer afford to view the Earth as an infinite source of materials for exclusive human use. Many of the Earth's resources upon which human beings depend are finite. The Earth has a limited supply of these resources. We ignore this imperative at our own risk.

Many observers believe that we need an attitude that seeks the cooperation rather than the domination of nature. Our efforts to dominate and control nature are often in vain, whereas cooperation may be one of the keys to our long-term success.

Finally, it is time to rethink our position in the ecosystem. We are not apart from nature, but a part of it. Our lives are dependent on the environment. What we do to the environment we do to ourselves. The logical extension of this simple truth is that planet care is the ultimate form of self care.

Humans are not the crowning achievement of nature, but rather members of a club comprised of all Earth's living creatures. To achieve a sustainable relationship, many observers argue that it is time to recognize and respect the rights of other species to exist and thrive alongside human culture. In this sense, natural resources may be viewed as the Earth's endowment to all species. Such a view may mean curbing our demands and finding new ways to live on the planet. In the long run, such changes will benefit all of us.

Focus on Principles, Problems, and Solutions

This book describes many important principles of ecology and resource management, concepts that will prove useful throughout a student's life. It also outlines many of the national and international environmental problems and offers a variety of solutions. These solutions take three basic forms: legislative (new laws and regulations), technological (applying existing, new, and improved technologies), and methodological (changing our methods). Applying these solutions falls to all of us, not just government officials. Therefore, the authors think that individuals, educators, business people, and government officials all have an important role to play in solving the environmental crisis and in building a sustainable society.

On the personal level, what we do or what we fail to do can have a remarkable impact on the future, and we encourage you to take active steps to find ways to help rather than harm.

Improvements in the Fifth Edition

This fifth edition of *Natural Resource Conservation* has undergone a substantial revision. We have updated our material and expanded our coverage of pressing issues to bring you the latest in natural resource issues. Given the growing importance of global warming, ozone depletion, and acid deposition, we have added a new chapter on international and global air pollution. We have expanded our coverage of fisheries management, and added material on coastlands and estuaries to our coverage of the ocean. Back by popular demand is a chapter on range management.

Many new photographs and drawings have been added to the fifth edition. The new design and the addition of color make this edition particularly appealing and more useful.

Learning Aids

To help students focus on key terms and concepts, we have included in each chapter three learning aids: key words and phrases, chapter summaries, and discussion questions.

KEY WORDS AND PHRASES. At the end of each chapter is a list of key words and phrases. We recommend that students read this list before reading the chapter. Afterward, take a few moments to define the terms and phrases.

RAPID REVIEW. Each chapter in the book also contains a summary of important facts and concepts, the Rapid Review. Summaries will help students review material before tests. Before reading the chapter, we think it is a good idea for students to read through the summary or study the major headings and subheadings for orientation.

DISCUSSION QUESTIONS. Discussion questions at the end of each chapter also provide a way of focusing on important material and reviewing concepts and crucial facts. We have written many questions to encourage students to tie information together and to draw on personal experience.

Furthering Your Education

To help students deepen and broaden their knowledge, we have provided a number of case studies and suggested readings.

CASE STUDIES. Case studies delve into controversial issues or detailed information that may be of interest to students pursuing a career in natural resource management.

SUGGESTED READINGS. The Suggested Readings list articles and books that we think are worthwhile reading for students who want to learn more about the environment.

Acknowledgments

This book is the result of the hard work of many people whom we would like to thank heartily. Numerous reviewers graciously gave of their time to comment on the manuscript and suggested many useful changes. We thank Wanna D. Pitts, San Jose State University; Conrad S. Brumley, Texas Tech University; Eric Fritzell, University of Missouri; Frederick A. Montague, Jr., Purdue University; Jim Merchant, University of Kansas; Gary Nelson, Des Moines Area Community College; and Ray DePalma, William Rainey Harper College.

Many thanks to the staff at Macmilllan, especially our long-time editor and close friend, Bob Rogers, who has pushed hard to make this book the best it could be and who has always offered friendly advice and encouragement. We would also like to thank Mary Dersch, who generated the new artwork for this edition; our photo researcher, Yvonne Gerin, for her hard work and good natured persistence in researching photographs; and Helen Greenberg, who edited the manuscript. The production staff at Publication Services, especially Don DeLand, deserves a large debt of gratitude for their hard work, attention to detail, and cheerfulness despite a tight production schedule.

Finally, we would like to thank our wives for their love and support during the writing and production of this book.

O. S. O.
D. D. C.

Brief Contents

Detailed Contents

Natural Resource Conservation

1

Introduction

The late Aldo Leopold, the senior author's ecology professor, once defined **conservation** as "a state of harmony between man and the land." For Leopold, conservation required equal portions of reflection and action. He wrote: "The real substance of conservation lies not in the physical projects of government, but in the mental processes of citizens." Leopold believed strongly that effective conservation depends primarily on a basic human respect for natural resources. He called such respect a **land ethic**. Each of us, he said, is individually responsible for maintaining "the health of the land." A healthy land has "the capacity for self-renewal." "Conservation," he concluded, "is our effort to understand and preserve that capacity." It is this concept of conservation that has guided and influenced the writing of this book.

THE CRISIS ON PLANET EARTH

Effective conservation in the United States and other countries is becoming more and more urgent, for human society is rapidly degrading the natural environment. The damage is so severe that many experts believe that the long-term future of society is in jeopardy. Ironically, humankind prides itself on conquering outer space and on its many new technologies that make space exploration and modern medicine possible. Yet, after two centuries of technological progress, we still fail to manage well the space around us here on planet Earth (Figure 1-1). This has led to an environmental crisis resulting from three interrelated problems: (1) rapid population increase, (2) excessive consumption of resources, and (3) pollution.

Population Increase

At the current rate of growth, global population will surge from nearly 5.2 billion in 1989 to roughly 8 billion by 2020 (Figure 1-2). This cancerous growth of the human population clouds the future on planet Earth and is an underlying cause of our resource-environmental crisis. An increase in population means an increase in the pollution of air, water, and land. It means an accelerated depletion of natural resources, many of which are already in short supply or are declining in quality. It means that massive starvation, as in Africa today, will spread to other parts of the world. It means that greater numbers of people, living in overcrowded conditions, will suffer from increasing emotional stress and will make increasing demands on wilderness and recreation areas in order to "get away from it all." Drug abuse, mental illness, crime, and suicide will be more common. Each surge in population will bring a corresponding decline in our overall standard of living. Unless population growth is halted within the very near future, even the most soundly conceived and effectively implemented conservation and environmental practices will be to no avail.

After nearly 4 million years of human history, global population has turned the bend of the J-curve and is now moving almost straight up. By this time tomorrow, there will be 234,000 more people on this planet; by next week, 1.6 million more; and by next year, an additional 87 million. On Memorial Day, our nation honors the memory of those Americans who have given their lives for their country on the world's battlefields. The fatalities have indeed been numerous— 57,000 in the Vietnam War alone. Yet the rate of pop-

FIGURE 1-1 Despite their extraordinary mental abilities, humans are directly responsible for many serious environmental problems.

FIGURE 1-2 Rapidly growing global population strains the limits of our resources. Urban populations concentrate millions of people in limited space, resulting in elevated pollution levels.

ulation growth is so high that all the battlefield deaths of soldiers the world over since the discovery of America by Christopher Columbus will have been replaced in only 6 months.

The people added to the world's population each year must be fed. For a number of political, social, economic, and ecological reasons, however, food is not available. During the hour it takes the average American family to polish off its Thanksgiving turkey (and cranberry sauce, and apple pie, and so on), 4,000 people took their last breath—dying either directly or indirectly from a lack of food. One year from now, an estimated 15 million people will have starved—a population equal to that of Pennsylvania and Kentucky combined. Another 25 million will have died from infectious and parasitic diseases worsened by malnutrition.

Excessive Resource Consumption

The world's industrialized nations are consuming non-renewable resources (coal, oil, gas, copper, zinc, and cobalt, for example) at an accelerating pace. The United States ranks first in per capita consumption. *Although our nation has only 5 percent of the global population, it consumes 30 percent of the world's resources.*

Many demands made by Americans on natural resources are excessive and do not contribute substantially to human happiness. Americans are the most

overfed, overhoused, overclothed, overmobilized, and overentertained people in the world. Our enormous consumption of cars, color television sets, dishwashers, air conditioners, golf carts, home computers, swimming pools, speed boats, and video cassette recorders certainly does not stem from need.

Through such excessive production and consumption, called **throughput** by economists, the United States and other highly industrialized nations are accelerating the depletion of our planet's resources.

Pollution

The United States, the world's most *affluent* nation, has also become the most *effluent* (Figures 1-3 and 1-4). Like other industrialized nations, we have degraded our environment with an enormous variety and volume of contaminants. We have polluted lakes, streams, oceans, and groundwater with sewage, industrial wastes, radioactive materials, heat, detergents, fertilizers, pesticides, and plastics. Millions of tons of sulfur dioxide and carbon dioxide are spewed into the air each year from the combustion of fossil fuels, such as

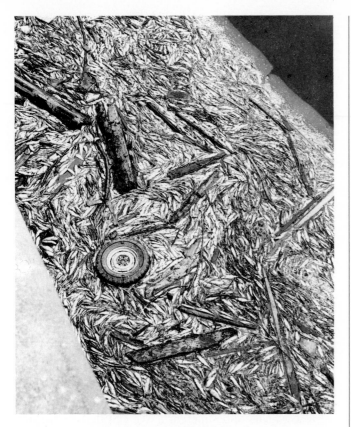

FIGURE 1-3   America has polluted her lakes and streams with sewage, industrial wastes, radioactive materials, heat, detergents, agricultural fertilizers, and pesticides. Massive fish kills have been the result.

coal and oil, and are causing serious climatic effects—not only in the United States, but in other nations as well. Our increasing dependence on nuclear power, as well as on nuclear arms, has led to the accumulation of large amounts of radioactive waste, some of which threatens human health and life.

QUALITY OF HUMAN LIFE ON PLANET EARTH

Can planet Earth support the reasonably high standard of living many of us now enjoy, by the year 2050? Or by the year 2100? This important question is almost impossible to answer with any degree of certainty. The problem is that there are so many interacting variables: population levels, resource availability, degree of environmental pollution, climatic patterns, industrial production, national and international politics, social attitudes, changing patterns of war and peace, and so on. In fact, the task we face in maintaining a reasonably high standard of living is much more formidable than that of developing the atomic bomb or putting a person on the moon!

Some years ago, a research group at the Massachusetts Institute of Technology published a book entitled *The Limits to Growth*. This book summarized their computer studies of the projected future of humans on Earth. The scientists wanted to determine the changes in environmental quality that might take

FIGURE 1-4   Industrial smokestacks have spewed large volumes of pollutants into our nation's atmosphere.

place through the year 2100, assuming that population growth, resource depletion, pollution, industrial production, and so on continue at exponential rates—in other words, moving almost straight up the J-curve. The graphed projections that appeared on their computer printout sheets are of extreme interest, and highly disturbing.

Figure 1-5 shows that the global population climbs until about 2050. Food production per capita, however, drops long before population peaks. Industrial output per capita follows a similar pattern. By the year 2030, the quality of human life has deteriorated. Several decades later, many natural resources will either be so severely depleted (fertile soil, oil, and metals) or so seriously polluted (air, water, and land) that both food and industrial production drop off sharply. Aggravating the problem then will be the continuing upsurge of global population. Eventually, after the year 2050, well within the lifetime of your children, there will be a massive reduction in the human population, primarily as the result of starvation. The prospects for human survival beyond 2100 appear poor, simply because the global stock of natural resources, upon which humans have depended during their 4-million-year tenure on this planet, will have reached the point of exhaustion.

Viewpoint of the Optimists

These somber projections have been criticized by those who believe that technology will solve our resource and environmental problems. History is full of examples

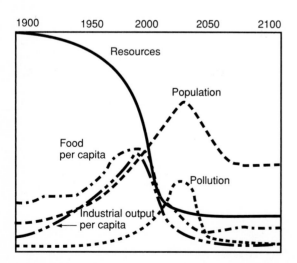

FIGURE 1-5 Computer predictions of different variables (food, population, industrial output, pollution, resources) if current trends continue. This graph shows that if population continues to grow, resources will decline dramatically. Pollution levels will increase. The combined effect is a decline in human population and considerable environmental damage.

showing that necessity is the mother of invention. The optimists suggest that the Western world is on the brink of another technological revolution. After all, isn't the current crisis the greatest in human history? If small crises result in small innovations, then certainly today's composite population-resources-pollution dilemma may be the necessary stimulus for the greatest technological breakthroughs of all time. These optimists confidently claim that "a breakthrough a day will keep the crises at bay." Wherever something has gone awry, technology will provide a "fix." Athelstan Spilhaus of the University of Minnesota is a leading spokesperson for this school of thought. He has suggested, for example, that "energy is the ultimate currency of civilization"; in other words, if enough cheap energy is available, all things can be accomplished, pollution will be controlled, food will be available for all, and clothing and shelter for the needy millions will be provided. Indeed, the nuclear power enthusiasts are predicting unlimited energy supplies once the breeder reactor has been perfected (see Chapter 21). To increase food production, the optimists suggest a variety of schemes ranging from fish farming to synthesizing food in test tubes; from yeast and algal culture to irrigating deserts; from draining swamplands to using genetic engineering to produce miracle wheats and supercorn. We can derive oil from worn-out rubber tires, say the optimists, refine methane gas from manure, and obtain construction materials from broken glass and fly ash. According to these optimists, we can always depend on human ingenuity and skill to "pull another rabbit out of our technological hat."

Viewpoint of the Pessimists (or Realists?)

Unfortunately, say the pessimists, technology will not solve all of our problems. For one, there isn't enough time to find technological fixes to problems that need solutions today.

Why is time so crucial? The key to the answer is the word **exponential**. Remember the J-curve? It represents exponential growth—of population, of resource depletion rates, of pollution. Such growth increases *geometrically*, as symbolized by the numerical sequence 1, 2, 4, 8, 16, and so on. This is in contrast to *arithmetic* growth, which is symbolized as 1, 2, 3, 4, 5, 6, and so on. The rapidity of exponential growth is best understood through an analogy.

Suppose that there is a cancerous tumor in the windpipe that carries oxygen to your lungs—a tumor that doubles in size each day. Assume that it will take only 30 days for this cancer to close off your windpipe completely and cause your death from suffocation. On Day 29 you are rushed to the hospital for emergency surgery. The surgeon examines the tumor and discovers that it has blocked off half of your windpipe. Now, if he is unfamiliar with the dynamics of exponential growth, he will probably suppose that he has plenty of time to remove the tumor and save your life. Wrong. He has just one day left.

In this analogy, the windpipe represents the fragile and highly vulnerable life support systems for humans. The cancerous tumor represents the exponentially growing global population, resource consumption, and pollution. Even though the world's best scientists, technologists, ecologists, sociologists, and economists struggle valiantly to remove this rapidly growing environmental cancer, it will be too late. *Day 29 is rapidly approaching!*

Viewpoint of the Moderates

Which viewpoint, optimistic or pessimistic, is closer to the truth? Unfortunately, we cannot be sure. Perhaps, however, as in many other instances, a moderate viewpoint is more correct. The moderates view our current resource-environmental posture with justifiable concern. Yet they feel that there is still sufficient time, if we start *now* to shift from today's **spendthrift society** to a **sustainable society**—one that is much less damaging to resources and the environment.

Many political scientists, sociologists, economists, and ecologists are convinced that eventually our lifestyles will simplify. We can achieve a sustainable society shown in Figure 1-6, with an emphasis on cultural, intellectual, moral, and spiritual values rather than on material wealth. Lifestyles in this sustainable society, which can be attained by 2025, would be much

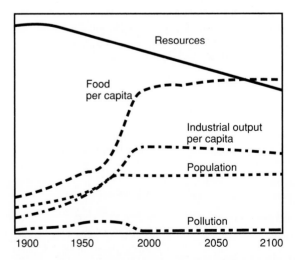

FIGURE 1-6 If strenuous attempts are made now to stabilize population size (1990–1995), a sustainable, steady-state type of society may be achieved by 2025. The finite resource base will continue to fall, however, suggesting the need for renewable resource use.

simpler than those of today. The average American, for example, would get along without some of the traditional status symbols, such as a large, energy-wasteful home, a second or third family car, a recreational vehicle, and a speed boat. This lifestyle, however, would be ecologically sound rather than ecologically suicidal and probably might offer us a better chance of finding real happiness. Attaining a sustainable society may ultimately depend on sharing knowledge and, possibly, on a redistribution of our planet's limited resources so that all of its inhabitants get their *fair share*. This idea, admittedly, is not without its critics (Chapter 6).

If resource redistribution is not brought about, it is likely that the frustrated hopes of the poor nations will lead to more political unrest, riots, revolution, and even nuclear war. The British philosopher Bertrand Russell noted that "nothing is more likely to lead to an H-bomb war than the threat of universal destitution through overpopulation." Newspaper columnist Smith Hempstone makes the following somber prediction: "Neither democracy nor peace will survive in areas where the roots of both are weak. Governments will fall like tenpins and hungry nations will go to war in an effort to seize what they cannot produce." A nuclear exchange, of course, could impose a *simple* life on humankind. However, it would not be characterized by happines, but rather by a primitive level of existence, with remnant populations literally scratching for survival on what is left of planet Earth.

Our task—to achieve a true sustainable, spaceship type of society—is difficult and challenging. It requires the dedicated, highly coordinated, and long-sustained efforts of many different types of people, from factory workers to business executives, from college students to farmers, from scientists to politicians, from food specialists to geographers. It requires imaginative and inspirational leadership from government leaders at all levels, from small-town mayors to presidents of the United States and commissars of the Soviet Union, from village tribal chiefs in Africa to benevolent despots in South America. Some of the required changes have already begun.

A BRIEF HISTORY OF THE RESOURCE CONSERVATION AND ENVIRONMENTAL MOVEMENTS

Conservation in the Nineteenth Century

Although progress toward conservation was relatively slow in the 19th century, several notable advances in the United States were made. In the early 1800s, George Washington and Thomas Jefferson used effective methods to control soil erosion on their farms. In 1864 the diplomat-naturalist George Perkins Marsh authored *Man and Nature*—a book that did much to draw attention to the fragile nature of our resources and how they can be abused by humans. It served as a catalyst for the fledgling conservation movement. Congress established three national parks: Yellowstone, the world's first, in 1872, followed by Yosemite and Sequoia in 1890. In 1891, 28 forest reserves were established—later to be designated as the nation's first national forests. In 1892 the noted naturalist John Muir founded the Sierra Club, an organization that today is one of our country's most politically active conservation groups.

Conservation in the Twentieth Century

By far the most significant advances in natural resource conservation have been made in this century. They have occurred primarily in three "waves." The first (1901–1909) developed under the dynamic and forceful leadership of President Theodore Roosevelt; the second (1930s) occurred during the presidency of Franklin D. Roosevelt; and the third (1970–1980) was given impetus by the Nixon, Ford, and Carter administrations (Table 1-1).

THE FIRST WAVE (1901–1909). The White House Conference on Natural Resources called by President "Teddy" Roosevelt in 1908 was a high-water mark for the cause of conservation (Figure 1-7). Several developments influenced Roosevelt's decision to call the conference. Among them were (1) the deep concern among scientists over the severe depletion of timber in the Great Lakes states; (2) the study of arid western lands by Major J. W. Powell in the 1870s, which had stimulated great interest in the possibilities of irrigation farming and converting deserts to vegetable gardens; (3) the 1907 report by the Inland Waterways Commission pointing out that the excessive use of water would

FIGURE 1-7 President Theodore Roosevelt, outdoorsman, big-game hunter, and ardent conservationist, at Yosemite National Park.

inevitably have a negative impact on other resources, such as timber, soils, and wildlife; and (4) a growing apprehension in 1908 that our nation's resources were being grossly mismanaged and that severe economic hardship would be the inevitable result.

Invited to the White House conference were governors, congressional leaders, scientists, anglers, hunters,

Table 1-1 The Three Waves of Conservation Progress

	First Wave (1901–1909)	**Second Wave (1933–1941)**	**Third Wave (1962–1980)**
Presidents	Theodore Roosevelt	Franklin D. Roosevelt	Richard Nixon, Gerald Ford, and Jimmy Carter
Constructive Action	Report of the Inland Waterways Commission	Prairie States Forestry Project	Wilderness Act of 1964
	White House Conference on Natural Resources of 1908	Establishment of shelter belts	Clean Air Act of 1965
		National Resources Board established	Solid Waste Disposal Act of 1966
	National Conservation Commission established	Second *Natural Resources Inventory*	Species Conservation Act of 1966
		Civilian Conservation Corps established	Wild and Scenic River Act of 1968
	First *Natural Resources Inventory*	Soil Conservation Service established	National Environmental Policy Act of 1969
		Tennessee Valley Authority established	Environmental Teach-In (1970)
		First North American Wildlife and Resources Conference	Legislation of the Decade of the Environment (Table 1-2)

and resource experts from several foreign nations. As a result of the conference, a 50-member National Conservation Commission was formed, composed of scientists, legislators, and businessmen; inspirational leadership was provided by Gifford Pinchot, a professional forester. The commission completed our nation's first comprehensive **Natural Resources Inventory**. The White House conference also resulted indirectly in the formation of 41 state conservation departments, almost all of which are still operating vigorously today.

THE SECOND WAVE (1933–1941). Franklin D. Roosevelt is a notable example of "the right man in the right place at the right time." When he assumed the presidency in 1933, there was an urgent need for an imaginative program to create jobs. Roosevelt's administration not only created employment, it solved many natural-resource problems plaguing our nation. Here are some examples:

1. The **Prairie States Forestry Project** was begun in 1934. Its goal was to establish shelter belts of trees and shrubs in farmland along the one-hundredth meridian extending from the Canadian border of North Dakota south to Texas. This project did much to reduce soil erosion.

2. The National Resources Board appointed by Roosevelt completed our nation's second comprehensive **Natural Resources Inventory** in 1934. In its report, the board identified serious resource problems plaguing the country, and described methods for solving them as well.

3. The **Civilian Conservation Corps** (CCC), which was established in 1933 and functioned until 1949, was organized into 2,652 camps of 200 men each. Many were located in the national parks and forests. The forest workers constructed fire lanes, removed fire hazards, fought forest fires, controlled pests, and planted millions of trees. The park workers constructed bridges, improved roads, and built hiking trails. In addition, the CCC made lake and stream improvements and participated in flood-control projects.

4. In 1935 the **Soil Conservation Service** (SCS) was established. The time was ripe for such a program. The frequent occurrence of severe dust storms over the Dust Bowl of the Great Plains bore testimony to the vulnerability of the nation's soils. The SCS conducted soil conservation demonstrations to show farmers the techniques and importance of erosion control.

5. The establishment of the **Tennessee Valley Authority** (TVA) in 1933 was a bold experiment, unique in conservation history, to integrate the use of the resources (water, soil, forests, wildlife) of an entire river basin. Although highly controversial at the time, it has received international acclaim and has served as a model for similar projects in India and other nations.

6. The **North American Wildlife and Resources Conference** was convened by President Roosevelt in 1936. Attended by wildlife management specialists, hunters, anglers, and government officials, it set out to develop an inventory of the nation's wildlife resources, and a statement of wildlife and other conservation problems, including policies by which those problems might be solved. This conference meets annually to this day.

THE THIRD WAVE (1960–1980). During the 1960s the U.S. conservation and environmental movement really "took off." Several highly influential books and essays were written during this time that sensitized the general public to the gravity of the nation's problems. Rachel Carson's *Silent Spring* (1962), a runaway best seller, alerted the general public to the potentially harmful effects of pesticides, such as DDT, on both wildlife and humans. Noted ecologist Paul Ehrlich, of Stanford University, authored *The Population Bomb*, which warned of the environmental degradation that would result if society could not control the worldwide surge of population. Garrett Hardin's classic essay, "The Tragedy of the Commons," proposed that any resource shared by many people would eventually be exploited and degraded.

In 1969 Senator Gaylord Nelson (D-Wis.) called for a nationwide "environmental teach-in" in an attempt to marshall the energies of the nation's college students "to halt the accelerating pollution and destruction of the environment." Ever sensitive to public opinion, Congress responded by enacting so many important laws to upgrade our resources and control pollution from 1970 to 1980 that this period has been called *the decade of the environment*. A partial list of these acts is shown in Table 1-2.

We must remember, of course, that the mere existence of a law—to control air pollution, for example—does not mean that we will automatically have clean air. Even the most superbly orchestrated act must be *enforced* if its purpose is to be realized. And effective enforcement requires money for personnel and equipment.

AN ENVIRONMENTAL BLUEPRINT FOR PRESIDENT GEORGE BUSH AND THE U.S. CONGRESS FOR 1989–1993

Shortly after President George Bush was elected, a number of leading conservationists and environmentalists

Table 1-2 Major Environmental Acts Passed During the Decade of the Environment (1970–1980)

Air Quality
Clean Air Act of 1970, 1977

Control of Noise
Noise Control Act of 1972
Quiet Communities Act of 1978

Control of Toxic Substances
Toxic Substances Control Act of 1976
Resource Conservation and Recovery Act of 1976

Control of Solid Wastes
Solid Waste Disposal Act of 1965
Resources Recovery Act of 1970

Energy
National Energy Act of 1978

Land Use
National Coastal Zone Management Act of 1972
Forest Reserves Management Acts of 1974, 1976
Federal Land Policy Management Act of 1976
National Forest Management Act of 1976
Surface Mining Control and Reclamation Act of 1977
Endangered American Wilderness Act of 1978

Water Quality
Federal Water Pollution Control Act of 1972
Ocean Dumping Act of 1972
Safe Drinking Water Act of 1974
Toxic Substances Control Act of 1976
Clean Water Act of 1977

Wildlife
Federal Insecticide, Fungicide, and
  Rodenticide Control Act of 1972
Marine Protection, Research and Sanctuaries Act of 1972
Endangered Species Act of 1973

presented him with a *Blueprint for the Environment*— an 800-page document prepared by 18 of the country's foremost environmental organizations. It was hoped that President Bush would respond by asserting strong leadership in tackling the crucial environmental problems facing our nation and the world. Of course, an equal commitment by the Democratic-controlled Congress is just as essential if appropriate environmental legislation is to be crafted. Both Republicans and Democrats must form a working partnership in this crucial effort. Among the items in the *Blueprint for the Environment* are the following:

1. *Air pollution*
   a. Promote international agreements for control of global warming (greenhouse effect), acid rain, and the thinning of the stratospheric ozone layer.
   b. Press for passage of a reauthorized Clean Air Act.
   c. Develop a coordinated program to monitor and regulate indoor pollution.

2. *Population problem*: Support an international agreement to reduce the rate of population growth by 50 percent by the year 2000.
3. *Soil erosion*: Develop creative strategies for the control of soil erosion, a crucial problem in at least 25 percent of the country's cropland.
4. *Water pollution*: Develop a unified national program to control the ever-increasing contamination of our groundwater.
5. *Forests*
   a. Block a proposal to build 580,000 miles of roads in our national forests by 2030. Such road construction would be highly destructive to the environment and would subsidize the operations of private logging firms at the expense of American taxpayers.
   b. Provide financial and technical assistance to Third World countries in the reforestation of 320 million acres. Such a project would have multiple benefits, one of which would be the slowing up of global warming due to the greenhouse effect.
6. *Wildlife*: Halt the destruction of wetland habitats, indispensable for waterfowl and marsh birds.
7. *Pesticide problem*: Speed up the EPA's review and certification of more than 600 basic pesticide ingredients now in use and being widely dispersed in the human and wildlife environments.
8. *Ocean pollution*: Ban all ocean dumping of domestic and industrial wastes.
9. *Hazardous waste problem*: Accelerate the cleanup of hazardous waste dumps (under the Superfund Act of 1980) to protect our groundwater from toxic contamination.
10. *Council of Environmental Quality (CEQ)*: Restore the influence the CEQ enjoyed in the 1970s. The CEQ advises the president on the nation's environmental condition, and informs him of programs by which it can best be improved.

CLASSIFICATION OF NATURAL RESOURCES

Conservationists recognize two major kinds of resources: renewable and nonrenewable (Table 1-3). **Renewable resources** include soils, rangelands, forests, fish, wildlife, air, and water. Although these resources can be renewed by natural processes, they can also be depleted due to overuse by humans. Renewal can be facilitated or managed by humans. Some resources may be renewed much more rapidly than others. For example, it may take 1,000 years for just 1 inch of fertile topsoil to form. A pine forest may develop from the

Table 1-3 Classification of Natural Resources

Renewable

Resources whose continued harvest or use depends on proper human planning and management. Improper use and/or management results in impairment or exhaustion, with resulting harmful social and economic effects.

1. **Fertile soil.** The fertility of soil can be renewed, but the process is expensive and takes time.

2. **Products of the land.** Resources grown in or dependent on the soil.
   a. Agricultural products. Vegetables, grains, fruits, and fibers.
   b. Forests. Source of timber and paper pulp. Valuable as a source of scenic beauty, as an agent in erosion control, as recreational areas, and as wildlife habitat.
   c. Rangeland. Sustains herds of cattle, sheep, and goats for the production of meat, leather, and wool.
   d. Wild animals. Provide aesthetic values, hunting sport, and food. Examples are deer, wolves, eagles, bluebirds, and fireflies.

3. **Products of lakes, streams, and oceans.** Black bass, lake trout, salmon, cod, mackerel, lobsters, oysters, and seaweed.

Nonrenewable

Amount of resource is finite. When destroyed or consumed, such as the burning of coal, the resource cannot be replaced.

1. **Fossil fuels.** Produced by processes that occurred millions of years ago. When consumed (burned), heat, water, and gases (carbon monoxide, carbon dioxide, and sulfur dioxide) are released. The gases may pose serious air pollution problems.

2. **Nonmetallic minerals.** Phosphate rock, glass sand, and salt. Phosphate rock is of crucial importance as a source of fertilizer.

3. **Metals.** Gold, platinum, silver, cobalt, lead, iron, zinc, and copper. Without these, modern civilization would be impossible. Zinc is used in galvanized iron to protect it from rusting; tin is used in toothpaste tubes; and iron is used in cans, auto bodies, and bridges.

---

seedling stage to maturity in 100 years. On the other hand, a herd of deer, under optimal conditions, could build up from 6 head to 1,000 head in only 10 years!

Nonrenewable resources occur in a fixed amount. They cannot be renewed by natural processes rapidly enough to be usable by current human society. They include fossil fuels (coal, oil, natural gas), nonmetallic minerals (phosphates, magnesium, etc.), and metallic minerals (copper, aluminum, etc.).

APPROACHES TO NATURAL RESOURCE MANAGEMENT

During the past two centuries, four resource management approaches have been used in the United States: (1) exploitation, (2) preservation, (3) the utilitarian approach, and (4) the ecological or sustainable approach.

Exploitation

The exploitation management approach suggests that a given resource should be used as intensively as possible to provide the greatest profit to the user. This philosophy prevailed early in our nation's history. No concern was given to such adverse effects as soil erosion, water pollution, or wildlife depletion. For example, the slogan of the early loggers of the 1800s who exploited our primeval forests was: "Get in, log off the trees, and get out." When the trees were gone, the loggers moved westward and repeated the process. Why not? The nation's forests seemed inexhaustible.

Preservation

The preservation management approach suggests that resources should be preserved, set aside, and protected. A forest, for example, should not be used as a source of timber. It should be preserved in its natural state as a wilderness. In the 1880s, the naturalist John Muir, who founded the Sierra Club, proposed that federal lands of unique beauty should be withdrawn from exploitation by timber, grazing, and mining interests and converted into national parks. As such, they would be preserved virtually unchanged for the enjoyment of future generations. Partly as a result of Muir's influence, Congress established Yosemite and Sequoia National Parks in 1890.

Utilitarian Approach

The utilitarian approach to resource management began during the 1930s. One important utilitarian concept is that of **sustained yield**. This concept suggests that renewable resources (soil, rangelands, forests, wildlife, fisheries, and so on) should be managed so that they will never be exhausted, but will be replenished and thus will be able to serve future generations. When a forest has been logged off, the site must be reseeded naturally or artificially so that a new forest can develop. Similarly, when fish are harvested from a lake or stream, they must be replaced either by natural reproduction or by stocking with hatchery-reared fish.

Ecological Approach

Ecology is the study of the interrelationships between organisms and their environment. Modern conservation strategies often operate within an ecological framework. More than 100 years ago, the American diplomat-naturalist George Perkins Marsh observed how humans had abused agricultural lands in Europe and Asia. He further observed how this abuse resulted in soil erosion, dust storms, water pollution, and the erosion of a nation's economic well-being. Upon returning to the United States, Marsh wrote *Man and Nature* (1864), mentioned earlier. In it he argued that humans cannot degrade one part of the environment without harming other parts. Marsh argued that although highly varied and infinitely complex, our natural environment is

The Importance of Environmental Education

The quality of the environment and the quality of life we enjoy are directly related. We humans have the power to control the quality of the environment, but too often the use of our power damages the environment, often irreversibly. Today many people realize that we must defend the environment and even reverse damage for present and future generations of all living things. Every citizen of planet Earth must accept responsibility for this goal and become an active participant in achieving this goal.

Society prepares its citizens to carry out their responsibilities through its system of education. Education *must* work to help each citizen develop an awareness of and a sensitivity to the environment and its problems. Furthermore, education *must* help each citizen acquire the knowledge and understanding needed to solve problems. And, education *must* foster positive attitudes and patterns of conduct toward the environment.

Environmental education must consider all aspects of the environment—natural and built, technological, social, economic, political, cultural, and aesthetic—

and acknowledge their interdependence. Environmental education must emphasize an enduring continuity, linking actions of *today* to consequences for *tomorrow*. It must also emphasize the *need to think globally*.

To accomplish the above, environmental education programs must be continuous, must pervade all subject areas at all levels, and must offer students experiences that are as concrete and direct as possible. Students must become involved in an active problem-solving process, investigating real environmental issues and problems in their own community.

Environmental education must aid young citizens in developing a sense of responsibility and a commitment to the future, and must prepare them to carry out the role of defending and improving the environment upon which all life depends.

Adapted from: *A Guide to Curriculum Planning in Environmental Education.* David C. Engleson. Madison, Wis.: Wisconsin Department of Public Instruction, 1985.

---

a dynamic and organic whole. Today's conservationists realize that Marsh was correct. More and more effort is being made to understand and protect nature's ecological systems.

The ecological approach to resource management embraces the concept of **multiple uses**. A forest, for example, is not only a source of timber, as the utilitarians suggest, but has many other values as well, such as wildlife habitat, scenic beauty, and flood and erosion control. The forest must, therefore, be managed so that these other values can be realized.

A forest ecologist would ask the following questions regarding the effects of the proposed timber harvest:

1. Will water runoff be accelerated? If so, will this result in flood damage in the valley towns? Will valley farmers have enough water for their crops and livestock?
2. Will the resultant soil erosion destroy trout spawning beds in the streams below the cut?
3. Will soil fertility at the site be reduced because of erosion and jeopardize the healthy development of seedlings on the logged-off site?
4. What will happen to deer, grouse, and other wildlife when the forest that provided food, cover, and breeding sites is removed?

5. Will the scar left after the stand has been logged off cause visual pollution for the thousands of motorists who travel along the nearby highways?
6. What effect will this timber harvest, and thousands like it throughout the world, have on the buildup of carbon dioxide in the global atmosphere and the progressive warming of the planet?

To summarize, then, in the ecological approach to conservation, resources (soil, rangelands, forests, wildlife, fisheries) should be used without adversely affecting the physical and biological environments. Much of this book focuses on resource managers' attempts to realize this difficult objective. As we shall see, in some cases, they are successful; in others, they are not.

ENVIRONMENTAL EDUCATION

If our nation, and indeed the entire community of nations on Earth, is to achieve a long-term, sustainable relationship with its renewable resources and the environment as a whole, it is imperative that understanding and appreciation of the sun-soil-air-water-organism complex be fostered at the preschool, primary, and secondary school levels. The old aphorism "As the twig is bent, the tree inclines" is appropriate here. Sociologists argue that many adult attitudes are shaped by the age of six. Many European grade schools are far ahead of American schools in the quality of their environmental education. Several years ago, at a Convocation of Ecology and the Human Environment of the St. Albans School in Washington, D.C., Admiral H. G. Rickover, U.S. Navy, remarked:

> During a visit to Switzerland for the purpose of familiarizing myself with their educational system, I was much impressed by the way ecology was taught in a one-room village school house. It was part of the curriculum through all the primary grades, being presented at first very simply—but always graphically; later, on a more complex level; and always alongside the three R's and history and government, so that the children absorb it as part of their general education. . . . I wonder, too, whether ecology, properly presented at the higher secondary school levels, might not help dissipate the tendency in contemporary thinking of regarding technology as an irresistible force with a momentum of its own that puts it beyond human direction and restraint.

Since Admiral Rickover made these remarks, more and more ecological education has been introduced into the American school curricula. Nevertheless, we still have a long way to go. (The philosophy behind teaching conservation and environmental education is given in the box "The Importance of Environmental Education.")

RAPID REVIEW

1. The global environmental crisis is the result of three major factors: (a) rapid population increase, (b) depletion of natural resources, and (c) pollution.

2. The global population will surge from 5.2 billion in 1987 to 8 billion by 2020.

3. Each year, 15 million people starve to death.

4. Although the United States has only 5 percent of the world's population, it consumes 30 percent of the world's resources.

5. The United States is degrading the environment more rapidly than any other nation on Earth.

6. The major thrust of this book is (a) to identify our nation's resource and environmental problems and (b) to consider the methods by which those problems might be controlled.

7. The book *The Limits to Growth* suggests that the world's population, resource, and pollution problems place limits on the level of agricultural, industrial, and economic growth possible.

8. Because population, resource, and pollution problems are increasing at an exponential rate, the chance that technological breakthroughs will solve them is rather remote.

9. Natural resources can be placed in two broad categories—renewable and nonrenewable. Renewable resources are represented by soil, rangelands, forests, fish, wildlife, air, and water. Nonrenewable resources include fossil fuels and metallic and nonmetallic minerals.

10. In a broad sense, conservation can be defined as "a state of harmony between man and the land."

11. The most significant conservation developments in the United States were made in this century in three waves: under the leadership of Teddy Roosevelt (1901–1909), during the presidency of Franklin D. Roosevelt in the 1930s, and under the impetus provided by the Nixon, Ford, and Carter administrations during the environmental decade of the 1970s.

12. Although the conservation movement progressed rather slowly during the nineteenth century, some advances were made. They included (a) the publication of *Man and Nature* by George Perkins Marsh, (b) the establishment of 28 federal forest reserves, later designated as national forests, and (c) the founding of the Sierra Club by John Muir.

13. So many environmental laws were passed by Congress from 1970 to 1980 that this period has been called the *decade of the environment.*

14. Among the serious conservation-environmental problems that face our nation are (a) soil erosion, (b) shrinking supplies of water, (c) wetland destruction, (d) unregulated hazardous waste dumps, (e) groundwater contamination, (f) acid precipitation, and (g) depletion of the ozone layer in the stratosphere.

15. Four basic approaches to conservation in the United States have been (a) exploitation, (b) preservation, (c) the utilitarian approach, and (d) the ecological approach.

KEY WORDS AND PHRASES

Blueprint for the Environment (1989–1993)	Environmental Protection Agency (EPA)
Civilian Conservation Corps (CCC)	Environmental Teach-In
Conservation	Exploitation approach to conservation
Decade of the environment	Exponential growth
Ecological approach to conservation	Leopold (Aldo)
	The Limits to Growth
	Man and Nature
Ecology	Marsh (George Perkins)

Muir (John)
National Resources Board
Natural resource classifi-
cation
Nonrenewable resource
The North American
Wildlife and Resources
Conference
Population growth
Prairie States Forestry
Project
Preservation approach to
conservation
Renewable resource
Resource consumption
Silent Spring

Soil Conservation Service
(SCS)
Spendthrift society
Sustainable society
Tennessee Valley Author-
ity (TVA)
The Population Bomb
*"The Tragedy of the
Commons"*
Utilitarian approach to
conservation
Waves of the conservation
movement
White House Conference
on Natural Resources

QUESTIONS AND TOPICS FOR DISCUSSION

1. Define conservation.

2. Discuss the major theme of *The Limits to Growth*.

3. Describe four major advances in the conservation movement that occurred during the administration of Franklin D. Roosevelt.

4. Name five major environmental acts that were passed during the decade of the environment (1970–1980).

5. Does the passage of the Clean Air Act necessarily guarantee nonpolluted air for the United States? Discuss.

6. Discuss the basic difference between renewable and nonrenewable resources. Name four resources of each type.

7. Name and describe the four basic approaches to conservation in the United States.

SUGGESTED READINGS

Brown, L. R., C. Flavin, and S. Postel. "No Time to Waste." *Worldwatch*, Vol. 2, No. 1, pp. 10–19, 1989. List of policy issues that President George Bush must address to aid in controlling global threats to the environment.

Brown, L. R., W. U. Chandler, C. Flavin, J. Jacobson, C. Pollock, S. Postel, L. Starke, and E. C. Wolf. *State of the World*. A Worldwatch Institute Report on Progress Toward a Sustainable Society. New York: Norton, 1987.

Carson, R. *Silent Spring*, Boston: Houghton Mifflin, 1962. A classic. Alerted the public to the harmful consequences of the use of pesticides on wildlife and humans.

Chiras, D. D. *Beyond the Fray: Reshaping the American Environmental Response*. Boulder, CO: Johnson Books, 1990. The junior author's critique of the present-day environmental movement with suggestions to strengthen it.

Ehrlich, P. R. *The Population Bomb*. New York: Ballantine Books, 1968. A classic. Alerted the public to the urgent need to control the population "explosion" so that massive starvation and environmental abuse are prevented.

Hardin, G. "The Tragedy of the Commons." *Science*, Vol. 162, pp. 1243–1248, 1968. A classic. Convincingly demonstrates that any resource that is common property, such as land, water, or air, eventually tends to be exploited and abused.

Hillary, E., ed. *Ecology 2000: The Changing Face of Earth*. New York: Beaufort, 1984. Highly readable collection of articles on the environmental crisis.

Meadows, D. H., D. L. Meadows, J. Randers, and W. W. Behrens. *The Limits to Growth*. New York: Universe, 1972. A wonderfully readable book that discusses computer modeling studies presented in this chapter.

Repetto, R. and W. B. Magrath. *Natural Resources Accounting*. Washington, D.C.: World Resources Institute, 1988. An investigation into the true economic value of our natural resources.

World Resources—1988–1989. Washington, D.C.: World Resources Institute, 1988. A highly authoritative survey of the status of natural resources in the United States and the world.

2

Lessons from Ecology

Ecology is *the study of the interrelationships between organisms and their environment*. An understanding of certain basic ecological concepts will help you to appreciate the problems facing conservationists and environmentalists and to understand the ways in which the problems might be brought under control.

LEVELS OF ORGANIZATION STUDIED BY ECOLOGISTS

As anyone who has ever taken a course in biology knows, one of the outstanding characteristics of any living organism is its organization. In ascending order of complexity, the organizational levels of the human body are the atom, molecule, cell, tissue, organ, organ system, and organism. Although ecologists are certainly concerned with each of these levels, most of their attention is focused on levels above that of the organism: the *population, community,* and *ecological system* or *ecosystem*, as seen in Figure 2-1.

Population

When the layperson uses the term **population**, it invariably refers to the number of humans in a given locality. Ecologists, however, use the term to include any organism, human or nonhuman, within arbitrarily set boundaries. Thus, they may refer to populations of white pine in the Chequamegon National Forest, trout in the Brule River, or fleas on Fido.

Community

The layperson uses the word **community** to refer to a town or city. Ecologists, on the other hand, define a community as *all living organisms occupying a given locality*. They refer to the community of a woodlot, lake, prairie, marsh, or even that of a rotting log or drop of pond water. The community of your backyard might contain millions of organisms from soil bacteria and earthworms to thrushes and oaks.

Ecosystem

A community of organisms does not operate in a vacuum. It operates in an environment. And this environment is composed of both living (biotic) and nonliving (abiotic) parts. The community of organisms can cause changes in the environment; the environment, in turn, may have effects on the community. The ecologist refers to the community plus the environment with which it interacts as an **ecological system**, or **ecosystem**. As shown in Figure 2-2, ecosystems may be either *balanced* or *unbalanced*.

As we will see in later chapters, most measures applied by conservationists involve ecosystem manipulation. A good example is the removal of snow cover from an icebound lake to prevent the winter kill of fish. This permits sunlight to penetrate the ice, making it available to aquatic plants for photosynthesis. The resultant increase in dissolved oxygen may prevent massive fish mortality. This relatively simple example includes interactions between nonliving components such as

FIGURE 2-1A Levels of organization: Population.

POPULATION

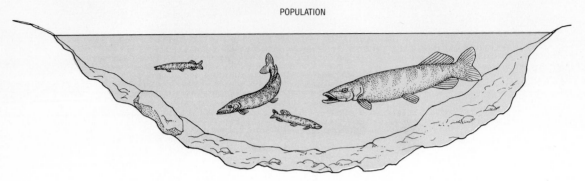

FIGURE 2-1A Levels of organization: Population.

water, solar energy, and oxygen and the biotic components represented by aquatic plants, fish, and humans.

Although it is convenient to consider ecosystems as separate entities, they are isolated only on the pages of ecology textbooks. In the actual living world, there is frequently some movement from one ecosystem to another, whether immediately adjacent or thousands of miles distant. The movement of energy and chemicals from one ecosystem to another is accomplished by biological (animal migration), meteorological (dust storms and hurricanes), and geological (flowing rivers and volcanic eruptions) processes. Thus, topsoil may be blown from an Oklahoma wheat field to the Atlantic Ocean, or it may be washed by spring rains into a nearby stream. Phosphorus originating in deep marine sediments may eventually be transferred to terrestrial ecosystems in bird droppings. How? Sea birds feed on fish, which, in turn, are nourished by crustaceans that eat algae, which absorb phosphorus from the ocean. In a sense, therefore, all the ecosystems on Earth are tied together

to form one all-encompassing ecosystem known as the **ecosphere**. The ecosphere is a thin envelope of life on the surface of this planet.

PRINCIPLES OF ECOLOGY
The Law of Conservation of Matter

One of the basic laws of physics (and ecology) is the **law of conservation of matter**. It states: *Although matter can be changed from one form to another, it can neither be created nor destroyed by ordinary physical and chemical changes.* This law relates directly to the massive pollution problems facing our nation. We are consuming natural resources at a record-breaking pace to support a lifestyle enjoyed by few other nations on Earth. But in the process, we are also generating wastes at a record-breaking pace. The law of conservation of matter should remind us that waste remains, in one form or another, forever. Take as an example the solid waste that

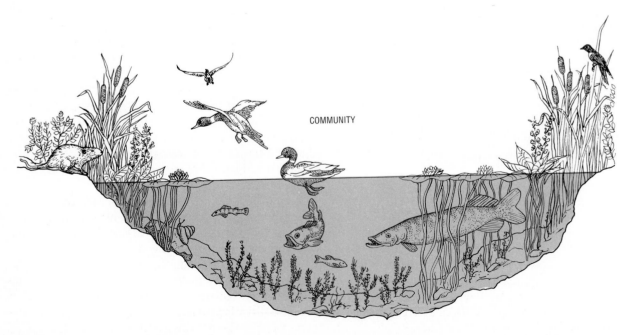

COMMUNITY

FIGURE 2-1B Levels of organization: Community.

FIGURE 2-1C Levels of organization: Ecosystem.

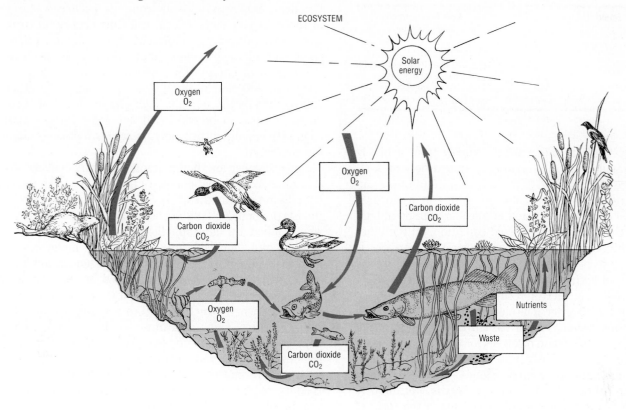

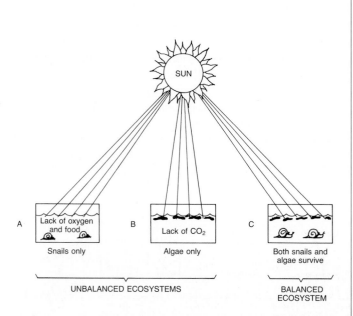

Balanced and unbalanced ecosystems. In aquarium A, the snails die because of lack of food and oxygen. In B, the algae die from lack of carbon dioxide necessary for photosynthesis. In C, the aquarium occupied by snails and algae, all organisms survive. There is sufficient food and oxygen for the algae-consuming snails; the algae are able to photosynthesize because they have an adequate supply of carbon dioxide (released by the snails).

accumulates in the average community. In order to prevent land pollution, wastes might be buried in a landfill.

That sounds great, but if the landfill is not properly situated or designed, some of the waste may leach into a nearby stream, causing water pollution and destroying aquatic life. You say, "Why not burn the waste?" That should do it. The waste certainly would be reduced in volume—to a few ashes—but in the act of burning, we generate large amounts of fly ash, smoke, and gases (carbon monoxide and sulfur dioxide, for example), air pollutants that could be harmful to our health. So, no matter what waste disposal method we try, pollution (matter) is still very much with us. Perhaps the best approach would be to consider solid waste as a natural resource in disguise, which could be recycled and used over and over again.

The Laws of Energy

The leap of a tiger, the beat of a heart, the scream of an eagle, the turn of a wheel, the dip of a canoe paddle—all of these seemingly diverse events have something in common: they require energy, and they represent change, or work. Just what is **energy**? Physicists define it as *the ability to do work or cause change.* Unlike matter, such as nitrogen, carbon, and phosphorus, *energy cannot be recycled.* Instead, energy flows through systems, whether the system is a single organism, like a college student, or the entire ecosphere.

Table 2-1 Concept of Entropy

High Organization Low Entropy		Low Organization High Entropy
Gasoline	→	Movement of car
Electricity	→	Light and heat from study lamp
Waterfall	→	Water flowing downstream
Volcanic eruption	→	"Rain" of volcanic ash
Candy bar (sugar)	→	Body heat

Energy tends to move spontaneously from a highly concentrated or highly *organized* state (food or fuel) to a more *dispersed* or disorganized state (motion and heat). Energy in a concentrated state can perform a great deal of useful work and is considered to be of high quality. Energy in the dispersed condition, on the other hand, cannot perform as much work and therefore is considered to be of relatively low quality.

If the energy in a particular system is largely in a dispersed condition, we would say that the system shows a high degree of disorder. The measurement of the degree of disorder of a system is known as **entropy** (Table 2-1). All systems, from tigers and oak trees to volcanoes and thunderstorms, spontaneously move toward disorder. Living organisms can be considered "islands" of order living in an "ocean" of disorder. However, energy is continuously being lost from the bodies of organisms in the form of *heat*. Therefore, to retain organization, organisms must have access to a continuous inflow of high-quality energy. In the case of animals, this inflow is achieved by the consumption of energy-rich foods. In the case of plants, the energy inflow is represented by the solar energy captured by chlorophyll during photosynthesis.

FIRST LAW OF ENERGY. Pertinent to our study of food chains, food webs, and energy pyramids in the next few pages are the laws of energy. The **first law of energy** states: *Although energy cannot be created or destroyed, it can be converted from one form to another.* We might ask: "What are some of the forms in which energy exists?" When you opened this book a few minutes ago, the contraction of your arm and hand muscles repre-

sented the *energy of motion*, or *kinetic energy*. But this kinetic energy was derived from the *chemical energy* of the food you recently ate. And this energy, in turn, was derived directly or indirectly from *solar* or *radiant energy* during the process of photosynthesis. In this brief description of energy flow, we have identified kinetic, chemical, and radiant energy. But there are also other forms, such as *nuclear* and *heat energy*. Each of these energy forms can be converted into other forms. With each conversion, surprisingly, *energy is neither created nor destroyed*.

Let's consider another example of energy conversions (Figure 2-3). The fuel energy of the coal we burn today actually represents the energy of sunlight that shone on the Earth about 300 million years ago. This solar energy was trapped by chlorophyll, converted into chemical energy, and "locked" into the organic molecules of plants. Eventually, those plants were converted into coal. Today, when this coal is burned by the electrical power industry, the coal's chemical energy is converted into heat energy, which is used to generate steam. The steam, in turn, spins a turbine (kinetic energy), which then converts the kinetic energy into electrical energy. Eventually, when you turn on the study lamp in your dormitory room (to study ecology), the electrical energy is converted into radiant energy. In this example, energy was progressively changed from *radiant* to *chemical* to *heat* to *kinetic* to *electrical* and back to *radiant* energy. And in all those conversions, energy was neither created nor destroyed.

SECOND LAW OF ENERGY. As stated before, the quality of energy varies greatly. Thus, the energy in sunshine, food, or fuel (coal, wood, or oil) is highly concentrated and of high quality. On the other hand, the energy in heat is more dispersed and is of low quality. The **second law of energy** states: *Whenever energy is converted from one form to another, a certain amount is lost in the form of heat.* (In terms of quality, energy is constantly flowing downhill.) Note that *lost* does not mean the same as *destroyed*. When we say that energy is lost, we simply mean that it no longer can perform

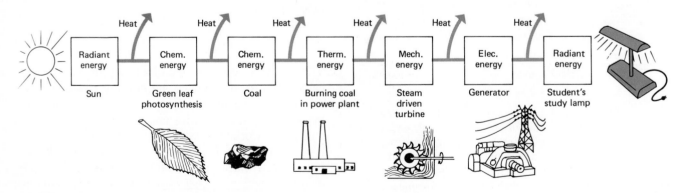

FIGURE 2-3 Different forms of energy. Energy can be changed from one form to another. However, with each change a certain amount is lost as heat.

useful work. Now let's examine once more the energy conversion series described. Only about 1 percent of the solar energy that bathes a plant leaf actually is converted to chemical energy during photosynthesis. Most of it is reflected or is converted into heat energy and simply warms up the surface of the leaf. That heat is low-quality energy; it cannot perform useful work and, therefore, in a sense is lost. Heat is lost in each successive conversion in the series. During the conversion of electrical energy to radiant (light) energy, again heat is lost—as everyone who has accidentally touched a hot light bulb knows (Figure 2-3).

Now let's consider an example dealing with the internal combustion engine in your car. Only about 25 percent of the high-quality chemical energy consumed by the engine is converted into high-quality kinetic energy that propels you along the highway. About 75 percent of the energy in the gasoline is converted to low-quality heat energy—useless as power but nice to have for warming your car during a midwinter trip. Eventually this heat energy radiates from the car and cannot be used again.

The second energy law also operates in living systems. For example, during photosynthesis, high-quality solar energy is converted to high-quality chemical energy by green plants. When you eat plants, whether beans or bananas, the chemical energy of the food is eventually converted by your body to the high-quality chemical energy stored in your body tissues. Sooner or later, your body converts it into high-quality kinetic energy that powers such life-sustaining activities as breathing, the beating of the heart, and the muscle contractions of such organs as the stomach, intestine, and throat. However, here again, with each conversion, from solar energy to chemical energy and from chemical energy to kinetic energy, a certain amount of energy is lost as heat. Of course, in the latter conversion, the heat serves to help keep your body temperature at about 37 °C (98.6°F). Eventually, however, it radiates into the surrounding atmosphere and is lost.

Matter and Energy Laws: Their Ultimatum

The activities of all organisms, from beans to bananas, from hummingbirds to humans, are under the control of the basic matter and energy laws we have just discussed. These laws also control the activities of all ecosystems on spaceship Earth. In addition, they affect a whole series of resource and other environmental problems from bark beetle outbreaks in a pine forest in Colorado to the toxic contamination of well water on Long Island. These laws provide us with a key to understanding (1) the urgency of our nation's environmental problems and (2) how those problems can be solved or brought under control.

The matter and energy laws, moreover, provide us with a stern ultimatum: "You must shift from

a high-entropy, ecologically unsound, nonsustainable society to a low-entropy, ecologically sound, sustainable society. Unless you do this soon, it is inevitable that your system will collapse." We can no longer continue to use a system that is characterized by faster and faster rates of matter and energy flow. The ultimate result will be an increasing degree of entropy. For centuries, industrialized societies have believed that progress could only be achieved by the intensive conversion of resources into the products (cars, bridges, computers) desired by human beings. Unfortunately, this long-cherished belief completely ignores the all-pervasive, unchanging matter and energy laws.

Indeed, those laws compel us to convert to a system that emphasizes resource conservation and reuse, pollution control, and low levels of entropy. *We cannot continue to act as if we rule nature; we must act as though nature rules us.* It is a curious paradox that while the world's industrialized nations have raised their standard of living, they have unavoidably lowered their standard of environment.

We cannot look at nature and wonder what we can get out of it and how fast. Rather, we must regard nature with the respect it deserves as the source of life and bounty for all humankind. We must learn to adapt ourselves to nature's basic ecological laws rather than heavy-handedly disrupt its exquisitely intricate and delicate workings, and in the process eventually destroy ourselves.

The Elemental Cycles

Suppose that the following figure represents the mass of planet Earth:

Now suppose that we draw another figure to represent the total amount of living substance (protoplasm) that has ever existed since the first living organism evolved 3.7 billion years ago. This sphere, of course, would include your own body, as well as those of Stone Age people, ancient tree ferns, and dinosaurs. How big do you think this ball of protoplasm would be? You might be suprised to know that it would be considerably larger than the Earth:

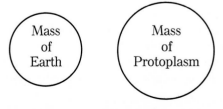

Of the 103 elements known to science, only about 35 contribute to the formation of protoplasm. Carbon, hydrogen, oxygen, and nitrogen form about 96 percent of the human body; elements such as sodium, calcium, potassium, magnesium, sulfur, cobalt, zinc, iron, iodine, and many others occur in smaller amounts. All the elements forming the bodies of living organisms were derived either from the top few inches of the Earth's crust (soil); from the rivers, lakes, oceans, and aquifers on or near the surface of the Earth; or from the thin atmospheric "blanket" of air that envelops the Earth. If this is true, then the only way we can explain a cumulative ball of protoplasm larger than the planet Earth is to assume that the elements forming the protoplasm were used over and over again. In other words, a given atom of, say, nitrogen, which was once part of a dinosaur's jawbone, might eventually have formed part of a professor's brain and, at some time in the future, may form part of a steak you will have for dinner one evening. The circular flow of an element from the nonliving (abiotic) environment, such as rocks, air, and water, into the bodies of living organisms and then back into the nonliving environment once again is known as an **elemental cycle**.

For eons, elemental cycles have been in equilibrium. In other words, the *same* amount of an element had been moving into the various elemental reservoirs as had been moving out. However, in the last 200 years or so, humans have caused imbalances of some elemental cycles. The result has been the buildup of large concentrations of certain elements, such as carbon, nitrogen, and phosphorus, in certain parts of the cycle where they can be harmful to humans and other organisms.

THE NITROGEN CYCLE.   In pure form, nitrogen is a colorless, tasteless, odorless gas (N_2). Atomic nitrogen (N) is an essential component of many important compounds, such as chlorophyll in plants, hemoglobin, insulin, and deoxyribonucleic acid (DNA, the heredity-determining molecule) in animals.

Nitrogen gas is extremely abundant. It constitutes about 80 percent of the atmosphere. There are about 31,000 metric tons of nitrogen in the air column above each 0.4 hectares (1 acre) of the Earth's surface. One would suppose, therefore, that securing adequate supplies of nitrogen would be relatively simple for living organisms. The problem is, however, that nitrogen gas is chemically inactive. It does not combine readily with other elements, and it cannot be used by most organisms in this form.

How, then, can we and the great majority of living organisms make use of gaseous nitrogen to synthesize life-sustaining proteins? First, the nitrogen has to be *fixed*—converted to a usable form. There are several mechanisms by which nitrogen is fixed in nature.

One type of nitrogen fixation is **atmospheric fixation**. In this process, the energy of lightning or sunlight causes the nitrogen to combine with oxygen to form nitrate (NO_3). About 7.6×10^6 metric tons of nitrate are formed annually in this way. This nitrate is then washed to earth by rain and snow and is absorbed by the roots of growing plants.

A second type of nitrogen fixation is **biological fixation**. It is much more important than atmospheric fixation. About 54×10^6 metric tons of nitrogen are fixed annually by biological fixation. It is accomplished by microscopic organisms such as bacteria and blue-green algae, which occur abundantly in soil and water. In this process, nitrogen is combined with hydrogen to form ammonia (NH_3). Then other bacteria convert the ammonia to nitrate, which is usable by plants. Many types of nitrogen-fixing bacteria live inside the root systems of about 190 species of plants, including **legumes** (alfalfa, peas, beans, soybeans, and clover), some pines and alders (Figure 2-4). The nitrogen-fixing bacteria

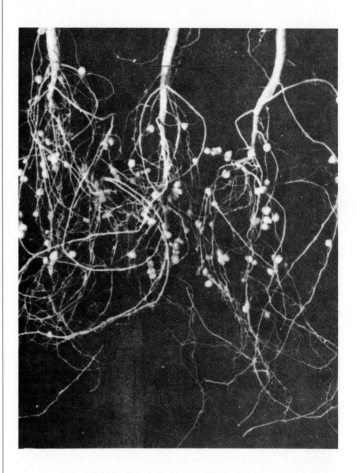

FIGURE 2-4 Root modules on soybean plants and other legumes incorporate atmospheric nitrogen. Bacteria living inside the nodules convert that nitrogen to forms the plant can use to make amino acids and other biologically important molecules.

in legume plants produce more fixed nitrogen than is needed by the bacteria and the legumes. This surplus is then released into the soil. As a result, a farmer may increase the nitrogen content (and hence fertility) of a given acre by 90 kilograms per hectare (80 pounds per acre) per year simply by growing legumes. Similarly, the fertility (and hence fish production) of certain mountain lakes may well depend on the nitrogen-fixing bacteria living in the roots of the alders fringing its shores.

A third type of nitrogen fixation is **industrial fixation**, a process in which nitrogen is combined with hydrogen to form ammonia. Later the ammonia is converted into ammonium salts that can be used as fertilizers. Such commercial production of fertilizer, which requires large amounts of energy (natural gas), has increased enormously since World War II.

Let us now, with the aid of Figure 2-5, follow nitrogen through a hypothetical cycle:

1. Nitrogen diffuses from the atmosphere into the air spaces of soil.

2. It enters the root swellings (nodules) of an alfalfa plant, where the nitrogen-fixing bacteria are located.

3. The nitrogen-fixing bacteria combine the nitrogen with hydrogen to form ammonia and eventually incorporate the nitrogen into amino acids, the building blocks of proteins.

4. The alfalfa plant then builds up its own protein from the surplus ammonia not used by the bacteria.

5. A cow (or other consumer) feeding on the alfalfa digests the plant protein, using the amino acids to make its own proteins.

6. The cow uses protein to build muscle, make milk, and to produce enzymes. Some protein is broken down in the cells of the cow, releasing amino acids. When they are broken down, nitrogen-containing urea is formed. It is excreted in the urine. The cow's feces are also rich in nitrogen; undigested protein and bacteria in the cow's digestive tract are the source of this nitrogen.

7. The urea and large, complex, nitrogen-containing protein molecules in the wastes (or carcass) are then

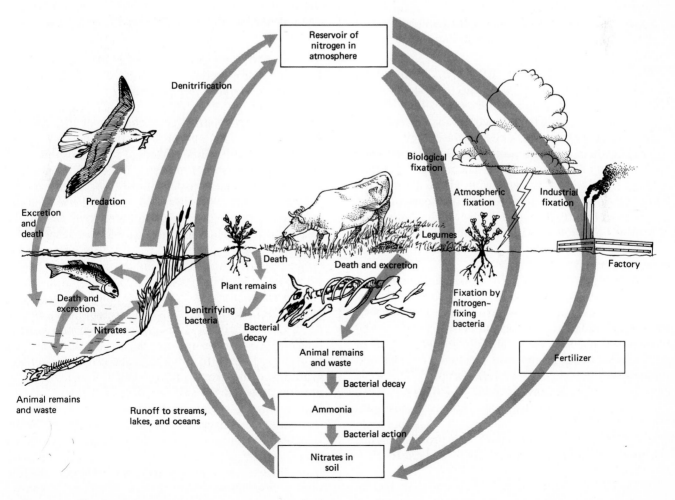

FIGURE 2-5   The nitrogen cycle.

eventually broken down (decomposed) by successive groups of soil bacteria into nitrates, a process called **nitrification**.

8. A plant, such as corn, wheat, or oak, can now absorb the soluble nitrates through its roots and use them to build up its own essential protein compounds, thus starting the cycle over again.

Nitrogen can flow from one ecosystem to another. For example, it may flow from a terrestrial ecosystem to an aquatic ecosystem and back to a terrestrial ecosystem again, as shown in Figure 2-5. Thus:

1. The soluble nitrate salts formed by the decay of a rabbit carcass may be washed into a stream and eventually carried to the ocean.
2. The nitrates may be absorbed by marine algae.
3. The algae may be consumed by crustaceans that, in turn, are eaten by fish that, in turn, are consumed by cormorants.
4. The cormorants then fly back to their nesting colony on the California coast and feed some of the partially digested fish to their young. Or the adult bird may excrete some waste as it flies over California farmland, thus contributing slightly to its fertility.

The flow of nitrogen is truly *circular*, therefore, it must eventually pass back into the atmospheric reservoir from which it originally came. How is this accomplished? **Denitrifying bacteria** in the soil and water break down nitrates. They use the energy released to sustain their own life processes. Gaseous nitrogen (N_2) is given off as a byproduct. The nitrogen gas then escapes into the atmosphere from which it originally came. This process, by means of which gaseous nitrogen is converted to nitrogen gas, is known as **denitrification**. Nitrogen is also released into the atmosphere whenever organic material, like trees, grasses, and animals are consumed by fire.

Researchers in Florida have shown that some chlorinated hydrocarbon pesticides are detrimental to the soil bacteria responsible for nitrification. This suggests that pesticides should be used cautiously, for if populations of soil bacteria are greatly diminished, the nutrient cycle on which plants, and eventually animals and humans, depend could be severely disrupted. The noted ecologist Paul R. Ehrlich of Stanford University views the phenomenon with considerable gravity. In his opinion, "our general lack of attention to the possible long-range effects of these and similar subtle problems in our environment could ultimately prove to be fatal to mankind."

By the year 2000, scientists estimate that 100×10^6 metric tons of nitrogen fertilizers will be produced annually. At the present time, as much nitrogen is being fixed by industry in fertilizer production as was fixed biologically before the advent of modern agriculture. Another form of fixation, which is completely accidental, occurs when fossil fuels are burned. In such instances, atmospheric nitrogen combines with oxygen (a reaction driven by the heat of combustion) to form nitrogen dioxide, which is later converted to nitrates and nitric acid. Nitrates may nourish terrestrial and aquatic plants, while nitric acid can poison many life forms.

For thousands of years before commercial fertilizer production and the modern automobile, the nitrogen cycle was in **dynamic equilibrium**, a steady-state in which the amount of nitrogen leaving the atmosphere by nitrogen fixation was balanced by the amount of nitrogen entering the atmosphere as a result of denitrification. But the fixation of increasing amounts of nitrogen by industrial processes has caused an imbalance; the excess nitrate has been washed from terrestrial to aquatic ecosystems and has caused **eutrophication**. This form of pollution, which is discussed at length in Chapter 8, is characterized by explosive growth of aquatic plants that render lakes unsightly, decrease their recreational value, and cause the replacement of valuable game fish with less desirable species.

THE CARBON CYCLE. Carbon is the key element in the molecular structure of all organisms, from bacteria to humans. It forms 49 percent of the dry weight of the human body. It is an indispensable element in all the organic compounds characteristic of life, such as carbohydrates, fats, and proteins. Carbon exists in several different **reservoirs**, including the atmosphere, the bodies of organisms, the ocean, ocean sediments, and as calcium carbonate (rocks, shells, and skeletons), as shown in Figure 2-6. Although the actual *size* of atmospheric and organismic reservoirs is relatively *small*, the rate of flow of carbon into and out of those reservoirs is relatively *high*.

Six tons of carbon occur in the air column above each acre of the Earth's surface. One acre of lush vegetation can remove 20 tons of carbon from the atmosphere annually. After moving through the pores in the leaf of a plant, such as clover, the carbon is combined with hydrogen to form sugar and other organic molecules. Energy to drive this process, called **photosynthesis**, comes from sunlight. When the clover leaves are consumed by an animal, such as a deer, the carbon-containing organic compounds of the clover are digested and converted into deer protoplasm. When humans eat venison, the digested meat is eventually transformed into human protoplasm. In all these organisms, clover, deer, and humans, some carbon is released during **respiration**—a process in which an organism burns the organic fuel (carbohydrates, protein, and fats) in its cells and extracts the energy. In plants, the carbon

FIGURE 2-6   The carbon cycle.

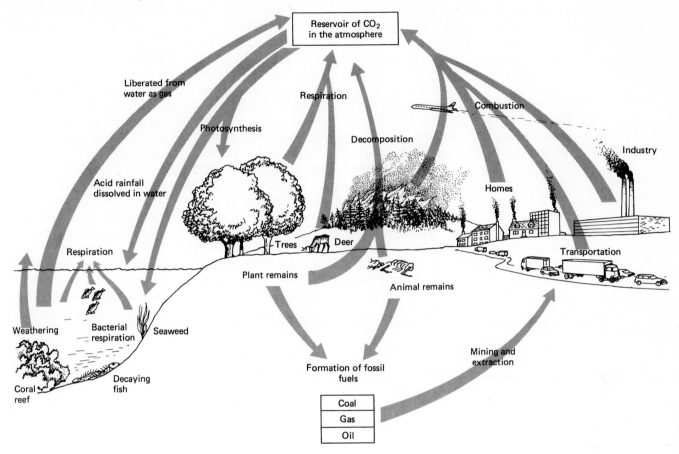

is released (as carbon dioxide) to the atmosphere via pores in the leaves; in animals, the carbon dioxide is exhaled from the lungs. The carbon-containing remains of dead organisms (clover, deer, humans, and so on) or the wastes (feces and urine) of animals are broken down by the bacteria and fungi that occur abundantly in soil, air, and water. Such decomposition releases carbon into soil and air.

About 250 to 300 million years ago, during the Carboniferous Period, giant tree ferns and other plants grew in areas now known as Pennsylvania, West Virginia, Ohio, Kentucky, Tennessee, Indiana, Illinois, Wyoming, New Mexico, Colorado, and South Dakota. Many of those plants were buried by sediment and therefore escaped decomposition. They were eventually converted into coal. In a somewhat similar fashion, both plant and animal bodies were converted to crude oil and natural gas. The carbon in these fossil fuels was removed from circulation. Two hundred years ago, however, humankind discovered the remarkable potential of fossil fuels. Society today depends almost entirely on these fuels. As discussed in Chapter 18, our accelerated combustion of fossil fuels has resulted in a 21.5 percent increase in the amount of carbon in the atmosphere from 1870 to 1988. This increase may re-

sult in climatic changes that will be harmful to human welfare.

The oceans, which cover 70 percent of the Earth's surface, also serve as a carbon reservoir. Carbon dioxide is continuously being exchanged between the atmosphere and the ocean. When atmospheric carbon dioxide increases, more is dissolved in the ocean. Conversely, when atmospheric carbon dioxide decreases, more carbon dioxide is liberated from the ocean. By this mechanism, the carbon dioxide in the atmosphere has been maintained at a fairly constant level for thousands of years — at least until the last century.

The carbon dioxide dissolved in the ocean may move through an algae-crustacean-fish food chain. The fish, in turn, may be eaten by such organisms as sharks, tuna, waterfowl, whales, or humans. Some of this carbon is returned to the ocean by the respiration of marine organisms, and some is used by clams, oysters, scallops, and corals to build limestone shells and skeletons. Tremendous quantities of carbon are locked up in coral reefs off the coasts of California and Florida. The Great Barrier Reef off the Australian coast—a mass of limestone 56 meters (180 feet) thick and (2,100 kilometers (1,260 miles) long—is composed of billions of coral skeletons.

Eventually, as a result of weathering processes that operate for millennia, small amounts of the carbon from coral reefs and the shells of clams and oysters are returned to the ocean waters.

THE PHOSPHORUS CYCLE.   Roughly 1 percent of the human body is composed of phosphorus. It is an essential component of such compounds as DNA, and adenosine triphosphate (ATP)—the energy-rich molecule that powers virtually all organisms.

Let us now trace the circular flow of a given phosphorus atom with the aid of Figure 2-7. We begin with its reservoir in phosphate rock. Because of the process of weathering, some of the phosphate dissolves in raindrops and is washed into the soil. There it represents a potential plant nutrient, just like nitrogen. The phosphorus atom passes into the plants and then into the animals that feed on them. When the plant or animal dies, its body is decomposed by bacteria and fungi. Phosphate is released to the soil as a result. Some of this phosphate-containing soil may then be washed into a stream after a rainstorm. The stream may transport it to a lake or to the ocean. In these aquatic ecosystems, the phosphorus may be absorbed by algae and rooted plants. From these plants, it moves through the

aquatic food web from crustaceans to fish. When marine organisms die and decompose, phosphorus-containing materials are transported to the ocean. Marine animals also excrete wastes, releasing them into the ocean. Phosphorus in sea water often settles to the ocean floor, forming part of the sediment. Over a period of millions of years, these sediments may eventually form phosphate rock. Ultimately, by some geological process such as upheaval, the rock may become exposed to the atmosphere. Then, by the action of weathering and erosion, some of the phosphorus in the rock may become part of the soil once again.

For eons, the amount of phosphorus moving *from* its phosphate rock reservoir into the bodies of living organisms was in equilibrium with the amount moving from living organisms *into* the phosphate rock reservoir. The total amount of phosphorus in circulation was relatively small. However, in the last few decades the intensive fertilization of agricultural lands to feed a mushrooming human population, as well as the use of phosphorus-containing detergents, has caused an imbalance in the phosphorus cycle. The loss of phosphorus from agricultural lands from erosion is estimated to be about 34 metric tons per square kilometer per year. The increased levels of phosphorus in our lakes and

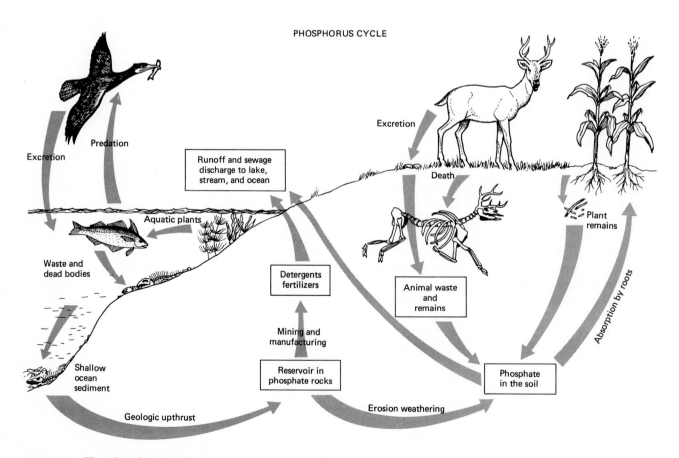

FIGURE 2-7   The phosphorus cycle.

streams has been a significant factor in their eutrophication, a condition caused by excess nutrients (Chapter 8).

THE FLOW OF ENERGY THROUGH ECOSYSTEMS

The sun is the source of virtually all energy on Earth. It heats the Earth and causes winds. It evaporates water, allowing rainfall. It nourishes plants and all life dependent on them.

The sunshine that warms you on your way to class reached your skin only 8 minutes after leaving the sun's surface, roughly 155 million kilometers (93 million miles) away. The sun releases many forms of energy. The total range of radiant energy released from the sun is known as the **electromagnetic spectrum** (Figure 2-8). Note that the visible light (sunshine) we are familiar with forms only a small portion of the entire spectrum. The types of energy represented in the spectrum range from low-energy radio waves to high-energy gamma rays. This energy may be thought of as coming to the earth in the form of waves. The distance between two successive wave peaks is the **wavelength**. Both the level of energy and the wave frequency (number of waves per unit distance) increase from the radio wave to the gamma ray end of the spectrum. The potentially harmful effects of ultraviolet rays, X-rays, and gamma rays will be discussed later in this book.

Solar Energy Flow

Let us now examine the fate of solar energy once it has been received by our planet (Figure 2-9). Only 66 percent of the incoming solar energy is absorbed by the Earth's atmosphere, land, water, and vegetation. The remainder is reflected back into space by dust particles, clouds, and the Earth's surface. This reflectivity is known as the **albedo**. Improper soil management practices that cause soil erosion and the formation of dust storms would therefore have a cooling effect because of the increased albedo. A similar effect would be caused by a volcanic eruption or the release of soot and fly ash from the smokestacks of factories.

About 22 percent of the solar radiation absorbed by the Earth drives the water cycle. This energy moves the water, by evaporation, from the oceans into the atmosphere, where it is released as rain, falls to Earth, and eventually flows back to the oceans.

Almost all of the solar energy absorbed by the Earth is eventually degraded into low-quality infrared (heat) energy in accordance with the second energy law. This energy then leaves the Earth's surface and radiates into space. The ability of the Earth to release this energy is known as its **emissivity**. Certain chemicals in the atmosphere, such as carbon dioxide molecules, block the release of some of this energy. The result is a warming effect. The accelerated consumption of fossil fuels during the last 50 years in the United States has had such an influence.

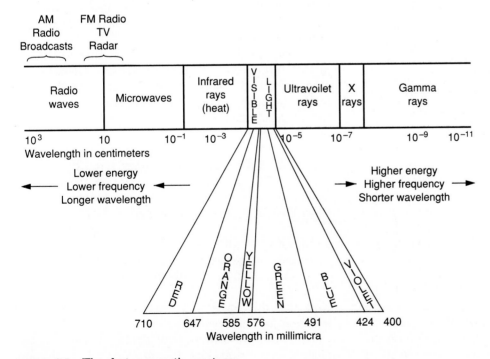

FIGURE 2-8 The electromagnetic spectrum.

FIGURE 2-9   The global flow of energy.

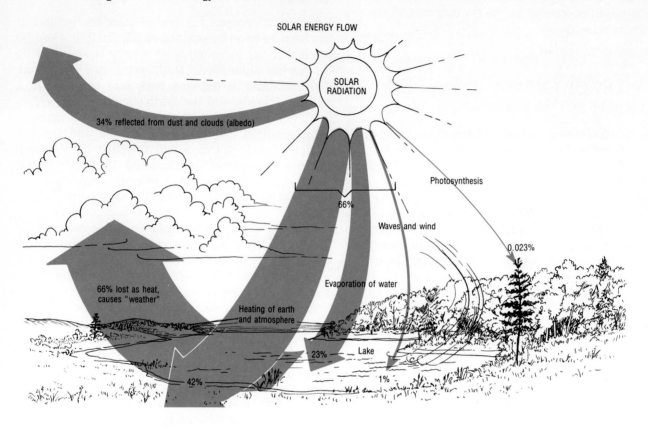

SOLAR ENERGY FLOW

SOLAR RADIATION

34% reflected from dust and clouds (albedo)

Photosynthesis

66%

Waves and wind

0.023%

66% lost as heat, causes "weather"

Evaporation of water

Heating of earth and atmosphere

23%   Lake

42%   1%

Photosynthesis and Respiration

All the energy that powers the activities of life—from the growth of a cabbage to the beating of the human heart—can be traced back to its original source, the sun. Sunlight energy is first captured by plants during photosynthesis, the process by which solar energy is used in the conversion of carbon dioxide and water into sugar. With a few minor exceptions, this process can occur only in the presence of chlorophyll, a green pigment found in algae, some bacteria, and plants (Figure 2-10). In a sense, the solar energy is trapped by the chlorophyll and channeled into sugar molecules in the form of chemical energy. The general equation for photosynthesis is

$$\text{solar energy} + \underset{\substack{\text{(carbon} \\ \text{dioxide)}}}{6CO_2} + \underset{\text{(water)}}{6H_2O} \rightarrow$$

$$\underset{\text{(sugar)}}{C_6H_{12}O_6} + \underset{\text{(oxygen)}}{6O_2} + \text{chemical energy}$$

Some of the released oxygen may be used directly by the plant or may pass from the leaf through microscopic pores into the atmosphere. Here the oxygen may be used by other organisms, from bacteria to humans. There is considerable concern among some ecologists that the progressive contamination of the oceans with

pesticides and industrial wastes may sharply reduce the photosynthetic activity of marine algae and therefore greatly diminish the Earth's supply of atmospheric oxygen. Another harmful result, of course, would be sharply limited food supplies for a rapidly expanding population of human consumers, which could reach 8 billion by the year 2020.

Primary production is the total amount of organic matter produced by photosynthesis. Globally, it amounts to 243 billion metric tons yearly. Since organic matter contains energy, primary production can also be thought of as the amount of solar energy captured by plants and other photosynthesizers.

All living plants and animals break down the products of photosynthesis in a complex series of chemical reactions. This process, called **respiration**, yields energy needed by cells to carry on their many activities. The general equation for respiration is

$$\underset{\text{(sugar)}}{C_6H_{12}O_6} + \underset{\text{(oxygen)}}{6O_2} \rightarrow \underset{\substack{\text{(carbon} \\ \text{dioxide)}}}{6CO_2} + \underset{\text{(water)}}{6H_2O} + \text{energy}$$

Note that this equation is exactly the opposite of the equation for photosynthesis.

Thus, the *raw materials* of photosynthesis—carbon dioxide and water—are the *products* of respiration. The *products* of photosynthesis—glucose and oxygen—

FIGURE 2-10   The food factory. Leaves absorb carbon dioxide and sunlight and use them to make organic molecules in plants during photosynthesis. Water taken up by the roots is a valuable participant in photosynthesis.

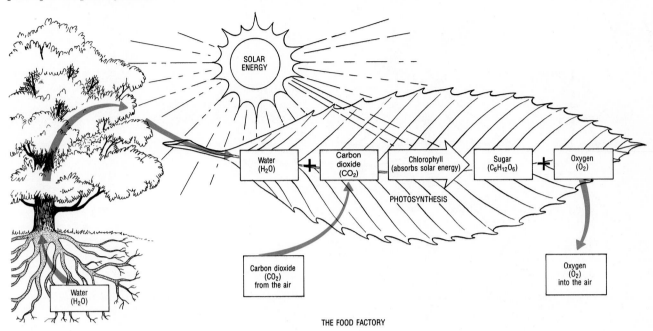

THE FOOD FACTORY

are the *raw materials* of respiration. All plants, of course, must respire, and therefore "burn up" glucose. For that reason, ecologists distinguish between **gross production**, which is the *total* amount of energy captured by the plant during photosynthesis, and **net production**, which is the chemical energy that remains after respiration. The net production may serve as food for plant-eating animals. Unlike green plants, animals are able to capture energy only by consuming other organisms.

Food Chains

A **food chain** is the sequence of organisms through which energy and nutrients move. A representative food chain that might operate in a wet meadow is

grass   →   grasshopper →
(producer)   (primary
                consumer)
                (herbivore)

                frog   →   snake   →   hawk
              (secondary   (tertiary   (quarternary
               consumer)   consumer)   consumer)
                     ‾‾‾‾‾‾‾‾‾‾‾‾‾‾‾‾‾‾‾‾‾‾‾‾
                          (carnivores)

In this food chain, grass is classified as a **producer** because it produces organic food molecules that nourish all other organisms. Any food chain that has a green

plant as its first link is known as a **grazing food chain**. The chemical energy in plant material (derived from the sun) is available to other "higher" members of the food chain (Figure 2-11). This is indeed the energy that either directly or indirectly powers the activities of all organisms on Earth. The grasshopper in this food chain is classified as an **herbivore** because it is a plant eater. It is also called a **primary consumer**. The flesh-eating frog, snake, and hawk are all classified as **carnivores**. They are also called **secondary**, **tertiary**, and **quaternary consumers**, respectively.

Another type of consumer, not represented in our food chain diagram, is the **detritus feeder**. These organisms obtain their energy and nutrients from detritus—waste materials and the dead bodies of plants and animals. Detritus feeders in a forest are represented by bacteria and fungi (mushrooms and molds), as well as by such animals as maggots and termites. As a result of their activities, the large, complex molecules in plant and animal remains are broken down (decomposed) into smaller molecules such as nitrates. These compounds may then enrich the soil and be used as nutrients by future generations of plants (producers). In some shallow lakes, detritus is abundantly represented by decaying vegetation. This material, in turn, is eaten by crayfish and snails, which in turn are consumed by fish.

Any food chain that has its base in the dead remains of plants and animals is known as a **detritus food chain** (Figure 2-12). Roughly 90 percent of the biomass in an oak woods eventually dies and enters detritus

FIGURE 2-11   Food chain for a wet meadow and the web of which it is a part. Food web is highly simplified.

food chains. In the open water of a lake, on the other hand, the situation is reversed. There the floating algae represent the principal producers. Roughly 90 percent of the algal producers are consumed by small crustaceans and thus serve as the food base for grazing food chains.

Food Webs

In actuality, a food chain virtually never exists as an isolated entity. Consider the food chain corn-pig-human, for example. A pig eats other foods besides corn, such as rats, mice, insects, grubs, earthworms, baby chicks, grass, weeds, and garbage. Similarly, in addition to pork, humans consume everything from artichokes to zweiback, from kippered herring to pheasant under glass. In nature, therefore, food chains exist primarily as separate strands of an interwoven **food web**, an interconnected series of food chains.

The grass-grasshopper-frog-snake-hawk food chain of a wet meadow joins with a few other food chains to form a more complex food web, as shown in Figure 2-11. In all probability, this food web is still grossly oversimplified because the complete food web of a wet meadow includes hundreds of species.

As a general rule, the greater the number of alternative channels through which energy can flow, the greater the stability of the food web and the ecosystem. Why should a complex food web have stability? In our wet meadow, foxes prey on rabbits, mice, grasshoppers, sparrows, frogs, and snakes. Now suppose that the rabbit population was reduced, possibly because of adverse weather during the breeding period. Under those conditions, the fox population would shift the predatory pressure it had exerted on rabbits to some (or all) of its alternative prey without suffering from nutritional hardship. Reduced predatory pressure on the rabbit population, in turn, might permit it to rebound quickly when breeding conditions are favorable. If the fox did not have other prey, however, rabbits might have been exterminated, or the foxes would have left the area or died.

Many of the ecological problems humans have unwittingly brought on have resulted from our attempt to simplify ecosystems, making them extremely unstable. The Irish potato famine of the 1840s is an illuminating example. The potato was introduced to Ireland in the late sixteenth century. For many years it was a staple of the Irish and yielded more calories per acre than any other crop. However, in 1845 a disease called the potato blight, caused by a fun-

FIGURE 2-12 Detritus food web of an oak woods. Highly simplified.

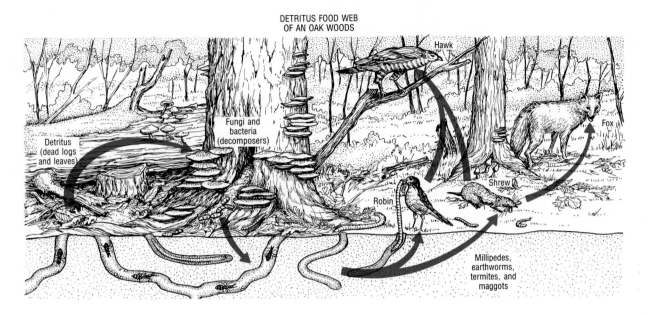

DETRITUS FOOD WEB
OF AN OAK WOODS

Hawk

Fungi and
bacteria
(decomposers)

Fox

Detritus
(dead logs
and leaves)

Shrew

Robin

Millipedes,
earthworms,
termites, and
maggots

gus, devastated potato crops over a 5-year period. Since the Irish were highly dependent on the potato as a food source, and since few alternative foods were available, more than 1 million people died from starvation or disease. Another 1 million Irish left the country. The overall effect of the blight was a 25 percent decline in Ireland's population in just 5 years—largely due to the ecosystem simplification—the planting of huge crops that allowed disease organisms to proliferate.

PYRAMID OF ENERGY. Suppose that we consider, for a moment, the food web of a lake ecosystem, as shown in Figure 2-13. Each feeding level in that community is known as a trophic level. Thus, all the producers (algae, rooted plants, water lilies, cattails, and so on) form the first trophic level. All the plant eaters, known as primary consumers, or herbivores, such as crustaceans and insects, form the second trophic level. The secondary consumers (carnivores), such as fish, feed on the primary consumers and form the next trophic level, and so on.

Not all the energy in a given trophic level ends up in the next level. In fact, as a general rule, only about 10 percent of the energy in one trophic level is transferred to the next. Thus, the primary consumers (her-

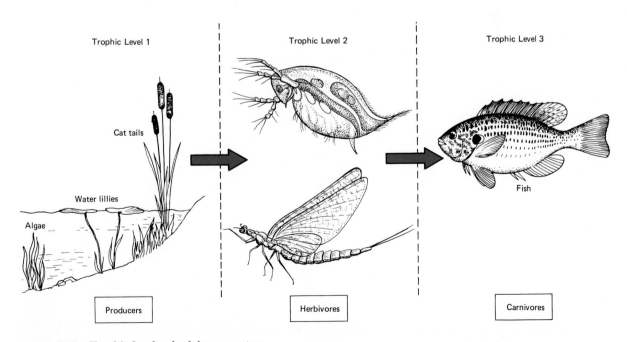

Trophic Level 1

Trophic Level 2

Trophic Level 3

Cat tails

Water lillies

Algae

Fish

Producers

Herbivores

Carnivores

FIGURE 2-13 Trophic levels of a lake ecosystem.

FIGURE 2-14 Energy pyramid for a lake ecosystem.

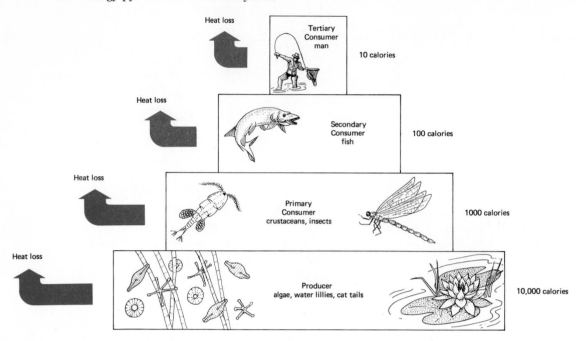

bivores) contain only 10 percent of the food energy in the producer (green plant) level. Similarly, the secondary consumers (carnivores), in turn, contain only 10 percent of the food energy present in the primary consumer level. As a result, the energy contained in the various trophic levels of a food web may be represented in the form of an **energy pyramid**, as shown in Figure 2-14.

So far, our description of tropic levels has been greatly simplified for clarity. You must not get the idea that a given species of organism can belong to only one trophic level. For example, although some fish are either exclusively herbivorous or exclusively carnivorous, other fish, such as the carp, are **omnivorous**—they feed on both plants and naimals. Therefore, the carp are both the primary and secondary consumers in the food web of a lake.

Reasons for Low Efficiencies. The curious student will now ask: "Why does each consumer level contain only about 10 percent of the food energy of the lower level?" Let's see if we can answer. There are four main reasons for the low efficiencies. First, most organisms have acquired adaptations to avoid being eaten by others. Plants deter herbivores with spines, thorns, thick protective bark, irritating secretions, or foul odors. Animals such as insects, trout, and antelope fly, swim, or run from the approaching predator at high speed. Some animals rely on protective coloration to escape detection by predators. This adaptation is well exemplified in certain species of moths whose colors make them almost invisible against the bark of a tree. Similarly, many ground-nesting birds, like pheasants and grouse, are extremely difficult to detect while they

are incubating their eggs, even a few feet away. If an organism escapes predators, it will eventually die from some other cause, such as disease or starvation. Its carcass will then be decomposed by bacteria and/or fungi and will then enter the detritus food web.

Second, the low efficiency in energy transfer from one trophic level to another can be explained by the fact that not all the body of the food organism is digestible or accessible. For example, an owl that has eaten a mouse cannot digest the bones and fur. This material is formed into a pellet and later ejected through the mouth. Similarly, many herbivores, such as porcupines, beaver, deer, and rabbits, cannot digest the cellulose in plant cell walls. Therefore, many cellulose fibers are voided from the body as waste.

Third, not all material is accessible. As a rule, the roots of plants are not eaten by herbivores and thus retain much of the energy captured from the sun.

Fourth, the low efficiency in energy transfer can be partially explained by the fact that all organisms respire. You will recall that respiration is the process by which organisms oxidize, or burn, energy-rich organic compounds to release the energy they need to power their life activities. Respiration itself is a relatively inefficient process. For example, only about 40 percent of the energy in a given sugar molecule may actually work for an organism. The remainder is largely converted to useless heat that escapes into the environment.

PYRAMID OF BIOMASS. Ecologists refer to the dry weight of the living substance (protoplasm) in an organism, a population, or a community as its **biological**

FIGURE 2-15 Biomass pyramid. It takes 1,000 kilograms of corn to produce 100 kilograms of pork needed to produce 10 kilograms of human biomass.

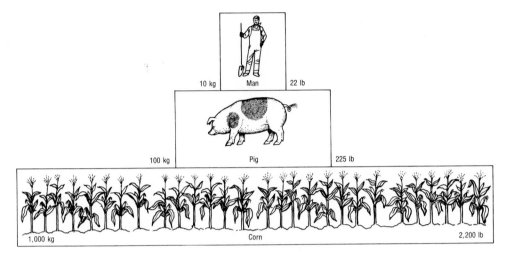

10 kg	Man	22 lb
100 kg	Pig	225 lb
1,000 kg	Corn	2,200 lb

mass, or **biomass**. In typical food webs based on small green plants and ending in predators like hawks, there is a *progressive reduction in the total biomass represented at each succeeding trophic level*. This, of course, is the result of the progressive reduction in food energy available for biomass synthesis at each succeeding trophic level.

A good example is the corn-pig-human biomass pyramid. For example, 1,000 kilograms (2,203 pounds) of corn are needed to produce 100 kilograms (220 pounds) of pork and ham, which in turn can be converted into 10 kilograms (22 pounds) of human flesh (Figure 2-15).

In some cases, the biomass pyramid may be *upside down*. This occurs in some aquatic ecosystems where the food webs are based on billions of microscopic algae. The algae reproduce very rapidly, doubling their numbers every few days. The consumers, however (crustaceans), feed on the algae almost as rapidly as they are produced. As a result, the algal (producer) trophic level has less biomass than the crustacean (consumer) trophic level (Figure 2-16).

PYRAMID OF NUMBERS. In typical food webs based on small green plants or algae and ending in predators like hawks and fish, the numbers of individuals are frequently greatest at the producer level, fewer at the herbivore level, and fewest at the carnivore level.

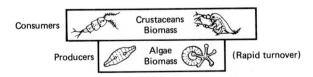

FIGURE 2-16 Inverted biomass pyramid of a lake ecosystem.

When graphically represented this forms a **pyramid of numbers**. Figure 2-17A illustrates the pyramid of numbers in the food web of 0.4 hectare (1 acre) of bluegrass in Michigan. In food webs ending in parasites, the pyramid of numbers is upside down. This is evident in the dog-flea-protozoan food chain, where the protozoans are parasites of the parasitic fleas (Figure 2-17B). However, because number pyramids do not provide accurate pictures of either biomass or energy content in the trophic levels, they are of somewhat limited value.

PYRAMID OF ENERGY AND HUMAN NUTRITION. The second law of energy imposes a limit on food chain length. Most terrestrial food chains have only three or four links. In the unusually long food chain clover-grasshopper-frog-snake-hawk, which might operate in a wet meadow, the hawk uses only 0.0001 percent of the incoming solar energy. Some marine food chains leading from algae to tuna are so long that 100,000 kilograms of algae would be required to produce a single kilogram of tuna usable by humans.

Knowledge of these energy relationships enables us to understand the striking difference between Indian and American diets, for example. If, as an American, you live to be 70, you probably will have consumed 10,000 pounds of meat, 28,000 pounds of milk and cream, and additional thousands of pounds of grain, sugar, and speciality foods. However, a 70-year-old Indian probably would have eaten only 1 percent as much meat as you. In overpopulated nations like India and China, it is no accident that human food chains frequently have only two links, in which herbivorous *humans* have replaced the herbivorous *cow, sheep,* or *pig* (Figure 2-18). More energy is available to the Asian (or to the New York

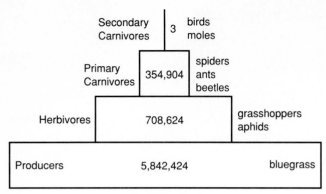

A. Pyramid of numbers

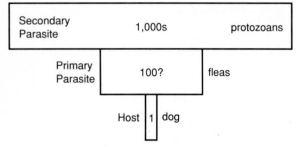

B. Inverted pyramid of numbers

FIGURE 2-17 Two kinds of number pyramids. The upper pyramid (A) is for a weedy field. The lower pyramid (B) is for a dog-parasite system, and is inverted.

ECOLOGICAL PRINCIPLES

The Law of Tolerance

The survival of any organism depends on essential factors in its physical environment, such as water, temperature, oxygen, and nutrients. The concentrations of these factors may vary greatly. For each factor, a given species has a **range of tolerance** that is determined by its genetic makeup and its ability to adapt to the environmental conditions. The organism is adversely affected when the factor approaches values beyond its tolerance limits. Consider your tolerance for air temperature, for an example. If the air temperature gets too high, you sweat and feel uncomfortable. If it gets too low, you shiver and again are uncomfortable. However, if the air temperature is about 23°C (70°F), you operate most efficiently and feel comfortable. Figure 2-19 shows the house fly's range of tolerance for air temperature.

Let's give another example. You require 4 grams of iodine in your diet each year. The reason? It is needed in the synthesis of the hormone thyroxine, which plays an important role in regulating your body's metabolism and, therefore, your body temperature, heart rate, and physical and mental development. An absence of iodine in your diet would surely result in death. On the other hand, if you mixed a few pounds of iodine into your breakfast cereal tomorrow morning, your early death would be virtually assured. The concept that either too *little* or too *much* of a given factor may adversely affect an organism is known as the **law of tolerance**.

The tolerance of a given species for an environmental factor may for with the age of the organism. Thus, newly hatched salmon are much more vulnerable to such water contaminants as heat, toxic metals, and pesticides than are adults.

slum dweller) by moving down the chain—closer to the producer base. Americans still live in a "land of milk and honey" (as well as pork chops and tuna). However, the time may well come, as a result of our mushrooming population (expected to reach 268 million by the year 2000), when we will be faced with the ecological ultimatum: "Shorten our food chains or tighten our belts."

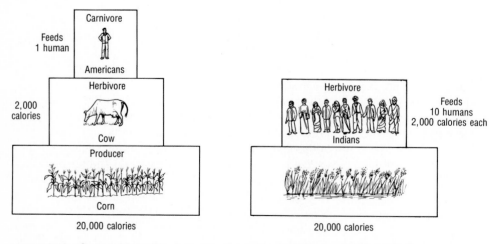

FIGURE 2-18 Comparison of food chains of Americans and poor people of India.

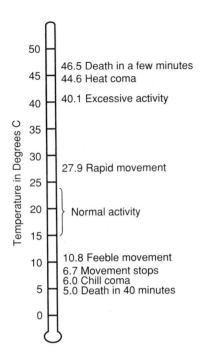

FIGURE 2-19 Range of heat tolerance in the house fly.

Tolerance may also vary with the genetic makeup of the organism. For example, when DDT is first sprayed on a population of house flies, almost all of them are destroyed. However, those that survive because they are genetically resistant will produce resistant offspring. Higher doses of DDT may kill many of these offspring. Once again, however, survivors genetically resistant to DDT will produce a new generation of DDT-resistant flies. Eventually, after many generations of flies have been sprayed with DDT, a generation develops that is highly resistant to the chemical.

The Niche

The **habitat** of an organism is its "address"—the place where it lives. For example, the habitat of the red-winged blackbird is a cattail marsh; a cold water stream is the habitat of a trout. An organism's **niche**, on the other hand, includes its habitat and its total functional role in its particular ecosystem. A description of an animal's niche would include answers to the following questions:

1. What is the animal's range of tolerance to temperature, humidity, solar radiation, and wind velocity?
2. What type of food does it consume?
3. With which species (other than its own) does it compete for food, nesting or breeding sites.
4. Where does it produce its young? In a den? In a nest?

5. If it is a fish, where does it lay its eggs? On the stream bottom? On aquatic vegetation? Or do the eggs simply float on the water's surface?
6. If it is a nest builder, what types of materials does it use in nest construction?
7. What parasites plague the animal?
8. To what type of predators is the animal vulnerable?
9. How does the animal escape from predators? By "freezing," by its coloration, by hiding under vegetative cover, by fighting, or by swimming, running or flying away?
10. What type and volume of waste does the animal excrete?
11. How does this waste affect the surrounding plant and animal life?

By understanding an organism's niche, humans can better manage and live with other species.

Let us now examine an important principle based upon the concept of the niche.

The Competitive Exclusion Principle

The **competitive exclusion principle** states that *no two species of plants or animals can occupy the same ecological niche indefinitely*. Sooner or later, the population of one of the species will decline to zero. There are two reasons for this. First, competition between the species would be intense. Plants would compete for sunlight, soil moisutre, nutrients, and so on. Animals would compete for food, breeding sites, cover, and so on. Second, the two species would not be equally well adapted to occupy that particular niche. For example, one species of plant may be more effective in absorbing soil moisture because of its longer roots or may be more efficient in photosynthesis. In the case of predators, one species may be able to pursue prey more effectively than another species because of its keener vision and longer legs. In each case, the population of the less well adapted species would eventually decline and be eliminated by the better adapted organism.

Consider an example. The shag and cormorant are fish-eating birds that nest on cliffs of the British coast and feed in nearby waters. Since they coexist in the same area, they seem to contradict the competitive exclusion principle. However, intensive studies have shown that they actually do not occupy the same ecological niche. The shag, for example, feeds primarily on eels and herring-like fish that it finds in the upper waters. The cormorant preys on shrimp and flatfish that live on or near the ocean bottom. Moreover, the shag nests at lower levels on the cliffs than the cormorant.

FIGURE 2-20   Stages of a primary succession that begins on bare rocks and ends in an oak forest. This succession could take 1000 years.

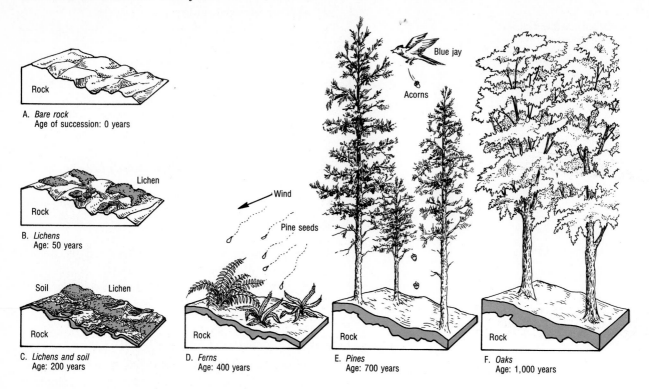

A. *Bare rock*
Age of succession: 0 years

B. *Lichens*
Age: 50 years

C. *Lichens and soil*
Age: 200 years

D. *Ferns*
Age: 400 years

E. *Pines*
Age: 700 years

F. *Oaks*
Age: 1,000 years

In actuality, very few well-documented examples of the competitive exclusion principle have been reported. One such example involves competition between field-living house mice and meadow mice that were coexisting in a field in California. These two species competed for the same space, food (weed seeds), and breeding sites. However, the meadow mouse was much more aggressive in this competition. As a result, the house mouse population declined sharply from about 825 per hectare (330 per acre) to zero in only 14 months.

Biological Succession

Biological succession is *the replacement of one community of organisms by another in an orderly and predictable manner.* In a plant succession the plants of a successional stage cause changes in sunlight intensity, wind velocity, humidity, and temperature, as well as in the structure, depth, moisture, and fertility of the soil. These changes result in the replacement of the original stage by a stage better adapted to the modified environment.

PRIMARY SUCCESSION.   A succession occurring in an area not previously occupied by organisms is known as a **primary succession**. It must start from scratch, so to speak. It may become established on a jagged outcrop of granite, on a lava-covered slope, on rubble left in the

wake of a landslide, or even on the slag heaps of an open-pit mine.

We will trace a primary succession that might occur on a rocky surface in the deciduous forest of the eastern United States (Figure 2-20). The first stage is the **pioneer community**. Organisms of this stage are adapted to withstand great extremes of temperature and moisture. A typical pioneer organism that might become established on a bare, windswept, rocky outcrop is the lichen, whose wind-dispersed reproductive bodies—spores—might be blown into the area. The lichens gradually form a grayish-green crust on the rocks. Even if the rock is completely dry, the lichen spores will develop if adequate atmospheric moisture is available. Once established, lichens begin to modify the immediate environment around them. Weak carbonic acid (H_2CO_3) produced by the lichen begins to dissolve the underlying rock. Lichens growing side by side form a trap in which particles of windblown sand, dust, and organic debris begin to accumulate. When an occasional lichen dies, bacteria and small fungi cause its decay. The resultant organic material and the excreta of minute lichen-eating insects that have invaded the microhabitat enrich the relatively sterile soil that has accumulated. This soil now acts as a sponge, rapidly absorbing water from dew or rain. Once sufficient soil has accumulated, mosses and ferns may become established, also by means of wind-distributed spores. Ferns eventually shade out the lichens and replace them in the succession. The soil

FIGURE 2-21 Stages of a secondary succession that begins on abandoned farmland and ends, after only 70 years, in a hardwood forest.

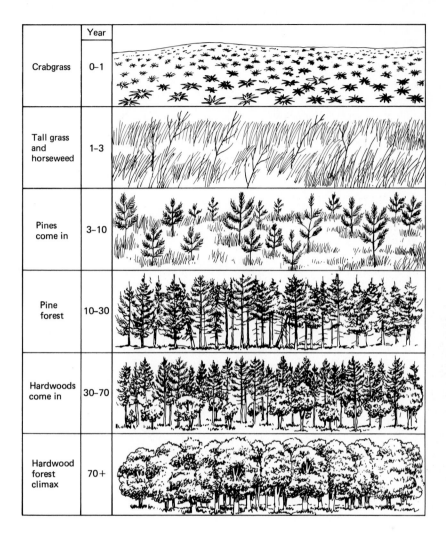

	Year	
Crabgrass	0–1	
Tall grass and horseweed	1–3	
Pines come in	3–10	
Pine forest	10–30	
Hardwoods come in	30–70	
Hardwood forest climax	70+	

becomes further enriched each fall with the decay of the ferns. Eventually, as the decades pass, windblown pine seeds from a hilltop pine forest may fall in the area. They may have been dropped by seed-eating birds, such as the pine siskin, as they flew overhead. The young sun-loving pine seedlings, in turn, compete with the ferns. Eventually the pines shade out the ferns and replace them in the succession.

With the passage of time, gray squirrels may enter the area to bury acorns brought in from a neighboring oak woods. Acorns may also be accidentally dropped by a wandering raccoon or by a blue jay during a flight over the young pines. The acorns germinate readily in the relatively fertile soil, which by now has been developing for centuries since the succession began. The young oak seedlings grow well in the shade under the pine canopy. The oaks (and other species such as hickory, red maple, and red gum) have long roots and therefore can make use of soil moisture that is unavailable to the shallow-rooted pines. As an occasional pine dies, its position in the forest community is filled by an oak. Over time, an oak forest, with its characteristic complement of plants

and animals, will become established, as the stable terminal community, or **climax community**, of the succession (Figure 2-21). Thus, after hundreds of years, the bare, windswept rock outcrop is replaced by a mature oak forest.

SECONDARY SUCCESSION. Succession in an area that was previously occupied by organisms is called **secondary succession**. It is much more common than the primary succession. It occurs when a given ecosystem is partially destroyed and is therefore moved back to an earlier stage of succession. For example, a secondary succession may start in a burned-over forest or in a lake that had been accidentally poisoned with waste from a chemical plant. At the present time, secondary succession is slowly starting on the lava-covered slopes of Mount St. Helens, the volcanic mountain that erupted May 18, 1980 (see the box "Life Returns to Mount St. Helens"). With the help of Figure 2-22, let us examine the secondary succession that develops in abandoned cotton fields in the Piedmont region of Georgia.

FIGURE 2-22 Summary of some major trends occurring during an ecological succession. The number of species, complexity of food chains, and degree of vegetational stratification (layering) increase as the succession proceeds. However, rates of growth and net production decrease.

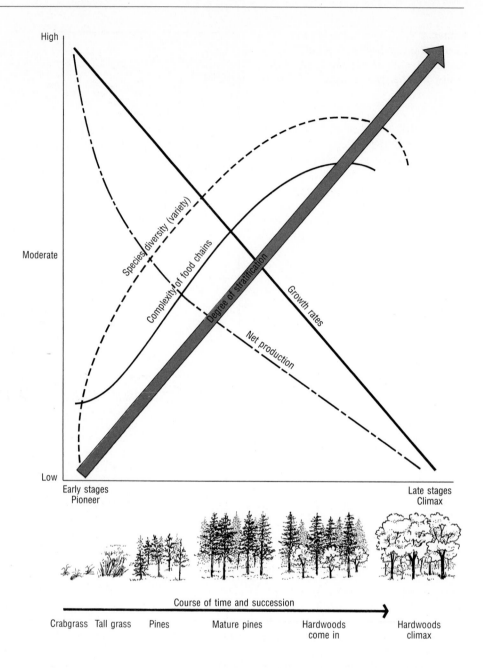

During the first year following abandonment, the land is populated by two pioneer species: crabgrass and horseweed. During the second year, they are replaced by aster. Tall grass, in turn, replaces the aster by the third year. Shrubs and young pines become established in about the fifth year and gradually shade out the tall grass. The pine forest dominates the succession until it is about 50 years old. At this point, sun-loving pine seedlings can no longer survive in the dense shade on the forest floor. They are replaced by the shade-loving seedlings of oaks and hickories. With the passage of time, mature pines die, one by one, and their place is taken by young oaks and hickories. About 100 years after the succession began, the pines are shaded out by the oaks and hickories. The latter species eventually form the climax stage of the succession. Note that this secondary succession required only 100 years to move from the pioneer stage to the climax because of the presence of soil. By contrast, a primary succession that starts on bare rock or sand may require 500 to 1,000 years before the climax stage is reached.

Although we have stressed the succession of plants because vegetational changes are more basic and conspicuous, it should be emphasized that a succession of animals in the community occurs as well. This is understandable, because the occurrence of a given species of animal in a particular stage of a succession depends on such factors as food, water, protective cover against predators and storms, breeding sites, temperature, and humidity, all of which change as the succession

Life Returns to Mount St. Helens: A Dramatic Example of Succession

Mount St. Helens erupted on May 18, 1980 (Figure 1). It was one of the most spectacular volcanic eruptions witnessed on the planet. Mortality to both plant and animal life was awesome. Some ecosystems were literally knocked back to ground zero and had to start from scratch. Roger del Moral described the dramatic comeback of life in an article entitled "Life Returns to Mount St. Helens." Excerpts from his article follow.

At 8:32 A.M. superheated groundwater close to the magma flashed into steam, resulting in a lateral explosion that pulverized rocks and trees and sent a hurricane-force . . . bolt of ash off the north face and across the Toutle River Valley to the north and west. Temperatures in this inferno were estimated to exceed 900°F. Comparable to a 400-megaton blast, the explosion blew down trees in a 160° arc up to 14 miles north of the crater. As the summit of the mountain collapsed, two vertical columns of gas and steam were injected more that 65,000 feet into the air. The ash was eventually deposited, in layers up to five inches thick, over 49 percent of Washington State and beyond.

The number of animals killed as a direct result of the explosion was high. Subterranean animals, such as pocket gophers, appear to have survived in many places even within the blast zone, but mammals and birds living above ground had no protection from the blast. The Washington Department of Game estimates that among the more important casualties were 5,200 elk, 6,000 black-tailed deer, 200 black bears, 11,000 hares, 15 mountain lions, 300 bobcats, 27,000 grouse, and 1,400 coyotes. . . . The eruption also severely damaged 26 lakes and killed some 11 million fish, including trout and young salmon.

Larger vertebrates may form a crucial link in the process of vegetation recolonization. Where heavy ash or mudflows dried to form a hard, uniform crust, there are few cracks to shelter germinating seeds. But large animals wandering in search of food or water make tracks that trap seeds.

Higher terrestrial life may be scarce in the blast zone but dead organic matter is abundant, and such a resource is never unexploited for long. Here, where many humans died, where entire ecosystems ceased to exist in a matter of seconds, Dave Hosford of Central Washington State College has found a mushroom growing from the ash, slowly decomposing organic matter found there and beginning a terrestrial succession.

Of all the regions on the mountain, the most severely affected was the blast zone immediately north of the crater, including Spirit Lake. Every type of volcanic behavior displayed by the mountain has assailed this terrain. All life was seemingly obliterated. Trees were pulverized and soil vaporized. Yet, even here life is returning.

FIGURE 1 Mount Saint Helens after its historic 1980 eruption. Barren land in the foreground will slowly revegetate and over decades return to its previous condition.

proceeds. In the Georgia study, marked changes in breeding bird populations were observed in the various stages.

Mammalian communities show a similar change in species composition and density with the progress of succession. Thus, in the secondary succession we have just described, cottontails and grass snakes of the grass stage were succeeded by such oak-hickory inhabitants as the oppossum, raccoon, and squirrel. A summary of some of the major trends occurring in a succession is shown in Figure 2-22.

FIGURE 2-23 The biomes.

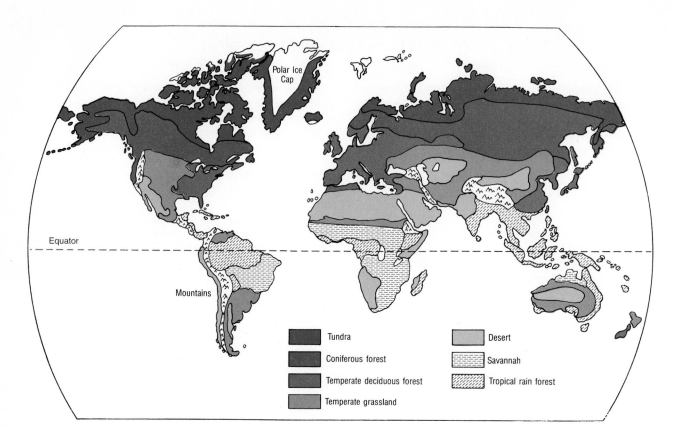

Tundra

Desert

Coniferous forest

Savannah

Temperate deciduous forest

Tropical rain forest

Temperate grassland

The Biomes

Anyone who has driven from New England to California is acutely aware of the marked changes in landscape that unfold from the evergreen forests of Maine to the beech-maple woodlands of Ohio, from the windswept Kansas prairie to the hot Arizona desert. Each of those distinctive areas represents a different **biome**. The biomes of the world are shown in Figure 2-23 and summarized in Table 2-2. We may define a biome as *the largest terrestrial community that can be easily recognized*. The role of climate in determining biome type is shown in Figure 2-24.

TUNDRA. The Siberian word **tundra** means "north of the timberline." The term is highly appropriate because it extends from the timberline in the south to the belt of perpetual ice and snow in the north. The surface rolls gently. The tundra, about 10 percent of the earth's land area, extends around the globe in the northern latitudes. Because of its relative simplicity, the ecology of the tundra is better understood than that of other biomes. The principal limiting factors are the small amount of solar energy and the bitter winter cold. During June and July the tundra on the edge of the Arctic Circle is a "land of the midnight sun." In January, however, this same region is a "land of daytime darkness," for

the sun never rises. Annual precipitation is under ten inches, most of which falls in summer or autumn as rain. Snowfall is scant. Because of the cold weather and the short six-week growing season, the vegetation in the northern tundra is sparse. As a result, this region is sometimes referred to as an Arctic desert. In fact, plant productivity in the tundra is just slightly higher than in the desert biome (Figure 2-25). The low temperature slows down the chemical and biological activities that are necessary for the formation of mature soils. The upper level of the permanently frozen soil (or **permafrost**) occurs at a depth of about 15–45 centimeters (6–18 inches). In spring and summer the thawed-out ground turns into a quagmire. The meltwaters of late spring form thousands of tiny lakes because of poor drainage and low evaporation. Dwarf willows are characteristic producers. Although only a few meters high, some of these willows may be more than 100 years old. Representative consumer species include herbivores such as the lemming, ptarmigan, caribou, and musk ox. The snowy owl and Arctic fox are characteristic carnivores in the area (Figure 2-26).

The tundra is a fragile ecosystem. One reason is the very slow rate of recovery from human disturbance. Thus, wagon wheel tracks that were formed more than 100 years ago are still plainly visible. The tundra may

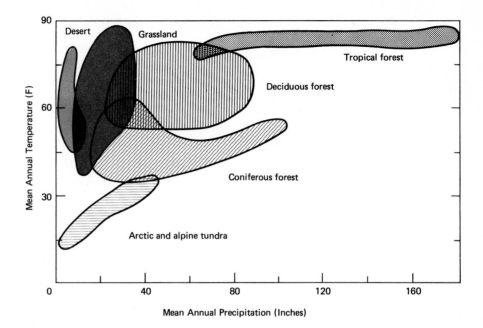

FIGURE 2-24 Influence of temperature and rainfall in determining biome types.

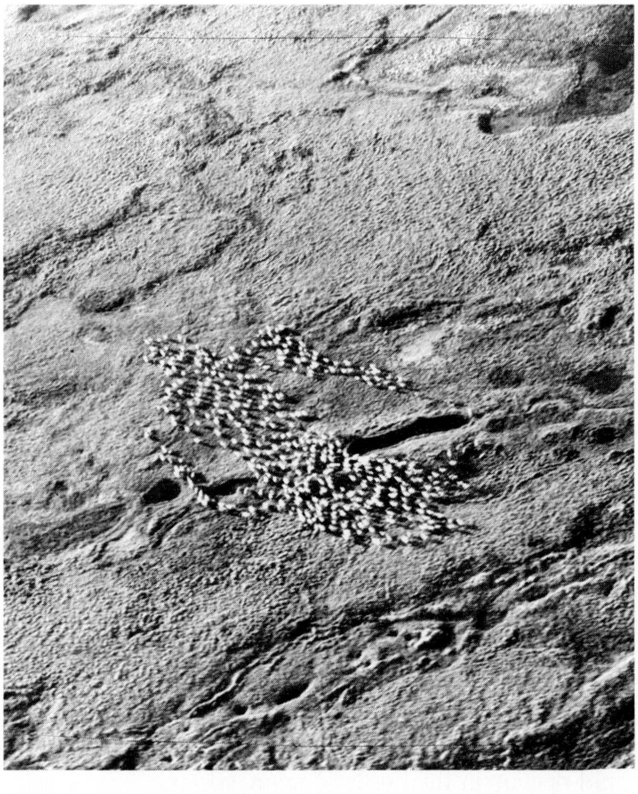

and valuable wildlife habitat and has caused excessive soil erosion. In addition to oil, the tundra contains two-thirds of the North American continent's known reserves of coal, and substantial amounts of zinc, lead, and copper. These resources could be exploited in the not too distant future, creating an ecological nightmare.

NORTHERN CONIFEROUS FOREST. As shown on the global biome map (Figure 2-23), the **northern coniferous biome** forms an extensive east-west belt just south of the Arctic tundra in North America, Sweden, Finland, Russia, and Siberia. Characteristic *physical features* include an annual rainfall of 37 to 100 centimeters (15 to 40 inches), average temperatures of −6.6°C (20°F) in the winter to more than 21°C (70°F) in the summer, and a 150-day growing season. Dominant climax vegetation includes black spruce, white spruce, balsam fir, and tamarack. The evergreen trees are well adapted to survive; their branches are so flexible that they bend under the burden of a heavy snowfall without snapping. Lightning-triggered crown fires are fairly common because the dead, dry needles, which persist on the branches, are easily ignited. Over 50 species of insects are adapted to feed on the conifers. The populations of some species, such as spruce budworm, tussock moth, pine bark beetle, and pine sawfly, may suddenly erupt, causing considerable mortality of spruce, fir and pine. White birch and quaking aspen are representative of the earlier successional stages. Typical animals include the moose, snowshoe hare, lynx, pine grosbeak, and red crossbill.

FIGURE 2-25 The caribou, characteristic herbivore of the tundra. Note the low-lying vegetation, composed primarily of lichens, grasses, and mosses.

be very seriously disturbed in the next few years as a result of our never-ending quest for energy. In 1968 the richest oil deposit in the Western Hemisphere was discovered on Alaska's North Slope. A 1,262-kilometer- (789-mile)-long pipeline was constructed to transport this oil to the port of Valdez on Alaska's southern coast. This caused the destruction of much vegetation

DECIDUOUS FOREST. The global biome map (Figure 2-23) also shows that the **deciduous (broad-leafed) forest biome** originally covered eastern North America,

all of Europe, and parts of China, Japan, and Australia. In the United States, the deciduous forest biome attains its greatest development east of the Mississippi River and south of the northern coniferous forest. In precolonial times, the deciduous forest was virtually continuous and unbroken. Today, however, as a result of settlement, agricultural development, logging, mining, and highway construction, the biome has been reduced to a small fraction of its original area. Fingers of deciduous forest extend westward into the prairie country along major river valleys in response to increased levels of soil moisture. Because of abundant precipitation (at least 75 centimeters [30 inches]) and the fairly long growing season, plant productivity is the highest of any biome in North America, except the rain forest. Characteristic trees are oak, hickory, beech, maple, black walnut, black cherry, and yellow poplar. Representative consumers include the gray squirrel, skunk, black bear, and white-tailed deer.

TROPICAL RAIN FOREST. The **tropical rain forest biome** is located in the equatorial regions wherever there is more than 200 centimeters (80 inches) of rainfall annually. As shown in Figure 2-23, rain forests are located primarily in Central America, in South America along the Amazon and Orinoco rivers, in the Congo River basin of Africa, in Madagascar, and in Southeast Asia. The day-night temperature variations are greater than those of summer-winter. Heavy rains may fall *daily* throughout much of the year, so moisture drips almost continuously from the canopy. Because so much sunlight is screened out by the canopy, the forest floor is relatively dark and poorly vegetated. To some, the rain forest is a "green cathedral"; to others, it's a "humid hell."

Plant life is highly diverse in the rain forest. Two hundred species of trees may be found in 1 hectare (2.47 acres) compared to only 10 species per hectare in the temperate deciduous forests of the United States. The forests are highly layered, or stratified, with the tree crowns occurring at three or even four different levels.

Animal life is abundant and highly diverse. At least 369 species of birds have been identified in just 2 hectares of Costa Rican rain forest—more than are found throughout Alaska. Some insects are extremely large. In the Amazon rain forest, the wingspread of one species of moth is nearly 1 foot, and some spiders are large enough to feed on birds caught in their webs!

Unfortunately, humans are cutting the rain forest, leaving only small fragments in many countries. The reasons are many: (1) to develop settlements, (2) to acquire wood, and (3) to establish farms and pasture. Agricultural ventures usually result in failure, not only because the soil is very infertile, but also because it frequently contains iron compounds that bake brick hard under the tropical sun. Deforestation has contributed to the atmospheric buildup of CO_2 and the warmup of the planet (Chapter 18).

TROPICAL SAVANNAH. A **savannah** is a warm-climate grassland characterized by scattered trees. As shown in the global biome map (Figure 2-23), savannahs are located primarily in South America, Africa, India, and Australia. Rainfall averages 100 to 150 centimeters (40 to 60 inches) per year. Wet seasons alternate with dry seasons, and fires are common during the prolonged dry spells. Plants and animals must be drought and fire resistant. As a result, the diversity of species is not great.

The African savannah is characterized by the picturesque baobab and thorny acacia trees. This savannah supports the greatest variety and largest number of hoofed herbivores in the world, including the zebra, giraffe, wildebeest, and many species of antelope. In the struggle to produce more food, many people in Africa and India have converted extensive acreages of savannah into farms and livestock pasture. Those disturbances, along with illegal hunting, have caused a rapid decline in the herds of many species.

GRASSLAND. On a global basis, as shown in Figure 2-23, the principal **grasslands** include the **prairies** of Canada and the United States, the *pampas* of South America, the *steppes* of Eurasia, and the *veldts* of Africa. Major grasslands occur in two regions in the United States: the Great Plains, a vast area extending from the eastern slopes of the Rockies to the Mississippi River, and the more moist portions of the Great Basin lying between the Sierras to the west and the Rockies to

Table 2-2 Biome Summary

Biome	Climate	Typical Plants	Typical Animals
Tundra	Temp.: −57–16°C Precip.: 10–50 cm	Lichens, mosses Dwarf willows	Ptarmigan, snowy owl, lemming, caribou, musk ox, Arctic fox
Coniferous forest	Temp.: −54–21°C Precip.: 35–600 cm	Black spruce, white spruce, balsam fir, white birch, aspen	Spruce budworm, tussock moth moose, snowshoe hare, lynx
Deciduous forest	Temp.: −30–38°C Precip.: 60–225 cm	Oak, hickory, beech, maple, black walnut, yellow poplar	White-tailed deer, gray squirrel, skunk, opossum, black bear
Grassland	Temp.: 40–60°C Precip.: 30–200 cm	Little and big bluestem, grama grass buffalo grass	Meadowlark, burrowing owl, pronghorned antelope, badger, jackrabbit, coyote
Desert	Temp.: 2–57°C Precip.: 0–25 cm	Prickly pear cactus, saguaro cactus, creosote bush, mesquite, sagebrush	Diamond-backed rattlesnake, Gila monster, roadrunner, kangaroo rat, wild pig
Savannah	Temp.: 13–40°C Precip.: 25–90 cm	Baobab tree, acacia tree, grasses	Zebra, giraffe, wildebeest, elephant, antelope
Tropical rain forest	Temp.: 18–35°C Precip.: 125–1250 cm	Great diversity	Great diversity

the east. In north temperate latitudes, grasslands are the vegetational expression of an average annual precipitation that is excessive (over 25 centimeters [10 inches]) for the development of desert vegetation and inadequate (under 75 centimeters [30 inches]) for the development of forest. Winter blizzards and summer drought can be severe. There is evidence that devastating fires periodically have burned the prairie.

The dominant vegetation includes the big bluestem, little bluestem, buffalo grass, and grama grass. The horned lark, meadowlark, and burrowing owl are characteristic birds in that grassland. Dominant mammals include the pronghorned antelope, badger, white-tailed jackrabbit, coyote, and pocket gopher (Figure 2-27).

It must be emphasized that only scattered remnants of the climax grassland biome remain. Humans have replaced the original wild grasses with cultivated "grasses" such as corn and wheat. In addition, humans have almost eradicated the bison and replaced it with domesticated herbivores such as cattle and sheep.

DESERT. As shown in the global biome map (Figure 2-23), the world's deserts are primarily located in the United States, Mexico, Chile, Africa (Sahara), Asia (Tibet and Gobi), and Australia. American deserts are located in the hotter, drier portions of the Great Basin and in parts of California, New Mexico, Arizona, Texas, Nevada, Idaho, Utah, and Oregon. Deserts occur primarily to the leeward of prominent mountain ranges, such as the Sierra Nevada and the Rocky Mountains. The prevailing warm, humid air masses from the Pacific Ocean cool as they move up windward slopes and release their moisture as rain or snow. The region to the leeward of the mountains lies in the "rain shadow," where precipitation is minimal. A desert community generally receives less than 25 centimeters

FIGURE 2-27 Resident of the grassland biome. The prairie dog at the edge of its crater-like burrow entrance. The mound of earth not only serves as a lookout post but also prevents flash-flooding of its burrow.

(10 inches) of annual precipitation. Rainfall, moreover, may not be uniformly distributed, but may fall periodically in cloudbursts that cause flash floods and severe erosion. An extremely high evaporation rate aggravates

FIGURE 2-28 Biome productivity.

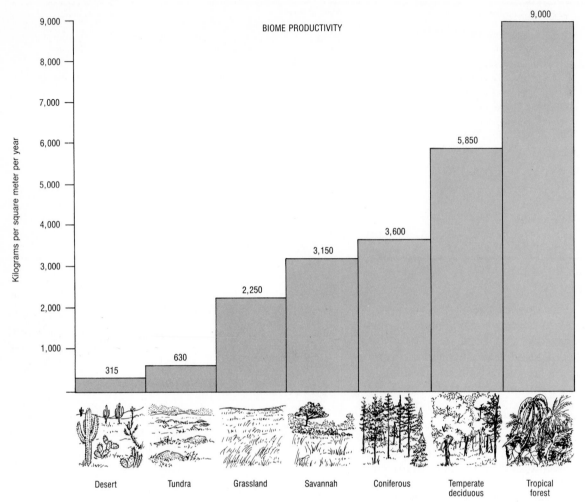

BIOME PRODUCTIVITY

the severe moisture problem. For example, the water that theoretically *could* evaporate from a given hectare in one year may be 30 times the actual amount received as precipitation.

Summer temperatures range from about 9.9°C (50°F) at night to about 48.40°C (120°F) during the day. Desert floor temperatures reach 62°C (145°F) in summer. Only organisms that have evolved specialized structural, physiological, and behavioral adaptations to extreme heat and dryness can survive in the desert. Characteristic producers are prickly pear cactus, saguaro cactus, creosote bush, and mesquite.

Conspicuous among desert consumers in the United States are the rattlesnake, Gila monster, roadrunner, jackrabbit, kangaroo rat, and wild pig.

ALTITUDINAL BIOMES.   As shown in Figure 2-28, the productivity of the biomes varies considerably (Figure 2-28), depending on temperature and precipitation. By traveling several thousand miles from Texas northeastward to northern Canada, you pass through a series of different biomes—desert, grassland, deciduous forest, coniferous forest and tundra. These biome changes, of

course, reflect progressive changes in temperature and precipitation. Such a series of biomes also exists on the slopes of tall mountains, such as the 4,200-meter (14,000-foot)-high Colorado Rockies. Here again, the gradual changes in biome type are dictated by climatic factors, which in this case change progressively with *altitude* rather than latitude (Figure 2-28).

RAPID REVIEW

1. Ecology is the study of the interrelationships between organisms and their environment. Ecologists focus their studies primarily on three levels of organization: the *population*, the *community*, and the *ecological system*, or *ecosystem*. A population is the total number of individuals of one *species* in a given area. A community includes all living organisms in a given area. An ecosystem is the community and the environment with which it interacts.

2. The circular flow of an element from the nonliving environment into the bodies of living organisms

and then back into the nonliving environment is known as an *elemental cycle*. For millions of years before the advent of human technology, the elemental cycles were delicately balanced. However, in recent years, our technology has caused many elemental cycles to become unbalanced. In other words, we have accelerated the movement of a given element from one point to another in its cycle. The result is the *pollution* of air, water, and land.

3. The first law of energy states: Although energy cannot be created or destroyed, it can be converted from one form to another. The second law of energy states: Whenever one form of energy is converted to another, a certain amount is lost as heat.

4. Photosynthesis is the process by which green plants convert the raw materials carbon dioxide and water to glucose and other organic molecules in the presence of sunlight. The green pigment in plants, known as *chlorophyll*, serves as a catalyst in the process.

5. A *food chain* is a sequence of organisms through which nutrients and energy move. A network of food chains is known as a *food web*.

6. The stability of a food web increases in proportion to its complexity. Green plants convert energy from the sun to organic food energy that can be used by other organisms. Because of this process, green plants are called *producers*. Plant-eating animals, such as the rabbit, are called *herbivores*, or *primary consumers*. Animals like the wolf, which feed on other animals, are known as *carnivores*, or *secondary consumers*.

7. The total dry weight of living substance (protoplasm) in a given organism, population, or community is known as the *biological mass*, or *biomass*. There is a progressive reduction in biomass in each succeeding feeding level, or *trophic level*, of a given food web. This is known as the *pyramid of biomass*.

8. *Energy* is the capacity to do work. Unlike the elements, energy cannot be recycled. Living organisms are only about 10 percent efficient in converting the energy of their food into the energy of their own biomass. As a result, there is a progressive reduction in the amount of food energy represented by the successive trophic levels (feeding levels) of a given food web. This is known as the *pyramid of energy*. In other words, more energy is available to plants than to herbivores, and more energy is available to herbivores than to carnivores. More food energy would be available to human beings if we would move down the food chain—closer to the producer base.

9. For each organism there exists a specific tolerance range for any essential environmental factor, below or above which the organism is adversely affected. This principle is known as the *range of tolerance*.

10. The replacement of one community by another under constant climatic conditions is known as *ecological succession*. The initial stage of a succession is known as a *pioneer community*. This community usually can withstand considerable extremes in temperature and moisture. The final stage of a succession is known as the *climax community*. This stage is stable. In theory it will persist indefinitely unless the climate changes or some geological process or human action destroys it. A succession that becomes established in an area where living organisms were not previously present, such as bare rock or a lava flow, is known as a *primary succession*. However, a succession that becomes established in an area that once supported life, such as a burned-over forest or an abandoned corn field, is known as a *secondary succession*.

11. A *biome* is the largest terrestrial community that is easily recognized by a biologist. It is the biological expression of the interaction of climate, soil, water, and organisms. Representative biomes discussed in this chapter were the following: tundra, northern coniferous forest, deciduous forest, tropical rain forest, grassland, tropical savannah, and desert. Each biome is characterized by a unique assemblage of plants and animals. On the slopes of tall mountains, such as the Rockies, a series of *altitudinal biomes* can be recognized.

KEY WORDS AND PHRASES

Altitudinal biomes	Ecosystem
Atmoshperic fixation	Electromagnetic spectrum
Biological fixation	Elemental cycle
Biomass	Entropy
Biome	Energy
Carnivore	Eutrophication
Chlorophyll	Food chain
Climax community	Food web
Community	Fossil fuel
Competitive exclusion	Herbivore
principle	Industrial fixation
Coniferous forest biome	Kinetic energy
Decomposer	Law of conservation of
Denitrification	matter
Desert	Laws of energy
Detritus feeder	Legume
Dynamic equilibrium	Limiting factor
Ecological succession	Mechanical energy
Ecology	Mount St. Helens
Ecosphere	Net production

Niche
Nitrification
Nitrogen cycle
Nitrogen fixation
Omnivore
Permafrost
Phosphorus cycle
Photosynthesis
Pioneer community
Population
Primary consumer
Primary production
Primary succession
Producer
Pyramid of biomass

Pyramid of energy
Pyramid of numbers
Radiant energy
Reservoir
Respiration
Savannah
Secondary consumer
Secondary succession
Succession
Stomata
Stratification
Trophic level
Tropical rain forest
Tundra

QUESTIONS AND TOPICS FOR DISCUSSION

1. *Levels of organization.* Define and give an example of each of the following: community, population, ecosystem.

   a. *Ecosystem.* Do large cities have the characteristics of a balanced ecosystem? In other words, could a city continue to exist completely isolated from all other ecosystems? Why or why not?

   b. *Ecosystem.* For many years, a lake has been operating as a balanced ecosystem. Suppose now that a disease kills off all the plants. What effect would this have on the animals in that ecosystem? Suppose that instead of killing off all the plants, a disease destroyed all the bacteria in the lake. What effect would this have on the lake ecosystem? Discuss your answer.

   c. *Ecosystem.* Describe and discuss the structure and function of the ecosystems represented by your college campus. Does the campus represent a balanced ecosystem? Why or why not? What sorts of disturbances would tend to promote imbalance?

2. *Elemental cycles.* Make labeled diagrams of the *shortest* nitrogen, carbon, and phosphorus cycles you can devise.

   a. *Nitrogen cycle.* Describe three ways in which nitrogen can be fixed.

   b. *Carbon cycle.* Trace a given carbon atom from the air that existed over Pennsylvania 250–300 million years ago to the fried egg you had for breakfast this morning.

   c. *Elemental cycle.* In one sense, pollution can be defined as an imbalance of an elemental cycle. Explain. In this context, can you give one example each of land, air, and water pollution?

3. *Range of tolerance.* Discuss the range of tolerances that you have for various physical conditions to the daily environment to which you are exposed. Find a newspaper clipping describing recent human fatalities that resulted because tolerance ranges were exceeded.

4. *Second law of energy.* Trace the radiant energy from your study lamp backward in time to its ultimate source in solar energy.

5. *Photosynthesis.* Compare photosynthesis with respiration. Does a green plant give off oxygen both day and night? Does a green plant take in carbon dioxide both day and night?

6. *Food chains.* Distinguish between grazing food chains and detritus food chains. Given an example of each type. Which type is more easily observed? Which type of food chain is most important in a forest ecosystem? Which type is most important in a marine ecosystem?

7. *Food web.* How many different species of organisms can you identify that are living either in your dormitory or in your home? Identify their trophic level. In other words, are they producers, herbivores, carnivores, omnivores, or detritus feeders? Compare your results with those of other members of your class.

8. *Food web.* List all the food organisms you consumed, in part or in entirety, during your last three meals. Now construct a food web, using this list and yourself as a starting point. You may include other organisms not actually represented in your meals. Identify the trophic level of each species in the web.

9. *Pyramid of biomass.* The total biomass of the animals living in the English Channel is five times greater than that of the plants. Can you offer any explanation for this seeming contradiction of the biomass pyramid concept?

10. *Trophic levels.* Suppose that you are in charge of a unique wildlife refuge that is completely isolated from other ecosystems. This refuge is composed of one kind of producer (grass), one kind of herbivore (rabbits), and one kind of carnivore (hawks). Assume that one rabbit weighs as much as one hawk. Assume further that the rabbits consume only grass and that the hawks feed only on rabbits. Suppose that you originally stocked the refuge with three rabbits and six hawks, in other words, a 2:1 ratio of hawks to rabbits. After about 5 years, would you expect that this same ratio would exist? Why or why not? What ratio would you expect?

11. *Energy flow.*

    a. As we have learned in this chapter, elements are recycled through ecosystems but energy is not. Suppose, however, that energy was recycled and elements were not. What would be the effects on ecosystems? Discuss your answer.

b. Suppose that the sun stopped shining. What effect would this have on life on Earth? Would life still be possible? Discuss your answer.

12. *Pyramid of energy.* Suppose that 20,000 calories of solar energy are available to grass for photosynthesis. Suppose that grass converts 1 percent of the solar energy available to it. Suppose further that animals can store 10 percent of the food energy they consume in their own protoplasm. How many food calories would you get if you consumed the grass? If you lived on beef derived from grass-eating cattle? How much food energy would be available to a hawk at the end of a grass-grasshopper-frog-snake-hawk food chain? What percentage of the original 20,000 calories would be stored in the body of the hawk?

13. *Ecological succession.* Describe three sites at which a primary succession might start. Describe three sites at which a secondary succession might become established.

14. *Ecological succession.* Construct a chart listing four basic differences between the pioneer and climax stages of an ecological succession.

15. *Ecological succession.* Suppose that a square mile of oak woods in Ohio is removed and replaced with a huge slab of polished marble. One thousand years pass. Will the marble slab still be visible? Why or why not? Give a detailed explanation of the probable events that occurred.

16. *Biomes.* Describe the physical features of the tundra biome. Why is it sometimes called an *Arctic desert*? Why is it considered a fragile ecosystem? Would it be a good place to study succession? Why or why not? Explain.

17. *Biomes.* Which of the biomes discussed in the chapter has the greatest diversity of animal life? Which features of the biome make this diversity possible?

SUGGESTED READINGS

Campbell, N. A. *Biology*. Second edition. Menlo Park, Calif.: Benjamin Cummings, 1990. See Chapters 46–49 for more aspects of ecology.

Ehrlich, P. R., and J. Roughgarden. *The Science of Ecology*. New York: Macmillan, 1987. Comprehensive textbook on ecology by leaders in the field.

3

The Human Population Problem

Humans have unique abilities. One of the most distinguishing is our ability to assess problems, devise solutions, and put those solutions into operation. However, at this crucial period in human history, we have not yet effectively applied our talents to solving the problem of our rapidly expanding global population. If uncontrolled, our soaring population may bring calamity to the human species. Remember the Armenian earthquake disaster in 1988? That catastrophe took about 50,000 lives. But because of the rapid rate at which the human population bomb is ticking, those lives will be replaced in only 5 hours! With each passing second, three more babies take up the struggle for survival on this already crowded planet. That adds up to over 5,000 more humans in the time it takes you to watch the evening news. Whether the birth takes place in a modern maternity ward in urban America or on the floor of an African hut, each newborn taxes the earth's dwindling stock of resources.

Currently the global population is increasing at a rate of more than 234,000 per day, equal to another Syracuse, New York, or Richmond, Virginia. To give each person in this daily increase a glass of milk would require milk from 15,000 cows; to give each a loaf of bread would take more than 300 acres of wheat. In 1988 alone, it was necessary to provide food, water, shelter, and living space to sustain 87 million additional people—equal to nine New York Cities or two Englands. Every 3 years, the global environment and its resources

must somehow support another 250 million people—equal to another United States! At present, the earth's population is increasing at the rate of 1.8 percent annually—a rate at which it will double, from 5.2 billion (1987) to 10.4 billion (2026) in only 39 years (Figure 3-1).

It is sobering to note that global population growth has been greater in this decade than in any previous one in history; more than 800 million people were added to the planet during this period. Almost 90 percent of them were in the less developed countries (LDCs) of Asia, Africa, and South America (Figure 3-2). Living standards in these nations are already inadequate. The increased population pressure is already straining their environments and their economic, social, and political structures. In Mexico and Central America, where unemployment rates reach almost 50 percent, the sharply increasing population will triple the number of people looking for work in less than 50 years. Even the United States is experiencing substantial population growth—equal to four Washington, D.C.s, every year, another New Jersey every 3 years, and one more California every decade!

Since 1970, the global population growth rate has slowly decreased. Most of the slowdown has occurred in the (LDCs) of Asia and South America. **Zero Population Growth (ZPG)** has actually been attained in some European countries. However, *the global growth rate decrease does not mean that the earth's population will*

44

FIGURE 3-1   Population "crush" on planet Earth.

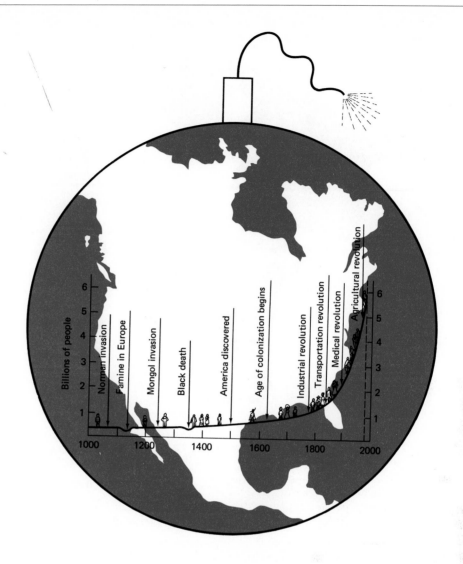

stop growing (Figure 3-3). For example between 1987 and 2020, the world population will increase by nearly 3 billion people.

BIRTH AND DEATH RATES

Before we look at the impacts of the exploding human population and suggest some strategies to control it, we will discuss some measurements used to describe populations.

The **birth rate** is the number of persons born per 1,000 individuals in a given year. The **death rate** is the number of persons per 1,000 individuals who die in a particular year. The difference between the birth and death rates is known as the **rate of natural increase** (or **decrease**). If the death rate is higher, the population will decrease; if the birth rate is higher, the population will increase (see Figure 3-4 for data on the United States). The global birth rate in 1989 was 28, while the death rate was 10. Therefore, the rate of natural increase was 18 per 1,000.

Figure 3-5 shows the population growth rates for the more developed countries (MDC's) and LDCs. Note that the population of the LDCs is increasing much more rapidly than that of the MDCs (Figure 3-6).

The **population growth rate** of a nation can be calculated as a percentage as follows:

percent annual growth rate =

birth rate − death rate × 100

Therefore, the *percent annual growth rate* for the world in 1989 is determined as follows:

$$\frac{28}{1000} - \frac{10}{1000} = \frac{18}{1000}$$

$$\frac{18}{1000} \times 100 = 1.8 \text{ percent}$$

Note the global population growth curve in Figure 3-6. The number of humans increased slowly at first but

FIGURE 3-2 The world's ten largest urban areas—1985.

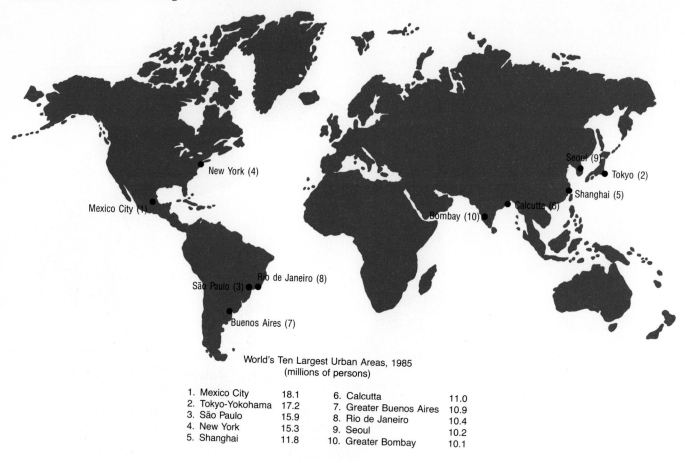

World's Ten Largest Urban Areas, 1985
(millions of persons)

1. Mexico City	18.1	6. Calcutta	11.0
2. Tokyo-Yokohama	17.2	7. Greater Buenos Aires	10.9
3. São Paulo	15.9	8. Rio de Janeiro	10.4
4. New York	15.3	9. Seoul	10.2
5. Shanghai	11.8	10. Greater Bombay	10.1

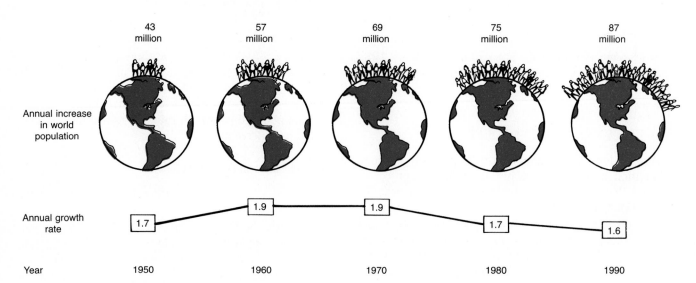

FIGURE 3-3 Despite the fact that the world's annual population growth rate is decreasing, the number of people in the world is still increasing rapidly.

FIGURE 3-4 Components of population change in the United States, 1960–1985. U.S. population growth is a product of birth rates, death rates, and net immigration.

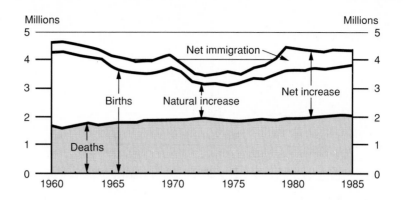

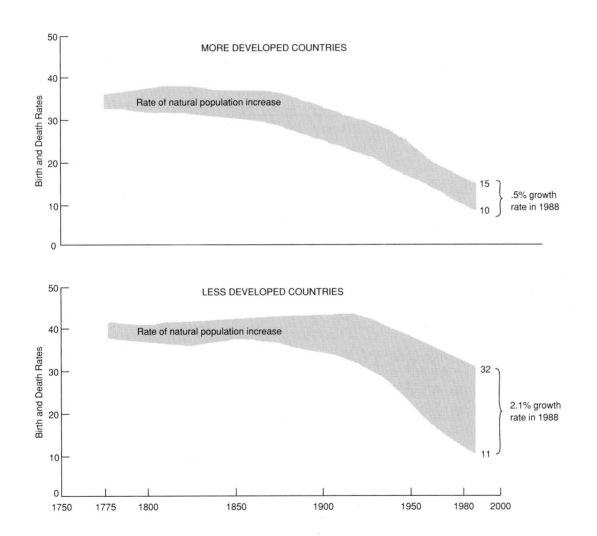

FIGURE 3-5   Comparison of population growth rates in developed and less-developed countries.

FIGURE 3-6 Comparison of population increase in developed and less-developed countries, 1750–2100.

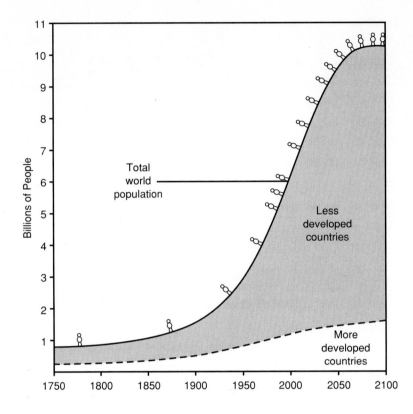

then accelerated rapidly. Such extremely rapid growth is called **exponential**.

Exponential growth occurs any time a quantity or an activity grows by a fixed percentage. A bank account growing at 4.5 percent a year is growing exponentially *if* the interest is retained. As shown in Figure 3-6, exponential growth follows a J-shaped curve. The slow initial growth is followed by a rapid upswing in absolute numbers. No matter if it's a population or resource use or pollution, the rapid upswing can be difficult to deal with.

To determine how long it takes a given population to double in size, you can divide 70 by the percent annual growth rate. The result is the doubling time. For the global population (as of 1989) **doubling time** is

$$\frac{70}{1.8} = 38.9 \text{ years}$$

REDUCING DEATH RATES: POPULATION IMBALANCE

Many regard today's medical technology and improved sanitation as a wonder, a boon for humans. However, advanced medical technology and sanitation are largely responsible for the present surge in human numbers. Before the advent of modern medicine, human mortality rates were much higher. Three centuries B.C., Aristotle noted that "most babies die before the week is out."

At one time, humankind was extemely vulnerable to the lethal attacks of infectious parasites such as viruses, bacteria, and protozoa. Medieval lands were scourged with killing plagues, which killed over 25 million people in Asia and Europe. Smallpox spread like wildfire and killed one out of every four afflicted persons until Jenner developed his vaccine at the close of the eighteenth century. A child born in 1550 had a life expectancy of only *8.5 years*. In 1900 the prime killer was tuberculosis, with pneumonia running a close second. As late as 1919, the influenza virus took a toll of 25 million people.

Since then, the mortality picture has drastically changed. Tuberculosis and pneumonia are controlled with antibiotics, and effective vaccines have been developed against smallpox, tetanus, diphtheria, whooping cough, and many other diseases. Largely because of modern medicine, the world death rate of 25 per 1,000 in 1935 fell to about 10 per 1,000 by 1989. Disease was also held in check by improved sanitation—sewage systems that diverted human waste from drinking water supplies.

Early in the twentieth century, the mosquito-borne disease malaria was either directly or indirectly responsible for 50 percent of all heman mortality. This disease was held in check by insecticides such as DDT. Consider Ceylon. Because of the intensive malarial-control campaign launched there in 1946, the Ceylonese mortality rate was reduced form 22 to 13 per 1,000 in only six years.

Will AIDS Correct the Imbalance?

In the mid-1980's, a new human disease, known as **acquired immune deficiency syndrome (AIDS)**, began spreading rapidly through the African population and then throughout the rest of the world. Caused by a virus, this disease is transmitted during sexual intercourse, drug injections, and blood transfusions, as well as from an infected pregnant woman to her fetus. The AIDS virus destroys the person's defense against infectious diseases such as tuberculosis and pneumonia. This lethal disease is spreading rapidly. For example, even though there were only about 150,000 cases worldwide in 1988, it is expected that there will be an additional 1.1 million cases by 1992! A cure for this disease may not be developed for 20 years. By that time, AIDS may have killed 20 percent of the black population of Africa and millions of people on other continents as well. Ultimately, AIDS may kill at least as many people as were killed by the Black Death in the 14th century (See Figure 3-1). This devastating disease may eventually bring our global population more in balance with the resource supply upon which it depends.

Demographic Transition: Helping to Reestablish the Balance

Disease can help stabilize populations but so can other factors. One of those is the **demographic transition**. Demographic transition is the name given to a particular type of change in a population. It occurs when a country goes from high birth and death rates to low birth and death rates, as shown in Figure 3-7. This transition usually occurs when a nation becomes industrialized. Virtually all of the industrialized European nations, as well as the United States, Canada, and Japan, have undergone the demographic transition. Note the four characteristic stages of the demographic transition shown in Figure 3-7, using Finland as an example. In stage 1 (preindustrial), the Finnish people had large families because many children were required to work the farm and to provide financial security for parents in their old age. In stage II, death rates fell because of improving economic and social conditions. At this time, the discrepancy between birth rates and death rates resulted in rapid population growth. It was not until stage III that birth rates began to fall. The decline in birth rates during stage III may have several explanations:

1. An increasing percentage of families moved from rural areas to urban areas, where a large number of children are no longer needed to help with farm chores.
2. Increasing educational and employment opportunities for women caused them to delay marriage and, therefore, to have fewer children.
3. The high standard of living demanded by a married couple made it financially impossible for them to have many children.

The decline in birth rates is caused by industrial development. Unfortunately, many of the LDCs are stuck in stage II (transition) with low death rates and high birth rates, resulting in rapid population growth. Many LDCs, like Ghana, Chad, and India, simply cannot depend upon industrial development to carry them

FIGURE 3-7 Characteristic features of the demographic transition.

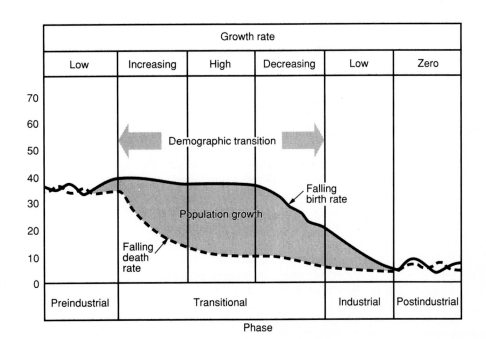

FIGURE 3-8   Characteristic population age structure profiles for (a) rapidly growing, (b) stable, and (c) declining populations.

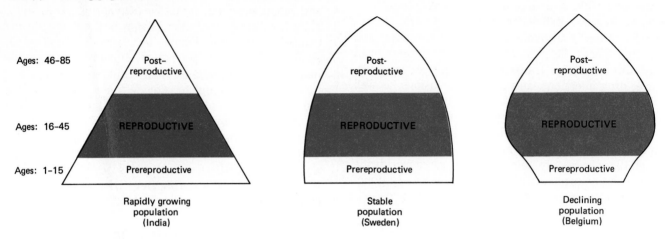

through the demographic transition and bring about a reduction in birth rates. Why? There are several reasons:

1. They lack the large number of highly trained people upon which industrial development depends.
2. They lack the essential energy base represented by such resources as coal, oil, and natural gas.
3. They simply do not have enough *time*. Substantial industrial development cannot be accomplished in less than several decades, even with trained personnel and abundant energy resources. With the populations of many of these nations doubling every 33 years or less, time is running out!
4. Many countries also lack the financial resources needed to develop economically.

AGE STRUCTURE OF A POPULATION

The **total fertility rate (TFR)** is the number of children a woman produces in her life. Since 1972, the TFR of American women has been well below the **replacement level fertility**, the number of children born that exactly replaces the number of people who die. If this is true, why do population experts predict that our nation's population will continue to increase well into the twenty-first century? This seeming contradiction can be explained by the age structure of our population. The **age structure** is the number of individuals occurring in each age class within the population.

By examining the profile of an **age-structure diagram**, it is possible to determine whether a given population is growing rapidly, growing slowly, or remaining stable (See Figure 3-8). An age-structure diagram for a typical LDC has a very broad base and a narrow apex—a shape characteristic of a rapidly growing population. Indeed, the doubling time for these population is about 20 to 40 years. Typical age-structure diagrams for an MDC like the United States have a somewhat narrower base and steeper sides. They are characteristic of a slowly growing population whose doubling time is 40 to 120 years. The age-structure diagram for most European countries has a still narrower base, which indicates an extremely slow growth rate, with doubling times of 121 to 3,000 years.

When considering age structure, it is useful to divide the population into three major age groups: *prereproductive* (ages 1 to 15), *reproductive* (ages 16 to 45), and *postreproductive* (ages 46 to 85 +). Current population growth, of course, depends on the number and fertility of the females in the age group 15 to 45. *Future* population growth, on the other hand, depends ultimately on the females who are now in the age group 1 to 15. (A comparison of population profiles for the years 1960 and 1988 in the United States is shown in Figure 3-9).

Consider, as an example, the U.S. "baby boom" during the years 1955–1959, as indicated by the broad base in Figure 3-10. As the years passed, this population bulge gradually moved upward in the age-structure pyramid. Eventually, many of the females in the baby-boom population attained reproductive age.

It is the size of this pre-reproductive group that tells the future of a population, especially today. At the present time, 33 percent of the world's population is under 15 years of age. (In Mexico the figure is 42 percent!) Thus, we have a built-in mechanism for explosive population growth in the near future. From the standpoint of population control, this is an extremely distressing situation. After all, there are already more women of childbearing age on this planet than there have ever been—about 800 million.

FIGURE 3-9 A comparison of U.S. age-sex population profiles for 1960, when the population was growing rapidly, and for 1988 when the population was stabilizing.

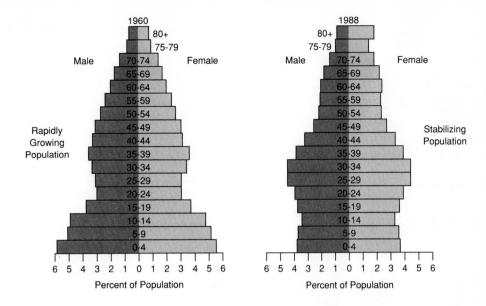

TWO KINDS OF OVERPOPULATION

Two basic types of overpopulation threaten the fragile life support systems of our planet. One is called Malthusian, the other is technological.

Malthusian Overpopulation

Malthusian overpopulation occurs in the LDCs. This type of overpopulation is named after Robert Malthus, a British economist, who stated in 1798 that populations tend to increase faster than food supplies. The only way population will come into balance with the available food supply, according to Malthus, is by a massive die-off caused by starvation, disease, war, or some other calamity. The most important factor in Malthusian overpopulation is population size. It is simply a matter of too many stomachs and not enough food. For example, at present growth rates, the populations of Kenya, Nigeria, Tanzania, and Uganda will double in only 23 years. Such a population surge results in the malnutrition and starvation of 800 million people worldwide today.

The effects of Malthusian overpopulation are grimly described in the following extract by Lee Ranck, an executive of an international relief organization. The following is merely one of many similar tragedies that he often observed while on an extended tour through several of the approximately 100 LDCs, where a majority of people live in appalling poverty and chronic malnutrition (see Figure 3-11).

Hunger is more than cold facts and awesome statistics. Hunger has a face. I know. I have looked into it. Hunger is a Bengali face—a little mother named Jobeda whom I found in the shade of a tattered leanto in a refugee camp in Dacca. A small withered form lying close beside her whimpered and stirred. Instinctively she reached down to brush away the flies. Her hand carefully wiped the fevered face of her child. At six years acute malnutrition had crippled his legs, left him dumb, and robbed him of his hearing. All that was left was the shallow, labored breathing of life itself, and that, too, would soon be gone. But death is not stranger to Jobeda. She has seen starvation take away her husband and five of her seven children. . . .

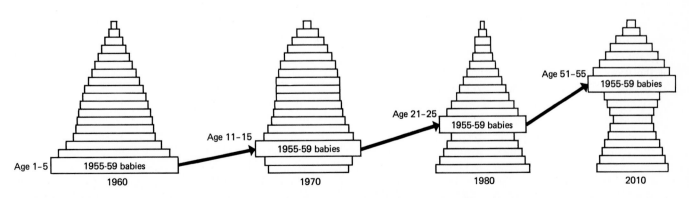

FIGURE 3-10 The U.S. "baby boom" bulge of 1955–1959 moves up the population profile as the decades pass.

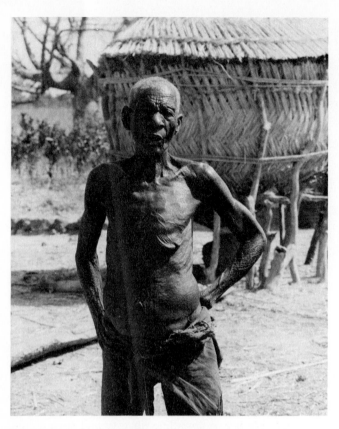

FIGURE 3-11 An aged woman suffering from undernourishment in famine-plagued Africa.

Today 100,000 people will die either directly or indirectly from starvation and malnutrition. Tomorrow 100,000 more. Although the causes of these deaths are multiple, certainly the basic cause is Malthusian overpopulation: too many human stomachs and not enough food, a problem discussed at length in Chapter 6.

Technological Overpopulation

The second type of overpopulation taxing the earth's life support systems is **technological overpopulation** (Figure 3-12). It is characteristic of the MDCs (the United States, Japan, West Germany, the Soviet Union, and others). Here the most important factors when considering environmental impact are the resources used and the pollution generated per person. The United States and other MDCs are using more than their fair share of the world's resources. A relatively small population may therefore cause considerably more damage. Instead of dying from starvation, people are killed by the pollutants their technology has generated.

The effects of technological overpopulation are not hard to find. They are visible all around us—right here in the United States. Following are some examples:

1. Between 1987 and 2000, Americans will generate over 1 billion tons of solid waste. Each of us is

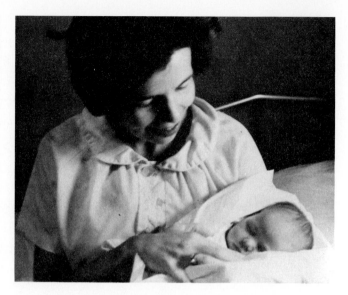

FIGURE 3-12 The population of the United States is increased by one! The average number of children per family in the United States has dropped from 3.5 in the 1960s to 1.8 in 1988.

responsible for over half a metric ton of garbage a year!

2. Over 20 million metric tons of sulfur dioxide released into the air from the stacks of power plants and other sources, is forming **acid precipitation**. Acid precipitation is destroying the fish populations of hundreds of lakes, leaching valuable nutrients from farmlands, and stunting the growth of forests and food crops the world over.

3. Each year, more than 450 million kilograms (1 billion pounds) of phosphorus are washed from fertilized American farmlands into lakes and streams. The result is widespread degradation characterized by the explosive growth of algae and weeds, lowered levels of dissolved oxygen, fish kills, foul smells, and the defilement of scenic beauty.

4. "Buckshot" urbanization results in the loss of 400,000 hectares (1 million acres) of top-quality farmland in the United States each year.

5. Massive bulldozers and other earth-moving equipment have laid bare the soil during highway and building construction projects. The result is accelerated erosion. Poor soil management on U.S. Farms and ranches results in additional soil erosion totaling nearly 3 billion metric tons per year.

6. The operation of nuclear power plants, as well as the development and testing of nuclear weapons, have resulted in a serious waste problem. Tens of thousands of kilograms of high-level radioactive waste are now in temporary storage, awaiting a safe permanent disposal site.

7. In the Love Canal region of Niagara Falls, New York, the ground and surface water were so badly polluted by toxic chemicals from a waste dump that the federal government designated it a disaster area. Eight hundred families were forced to move elsewhere because of the imminent danger to their health.

8. Each year U.S. factories produce an estimated 270 million metric tons of waste considered hazardous by state and federal standards—over 1 metric ton per person!

9. Habitat destruction, pollution, and/or overhunting have caused severe population declines of wildlife, such as the red wolf, peregrine falcon, and California condor.

Taken together, these events represent an environmental horror as serious as the starvation and malnutrition problem in the poor nations of the world. In a sense, the problems in the United States (and other industrialized nations) are also the result of **overpopulation**—too many people for the available resources. Americans demand a lifestyle that cannot be supported without intensive consumption of resources and considerable environmental contamination.

Throughout the remainder of this book, you will see these two types of overpopulation in discussions of soil erosion, air and water pollution, wildlife extinction, the energy crisis, the toxic chemical problem, or global starvation.

METHODS OF BIRTH CONTROL

As we view (and feel) the crush of people on this planet, it may come as an ironic surprise that humans have practiced various methods of birth control for centuries. (Obviously, they weren't very effective!) Contraception was advocated on ancient Egyptian papyri dating back to 5,000 B.C. A great variety of techniques were tried. For example, a combination of wool fibers and alligator dung was used by women as a vaginal barrier to sperm. Men often used condoms fashioned from animal bladders. Foul-tasting concoctions made from bark fibers, weeds, and ground gall bladders were gulped down prior to intercourse in the erroneous belief that conception would be prevented.

Of the world's 800 million couples of childbearing age, 1 out of 4 practice some form of birth control. Of course, a much greater variety, as well as more effective methods, are available today than in ancient times. Many have been developed in the past 30 years. A major breakthrough was the development of the **pill**—a chemical contraceptive that prevents the female from ovulating. It is the most widely used contraceptive in the MDCs, such as the United States and England. The worldwide rate of use ranges from 0 percent to Mauri-

tania (Africa) to 13.5 percent in the United States and a high of 40 percent in Austria.

Another type of contraceptive is a plastic or nylon loop that is inserted into the uterus. Known as **intrauterine devices (IUDs)**, they apparently prevent the embryo from embedding in the uterine lining. IUD manufacturing plants have been built in some of the LDCs so these contraceptives can be readily available on a mass basis. The senior author has an acquaintance who wears IUDs as earrings to coffee parties in order to emphasize her position on the importance of birth control! The rate of IUD use among women of childbearing age ranges from 0 percent in Mauritania (Africa) to 4.8 percent in the United States to 30 and 37 percent in China and Cuba, respectively.

Sterilization is another major method of contraception. Basically, it involves cutting the sperm ducts in the male or the egg tubes in the female. Its worldwide use among couples of childbearing age ranges from 0 percent in the Ivory Coast (Africa) to 28 percent in the United States to a high of 35 percent in Canada. Sterilization has become more popular in the United States in recent years. Among LDCs, it is the method of choice in India, El Salvador, and Korea.

Abortion

In case of contraceptive failure a woman may terminate her pregnancy by an abortion rather than give birth to an unwanted child. An **abortion** is a premature expulsion of the fetus from the womb that results in fetal death. Many abortions occur naturally, and fortunately so, because almost 40 percent of these aborted fetuses would otherwise have developed into either physically or mentally impaired individuals. Some abortions, on the other hand, are caused by human intervention and result in the death of a fetus that otherwise would probably have developed into a normal, healthy baby.

The legalization of artificial abortion has become an effective method of birth control. The U.S. Supreme Court legalized abortions in 1972. There are obviously strong ethical, moral, and religious arguments against the legalization of abortion. What right does a human who is living today have to take the life of another human, who, except for the violent act of abortion, would be alive tomorrow? In the eyes of many eminent persons in the law, medicine, and religion, except in the case of incest or a life threat to the mother, the willful act of abortion is murder. This is the view currently held by President Bush. In 1989, the Supreme Court upheld the state's rights to restrict abortions using state monies, which has touched off what could prove to be a long, drawnout battle over abortions.

On a global basis, abortion is the third most widely used method of birth control after sterilization and the pill. In fact, were it not for the practice of abortion, the resources of this planet would have to sustain another

50 million people every year. Abortion is being used primarily by the women of Asia, Africa, and Latin America. Abortion rates are high in Latin America, even though the act is illegal. Unfortunately, many of the illegal abortions are self-induced with wires, coat hangers, or pointed sticks, and are 75 times more dangerous to the mother than legal abortions performed by the medical profession.

New Methods

There is an urgent need for more effective long-term birth control methods that are especially suited to the rural poor of the LDCs. Several new antifertility technologies are likely to be available in the 1990s.

In 1988 a French pharmaceutical firm developed an abortion pill called **RU-486**. When used within 10 days after a woman misses her period, RU-486 will induce a relatively safe abortion. Another development is a plastic ring that is inserted into the vagina. It gradually releases hormones that prevent conception. Hormone injections, such as Depo-Provera, that prevent pregnancy for 1–3 months, have recently been approved for use in at least 90 countries. *Norplant* is another contraceptive that holds considerable promise. It consists of time-release capsules filled with steroids that are implanted under the skin. A single Norplant implant ensures the woman's inability to conceive for at least 5 years! Indonesia, Thailand, and China are among the 12 nations for which Norplant has been approved for use as of 1989.

POPULATION TRENDS IN THE MDCs

This is the bright side of the global population picture. The TFR has steadily decreased in the MDCs of Western Europe, Canada, and the United States. At the current rate of growth it would take almost 100 years for the population of North America to double, and about 350 years for that of Europe.

A number of MDCs in Europe have already completed the demographic transition. As a result, their populations have either stabilized at ZPG (Belgium, Denmark, East Germany, Italy, and the United Kingdom) or are actually declining (Austria, France, Hungary, and West Germany).

What is the population picture in the United States? Unfortunately, according to Paul Ehrlich, population expert at Stanford University, our population will increase substantially, at least until the end of the century. Fortunately, however, the *long-term* population trends for our nation are much more encouraging. After all, since 1972, average TFR for the United States has been about 1.8. This is substantially below 2.1, the replacement rate. This means that eventually our pop-

ulation will indeed level off. However, we must remember at present our annual net immigration rate is about 500,000 to 1,000,000. If we assume that this rate of immigration will continue, our nation will probably not be able to attain ZPG until about 2050—when most of the students reading this material will be elderly. In 1989 the U.S. Population Census Bureau estimated that our nation's population would gradually rise from 247 million to a peak of 302 million by 2038 and then begin to decline.

POPULATION TRENDS IN THE LDCs

This is the discouraging side of the global population picture. Dozens of nations in Central and South America, Africa, and Asia have been caught in the **demographic trap** in which death control has occurred without birth control. In most of these nations, which represent more than half of the global population, natural resources are being overtaxed, and per capita food supplies and income are declining.

Large Family Size

In contrast to the MDCs, where the desired number of children per family ranges from zero to three, the LDCs of Asia, Africa, and Latin America, with a few exceptions such as China, prefer to have much larger families. For example, couples are having, on average 6.1 children in Syria and Ghana (Africa), and 6.3 in the Sudan (Africa) and Jordan. In the African nation of Mauritania average family size is 9.2—the largest desired family size for any nation on earth.

There are a number of ingrained cultural reasons for this desire for large families. First, children are needed to help with household tasks, such as gathering wood and dried cow dung for fuel or bringing water from distant streams. Second, children are needed to provide security to the parents in old age. Most MDCs such as the United States, England, and Sweden, have well-developed social security programs to support their older citizens when their wage-earning years are over. However, in the LDCs, for the most part, such programs are lacking. A third reason for large family size in the LDCs has to do with the macho image desired by many males. The larger the family, the greater the status of the father. Many children are fathered out of wedlock as well. A man named Denja, from the province of Nyanza, in Kenya (Africa), boasts of being the father of 497 children! Yet another reason for large family size in the LDCs is that birth control methods such as chemical contraceptives, sterilization, and abortion are strictly forbidden by the religion of the prospective parents. For example, in Mexico, Kenya, and the Philippines, where populations are soaring, the Catholic Church is firmly opposed to any artificial method of birth control. A similar stand has been taken by the Muslim fundmentalists in Pakistan, Egypt, and Iran.

Lester Brown, president of the Worldwatch Institute, a highly respected environmental organization, views the continued population surge as a dire threat to the world's resources and the quality of human life. He strongly urges that the number of children per family the world over should be no more than two, and in some nations only one. To this end, the governments of the LDCs must launch effective mass education programs on birth control, not only in cities but in the rural areas, where the great majority of the people live. Although such efforts have begun in some nations, they must be greatly expanded and intensified.

Efforts to develop strong family planning programs in the LDCs were recently evaluated by two sociologists, Robert J. Lapham and W. Parker Mauldin. The programs of 100 nations were measured on a scale from 0 (non-existent) to 120 (maximum possible). The average score for all Asian nations was 83 (strong), for Latin America 56 (moderate), for the Middle East and North Africa 31 (weak), and only 17 (very weak) for sub-Saharan Africa. Of the 100 LDCs China had the highest score, 101 (very strong), while Libya, Laos, and Mongolia rated zero.

Population Problems in Africa

No continent has suffered more from the adverse impact of rapid population increase than Africa. Consider the following demographic features of this continent:

1. The African population will increase from just under 500 million in 1980 to 1.5 billion in 2025—a threefold increase in only 45 years!

2. At current growth rates, the nations of Kenya, Rwanda, Uganda, Liberia, and Nigeria will double their populations in less than 24 years.

3. The average annual population growth will remain dangerously high (about 3 percent) at least until the year 2000.

4. Even if strong population curbs could be initiated *immediately*, the continent's population will continue to soar far into the next century.

5. The population in Africa has greatly exceeded the carrying capacity of the continent. Excessive demands have been made on soil, water, rangelands, forests, and wildlife. As a result of the degradation of these resources, the quality of life for many Africans has sharply decreased. Nigeria, for example, experienced an overall 28 percent reduction in per capita income during the period 1980–1986.

Consider Kenya, an African nation where population growth has reached critical proportions. The estimated birth rate for the period (1985–1990) is 54.2, *the highest in the world*. In 1986 the TFR was 8 at a time when the global TFR was only 3.6. With a growth rate of 4.1 percent, Kenya's doubling time in 1989 was only 17 years compared to 41 years for the world as a whole. This high rate of population growth has largely been responsible for an 8 percent *decrease* in per capita income during the period 1980–1986.

There is hope, however. In 1977 the Kenyan government implemented a Family Planning Program. This project has already yielded some encouraging results: (1) average desired family size has dropped from 7.2 to 6.2 since 1977; (2) 80 percent of the women are now aware of at least one method of birth control; (3) the proportion of women using contraceptives rose from 7 percent in 1977 to 17 percent in 1984 and is increasing steadily; and (4) two-thirds of the married women are interested in limiting their family size.

Nevertheless, by 2000 the population of Kenya will likely reach 38 million—roughly 52 percent higher than the 24 million of 1989!

Control of Population Growth in China

China's great famine of 1958–1962, in which 30 million people starved to death, was a grim warning to its leaders that the theory advanced by Robert Malthus is probably correct. However, it was not until the late 1970s that the nation's State Birth Planning Commission initiated the most comprehensive, the most rigidly enforced, and probably the most effective population control program in human history. The results have been impressive: The TRF has been reduced from 5.9 in the late 1960s to the replacement level of 2.1 today; the crude birth rate has fallen from 36.9 to 18.4, and the annual population growth has declined from 2.6 to 1.1.

Let's examine the major features of this remarkably successful program:

1. A mass education program was launched to foster public understanding of the adverse future effects on living standards if China's population was not curbed. Long-term projections were made public concerning how much food, water, energy, and other resources each person would have if China continued on its course into the demographic trap.

2. The education program included a strong emphasis on postponing marriage to reduce the average family size.

3. Another educational objective was to make the one-child family the norm among recently married couples.

4. Couples who made the commitment to a one-child family received multiple benefits, including (a) cash payments, (b) free family-planning education, (c) larger old-age pensions, so that extra children would

not be needed to provide security to the parents in their later years, (d) better housing and employment, and (e) free schooling for children.

5. Family-planning education was made readily available and publicized widely throughout all available media.

6. Abortions, sterilizations, the fitting of IUDs, and the dispensation of birth control pills were done by local people who had been specially trained as nurses or paramedics.

7. Penalties were imposed on couples who had more than two children after entering the program. Among the penalties were (a) an increase in taxes, (b) compulsory sterilization for either the father or the mother, (c) the return to the state of all financial benefits awarded to the couple because of their agreement to curb family size to the state, (d) intense peer pressure for a woman pregnant with her third child to have an abortion, and (e) reduction of food, employment, and educational benefits for both parents and children.

China's family planning program gained momentum rapidly, especially in the urban areas. By 1982, for example, 70 percent of the couples in China's three largest cities—Shanghai, Beijing, and Tientsin—with an aggregate population of more than 20 million, had agreed to have no more than one child. The goal of the Birth Planning Commission is to achieve ZPG by 2000, with a population of 1.2 billion, followed by a decline to 800 million by 2100.

Although China's population control program has been eminently successful from a technical standpoint, many democratic nations, including the United States, have been deeply concerned that the Chinese government makes sterilization mandatory after a woman has had her second child. The United States has funded population control programs in the LDCs for many years through such organizations as the World Bank, the Agency for International Development, and the United Nations. However, because of China's coercive sterilization and abortion policy, the U.S. government has withdrawn all support for the United Nations Fund for Population Activities, an agency that provides financial assistance to China's population control program—and many others as well.

HUMAN POPULATION AND THE EARTH'S CARRYING CAPACITY

Ecologists define **carrying capacity** as the ability of a particular environment to support a certain population of a species for an extended period of time. For example, they might determine that the carrying capacity of a particular forest for deer is 1,000 head.

It is imperative that the human species not exceed the carrying capacity of the earth to sustain it. Unfortunately, no one knows the earth's carrying capacity for *Homo sapiens*. Some experts believe that this planet could sustain at least 10 to 50 billion people. Others think the number is closer to 500 million.

At the risk of a gross oversimplification, let us assume that our global population can follow two alternative paths, as shown in Figure 3-13. In scenario A, our population continues to grow exponentially and overshoots the earth's carrying capacity by a wide margin. This would eventually result in a die-off (caused by starvation, disease, pollution, and resource pollution), which would reduce our population to the carrying capacity level. It is important to understand that simply expanding food production may permit more people to be sustained over the short term. However, the long-term result would be a human ecosystem that would be severely out of balance. For in the process of producing more and more food to fill more and more stomachs, we would severely deplete our natural resources, generate massive amounts of air and water pollution, and cause the extinction of many forms of wildlife.

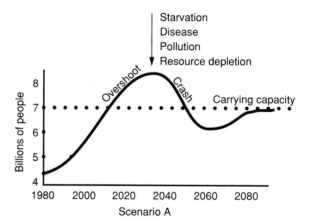

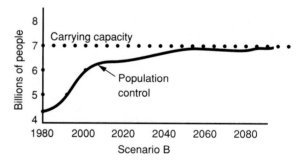

FIGURE 3-13 Population growth and carrying capacity. Scenario A. Population overshoots carrying capacity. Eventually there is a massive die-off due to starvation, disease, pollution, and resource depletion. Scenario B. Before the population reaches carrying capacity intensive efforts are made at population control (family planning, use of contraceptives, delayed marriage, and so on). As a result, population gradually reaches carrying capacity and die-off is prevented.

The preferred alternative, shown in Scenario B, is a gradual reduction in the rate of population growth, long before it reaches the carrying capacity level, by means of the strategies discussed earlier in this chapter. Eventually, our population would stabilize at the level of the carrying capacity, at which point the human species and the environment with which it interacts would become part of an ecological system that could be sustainable far into the future.

RAPID REVIEW

1. The global population is increasing at the rate of 234,000 per day—equal to the daily increase of another Syracuse, New York.

2. Each year, the world's population is increasing by 87 million—equal to nine New York Cities or two Englands.

3. The *birth rate* is the number of persons born per 1,000 individuals in a given year.

4. The *death rate* is the number of deaths per 1,000 individuals in a given year.

5. The *rate of natural increase* (or *decrease*) is the *difference* between the birth and death rates. The world's rate of natural increase at present is about 18 per 1,000.

6. The percent annual growth rate for the world population at present is about 1.8.

7. The doubling time for the global population at present is about 39 years.

8. Unless a cure for AIDS is found, the disease is expected to destroy 20 percent of the African black population by 2010.

9. When nations become industrialized, they undergo a *demographic transition*. This is characterized by a reduction in both birth and death rates. Many of the LDCs are stuck in stage II of the demographic transition, which is characterized by a falling death rate combined with a high birth rate.

10. The *age structure* of a population is the number of individuals occurring in each age class.

11. The age-structure diagram of a rapidly growing population has a broad base, wheras the diagram of one that is growing very slowly has a narrow base.

12. At the present time, 33 percent of the world's population is under 15 years of age.

13. *Malthusian overpopulation* means too many people for the available food supply. It is characteristic of the LDCs of Asia, Africa, and South America.

14. *Technological overpopulation* refers to an overabundance of people, usually in industrialized countries, who, because of their use of advanced technology, have a harmful effect on the environment.

15. Environmental damage caused by technological overpopulation includes depletion of resources, pollution of air, land, and water; defilement of scenic beauty; wildlife extinction; and the release of chemicals that may be hazardous to human health.

16. Advances in medicine (including modern surgical techniques, the development of vaccines and antibiotics) and sanitation have, ironically, contributed to the present population explosion on earth.

17. Of the world's 800 million couples of childbearing age, 1 in 4 practice some method of birth control.

18. The U.S. Supreme Court legalized abortions in 1972, but in 1989 they voted to uphold the states' rights to restrict state-funded abortions. Many fear that abortions will become more and more difficult to obtain.

19. On a global basis, abortion is the most widely used method of birth control after sterilization and the pill.

20. The United States has an influx of about 500,000 legal and 100,000 to 400,000 illegal immigrants yearly.

21. Since 1972, the average TFR for the United States has been about 1.8, substantially below 2.1, the rate at which the number of people born replace the number who die.

22. The United States will probably not attain ZPG until 2050.

23. Populations are declining in Austria, France, Hungary, and West Germany.

24. At current growth rates, Kenya, Rwanda, Uganda, Liberia, and Nigeria will double their populations in less than 24 years.

25. The major features of China's population control program, which will have reduced the TFR to replacement level (2.1) as of 1990, are the following: (a) mass education on family planning, (b) delayed marriage, (c) multiple educational, health, and economic benefits for one-child families, (d) family planning services provided by specially trained local people, and (e) mandatory sterilizations or abortions for families having more than two children.

KEY WORDS AND PHRASES

Abortion
Acid rain
Acquired immune defi-
    ciency syndrome (AIDS)
Age-structure diagram
Baby boom
Birth rate
Carrying capacity
China
Contraceptives
Death rate
Delayed marriage
Demographic transition
Demographic trap
Doubling time
Exponential growth
Extinction
Family planning
Immigration
Intrauterine device (IUD)
Less developed countries
    (LDCs)

Love Canal
Malthusian overpopula-
    tion
More developed countries
    (MDCs)
Norplant
Percent annual growth
    rate
Pill
Radioactive waste
Rate of natural increase
Replacement rate
RU-486
State Birth Planning
    Commission (China)
Sterilization
Technological overpopu-
    lation
Total fertility rate (TFR)
Zero population growth
    (ZPG)

QUESTIONS AND TOPICS FOR DISCUSSION

1. Construct a simple graph that indicates (roughly) the buildup of the human population since humans appeared on earth.

2. Compare public health conditions that prevailed in medieval times with those of today. What were the major causes of mortality then? What are the major causes today?

3. What is the global birth, death, and natural increase?

4. How is the percent annual growth rate determined?

5. How do we determine how long it would take for a population to double?

6. List three reasons why birth rates tend to decrease when the standard of living rises.

7. The United States receives an influx of about 500,000 to 1,000,000 immigrants yearly. Do you approve of such an influx? Why or why not? What benefits might result? What might be the disadvantages to the United States?

8. Does a decrease in the fertility rate of a nation necessarily indicate that that nation's population is decreasing as well? Why or why not?

9. Describe the shape of age-structure diagrams for (a) rapidly growing populations, (b) slowly growing populations, (c) stable populations, and (d) declining populations.

10. Would a study of age-structure diagrams of the U.S. population be of benefit to automobile manufacturers? The agricultural industry? School administrators? Why?

11. Give five examples of environmental stress caused by the technological overpopulation experienced by the United States today.

12. Compare the population trends of the MDCs and LDCs.

13. Discuss the major features of China's population control program.

14. Discuss future population growth in terms of the carrying capacity of the earth.

SUGGESTED READINGS

Brown, L. R., and J. Jacobsen. *Our Demographically Divided World—1986.* Washington, D.C.: Worldwatch Institute, 1987. A detailed look at the current population crisis.

Brown, L. R., and E. C. Wolf. "Reclaiming the Future," in: *State of the World—1988.* New York: Norton, 1988. Advances the thesis that science is failing to assess the impact of human activity on the global environment.

Haub, C. "Trial by Numbers." *Sierra*, Vol. 73, pp. 30, 35, 1988. The "burst" of the population "bomb" is yet to come. Highly readable.

Mellor, J. W., and S. Gavian. "Famine: Causes, Prevention and Relief.", *Science*, Vol. 235, pp. 539–544, 1987. The population surge compounds starvation problems in the United States.

Repetto, R. *Population, Resources, Environment.* Washington, D.C.: World Resources Institute, 1988. The author examines the economic and environmental consequences of rapid population growth in the LDCs.

Steinhart, P. "Personal Boundaries." *Audubon*, Vol. 88, pp. 8, 10–11, 1986. High densities of people cause loss of human dignity in LDCs.

U.S. Bureau of the Census. *Current Population Reports.* Washington, D.C.: U.S. Government Printing Office, 1988. These are up-to-date statistics on population dyanmics of the United States.

Zhipei, Z. "China's Population Program." (Letter). *Science*, Vol. 238, pp. 1025–1026, 1987. Interesting comments on China's population program by a member of China's State Family Planning Commission.

4

The Nature of Soils

"Civilization is only skin deep"—so the saying goes. In this chapter we examine the "skin"—the soil—that forms a thin layer around the surface of the earth. It is this soil upon which human survival depends.

VALUE OF SOIL

Most city dwellers equate soil with "dirt," but to the farmer, soil is the essence of survival. The farmer's economic well-being is inextricably linked with the fertility of the soil. It may mean the difference between a squalid four-room shack and a comfortable ranch house, between an old "klunker" and a new car, or between eighth-grade schooling and a university education for the children.

Empires and nations, like individuals, are dependent on the soil. To the extent that a nation's soil resources are fertile and abundant, that state will have vigor and stability. When that resource is exhausted because of the mounting demands of a swelling population or mismanagement, the nation's survival is in danger. Some historians believe that the decline and fall of the mighty Roman Empire may be attributed as much to the deterioration of the soils in the Roman granary of northern Africa as to political corruption and the invader's prowess. Throughout the annals of recorded human history, soil has been valued highly and has been as attractive a war prize as armaments, buildings, industries, or slaves. During the long search for fertile soil, hitherto peaceful, responsible empires have turned into militant aggressors.

Soil Formation

The development of a mature soil is a complex process that may require centuries to complete (Figure 4-1). Major factors involved include (1) climate, (2) type of parent material, (3) living organisms, (4) topography, and (5) time.

CLIMATE. *Physical Weathering (Disintegration).* Physical weathering is the process by which rocks break up into smaller and smaller pieces. No chemical changes are involved. Rapid heating and cooling may cause expansion and contraction, which cause rocks to split and shatter. This is particularly common in the desert biome, where the day-night cycle, especially in summer, is characterized by major temperature shifts. Thus, the temperature of the floor of the Arizona desert may register 60°C (140°F) at noon and then drop to 18°C (64°F) by midnight. Freezing and thawing are characteristic of northern latitudes as well. During a winter thaw, the water from melted snow enters the cracks and pores of surface rocks. A subsequent freeze results in a flaking of the rock due to the force of the expanding ice.

Chemical Weathering (Decomposition). Chemical weathering is the process by which rocks decompose due to chemical changes (Figure 4-1). Chemical activity proceeds more rapidly in a warm climate than in a cool one. For example, it takes twice as long for soil to develop from limestone in northern Michigan as it does in Indiana. Both water and oxygen react with rock, causing it to soften and break up. The water, which is slightly acidic, gradually eats away at limestone or sandstone and hastens its decomposition.

FIGURE 4-1   Some agents of soil formation.

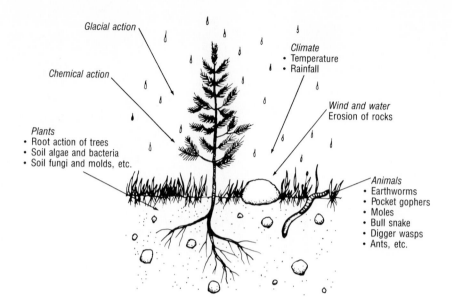

Glacial action

Chemical action

Climate
• Temperature
• Rainfall

Wind and water
Erosion of rocks

Plants
• Root action of trees
• Soil algae and bacteria
• Soil fungi and molds, etc.

Animals
• Earthworms
• Pocket gophers
• Moles
• Bull snake
• Digger wasps
• Ants, etc.

TYPE OF PARENT MATERIAL.   Soil forms from a variety of **parent materials** including granite, limestone, or shale. The parent material from which a soil develops may be the underlying **bedrock**. Such soils are said to be **residual**. The type of bedrock largely determines the texture and fertility of the residual soil. Thus, soils derived from sandstone are coarse, sandy, and low in nutrients. Soils that have developed from limestone are fine-grained and highly fertile. Most soils, however, are not residual, but have been derived from parent materials that have been transported considerable distances by ice, wind, or water.

Glacial Transport.   During the Pleistocene Period (1 million to 10,000 B.C.), four massive glacial advances moved southwestward from Canada into the northeastern states as far as Ohio, Indiana, Illinois, and Iowa. The massive dome-shaped glaciers sheared off hilltops and mountain peaks, gouged out depressions, and pulverized large boulders (Figure 4-2). Rocks, gravel, sand, silt, and clay accumulated underneath the moving glacier. Consequently, when the ice finally melted, a mantle of **glacial drift** remained, which served as fresh parent material for the development of future soils. Glaciation has generally enhanced the value of soils for agriculture by increasing soil fertility and by leveling the land.

Water Transport.   Rivers play an important role in building soil. Have you ever walked along a stream, picked up a flat stone and "sailed" it across the water to make it skip? It was the action of the water, operating for many years, that had smoothed down your "skipping" stone. The grains that were eroded from the rock and stone were transported downstream. These grains eventually became part of the load of sand, silt, and clay that the stream carries in suspension. Much of that material may ultimately be carried to the ocean at the

river's mouth to form a delta (Figure 4-3). The Mississippi River alone discharges 210 million metric tons of sediment into the Gulf of Mexico each year. When the major rivers of the world, such as the Mississippi, Nile, and Amazon, periodically overflow their banks, a nutrient-rich load of sediment is deposited along the river shore. The soil formed in this way is called **alluvial** soil (Figure 4-4). It supports almost one-third of the world's agriculture.

Wind Transport.   Parent material that is blown by the wind is called **loess** (Figure 4-5). Enormous amounts of loess were deposited in the Midwest about 17,000 years ago. These deposits are up to 30 meters (100 feet) thick. The soils derived from loess are of major importance to U.S. agriculture. Corn grows tall in the fertile loess soils of Iowa and Illinois. Loess has made possible the thousands of wheat farms in Nebraska and Kansas that form much of our nation's "breadbasket."

ORGANISMS.   The development of a mature soil also depends on the activity of a great number and diversity of organisms. Perhaps the most important soil organisms are the bacteria. They influence soil structure, aeration, moisture content, and fertility in ways that will be discussed later in this chapter. Lichens and mosses that have become established on rock also contribute to soil formation by trapping wind-blown organic debris such as plant fibers, seeds, dead insects, animal wastes, and so on, to a depth sufficient to form a film over the rock's surface. Lichens also secrete a very dilute carbonic acid (H_2CO_3) that slowly dissolves the rock, thus adding inorganic material to the developing soil. Finally, upon their death, the lichens and mosses decompose, releasing nutrients that enrich the soil.

Rock may be splintered by the roots of trees and other plants. Rooted vegetation absorbs mineral nutrients

FIGURE 4-2 Glacial action in soil formation. Note the striations on this rock formation in Wyoming. These striations, as well as the rounded shape of the rock, were caused by glacial movement thousands of years ago.

from lower levels. These nutrients then are deposited on the ground surface when leaves, fruits, and nuts fall, and when the plant dies, helping form soil. Earthworms, beetle larvae, bull snakes, pocket gophers, moles and ground squirrels burrow through the soil, aiding in the movement of air and water through the ground (Figure 4-6). Soil fertility is improved by animal wastes, especially those of earthworms, insects, birds, and mammals. And those nutrients eventually are absorbed by crops consumed by humans.

FIGURE 4-3 Water transport of soil is shown in this aerial view of the Missiquoi River watershed in Vermont. The delta of the river, which was formed by the water transport of thousands of tons of silt, is shown in the foreground.

DISTRIBUTION OF ALLUVIAL SOIL

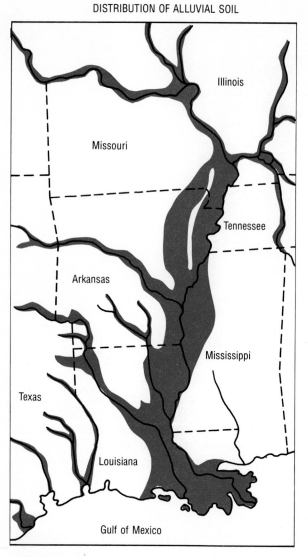

FIGURE 4-4   The flood plain and delta of the Mississippi River, it is the largest continuous area of alluvial soil in the United States.

TOPOGRAPHY.   The **topography**, or shape, of the land surface also plays an important role in determining the thickness and fertility of soil. For example, on steeply sloping surfaces, a relatively thin, infertile soil develops, which is virtually incapable of supporting vegetation. The reason is that the newly formed soil is washed down the slope by runoff waters almost as quickly as it develops. Conversely, on the relatively flat valley floor, a much thicker, more fertile soil develops because the valley receives soil particles, nutrients, and organic material that erode from the surrounding hills.

TIME.   When this planet first formed, about 5 billion years ago, it was completely devoid of soil. With the passage of time, however, physical, chemical, and (when organisms appeared on earth) biological process-

es, resulted in the formation of the first thin "envelope" of soil around the globe. The time required for a given soil to develop depends, in part, on the relative hardness of the parent material. Soil scientists estimate that 1 inch of topsoil derived from hard granite requires 1,000 years or more to develop. On the other hand, soft substrates like volcanic ash or shale may develop into crop-supporting soils in just a few decades.

THE CHARACTERISTICS OF SOIL

The major characteristics of soils are texture, structure, acidity, nutrient content, gas content, and moisture content. An understanding of these characteristics is an essential prerequisite to the study of soil profiles, soil types, soil productivity, and soil management.

Texture

Texture is the size and shape of the individual soil particles, as well as the proportions in which they occur. For convenience and efficiency, the U.S. Department of Agriculture (USDA) classifies soil particles in categories of diminishing size as **gravel, sand, silt,** and **clay**. It should be emphasized that these textural classes are relatively stable. Despite the dynamic nature of soil, despite the continuous physical, chemical, and biological activities that are continuously transforming it, and despite the soil-management activities of the farmer, gravel will not change to sand, nor silt to clay, within the average human life span.

CLAY.   Clay particles are so small (less than 0.004 millimeter) that they are not visible under an ordinary microscope. Each clay particle has the shape of a flat, many-sided wafer. The plasticity and cohesiveness of moistened clay permit it to be fashioned into pots, bowls, and vases. Because of their stickiness when wet, clay soils are worked only with difficulty and are therefore called **heavy** soils, in contrast to the easily worked **light** soils that are composed primarily of sand. When clay soils dry out, the particles contract and form hard clods. When it is baked by the sun, clay soil keeps out water almost as effectively as tile, which, of course, is clay baked by humans.

The total amount of air space in clay is somewhat greater than in sand. However, because much of the air space is represented by extremely minute pores, the actual rate of water and air movement through clay is much slower than through sand. Water is held so tenaciously that most plant root systems cannot absorb it. Moreover, because young plant rootlets cannot readily penetrate poorly oxygenated clay, soil composed exclusively of clay is unsuitable for crops.

FIGURE 4-5 Distribution of loess in central United States. Some loess also occurs in Idaho, Washington, and Oregon.

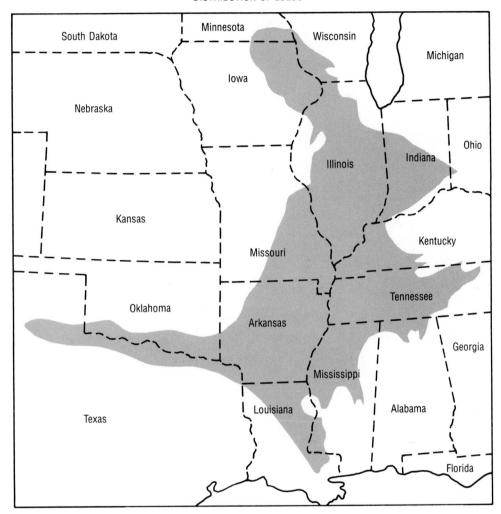

DISTRIBUTION OF LOESS

Clay is an important reservoir of plant food, a function that largely depends on two characteristics of clay particles: (1) their very *large surface area*, and (2) their *negative electrical charge*. Soil scientists, estimate that the aggregate surface area of the clay particles in the topsoil of only 2 hectares (5 acres) of an Iowa cornfield down to a depth of 30 centimeters (1 foot) is roughly equal to the *entire surface area of the North American continent*. The negatively charged surface of the clay particle attracts positively charged atoms (cations) of nutrient elements such as calcium, potassium, magnesium, phosphorus, zinc, and iron (Figure 4-7). These nutrients form a loose chemical bond with the clay particles. This process is called **adsorption**. From the standpoint of soil fertility, adsorption is of fundamental importance because it prevents the leaching (removal) of nutrients from the soil by the action of water. Nutrient ions on clay particles are replaced by hydrogen ions from the surface of the plant roots. The nutrient ions are then free to be taken in by the plant. Just 10 grams of dry Iowa topsoil may have 1.2 *quintillion* ion exchange sites that can hold nutrients for use of crops!

On the other hand, clay particles do not retain negatively charged nitrate (NO_3) or nitrite (NO_2) ions very well. As a result, nitrates are easily leached from the soil by rainfall or washed away by runoff waters. The nitrates may fertilize lake and pond waters and eventually convert open-water game fish lakes to weed-choked lakes containing less desirable species of fish. The accumulation of nutrients in a lake is called **eutrophication** and is discussed later. The reduction in the use of artificial fertilizers by farmers should ease this problem.

FIGURE 4-6 Characteristic organisms found in the soil that are important to its development.

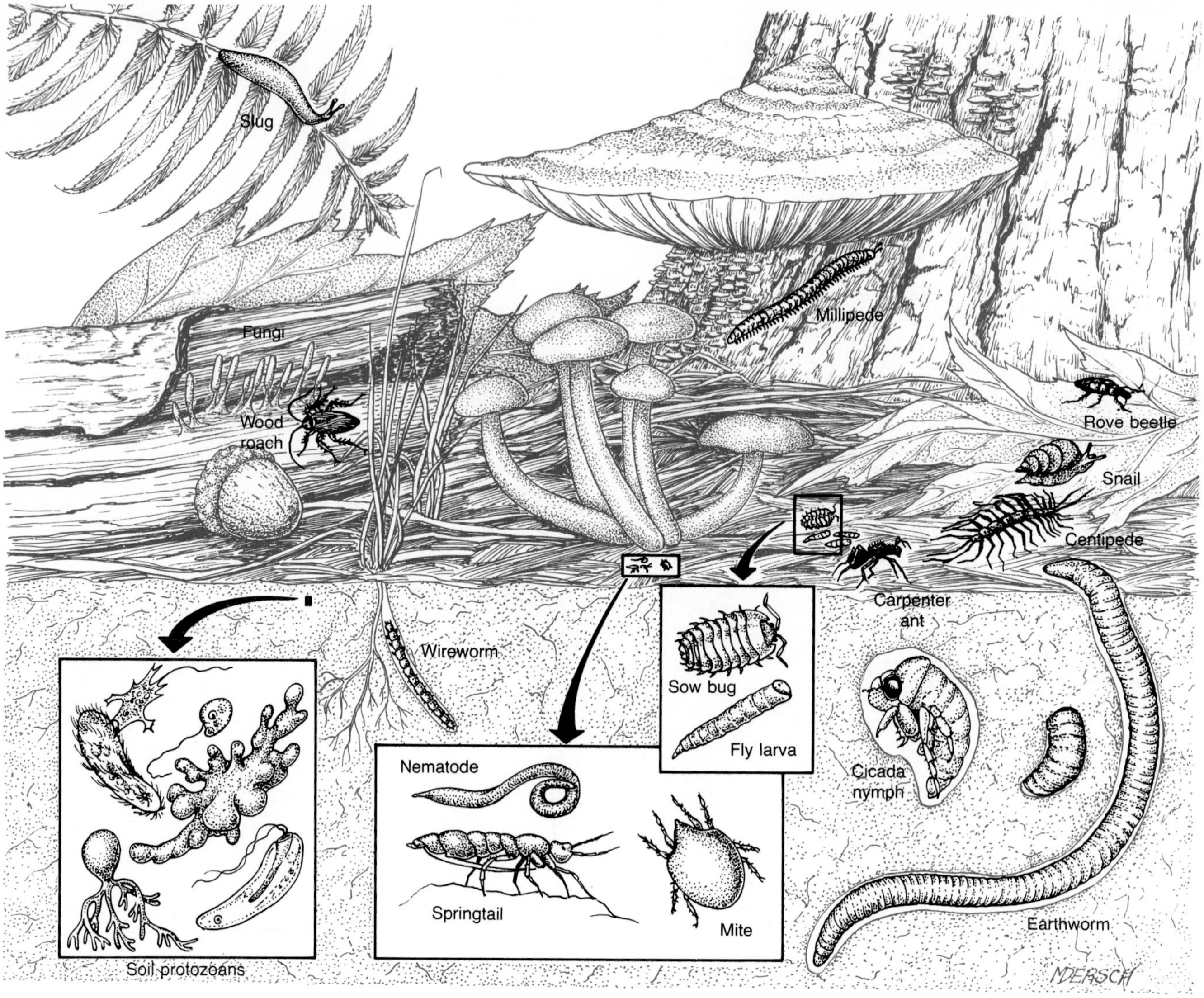

LOAM. Very few agricultural soils are composed exclusively of one textural class; usually they are a mixture in which all four of the major classes (gravel, sand, silt, and clay) are represented in varying proportions (Figures 4-8 and 4-9). The most desirable soil from an agricultural standpoint is **loam**, which is a mixture of heavy and light soil materials in the following proportions: sand, 30 to 50 percent; silt, 30 to 50 percent; and clay, 0 to 20 percent.

Structure

Soil structure is defined as the arrangement or grouping of a soil's primary particles (gravel, sand, silt or clay) into aggregates. These aggregates may have a variety of shapes, such as granular, blocky, prismatic, and so

on, as shown in Figure 4-10. The aeration, moisture content, fertility, and erosion resistance of a soil are all to some degree dependent upon its structure. Plowing, cultivating, liming, and manuring often improve a soil's productivity, primarily by changing its structure. Other factors affecting soil structure include alternate freezing and thawing, wetting and drying, plant root penetration, burrowing by animals like worms and pocket gophers, the addition of slimy secretions from animals, the bacterial decay of plant and animal remains, and compaction by farm equipment and off-road vehicles.

GOOD STRUCTURE. When farmland has a good soil structure, crop production is enhanced. When you squeeze a handful of such soil, it has a spongy or

FIGURE 4-7   Ion exchange between clay and plant roots. The positive ions of nutrient elements such as potassium (K), calcium (Ca), and magnesium (Mg) are attracted to the negatively charged surface of the clay particle. Note that these nutrient ions are replaced by hydrogen ions from the root systems of plants and then are absorbed by the plants. It is the role of the clay particle that makes it so valuable to the farmer in crop production.

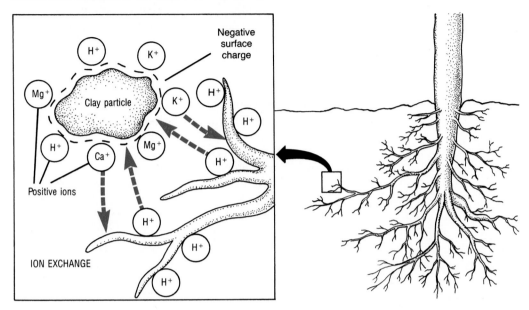

crumbly quality. Soil with good structure has an abundance of pores through which life-sustaining water and oxygen can move to plant root systems. Such soil allows water to infiltrate after a rainfall or snow melt. As you walk over this type of soil, you can sense a springiness underfoot. This soil is resistant to the erosive effects of wind and water. Soil structure can be improved by adding organic matter, by manuring, and by plowing under cover crops and crop residues such as stubble.

POOR STRUCTURE.   A soil with poor structure has a minimum number of pore spaces for air and water because of the closely packed soil aggregates. Individual soil aggregates tend to fall apart. Such soil has little resiliency. Because water infiltration is greatly reduced, in arid regions irrigation water may not penetrate deeply enough to sustain crops. In areas of abundant rainfall, however, poorly structured soils cause drainage problems on low-lying sites, whereas on uplands they result in severe runoff and erosion.

FIGURE 4-8   Soil texture designation based on percentages of sand, silt, and clay.

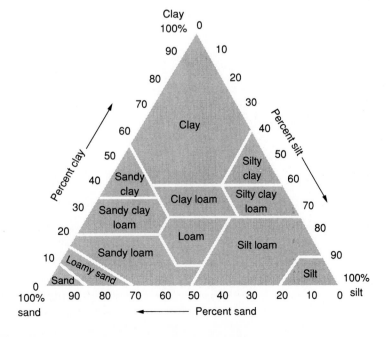

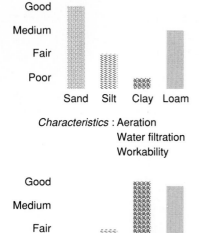

Characteristics : Aeration
                 Water filtration
                 Workability

Characteristics : Ability to hold water
                 Ion exchange capacity

FIGURE 4-9 Characteristics of sand, silt, clay, and loam. Note that only loam rates either medium or good for all five characteristics upon which crop production depends.

Acidity (pH)

The acidity or alkalinity of a soil depends on the relative amounts of hydrogen (H^+) and hydroxide (OH^-) ions. When hydrogen ions outnumber hydroxide ions, the soil is acidic; in the reverse condition, the soil is basic. Many of the hydrogen ions in the soil are produced when carbon dioxide gas (CO_2) in the air combines with water to form hydrogen (H^+) and bicarbonate HCO_3^- ions.

Soil scientists use the pH scale to signify hydrogen ion concentration. The pH scale ranges from 0 to 14. A pH of 7 is neutral, a condition in which the number of hydrogen ions equals the number of hydroxide ions. Soils with a pH above 7 are alkaline; those with a pH below 7 are acidic.

Soils vary in pH from 4.5 (strongly acid) to 9 (strongly alkaline) (Figure 4-11). Most vegetables, grains, trees, and grasses grow best in soils that are very slightly acid, having a pH of about 6.8. Soils under hardwood (oak, maple, beech, and so on) forests are usually more alkaline than soils under coniferous (spruce, fir, pine, and so on) forests.

With the help of a soil scientist from the local Soil Conservation Service District, the farmer or city dweller can determine the pH of his or her land. Lime may be applied if the soil is too acidic (Figure 4-12). To raise the pH of a 7-inch layer of soil over a 100 square-meter

FIGURE 4-10 Note the variety of shapes occurring in soil aggregates and the relative rates at which water can move through them.

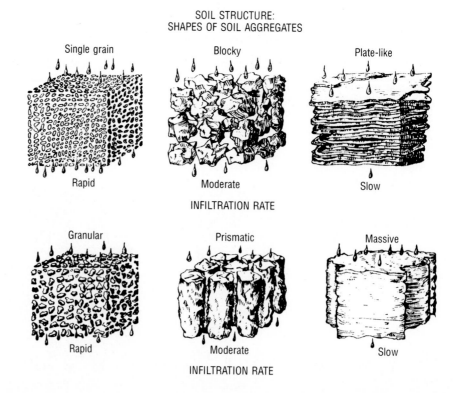

FIGURE 4-11   The pH scale. The pH
of certain well known substances are
shown on the left. The preferred soil
pH of some plants are shown to the
right.

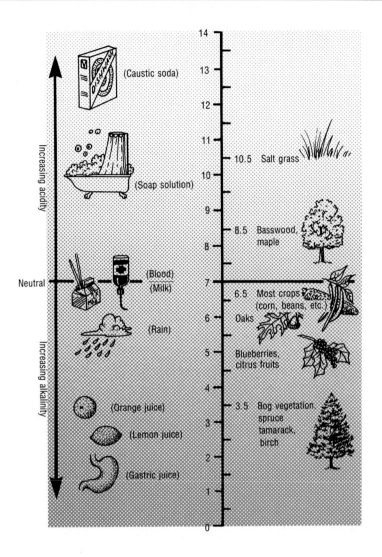

(1,000-square-foot) area from 5.5 to 6.5 would require
66 kilograms (30 pounds) of finely ground limestone.

ACID DEPOSITION.   One of the most serious environmental problems facing our nation is the deposition of
acid rain, snow, and fog that may have many harmful effects on terrestrial and aquatic organisms (Chapter 18). The severity of the effects depends, to a large
degree, on the soil pH. If the soil is alkaline (high
pH), the acids deposited in rain, snow, fog, and other

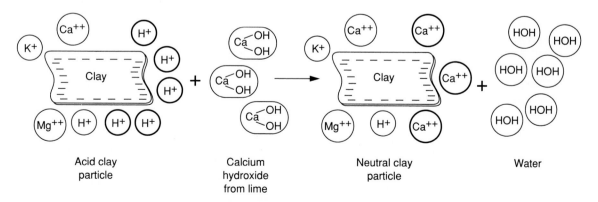

FIGURE 4-12   How lime makes acid soil neutral. The hydroxide ions from the lime reacts with
hydrogen ions on the clay particle to form water, which is neutral.

forms are often neutralized, although acids may damage plants directly. Where soil is poorly developed or alkalinity is naturally low, acids can wreak havoc on plants.

THE COMPOSITION OF SOIL

As shown in Figure 4-13, a well-worked loam soil is usually composed of about 50 percent solids (minerals and organic matter) and 50 percent air space. Under the best conditions for crop yields, the air space is occupied by equal amounts of water and air.

Organic Matter

The organic matter of the soil is largely derived from the decomposing bodies of plants and animals, as well as animal wastes. The darkly colored material that forms as the decay process proceeds is known as **humus**. Maintaining humus is an indispensable tool of good soil management. Humus: (1) improves soil structure, (2) increases pore space so that air and water can penetrate more readily, (3) increases the workability of the soil, (4) reduces erodibility of the soil, (5) minimizes leaching of nutrients, and (6) provides a suitable medium for valuable soil organisms, such as bacteria and earthworms.

Mineral Nutrients

Of the 92 chemical elements that occur in nature, 16 are required by plants for health, growth, and reproduction. Such essential elements are called **nutrients**. If they are

required in large amounts by plants, they are called **macronutrients**. Some nutrients are used in only small quantities and are known as **micronutrients**. For example, 70 grams of the micronutrient molybdenum is sufficient to satisfy the needs of 1 hectare (2.5 acres) of clover. Nutrients required by crops are listed in Table 4-1. The soil gains nutrients from (1) nitrogen fixation, (2) decomposition of plant and animal remains, (3) animal wastes, (4) weathering of parent materials, and (5) fertilizer (Figure 4-14). The soil loses nutrients by (1) root absorption, (2) leaching due to the downward movement of water, and (3) soil erosion.

As mentioned in Chapter 2, legumes like beans, peas, and alfalfa are natural hosts for nitrogen-fixing bacteria. In contrast, grains such as corn, wheat, barley, and oats do not host nitrogen-fixing bacteria and are thus incapable of adding nitrogen to the soil. Geneticists are now conducting intensive research in an effort to develop new strains of corn and other grains that can host the nitrogen-fixing bacteria. A dramatic breakthrough in this research could save U.S. farmers billions of dollars in fertilizer costs annually.

NUTRIENT AVAILABILITY. Crops require many nutrients (Figure 4-15). Even though a given nutrient may be present in soil in seemingly adequate amounts, it may not occur in a form *available* to a given plant. For example, even though there is enough potassium in most soils to last for thousands of years, farmers must add potassium fertilizer to maintain good yields. Only one-fiftieth of the potassium in the soil is actually available to plants. Availability is largely determined by the pH of the soil (Figure 4-16). A major reason for adding lime to correct soil acidity is to make important nutrients available for plant absorption.

Gas Content

Soil "inhales" and "exhales" continuously. Oxygen, which is present in greater concentration in the atmosphere than in the soil, diffuses into the soil pores. Carbon dioxide moves from the soil into the atmosphere. This constant "breathing" action of the soil is dependent upon the numerous soil pores, which serve as microscopic air reservoirs and passageways. When soil is extremely dry because of an extended drought, the pores are filled with air. However, after a violent thunderstorm, they are often filled with water, and plants may suffer from oxygen deficiency. Such an oxygen shortage slows the development of the root system upon which plants depend for the absorption of nutrients and water. Oxygen-deficient soils may also have lower soil fertility. This results from inhibition of the bacterial activity necessary for converting nitrogen to a form that is usable by crops.

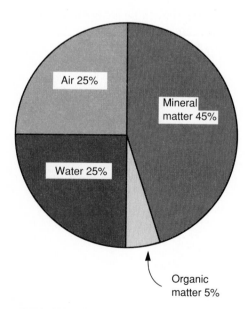

FIGURE 4-13   The composition of average soil. Mineral and organic matter constitute 50% of a well-worked warm soil.

Table 4-1   Major Functions of Some Plant Nutrients

Macronutrients

Nitrogen	Phosphorous	Potassium
1. Gives plants a dark green color	1. Stimulates root formation and growth	1. Imparts plant vigor and disease resistance
2. Makes vegetables more juicy	2. Encourages flower development, pollination, and seed formation	2. Produces strong stems
3. Increases leaf and stem growth	3. Improves winter hardiness	3. Improves winter hardiness
4. Aids in seed production in range grasses	4. Aids in formation of legume nodules	4. Increases grain size
5. Increases the quality of bread made from wheat		5. Aids in sugar transport
6. Required for protein synthesis		

Micronutrients

Iron	Boron
1. Very important for chlorophyll formation	1. Essential for pollination and reproduction
2. Vital in enzyme activity	2. Important in flower and seed formation
	3. Aids in providing tissues with oxygen

Manganese	Molybdenum
1. Assists in chlorophyll formation	1. Essential for nitrogen-fixing bacteria in root modules of legumes
2. Accelerates seed germination	2. Important in protein synthesis
3. Increases vitamin content	3. Important in vitamin formation
	4. Important in speeding up certain types of chemical reactions

Moisture

Water serves several important plant functions. It is an essential raw material for photosynthesis; it is the solvent medium by which minerals are transported upward to the leaves and sugar is transported downward to the roots; and it is an essential component of protoplasm, forming 90 percent of the weight of actively growing organs such as buds, roots, and flowers. The amount of water in the soil is critically important to crop health and survival. The amount of soil water present is indicated by the terms **saturation, field capacity,** and **wilting point** (Figure 4-17). At **saturation**, the pore spaces are completely filled with water to the exclusion of air. This condition frequently occurs after a severe thunderstorm or intensive irrigation. The roots of most crops cannot use this water because they cannot function in the absence of oxygen. At **field capacity**, half of the pore space is filled with water and half with air. Since plenty of oxygen is available to the roots, this water can be readily absorbed. At the **wilting point**, the only moisture left in the soil is in the form of a thin film that lines the pore spaces. This film is held so tenaciously by the soil aggregates that it is extremely difficult for roots to absorb it—a condition experienced by many farmers and backyard gardeners, who have seen their beans and lettuce shrivel during a midsummer drought.

THE SOIL PROFILE

When one looks at the exposed face of a road cut or the side of a stone quarry, it is apparent that many soils are organized into horizontally ranged layers, or **horizons**. Each of these horizons is characterized by a specific thickness, color, texture, structure, and chemical composition. A cross-sectional view of the various horizons is known as the **soil profile** (Figure 4-18).

The major layers from the ground surface downward to bedrock are designated as **horizons A** (topsoil), **B** (subsoil), **C** (parent material), and **D** (bedrock). These

FIGURE 4-14   Nutrient sources of crops.

HOW SOIL GAINS AND LOSES NUTRIENTS

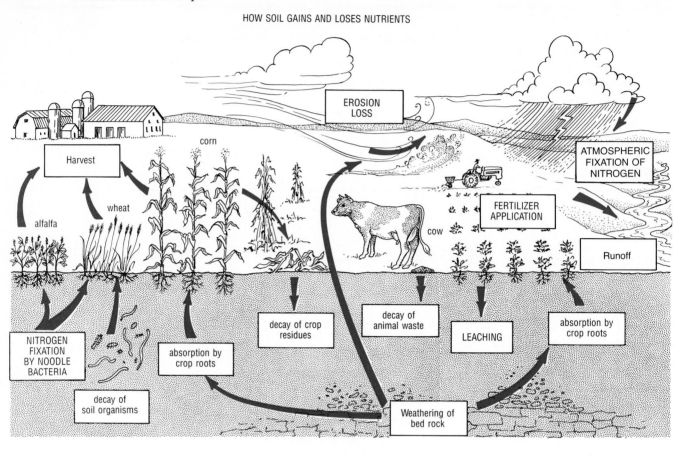

FIGURE 4-15   Nutrients required by crops.

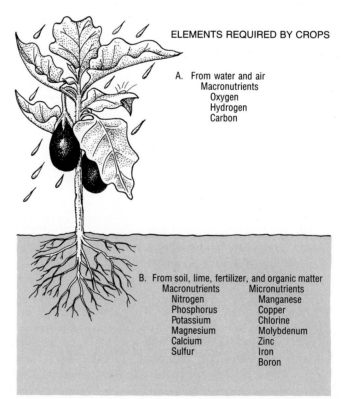

ELEMENTS REQUIRED BY CROPS

A. From water and air
       Macronutrients
           Oxygen
           Hydrogen
           Carbon

B. From soil, lime, fertilizer, and organic matter

Macronutrients	Micronutrients
Nitrogen	Manganese
Phosphorus	Copper
Potassium	Chlorine
Magnesium	Molybdenum
Calcium	Zinc
Sulfur	Iron
	Boron

FIGURE 4-16   Relative availability of certain plant nutrients as a function of soil pH.

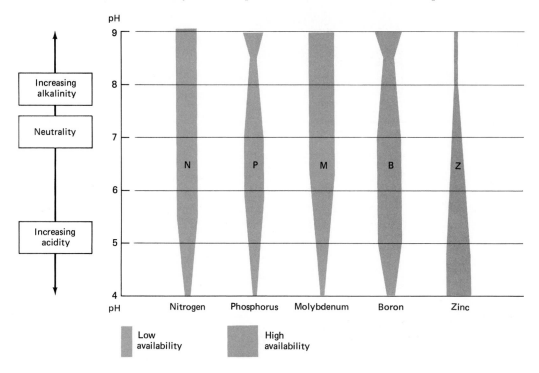

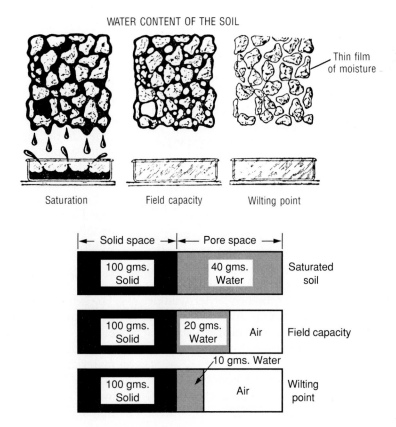

FIGURE 4-17   Water content of the soil varies considerably. Note variations in air content.

WATER CONTENT OF THE SOIL

FIGURE 4-18   Soil profile (highly simplified).

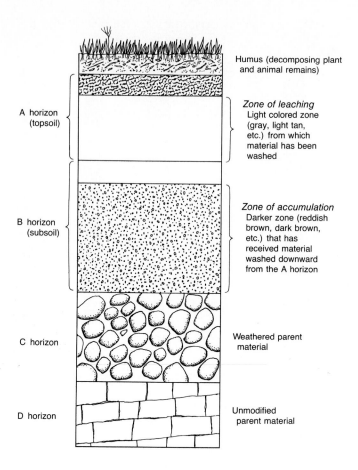

Humus (decomposing plant
and animal remains)

A horizon
(topsoil)

Zone of leaching
Light colored zone
(gray, light tan,
etc.) from which
material has been
washed

B horizon
(subsoil)

Zone of accumulation
Darker zone (reddish
brown, dark brown,
etc.) that has
received material
washed downward
from the A horizon

C horizon

Weathered parent
material

D horizon

Unmodified
parent material

horizons may not exist in all soil types. For instance, in immature soils, where weathering has not fully progressed, some horizons may be missing. In certain soils derived from water-borne sediment (**alluvial soils**), or in soils that have been thoroughly mixed by the burrowing of mammals, the stratified pattern may be absent.

The soil profile is the end product of the action of vegetation, temperature, rainfall, and soil organisms on parent rock materials operating for many thousands of years. The soil profile, therefore, tells us a great deal about soil **history**. It represents a kind of soil **autobiography**. From a practical standpoint, the soil profile is of great importance, for it can tell the soil scientist immediately whether the soil is suited for agricultural crops, for rangeland, for timber, or for wildlife habitat and recreation. The profile also reveals the suitability of the soil for various urban uses, such as home sites, highways, sewage-disposal plants, sanitary landfills, and septic tank fields.

Let us examine the basic characteristics of a soil profile, beginning with the uppermost horizon and moving downward to bedrock (Figure 4-18).

A Horizon

Human survival depends on the thin layer of **topsoil** that covers much of the earth. In the United States, its thickness ranges from 2.5 centimeters (1 inch) on the slopes of the Rockies to almost 600 centimeters (2 feet) in Iowa corn country. This layer is rich in humus. It is from the topsoil, or A horizon, that crop roots absorb vital water and nutrients. It is within this layer that most soil organisms live. The lower part of the A horizon is called the **zone of leaching** because much material is dissolved and carried downward to the B horizon by water.

B Horizon

The B horizon, commonly called the **subsoil**, is a zone of accumulation that receives and stores soluble salts and organic matter that are leached downward from the A horizon. There is also an upward movement of parent materials from the C horizon below. After many years of abusive farming, the topsoil may be completely eroded away. The B horizon, which now lies at the surface, may become a barren wasteland in many cases.

C Horizon

The C horizon is composed of weathered **parent material**. Usually this material was transported to the site by glaciers, wind, or water. In a few cases, the parent material in this horizon is derived from underlying bedrock. The parent material in the C horizon determines many soil characteristics—its texture, water absorption ability, nutrient levels, acidity, and so on. For example, if the parent material is granite, the soil tends to mature slowly and to be acidic. In central Canada, less than 2.5 centimeters (1 inch) of topsoil has developed from granite in the past 10,000 years. The acidic nature of the soil in this region makes the lakes very vulnerable to the harmful effects of acid deposition—a serious environmental problem to be discussed in detail later (Chapter 18). On the other hand, if the parent material is limestone, the soil develops rapidly and tends to be alkaline. Soils that develop from limestone usually tend to be more productive than those derived from granite.

D Horizon

The D horizon consists of the unweathered parent material, **bedrock**. As bedrock weathers, it contributes parent material to the C horizon above. The D horizon is absent, of course, in loess and alluvial soils, where the parent was transported by wind or water instead of being derived from bedrock.

SOIL CLASSIFICATION: THE ORDERS

There are thousands of kinds of soils in the United States. The study and understanding of their importance in supporting such renewable resources as crops, range grasses, forests, and wildlife would be severely hampered without some system of classification. In 1975 the U.S. Soil Conservation Service published a soil classification system. It recognizes 10 major groups known as **orders**. The name of each order ends in **sol**, which is derived from the Latin word *solum*, meaning soil. These orders are established on the basis of such features as (1) nature of the parent material, (2) horizon pattern, (3) texture, and (4) chemical content. The major features of several important orders are summarized in Table 4-2. The distribution of the major soil orders in North America is shown in Figure 4-19.

Spodosols

Spodosols develop in a cool, relatively humid climate under coniferous forest vegetation in Canada, in the

Table 4-2   Soil Order Summary

Order	Natural Vegetation	Climate	Color of Topsoil	Comments
Spodosol	Coniferous forest	Cold and humid	Lower part is gray or ash-like	Best used for timber, wildlife habitat, and recreation, rather than farming. However, grows potatoes in Maine with proper fertilization, as well as vegetables in Michigan, Wisconsin, and Florida.
Alfisol	Decideous forest	Mild and humid	Gray to brown	Together with mollisols, supports most of world's crop production. Fertility depleted after intensive farming and must be restored.
Ultisol	Forest, savannah, swamp	Warm and humid	Reddish or yellow	Strongly leached, moist soils; responds to good management
Mollisol	Grassland	Semiarid	Black or dark brown	Together with alfisols, support most of the world's crop production. Soft, crumbly, thick A horizon. Highly fertile.
Aridisol	Cactus, mesquite, sagebrush	Hot and dry	Reddish to light gray or brown	Little organic matter. Thin topsoil. Frequent droughts. Crop production dependent on irrigation.
Oxisol	Tropical rain forest	Tropical. High rainfall	Reddish, light colored	Reddish-brown iron compounds in subsoil. Nutrients rapidly leached from A horizon by rainfall. Soil becomes rock-hard when exposed to sun and air for a long time.

FIGURE 4-19   Major soil orders of North America.

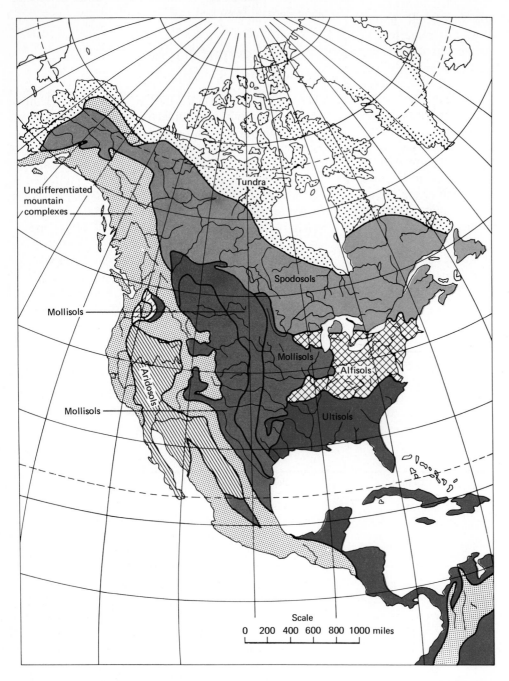

northern lake states, in the uplands of New England, and at high elevations in the western mountains (Figure 4-19). The litter of forest needles, cones, and branches decomposes to form a dark brown, extremely acidic humus. Percolating water and organic acids carry soluble carbonate and sulfate salts, as well as aluminum and iron compounds, downward from the A to the B horizon. This leaching causes the lower part of the A horizon to assume a gray, ash-like appearance. (The term *spodosol* is derived from the Greek word *spodos*, meaning wood ash, and the Latin *solum*, meaning soil.) The town of White Earth, Minnesota, received its name because of the light color of its spodosols. The lower portion of the B horizon, on the other hand, has a distinctive coffee-brown color because of the accumulation of iron compounds and organic materials. Since these soils are infertile, they are not suitable for crop production. Many an ambitious farming

FIGURE 4-20 The alfisol soil, which developed on the floor of this oak woods, was exposed by removing the leaf litter. This soil is blackish brown and springy under foot. It is rich in organic material and has good structure. Alfisol now supports much of the agriculture in northeastern United States.

venture based on tilling the spodosols of northern Michigan and Wisconsin in the early part of this century failed because of the relatively short growing season and the extremely acidic and infertile soil. This is corroborated by the presence of many abandoned farmhomes now being swallowed up by second-growth forest. Much of the once-farmed land is now covered with pine plantations. An outstanding exception to the general failure of spodosols as agriculturally productive soils is the famous potato-growing area in Aroostook County, Maine, where intensive fertilization and liming are practiced.

Alfisols

The **alfisols** are named after the symbols for aluminum (Al) and iron (Fe) because these elements are characteristic components of these soils. They occur just south of the spodosols in the north-central and northeastern parts of the United States (Figure 4-19). The alfisols developed under a deciduous forest (maple, beech, oak, hickory, and so on) cover (Figure 4-20). The extensive leaf litter, derived from herbs, shrubs, and trees, sometimes amounting to 2.5 metric tons per hectare (1 ton per acre) annually, decomposes much more readily and releases more calcium than the hard mat of needles that forms under coniferous (spruce, fir, pine) forests. As a result, the alfisols are less acid and more fertile than the spodosols. These are the soils on which America's pioneer farms depended. Although the fertility of such soils is quickly depleted, the climate favors farming. Therefore, when proper soil conservation practices are

maintained, a great spectrum of agricultural activity can be supported, from the raising of grains, tobacco, potatoes, and fruit to the development of lush pastures for beef and dairy cattle.

Ultisols ("Ultimate Soils")

Many of the **ultisols** are characterized by iron oxide compounds in the subsoil, which have a red or yellow color. They occupy an extensive area in the southeastern United States, ranging from Maryland to Florida and westward to the Mississippi River Valley (Figure 4-19). The virgin soils developed under a mixture of coniferous and deciduous cover. They are more highly weathered than any other soil in the United States. Because of the high average temperatures and the abundant rainfall, the accumulated leaf litter is rapidly decomposed by fungi and bacteria, allowing only a thin layer of topsoil to develop. Much of the area occupied by the ultisols is hilly and subject to severe erosion. Forests are much more extensive on these soils than in the alfisol regions to the north. Although the soil is inherently infertile, the land is amenable to the plow and the cultivator and is located in a region with a long growing season and abundant rainfall. Therefore, with proper techniques of erosion control and fertilization, the soils can be reasonably productive. In fact the higher-quality ultisols rank just below the mollisols and alfisols as first-class agricultural soils. Ultisols can produce a variety of crops, ranging from cotton, corn, tobacco, and peanuts to pasture for beef and dairy cattle.

Mollisols ("Soft Soils")

The term **mollisol** refers to the soil's soft, crumbly texture. The extremely fertile, blackish-brown topsoil may be up to 1.2 meters (4 feet) thick. The mollisols extend in a north-south belt in the Great Plains from the Dakotas south to Texas. They occupy 25 percent of the area of the United States—more than any other soil order (Figure 4-21). Calcification of the subsoil, resulting from the leaching of soluble calcium carbonate from above, is a dominant characteristic. However, because of an annual rainfall of only 37 to 62 centimeters (15 to 25 inches), usually in the form of brief summer thundershowers, leaching does not carry the calcium through to the C horizon. Instead, it is deposited in the lower subsoil, where it precipitates out and forms a grayish or yellowish band (Figures 4-22 and 23). The topsoil of the mollisols, characterized by a rich organic and nutrient content, is intrinsically *more fertile than any other soil in the United States*. In part, this is because of the dense mesh of roots extending down through the A horizon. It has been estimated than a single rye plant (which is actually a cultivated grass) only 50 centimeters (20 inches) tall may have more than 14 million branches in its root system. If laid end to end, these branches would form a line over 480 kilometers (300 miles) long! When a grass plant dies, its root system decomposes *in place* and releases nutrients that are immediately available to future plant generations.

Typical mollisol soils contain about 1,350 metric tons of humus per hectare (540 tons per acre) compared with only 112 metric tons per hectare (44.8 tons per acre) for spodosol soils. The relatively undependable, low annual rainfall limits ths soil's productivity, however. During

FIGURE 4-22   Profile of mollisol soil formed from glacial till in the South.

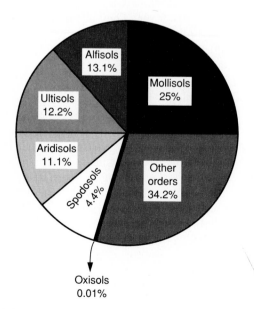

FIGURE 4-21   U.S. area occupied by soil orders.

wet years, bumper crops are commonplace, but during years of excessive heat and drought, crop failures may be extensive, as was the case in 1988 when thousands of ranchers and farmers went bankrupt. Major northern crops produced on these soils are high-quality corn, wheat, barley, oats, and rye. Sorghum is a prominent southern crop.

Aridisols ("Dry Soils")

The term **aridisol** is derived from the Latin word *aridus*, meaning dry. In the United States, the aridisols occur primarily in the deserts of the Southwest. A number of the world's great deserts, such as the Sahara of Africa and the Gobi of China, are largely composed of aridisols. Because the plants in these deserts are widely spaced, with extensive areas of bare soil between them, wind and water erosion may be severe and may leave a layer of stones called the **desert pavement**. Organic

FIGURE 4-23 Mollisol soil profile (highly simplified).

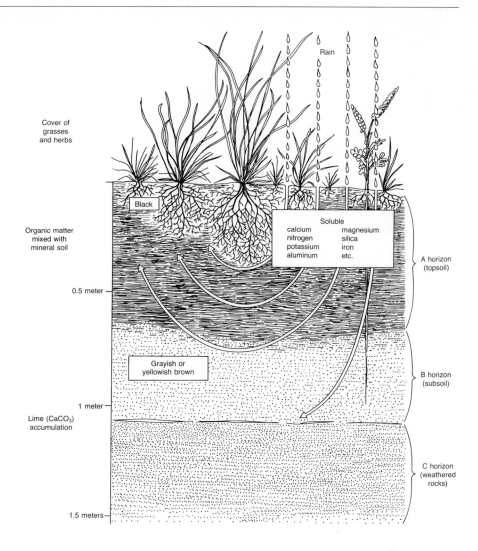

matter in the thin band of topsoil is rather scarce. However, because leaching is minimal, the nutrient content of the soil is surprisingly high. With the aid of irrigation, the aridisols of California's Imperial Valley have "burst into bloom" with a great variety of high-value crops ranging from citrus to celery, form walnuts to dates. Because these soils drain so poorly, though, salts can build up in the surface and impair crop production. This process is called **salinization**.

Oxisols ("Oxide Soils")

The **oxisols** characteristically occur under forest cover in the tropics. They are widely distributed in South America and southern Africa. However, in the United States, they are confined to Florida and occupy only 0.01 percent of the area of our country. When you think of a tropical forest, you picture lush jungles of vegetation. And that luxurious plant growth, in turn, must be possible only because the soil is very fertile. Right? Wrong. In a sense, the nutrients are locked up in the **vegetation**. Actually, most oxisols are highly infer-

tile; the topsoil is extremely thin. Much of the dead plant and animal material on the forest floor is rapidly decomposed by fungi that live partly inside and partly outside the living plant roots. As a result, the nutrients that are released during decomposition are immediately absorbed by the plant. The heavy rainfall quickly washes away any nutrients that might be left in the soil.

Another problem with oxisols is the high iron content in the B horizon. Suppose, for example, that hopeful farmers remove the trees and plant crops in the infertile, iron-rich soil. What will be the result? After a few years, the oxisols will bake brick hard in the "kiln" of the hot equatorial sun. Such brick-like soil was actually used by the ancient Khmer civilization of Cambodia to construct the magnificent temples at Angkor Wat. Even today, modern buildings are being constructed in Thailand with such oxisol "bricks." The hardness and durability of oxisols may be good for temples, but certainly not for growing crops! Despite the drawbacks of oxisols, however, it must be remembered that millions of people in the tropics depend on them for food and fiber.

RAPID REVIEW

1. Soil is one of the most important components of terrestrial communities. Its development is complex, involving the interaction of physical, biological, chemical, and climatic processes.

2. Physical processes in soil formation include rapid heating and cooling, and thawing and freezing.

3. The dissolving of rock by water is an important chemical process in soil formation.

4. Soil bacteria influence the aeration, moisture content, and fertility of soil.

5. In addition to the action of soil bacteria, other biological processes involved in soil formation include (a) the splitting of rock by plant roots, (b) the fragmentation of rocks by hoofed animals, (c) the burrowing of earthworms, pocket gophers, and ground squirrels, and (d) the pumping of nutrients to the soil surface by rooted vegetation.

6. The parent material from which some soil is derived may be the underlying bedrock. However, more than 95 percent of the parent materials in the United States have been transported by the action of wind, water, and glaciers.

7. Alluvial soils develop from parent material that has been transported by water. It is extremely fertile.

8. Alluvial soils support almost one-third of the world's agriculture.

9. Loess soils develop from parent material that has been transported by wind.

10. Huge yields of wheat and corn are produced on loess soils in Kansas, Nebraska, Iowa, and Illinois.

11. All factors being equal, the warmer and wetter the climate, the more rapid the process of soil development.

12. Soil particles are classified as gravel, sand, silt, or clay on the basis of size.

13. Pure clay is not a good soil for growing crops because air and water move through it very slowly.

14. Clay serves as an important reservoir for plant nutrients. The negatively charged surface of the clay particle attracts positively charged atoms of such nutrients as calcium, potassium, and magnesium.

15. Clay particles do not retain negatively charged nitrate particles. As a result, nitrates are easily washed from clay soils by rainfall.

16. The most desirable agricultural soil is *loam*—a mixture of sand, silt, and clay.

17. Soil *texture* refers to the size and shape of the individual soil particles, as well as to the proportions in which they occur.

18. Soil *structure* is the grouping of the primary particles, such as gravel, sand, silt and clay, into soil *aggregates*.

19. The pH of soils varies from 4.5 (strongly acid) to 9 (strongly alkaline). Most plants grow best in soil with a pH of about 6.8 (mildly acid).

20. Alkaline soils tend to minimize the harmful effects of acid deposition on ecosystems.

21. Roughly 50 percent of the soil volume is pore space.

22. Oxygen continuously moves from the atmosphere into the soil, whereas carbon dioxide moves from the soil into the atmosphere.

23. The major soil layers from the ground surface downward are known as the *A*, *B*, *C*, and *D* horizons.

24. The *soil profile* is the end product of the action of temperature, rainfall, vegetation, and soil organisms on parent materials through time, frequently measured in thousands of years.

25. Soils are divided into 10 major groups called *orders*.

26. Because of their infertility, *spodosol* soils are not well suited for agriculture.

27. *Alfisols* occur south of the spodosols in the eastern United States. The characteristic plant cover is deciduous forest. They are suitable for farming when proper soil conservation methods are practiced.

28. *Ultisols* occur in the southeastern United States. The subsoil has a red or yellow color due to the presence of iron compounds. With proper fertilization and erosion control practices, corn, cotton, tobacco, and peanuts can be produced successfully in this soil.

29. *Aridisols* develop in the desert biome. The characteristic vegetative cover is cactus and sagebrush. Aridisols can best be used as rangeland. Overgrazing, however, must be carefully controlled.

30. The *oxisols* occur in tropical forest regions. The topsoil is thin and rather infertile. When the forest is cleared, the soil eventually bakes brick hard under the equatorial sun and becomes useless for agriculture.

31. *Mollisol* soils are characterized by an extremely fertile, blackish-brown topsoil that may be up to 1.2 meters (4 feet) thick.

32. The productivity of mollisols is limited by an unpredictable and low average rainfall.

33. Most of the nutrients in tropical forests are locked up in the vegetation; as a result, the soil itself is infertile.

KEY WORDS AND PHRASES

A horizon	Hydroxide ions (OH^-)
Acid rain	Limestone
Acidity	Loam
Adsorption	Loess
Alfisol	Mollisol
Alluvial soil	Nutrients
Anions	Oxisol
Aridisol	Parent material pH
Bedrock	Permanent wilting point
B horizon	Physical weathering
Bicarbonate ion	Sand
Calcification	Saturation
C horizon	Silt
Chemical weathering	Soil order
Clay	Soil profile
D horizon	Soil structure
Eutrophication	Soil texture
Field capacity	Spodosol
Glacial drift	Subsoil
Glaciers	Topsoil
Granite	Ultisol
Gravel	Wilting point
Humus	Zone of accumulation
Hydrogen ions (H^+)	Zone of leaching

QUESTIONS AND TOPICS FOR DISCUSSION

1. Discuss the ecological implications of the biblical statement: "In the sweat of thy face shalt thou eat bread, till thou return unto the ground, for out of it wast thou taken; for dust thou art, and unto dust shalt thou return."

2. Is there any correlation between soil fertility and the power and influence of nations like the United States and the Soviet Union? Discuss your answer.

3. Describe five biological processes involved in the development of soils. What is the importance of each?

4. List three forces that play an important role in the transport of parent materials for soil development.

5. Discuss the role of glaciers in the development of the soils of Minnesota, Wisconsin, and Michigan.

6. How could a climatic change eventually cause a change in the type of soil occurring in a given region?

7. List five major properties of soils.

8. A farmer has a couple of hectares of land that is almost pure sand. If he fertilizes the soil well, carefully plants seeds, keeps the young plants well watered, and diligently removes weeds from his acreage, will he eventually be successful in growing a crop? Discuss your answer.

9. What characteristics of clay are undesirable for crop production? What characteristics are desirable?

10. What does pH mean? What pH is desirable for most trees and food crops?

11. Suppose that a farmer has soil with a pH of 5.0 but wishes to raise a crop that requires a pH of 6.0. What can he do?

12. What is meant by the statement "Soil inhales and exhales"?

13. Give three reasons why a plant cannot survive without water.

14. Discuss the statement "A soil profile represents a kind of autobiography." Is this statement valid? Why or why not?

15. What is the basis for naming a soil order? Give an example.

16. Compare the profiles of spodosol and mollisol soils. What are the major differences?

17. A Brazilian farmer living in the Amazon river valley cleared his land of forest cover and started to farm it. Were his prospects of long-term success very good? Why or why not?

18. Compare the aridisols and ultisols with respect to distribution in the United States, crop-producing potential, appearance, and fertility.

SUGGESTED READINGS

Brady, N. C. *The Nature and Property of Soils*, 9th ed. New York: Macmillan, 1984. This is a classic work on soils. It provides both comprehensive and in-depth treatment.

Ehrlich, P. R., and J. Roughgarden, *The Science of Ecology*. New York: Macmillan, 1987. Contains a section on the importance of soil in relation to the human ecosystem.

Jenny, H. *The Soil Resource: Origin and Behavior*. New York: Springer-Verlag, 1980. Superlative treatment at a sophisticated level.

Singer, M. J., and D. N. Munns. *Soils: An Introduction*. New York: Macmillan, 1987. Excellent introductory textbook.

U.S. Department of Agriculture. *Soil Taxonomy. Handbook 436*. Washington, D.C.: U.S. Government Printing Office, 1975. Describes the latest soil classification system.

5

Soil Conservation and the American Farm

The modern American farm is an important type of land use system, consisting of natural and human-made components (Figure 5-1). It has living components such as farmers, crops, insect pests, rodent pests, and so on. Nonliving components include soil minerals, rainfall, solar energy, fertilizers, pesticides, irrigation canals, tractors, and fossil fuels. These living and nonliving components interact in many ways. Numerous activities take place in this system, such as plowing, fertilizer application, photosynthesis, irrigation, erosion, and crop destruction by insects and rodents.

FARMING IN AMERICA

Need for Greater Food Production by American Farmers

The average farmer in the United States now produces enough food to satisfy the needs of about 55 people. But farmers must do even better in the years to come. First, farmers must produce more food to meet rising domestic demands. Second, farmers may need to increase food production to make more food available for export. Such exports are vital to our nation's economic well-being. Third, greater food yields are necessary to prevent hunger and starvation in the less developed nations of Africa, Asia, and South America while these countries find ways to control their population growth and to become self-sufficient in food production.

Problems Facing the American Farmer

Although farming may appear to involve little more than planting seeds and watching them grow, it is in fact a highly technical and sophisticated activity. It involves a complex web of interacting factors threatened by a number of problems, including the following:

1. *Buckshot urbanization.* American agriculture faces a serious dilemma. At the same time that it is under pressure to increase production, much prime farmland is being covered over by suburban homes, shopping centers, factories, and highways. Concrete is invading the cornfields. Highway "cloverleafs" are replacing the clover. Much of this urbanization is occurring in a hit-or-miss "buckshot" pattern. For every acre that is destroyed for crop-growing, another acre is rendered useless because of its isolation from adjoining farmlands. Because of this insidious process, our nation is losing 3,200 hectares (8,000 acres) of agricultural land per day—and this loss is permanent. Buckshot urbanization has been particularly destructive in the industrial states east of the Mississippi River. Maryland, for example, is losing 12,000 hectares (30,000 acres) per year. New England has lost

80

FIGURE 5-1   Cropland distribution in the United States. Each dot represents 25,000 acres.

about 50 percent of its best acreage. Florida could lose all of its high-quality farmland by the year 2000.

2. *Soil erosion.* Soil erosion has either destroyed or seriously impaired about 60 million hectares (150 million acres), or 15 percent of our nation's total cropland area. In an important address to the American Farm Bureau, Douglas M. Costle, then head of the EPA, emphasized how seriously accelerated erosion is affecting crop yields: "Soil scientists generally agree that even deep soils cannot sustain losses of more than 12 tons per hectare (five tons an acre) per year without harming productivity. Yet erosion losses nationally, from all sources, are estimated at between 22-29 tons per hectare (9 and 12 tons an acre) per year! In some cases 60 tons or more are recorded." A recent study of American farms showed that nearly half of our soil is eroding faster than it can be regenerated.

3. *High fuel costs.* Modern American agriculture depends on huge inputs of energy derived from increasingly costly fossil fuels, such as oil and natural gas, which are already in short supply. Over 50 percent of the world's known reserves of oil will be consumed by the year 2000. At that point the demand is likely to exceed the supply and costs are bound to climb, making agriculture even more costly.

4. *Flood and sediment damage,* caused in part by overgrazing, clear cutting of forests, strip mining, stream channelization, and construction projects, destroys $1.3 billion worth of crops and pastures annually.

5. *Limited water supplies.* Water needed for irrigation will sharply fall in the near future because of the competing demands of expanding urban populations, industrial development, and heavy irrigation demands.

6. *Salinization.* Because of poor soil drainage and improper irrigation practices, some farmland in California is now producing only one major crop: Imperial Valley "snow"—a whitish crust of aluminum sulfate. This salt is deposited when irrigation water evaporates from poorly drained land. Salts have reduced crop yields and destroyed 3.2 million hectares (8 million acres) of farmland in the West.

7. *High fertilizer costs.* As a result of the nutrient depletion of soils, American agriculture has been increasingly dependent on costly synthetic fertilizers. Since 1950 the nation's farmers have boosted their annual use of fertilizer at least sixteenfold. However, this has caused extensive, severe water pollution problems.

8. *Harmful effects of pesticides.* The intensive application of persistent pesticides, such as DDT, to croplands has resulted in soil contamination with residues. Some of those pesticides adversely affect the process of nitrification by which soil bacteria convert nitrogen to a form that is usable by crops. They also may enter food chains and impair the health of wildlife and humans.

9. *Atmospheric pollution* is inflicting about a $350 million annual loss on the agricultural industry. At least 36 commercial crops are affected. Pollution from the flood of vehicles along our interstate highways and powerplants has seriously diminished yields on nearby farms.

10. *Soil compaction.* Because of the continued intensive use of heavy machinery such as tractors and harvesters, agricultural soils in many areas are becoming increasingly compacted. The ability of such

FIGURE **5-2** Geological erosion caused by water—the Grand Canyon of the Colorado River.

soils to hold water and air is markedly reduced. As a result, crop yields decline.

Although this chapter deals primarily with soil problems in the United States, we should emphasize that these problems are experienced by almost *all* nations. For example, two-thirds of India's farmland has been either partly or completely destroyed by erosion. Pakistan is losing many hectares of cropland every day as a result of irrigation-induced salinization. Misguided farming ventures in the tropics of South America, Africa, and Asia have failed miserably because of the eventual hardening of the iron-rich soil into a brick-like "pavement" that is virtually impenetrable to crop root systems. Yet, paradoxically, never before in history have we been so dependent on the soil. One of every seven people in the world are either malnourished or go to bed hungry. This very day, about 33,000 unfortunates will quietly starve to death; tomorrow, 33,000 more. And the situation will probably worsen dramatically, for by the year 2000 the number of people in the world will have increased by 1 billion from 1988. Never in history has it been so urgent for us to develop a sense of stewardship toward our soil heritage.

THE NATURE OF SOIL EROSION

During the three-century history of soil deterioration in the United States, erosion has played a dominant role. The word **erosion** is derived from the Latin word *erodere,* meaning "to gnaw out." Erosion is, thus, the process by which rock fragments and soil are detached from their original site, transported, and then eventually deposited at a new location. The principal agents of erosion are wind and water.

Geological, or Natural, Erosion

Geological erosion is a process that has occurred at an extremely slow rate ever since the earth was formed nearly 5 billion years ago. Scientists estimate that water erodes a rocky surface at the rate of one-fourth to one-fiftieth of a millimeter per year—the rate depending, of course, on the force of the water and the nature of the rock. The mountains, valleys, canyons, coastlines, and deltas on the earth's surface have been sculptured by water and wind erosion working over eons. The Appalachian Mountains were once as tall and rugged as the Rocky Mountains, but since their formation 200 million years ago, they have been gradually worn down by erosive forces. Were it not for geological erosion, New Orleans would be resting on the bottom of the Gulf of Mexico, for the delta on which it is built was formed by a deposit of soil transported by the Mississippi River from sites as far as 1,600 kilometers (1,000 miles) away. The Grand Canyon originated as a shallow channel 100 million years ago. It was ultimately scoured to its awesome 1-mile depth by rain and the churning waters of the Colorado River (Figure 5-2).

Accelerated Erosion

Geological erosion, then, has continued to operate at a slow, deliberate pace for millions of years. However,

FIGURE 5-3 Comparison of top soil thickness in 1780 and today.

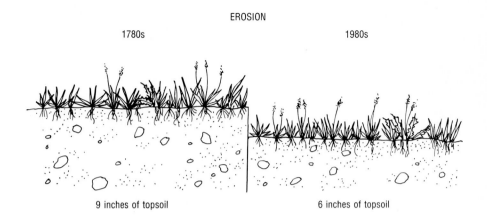

EROSION

1780s   1980s

9 inches of topsoil   6 inches of topsoil

with the appearance of humans, an artificial type of erosion began that has operated at a much faster rate than natural erosion. (The severity of erosion in the United States is shown in Figures 5-3 and 5-4.)

No one knows how much soil is eroded from U.S. farms and ranches, but the best estimates indicate that each year about 2.7 million metric tons (3 million tons) are washed away by water alone—an average loss of more than 342 metric tons per square kilometer (1.4 metric tons per acre). It is with this accelerated erosion that the conservationist is primarily concerned, and for good reason.

Accelerated erosion can also be caused by wind, especially after the land has been laid bare by farming, logging, strip mining, or construction activities. Some of the most destructive wind erosion our nation has ever experienced occurred on the Great Plains during the 1930s. Because of the frequency and severity of the dust storms in this region, it was called the **Dust Bowl**.

FIGURE 5-4 Accelerated erosion caused by humans resulted in these huge water-carved gullies on a North Carolina farm.

THE DUST BOWL

Fifty centimeters (20 inches) of annual precipitation is considered marginal for crop production. The arid and semiarid Great Plains frequently have less. During periods of severe drought, rainfall may be considerably less than 26 centimeters (5 inches) annually. Throughout history, the Great Plains experienced alternating periods of drought and adequate rainfall. Although major droughts appear to have recurred at roughly 22-year intervals, the precise time of their occurrence has not been predictable (Figure 5-5). Drought visited the Great Plains in 1890 and again in 1910. During each dry spell, crops withered and died. Farms and ranches were abandoned, only to be reoccupied during the ensuing years of adequate rainfall.

Then came the Big Drought. For five years, from 1927 to 1932, there was hardly enough rain to settle the dust. On the ranches, the buffalo grass and other prairie grasses lost their vigor and withered. Overstocked pastures were clipped to ground level by scrawny cattle. Much livestock was mercifully slaughtered.

Droughts had visited the plains before; so had windstorms. But never before in the history of the North American prairie had the land been more vulnerable to their combined assault. Gone were the profusely branching root systems of the buffalo grass, the grama grass, the big bluestem, and the little bluestem, which had originally kept the rich brown soil in place. Gone was the decomposing organic material that aids in building stable soil aggregates and the soil cover of grass mat and sagebrush. On the ranches, soil structure deteriorated under the concerted pounding of millions of cattle. On the wheat and cotton farms, soil structure broke down under the abuse inflicted by the heavy machinery. The stage was set for the "black blizzards" (Figure 5-6).

In the spring of 1934 and again in 1935, winds of gale velocities swept over the Great Plains. In western Kansas and Oklahoma, as well as in the neigh-

FIGURE 5-5 A 75-year record of rainfall and temperature in the wheat-growing states of Kansas, Nebraska, North Dakota, South Dakota, and Oklahoma. The graph indicates a drought cycle of about 22 years. The Dust Bowl era was characterized by extreme drought.

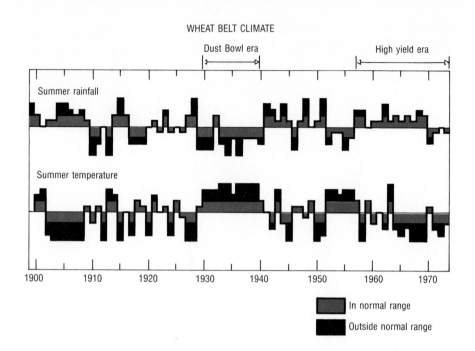

boring parts of Texas, Colorado, and Nebraska, the wind whirled minute particles of clay and silt far upward into the prairie sky. Brown dust clouds up to 2,000-meters (7,000-feet) thick filled the air, with an upper edge almost 3.3 kilometers (2 miles) high (Figure

5-7). One storm of May 11, 1934, lifted 300 million tons of fertile soil into the air. (This roughly equals the total soil tonnage scooped from Central America to form the Panama Canal.) In many areas, the wilted wheat was uprooted and blown into the air. In the

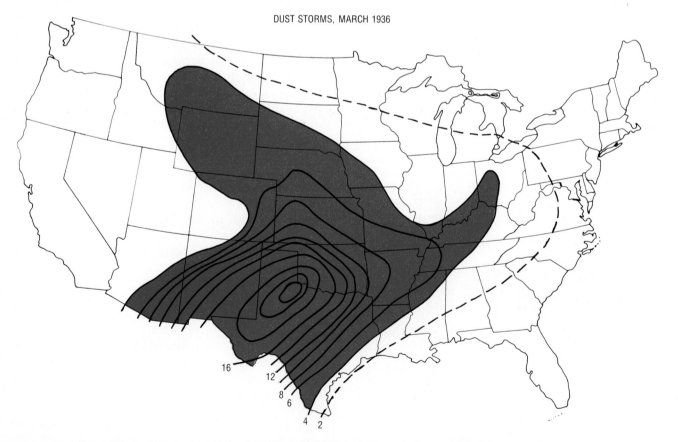

FIGURE 5-6 Concentration of dust storms of 1936 in the High Plains of Texas, Oklahoma, Colorado, and Kansas.

FIGURE 5-7 Dust storm approaching Springfield, Colorado, on May 21, 1937. This storm reached the city limits at exactly 4:47 a.m. Total darkness lasted about one-half hour.

Amarillo, Texas, area during March and April 1935, 15 wind storms raged for 24 hours; 4 lasted for over 55 hours.

Dust from Oklahoma prairies came to rest on the deck of a steamer 330 kilometers (200 miles) out in the Atlantic. Dust sifted into the plush offices of Wall Street and smudged the luxury apartments of Park Avenue. When it rained in the blow area, the drops would sometimes come down as dilute mud. In Washington, D.C., mud splattered buildings of the Department of Agriculture, a rude reminder of the problem facing it and the nation. A thousand miles westward, people stuffed water-soaked newspapers into window cracks to no avail (Figure 5-8). The dust sifted into kitchens,

forming a thin film on pots and pans and fresh-baked bread. Blinded by swirling dust clouds, ranchers got lost in their own backyards. Motorists pulled off to the side of the highways. Hundreds of airplanes were grounded. Trains were stalled by huge drifts. Hospital nurses placed wet cloth on patients' faces to ease their breathing. In Colorado's Baca County (March 1935), 48 relief workers contracted "dust pneumonia," 4 of whom died.

When the winds finally subsided, ranchers and farmers wearily emerged to survey the desolation. Five to 30 centimeters (2 to 12 inches) of fertile clay and silt soils had been carried to the Atlantic seaboard (Figure 5-9). The coarser sand, too heavy to be airborne, bounced across the land, sheared off young wheat, and finally accumulated as dunes to the leeward side of homes and barns. Heavily mortgaged power machinery became shrouded in sand.

The dust storms of the 1930s inflicted both social and economic suffering. Yet a few ranchers and farmers were philosophical about their misfortunes and even cracked jokes about the birds flying backward "to keep the sand out of their eyes" and about the prairie dogs "digging burrows 100 feet in the air." However, for most Dust Bowl victims, the dusters were not funny. Many victims were virtually penniless. The 300 million tons of topsoil removed in a single storm on May 22, 1934, represents the equivalent of taking 3,000 farms of 100 acres each out of crop production. Up to 1940, Dust Bowl relief alone cost American taxpayers over $1 billion; $7 million (more than was paid for Alaska) was pumped into a single Colorado county. The only recourse for many of these ill-fated farmers was to find a new way of life. They piled their belongings into rickety cars and trucks and moved out—some to the Pacific

FIGURE 5-8 Abandoned Oklahoma farmstead, showing the disastrous results of wind erosion.

FIGURE 5-9   Wind erosion in the Great Plains.

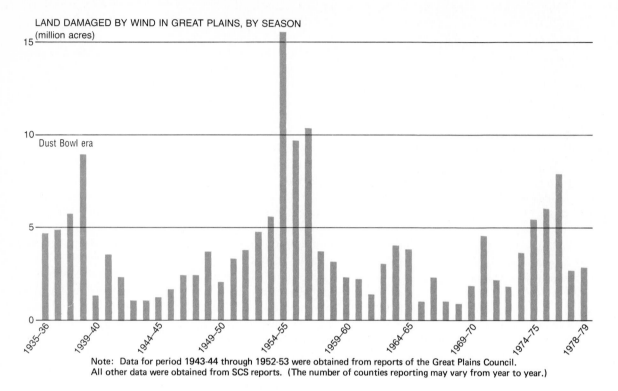

Note: Data for period 1943-44 through 1952-53 were obtained from reports of the Great Plains Council. All other data were obtained from SCS reports. (The number of counties reporting may vary from year to year.)

coast, some to the big industrial cities of the Midwest and East. However, our nation was still in the throes of a depression, and many an emigrating family found nothing but frustration, bitterness, and suffering at the end of the road.

THE SHELTERBELT PROGRAM

In an attempt to prevent future Dust Bowls, the federal government launched a massive shelterbelt system in 1935. More than 218 million trees were planted

FIGURE 5-10 This North Dakota farm is well protected from wind and snow by a 17-year-old windbreak of confiers, fruit trees, and shrubs.

on 30,000 farms across the Great Plains from North Dakota south to Texas. The green checkerboard patterns formed by the 32,000 kilometers (20,000 miles) of windbreaks have added color and variety to the prairie landscape (Figure 5-10). In the Central Plains a typical shelterbelt consists of one to five rows of trees planted on the western margin of a farm in a north–south line, to intercept winter's prevailing westerly winds. Conifers such as red cedar, spruce, and pine provide the best year-round protection. By planting a few rows of grain between the rows of trees, farmers can further reduce wind erosion. A properly designed shelterbelt of adequate height and thickness can reduce a wind velocity of 50 kilometers (30 miles) per hour to only 13 kilometers (8 miles) per hour to leeward of the trees (Figure 5-11).

Although windbreaks occupy valuable land that otherwise could be used for crop production, are relatively slow to grow, and must be fenced from livestock until the stands are well established, the accrued benefits far outweigh these minor disadvantages. In addition to controlling wind erosion, properly designed windbreaks provide aesthetic benefits, increase soil moisture by reducing evaporation and trapping snow, and provide a habitat for wildlife. Moreover, the fuel requirement for heating and cooling nearby homes is reduced by about 28 percent. Unfortunately, a number of shelterbelts planted in the 1930s are now being removed— in some cases so that the farmer can use the wood as fuel, in other cases to make room for crops and to facili-

tate the use of heavy farm machinery and sprinkler irrigation systems. Roughly 25 percent of the shelterbelts in Oklahoma had been removed by the early 1980s.

SOIL EROSION TODAY

The Dust Bowl period was devastating to our nation's soil resource, to our economy, and to the emotional well-being of millions of Americans. In the fifty years that we have passed since that critical period in American agriculture, the federal government has spent tens of billions of dollars to control erosion. Scientists at many major universities have conducted erosion-control research with tax-money support. Hundreds of scientific publications have been written on the subject. The USDA has established more than 3,000 Soil Conservation Districts whose prime function is to assist the farmer with erosion problems. So, after devoting all this time, energy, and money to soil erosion control, we, as taxpayers, are justified in asking: "Is the American farmer doing any better in controlling erosion today than during the Dust Bowl years?" Unfortunately, the answer is an emphatic "no." In fact, soil erosion today, almost incredibly, is even more severe than it was in the 1930s (Figure 5-12).

Black blizzards are still very much with us. For example, in 1977, a major dust storm caused extensive damage in the San Joaquin Valley of California. More than

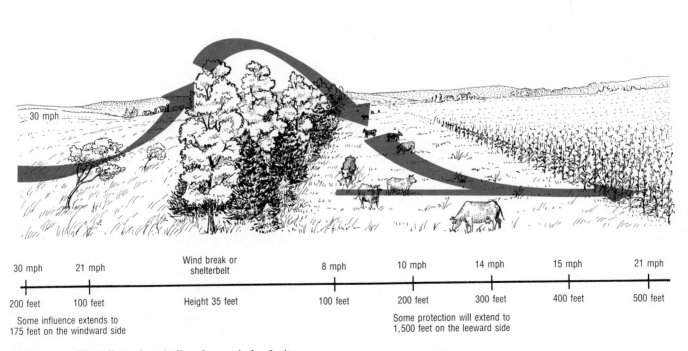

Wind currents in confusion

30 mph	21 mph	Wind break or shelterbelt	8 mph	10 mph	14 mph	15 mph	21 mph
200 feet	100 feet	Height 35 feet	100 feet	200 feet	300 feet	400 feet	500 feet

Some influence extends to 175 feet on the windward side

Some protection will extend to 1,500 feet on the leeward side

FIGURE 5-11 The effect of a windbreak on wind velocity.

FIGURE 5-12 Soil erosion rates in the United States caused by water.

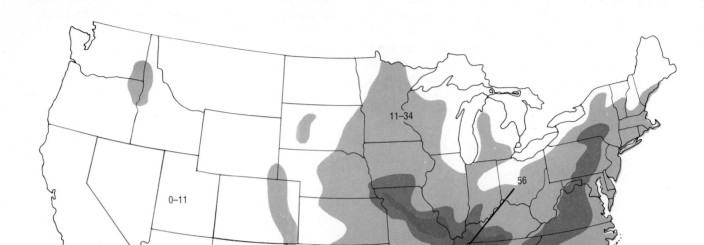

0–11 mg/ha per year

11–34 mg/ha per year

34–56 mg/ha per year

56 mg/ha per year

20 million metric tons of fertile soil was windstripped from a 2000-square-kilometer (800-square-mile) area of grazing land within 24 hours. Major natural factors contributing to the dust storm were severe drought and wind velocities of more than 160 kilometers (100 miles) per hour. Even more important, however, were anthropogenic (human-related) factors such as severe overgrazing and the lack of windbreaks. Moreover, a considerable amount of land had just been plowed in preparation for planting. Another predisposing factor was the removal of vegetative cover due to urban expansion, oil field development, and the recreational use of motorcycles and other off-road vehicles.

One highly destructive agricultural practice that is contributing to our nation's high rate of soil loss is **plow-out** or **sodbusting**—the conversion of previously uncultivated land to cropland. Much of this sodbusting has occurred in the past fifteen years. As the Council on Environmental Quality reports, the most dramatic examples of plow-out are those affecting prairie grasslands in the western Great Plains. In several states, this has become a highly emotional issue. Short-term gains that may result from sodbusting are often negated within three to five years by wind erosion, loss of moisture, and loss of organic material. The land may not

recover for decades. A number of counties in Colorado and Montana have already passed ordinances to limit plow-out, and in 1985 the federal government passed legislation to reduce sodbusting.

Soil erosion is sharply reducing the American farmer's capacity to produce food and fiber at a time when both domestic and foreign demands for our crops are reaching an all-time high. Some important wheat-growing regions are suffering such severe erosion that their productivity will end by the year 2000. Crop production in the United States grew at the rate of 2.1 percent per year from 1939 to 1965. Recently, however, the growth rate has been reduced to only 1.7 percent. This is largely the result of wind and water erosion losses. At present, nearly one-half of our cropland is losing topsoil at an excessive rate (Figure 5-12). For every kilogram of wheat harvested in eastern Washington, 20 kilograms (9 pounds) of topsoil are lost due to erosion. In many of the Midwestern states, such as Iowa and Illinois, 2 bushels of soil are lost for each bushel of corn harvested. To transport the soil lost annually in the United States would require a train of boxcars more than 1 million kilometers (633,000 miles long)—sufficient to circle the earth at the equator 24 times. To compensate for the nutrient losses caused by erosion would require an annual expenditure of $1.6 billion for fertilizer.

Topsoil depth in the United States ranges from a few centimeters to more than 1 meter. The USDA has determined that soils with a thick layer of top soil can withstand erosion losses of 12 metric tons per hectare (5 tons per acre) per year without losing their ability to support crops. This amount of soil, they say, is normally regained by the natural processes of soil formation. (Some critics disagree, saying that the tolerable rate of soil erosion should be *much* lower. The tolerable rate should not exceed natural soil replacement, otherwise farmers are losing topsoil.) Unfortunately, on 44 percent of our nation's croplands, soil losses are greater than 12 metric tons per hectare. For example, in some areas of Washington, Oregon, and Idaho, 120 to 250 metric tons per hectare per year are lost because of farming on steep slopes and highly erodible soil types.

Under the Soil and Water Resources Conservation Act of 1977, the USDA was charged with making a comprehensive appraisal of the quantity and quality of U.S. soil resources. It was found that these soils differ greatly in their susceptibility to erosion. Some types are 1,000 times more erodible than others. Cropland planted to corn showed losses that ranged from about 20 metric tons per hectare (8 tons per acre) per year on 17 million acres to more than 500 metric tons per hectare (200 tons per acre) per year on 49,000 acres.

FACTORS AFFECTING THE RATE OF SOIL EROSION

Rainfall and Runoff

Annual precipitation in the United States ranges from almost nothing in some parts of Death Valley, California, to 360 centimeters (140 inches) in parts of Washington State. The amount of precipitation a region receives greatly affects erosion rates. However, even more important is the seasonal rainfall pattern.

A town in Florida once experienced a deluge of 60 centimeters (24 inches) of rain in only 24 hours. The soil

loss resulting from runoff waters must have been severe. On the other hand, had this 60-centimeter rainfall been the result of daily 1-inch drizzles occurring over 24 consecutive days, the erosion threat would have been negligible because the soil would have had sufficient time in which to absorb the water. Surprisingly, even in the arid deserts of Nevada and Arizona, where annual rainfall averages 13 centimeters (5 inches), excessive erosion occurs because the entire annual precipitation occurs in a few torrential cloudbursts. As a result, the desert floor is dissected by canyons gouged out by runoff waters.

Soil Erodibility

Soil structure, discussed in Chapter 4, greatly influences its erodibility. The structure of a soil can be improved by plowing under a crop of clover or alfalfa (green manuring) or simply by adding decaying organic material, such as leaves, or barnyard manure. In Iowa, soil loss from nonmanured land was over five times that from heavily manured land. The addition of organic material improves the soil's water-absorbing ability. This trait, in turn, results in a more dense, vigorous growth of corn. The vegetative mantle further protects the soil (Figure 5-13). The developing corn root system also penetrates the soil particles more vigorously and binds them in place, reducing erosion.

Topography

The slope of the terrain greatly affects the intensity of surface runoff and soil erosion. Steepness of slope is indicated in terms of percentages. Thus, a 10 percent slope is one that drops 10 meters over a horizontal distance of 100 meters. In potato-growing Aroostook County, Maine, where slopes may be as steep as 25 percent, more than 60 centimeters (24 inches) of topsoil has already been removed by erosion since farming began. On farms planted to row crops like corn and cotton, a doubling of the slope results in a tripling of soil erosion by water.

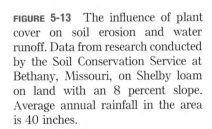

FIGURE 5-13 The influence of plant cover on soil erosion and water runoff. Data from research conducted by the Soil Conservation Service at Bethany, Missouri, on Shelby loam on land with an 8 percent slope. Average annual rainfall in the area is 40 inches.

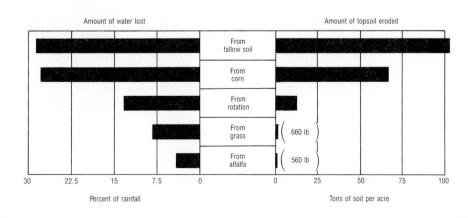

FIGURE 5-14 Contour farming in Bell County, Texas. The pattern of farm conservation is reflected in the fields of this Texas farmer, who uses contour farming to reduce rainwater runoff and its erosive effects on soil. The different shades are caused by different crops (strip-cropping); the pattern conforms to the contour of his fields, with the highest elevation where the smaller rings are. Besides slowing water so that it can soak into the soil better, such measures reduce siltation, the most common cause of water pollution in the United States, according to the U.S. Department of Agriculture.

CONTROLLING EROSION

Erosion Control Practices

By altering the factors that contribute to soil erosion, soil erosion can be controlled. Erosion control practices include (1) contour farming, (2) strip cropping, (3) terracing, (4) gully reclamation, (5) shelterbelts (discussed earlier), (6) removal of cropland from production, and (7) conservation tillage.

CONTOUR FARMING. This erosion control practice may be defined as plowing, seeding, cultivating, and harvesting *across* the slope, rather than *with* it (Figure 5-14). It was used by Thomas Jefferson, who wrote in 1813, "We now plow horizontally, following the curvature of the hills . . . scarcely an ounce of soil is now carried off." Jefferson, however, was an exception. In the early days of American agriculture, the farmer who could plow the straightest furrows (usually up and down slopes) was considered a master plowman and was praised by his neighbors.

An experiment conducted on a Texas cotton field with a 3 to 5 percent slope revealed that the average annual water runoff from a noncontoured plot was 12 centimeters (4.6 inches), whereas that for a contoured plot was 65 percent less, or 4 centimeters (1.6 inches). The lower the water runoff the lower the erosion rate.

STRIP CROPPING. On sloped land, planting crops on contoured strips is an effective erosion deterrent (Figure 5-15). When viewed from a distance, such farmland appears as a series of slender, curving belts of color. A row crop, such as corn, cotton, tobacco, or potatoes, and a cover crop of hay or legumes are alternated along the contours. Strip cropping is frequently combined with crop rotation, so that a strip planted to a soil-depleting corn crop one year will be sown to a soil-enriching legume crop the next.

TERRACING. Terracing has been practiced by humans for centuries. It was used by the Incas of Peru and by the ancient Chinese. Plagued with relatively dense populations and a scarcity of arable land, those civilizations were forced to till extremely steep slopes, even mountainsides, in order to prevent widespread hunger. The flat, steplike bench terraces that those ancient agriculturists constructed, however, are not amenable to today's farming methods. To be effec-

FIGURE 5-15 Strip cropping in Wisconsin. Alternating strips reduce erosion, pesticide demands (because of increased diversity), and help enhance soil fertility.

tive, terraces must check water flow before it attains a velocity of 1 meter per second (3 feet per second) to loosen and transport soil (Figures 5-16 and 5-17). In the United States, two major types of terraces are constructed to control erosion: the ridge terrace and the channel terrace.

1. *Ridge terrace.* This type of terrace is formed simply by constructing a ridge of earth at right angles to the slope—in other words, across the path of water runoff. It is the terrace typically used on the Great Plains. Two types of ridge terrace are shown in Figure 5-16.

2. *Channel terrace.* This type of terrace is formed by digging a channel across the slope. It is frequently used in the Tennessee and Ohio Valleys, as well as the Southeast and the Mid-Atlantic states, where rainfall is high but the water-absorbing capacity of the soil is poor.

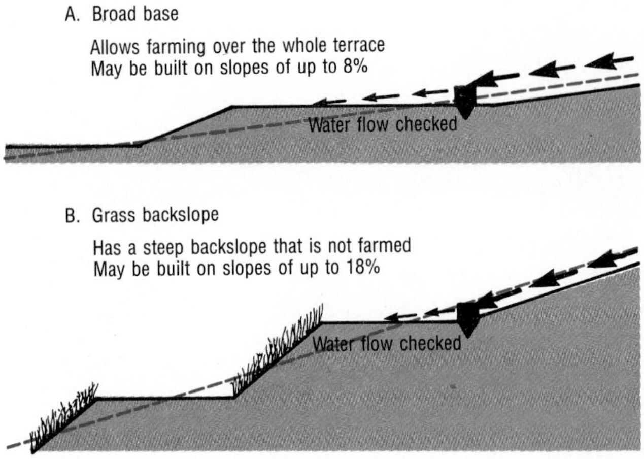

GULLY RECLAMATION. Gullies are especially common in the Southeast due to a long history of soil abuse and intense rains. Gullies are danger signals indicating that land is eroding rapidly and that the area may become a wasteland unless erosion is promptly controlled. Some gullies work their way up a slope at the rate of 5 meters (15 feet) a year (Figure 5-18A). In North Carolina, a 45-meter (150-foot)-deep gully was gouged out in only sixty years, swallowing up fence posts, farm implements, and buildings in the process.

If relatively small, a gully can be plowed and then seeded to a quickly growing "nurse" crop of barley,

A. Broad base
Allows farming over the whole terrace
May be built on slopes of up to 8%

Water flow checked

B. Grass backslope
Has a steep backslope that is not farmed
May be built on slopes of up to 18%

Water flow checked

FIGURE 5-16 Terrace types. A comparison of the broad base and grass backslope terraces.

oats, or wheat. In this way, erosion will be checked until sod can become established. In cases of severe gullying, small check dams of manure and straw constructed at 6-meter (20-foot) intervals may be effective. Silt collects behind the dams and gradually fills the channel, allowing plants to take root. Dams may be constructed of brush or stakes held securely with a woven wire netting. Earth, stone, and even concrete dams may be built at intervals along the gully. Once dams have been constructed and water runoff has been restrained, soil may be stabilized by planting rapidly growing shrubs, vines, and trees. Willows are effective. Not only does such pioneer vegetation discourage future erosion, but it obliter-

FIGURE 5-17 A system of parallel terraces controls water erosion on a farm near Templeton, Iowa.

FIGURE 5-18A   Gully erosion on a Minnesota farm.

FIGURE 5-18B   To prevent further erosion the area was planted with protective vegetation, primarily locust trees. Five growing seasons later, the locust trees averaged fifteen feet in height and not only served to control erosion, but provided wildlife cover and beautified the landscape.

ates the ugly scars and provides food, cover, and breeding sites for wildlife (Figure 5-18B).

REMOVING CROPLAND FROM PRODUCTION. In 1985 Congress passed the **Food Security Act**. It calls for the removal of 18 million hectares (45 million acres) of marginal cropland from the cropland base. The cropland taken out of production is that which is most vulnerable to erosion when cultivated. This land will be planted to trees, shrubs, and grasses to stabilize the soil.

A major objective of this act is to control erosion on 45 million acres of highly erodible cropland. Under the terms of the act, the farmer makes a contract with the USDA to withdraw erodible farmland from crop production for ten years and to establish vegetation cover (grass, shrubs, trees) on this land to stabilize the soil. The USDA, in turn, makes "rental" payments to the farmer during this period. Payments average about $42 per acre per year. Not only are the plantings valuable in checking erosion, they are useful in providing food

and cover for wildlife as well. The erosion rates on the 1.5 million hectares (3.8 million acres) withdrawn by the end of 1986 was over 62.5 metric tons per hectare (25 metric tons per acre).

Enforcement of the erosion control provisions of the Food Security Act poses a formidable challenge to the USDA. However, this problem may be solved by the work of USDA scientists at Kansas State University, who in 1989 developed regionally adaptable computer models of erosion rates. The models, it is hoped, will enable the USDA to know instantly how much soil erosion a particular farming practice on a certain soil type will cause in a specific type of climate anywhere in the United States. Suppose, for example, that the USDA learns, with the aid of computer models, that Mr. Brown's uphill-and-downhill plowing method on silty loam in northern Illinois is causing the erosion of 74 tons per hectare (30 tons of soil per acre) annually—62 tons per hectare (25 tons per acre more) than is considered acceptable. If Mr. Brown refuses to shift to contour plowing, the USDA could reduce or even eliminate his federal subsidies, as required by the Food Security Act.

CONSERVATION TILLAGE.   Before we discuss the revolutionary agricultural development known as **conservation tillage**, we must describe the traditional procedures involved in tilling the soil:

1. One pass is made over the field with a plow. During this process, the crop residues remaining after the previous harvest are plowed under and the upper 15 centimeters (6 inches) of the soil up inverted and broken up.
2. One or two passes over the field are then made with a harrow to break up any clods and to prepare a seedbed for the next crop.
3. After row crops like corn or cotton have sprouted, a cultivator is used to remove weeds that compete with the crop for moisture and nutrients.

In contrast, conservation tillage restricts plowing of the soil to reduce erosion. Such restriction may vary from slight to complete. If tillage is omitted completely, the term **no till** is applied. Conservation tillage has spread rapidly from only 2 percent of our nation's harvested croplands in 1962 to more than 20 percent in the 1980s. Experts predict that by the year 2000, 75 percent of our farmlands will be under some form of conservation tillage (Figure 5-19).

In the no-till form of conservation tillage, special machinery is used that cuts narrow slits into the ground in which the seeds of the next crop are planted. This is all done in a single pass over the field. No seedbed preparation is necessary. Corn and soybeans, for example, can be sown directly in wheat stubble. Up to 75

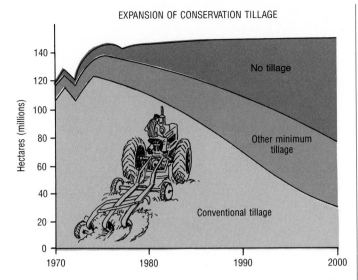

EXPANSION OF CONSERVATION TILLAGE

No tillage

Other minimum tillage

Conventional tillage

FIGURE 5-19 Decline in conventional tillage and growth in conservation tillage in the United States from 1970 to 2000 (projected).

percent of the residue from the previous crop harvest remains on the surface, compared to only 3 percent with conventional tillage.

Research conducted on farms in Illinois has shown that no-till farming controls erosion even on slopes as steep as 9 percent. On many farms, the layer of crop residues on the surface can reduce soil loss from erosion by 90 percent. In fact, a recent experiment conducted by the Soil Conservation Service (SCS) in Georgia showed that no-till farming reduced erosion losses from 58.5

metric tons per hectare (26 tons per acre) per year to only 0.2 metric ton per hectare (0.1 ton per acre)—more than a 99 percent reduction.

Conservation tillage provides a number of other benefits. There also are some disadvantages. The pros and cons of this revolutionary farming technique are summarized in Table 5-1.

The Soil Conservation Service and Its Program

The black blizzards of the 1930s alerted a hitherto apathetic nation to the plight of its soil resources more forcefully than thousands of urgent speeches.

The federal government finally faced up to the soil erosion problem. It has spent about $30 billion on soil conservation programs in the last 45 years. In 1934 the newly organized Soil Erosion Service (SES) set up 41 soil and water conservation demonstration projects. The labor force for these projects was supplied by Civilian Conservation Corps (CCC) workers drawn from about 50 camps. The projects impressed Congress so much that it established the Soil Conservation Service (SCS) in 1935. The major function of the SCS has been to provide technical assistance to farmers and ranchers so that they can better utilize land with methods that are as consistent with the needs of the soil as with those of the landowner.

The administrative and operative unit of the SCS program is the SCS district, which is organized and run by farmers and ranchers. Each district is staffed by a professional conservationist and several aides who

Table 5-1 Pros and Cons of No-Till Farming

Pros	Cons
1. Labor may be reduced by 30 to 50 percent. The only passes over the field are for planting and fertilizing, pesticide application, and harvesting.	1. Farmers require greater management skills.
2. Use of diesel fuel is reduced by 30 to 50 percent. Farmers in Texas have saved over 2 million gallons of fuel a year.	2. Special equipment is needed to plant seeds directly in crop residues.
3. Wear and tear of farm equipment is reduced.	3. Not suitable for all crops.
4. Soil erosion is generally reduced by 90 percent.	4. Seeds may not make contact with soil if the seed planter is not perfectly level. As a result, seed germination can be lowered.
5. Soil retains more moisture because of reduced rates of evaporation and surface runoff.	5. Plant diseases, such as fungi, may be more abundant because of the higher soil moisture levels.
6. Sediment pollution of lakes and streams is reduced.	6. Populations of crop-destroying insects and rodents are often greater.
7. Fertilizer pollution (eutrophication) of lakes and streams is lessened.	7. Weed populations are often greater; therefore, competition with crops for available nutrients and moisture can be more intense. More herbicides are needed to control these weeds.
8. Crop yields often increase.	8. More energy is consumed (by manufacturers) to produce the additional pesticides.
9. Double cropping, the growing of two different crops in the same growing season, is possible. Thus, soybeans can be planted immediately after a wheat harvest on the same field.	9. Anaerobic (no-oxygen) conditions may prevail in certain pockets of soil. This, in turn, increases the rate of nitrogen loss because denitrifying bacteria are more active.
10. Crop residues provide food and cover for wildlife.	
11. Air pollution is diminished because of the decrease in fuel consumption.	

The Universal Soil Loss Equation

The Universal Soil Loss Equation (USLE) was developed by soil scientists after many decades of research. The equation is:

$$A = RKLSCP$$

where

> A = number of metric tons (tons) of soil lost per hectare (acre) per year
>
> R = rainfall and runoff
>
> K = erodibility of soil
>
> L = length of slope
>
> S = steepness of slope
>
> C = cover type (grass, wheat, forest, etc.)
>
> P = practice used in erosion control (strip cropping, contour farming, etc.)

By using the equation, farmers can estimate soil loss for any farm in the United States. Values for erosion factors $RKLSCP$ can be obtained from any state SCS office.

Suppose that a farmer in southern Ohio, whose soil is a silty loam, would like to know his erosion losses. From tables available from the SCS office he determined that on his farm:

$$R = 150$$
$$K = 0.33$$
$$LS = 0.40$$

Suppose now that the farmer's land is almost devoid of cover from the time of the harvest in autumn to the planting of the next crop the following spring. In this case, $C = 0.9$. Suppose further that the farmer does not use any soil erosion control practices, such as terracing or strip cropping. In this case, $P = 1.0$. The expected soil loss on this Ohio farm can then be calculated by using of the equation:

$$A = (150)(0.33)(0.40)(0.90)(1.00) = 17.8 \text{ tons per acre annually, or } 40.2 \text{ metric tons per hectare}$$

Obviously, erosion is excessive on the farmer's land, the rate being roughly 3.5 times the tolerable limit of 11.2 metric tons per hectare (5 tons per acre) per year. Since factors $RKLS$ remain fairly constant, the only practical way for him to reduce erosion losses on his farm would be to reduce the values of C (cover) and P (practices). He decides to substitute conservation tillage for traditional tillage on his farm. In this way, some crop residues are always on his land, even between the harvest and the next planting. As a result, the value for C drops to 0.1 in the USLE. The farmer further decides to till and plant on the *contour*. Adoption of this practice, in turn, reduces the value of P to 0.4 in the USLE.

Now let us recalculate the soil loss on this Ohio farm after substituting the new values for C and P in the USLE:

$$A = (150)(0.33)(0.40)(0.10)(0.40) = 1.8 \text{ metric tons per hectare } (0.79 \text{ ton per acre}) \text{ per year}$$

It is clear that conservation tillage and contour farming have been extremely effective, reducing erosion losses on the farm from 40 to 1.8 metric tons per hectare (17.8 to 0.79 ton per acre) annually.

---

work directly with farmers on their land. The highly diversified types of assistance provided by the SCS to the farmer are indicated by the kinds of specialists on its staff: agricultural engineers, botanists, chemists, ecologists, foresters, irrigation engineers, land appraisers, land use specialists, soil scientists, and wildlife biologists. Any farmer in an SCS district can request assistance to set up and maintain a sound conservation program on his or her farm. Participation in the SCS program is voluntary. Today nearly 3,000 SCS districts have been organized, embracing roughly 2 million hectares (5 million acres) and 96 percent of the nation's farms and ranchlands. In 1980 the SCS assisted more than 900,000 farmers and ranchers. This assistance included:

1. Soil surveys on 24 million hectares (60 million acres)
2. Conservation tillage on 24 million hectares (60 million acres)
3. Control of salinization (due to improper irrigation practices) on 6,400 hectares (16,000 acres) in the Colorado River Valley
4. Identification of prime farming areas on 500 different county soil maps
5. Construction of several thousand terraces and farm ponds.

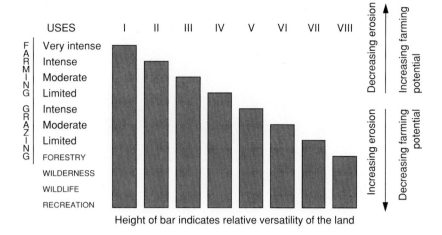

FIGURE 5-20 Land classification and capability. Class I land suitable for very intense farming and grazing. Class VIII land suitable for forestry and other uses. Increasing usage will increase erosion.

In addition, the SCS established plant cover on the lava-covered slopes of Mt. Saint Helens in Washington.

Each year more than 400,000 hectares (1 million acres) of agricultural land, lying primarily on the "edge of town," are converted to urban use. Jaguars and Mustangs roar where cattle once roamed. As a result, the SCS has found a new challenge. As one spokesman has expressed it, "The country's 3,000 soil and water conservation districts have inherited the problems and opportunities of exploding suburbia. A common experience has been the replacement of two or three problems of individual farmers by the soil and water ailments of thousands of new homeowners." The SCS has prepared soil survey maps to meet not only the needs of prospective homeowners, but also those of highway engineers and public utilities. Soils data are very useful to urban planners in helping them to select and develop desirable spatial distribution patterns for industrial, commercial, residential and recreational development.

One of the most significant accomplishments of the SCS early in its history was the development of a **land capability classification**. In this scheme, land is classified into eight categories. Class I land is most suitable for crop production, being flat, fertile, and not vulnerable to erosion. Classes II and III may be used for growing crops, but proper erosion control measures must be practiced. Class IV land is suitable for grazing livestock. Classes V, VI, and VII may be used as rangeland or forest. Class VIII land, being stony, infertile, and/or hilly, is suitable only as a wildlife habitat, wilderness, and/or recreation (Figures 5-20 and 5-21). This system helps farmers develop farming plans that put the land to

FIGURE 5-21 Land capability of this farm is indicated by Roman numerals according to the official USDA System.

FIGURE 5-22   Conservation program for a Georgia cotton farm.

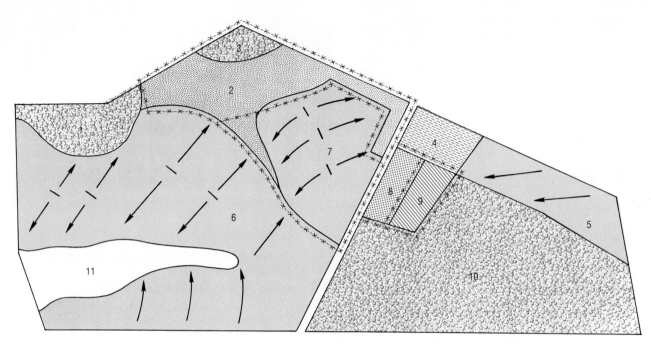

Field number	Acres	Recommended Use	Recommended Land Management
1	2.5	Woods	Thin and cull; cut annually for sustained yields
3	1.5		
10	22.0		
2	5.0	Costal Bermuda and Crimson Clover	Construct fence; lime and fertilizer as determined by soil analysis
8	2.0	Common Bermuda and Crimson Clover	Lime and fertilizer
9	2.0	Fescue and Ladino Clover	Construct fence; lime and fertilizer as determined by soil analysis
4	2.0	Farmstead	
11	5.0	Permanent sod	Lime and fertilizer
6	39.0	Rotation cropland	Build up terraces; establish 4-year rotation of small grain with row crops
7	9.0	Rotation cropland	Fence to permit grazing small grain; build up terraces; lime and fertilizer as needed
5	5.0	Rotation cropland	Build up terraces; establish 4-year rotation of small grain with row crops; lime and fertilizer as needed

best use. It's important to note, however, that this system often relegates wildlife to some of the least suitable habitat.

The Development of an SCS Farm Plan

If a farmer requests technical assistance from this SCS district, four steps are followed in executing the conservation plan for the farm.

First, the technician and the farmer make an intensive survey of the farm. On the basis of such criteria as slope, fertility, stoniness, drainage, topsoil thickness, and susceptibility to erosion, the technician maps each parcel of land on the basis of its capability. Each plot is given a capability symbol in the form of a Roman numeral or color. This capability map is then superimposed on an aerial photograph.

Second, the farmer draws up a **farm plan** with assistance from the technician. This plan involves decisions on how each acre will be used and how it will be improved and protected. For example, should a given acre be used for crops, pasture, forests, or wildlife area? Usually alternative uses and treatments are considered.

Third, the treatment and uses called for in the plan are actually *applied*. Although much of this application can be completed by the farmer alone, he or she may find it helpful to enlist the aid of the SCS technicians for more complex conservation measures like terracing and strip cropping. Recommended management practices for a Georgia cotton farm are shown in Figure 5-22.

The final and most important phase of the program is its *maintenance* from year to year with the assistance of conservation technicians. As time passes, agricultural geneticists might develop a new strain of rust-resistant wheat or tick-resistant breed of cattle. A new subspecies of bluegill may be discovered that thrives in farm ponds, or perhaps a new method of tilling wetlands will become available. These new developments can gradually be incorporated into the overall conservation program.

SOIL FERTILITY

Loss of Soil Nutrients

LOSS BY CROPPING. Before settlers came to North America, this vast continent was populated by ten million native Indians, far fewer people than inhabit the Chicago area today. Although the Indians raised a few crops (corn, pumpkins, beans, squash, and potatoes), for the most part they depended on hunting, fishing, and gathering berries, fruits, and nuts. The Indians had little effect on the prairies and forests. Generation after generation of big bluestem grass, oak, hickory, beach maple, spruce, fir, and pine lived and died on the lands the Indians inhabited. During their life span, these plants absorbed large quantities of life-sustaining nutrients from the soil, channeling them into billions of tons of wood, bark, leaves, flowers, roots, and seeds. As organisms died, however, the nutrients were returned to the soil. Soil fertility was also replenished by the wastes and decaying bodies of animals.

Then came the settler's agriculture, which replaced forest and prairie vegetation with corn, wheat, cabbage, beans, and potatoes. Consequently, the normal circular flow of soil elements was greatly disrupted. Where once they were recycled, many soil nutrients began to move down a one-way street—first being channeled into plant or animal crops, then into human digestive tracts and biomass, and then finally, as human waste, being flushed by sewage systems into rivers, lakes, and oceans. Livestock manure returned soil nutrients in some regions, especially before the advent of the farm tractor, but it was not sufficient to halt the nutrient loss. As soil scientist Firman Bear so aptly states, "in many areas of the United States, the land has been turned into a nearly lifeless organic medium that must be nursed along like an invalid at the threshold of death."

LOSS BY EROSION. Erosion has also exacted a heavy toll on soil fertility. It removes millions of tons of nitrogen and phosphorus from American farms and ranches annually—the equivalent of $1.6 billion worth of fertilizer. Each year, erosion from wind and rain deprives future generations of crops of more than 6 billion metric tons of potentially valuable topsoil.

Temporary Restoration of Soil Fertility

USE OF LEGUMES AND CROP ROTATION. An acre of farmland probably loses 27 to 32 kilograms (60 to 70 pounds) of nitrogen yearly in the form of crops that have been harvested, as well as 9 to 11 kilograms (20 to 25 pounds) because of soil erosion. Thus, roughly 36 to 43 kilograms (80 to 95 pounds) of nitrogen per acre are required annually to prevent a deficit. This deficit can be met with **legumes**. Several species can be used, including alfalfa, clover, soybeans, and vetch. Some of the nitrogen fixed by the nodule bacteria is added to the soil and becomes available to the next crop in the rotation.

Effective crop rotation promotes soil fertility and minimizes erosion. A typical three-year rotation pattern might involve a wide-row, cultivated, soil-depleting crop (corn or cotton) the first year; a narrow-row, noncultivated, silt-depleting crop of wheat, barley, or oats the second year; and a dense, noncultivated cover crop (grasses or legumes) the third year. The grass-legume crop of the terminal rotation year would cover the soil with an almost continuous shield of leaves and stems; it would receive the full impact of rainfall and minimize erosion. Moreover, the nitrogen-fixing bacteria of the root nodules would fix about 220 kilograms of nitrogen per hectare (200 pounds per acre). When properly practiced, crop rotation would do much to build up impoverished soils or to maintain the fertility of good soils.

Regrettably, in recent years, the intensive use of commercial fertilizers has enabled farmers to shift from the soil-conserving practice of crop rotation to the soil-abusing practice of planting the same cash crop year after year on the same acreage. The long-term results of such malpractice are always soil erosion and nutrient depletion.

USE OF ORGANIC FERTILIZERS. When the American Indian put a fish head in each hill of corn, he was using a form of organic fertilizer. About 1.8 million metric tons of organic wastes are produced in the United States each year (Figure 5-23). Much of this waste could be used as fertilizer, including slaughterhouse and cannery waste, steam-treated garbage, and sludge from human sewage.

In addition to providing nutrients, organic fertilizers (1) reduce erosion, (2) help retain soil moisture, (3) aerate soil, (4) stimulate the growth and reproduction of soil bacteria, and (5) buffer the soil against sudden shifts in acidity and alkalinity.

Animal Manure. More than 157 million metric tons of manure are generated by livestock in the United

FIGURE 5-23 Even "city slickers" know the value of cow manure. Hundreds of bags of this "brown gold" is on display at a garden center in Wisconsin. This organic fertilizer not only serves as a source of nutrients, but improves soil structure and decreases erodability as well.

States each year. The manure a corn-fed dairy cow returns to the soil via its waste amounts to 75 percent of the nitrogen, 80 percent of the phosphoric acid, and 90 percent of the potash obtained from its feed. Manure added to the soil helps return the nutrients and increase crop production. Applying 12.5 metric tons of manure per hectare (5 tons per acre) in Michigan, for instance, increased the yield to 115 bushels of corn per hectare (46 per acre), from 87 bushel per hectare (35 per acre) yield of nonmanured land—a 31 percent increase.

Another source of organic fertilizer is the excrement, or guano, of wild birds and bats. For many years, 4 to 5 million fish-eating cormorants have maintained dense breeding colonies on the Chincha Islands off the coast of Peru. Over the centuries, the guano of those birds has hardened and accumulated to a depth of over 33 meters (100 feet). Rich in both nitrogen and phosphorus, the deposits have been mined and shipped all over the world as fertilizer.

Human Waste. Even though most countries use human waste to increase soil fertility, this practice is not very popular in the United States. Only about 23 percent of the human sewage sludge produced in this country is spread on cropland as organic fertilizer. Chicago is exporting its human sewage sludge to fertilize sandy farmlands 96 kilometers (60 miles) away. By the year 2015, nitrogen- and phosphorus-rich sludge from millions of Chicagoans will have been piped or sprayed on 25,000 hectares (62,000 acres) to raise corn and

pasture for cattle on previously infertile soil. A few sewage disposal plants convert their sludge into commercial products. For example, Milwaukee has marketed a sludge product, called Milorganite, that is used as both a fertilizer and a soil conditioner.

Green Manure. The process of plowing under immature crops to improve soil productivity is known as **green manuring**. Its effect on soil is similar to that of animal manure. With the latter becoming more scarce in some areas as farms become more mechanized, green manure has assumed an especially significant role. Rye, oats, and soybeans are all excellent crops for this practice.

USE OF INORGANIC FERTILIZERS

Nitrogen Fertilizers. Nitrogen forms up to 0.3 percent by weight of dark brown prairie topsoil—a total of 4.5 metric tons per hectare (2 tons per acre). When such soil is subjected to intensive cropping or severe erosion, however, the initially abundant nitrogen may be rapidly depleted.

The greatest single inorganic source of nitrogen currently used in U.S. agriculture is produced by the Haber process, in which nitrogen and hydrogen are combined under pressure in the presence of a catalyst to form ammonia.

Balanced Fertilizers. A balanced fertilizer is a mixture (in varying ratios) of nitrogen, phosphorus, and potassium. A bag of balanced fertilizer must carry a printed guarantee of the nutrients it contains. The guarantee is usually stated in percentages. Thus, a 5-10-5 mixture contains 5 percent total nitrogen, 10 percent phosphoric acid, and 5 percent water-soluble potash.

Disadvantages of Synthetic Fertilizers

Synthetic fertilizers have helped farmers to increase crop production. However, these chemical additives are a mixed blessing, for the following reasons:

1. *Intensive use of energy.* The syntheses of fertilizer requires enormous amounts of energy. In fact, in a given year, American fertilizer manufacturers consume more energy than is used by all farmers in the United States in tilling the soil and in planting, cultivating, and harvesting crops.

2. *Reduction in soil oxygen.* Synthetic fertilizers may also have subtle adverse effects on soil structure. The result is reduced soil space for oxygen. This, in turn, reduces the efficiency of a given crop in making use of the fertilizer, since roots function best when oxygen is readily available.

3. *Water pollution.* Synthetic fertilizers, which are unused by crops, may be washed into lakes and streams, where they contribute to a process called **eutrophication**. It is characterized by an explosive

growth of water plants and levels of dissolved oxygen, which adversely affect fish and other aquatic species. (For more on this problem, see Chapter 8.)

4. *Human illness.* The exorbitant use of nitrate fertilizers in the United States has also been indirectly responsible for an increased rate of **methemoglobinemia**, a serious blood disease of infants that may be lethal. The excessive nitrate not absorbed by crops may be carried into the groundwater and may eventually contaminate private or municipal wells. Nitrate itself is not highly deleterious. However, when it enters an infant's intestines, nitrate is converted into **nitrite**. The nitrite then combines with hemoglobin (the red-blood cell pigment) to form methemoglobin, which carries less oxygen than hemoglobin. In severe cases, mental impairment results because the brain does not get enough oxygen. Occasionally, this disorder causes an infant to suffocate.

   The streams of California's Central Valley have perhaps the highest nitrate level in the nation. Public health authorities in the area have therefore suggested that babies be given only bottled water. Illinois, Missouri, Minnesota, and Wisconsin have all reported numerous cases of methemoglobinemia.

5. *Limited reserves of phosphates.* Artificial fertilizers, widely used in the United States, face an uncertain future. The phosphorus used in balanced fertilizers is obtained from phosphate rock. The most important source of this rock in the United States has been the Bone Valley in central Florida. Unfortunately, this source, as well as all other phosphate reserves in the world, will be exhausted within forty years. At that time, the high level of food production that has characterized the American agroecosystem could come to an end.

BUCKSHOT URBANIZATION AND ITS CONTROL

The "baby boom" that followed World War II caused an upsurge in our nation's population. This eventually resulted in a critical need for extra housing; as a result, more homes were built from 1940–1970 than in the past 200 years. Unfortunately, 20 million of these new homes were built on prime farm land, land that in many cases had been purchased by developers from financially troubled farmers. This process is continuing. Today 58 percent of the most agriculturally productive counties in the United States are located in the "urban fringe."

A good example of such scattered or *buckshot* urbanization is occurring 50 kilometers (30 miles north) of San Francisco in Marin, Napa, and Sonoma counties. This region is widely known for its dairy farms, apple orchards, and vineyards. Today the city of Novato now covers land that once supported the largest apple orchards in the world. The dairy farms in Marin County have also been victims of buckshot urbanization. The number of dairy farms has plummeted from 250 in 1950 to a mere 70 today. From 1967–1977, the area of fertile farmland in the United States lost to buckshot urbanization equaled the states of Connecticut, Delaware, Massachusetts, New Hampshire, Rhode Island, and Vermont combined. This process continues unabated. How can this problem be controlled? There are several possible strategies:

1. Governments could provide tax incentives to farmers to encourage them to refrain from selling their land to developers.

2. A given strip of farmland on the fringe of an urban area could be zoned for agricultural use only. The land would be taxed on the basis of its assessed agricultural value, rather than on its potential value as a site for future development. In the past, many farmers have had to sell out and abandon farming because of high taxes.

3. Governments could form a land trust to purchase agricultural easements that would protect the land forever. Under this strategy, the farmer would receive financial compensation from the trust for resisting the sale of the farm to developers. The farmer could sell the farm, but the new owner could use it only for agriculture. The American Farmland Trust, a national organization, has had considerable success with this strategy.

WHY DON'T AMERICAN FARMERS DO A BETTER JOB OF SOIL CONSERVATION

It is extremely difficult for an American citizen who is not a member of the agricultural community to understand why our nation's farmers have permitted their soils to deteriorate. After all, the technical knowledge needed to prevent erosion is widely available, and professional assistance to apply that knowledge can be obtained from the farmer's SCS district. What factors have contributed to the sorry plight of our nation's soils?

1. *Soil conservation measures are expensive.* For example, contour farming requires much more tractor time (as well as costly diesel fuel) than straight row farming. It takes considerably more time (and skill) for the farmer to follow the curving topographical pattern than to plow straight up and down the hills. It is estimated that the application of soil conservation measures may add 10 to 20 per-

cent to the farmer's operating expenses—at a time when the profit margins on most farms are razor thin.

2. *Soil conservation measures result in reduced income in the short term.* Suppose, for example, that the farmer was growing wheat on a steep, severely eroding hillside and replaced the wheat with erosion-controlling grass. The annual income for that farmer from the grassed area would be nil.

3. *The farmers' independent spirit.* As a result of their fiercely independent nature, farmers often resist applying effective soil conservation measures on a cost-sharing basis with the federal government if, in the process, they lose some freedom in the way they operate their farms. They may therefore reject a government-designed plan even though it would benefit them financially.

4. *Tenant farming.* An owner-operator may be willing to invest time, energy, and money in effective soil conservation measures, even if the payoff in enhanced crop yields may not materialize for several years. However, a tenant farmer, who often rents a given farm on a year-to-year basis, does not have the same motivation.

5. *Federal funding is limited.* Federal funds for cost-sharing programs designed to upgrade soils are shrinking. Consider the Agricultural Conservation Program (ACP), for example. It is the oldest, largest, and best-known of all such programs. Nevertheless, its annual budget was sharply reduced by the Reagan administration, from $245 million in 1979 to only $160 million by 1986—a 39 percent decrease.

6. *Some federal erosion control programs are not meeting their principal objective: curbing soil losses on the most erosion-vulnerable lands.* For example, in the early 1980s, more than 52 percent of cost-shared erosion control practices were on lands where the erosion rate was less than 12.5 metric tons per hectare (5 metric tons per acre) per year. Only 20 percent of the funds were being spent on lands that were eroding by more than 35 metric tons per hectare (14 metric tons per acre) per year and that were responsible for 86 percent of our nation's erosion losses.

7. *Modern farm machinery promotes erosion.* Tractors used by today's farmers are big, fast, and impressive. However, they cannot turn on a dime. To be efficient, they must work on long, straight rows. In order to accommodate these huge tractors, farmers have to combine some of their small fields into one huge field measuring perhaps a half-mile on one side. Unfortunately, terraces and shelterbelts get in the way of these large tractors; they also make it inconvenient for the farmer to use modern cen-

ter-pivot irrigation systems. As a result, thousands of miles of shelterbelts and terraces have been sacrificed on the altar of modern farming technology.

8. *American farmers are in the business of feeding the world.* From time to time, federal farm policymakers put pressure on the American farmer to maximize production so that huge food exports can be made. Such sales, of course, help the United States maintain a favorable balance of trade and are vital to a strong national economy. In the early 1980s, roughly 40 percent of our nation's farmland was devoted to export production. However, such production in possible only at the cost of considerable abuse to the land.

9. *The farmer's payoff for instituting soil conservation measures is not immediate, but may take years.* Crop yields will not increase until the soil's quality is built up. As a result, many farmers choose to invest in fertilizers that pay off in increased yields *the same year.* To the average farmer, who is strapped financially, it makes much more sense to spend $1 on fertilizer in April 1990 and get a $1.10 return on the investment in September 1995 than to invest $1 in soil conservation practices in 1990 and wait until 2000 to get a $1.10 return—maybe.

10. *The farmers may see no future for their farms.* The average age of the average American farmer is increasing. At present, it is about 50-55 years. And at that age, farmers are possibly becoming more interested in retirement than in raising the productivity of their soil. In any event, they may have promised to sell their land to developers or to a mining company interested in the coal underneath the soil. And if this land is going to be covered some day with homes, paved roads, and shopping centers, or if it is going to be stripped for coal, the only policy that makes any sense to farmers may be to "mine" the soil of its nutrients right up to the day of sale.

11. *Farmers lack appreciation of the gravity of the soil erosion problem.* In a recent study in Nebraska, an overwhelming number of farmers did not believe that erosion rates of 10 to 15 tons per acre per year were serious. When questioned by soil conservation researchers as to the reason for their lack of concern, they answered: "Even though my farm is experiencing these rates of erosion, my crop yields have not declined." And, of course, they were right. But the only reason their yields remained high was that their increased use of fertilizers had temporarily offset the effect of the erosion losses.

12. *Soil conservation officials have not been able to make soil conservation relevant to the modern farmer.* Admittedly, the task is enormous, espe-

cially in the face of today's economic pressures. But the job must be done—and soon. As R. Neil Sampson writes: "The fact that the United States Department of Agriculture, after 100 years in business and over 40 years of soil conservation programs, still cannot provide a convincing analysis to demonstrate the full cost of soil erosion to either an individual farmer or to society (in general) is a disgrace. It is proof that such problems have not had a very high priority over the years."

THE FUTURE

Our nation's agriculture is in deep trouble. Its ability to produce food and fiber for Americans, let alone for many of the worlds hungry, is in serious jeopardy and conditions will worsen if current trends continue. You may say: "But how can that be? The supermarkets are packed with attractive fruits and vegetables, meats and fruit juices, pastries, cookies, and milk." True. Right now, American farmers are producing more food per acre than ever before. But they are doing it at a price— a price measured in greater vulnerability to erosion, a reduction in soil nutrient levels, and reduced ability of the soil to hold water and oxygen. In other words, for a few short years, we will witness a curious paradox: *American farm production is at an all-time high at the same time that the soil resource is deteriorating at record speed.* A growing number of soil scientists believe that if this trend continues, at some point crop yields will drop suddenly—perhaps by as much as 40 to 60 percent. It is obvious that such a decline in food production would trigger both a national and a global calamity.

Many historians believe that the United States is about to lose its position of power and leadership in the world. They list several reasons: lack of abundant oil supplies, lack of innovative technology, and lack of devotion to the work ethic. Perhaps another "lack" should be added to the list: lack of ability to protect and maintain the soil—the greatest food-producing resource on the face of the earth.

RAPID REVIEW

1. American farmers must increase their food production to (a) satisfy sharply increasing food needs in the United States, (b) to help nourish millions of hungry people abroad, and (c) maintain the economic well-being of our nation.

2. Agricultural production in the United States is hampered by several problems, including (a) buckshot urbanization, (b) soil erosion, (c) high fuel and pesticide costs, (d) flood and sediment damage, (e) limited supplies of irrigation water, (f) salinization, (g) harmful effects of pesticides, (h) air pollution, and (i) compaction of the soil.

3. The severe dust storms that ravaged the Dust Bowl in the 1920s resulted from a combination of factors, including severe drought, high-velocity winds, overgrazing, and poor soil management. In one storm alone, more than 300 million tons of soil were blown away. From 2 to 12 inches of topsoil were carried to the Atlantic seaboard. Millions of farmers and ranchers in states like Oklahoma, Colorado, Kansas, and Texas suffered severe economic hardship and were forced to seek employment in urban centers.

4. Even though the federal government has spent about $30 billion on programs to upgrade our nation's soil, it is actually in poorer condition today than it was in the 1930s. Soil erosion losses now amount to almost 6 billion tons annually. At a value of $7.50 per ton, this amounts to an annual loss of $48 billion.

5. One highly destructive practice that contributes to soil erosion is plowout, the conversion of previously uncultivated land into cropland. A number of counties in Colorado and Montana have passed ordinances to limit this practice.

6. Some of our soils are 1,000 times more erodible than others. Erosion losses range from 8 to 200 tons per acre per year.

7. The rate of water erosion is influenced by such factors as (a) volume and intensity of precipitation, (b) soil erodibility, (c) topography, and (d) erosion control practices.

8. Effective methods of erosion control include (a) contour farming, (b) strip cropping, (c) conservation tillage, (d) terracing, (e) shelterbelting, (f) gully reclamation, (g) removal of land from production, and (h) conservation tillage.

9. Conservation tillage may reduce soil erosion by 90 percent. By the year 2000, about 75 percent of our farmers will be using this practice. One major disadvantage of this method is that more pesticides are needed to control weeds and insects.

10. The Universal Soil Loss Equation (USLE) is $A = RKLSCP$, where A = number of tons of soil lost per hectare (acre) per year, R = rainfall and runoff, K = erodibility of soil, L = length of slope, S = steepness of slope, C = cover type, and P = practice used in erosion control. By using the USLE, fairly good estimates of soil loss can be made on any farm in the United States.

11. The SCS will provide technical assistance to farmers so that they can develop a conservation plan for their land. Almost 3,000 soil conservation districts have been organized. The major function of the districts is to provide technical and financial assistance to farmers so that they can effectively manage each acre of land according to its capability.

12. According to the Land Capability Classification scheme of the USDA, land is placed in eight different categories according to its productive potential. Classes I–III may be cropped. Class IV is suitable for grazing livestock. Classes V–VII may be used as rangeland or forest. Class VIII land is suitable only for wildlife habitat, wilderness, recreation, and scenic beauty.

13. Soil fertility on our nation's farmlands has been lost due to intensive cropping and erosion. It can be temporarily restored by the use of (a) legumes, (b) crop rotation, (c) synthetic fertilizers, and (d) organic fertilizers (green manure, animal manure, and human waste).

14. Despite the fact that our agricultural problems are well known, many farmers continue unsustainable practices. The reasons are many. Cost, reduced income, limited federal funding, resistance to outside interference, and the use of modern machinery are some of the most important ones.

KEY WORDS AND PHRASES

Accelerated erosion	Methemoglobinemia
Animal manure	Milorganite
Balanced fertilizer	Molybdenum
Black blizzard	Monotype
Broad-base terrace	No-till farming
Buckshot urbanization	Organic fertilizer
Conservation tillage	Plant manure
Contour farming	Plow-out
Crop rotation	Rill erosion
Dust Bowl	Runoff
Energy subsidy	Sheet erosion
Farm plan	Shelterbelt
Food Security Act	Sodbusting
Geological erosion	Soil and Water Resources Reclamation Act
Grass backslope terrace	Soil Conservation Service (SCS)
Green manure	
Guano	Soil erodability factor
Gully erosion	Strip cropping
Gully reclamation	Synthetic fertilizer
Haber process	Terracing
Heterotype	Universal Soil Loss Equation (USLE)
Land capability classification	
Legumes	

QUESTIONS AND TOPICS FOR DISCUSSION

1. Suppose that a farmer did not harvest the crop of corn, but abandoned the farm and let nature take over. Explain the vegetational changes that probably would occur during the next two or three years. (You may need to refer to Chapter 2.)

2. In what ways is a field of corn similar to a pioneer stage in a natural ecological succession? In what ways is it different?

3. Suppose that most Americans raised all the food they required in their own backyard family garden and by keeping a few chickens or pigs. In other words, suppose that the agricultural ecosystem gradually shifted from a few million big farms to 30 million small family farms. Discuss the pros and cons of this development.

4. Suppose that all commercial fertilizers were banned for agricultural use. Discuss the advantages and disadvantages of this development.

5. Suppose that all pesticides and herbicides were banned for agricultural use. Discuss the advantages and disadvantages of this development.

6. Our soil is in worse condition today than it was during the Dust Bowl era, even though roughly $30 billion has been spent by federal and state governments to upgrade it. Who is to blame? The farmers? The legislators? The soil scientists? The public? Discuss your answer.

7. Discuss the advantages and disadvantages of conservation tillage.

8. Some soil scientists project that, by the year 2000, if current trends continue, no further increase in food production by American farmers will be possible. Suppose, however, that the population of the United States and the world continues to increase at the present rate. Discuss the probable effect on our economy. What will be the source of the needed food supplies? How will the health of our people be affected? What will be the effect on food prices? What will be the effect on government stability? On international relations?

9. Discuss buckshot urbanization. Are there possible alternatives? If so, what are they? How would they be implemented?

10. Some years ago, a senator from South Carolina commented as follows on the malnourishment in Appalachia and in the ghettos of our big cities: "There has been hunger since the time of Jesus Christ and there always will be." Was he correct? Was his attitude correct? Discuss your answer. What are our responsibilities in preventing starvation in the United States? In the world?

11. Compare modern agricultural practices to the hunting and food-gathering practices of early humans in terms of their disruption of natural ecosystems.

12. Severe drought recurs in the United States at intervals of roughly 22 years. Were the black blizzards of the Dust Bowl era caused directly by drought? Could they have been prevented despite the drought? Discuss your answer.

13. Discuss the statement: "The only energy an ear of corn on your dinner table represents is the solar energy involved in photosynthesis that made the development of that ear possible."

14. What can Congress and the state legislatures do about buckshot urbanization? Why haven't they done more to date? Discuss the pros and cons of legislation that would outlaw buckshot urbanization completely.

15. Briefly list five benefits of conservation tillage.

16. In what way could conservation tillage indirectly cause water pollution?

17. What is the Universal Soil Loss Equation?

18. How can the farmer use this equation to control soil erosion on the land?

SUGGESTED READINGS

Brady, N. C. *The Nature and Property of Soils*, 9th ed., New York: Macmillan, 1984. This is a classic work on soils, providing a sophisticated treatment.

Brown, Lester R., et al. *State of the World—1988*. New York: W. W. Norton, 1988. Contains a vivid discussion of the soil, water, fertilizer, and energy problems thwarting adequate food production in a hungry world.

Goudie, Andrew. *The Human Impact on the Natural Environment*. Cambridge, Mass.: MIT Press, 1986. Chapter 4 has a vivid, interestingly written discussion of the erosion problem by an international authority.

Singer, Michael J., and Donald N. Munns. *Soils: An Introduction*. New York: Macmillan, 1987. Authoritative, highly readable, nicely illustrated text.

World Resources Institute. *World Resources—1988*. New York: Basic Books, 1988. One section of this book provides a global perspective on the food production problem.

6

Feeding a Hungry Planet

Of all the problems created by the current crush of people on earth, undoubtedly the one with the greatest potential for human disaster is hunger and malnutrition. Many of the consequences of overpopulation, so evident today, were first predicted in 1798 by Thomas Malthus, a British clergyman and economist. He argued that the fixed land base imposes limits on food production; human populations and their demand for food, he argued, would grow faster than food supplies. Without population control, he said, starvation, disease, and war would prevail to correct the ecological imbalance.

WORLD HUNGER

Today Malthus's glum predictions may be coming true. An estimated 40 million people, nearly half of them children, die each year from hunger and diseases worsened by hunger. The death toll is equivalent to that of 300 jumbo jets, each containing 400 passengers, fatally crashing each and every day of the year.

According to recent estimates of the World Bank, 730 million people—or one of every seven in the world—regularly consume less food than they need to stay healthy. Most of these people live in Africa, Asia, and Latin America (Figure 6-1). They suffer from two basic maladies: undernutrition and malnutrition.

Undernutrition is a quantitative phenomenon characterized by an inadequate amount of food—or calories—resulting in half-empty stomachs and gnawing hunger pains. Nutritionists assume that the average person must have a minimum of 2,200–2,400 calories daily.

Western Europeans and North Americans get 3,200 calories daily. We are among the fortunate. Compare our situation to that of the average Ethiopian, who consumes only 1,600 calories daily—only half of our intake (Figure 6-2). This 600-daily-calorie deficit undermines strength, causes severe mental and physical lethargy, and weakens resistance to a variety of diseases.

Chronic **malnutrition**, on the other hand, is a qualitative phenomenon characterized by a lack of certain important foods. This results in a deficient supply of one or more of the following: proteins, vitamins, or other key nutrients.

Malnutrition and undernutrition often go hand in hand. In many Third World nations, poor children suffer from a lack of protein and calories. As shown in Figure 6-3, these children are thin and wasted. They gnaw endlessly on their clothing to appease the insatiable hunger that plagues them day and night. Called **marasmus**, this disease afflicts infants under one year of age separated from their mother's breast milk, which is rich in proteins and calories.

Millions of children (under six years of age) in the Third World are suffering from the protein-deficiency disease kwashiorkor. **Kwashiorkor** is a West African word that means "the disease the child gets when another baby is born" because the mother can no longer feed the older child with her breast milk. Although the disease was first discovered in tropical Africa, it has since been identified among children of Central and South America, the Caribbean, the Middle East, and the Orient.

Frail kwashiorkor-afflicted children lie in their mother's arms weak and lifeless. Their limbs are thin and

FIGURE 6-1 Map of world hunger.

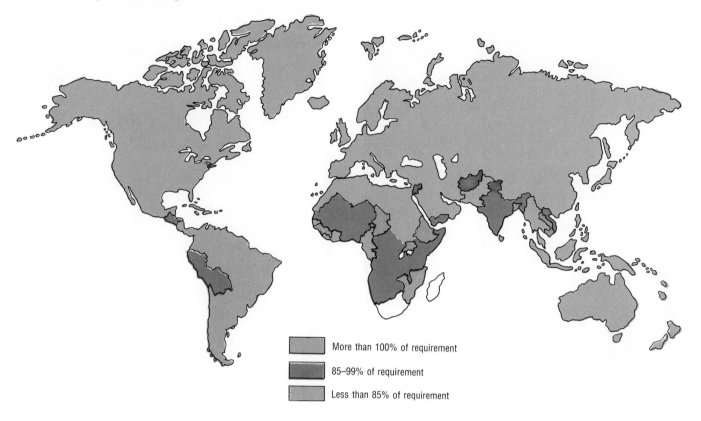

More than 100% of requirement

85–99% of requirement

Less than 85% of requirement

wasted (Figure 6-4). Their abdomens protrude because of the fluid that has accumulated inside. They suffer from skin ulcers and increased susceptibility to infectious diseases common in many parts of the developing world.

Protein deficiency retards physical as well as mental development, and even if a proper diet is available several years later, the brain damage cannot be reversed.

Kwashiorkor and marasmus are two clinically recognizable diseases. But for every child diagnosed with one of these diseases, there are a hundred children who suffer from milder cases of malnutrition and undernutrition.

FIGURE 6-2 The average American is overfed; the average person living in a poor nation is underfed. Hunger and starvation kill 42 million people a year.

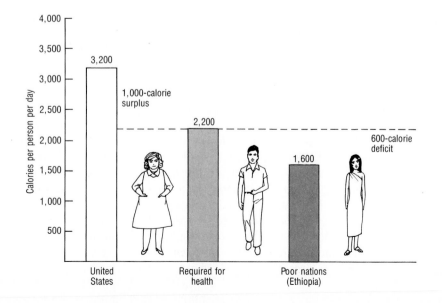

FIGURE 6-3 Death from starvation. Parvati Pura India. This village suffered from a local famine because of an extended drought. The two-year-old boy is almost dead from protein and caloric deficiency (marasmus).

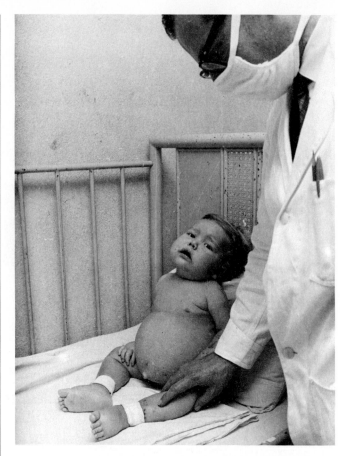

FIGURE 6-4 A Guatemalan child suffering from kwashiorkor (protein deficiency). Note the extreme lethargy and protruding abdomen.

By the year 2000, experts predict, the number of people afflicted by severe hunger could rise to 800 million or more. The most severe problems will occur in Latin America and Africa, where many countries are besieged by an explosion in human population. For them, starvation will be a way of life.

In Latin America, largely because of soaring population growth, food production per capita has fallen by 8 percent since its historical peak in 1981. In Africa, where the population is now growing by 2.8 percent per year, food supplies per capita have been declining since 1969. Despite abundant harvests in 1986, for instance, food production per capita was 14 percent lower than in 1969.

Food aid has helped to alleviate the widespread starvation and hunger in Ethiopia, Sudan, Chad, and other countries, but the land may be paying the price. In Ethiopia, for example, people struggling to feed themselves on the parched landscape have hastened the spread of deserts and accelerated soil erosion of farmland. Over a billion tons of topsoil are blown or washed away from Ethiopia's highlands each year. So severe is the population pressure that the land may never recover from the drought that has gripped the area for more than a decade. Ethiopia's agriculture has

steadily improved over the last two decades. More land has been plowed, and grain yields have nearly doubled. Regardless, the annual harvest provides 15 percent less grain per person than it did in 1950. Despite the publicity Africa has gained in recent years, two-thirds of the world's starving people are in South Asia.

The news on world food production is not all bad. In some areas, where horrible shortages were once common, food is now grown in abundance. In India, thanks to new high-yield grains, grain reserves are sufficient to offset two bad years of harvest. Indonesia, once the world's leading importer of rice, is now self-sufficient and exports its rice to hungry nations. China, once food poor, is teeming with food.

World agriculture faces several important challenges. *In poor nations where starvation is common, the immediate challenge is to feed the masses of hungry people.* The demands of future citizens must also be met. *In countries currently supplying their own needs, agriculture must be maintained and expanded to meet future needs without harming the renewable base upon which agriculture depends: the soil.* In the face of rapid population growth and rising costs, this task may be difficult. Feeding people now and feeding people in the future requires population control and a system of agriculture that is sustainable—one that does not squander topsoil or rob the soil of its nutrients. The next section looks at these goals and describes ways to achieve them.

INCREASING FOOD PRODUCTION

The world's population is expected to increase by over 1 billion people between 1988 and 2000. By 2020, the population is expected to climb another 2 billion, an increase of nearly 60 percent over 1988. Food production must climb accordingly just to maintain the status quo, which is woefully inadequate in many areas. But where will that food come from?

Food to feed the hungry planet can come from a variety of measures, including (1) improving soil management, (2) reducing farmland conversion, (3) exploiting farmland reserves, (4) expanding irrigation and improvements in irrigation efficiency, (5) increasing yields through plant breeding and genetic engineering, (6) using fertilizer more efficiently, (7) reducing pest damage, and (8) developing new food sources.

The food crisis, however, cannot be solved in the farm fields of the world alone. Careful population control strategies, most experts agree, must acompany efforts to produce more food. Political reforms can also go a long way toward solving hunger. Without population control and political improvements, the technical measures to be described will be nothing more than stopgap measures that merely postpone the day of reckoning predicted by Malthus nearly two centuries ago.

Improving Soil Management

Farmland throughout the world is eroding away at an alarming rate. Some 75 billion metric tons of soil are washed or blown away from farmland worldwide each year. Eroded soil loses its ability to support crops and contributes to declining agricultural productivity. In the long run, it could result in even more widespread starvation. Inadequate fertilization also adds to the problem by gradually impoverishing the soil of important nutrients.

Desertification, the spread of the desert in semiarid regions largely due to poor land management, also robs us of much arable land (Figure 6-5). If soil erosion and desertification continue at current rates, 75 million hectares (185 million acres), or about 5 percent of the world's arable land, will be taken out of production between 1975 and 2000. This estimate does not inclued the 7 million hectares (17 million acres) of grassland consumed annually by spreading deserts.

Thus, after population control, the first line of attack on world hunger must be improvements in soil management. Controls on soil erosion and nutrient depletion, discussed in Chapter 5, can go a long way toward increasing food supplies.

Desertification can be controlled by reducing grazing

FIGURE 6-5   Desertification caused by overgrazing and poor agricultural practices destroys millions of hectares of marginally productive land in the United States, South America, Asia, and Africa.

and farming and by revegetating land on the perimeters of the world's deserts. As a general plan of protection, good land with adequate water should be farmed using crop rotation, terracing, and other measures that conserve soil. However, moderately dry land should planted in crops that can withstand long dry spells, such as sorghum and fast-growing maize. Farmers should alternate these crops with species that restore soil fertility, such as groundnuts and cowpeas. Farmers could plant certain tree species that prosper in semiarid climates, add nitrogen to the soil, and provide food for livestock and fuel for local villages. Semiarid grasslands must also be carefully managed (see Chapter 11). Livestock herds must be either reduced or grazed on a rotational basis that gives grasslands time to recover. Devegetated grassslands can be planted with clover and alfalfa, legumes that help restore soil fertility and reduce erosion.

Reducing Farmland Conversion

In the Third World, urban sprawl, new villages, roadways, reservoirs, and other uses consume once-productive farmland at an alarming rate. Much the same is occurring in the developed world (Figure 6-6). Between 1975 and 2000, an estimated 150 million hectares (370 million acres) worldwide will be lost to nonfarm use. Only through careful land management and population control can this dangerous trend be halted. But land management, even in the developed nations, is often spotty and poorly applied. Expecting adequate planning in the poor, developing nations of the world may be unrealistic.

Tapping Farmland Reserves

Many countries have tried to boost agricultural production by farming new land. In an ambitious period from the mid-1950s to the mid-1970s, China, the Soviet Union, and the United States, for instance, all expanded their farms onto previously untilled land. But much of the expansion was on marginal land, which was often hard to farm, poor in nutrients, or highly erosive. In the United States, 50 percent of all the soil eroded from our cropland came from a paltry 10 percent of the land.

Starting in the late 1970s, the high cost of farming marginal land forced officials in these three countries to cut their losses. All began to withdraw marginal land from production. In the United States, the Food Security Act of 1985 provided a way to withdraw 18 million hectares (45 million acres) from production—about one-tenth of the U.S. land currently under cultivation.

Lester Brown, president of the Worldwatch Institute and world-renowned expert on agriculture, doubts that farmland in most major food-producing nations will expand much in the next decade or so. One reason is that, to meet energy demands, many developed countries will convert large tracts of farmland now dedicated to food production to **fuel crops**, like corn that can be converted to ethanol, a liquid fuel that may replace gasoline as oil supplies fall in the late 1990s and beyond.

The prospects for expanding food production in the Third World are mixed. In Southeast Asia, most of the cultivable land is already under cultivation. In Southwest Asia, more land may be farmed that is believed to be sustainable. In Africa, however, only 21 percent of the land area thought to be suitable for agriculture is currently being farmed. In South America, only 15 percent is being farmed. Expansion is feasible on both of these continents, but it should not be undertaken until careful land management is practiced on existing farmland. Ecologists warn that tropical rain forests, arid lands, and wetlands should not be converted to farmland, for reasons to be explained.

TROPICAL RAIN FORESTS. Tropical rain forests are blessed with abundant sunshine, rainfall, and perpetually warm days. These regions have supported dense forest for many centuries. To the untrained eye, the tropical forests might appear to be prime candidates for farmland conversion (Figure 6-7). The fact is however, that tropical rain forests stripped of trees and planted in crops make for some of the worst farmland known to humankind.

Unlike deciduous forests of the eastern United States, where leaves and other plant litter form a thick, spongy layer that decays over time, making the soil rich and productive, tropical rain forest soils are bare and nutrient poor. Fallen leaves and branches are quickly decomposed by bacteria, insects, fungi, and earthworms. The nutrients released by decomposition are rapidly snatched from the soil by the roots of the large trees that tower over the forest floor. Thus the soil that supports the most productive ecosystem on earth is, paradoxically, among the poorest known to humankind (Chapter

FIGURE 6-6 Cropland is destroyed by housing developments, highway and airport construction, new shopping malls, and other byproducts of urbanization. Prime agricultural land is often taken out of production because it is flat and suitable for building and is often located near expanding cities.

FIGURE 6-7 Shifting type of cultivation in central Sumatra. Agricultural land is opened up by cutting and burning the forests. The cleared area will then be intensively cropped for a few years until the fertility has been exhausted; then it will be abandoned and left exposed to erosion by wind and water.

4). Chopping down trees and planting crops is a prescription for disaster. What nutrients exist in the soil are quickly taken up by the crops or leached from the soil into the deeper layers, where they are inaccessible to crops. More commonly, nutrients are washed away by the rains that come so frequently, impoverishing a land that has little recuperative ability.

Another problem with tropical forest soils is that many are rich in an iron compound that, when exposed to sunlight, hardens the soil, creating a brick-like layer impervious to plants and farm equipment alike. Known as **laterites**, these reddish-brown soils may have caused the downfall of the Khmer civilization in Cambodia and the Mayas of Mexico. In more recent times, they caused the failure of an agricultural colony started by the Brazilian government in the heart of the Amazon basin.

Today tropical rain forests are falling at an alarming rate. Each year, an area of tropical forest the size of Great Britain is cleared for timber and other wood products. Farms and pastures are started on the denuded landscape but, almost without exception,

soon fail. Plans to expand agriculture at the expense of forests, most agree, must be stopped. (For more information on tropical rain forests, see Chapter 13.)

ARID LANDS. Many optimists look to the deserts and semiarid lands as a source of potential farmland. In their wildest moments, they envision plans to turn the vast parched Sahara to cropland. Few agriculturalists would deny that, with adequate water and fertilizer, the sandy soils of arid and semiarid lands could be made to produce crops. In Egypt the gigantic Aswan Dam on the Nile River has made possible an increase in crop production in the desert because irrigation water is now available year round. A huge aquifer lying 330 meters (1,000 feet) beneath the surface in the central Sahara supports an oil town with 50,000 residents and provides irrigation for 50,000 trees.

However promising these examples are, many irrigation projects are riddled with problems. High costs and low returns are key stumbling blocks. Adding to the purely economic barriers are salinization and waterlogging. Salinization today threatens every arid land region of the world where irrigation is used. In the intermediate or final stages of salinization, this land will fall into disuse. **Waterlogging** is the saturation of soil by irrigation, occurring in poorly drained fields. Water fills the pores in the soil and blocks oxygen penetration, killing plants. Plans to expand agriculture into arid lands, many experts believe, are a short-term answer that cannot last.

WETLANDS. Throughout the world, wetlands have been drained to provide living space and valuable farmland. **Wetlands** are lands that are wet part or most of the year. They include swamps, bogs, salt marshes, lagoons, bays, and mangrove swamps. The agriculturally productive fenland of Britain was once a swamp. Flourishing Israeli settlements now occupy the site of the formerly waterlogged Huleh marshes. Drainage has made crop production possible in Italy's Po Valley and in the Yazoo Delta of the Mississippi.

Inland and coastal wetlands, attractive as potential farmland, are also valuable and productive fish and wildlife habitats. Many species of waterfowl live and breed in wetlands. Many commercially valuable fish and shellfish depend on coastal wetlands. Destroying these areas, ecologists warn, impairs fish and wildlife and may also affect human civilization. Why? Because wetlands are also water purifiers that trap sediment and other pollutants. They act as sponges as well, holding back rainwaters and reducing flooding (Table 6-1).

Efforts to protect wetlands have been stepped up in many nations. In the United States, where nearly one-

Table 6-1 The Value of Our Wetlands

Wetland Function	How Wetlands Perform Function	Conservation Concern
Flood storage	Some wetlands store and slowly release flood waters.	Filling or dredging of wetlands reduces their flood storage capacity.
Flood conveyance	Some wetlands (particularly those immediately adjacent to rivers and streams) serve as floodway areas by conveying flood flows from upstream to downstream points.	If flood flows are blocked by fills, dikes, or other structures, increased flood heights and velocities result, causing damage to adjacent upstream and downstream areas.
Erosion control wave barriers	Wetland vegetation, with massive roots and rhizone systems, binds and protects soils. Vegetation also acts as wave barriers.	Removal of vegetation increases erosion and reduces the capacity to moderate wave intensity.
Sediment control	Wetland vegetation binds soil particles and retards the movement of sediment in slowly flowing water.	Destruction of wetland topographic contours or vegetation decreases wetland capacity to filter surface runoff and act as sediment traps. This increases water turbidity and siltation of downstream reservoirs, storm drains, and stream channels.
Pollution control	Wetlands act as settling ponds; they also remove nutrients and other pollutants by filtering and causing chemical breakdown of pollutants.	Destruction of wetland contours or vegetation decreases natural pollution control capability, resulting in lowered water quality of downstream lakes, streams, and other waters.
Fish and wildlife habitat	Wetlands provide water, food supply, and nesting and resting areas. Coastal wetlands contribute nutrients needed by fish and shellfish to nearby estuarine and marine waters.	Filling, dredging, damming, and other alterations destroy and damage flora and fauna and decrease productivity. Dam construction is an impediment to fish movement.
Recreation	Wetlands provide scenery, wild areas, habitat, wildlife, and water for recreational use.	Filling, dredging, or other interference with wetlands cause loss of areas for boating, swimming, bird watching, hunting, and fishing.
Water supply (surface)	Some wetlands store flood waters, reducing the timing and amount of surface runoff. They also filter pollutants. Some serve as sources of domestic water supply.	Filling or dredging causes accelerated runoff and increases pollution.
Aquifer recharge	Some wetlands store water and release it slowly to groundwater deposits. However, many other wetlands are discharge areas for a portion or all of the year.	Filling or drainage may destroy wetland aquifer recharge capability, thereby reducing base flows to streams and groundwater supplies for domestic, commercial, or other uses.

Source: Modified from Kustler, John A., 1983. *Our Natural Wetland Heritage—Wetlands, Their Use and Regulation* (Washington, D.C., U.S. Congress, Office of Technology Assessment, OTA-0-208, March 1984).

half of all coastal and inland wetlands have been drained, new laws prohibit futher drainage. The federal government, in fact, recently beefed up its control of wetland drainage for farmland, refusing federal crop insurance and other economic support for wetlands that farmers drain. Local enviromental groups are waging successful campaigns to prevent the loss of important swamplands. In Florida, a huge swamp along the Kissimmee River is being restored only a few years after a multi-million-dollar drainage project was completed. Further drainage here or abroad must be viewed with caution. The impacts on wildlife and fish, stream flow, and water quality may far outweigh the benefits accrued by converting them to farmland.

Limiting farmland expansion in many African nations may protect a vital economic resource: wildlife species that attract wealthy tourists from all over the world. Revenues from such activities could help support programs of improved soil management and population control, reducing the present crunch.

Increasing Irrigation and Irrigation Efficiency

Irrigation has helped boost cropland production enormously in the past four decades (Figure 6-8). Between 1950 and 1985, for instance, the amount of land under irrigation in the United States nearly tripled. In the 1950s and 1960s, irrigated cropland grew at the astounding rate of 4 percent per year. In the 1970s, however growth slowed; today it is less than 1 percent per year. Why has irrigation fallen off?

Agricultural scientists point to six major reasons: (1) the generally depressed farm economy, (2) groundwater depletion, (3) salt buildup in irrigated soils that renders them inhospitable to crops, (4) waterlogging, (5) increasing competition for ground water supplies, and (6) siltation of reservoirs that once supplied farmers with water.

Because these problems are likely to grow worse, many experts see little growth in irrigated land. Gains in production, they insist, must come from improvements in irrigation efficiency. Cement-lined ditches and

FIGURE 6-8 Irrigation made possible in Egypt by the Aswan Dam. An area of one million acres formerly dependent on the annual Nile floods for irrigation is now cultivated under a system of perennial irrigation based mainly on lifting water. The new irrigation system makes possible a 40 percent increase in crop production in Upper Egypt, because at least one additional crop can be grown per year. Photo shows a mechanized irrigation pump at Habu that has replaced the laborious methods of lifting water by a hand-operated or animal-driven waterwheel. Unfortunately, the increased food production can barely keep up with Egypt's population increase.

pipelines instead of open ditches to transport water, drip irrigation systems that irrigate row crops sparingly, and computer-controlled irrigation systems that monitor soil moisture and apply water only when it is needed are all potential solutions. Other more costly solutions to increase water supplies are discussed in Chapter 7.

Improving Yields Through Better Plants

Since the dawn of humankind, nearly 4 million years ago, humans have succeeded in domesticating only about 80 species of food plants. The "big three" are wheat, rice, and corn. Today, well over 50 percent of the world's cropland are devoted to them. It is only natural, therefore, that plant geneticists have channeled much of

their research into developing superior strains of these plants. The progress made in the first few decades of plant research promised to close the gap between food supply and demand in the developing world and has been dubbed the **Green Revolution**.

THE GREEN REVOLUTION. Plant geneticists have developed high-yield grains with higher protein content than their predecessors (Figure 6-9). Wheat and rice varieties, in fact, yield three to five times as much grain as their predecessors. New varieties of wheat grow faster as well, allowing farmers in areas with long growing seasons an additional planting each year.

The Green Revolution began in 1943 with the establishment of the International Maize and Wheat Improvement Center in Mexico. Sponsored by the Rockefeller and Ford foundations, the center set out to develop high-yield varieties of wheat and rice under the leadership of Norman Borlaug, an agricultural geneticist (Figure 6-10). After 25 years of intensive research, the center amassed an impressive record of new seed varieties, in addition to wheat and rice. Blight-resistant

FIGURE 6-9 A new rice strain for hungry India: IR5 (left), a new high-yielding variety of rice under test at a research station in Aduthurai. The plant to the right is the traditional variety.

FIGURE 6-10 One of the architects of the Green Revolution, Nobel Prize winning Dr. Normal E. Borlaug is shown recording the vigor and stage of growth of wheat plants on a selective breeding plot in Mexico. Dr. Borlaug was successful in developing the so-called miracle wheats that, at least temporarily, greatly boosted wheat production in Mexico and other underveloped nations around the world.

potatoes developed there increased the yield by an amazing 500 percent. Disease-resistant beans quadrupled the yield. Best publicized, however, was the new high-yield wheat, which boosted Mexico's grain production from 780 kilograms per hectare (700 pounds per acre) to 4,700 kilograms per hectare (4,200 pounds per acre), and new high-yield varieties of rice.

The new wheat and rice were specially developed for use in tropical and subtropical countries. Extremely responsive to fertilizer and irrigation water, these plants grew fast and heartily. The new strains are shorter and stouter, withstanding winds and harvesting better than the traditional long-stemmed strains. Their short growing seasons ensured two or three harvests per year.

It took Borlaug and his associates 30 years to develop the new "miracle" strains. But the promise of higher yields was heralded throughout the world and won Borlaug the Nobel Prize in 1971, a fitting recognition of his service to humankind.

The high-yield varieties spread more quickly and more widely than any other agricultural innovation in the developed countries. By the mid-1980s, nearly 50 percent of the wheat cropland and nearly 60 percent of the rice land was sown with high-yield seeds. The amount of rice and wheat grown in the developed world shot up by 75 percent between 1965 and 1980, even though the area planted to those crops increased by only 20 percent. The benefits of the green Revolution also spread to the developing countries. India, once crippled by food shortages, became self-sufficient (Figure 6-11). Mexico and Indonesia boasted similar progress.

Despite the obvious benefits of the new plant crops, however, critics note that the Green Revolution has not

FIGURE 6-11 Women in Bihar, India, harvesting a crop of high-yielding wheat that has been grown with improved irrigation.

been a panacea for world hunger. The new high-yield varieties have proved to be disappointing for a number of reasons.

Perhaps the most common criticism is that the Green Revolution mostly benefited well-to-do farmers who could afford to irrigate their farmland and buy the fertilizer necessary for the new high-yield varieties. In rural Africa, where food is desperately needed, the Green Revolution had virtually no influence. Worldwide, an estimated 1.4 billion people live by subsistence farming. They grow barely enough food for themselves and their families, and cannot afford the expensive seed or the costly fertilizer needed to make the new miracle seeds grow.

The high-yield varieties also proved inadequately equipped to ward off pests and disease. The genetists had, they found, inadvertently eliminated the natural resistance of wheat and rice, and had produced a generation of genetic lighweights. To protect their crops, therefore, farmers needed large amounts of pesticides, which further drove up the cost of farming. A farmer who could afford the seed might not have enough money to pay for costly fertilizer.

Another problem of the Green Revolution (and modern agriculture in general) is that it fostered the use of a limited number of genetic strains—a reduction in genetic diversity. Where dozens of strains had once been grown, huge fields containing one variety sprung up. The fewer the number of strains, the more devastating the emergence of a plant disease or hungry insect pest.

Many critics claimed that the Green Revolution was a failure. But their criticism was premature. Learning from their errors, geneticists developed new varieties of wheat and rice that grow under less favorable conditions. In Bangladesh, for example, one-half of the wheat crop is a new high-yield strain that is grown without irrigation. Research is continuing on crop strains that can withstand drought and are more resistant to frost, pests, and crop diseases. A frost-resistant strain of winter wheat has been developed and is now used in Canada, helping to increase wheat production. Perhaps one of the most promising developments for the rural poor of Africa and Latin America is the relatively new genetic research aimed at increasing the yield for staples such as yams, potatoes, and various legumes. The Rockefeller Foundation, a key participant in the Green Revolution, recently announced plans to concentrate its agricultural program on genetic improvement of such crops, a potential boon to the 1.4 billion rural subsistence farmers who grow them.

GENETIC ENGINEERING. Plant breeding, while successful in raising the productivity of food crops, is slow, tedious work. Until recently, 10 to 20 years were needed to develop desirable hybrids. Today a new technology, discovered in 1973, may greatly accelerate genetic enhancement. That technology is genetic engineering.

Genetic engineering is a complicated process in which scientists isolate and transplant **genes**, segments of the hereditary material of cells that determine the characteristics of an organism—for example, resistance to pests, drought tolerance, and protein content. By transplanting desirable genes from one strain to another, genetic researchers can create new strains that may outperform their predecessors. And, more importantly, they can accomplish these remarkable feats in a fraction of the time required by traditional methods.

Where do all the desirable genes come from? They may come from existing **cultivars**, strains that are currently under cultivation, often in remote parts of the world. Or they may come from the wild species, from which our cultivars were derived. As a result, nations throughout the world are scrambling madly into the vanishing wilds in search of the ancient relatives of corn, wheat, beans, and other plants that could benefit from a genetic boost. The USDA currently houses seeds from nearly half a million species of plants. Should they vanish from the wild, their genetic potential would not be lost (Figure 6-12).

The importance of genetic improvements cannot be overstated. In the past 60 years, for instance, corn harvests have increased more than four times—from 20 to 100–250 bushels per hectare—thanks to genetic

FIGURE 6-12 Scientist at the National Seed Storage Laboratory at Colorado State University checks seeds stored in liquid nitrogen. This technique allows for better long-term storage than previous measures.

infusions. With the tools of genetic engineering replacing the slower techniques of plant breeding, the world food supply could increase dramatically.

Increasing Fertilizer Use

Japan has less than 0.07 hectare (0.166 acres) of arable land per capita, one-thirteenth that of the United States. Only with the most intensive agricultural methods has this tiny island nation been able to feed its 123 million people. Japanese farmers have achieved amazing success, producing 5,300 calories per cultivated hectare (2,150 calories per acre) per day, almost three times the per-hectare-calorie production of American farmers. One key to Japan's agricultural accomplishments is the large amounts of fertilizer applied to the land: sardine-soybean-cottonseed cakes, animal wastes, green manure, human solid wastes, and artificial fertilizer.

Japan's success with soil enrichment can be repeated in many developing countries, although on a smaller scale. Even without modifying any farm method, 9,500 fertilizer trials conducted by U.S. agricultural specialists in 14 developing nations have shown an averall average yield increase of 74 percent. In the next 25 years, however, fertilizer use must increase sevenfold if rapidly growing populations are to be properly fed. How likely is this?

Between 1950 and 1986, world fertilizer use increased from 13 million to 118 million metric tons (Figure 6-13). The increased use of fertilizer was responsible for a dramatic increase in grain production—from 620 million metric tons in 1950 to nearly 1700 million metric tons in 1986. Despite these impressive gains, however, fertilizer use has begun to taper off. In the 1970s, it increased by an average of 6 percent per year. In the 1980s, though, growth fell to 3 percent per year. The long-term prognosis for fertilizer use is not very good.

Despite its many benefits, many Third World farmers simply cannot afford it. Nor can their much wealthier counterparts in the developed world. Heavily dependent on fossil fuel energy for its production and application, fertilizer is likely to get more expensive in years to come as world oil supplies taper off. Thus, some experts predict that fertilizer use will grow slowly in the next decade and may begin to decline somewhat in the late 1990s. What is needed more than increased use, they argue, is more efficient application of fertilizer.

Edward Wolf of the Worldwatch Institute, for instance, points out that many countries overfertilize their most productive areas. They would achieve far more benefit from applying that additional fertilizer to marginal land. In 1983, for instance, Chinese farmers applied most of their fertilizer to one-third of their cropland, which is their most productive land. Applying that fertilizer to the marginal cropland—the remaining two-thirds—would yield 3 to 15 times more grain per ton of added fertilizer than it does on the productive land.

In Africa, Latin America, and Asia, where farmers could benefit most from fertilizer use, farmers frequently cannot afford the luxury of fertilizer. Instead of food aid, therefore, wealthier nations might consider donating fertilizer to help hungry nations become self-sufficient. Alternatively, they might assist in building fertilizer factories and transportation networks needed to distribute fertilizer economically and quickly to rural areas. This would be costly and time-consuming.

Recent evidence shows that low doses of artificial fertilizer applied to nitrogen-fixing plants actually enhance the plant's ability to fix atmospheric nitrogen. Heavier doses, however, impair the plant's nitrogen-fixing ability. Thus, small donations of nitrogen fertilizer and technical assistance to help achieve a proper balance of artificial fertilizer and nitrogen fixation could help many nations improve production.

The use of organic fertilizer (discussed in Chapter 5), long practiced in many parts of the world, should also be encouraged. But in many Third World nations, one of the chief sources of organic fertilizer, cattle dung, has become more valuable as a fuel. Where it once enriched farmland, it now is dried and packed in cakes that are burned for cooking. Population pressures have reduced woodlands in many Third World nations, forcing peasants to use this alternative fuel. To return to the earlier methods, many countries are developing alternative fuels. Plans to develop sustainable forests near villages could help reduce the burning of dung and allow farmers to use it to enrich their fields.

Clearly, world hunger will not be solved just by pouring more fertilizer on the land. Fertilizer is a costly alternative and is bound to become more costly in the near future. But improvements in fertilizer application, the use of low doses of fertilizer in combination with nitrogen-fixing plants, crop rotation, better soil management, and the use of organic fertilizers can all

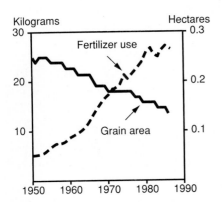

FIGURE 6-13 World fertilizer use and grain area per capita, 1950–1986.

FIGURE 6-14   Locust swarm threatens crops in Somalia. The operator of the spray plane on the left wished to spray this swarm with insecticides but the engine would not start because it was clogged with locusts. The locusts are so thick that they blot out the terminal building to the right of the picture.

help boost cropland production. These methods are part of a multifaceted plan needed to feed the world's people.

Reducing Pest Damage

Roughly 40 of every 100 kilograms of food grown throughout the world are destroyed by pests and disease organisms. Rats, insects, and fungi annually destroy enough food to feed one-third of India's population. One of every 14 people in the world will starve because of food deprivation imposed by agricultural pests.

RODENTS. The rat is one of humankind's greatest competitors. A single rat consumes 40 pounds of grain a year. The estimated 120 million rats in the United States alone destroy several billion dollars worth of food a year. In India, where rats may outnumber people by 10 to 1, up to 30 percent of the crops are ravaged by them.

DISEASE-TRANSMITTING INSECTS. In equatorial Africa, 23 varieties of tsetse fly, the transmitter of the protozoan that causes the dreaded sleeping sickness in humans and an equally serious disease in livestock, have effectively prevented livestock production in an area larger than the entire United States. The micro-scopic malarial parasite, **Plasmodium**, which is injected into the human bloodstream by mosquitos, has been a scourge to the farmers of Southeast Asia. It incapacitates millions of rice farmers at critical periods of transplanting and harvesting. To escape the malarial season in northern Thailand, for instance, farmers do not sow a second rice crop.

LOCUSTS AND OTHER INSECT PESTS. Crop-destroying insects cause billions of dollars of damage worldwide each year. Huge crops inadvertently improve the prospect for harmful pests. Migratory hordes of locusts have plagued farmers since the time of Moses and continue to devastate crops. One locust swarm near the Red Sea, so thick that it blocked out the sun, blanketed an area of over 5,000 square kilometers (2,000 square miles). Because of their great mobility, locusts may destroy crops over 1,600 kilometers (1,000 miles) and several nations away from their hatching sites (Figure 6-14). Swarms of locusts, for example, have been known to travel from Saskatchewan, Canada, all the way to Texas. (For more information on pests and pest control, see Chapter 15).

The effective control of agricultural pests in the developing nations would markedly boost food output. The United States and other developed nations have created sophisticated techniques of pest control, which are discussed in Chapter 15. Of special interest are the biological techniques that allow farmers to minimize the use of chemical pesticides, long known to have serious ecological impacts. Relatively simple measures, such as altering the time of planting to avoid the emergence of harmful insects or increasing crop diversity to miminize pest population growth, can dramatically increase agricultural productivity without the damaging side effects of pesticides.

Developing New Foods Sources

Much has been said about developing new food sources to feed the world's hungry people. Algae, yeast, and other food supplements rate high on the list. Despite the promise there new options offer, they are at best only of minor importance. Consider algae.

Algae have been grown for food in the United States, England, Germany, Venezuela, Japan, Israel, and the Netherlands for many years. One particular species, **Chlorella** can be grown in small ponds. **Chlorella** is rich in proteins, fats, and vitamins and apparently contains all of the essential amino acids required by humans. Each hectare devoted to algal culture could produce nearly 90 metric tons of dried algae. The protein content of this algal crop may be 40 times greater than the per-hectare protein yield of soybeans and 160 times greater than the yield of beef protein.

So why haven't food-producing nations gone berserk over algae the way they have over hamburgers? For one thing, algae are extraordinarily expensive to grow. Except perhaps in urban areas where abundant sewage is available to nourish the microscopic plants, the economic costs are so high that they cannot justify

widespread algal culture. Aside from the cost, new foods like algae face tremendous consumer resistance. Foods not integral to a culture often fail to catch on, making the financial risks of such ventures even greater. In the developing world, algal culture is an unlikely candidate for raising food production. However, more and more catfish, trout, and other tasty freshwater fish are grown in ponds in the United States and some Third World nations to help feed the people. In Colorado, the Rocky Mountain trout on the menu is likely to have been reared in a nearby fish pond.

NATIVE GRAZERS. Far more promising are schemes to raise native grazers: herbivores indigenous to regions, such as Africa, that are adapted to the local climate and the diseases there.

A number of years ago, a team of wildlife biologists compared the meat production of domesticated livestock raised in Africa with native populations of antelope, zebras, giraffes, and even elephants maintained in the wild (Figure 6-15). Their conclusions are illuminating.

First, wild herbivores make exceptional use of the available plant food base. Cattle, on the other hand, are very selective, consuming only certain, highly palatable grasses and ignoring other apparently less tasty forage. From the viewpoint of a range manager, cattle underutilize the available resources. Fences that protect them can also result in overgrazing of certain species of plants, eventually destroying the productive capacity of the land. In sharp contrast, when several native species graze a given area, they consume many different plants, making fuller use of the available forage: Antelope, for instance, feed on grasses and low-level foliage, giraffes

FIGURE 6-15 Giraffes and zebras in Southern Rhodesia. Such animals could be raised on large game ranches more profitably and efficiently than traditional livestock such as cattle and goats.

consume foliage higher up on grees, and elephants dine on bark and roots.

Second, wild herbivores are much better adapted to drought than domesticated livestock. For example, when a water hole dries out, they move to another, often many miles away. Cattle, restricted by fences, cannot wander off in search of water. Native species also require less water per pound than livestock. A zebra, for instance, can get along without water for 3 days, whereas the gemsbok does not require drinking water at all, but survives nicely on metabolic water (water produced when glucose is broken down by cells to produce energy) and the water in the plants it eats. Also along this line, native herbivores are much better able to avoid native predators. A cow is an easy target for a hungry lion. A native antelope has a good chance of escaping.

Third, wild herbivores are immune to the potentially lethal sleeping sickness transimitted by the tsetse fly. Introduced livestock, however, are not.

Finally, ranches that raise wild species for commercial meat production can expect a profit margin fully six times that of the traditional livestock ranch.

Livestock Improvements

Through animal breeding programs, agricultural scientists have developed new strains of cattle with meatier carcasses and new swine that grow faster and give birth to larger litters. Cows have been produced with a milk production vastly superior to that of the dairy cattle of developing nations. For example, American test breeds of Holsteins produce up to 900 kilograms (2,000 pounds) of milk a year, compared to the 140-kilogram (300-pound) per year production from the yellow cattle of China. A good part of that success results from artificial insemination, the injection of sperm from bulls selected for genetic superiority. Chickens with greater egg-laying capacity and more efficient feed-to-biomass conversions have been developed as well. Genetic engineering, discussed earlier in this chapter, may also enhance scientists' ability to come up with improved livestock.

Improved livestock strains could help alleviate world hunger. With the assistance of agricultural experts from the Food and Agriculture Organization (FAO) of the United Nations, Third World farmers could gradually acquire new strains that outproduce traditional livestock.

CAN WE FEED THE WORLD'S PEOPLE?

For hundreds, perhaps thousands of years, humankind has pondered a question as important today as it was 1,000 years ago: Can we feed the world's people?

Malthus suggested that the human population would always outstrip the food supply, creating hunger and starvation. But many people cannot accept this prognosis and dream of the day when all the world's people will be adequately fed.

That day may be decades away, despite the long list of potential solutions. Why? In large part, hunger is the result of poverty. Even in the chronically food-short nations, the rich can buy food while the poor starve to death. The peasants go hungry because they cannot buy or grow enough food. Some experts believe that not until the standard of living is raised in many Third World nations can hunger be wiped out. Even modest gains could go a long way. Thus, in addition to the measures described in the previous section, countries must find ways to raise the earning power of their poor. By reducing population growth, they can cut the explosion in the workforce. By developing small industries that use local resources for local consumption, they may be able to help peasants earn enough money to feed themselves and their children. Without increases in personal wealth, most experts agree, hunger will be with us for a long time.

Economic development by itself is not enough. Countries must also become self-sufficient in food production. Consider these facts: The FAO estimates that the world's total stock of surplus grains in 1987 could feed the hungry people of the world for two full years. But two-thirds of that food is in the developed nations, mainly in North America. The problem, therefore, is not that we can't grow enough food, but that not enough is grown where it is most needed or not enough is delivered to the people who need it most. The FAO estimates that 64 countries (29 of which are in Africa) will be unable to feed their populations in 2000.

Countries must strive for greater self-sufficiency in production. The rich industrial nations that today supply grain for many countries, often at low cost or free of charge, cannot be relied on indefinitely. Their grain will be diverted to produce fuel as oil supplies fall. Prices will rise, making it even more costly. Self-sufficiency is a must. Developed nations can lend a hand in making this important transition.

To eliminate hunger, many experts believe that we need an integrated approach: agricultural improvements like soil conservation and new plant varieties, small-scale economic development that benefits the hungry peasants, and population control. Together, these measures can move us a step closer to feeding the hungry planet and avoiding the ecological catastrophe already in the making.

RAPID REVIEW

1. The eighteenth-century British economist Thomas Malthus advanced the theory that because of the

limits set by the finite land supply, human populations tend to increase faster than the food supply. Eventually, therefore, the human population will experience a massive die-off that will bring it back in line with food production.

2. Malthus's glum predictions may be coming true. An estimated 40 million people, nearly half of them children, die each year from hunger and diseases worsened by hunger.

3. According to recent estimates of the World Bank, 730 million people are undernourished and malnourished. Most of them live in Asia, Africa, and Latin America.

4. Undernutrition is a quantitative phenomenon resulting from an inadequate intake of food. Malnutrition is a qualitative phenomenon characterized by inferior food quality that usually results in a deficient intake of proteins and vitamins.

5. Two clinically identifiable diseases are seen in many of the world's children. Marasmus is a disease that afflicts infants separated from their mother's milk. It is caused by a deficiency of protein and calories. Kwashiordor occurs in slightly older children and results from an inadequate intake of protein. For every child with kwashiorkor and marasmus, there are 100 children suffering from milder cases of malnutrition and undernutrition.

6. World agriculture faces two major challenges: (a) feeding people who are starving today and (b) meeting the demands of future citizens. Developing a sustainable system of agriculture is a must.

7. World population is expected to increase by 2 million people between 1988 and 2020. Food production must climb accordingly just to meet the demand of these new people. Fortunately, there are many ways to eliminate world hunger. The foremost strategy is population control.

8. Improving soil management on existing farmland can help improve food production. Better controls on soil erosion, efforts to stop the spread of deserts, and measures to halt nutrient depletion are all necessary.

9. Reducing farmland conversion can also help stem the rising tide of world hunger.

10. Expanding the amount of land under cultivation is a strategy of limited value, for many countries are already farming nearly all of their good land. In the United States and other nations, much of the land in reserve is marginal. This land is often too costly and enviromentally harmful to farm. In Africa and South America, large amounts of farmland lie in reserve. Before the reserves are tapped, however, more careful land management should be applied to existing farmland to avoid further losses. In addition, the use of tropical rain forests, arid lands, and wetlands should be avoided. Tropical rain forest soils are poor and highly erodible. Arid lands are easily damaged. Wetlands are an important biological resource better left undisturbed.

11. Irrigation has helped boost agricultural productivity, but growth in irrigation has slowed tremendously in recent years. Gains in production are more likely to come from improvements in irrigation efficiency—drip irrigation systems, cement-lined ditches, and pipes, for instance.

12. New plant species developed through plant breeding programs have resulted in a Green Revolution—an explosion in crop production. Rice and wheat crops now produce three to five times as much grain as their predecessors. Developed under the leadership of Norman Borlaug, the new varieties of rice and wheat have spread more rapidly than any other innovation in the history of agriculture. Despite the obvious benefits of the new crops, they have largely benefited wealthier farmers who could afford irrigation, fertilizer, and pesticides. As a result, new strains have been developed that grow without irrigation. Research is continuing on crops that can withstand pests and crop diseases. Work is also underway to develop higher-yield crops grown by subsistence farmers, such as yams, potatoes, and legumes. Genetic engineering may help speed up the development of high-yield plants and animals.

13. Fertilizer has played a key role in increasing agricultural productivity for over three decades. But the growth in fertilizer use has fallen considerably in recent years. While fertilizer will continue to help farmers expand the food supply, it will play a less central role. Far more important will be improvements in the efficiency of fertilizer use. Many countries overfertilize their best land and underfertilize their less productive lands. By shifting fertilizer from prime land to less productive land, farmers can greatly improve crop yields.

14. Pests destroy approximately 40 percent of the world's food supply each year. Through better pest control, farmers can raise food production. But pest control strategies must also be enviromentally safe.

15. Perhaps the least promising of all strategies is new food sources, such as algae and yeast. Far more promising are plans to raise native grazers. Native grazers fully utilize the plant food base, tend not to overgraze, are mobile, and are often resistant to diseases.

16. Despite the long list of potential ways to solve world hunger, little sustainable progress will be made without population control and measures to increase economic wealth.

17. What is needed is an integrated approach that includes the many measures discussed in this chapter and emphasizes self-sufficiency.

KEY WORDS AND PHRASES

Desertification	Kwashiorkor
Economic development	Laterites
Farmland conversion	Lester Brown
Farmland reserves	Malnutrition
Fuel crops	Marasmus
Genetic diversity	Native grazers
Genetic engineering	Norman Borlaug
Green Revolution	Salinization
High-yield strains	Self-sufficiency
Integrated approach	Thomas Malthus
International Maize and	Tropical rain forests
Wheat Improvement	Undernutrition
Center	Waterlogging
Irrigation	Wetlands

QUESTIONS AND TOPICS FOR DISCUSSION

1. Given what you know about the effects of over-population, debate the following statement: "Food surpluses from wealthy nations should be donated to poor, hungry nations, now and in the future. Through such donations, world hunger can be eliminated."

2. Thomas Malthus voiced dire warnings about world population growth nearly 200 years ago. What were they, and how valid are they today?

3. Define malnutrition and undernutrition. Why are these conditions particularly harmful to infants?

4. Describe the connections between overpopulation and hunger. In what ways can overpopulation worsen hunger?

5. What are the most immediate challenges facing the world in regard to food production?

6. Drawing on information from the previous chapters, describe a sustainable agricultural system. How does it differ from the system largely in place today? Describe ways that modern agriculture can be improved to make it sustainable.

7. Do you agree with the following statement? Why or why not? "The answer to world hunger is cropland expansion. We must plow all available land. There's plenty of good farmland left."

8. Give several reasons why the land on which tropical rain forests grow might appear to be a prime candidate for farmland conversion. Describe why these impressions are false.

9. Of what value are swamps, salt marshes, lagoons, and other wetlands? Why should or shouldn't they be drained to make more farmland?

10. List six reasons why the growth in farmland irrigation has slowed so dramatically in recent years.

11. What is the Green Revolution? In what ways was it initially successful, and in what ways was it unsuccessful? What new developments will help the world's subsistence farmers? How could genetic engineering help plant scientists increase crop yields?

12. Do you agree with the following statement? "Fertilizer has helped farmers the world over increase food production. By applying more fertilizer to cropland, especially in Third World nations, farmers can boost agricultural production." What are the limitations to this strategy? Can you suggest any more effective strategies?

13. Sketch the broad outlines of a master plan to increase food production worldwide.

14. Debate the following statement: "In large part, hunger is the result of poverty. To solve the hunger problem, we must raise the earning power of the world's people."

15. Do you agree with the following statement? "Poor countries must eventually become self-sufficient in food production. They cannot rely on the wealthy nations of the world to bail them out of their troubles."

SUGGESTED READINGS

Brown, L. R., Chandler, W. U., Flavin, J., Pollock, C., Postel, S., Starke, L., and Wolfe, E. C. *State of the World, 1985.* New York: W. W. Norton, 1985. See Chapter 2 for more on world agricultural problems.

Brown, L. R., Chandler, W. U., Flavin, J., Pollock, C., Postel, S., Starke, L., and Wolfe, E. C. *State of the World, 1987.* New York: W. W. Norton, 1987. See Chapters 7 and 8 for excellent but slightly technical discussions of world agricultural problems and solutions.

Carey, J. "Brave New World of Super-Plants." *International Wildlife* 16(6):16–18, 1986. Wonderfully readable discussion of the potential promise and peril of genetic engineering.

Ehrlich, A. H., and Ehrlich, P. R. "Why Do People Starve?" *The Amicus Journal* 9(2): 42–47, 1987. Sobering look at world hunger and food production.

Jackson, W., Berry, W., and Colman, B. *Meeting the Expectations of the Land*. San Francisco: North Point Press, 1984. Superb collections of essays on sustainable agriculture.

Oram, P. A. "Moving Toward Sustainability: Building the Agroecological Framework." *Environment* 30(9):14–17, 30–36, 1988. Good overview of some needed changes to help make agriculture more sustainable.

Postel, S. *Conserving Water: The Untapped Potential* World watch Paper 67. Washington, D.C.: World watch Institute, 1985. Detailed survey of numerous methods of conserving agricultural water.

Repetto, R. *Population Resources Environment: An Uncertain Future*. Population Bulletin 42(2). Washington, D.C.: Population Reference Bureau, July, 1987. A timely discussion of population and agriculture.

Sampson, R. N. *Farmland or Wasteland. A Time to Choose.* Emmaus, Pa.: Rodale Press, 1981. Comprehensive but readable account of agricultural problems and ways to solve them.

Vietmeyer, N. "Lesser-Known Plants of Potential Use in Agriculture and Forestry." *Science* 232: 1379–1384, 1986. Excellent article on valuable plant species that could be used to help raise agricultural productivity.

Wolf, E. C. *Beyond the Green Revolution: New Approaches for Third World Agriculture*. Worldwatch Paper 73. Washington, D.C.: Worldwatch Institute, October 1986.

Wolf, E. C., and Brown, L. R. "Seeds of Hope in a Dying Land." *Sierra* 87(2):104–107, 1985. Superbly written case study of the causes and devastating effects of hunger in Ethiopia.

7

Water

A severe water shortage is one of the most serious long-range environmental problems facing our nation. How can this be? After all, we receive 16 trillion liters (4.2 trillion gallons) of precipitation every *day*—about 16,800 gallons for every man, woman, and child. Although this is an enormous amount of water, the impending shortage is real. There are several reasons: (1) rapidly increasing population, (2) rising demand by agriculture, industry, and cities, (3) flagrant waste, (4) unequal distribution, and (5) pollution. Consider the following facts concerning our country's critical water situation:

1. *Agriculture*. Irrigated crop acreage in the United States has almost tripled during the last 30 years to about 20 million hectares (50 million acres). The capacity of the Ogallala aquifer, which extends from Nebraska to Texas, is being strained to the limit because of withdrawals by farmers, industries, and cities. In some areas, the water table (the upper limit of the groundwater) is dropping 1.5 meters (5 feet) per year.

2. *Industry*. Water is used by industry to cool equipment, for use in products, and to make steam to generate electrical power. In the United States, electrical power plants use 12 billion liters (3.2 billion gallons) a day. It takes 53.2 liters (14 gallons) of water to make a pound of sugar, 570 liters (150 gallons) for the Sunday newspaper, and 247,000 liters (65,000 gallons) to produce an automobile.

3. *Urban use and waste*. Eighty percent of our nation's population (196 million people) depend on 21,000 municipal systems for their water supply. The average American family uses 230 liters (60 gallons) each day. This level of use seems very wasteful, since European families use only half as much. We use water to wash everything from a ten-ton truck to a newborn baby. We use it to douse fires, flush sewage, and clean city streets. The rapidly increasing use of ground and surface water by booming cities in the arid Southwest such as Santa Fe, New Mexico, and Phoenix, Arizona, has reduced the amount available for irrigated farming. Great amounts could be made available by finding ways to reduce waste in these areas.

4. *Unequal distribution*. U.S. water problems are not caused by absolute shortages in supply. They are problems of distribution resulting from the intensive concentration of water-using people and industry. The accelerated migration of people to the Southwest, for example, has reduced water supplies in this region to the vanishing point. As a result, water may have to be transported long distances from water-rich regions, or strict conservation measures and recycling programs may have to be started.

5. *Pollution*. Contamination of lakes, streams, and groundwater contributes significantly to our nation's water shortage. Lead from old pipes has made water in parts of Boston unfit to drink. According to the EPA, a number of our rivers, such as the Mississippi River below Minneapolis–St. Paul, are so polluted that public health may be jeopardized. As of 1988, the groundwater in 23 states was contaminated with 17 health-threatening pesticides. This problem is especially severe in Florida, Wisconsin, and California.

Table 7-1 Water Cycle Facts

Location of Reservoir	Total Water Supply (%)	Renewal Time
On the land		
Ice caps	2.225	16,000 years
Glaciers	0.015	16,000 years
Freshwater lakes	0.009	10–100 years (varies with depth)
Saltwater lakes	0.007	10–100 years (varies with depth)
Rivers	0.0001	12–20 days
Subsurface		
Soil moisture	0.003	280 days
Groundwater		
To half-mile depth	0.303	300 years
Beyond half-mile depth	0.303	4,600 years
Other		
Atmospherere	0.001	9–12 days
World's oceans	97.134	37,000 maximum
Total	100.000	

These problems are already causing regional shortages that are bound to grow worse as our population increases. This intensively used, life-sustaining resource moves in a circular path through the human ecosystem, a phenomenon called the **water cycle** (Table 7-1). Familiarity with the water cycle is basic to an appreciation of the nature and complexity of the serious water conservation problems confronting the United States.

THE WATER CYCLE

Because of the cyclical nature of water movement, a given water molecule may be used over and over again throughout the centuries (Figure 7-1). For example, the bath water used by Cleopatra over 2,000 years ago has flowed to the sea and been mixed with ocean water. Some has already evaporated and fallen on the continents as rain. A few molecules from her bath may be present in your next bath. In a more serious vein, virtually all water on our planet is recycled. Even the 50 kilograms (110 pounds) of water in the body of the average college student is replaced many times during the school year.

The water cycle is powered by solar energy and gravity, the daily energy input being *greater than all the energy utilized by human beings since the dawn of civilization*. Solar energy lifts the water from the soil, plants, oceans, lakes, and streams during evaporation, while gravity pulls it down again as rain or snow. In actuality, all water is not continuously moving. It may be temporarily stored (for centuries), either within the earth's crust, on the earth's surface as polar ice caps or glaciers, or in the atmosphere (Figures 7-2 and 7-3). The time required for the complete replacement of the water at a particular phase of the cycle is known as the **replacement period**. Average replacement periods range from 9 days for water in

the atmosphere to 37,000 years for water in the deep oceans.

Oceans

When the astronauts peered down at the earth from outer space, it appeared blue, with just a few patches of green. This is understandable because oceans cover 70 percent of our planet. If the earth were a perfectly smooth sphere, the ocean water would be sufficient to submerge the entire globe to a depth of 242 meters (800 feet).

Precipitation

Water molecules at the ocean's surface are warmed by the sun; they rise into the atmosphere as a gas in a process called **evaporation**. As the water vapor rises, it gradually cools, condenses, and forms clouds. Water that has evaporated from a Louisiana rice field may eventually fall as rain on a college campus in Ohio. Our nation's average annual rainfall would be sufficient to cover the entire country (if it were perfectly level) to a depth of 1 meter (3.3 feet). In the United States, unfortunately, rainfall is very unevenly distributed both in time and in space. The average annual precipitation per state is shown in Figure 7-4. Death Valley receives only 4.3 centimeters (1.7 inches) annually, whereas the western slope of the Cascades, not far from it, gets 350–400 centimeters (140–150 inches).

When rain or snow originally forms high above the earth's surface, it is uncontaminated with foreign materials. However, as the raindrops and snowflakes fall earthward, they intercept various atmospheric pollutants, such as carbon dioxide, soot, dust, pollen, and bacteria. Where rain falls through air that is polluted with oxides of sulfur and nitrogen, as is the case in many industrial areas, it is converted into dilute sulfuric and nitric acids. The pH of this rain may be

FIGURE 7-1 The water cycle.

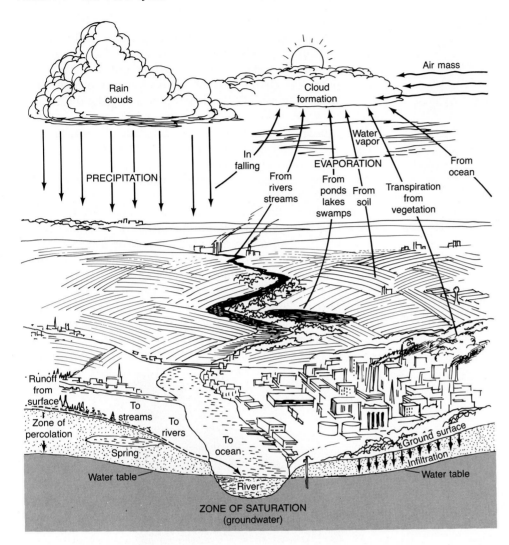

as low as 3, sufficient to corrode water pipes, accelerate the leaching of soil nutrients, and poison aquatic and terrestrial life. Eventually, all the contaminants in the water are carried to streams, lakes, and finally the ocean, which serves as the ultimate sink.

Bodies of Organisms

Each of the more than 10 million kinds of organisms on this planet, from the ameba to the blue whale, must take water into its body to survive. In most species, including humans, 70 percent of living biomass is composed of water. Plants absorb soil water through their root systems; a large oak needs 400 liters (100 gallons) per day. The body of the average human adult contains 50 liters (110 pounds) of water. It serves many functions. As a principal component of the blood, it is a transportation medium for many substances, including hormones, enzymes, vitamins, oxygen, and minerals. Water leaves

the body and passes back into the environment as urine and sweat. If the human body loses more than 12 percent of its water, death quickly follows.

Evaporation and Transpiration

Of the 0.75 meter (30 inches) of annual rainfall, about 0.5 meter (21 inches) is released into the atmosphere by evaporation and transpiration. Evaporation may take place directly from streams, oceans, moist soil, wet vegetation, and the bodies of animals and their wastes (Figure 7-5). Plants lose water through **transpiration**, the escape of water from a plant through pores in its leaves. This process is essential to the plant's survival, for it draws dissolved nutrients from the soil up through the stem (or trunk) to the leaves. One mature oak tree may transpire 380 liters (100 gallons) per day—more than 150,000 liters (40,000 gallons) in a year.

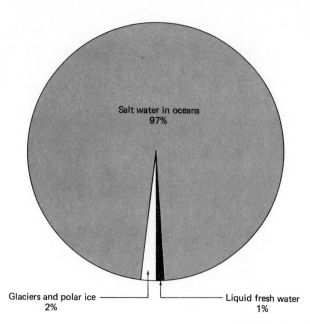

Salt water in oceans
97%

Glaciers and polar ice
2%

Liquid fresh water
1%

FIGURE 7-2   The oceans represent an enormous reservoir of water, forming 97 percent of all the water passing through the water cycle.

Surface Water

About 22 centimeters (9 inches) of the 76 centimeters (30 inches) of annual rainfall in the United States ends up in ponds, lakes, and streams, which are known as **surface water**. Some may filter down through the pores and channels of the earth's crust to form **groundwater** (Figure 7-6). Surface water and groundwater are of great concern to conservationists, for it is these sources that are usable for domestic, industrial, and recreational purposes. It is this water that we pollute with toxic chemicals, pesticides, human waste, and many other contaminants—a problem we discuss in the next chapter.

Stream flow in the United States averages 4,560 billion liters (1,200 billion gallons) a day. It may be in the form of a tiny mountain brook or a mighty river such as the Mississippi, which drains 40 percent of the land area in the United States and flows 3,800 kilometers (2,300 miles) across mid-America to the Gulf of Mexico. Surface runoff water, in the form of streams, ponds, and lakes, satisfies about 75 percent of our water requirements.

FIGURE 7-3   Glaciers represent a phase of the hydrologic cycle: about three-fourth's of the world's fresh water is locked up in glaciers and polar ice caps. They hold as much water as would flow through the world's rivers in about 1,000 years. Many of the lakes in the northeastern United States were formed from glacial meltwater. This is a view of the Mendenhall Glacier, Tongass National Forest, Alaska.

FIGURE 7-4 Average annual precipitation in the United States.

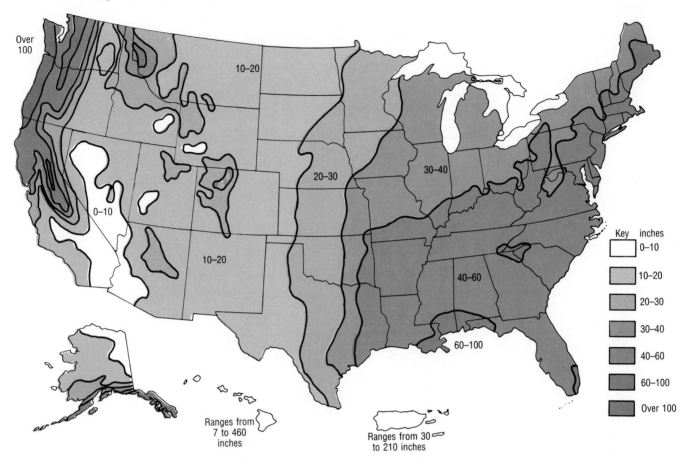

Groundwater

Some of the rainfall and snowmelt gradually seeps down through the soil in a process called **infiltration** (Figure 7-6). This water first moves through the **zone of aeration**. This zone, which includes both the topsoil and subsoil, is characterized by pore spaces that contain water and air. The soil moisture in this zone is known as **capillary water**. Some of this water is absorbed by plant root systems. It then passes up plant stems and tree trunks to the leaves. Most of this water then transpires from the leaves into the atmosphere. A small amount of the water in the leaves is used as a raw material in photosynthesis.

Much of the soil water continues to filter down through the zone of aeration into the **zone of saturation**. As the water moves through the soil many pollutants adhere to the surfaces of the soil particles. As a result, the water quality is often improved. Eventually, the downward movement of the water through the zone of saturation is stopped by a layer of impermeable rock. As a result, the water accumulates in the soil and gravel above the impermeable layer until all the spaces, pores, and cracks become filled with water. The upper level

of the zone of saturation is known as the **water table** (Figure 7-7). The water table may intersect the surface and form marshes, ponds, or springs. In other cases, the water table may be more than a mile deep.

Since time immemorial, humans have tapped groundwater by drilling wells below the water table. After heavy rainfall, the water table rises. (An exception would be flash floods in deserts, where most of the water runs off instead of infiltrating.) However, during periods of drought, the water table drops. In extreme cases, some wells may run dry (Figure 7-8).

Ninety-seven percent of the world's supply of liquid fresh water (2 million cubic miles) is held in porous and permeable layers of sand, sandstone, and limestone known as **aquifers**. In the United States, the groundwater in aquifers in the upper 0.5 mile of the earth's crust is equal to all the water that will run off into the oceans during the next 100 years! However, water in these great underground reservoirs moves very slowly and often comes from precipitation that fell hundreds of years earlier. For example, the aquifer that supplies a large amount of Chicago's water came from rain and snow that fell on the Great Plains far to the west a million years ago, and then slowly

FIGURE 7-5 What happens to the rain and snow? Water continuously evaporates into the atmosphere, most of it from the oceans. About 40,000 billion gallons per day (bgd) pass over the
United States as water vapor, even in times of drought. Roughly 1 gallon in 10—4200 bgd—
falls to the surface of the coterminous United States. That works out to an average of 30 inches
a year, of which 26 inches arrive as rainfall and the rest as snow, sleet, and hail.

But few places receive the average precipitation, which ranges from less than 4 inches a year
in the Great Basin to more than 200 inches a year along the Pacific Northwest coast.

More than two-thirds of the precipitation returns to the atmosphere, but nine inches (1300 bgd)
either soaks down to the water table or runs into lakes or streams, from which it eventually moves
to the ocean. Only a small fraction of the precipitation, 106 bgd, is consumed.

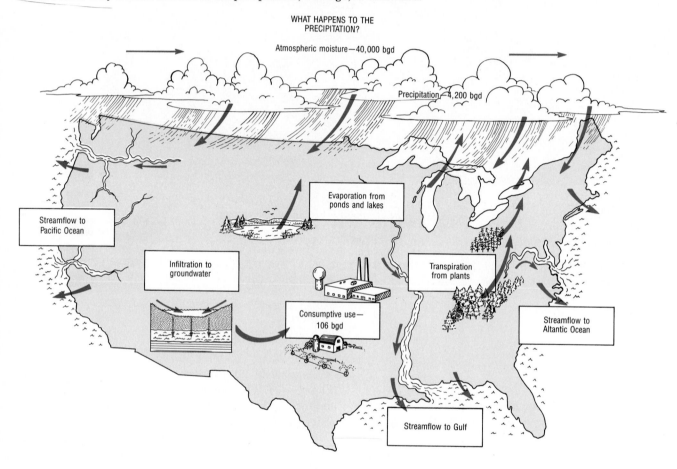

trickled through rocks at a rate of a few centimeters or
meters a year. The Ogallala aquifer, one of the largest
in the United States, lies under 572 square kilometers
(225,000 square miles) of land that extends through
eight states from Nebraska south to Texas (Figure 7-9).
This aquifer contains 2.5 million billion liters (650
trillion gallons). It provides drinking water for 2 million people, but it is being drained faster than it can
recharge. It makes possible a multi-billion-dollar economy based on irrigation farming that is fast running
into trouble.

WATER PROBLEMS

Drought

According to the U.S. Weather Bureau, a drought exists
whenever rainfall for a period of 21 days or longer
falls 30 percent below the average. The Great Plains
from Texas to Montana, averages about 35 consecutive
drought days each year and 75 to 100 successive days
of drought once in 10 years. Up to 120 *consecutive
rainless days* have been recorded for the southern Great
Plains, or Dust Bowl, region. The relative frequency of

FIGURE 7-6 Fate of water that has fallen on the ground as precipitation.

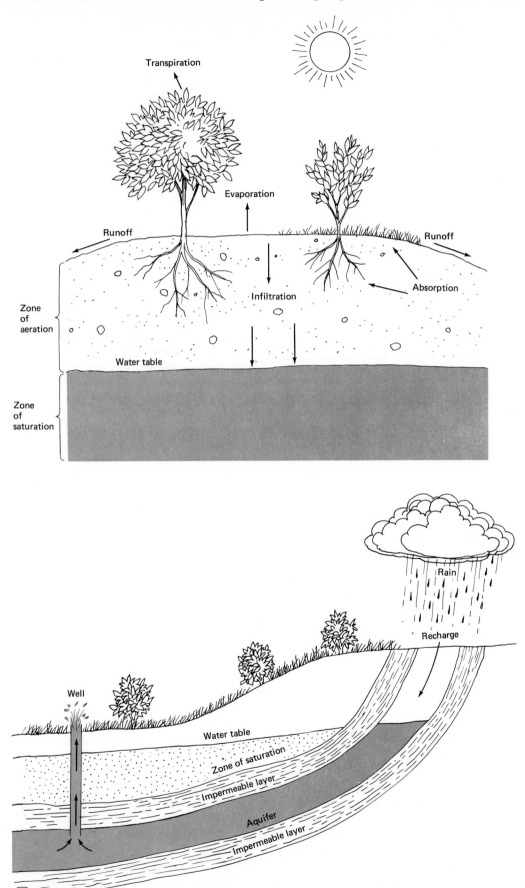

FIGURE 7-7 An aquifer serves as a source of well water. Continued water withdrawal would eventually deplete the supply if the rate of withdrawal exceeded the rate of recharge.

FIGURE 7-8 Effect of drought on water table levels and well water availability.

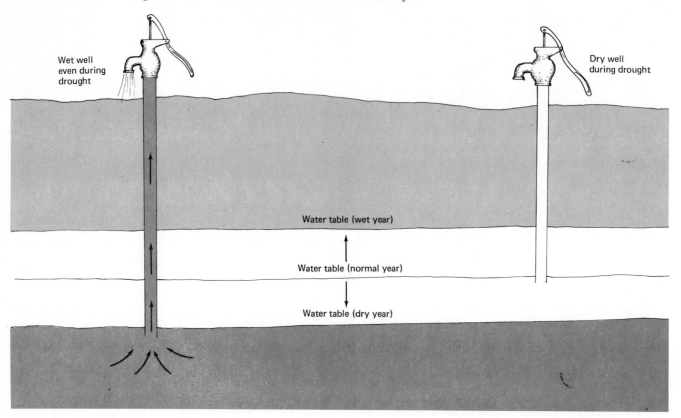

drought in various regions of the United States is shown in Figure 7-10.

J. Murray Mitchell, a research climatologist with the National Oceanic and Atmospheric Administration, studied drought patterns as revealed by tree rings. Going back to 1600 A.D., he found that the western states have experienced a prolonged, extended drought about every 22 years. Much to his surprise, Mitchell found that the drought cycle is correlated with sunspot patterns. Such information is extremely valuable for national planning. Unfortunately, however, Mitchell's research is not sufficiently refined to allow him to predict in what *state* the next drought will occur.

Floods

Not only are we plagued by water scarcity, we also are beset with the equally serious problem of *too much* water from time to time. Throughout history we have suffered from destructive floods (Table 7-2, Figure 7-11).

Paradoxically, however, in some parts of the world, human survival may depend on floods. The flourishing agricultural economy of Egypt, for example, was sustained for millennia by the recurrent flooding of the Nile. Each inundation was eagerly awaited by farmers, for when the Nile finally receded, it left behind extremely fertile topsoil carried from its upstream watershed.

THE UPPER MISSISSIPPI FLOOD. An unusual combination of factors involving excessive rainfall, massive snowmelt, and frozen ground set the stage for a once-in-a-century flood in the upper Mississippi River Valley during the spring of 1965. Swollen with spring runoff waters, the Mississippi River surged over its banks from Minneapolis south to its junction with the Missouri River at St. Louis, Missouri. Thousands of hectares of winter wheat were destroyed. More than 36,000 hectares (90,000 acres) of cropland were submerged in Illinois alone. The *Hiawatha*, a crack express train, was forced to halt its Minneapolis–Milwaukee run for the first time in history. At Hannibal, Missouri, a few resolute shop owners hung out "business as usual" signs, even though much of Main Street was open to motorboat traffic only. At Mankato State College in Minnesota, hundreds of student volunteers erected a sandbag barrier to restrain the floodwaters. Despite such emergency measures, the rising waters drove 40,000 people from their homes. Eventually the waters receded. A thick, smelly deposit of brownish ooze covered the wall-to-wall carpeting of many riverfront homes. Thousands of fish were stranded in stag-

The "Big Dry" of 1988

The "Big Dry" of 1988, as *Time* magazine called it, was the most destructive drought to wither our nation's croplands since the Dust Bowl era half a century ago. The dramatic late-summer scene that unfolded at Stanley, a tiny farming community in northwestern Wisconsin, illustrates the plight of the farmer. The figure of Father Jeremiah Cashman was silhouetted against the orb of the setting sun as he celebrated communion with dozens of grim-faced farm families. For each family, the prospect of an impending crop failure was a searing, gut-wrenching experience. The mass was the climax to an outdoor "pray-for-rain" service. After all, Indian rain dances had failed. Cloud-seeding experiments by rainmakers had failed. Now it was time to try prayer. Except for Father Cashman's voice, the only sounds were the crunch of his shoes on the parched earth and the brittle rasp of shriveled corn caught in a swelling breeze.

The drought cut our nation's corn production by 30 percent. The soybean harvest was 25 percent below normal. The summer of 1988 was abnormally dry in Canada, the Soviet Union, and China as well. As a consequence, the world's stores of grain experienced the sharpest 1-year decline in history. America's farm economy dried up, along with its croplands. In Wisconsin alone, the Big Dry forced at least 1,000 farmers to "lock up their barns" for the last time and search for a new way of life. The drought persisted in sections of the Midwest well into 1989 and shriveled up a multimillion-dollar crop of winter wheat.

Although perhaps not as damaging in a financial sense, the drought had a strong impact on urban dwellers as well. In major urban areas throughout the Midwest, summer rainfall levels were at record lows. Minneapolis, for example, had only 3 inches of rain for the months of May, June, and July. Sponge baths replaced tub soakers. Shower time was cut in half. In Nashville, Tennessee, attorney Frank Reeves showered in his front yard so that he could clean up and water his lawn at the same time. Said Reeves: "I think my lawn needs the water more than the city sewer." Reservoir levels dropped to record lows and forced some towns to ration water. (In early 1989, water use was still restricted along the Gulf Coast and in the Northeast.)

It is true that the mighty Mississippi "kept rollin' along" throughout the Big Dry. However, the volume and depth of the river were sharply reduced. On July 7, for example, the water level was so low that 130 towboats and 2,400 barges were stranded in Greeneville and Natchez, Mississippi. Many of the barges were loaded with grain, paper, and chemicals for northern markets. The stranded cargo would have filled a caravan of trucks more than 20 miles long. The Mississippi's greatest traffic jam was finally broken when the U.S. Army Corps of Engineers dredged an emergency channel. Nevertheless, the shallow river caused severe financial problems for the barge and towboat industry. Towboat operators alone expected to lose $200 million—20 percent of their annual income.

Wildlife populations were also seriously affected by the drought, especially those associated with aquatic habitats, such as fish and water fowl. River levels in many lakes, streams and marshs dropped to once-in-a-century lows. The result was sharply reduced dilution of pollution generated by industrial plants and municipal sewage systems. State and federal conservation officials reported adverse effects on fish populations in a number of badly polluted rivers. Developing embryos and newly hatched young were especially vulnerable. In some cases, a whole *year class* of young fish were destroyed in a particular stretch of stream.

The Big Dry of 1988 had disastrous effects on the reproduction of North American waterfowl populations. More than half of the ducks are reared on small breeding ponds in the prairie provinces of Alberta, Saskatchewan, and Alberta, and in the Dakotas, Minnesota, and Iowa. The drought caused more than 1 million of these ponds to go bone dry. The consequences were calamitous. The total duck population of the United States just prior to the fall migration was an estimated 66 million birds, 8 million less than in 1987 and the second lowest since records were kept.

What caused the record drought? Many experts think it is the result of global warming, a gradual rise in global temperature brought on by pollution from human sources. Carbon dioxide from fossil fuel combustion is one of the chief culprits (Chapter 18).

nant backwaters. The official toll was 16 drowned, 330 injured, and $140 million in property damage.

FLOOD CONTROL. Although we cannot prevent *all* floods, we can prevent some of the lesser ones and restrict the magnitude and destructiveness of others. Flood control measures include protecting the watershed, zoning flood plains, measuring snowpack to predict flood conditions, building levees, dredging, and constructing dams.

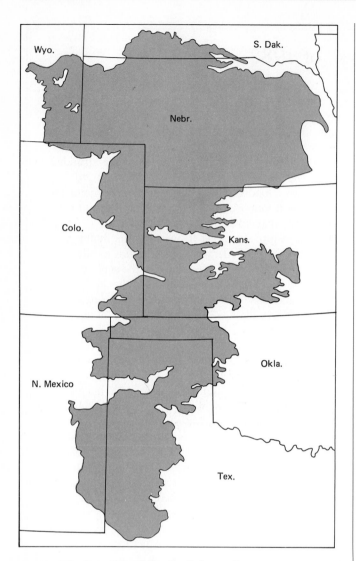

FIGURE 7-9 Location of the Ogallala aquifer.

Protecting the Watershed. A **watershed** is the area drained by a single watercourse. The largest watersheds, such as those of the Ohio, Missouri, Colorado, and Mississippi rivers, are known as **drainage basins**. All watersheds, large or small, have the basic function of converting precipitation into stream flow and groundwater. Even during a light shower of only 0.25 centimeters (0.1 inch) of rain, a 2.5-square-kilometer (1-square-mile) watershed would produce 6.6 million liters (1.7 million gallons) of stream flow.

Watershed protection is the preventive medicine of flood control. Watersheds are protected by the Watershed Protection and Flood Prevention Act. The small watershed program is administered by the USDA's Soil Conservation Service. According to the USDA, 8,000 (61.5 percent) of the 13,000 small watersheds (of fewer than 100,000 hectares or 250,000 acres) in this coun-

try have flood and erosion problems (Figure 7-12). Protection of large watersheds is primarily the concern of the Bureau of Reclamation, the U.S. Army Corps of Engineers, and the Tennessee Valley Authority (TVA). Although the primary objective of the act is flood control, it is operated under a multipurpose concept, and, where possible, it embraces problems of erosion, water supply, wildlife management, and recreation.

Vegetation impedes the flow of water and promotes its absorption by the soil, thus reducing flooding and soil erosion. This is well illustrated by the following episode. Some years ago, merry celebrations ushering in the New Year at La Crescenta, California, were abruptly ended when floodwaters rushed down from the adjacent hills of the San Gabriel Mountains, inflicting $5 million in damage and killing 30 people. When flood control experts investigated the watershed above La Crescenta, they discovered that the floodwaters originated from an 18-square-kilometer (7-square-mile) area in the San Gabriel Mountains *that had been burned over only a short time before*. However, the unburned watershed, with its vegetational sponge of chaparral, herbs, and grasses, thwarted the downhill rush of runoff waters; peak flows were roughly 5 percent of those of the burned areas. Whether it is California chaparral, Alabama alfalfa, or Wisconsin woodlands, any type of vegetational cover is useful in flood control.

Measuring Snowpack to Predict Floods. The U.S. Geological Survey measures the depth of the snowpack at more than 1,000 snow courses in the western mountains. Surveys can help warn officials of impending floods, allowing them time to take evasive actions. Several years ago, such a survey predicted that the imminent spring snowmelt in the Northwest would crest the Kootenai River at 10 meters (35.5 feet), sufficient to cause extensive flooding at Bonner's Ferry, Idaho. Alerted by this forewarning, federal troops evacuated all residents and reinforced the dikes. On May 21, the river crested at 10 meters (35.5 feet), as predicted. Flood damage was minimized, however, and not one life was lost.

Levees. Levees are dikes constructed of earth, stone, or mortar at varying distances from the river bank to protect valuable residential, industrial, and agricultural property from floodwaters. Levees along the Arkansas, Red, White, and Ouachita rivers in Arkansas have given a measure of protection to more than 0.8 million hectare (2 million acres) of fertile alluvial land. During the last 150 years, a mammoth system of over 3,500 levees and dikes has been constructed along the lower Mississippi River.

There are certain drawbacks associated with levees, however. In some situations, they may actually *increase* flood damage rather than reduce it. This is especially true in the United States because levees encourage peo-

FIGURE 7-10 Percentage of months in which areas in the United States experience severe or extreme drought.

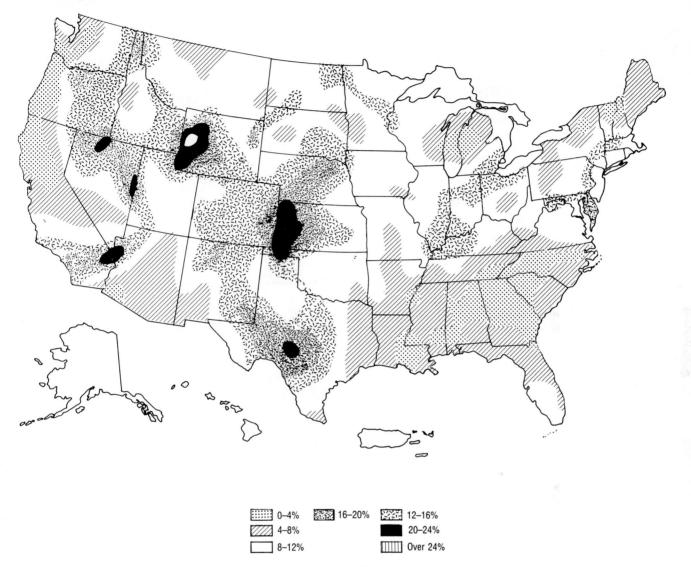

0–4%	16–20%	12–16%
4–8%		20–24%
8–12%		Over 24%

ple to settle on flood plains. This results from pressure exerted by real estate agencies and developers to change zoning on flood plains to develop more land.

Dredging Operations. Because of the huge amounts of soil that are washed into streams from surrounding watersheds, the channels tend to accumulate sediment, which, in turn, increases the probability of a flood. The enormity of this problem can be appreciated if we note that the Mississippi River, for example, transports roughly 2 million metric tons of sediment daily. To cope with this problem (as well as to deepen the channels for navigation), the Mississippi River and a host of others are periodically dredged by the U.S. Army Corps of Engineers.

The importance of dredging is emphasized by the 1852 Yellow River catastrophe in China. As the channel of this river became choked with silt, levees were built higher and higher, until the Yellow River was flowing above the rooftops. Eventually, a massive surge of floodwaters crumbled the retaining walls and drowned 2 million people.

Dams. Despite serious criticisms of dams, the United States has apparently committed itself to a vast program of superdam construction. The largest is the Hoover Dam on the Colorado River (Figure 7-13). The Colorado drains almost one-thirteenth of the U.S. land area. This enormous concrete dam was built to control the river, prevent flooding, and provide irrigation water and electrical power for thousands of farmers in the arid Southwest. The Hoover Dam stands 220 meters (726 feet) high. The impounded water forms Lake Mead, the largest reservoir in the world; 115 miles long, it has an area of 640 square kilometers (246 square miles). Its storage

Table 7-2 Examples of Flood Disasters

Date	Location	Deaths and Injuries	Property Damage
1811	Danube (Germany and Austria)	2,000 drowned	24 villages washed away
1861	Sacremento River (California)	700 drowned	300 villages destroyed; 2 million homeless
1889	Conemaugh River (dam burst) (Pennsylvania)	2,000 drowned at Johnstown, Pa.	$10 million
1900	Galveston, Texas (hurricane-spawned flood waters)	6,000 dead	3,000 buildings destroyed
1936–1937	Mississippi River	500 drowned 800,000 injured	$200 million
1942	Columbia River		$100 million
1955	Atlantic Coast (Hurricane Hazel)		$1.6 billion
1965	Upper Mississippi River	16 drowned, 330 injured	$140 million
1979	Zambezi River (Mozambique)	45 drowned	250,000 homeless
1979	Brazos River (West Texas)	22 drowned	
1980	Southeast Brazil	700 drowned	350,000 homeless
1981	Northern India	1,500 deaths	Extensive crop losses

capacity of nearly 3.7 hectarometers (30 million acre-feet) would be adequate to meet all the water requirements of New York City residents for 20 years.

Are dams effective in flood control? According to Brigadier General W. P. Leber, Ohio River Division Army Engineer, an Ohio River flood of several years ago would have caused additional damage costing $290 million had it not been for the coordinated system of 30 flood control reservoirs, plus 62 floodwalls and levees. He stated that flood crests were reduced by up to 3.2 meters (10.5 feet) by these flood control facilities. Several years ago, Los Angeles County, which has expe-rienced repeated floods from rain-swollen rivers, estab-lished a coordinated complex of control structures cost-ing nearly $600 million. It involves 60 headwater dams in the mountains, 15 retention reservoirs in the Los Angeles and San Gabriel rivers, and 6 major flood con-trol dams. This system has proven to be very successful in protecting 130 million hectares (325 million acres) from flooding.

Despite the value of big dams in flood control and in generating hydroelectric power, big dams create a number of problems (Table 7-3).

One major drawback associated with the construction

FIGURE 7-11 Emergency workers prepare to help people stranded by the floodwaters in Fort Wayne, Indiana.

FIGURE 7-12 Flooding problems areas. Flood damages are expected to increase in the future on 175 million acres of land that is flood prone. (A flood-prone area is land adjoining rivers, streams, or lakes, where there is a 1 percent chance of flooding during any given year.) Forty-eight million acres of flood-prone land are cropland, 102 million acres are pasture, range, and forest, and 21 million are other land, including built-up areas. Twenty-one thousand communities are subject to floods, including 6,000 towns or cities with populations exceeding 2,500. The potential damage caused by floods in any given year in the U.S. is about $4 billion. Because the number and value of buildings are increasing, flood damages will also increase.

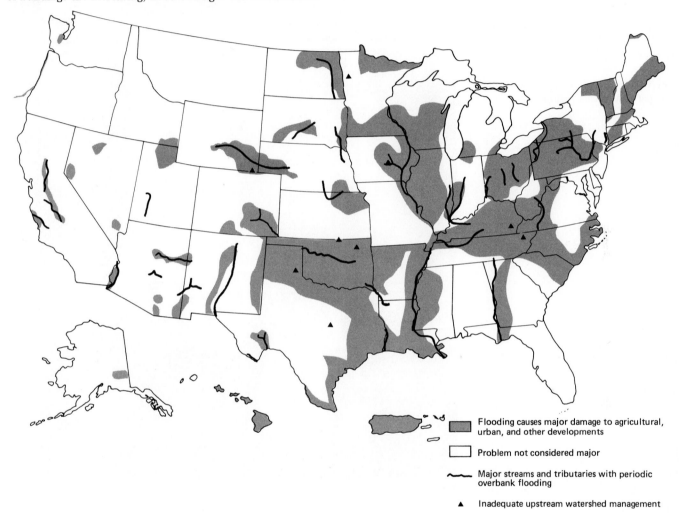

Flooding causes major damage to agricultural, urban, and other developments

Problem not considered major

Major streams and tributaries with periodic overbank flooding

▲ Inadequate upstream watershed management

of big dams is the speed with which reservoirs fill with sediment. The rate of filling depends, of course, on the soil types in the drainage basin, the topography, and the degree to which soil erosion is controlled. Because the Columbia River is relatively sediment free, dams such as the Grand Coulee and Bonneville might have a storage life of 1,000 years. However, the life span of dams constructed across muddier streams may be quite short. For example, the huge Lake Mead Reservoir behind Hoover Dam on the Colorado River in Arizona is filling with silt at a rate sufficient to destroy the operation of this multi-million-dollar structure in fewer than 250 years. The death of a Texas reservoir is shown in Figure

7-14. California's Mono Reservoir, which was designed to provide a permanent water source for the people of Santa Barbara, filled up with sediment in 20 years. In addition, biological succession proceeded so rapidly that a thicket of shrubs and saplings became firmly established. For all practical purposes, Mono Reservoir has been reclaimed by nature.

Evaporation losses from reservoirs in hot, arid regions where winds are prevalent can be considerable. The top 2 meters (7 feet) of water in Lake Mead, for example, evaporate every year. About 0.74 million hectare-meters (6 million acre-feet) are lost each year from 1,250 large western reservoirs, an amount sufficient

FIGURE **7-13** Hoover Dam, one of the world's largest dams. It is located on the Arizona-Nevada border, about 25 miles south-east of Las Vegas. The electric generators at the dam supply most of the power needs of southern California, Arizona, and Nevada. It restrains the turbulent waters of the Colorado River and is useful in controlling downstream floods. Water from Lake Mead, the 125-mile long impoundment behind the dam, irrigates one million acres and has increased crop production 120 percent in this region.

to supply all the domestic needs of 50 million people. Although such losses can be reduced on very small reservoirs in the West with roofs and covers, they still are quite substantial. The use of a surface film of hexadecanol could reduce evaporation losses by almost 20 percent, but the technique has some drawbacks. First, it is quite costly because the film tends to disperse and, therefore, must be repeatedly applied. Second, it has adverse effects on fish and other aquatic organisms because the level of dissolved oxygen declines. This results from increased water temperatures and from sealing off the reservoir from atmospheric oxygen.

On rare occasions, a dam will *collapse* because of faulty design. Such was the case with the mighty Teton Dam in Idaho (Figure 7-15). It was built by the U.S. Bureau of Reclamation, an agency that has constructed more than 300 dams, including the world-famous Grand Coulee and Hoover dams. However, on June 5, 1976, the bureau's record was sullied. Only hours after the first fissure appeared in the dam, the monstrous earthen structure gave way with a deafening roar and a mammoth wall of water surged down the valley. The resultant destruction was awesome. At least 14 lives were lost. Estimates of property damage approached $1 billion. Shortly afterward, the Secretary of the Interior and the governor of Idaho appointed a panel of distinguished engineers to investigate the cause of the Teton's failure. As reported in *Science*, the panel concluded that "under difficult conditions that called for the best judgment and experience of

Table 7-3 Disadvantages of Big Dams

1. Extremely expensive: hundreds of millions to billions of dollars. (*Example:* Hoover Dam on the Arizona–Nevada border: cost, $120 million.)

2. Prime agricultural land is flooded.

3. Scenic beauty is destroyed. (*Example:* The Rainbow Bridge National Monument in Arizona is threatened by the Glen Canyon Dam on the Colorado River.)

4. The resulting saltwater intrusion in coastal areas destroys cropland and pollutes freshwater aquifers. (*Example:* This has happened in both Florida and California.)

5. Drawdowns periodically eliminate the shallow-water areas where fish frequently spawn.

6. The natural habitat of endangered species is destroyed. (*Example:* The snail darter at the Tellico Dam.)

7. The upstream migration of adult salmon is blocked, interfering with reproduction.

8. There are excessive water losses from reservoirs because of evaporation. (*Example:* Lake Mead behind the Hoover Dam.)

9. The life of a dam is shortened because of the siltation of the reservoir. (*Example:* Mono Dam in California.)

10. The collapse of the dam is possible as a result of faulty construction. (*Example:* Teton Dam in Idaho.)

FIGURE 7-14 The "death" of the Lake Ballenger, Texas, reservoir. Although the original depth of this lake was 35 feet, it eventually had to be abandoned because of siltation.

the engineering profession, an unfortunate choice of design measures together with less than conventional precautions . . . ultimately led to its failure."

Stream Channelization. The SCS has built up a good reputation during many years of valuable service in soil erosion and flood control. However, in the past decade, a storm of criticism has swirled around its **chan-** nelization program: the deepening and straightening of streams to control flooding.

There are two main steps in channelization. First, all vegetation is bulldozed away on either side of the stream. The denuded area is then planted with a cover crop. Second, bulldozers and draglines deepen and straighten the channel; in essence, the stream is converted into a water-filled ditch.

The benefits of channelization are two. First, cropland on either side of the channelized portion of the stream

FIGURE 7-15 The "death" of a dam. An aerial view of the Teton Dam, Idaho, shortly after its rupture. We are looking upstream. The site of break is roughly in the center of this picture. The torrential waters released from the reservoir above the dam caused the deaths of at least 14 people.

FIGURE 7-16   Irrigated acreage of the United States. One dot equals 8,000 acres where irrigation facilities are in place.

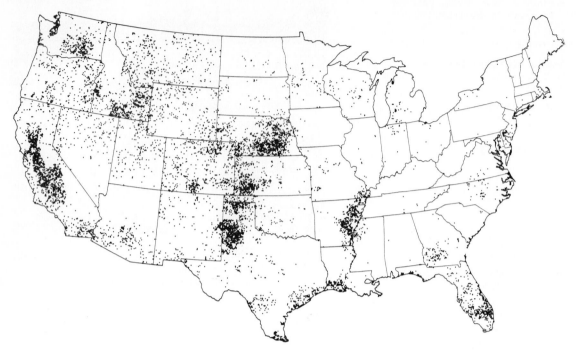

is protected from flooding. Second, small lakes with considerable recreational and wildlife potential are constructed by the SCS as an adjunct to the main channelization process.

Unfortunately the disadvantages of channelization are many.

1. A picturesque meandering stream is converted to an ugly eroding ditch.

2. Much valuable hardwood timber, already in short supply, is destroyed.

3. The diversity of the wildlife declines.

4. Water temperatures increase because of the removal of overarching trees that formerly intercepted the sunlight. This leads to numerous other problems, which are discussed in the next chapter.

5. Stream enrichment from leaf fall is considerably reduced.

6. Downstream flooding may actually increase.

In their long-range plans, the SCS proposed to channelize (and hence wreak gross environmental abuse on) several thousand small watersheds by the year 2000. That means degrading nearly half of our nation's small watersheds. Hopefully, the American public will not permit this bureaucratic ambition to be realized. In the long run, informed citizens, mounting pressure on vote-sensitive legislators, will prevail. There is no time to be lost.

Zoning of Flood Plains. The U.S. Army Corps of Engineers, the Bureau of Reclamation, and the SCS have spent more than $15 billion on **structural** flood control projects (dams, levees, sea walls, etc.) since 1925. However, despite this enormous expenditure of tax money, property damage from flooding continues to rise. Annual costs will increase from $3 billion in the least 1980s to $4 billion by 2000. More and more experts now believe that **nonstructural** flood control, involving flood plain **zoning**, is the most effective and economical strategy.

The **flood plain** is the low-lying area along a stream that is subject to periodic flooding. In a sense, the flood plain "belongs" to the river. Unfortunately, however, the flood plain has been taken over by humans. The flatness of the land, its natural beauty, and the availability of the river for cheap transportation have attracted community development. More than 2,000 cities in the United States, including Harrisburg, Pennsylvania, and Phoenix, Arizona, are located, at least partially, on flood plains. Most of these cities experience flooding every 2 to 3 years.

In 1973 Congress passed the Federal Flood Disaster Protective Act to regulate flood plain development and control flood damage. This law encourages the zoning of flood plains for use as parks, golf courses, bicycle trails, nature preserves, and parking lots. The construction of buildings on the flood plains is discouraged. Under the terms of the act, any home, store, or factory built in a hazardous area on the flood plain is denied federal flood insurance.

IRRIGATION

An extensive area of the desert biome and the more arid portion of the grassland biome are characterized by more or less permanent drought. There, through eons of interaction with the environment, plant and animal residents have evolved moisture-securing and moisture-conserving adaptations to survive. Humans, however, relative newcomers to this austere region, have not had to depend on long evolutionary processes to adapt to the environment. Instead, we have shaped the environment to fit our design. The most significant and dramatic example of our habitat-shaping talent in this region is modern irrigation.

Irrigation is an extremely complex and exacting operation that demands a high degree of planning, field preparation, and technical skill. It is a rather costly process. Nevertheless, the high market value of many crops and the long growing season that permits several crops per year make irrigation economically feasible. More than 10 percent of our nation's croplands, embracing 50 million acres, is now under irrigation. Four of every five acres irrigated are in the West (Figure 7-16). Until recently, the amount of irrigated farmland has increased steadily.

Methods of Irrigation

Irrigation water is either pumped or gravity fed through the main irrigation canal or pipe to laterals, which convey the water to individual farms. The laterals frequently follow field borders and fence lines. Up to 2.5 million liters (750,000 gallons) of water may be needed to irrigate a single acre in one growing season. The major methods are sheet, furrow, sprinkler, and drip irrigation.

SHEET IRRIGATION. The sheet method, usually used for hay, grain, and pasture crops, is suitable on land with a slight grade. The topsoil must be carefully prepared in advance so that water infiltrates properly. The water is drawn from laterals at the upper end of the slope. It gradually flows downslope in the form of a sheet (Figure 7-17). Soil erosion and leaching of nutrients can result from this method.

FURROW IRRIGATION. In the furrow method, water may be drawn from laterals by siphon tubes that empty into furrows between crop rows (Figure 7-18). This method is used primarily on row crops such as corn, cabbage, and sugar beets. Erosion can be lessened by contouring the furrows.

SPRINKLER IRRIGATION. The sprinkler method may be used in places where the previous methods are undesirable because of erosion due to the steepness of the slope. It involves costly equipment and is restricted primarily to crops of high cash value. Con-

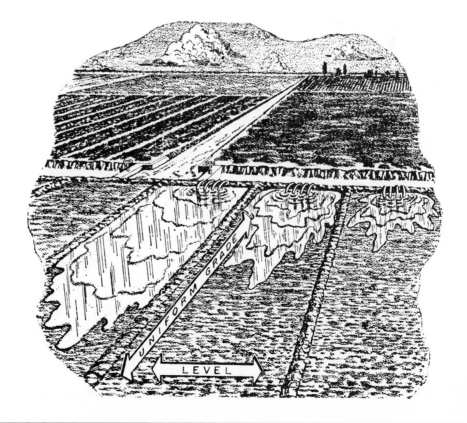

FIGURE 7-17 Sheet or flood irrigation. This field has been prepared for irrigation by building small levees around each leveled area. The areas are then flooded in rotation to irrigate them.

FIGURE 7-18 Furrow irrigation. Water is transferred from the lateral in the foreground to a series of parallel furrows to irrigate this lettuce crop in the Palo Verde Valley.

siderable amounts of energy are required to power the pumps.

Sprinklers may be either stationary or rotary (Figure 7-19A and B). Center pivot rotary sprinklers are very popular. Water is sprinkled from a raised lateral pipe that is in continuous slow rotary motion around a central pivot point. One model, known as the **big gun**, can propel a stream of water half the length of a football field. A circular area of 53 hectares (130 acres) can be irrigated in one revolution in 33 hours with a 400-meter (1,300-foot) pipe. Evaporation losses with all sprinkler systems may be considerable.

DRIP IRRIGATION. With the drip method, water is delivered through perforated or highly porous plastic pipes (Figure 7-20). The pipes may either be placed on the surface or buried underground. Water drips from the pipes. Erosion and water evaporation losses are minimal. Since drip irrigation requires 20 to 50 percent less water than sprinkler systems, it can help save water for some crops.

THE IMPERIAL VALLEY STORY. The story of the Imperial Valley is one of America's greatest success stories in irrigation (Figure 7-21). The valley, which is 170 kilometers (110 miles) long and 83 kilometers (50 miles) wide, lies in the Colorado Desert in southern California, just east of Los Angeles, with San Diego in its southwestern corner. Hundreds of thousands of years ago, this area was submerged by salt water from the Gulf of California. Gradually, however, it was built up, with millions of tons of fertile soil released by overflow of the Colorado River during its flow to the sea.

At the turn of the century, this valley was a hot desert wasteland. Annual rainfall, which is almost immediately vaporized because of hot, drying wind, is a paltry 3.75 to 7.50 centimeters (1.5 to 3 inches). However, where lizards and cacti lived, fruit and vegetable farms flourish, from which lettuce, tomatoes, watermelons, sugar beets, onions, asparagus, oranges, and dates are shipped throughout the United States. This has been made possible by the completion in 1940 of the 60-meter- (200-foot)-wide All American Canal, which carries water from the Colorado River 128 kilometers (80 miles) away to the fertile valley. The potential for crop production in this area always existed. There was abundant sunshine and a long growing season (up to 10 cuttings of alfalfa are made in a single year). The limiting factor was water, and that was overcome with imagination, resourcefulness, engineering skill, and billions of dollars of taxpayers' money.

Irrigation Problems

WATER LOSS. Many irrigated fields in the United States receive their water from reservoirs or streams located hundreds of kilometers away. The fruit-raising Central Valley of California, for example, gets its water from the Colorado River, 300 miles to the east. During transit considerable amounts of water are lost. According to the USDA, only 1 of every 4 gallons drawn for irrigation is actually absorbed by crop root systems. The remaining 3 gallons are lost to evaporation, to water-absorbing weeds, or to ground seepage (Figure 7-22). In some areas, seepage may be sufficient to raise the water table and form a marsh.

Salinization. Would you believe that bringing fresh water to a desert might be destructive to crops? Sounds incongruous, doesn't it? However, even fresh water is slightly salty, having acquired dissolved sodium, calcium, and magnesium salts as it flows down mountain slopes and through valley bottoms. When such water is brought by irrigation canals to hot deserts, where drainage down through the soil is very poor and the evaporation rate is very high, much of the water passes into the atmosphere. As a result, the salts are left behind on the ground as a white crust. Additional salt may be

FIGURE 7-19 Two types of sprinkler irrigation. In center pivot irrigation the perforated pipe moves slowly in a circle and may irrigate an area of about 150 acres.

TYPES OF SPRINKLER IRRIGATION

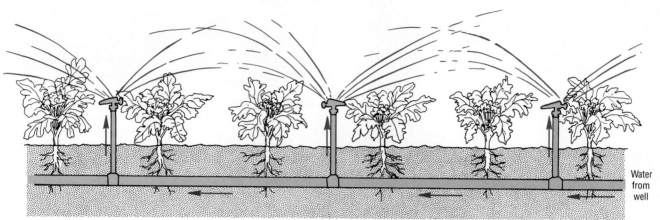

A. Buried Pipe

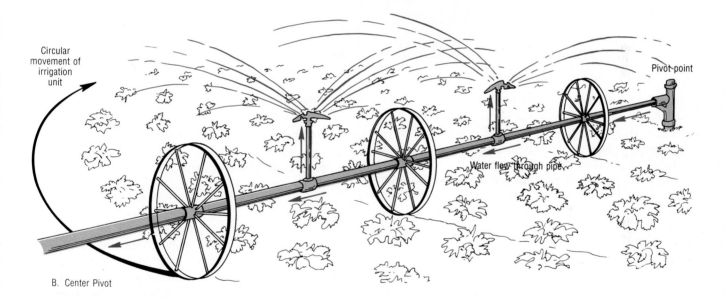

B. Center Pivot

FIGURE 7-20 Drip irrigation. This method is used primarily on fruit trees and high cash crops. Water is applied directly to the roots of the fruit tree. The perforated plastic pipes may either lie on the ground surface or be buried.

DRIP IRRIGATION

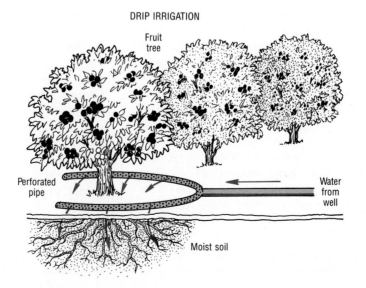

FIGURE 7-21 Irrigation transforms the desert! Water from the Colorado River conveyed by the All American Canal System makes it possible for crops to be produced in Imperial Valley, California. Note the stark contrast between the non-irrigated desert on the right and the irrigated fruit orchards on the left.

deposited because of the evaporation of groundwater that has been drawn to the surface by capillary action.

The buildup of salt in the soil is called **salinization**. As time passes, the salt deposits increase, becoming toxic to crops. Agricultural experts estimate that 30 percent of the West's irrigated land has salinity problems. After 20 years of irrigation, some land may have a salt load of more than 30 metric tons per hectare (80 tons per acre). Even in California's Imperial Valley, where crop harvests have been so bountiful, salinization has caused many farms to be abandoned.

Several solutions to salinization problems in California's San Joaquin Valley have been proposed:

1. Construct a system of underground drainage pipes to collect and dispose of the salty groundwater. These pipes connect to a master drainpipe that would extend 464 kilometers (290 miles) through the length of the valley. This drainpipe would then empty directly into a wetland ecosystem at Suisun Bay, northeast of Oakland, where the Sacramento and San Joaquin rivers meet. However, such drainage systems have their drawbacks. For example, in California's Central Valley, irrigation drainage water carries large amounts of selenium from the soil. This contaminated water caused extensive mortality to fish and waterfowl at the Kesterson National Wildlife Refuge in 1983 and is of continuing concern.

2. Use efficient irrigation methods to reduce water use and, therefore, salinization by 20 percent.

3. Develop salt-resistant strains of crops to replace traditional varieties.

4. Reduce irrigated crop acreage.

5. Convert areas plagued with recurring salt problems from cropland to grazing land.

Unfortunately, however, many farmers are resistant to these solutions.

Irrigation salinizes the soil but also adds potentially harmful salts to surface waters. The Colorado River receives large amounts of salty water that has been flushed from thousands of irrigated farms in western Colorado, Utah and Arizona. This water becomes progressively more salty as it flows southwestward across the Mexican border toward the Gulf of California. As a result of irrigation practices, the salinity of the lower Colorado has increased by 30 percent in the last 20 years. The Colorado's saltiness jeopardizes cotton production in the Mexicali district, where farmers have used the river as a source of irrigation water for decades. The economy of the region was threatened to such an extent that Mexican presidents frequently conveyed their concern to the U.S. government. The United States was eventually forced to construct a desalination plant near the Mexican border so that the water would be usable by Mexican farmers.

Depletion of Groundwater. The number of hectares irrigated by American farmers has increased sharply, from 6.4 million in 1940 to roughly 50 million in the late 1980s. In the High Plains, a vast region extend-

FIGURE 7-22 Irrigation of croplands is the biggest consumptive use of water in the United States. Seventy-five percent of the water is lost to transpiration and evaporation. Roughly 120 million acre feet of water are applied to 40 million acres of land in the western states. This is equal to about three feet of water for every irrigated acre. The salts in the original volume become concentrated in the 30-million acre-feet of water that remains after transpiration and evaporation. This remaining water may have a salt concentration of more than 2,000 parts per million. It must be drained from the croplands to prevent a toxic buildup.

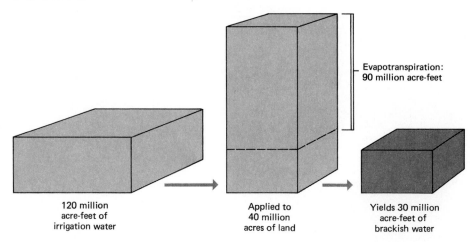

120 million acre-feet of irrigation water

Applied to 40 million acres of land

Evapotranspiration: 90 million acre-feet

Yields 30 million acre-feet of brackish water

ing from Nebraska south to Texas, most of the irrigation water is pumped out of the Ogallala aquifer. In 1946 there were only 2,000 irrigation wells in western Texas; today there are more than 70,000. The rate of withdrawal around Lubbock, Texas, is 50 times the rate at which the aquifer is naturally recharged by rain and stream flow.

As a result of the enormous overdraft for irrigation, groundwater levels have dropped significantly in some western states—more than 30 meters (100 feet) in portions of Kansas, Oklahoma, Texas, and New Mexico, and more than 120 meters (400 feet) in parts of Arizona. As a result, new wells must be drilled more deeply at considerable expense. And, of course, it takes more fossil fuel or electricity to pump water from the deeper wells. If this trend continues, irrigation farming will eventually become prohibitively expensive. West Texas could experience a 95 percent decline in irrigation and a 70 percent decrease in crop harvests by 2015. Serious declines in irrigation farming are expected over an 11-state area of the Great Plains and the Southwest by the year 2000 (Figure 7-23).

When large volumes of water are removed from fine-grained, porous aquifers, the weight of the overlying soil and rock occasionally causes compression or collapse of the aquifer. As a result, the earth above the aquifer sinks, or **subsides** (Figure 7-24).

Significant land sinking or **subsidence** has occurred in at least 11 states in the South and West due to groundwater overdrafts. Water mining caused the dramatic appearance of a sinkhole at Winter Park, Florida, in 1981. The huge pit was 37.5 meters (124 feet) deep and 120 meters (396 feet wide). It swallowed up a house, a swimming pool, six sports cars, and a camper. In the San Joaquin Valley of California, an 11,000-square-kilometer (4,200-square-mile) area sunk more than 0.3 meter (1 foot). Some regions subsided more than 9 meters (30 feet).

Subsidence causes damage to irrigation facilities such as canals and underground pipes. The Department of the Interior spent $3.7 million in a single year to repair the damage caused by subsidence to federal irrigation projects.

In the Galveston Bay region near Houston, Texas, subsidence over a 10,000-square-kilometer (4,000-square-mile) area resulted in widespread flooding of shoreline properties. When subsidence occurs under urban areas, damage may be very extensive: Sewer and water pipes burst, wells are destroyed, building foundations crack, and concrete highways buckle.

SALE OF WATER RIGHTS. Some farmers and ranchers in the arid states are discovering that their irrigation water is more valuable than wheat, fruits, vegetables, and beef cattle they produce. As a result, they are now beginning to sell their land and water rights to nearby communities that need the water. Consider the situation in the Salt Lake City area. Water requirements there by the year 2000 will jump an additional 50,000 acre-feet. Water sales to the towns by former farmers and ranchers will make possible the "production" of apartments and condos instead of beans and

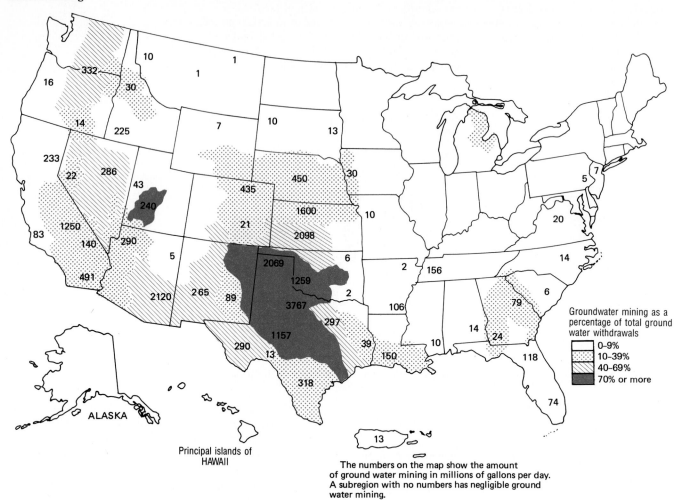

FIGURE 7-23 Groundwater mining in the United States. Shaded area indicates regions of most intense mining.

Groundwater mining as a percentage of total ground water withdrawals
- 0–9%
- 10–39%
- 40–69%
- 70% or more

The numbers on the map show the amount of ground water mining in millions of gallons per day. A subregion with no numbers has negligible ground water mining.

ALASKA

Principal islands of HAWAII

beef. Surface water is also growing more costly. For example, in Reno, Nevada, the cost of water from the Truckee River, which flows right past the town, surged from a mere $50 per acre-foot in 1976 to $2,500 per acre-foot in 1986—a 50-fold increase in a single decade!

HOW CAN WE INCREASE WATER SUPPLIES IN THE UNITED STATES?

Even if per capita use of water *remains the same*, total water use in the United States by the year 2000 will increase *substantially* because of our projected population increase of 25 million. However, our per capita use (taking into account all industrial, domestic and agricultural water required by the United States) is rising sharply as well—from 6,000 liters (1,500 gallons) per day in 1960 to an expected 7,800 liters (2,700 gallons) by 2000. Total municipal water use will rise from 84 billion liters (21 billion gallons) per day in 1960 to 172

billion liters (43 billion gallons) per day by 2,000, if trends continue.

Where will this additional water come from? There are several strategies that can be pursued. Among these methods are the following: (1) water conservation, (2) reclamation of sewage water, (3) further development of groundwater resources, (4) desalination of sea water, (5) development of salt-resistant crops, (6) development of drought-resistant crops, (7) rainmaking, (8) harvesting of icebergs, and (9) diversion of surface water to water-short regions.

Conservation

ON THE FARM. Nearly 47 percent of all water used in the United States is used by farmers, mainly for irrigation. Crop growth requires enormous amounts of water—600 liters (150 gallons) of water for 0.45 kilogram (1 pound) of cotton and 60,000 liters (15,000 gallons) for a bushel of wheat. Conservation on the

A. Before Land Sinking

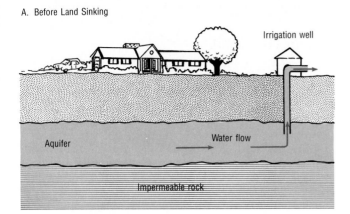

Irrigation well

Aquifer

Water flow

Impermeable rock

B. After Land Sinking

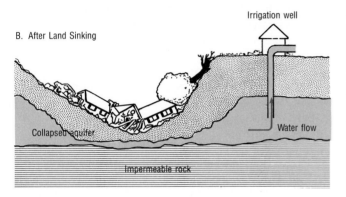

Irrigation well

Collapsed aquifer

Water flow

Impermeable rock

FIGURE 7-24 The land-sinking phenomenon caused by water mining.

FIGURE 7-25 Specialist taking soil moisture readings from delicate instrument operated by the Bureau of Reclamation. With such information available farmers will irrigate only when and where needed. Such irrigation efficiency will not only reduce the amount of water used but also the severity of salt buildup.

farm, mentioned in Chapter 6, can greatly expand our nation's water supplies.

Reducing Seepage Losses. Seepage loss can be minimized by lining canals with concrete, asphalt, or plastic or by replacing ditches with closed pipes. For instance, the city of Casper, Wyoming, now has larger supplies of water available for domestic and industrial purposes because irrigation canals in the surrounding farmland were relined.

Increasing Use of Drip Irrigation. At least 1.1 million acre-feet of water could be saved annually nationwide if farmers made maximal use of drip irrigation. By this method, water can be slowly released directly to crop roots by means of perforated plastic pipes. Water loss during irrigation can be cut in half. Unfortunately, however, not all crops can be irrigated by this method.

Using Heat Sensors. Infrared sensors have recently been developed by the U.S. Water Conservation Laboratory in Phoenix to detect the amount of heat being given off by crops (Figure 7-25). This device indirectly determines crop moisture content because plants become progressively warmer as they dry out. Farmers could use this instrument to find out whether a given crop requires irrigation. Unnecessary "flooding" of the crop would then be avoided.

IN INDUSTRY. For many years, industry has been flagrantly wasteful of water, especially in the water-rich Eastern states, where it has been assumed that water is virtually inexhaustible. Contributing to this opinion is water's extremely low cost. For example, one study showed that when water costs only 1 cent per 4,000 liters (1,000 gallons), a coal-fueled electric power plant uses 200 liters (50 gallons) of water for each kilowatt-hour of electricity produced. On the other hand, when the price of water rises to 1.25 cents per liter (5 cents per gallon), the same power plant reduces water use to 3.2 liters (0.8 gallon) per kilowatt-hour.

With a blend of newly developed technology and creativity, a number of industries are making great progress in conserving water.

As water-saving technology improves, the percentage of water saved will certainly increase. The U.S. Department of the Interior has predicted that by the year 2000, American industry will be recycling waste water so intensively that its water requirement will be only 40 percent of what it is today.

ON THE COLLEGE CAMPUS AND AT HOME. Hopefully, as a student in a resource conservation class, you have by now developed a sensitivity to, and an understanding of, the overriding importance of saving the earth's precious resources, among them water. Practical methods by which you, your fellow students, and your family could save water are described in the box entitled "Your part in saving water."

Water Wars in the Cactus Belt

The scarcity of high-quality groundwater may well be our nation's next environmental crisis, especially in the sagebrush and cactus country of the Southwest. Between 1950 and 1987, groundwater consumption in the United States tripled—from 120 to 360 billion liters (30 to 90 billion gallons) per day. In fact, water consultant Joe Lord of Fresno, California, believes that the country's water crunch will become so severe that it will make the Organization of Petroleum Exporting Countries (OPEC) oil embargo of 1973 look like a "tea party." Competition for the dwindling supplies of water in the West and Southwest is becoming increasingly fierce. Ongoing "water fights" are being waged between farmers and Indians, between farmers and urban dwellers, between water-rich and water-poor states, and between state governments and federal agencies. There is even international friction involving the United States and Mexico. A few examples follow.

1. In 1985 the Great Lakes Charter was signed by the governors of eight states bordering the Great Lakes and by the premiers of Ontario and Quebec. The unprecedented action represented a cooperative strategy to block a possible future diversion of Great Lakes water to the Southwest. Although such a "raid" on the Great Lakes would be prohibitively costly today, if water prices continue to soar, as they are doing now, such a scheme may be more attractive in the not-too-distant future.

2. Wyoming believes that it owns the water rights on the Wind-Big Horn River. Currently, however, those rights are being fiercely contested by two Indian tribes and the federal government.

3. A water battle is also being waged between Montana and the U.S. Bureau of Reclamation over water rights to the Missouri River.

4. The bustling boom town of El Paso, Texas, with a population of 500,000, needs more water to supply its mushrooming population and its expanding industries. For several years, the city's water engineers have proposed drilling 21 wells into the New Mexican side of the Hueco aquifer, a water-rich reservoir that straddles the border between the two states. Although El Paso would like to start pumping by 1999, the people of New Mexico have vowed that not one drop of their water will wind up in the faucets, sprinklers, and boilers of El Paso.

5. The Central Arizona Project is a system of pumps, tunnels, and aqueducts that transports urgently needed water to the rapidly growing cities of Tucson and Phoenix. Opened in 1985, the $2 billion system transports water 500 kilometers (300 miles) from the Colorado River. Unfortunately, however, much of the Colorado River water is already committed, by treaty, to seven other states and Mexico. There simply won't be enough water to go around, especially during periods of drought. As a result, Arizona has been the subject of considerable verbal sniping by the treaty states, which think that the Central Arizona Project is siphoning off water that is legally theirs under the terms of the treaty.

Reclamation of Sewage Water

Sewage effluent is 99 percent water, and when the 1 percent of pollutant is removed, the final water product may be purer than the original substance.

Processed sewage water is already being used for a variety of purposes. The Bethlehem Steel plant in Baltimore, Maryland, uses 600 million liters (150 million gallons) of sewage effluent daily to cool steel. Golf courses are sprinkled with it in San Francisco, Las Vegas, and Santa Fe. Treated sewage water is used to irrigate crops in San Antonio, Texas and Fort Collins, Colorado. Ornamental shrubs along highways in San Bernardino, California, are watered with it.

Los Angeles daily discharges 68 million liters (17 million gallons) of processed sewage water over sewage-spreading beds at the edge of town. Eventually, this water seeps into aquifers that supply the town's wells.

This water is of higher quality than the water from the Colorado River. Treated wastewater has also been used in southern California to stop salt water intrusion from the ocean. By the early 1960s, water table levels had been dropping steadily in the coastal region. As a result, salt water encroached at the rate of 1.6 kilometers (1 mile) per year. To check this invasion, a freshwater barrier was formed by injecting treated wastewater into a series of coastal wells.

Developing Groundwater Resources

There are 53,000 cubic miles of fresh water in the aquifers located in the upper 0.8 kilometer (half-mile) of the earth's crust. In an effort to alleviate the impending water deficit, aquifers will be tapped to depths of 150 to 600 meters (500 to 2,000 feet). These supplies must be carefully used to avoid depletion. the long-

FIGURE 7-26 California's State Water Project.

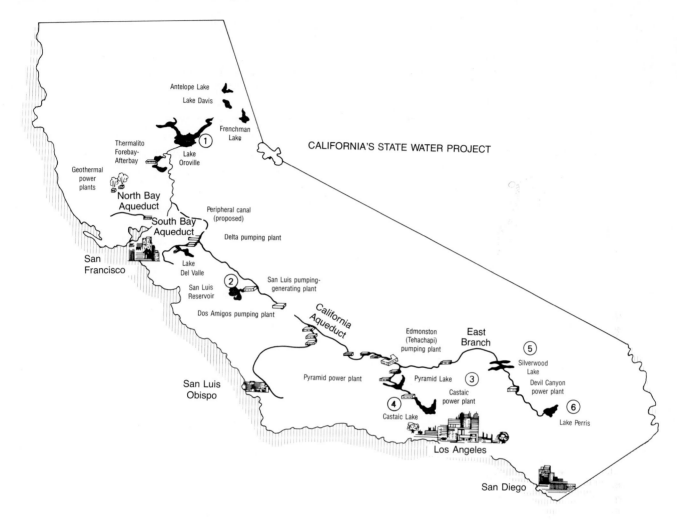

range economic viewpoint. In some situations, the proper decision may be to mine the water until the supply is exhausted; in other cases, it may be better to draw the water on a sustained-yield basis.

Intensive efforts are being made by the U.S. Geological Survey to locate and develop new aquifers. Radioactive tracer techniques are being used to determine the pattern and rate of aquifer water flow. Such data will enable scientists to predict how withdrawal from one site will affect groundwater at other points. These studies are already yielding results.

Desalination

"Water, water everywhere, but not a drop to drink" wailed the sailor in "The Ancient Mariner." It is a curious paradox that 70 percent of the earth's surface is covered by oceans, in some places up to 6 miles deep, yet a water shortage plagues civilization from New York to New Delhi. The problem, of course, is that sea water is salty.

As a result, a number of American communities are now operating desalination plants. The nation's first desalination plant was built in California. It produces 100,000 liters (28,000 gallons) of fresh water daily. About 75 installations have been established on the west coast of Florida alone. These plants, in aggregate, are capable of producing 430 million liters (114 million gallons) of fresh water per day.

Unfortunately, desalination is an expensive process. In general, it is much cheaper to pump fresh water—if it's available. However, if the fresh water source must be pumped more than 150 kilometers (90 miles) to the site of consumption, desalination becomes economically feasible.

Developing Salt-Resistant Crops

After 6 years of research, two scientists from the University of California–Davis announced the development of a new strain of barley that will grow well even though

Your Part in Saving Water

During a recent drought it was reported that one Californian stapled a stamp to an envelope to save saliva! Such extreme measures may be heroic but they are unnecessary. Here is a list of practical measures on how to save water at home that could save our nation billions of gallons of precious water every year.

Save in the Bathroom

1. Take shorter showers.
2. Don't use the toilet as a waste basket.
3. Don't let the water run while brushing your teeth.
4. Don't run the water while shaving. Plug and partly fill the basin to rinse your razor.
5. Repair leaks promptly.
6. If you replace your toilet, install a low-water unit.
7. A few drops of food coloring or dye tablets in your toilet tank can help you spot a leak. If color appears in the bowl, you have a leak. Fix it promptly.
8. Place bricks or plastic bottles in your toilet tank and save 1–2 liters every time you flush.
9. Install a low-flow shower head.

Save in the Kitchen

1. Wash only full loads in your washing machine and dishwasher.
2. If you wash dishes by hand, don't let the water run.

3. Cool your drinking water in the refrigerator, *not* by letting the water run.
4. Don't use water-wasting garbage disposals.
5. *Stop those leaks* (New York City alone wastes 800 million liters each day because of them). Leaking faucets and wasteful people are robbing Americans of scarce water supplies. A small leak (eighty drips per minute) wastes 26.5 liters (7 gallons) of water daily.

Save Water Outside Your Home

1. Use a broom, not a hose, to clean driveways, sidewalks, and steps.
2. Use an "on-off" spray nozzle on your hose.
3. Wash your car with a bucket of water; use a hose only to rinse.
4. Water your lawn and garden only during the cool of the day or during the evening. Older trees and shrubs often do not require irrigation. Plants are frequently overwatered.
5. Remove water-stealing weeds from the lawn and garden.
6. Use less fertilizer; it increases the need of plants for water.
7. Apply a mulch between rows in your garden to hold the soil moisture.

Source: California Department of Water Resources. *Save the Water*. Sacramento, California, 1982.

---

irrigated with *sea water*. Barley plants have been grown on a tiny windswept beach at Bodega Bay in northern California. They have achieved yields of 1,480 kilograms per hectare (1,320 pounds per acre), equal to the average global per acre yield of barley provided with fresh water. As one of the researchers, Emanuel Epstein, noted: "We have shown that sea water is not pure poison to crops." Their success is highly significant. Millions of acres of once prime agricultural land the world over (1.8 million hectares [4.5 million acres] in California alone) have been rendered worthless because of salinization. Until now, farmers have been advised to cease cropping salinized soils or to flush out the salt, at considerable expense, with huge volumes of fresh water. However, the new "saltwater barley" and other crops now under development might do well in these soils.

Developing Drought-Resistant Crops

Even if we are unable to increase water supplies for agriculture, we could nevertheless increase food production by developing new varieties of crops that are resistant to drought. George G. Still, a scientist for the USDA, is optimistic about the water-saving potential of such plant-breeding projects: "Sorghum is a very important grain crop in the arid portion of the Third World. . . . There is something inherent in the plant, the germ plasm or the genes, that causes sorghum to put itself on 'idle' during a dry spell and then go on and yield a crop when the rains come." With the aid of recently developed techniques in genetic engineering, it may be possible to breed plants that require considerably less water. To this end, the USDA plans to set up a $21 million research laboratory in Lubbock, Texas.

Rainmaking

Rainmaking is a novel approach to increasing our water supply. One technique involves seeding clouds with tiny crystals of silver iodide. The hope is that these crystals will serve as condensation nuclei around which moisture will collect until raindrops are formed. The U.S. Bureau of Reclamation is confident that the weather modification techniques now available can increase the water supply of the San Joaquin River Basin by 25 percent, that of the Upper Colorado River Basin by 44 percent, and that of the Gila River Basin (Arizona) by 55 percent. Nevertheless, the bureau is moving very cautiously with its Project Skywater Program. There are substantial problems involved—some legal, some political, some economic, and some environmental. One drawback is the high cost. Another problem is the possibility that cloud seeding merely means that one farmer's rainfall is another's drought. Still another problem is the lack of control over the amount and precise location of the precipitation. For example, a late July rainfall might benefit corn but might damage the alfalfa in a nearby field awaiting the baler. Increased rainfall might improve forage for a rancher's cattle but might raise havoc with a nearby citrus grower's orange crop. Even more serious, lack of control over precipitation might lead to flooding, soil erosion, property damage, and even loss of life.

Harvesting Icebergs

Billions of liters of fresh water are locked up in Antarctic icebergs. Some optimists believe that one day this water may be used to irrigate cropland in California. Researchers for the Rand Corporation predict that the use of the extensive icebergs in the Antarctic to support crops in our southwestern states is realistic both technically and economically. In their imaginative scheme, a number of iceberg blocks could be harvested and cabled together to form "trains." The trains would then be pushed into suitable ocean currents and guided north for more than 10,000 kilometers (6,000 miles) to a "parking" area off Los Angeles. Warm-water discharges from electric power plants along the coast would speed up the meltdown of the icebergs. The water would then be piped inland for either domestic, industrial, or agricultural use. The water would actually be much less salty than that of the Colorado River, which is being intensively tapped for irrigation farming today. By using such iceberg water, southern Californians could reduce their expensive withdrawals from the Colorado River by at least 1 million acre-feet per year. The estimated cost would be less than that of water obtained by desalination or from the Colorado River. Sounds attractive and exciting, doesn't it? However, before a single iceberg is guided north, the environmental effects of those icy mountains on coastal water temperatures, fish reproduction, and migration, as well as on climatic patterns, must be thoroughly studied.

Long-Distance Transport: The California Water Project

Although costly and controversial, water diversion projects are seen by some developers and government officials as a way to provide water to water-short regions. The California water project is an example of what can be done.

Looking down on the earth, a bluish sphere far below, America's moonbound astronauts could identify only two artificial structures: the Great Wall of China and the main aqueduct of the California Water Project (CWP). California has long been victimized by the curious fact that 70 percent of its potentially usable water falls on the northern third of the state (in the form of relatively abundant rainfall and the snowmelt of the High Sierras), while 77 percent of the demand is located in the semiarid southern two-thirds, where only 12 centimeters (5 inches) of rain fall per year.

The CWP was built to rectify this problem. The most complex and expensive water diversion project in the history of the world, the CWP includes 21 dams and reservoirs, 22 pumping plants, and 1140 kilometers (685 miles) of canals, tunnels, and pipelines (Figure 7-26). An expensive "faucet," the project cost well over $2 billion—enough money to build six Panama Canals.

Despite the obvious benefits derived from this colossal project, certain aspects have drawn criticism from environmentalists. They claim that the CWP was built at an excessive cost, not only in tax dollars but in energy costs, losses in scenic beauty, and the destruction of fish and wildlife habitat. Environmentalists also criticize the proposal to dam up other free-flowing wild rivers in northwestern California, such as the Eel, Klamath, and Trinity. In their view, too many of such unharnessed streams have already been sacrificed on the altar of irrigation and power production.

Regardless of these criticisms and the enormous cost to the people of California, the CWP is an accomplished fact and is helping to alleviate southern California's recurring water shortages.

Impressive as this project may be, it is likely to be one of the last of its kind. Conservation measures, water recycling, and recharging ground water may be able to provide a sustainable supply of water in a way that is much more environmentally sound.

RAPID REVIEW

1. A severe water shortage is one of the most serious, long-range environmental problems facing our

nation and the world. The causes of the shortage are (a) a rapidly increasing population, (b) increasing demands by agriculture, cities, and industry, (c) waste, (d) unequal distribution of water, and (e) pollution.

2. Water continuously moves from oceans-to-air-to-land-to-rivers-and back to-oceans in what is known as the **water cycle**. This cycle is powered by solar energy and gravity. The oceans contain more than 97 percent of the world's total water supply. On the average, the United States receives 75 centimeters (30 inches) of rainfall annually. Much water filters down into the soil and rocks to become **groundwater**. The uppermost level of the zone that is **saturated** with groundwater is called the **water table**. Ninety-seven percent of the world's supply of fresh water is held in porous layers of sand, gravel, and rock known as **aquifers**. The Ogallala aquifer, which extends from Nebraska south to Texas, provides drinking water for several million people and irrigation water for thousands of farms.

3. A **drought** exists whenever rainfall for 21 days or longer is 30 percent below average. The 1988 drought was one of the most serious in several decades.

4. Floods are a major problem the world over, costing billions of dollars a year.

5. Floods can be controlled by (a) protecting watersheds, (b) measuring snowpack to predict flood conditions, (c) building levees, (d) dredging rivers, and (3) building dams.

6. Big dams have several disadvantages. Among them are (a) high costs, (b) possible collapse, (c) reservoir evaporation losses, (d) flooding of prime agricultural land, (e) siltation of reservoirs, (f) saltwater intrusion in coastal areas, (g) destruction of scenic beauty, and (h) destruction of the habitats of rare species.

7. Stream channelization has multiple disadvantages: (a) wildlife habitats are destroyed, (b) stream bank erosion is accelerated, (c) the water table is lowered, (d) severe aesthetic losses are inflicted, (e) the recreational functions of streams are lost, and (f) the projects are excessively costly to the taxpayer.

8. Many experts believe that watershed protection and flood plain zoning are the most effective and economical method of flood control.

9. Irrigation permits a flourishing agricultural economy in arid portions of the Southwest that were once relatively nonproductive.

10. Four methods of irrigation are (a) sheet, (b) furrow, (c) sprinkler, and (d) drip or trickle.

11. Serious problems associated with irrigation include (a) water loss during transit along canals, (b) inefficient practices during the application of water to the crops, (c) salinization of the soil, and (d) depletion of groundwater.

12. Between 1950 and 1987, groundwater consumption in the United States tripled from 120 to 360 billion liters (30 to 90 billion gallons) per day.

13. Competition for the dwindling supplies of water in the West and Southwest is intensifying. Ongoing water fights are being waged between farmers and Indians, between farmers and urban dwellers, between water-rich and water-poor states, and between state governments and federal agencies.

14. Possible methods for alleviating the crisis of water scarcity are (a) water conservation, (b) reclaiming sewage water, (c) developing new sources of groundwater, (d) desalinizing sea water, (e) developing drought-resistant and salt-resistant crops, (f) rainmaking, (g) harvesting icebergs, and (h) transferring surplus water to water-short areas.

QUESTIONS AND TOPICS FOR DISCUSSION

1. Discuss four major factors that contribute to our nation's water crisis.

2. Discuss the movement of water through the water cycle. What powers the water cycle? What are the main water reservoirs? What are the renewal times for the atmosphere, rivers, lakes, glaciers, and oceans?

3. Is water, like energy, ever lost from ecosystems?

4. Discuss the statement "The United States does not really have a water *shortage*; it is plagued with a water *distribution* problem."

5. Trace a water molecule in a raindrop falling on your college campus through your own body and finally into another raindrop.

6. Drawing on your knowledge of ecological concepts, discuss the effect of floods on an aquatic ecosystem and on a woodland ecosystem.

7. Discuss the effects of drought on an aquatic ecosystem and on a woodland ecosystem.

8. Describe some of the positive and negative effects of dredging operations.

9. Discuss the statement "Big dams, like the Hoover, are engineering masterpieces that have been unqualified successes in boosting human welfare."

10. Suppose that the dams that now exist in the United States had never been built. What would have been the disadvantages? Would there have been any advantages? Discuss your answer in terms of the American economy, human safety, agricultural production, wildlife preservation, scenic beauty, and endangered species.

11. List the disadvantages of stream channelization to the agricultural ecosystem and to the stream ecosystem.

12. What causes salinization? Briefly describe five ways in which salinization could be controlled.

13. Does iceberg harvesting seem feasible to you? Why or why not?

KEY WORDS AND PHRASES

Aquifer
California drought
California Water Project
Capillary water
Delaware River Basin drought
Desalination
Drainage basin
Dredging
Drip irrigation
Drought-resistant crops
Evaporation
Flood plain zoning
Furrow irrigation
Ground subsidence
Groundwater
Hoover Dam
Hydrologic cycle
Imperial Valley
Infiltration
Irrigation
Irrigation water subsidies
Kesterson National Wildlife Refuge
Lake Mead
Levee
Mono Reservoir
Ogallala aquifer
Open-ditch irrigation
Precipitation
Rainmaking
Replacement period
Renewal time
Rotary sprinkler
Salinization
Salt-resistant crops
Saltwater intrusion
Seepage
Sheet irrigation
Snowpack
Sprinkler irrigation
Stream channelization
Subsidence
Surface water
Transpiration
Upper Mississippi flood
Water cycle
Water mining
Watershed
Zone of aeration
Zone of saturation

SUGGESTED READINGS

El-Ashry, M. T. *Water and the Arid Lands of the Western United States*. New York: Basic Books, 1988. The book examines the intense competition among farmers, cities, commercial interests, and industries for economically scare water.

Goudie, A. *The Human Impact on the Natural Environment*. Cambridge, Mass.: MIT Press, 1986. Excellent, well-illustrated survey of water problems from a global aspect.

World Resources Institute. *World Resources—1988–1989*. New York: Basic Books, 1988. Includes a survey of water resource problems in the United States and abroad.

8

Water Pollution

Widespread illness in Jackson Township, New Jersey, ranging from skin rash and kidney malfunction to premature death; a once clear lake near Chicago converted to pea green "soup"; the skeleton of a perch loaded with radioactive strontium; a stream bottom near Baltimore blanketed with sludge worms; maggot-infested fish rotting on a Lake Erie beach; eight youngsters contracting typhoid fever after eating a watermelon they found floating in the Hudson River; 140 million fish deaths in our nation's waters in a single year; the Cuyahoga River (Ohio) bursting into flames; 18,000 people in Riverside, California, stricken with fever and vomiting; the Mahoning River (Ohio) heated up to 140°F; an outbreak of hepatitis in New York and New Jersey; thousands of fish floating, belly up, in the Potomac River just below our nation's capital; the premature "death" of the Mono Dam Reservoir near Santa Barbara, California—all these seemingly diverse events have one thing in common: They were caused by water pollution (Figures 8-1 and 8-2).

KINDS OF WATER POLLUTION

Water pollution can be defined as *any contamination of water that lessens its value to humans and nature.* There are two broad types of water pollution facing our nation: point and nonpoint (Figure 8-3).

Point Pollution

Point pollution has its source in a well-defined location, such as the pipe through which a factory discharges waste into a stream. Although such pollution may be

FIGURE 8-1 A sign of the times. Although considerable progress has been made in cleaning up our nation's waters, signs such as this can still be seen.

very serious, it usually can be reduced with current technology if industry or government will finance appropriate measures.

FIGURE 8-2 Water pollution in the United States.

○ Saltwater seepage
□ Silting of reservoirs
■ Increasing salinity from evaporation

▨ Serious pollution
⋯ Less serious but
    important pollution

Nonpoint Pollution

Nonpoint pollution has its source over large areas such as farmland (pesticides, fertilizer, manure, sediment), grazing lands (animal wastes, sediment), stream banks (sediment), abandoned coal mines (acid drainage), construction sites (sediment), roadsides (lead, sediment, de-icing salts), and so on.

It may be surprising to learn that cities are nonpoint sources that release great volumes and varieties of water pollutants. Cities produce an incredible amount of runoff because of roof tops, streets, freeways, parking lots, shopping centers, and so on, which retard water absorption. Pollutant-laden water flows across such areas, rushes into street gutters and storm sewers, and then discharges into lakes, streams, and oceans.

Urban runoff carries a number of pollutants—nutrients from pet wastes and lawn and garden fertilizers; heavy metals (lead, zinc, copper); a variety of bacteria; phosphorus leached from fallen leaves; de-icing salts from streets; toxic organic compounds; gasoline from service station spills; sediment from construction sites for homes, schools, and freeway cloverleafs; and

so on. Nonpoint pollutants generally flow *directly* into the bodies of water they pollute.

Unfortunately, federal funding to control nonpoint pollution has been grossly inadequate. Bob Adler, attorney for the Natural Resources Defense Council, recently commented: "The irony is that Congress has spent $45 billion over the past 15 years to build sewage treatment plants but precious little to control nonpoint pollution—which the EPA and the states agree is half of our water pollution problem."

CONTROL OF POLLUTION

There are two major approaches to the control of any type of pollution, whether it occurs on water, on land, or in the atmosphere. **Input controls** prevent pollutants from being generated in the first place. This is the more desirable approach from both an ecological and an economic viewpoint. The other approach is **output control**. This is an after-the-fact method that attempts to control the pollutant and/or its effects after it has been produced (Figure 8-4).

FIGURE 8-3 Examples of point and non-point pollution.

TWO TYPES OF POLLUTION

Industrial waste
treatment facility

Sewage treatment plant

Point pollution

Leachates to
groundwater

Fertilizers,
pesticides,
sediment

To groundwater

Barnyard
runoff

Cropland
runoff

Nonpoint pollution

Sediment Pollution

America's aquatic ecosystems are being polluted with 1 billion tons of sediment annually. The Mississippi River alone carries 210 million metric tons of sediment into the Gulf of Mexico each year. To transport just one year's load would require a train of box cars 37,000 miles long—sufficient to circle the earth one and one-half times at the equator! It is a curious paradox that the very soil that makes the production of life-sustaining food possible suddenly becomes one of our nation's most destructive water pollutant when washed into our lakes and streams.

WHERE DOES SEDIMENT COME FROM? Much sediment comes from fields on which farmers have failed to use appropriate soil conservation measures. Such soil abuse has resulted in record-high concentrations of silt—up to 270,000 parts per million (ppm) in certain Iowa steams! On construction sites, where land is laid bare, 10 times as much sediment is eroded as from an equal area of cropland (Figure 8-5). Improper logging activities, in which large blocks of trees have been removed from steeply sloping land, contribute to sedimentation, especially in the Northwest. Strip-mining

operations, in which the soil mantle is scooped away by giant machines in order to expose the coal, also results in severe sediment pollution of streams, especially in Appalachia.

HARMFUL EFFECTS. Every day the American people lose about $1 million as a result of silt-polluted water. Sediment damages hydroelectric plants, clogs irrigation canals, and slows up barges on the Mississippi. Harbors and river channels must be routinely dredged because of sedimentation. Soil particles carry nutrients and toxic chemicals, such as pesticides, which in turn cause additional damage in aquatic ecosystems.

Suspended soil clouds the water to such a degree that millions of algae, an important base for aquatic food chains, die because they do not receive enough light for photosynthesis. This, in turn, reduces the levels of dissolved oxygen in the water. As a result, wastes discharged from canneries, slaughterhouses, and pulp mills tend to accumulate instead of being decomposed by oxygen-using bacteria. Sediment has destroyed many valuable clam beds in the Mississippi River. Silt-induced fish mortality is extensive (see Chapter 9).

FIGURE 8-4   Comparison of Input and Output Pollution Control.

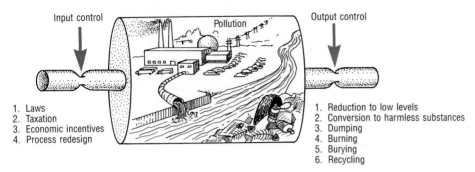

Input control   Pollution   Output control

1. Laws
2. Taxation
3. Economic incentives
4. Process redesign

1. Reduction to low levels
2. Conversion to harmless substances
3. Dumping
4. Burning
5. Burying
6. Recycling

Silt contaminates the nation's public water supplies as well. Over 7,000 billion liters (1,800 billion gallons) of silt-polluted water must be filtered annually so that Americans can have clean drinking water. The life span of thousands of reservoirs throughout the United States has been shortened as a result of sedimentation. The Mono Dam Reservoir near Santa Barbara was filled with mud a relatively short time after its construction, a phenomenon seen elsewhere (Figure 8-6).

CONTROL OF SEDIMENTATION

Input Control.   On croplands, sedimentation can be effectively reduced by the proper application of the erosion control strategies described in Chapter 5, such as conservation tillage, contour farming, use of shelterbelts, terracing, gully reclamation, and the removal of marginal land from production. Highly erodible sites should be avoided altogether.

On construction sites, efforts should be made to prevent workers from bulldozing any more soil than is absolutely necessary. Denuded areas should be seeded or sodded with grass as soon as possible. Seeding on steep road cuts can be done with a hydroseeder, a machine that blows a slurry of seeds, fertilizer, straw mulch, and water onto the slope (Figure 8-7). Steep slopes should be regraded to reduce their slope. Temporary catchment basins may be constructed to intercept runoff water and trap its sediment load.

Output Control.   Output control methods include the following: (1) The flow of muddy water can be directed to swamps and marshes, which can serve as natural sediment-removing filter systems, provided the runoff is not toxic to organisms that live in these habitats. (2) Rivers and harbors can be dredged. (3) Drinking water can be filtered at municipal water treatment plants.

Nutrient Pollution

The nutrient enrichment of an aquatic ecosystem is known as **eutrophication**. This process occurs naturally as a lake or river ages over a period of hundreds or even thousands of years. The release of excessive amounts of nutrients into aquatic ecosystems, as a result of human activities, speeds up the process and, therefore, is called

FIGURE 8-5 Unprotected soil being washed away by run off waters after heavy rainfall at site of new shopping mall to be built in 1989 at Eau Claire, Wis.

FIGURE 8-6 Sediment-choked reservoir near Price, Utah. Its use as a source of drinking water or recreation is terminated.

cultural or **accelerated eutrophication**. It is a serious pollution problem.

NATURAL EUTROPHICATION.
All aquatic organisms require carbon, hydrogen, oxygen, nitrogen, phos-

phorus, sulfur, and many other elements to survive. An essential element occurring in minimal amounts, is called a **limiting factor**—because it restricts both the individual and population growth of the organisms. In aquatic ecosystems, nitrogen and phosphorus are the most important limiting factors. Nitrogen usually is available in the form of nitrate (NO_3^{-1}) ions; phosphorus usually is available as phosphate (PO_4^{-3}) ions. Because phosphorus is usually less abundant, it is more important as a limiting factor than nitrogen.

When nitrogen and phosphorus become abundantly available, the productivity of an aquatic ecosystem often increases sharply. With the passage of time, therefore, most bodies of water become increasingly productive.

CLASSIFYING LAKES BASED ON THEIR PRODUCTIVITY.
Ecologists recognize three major types of lakes: oligotrophic (nutrient-poor), mesotrophic (middle-nutrient), and eutrophic (nutrient-rich). The characteristics of each lake type are summarized in Table 8-1. The **oligotrophic** type is represented by Lake Superior, Lake Huron, the Finger Lakes of central New York, and many glacial lakes in northern Minnesota, Wisconsin, and Michigan. Oligotrophic lakes are frequently beautiful, clear-water lakes, skirted by pine and spruce. Their waters are clear because of a scarcity of floating algae (phytoplankton), resulting from the low levels of dissolved nutrients. Food chains are largely based on bottom-dwelling producers (green plants) growing in shallow water near the lake margins. The total biomass per unit volume of water is much lower than in the other two lake types.

Mesotrophic lakes are characterized by a moderate amount of nutrients. Fertility, clarity, levels of dissolved

FIGURE 8-7 Workers use hydroseeder to propel a stream of water, grass seeds, and fertilizer to establish grass cover on steeply sloping land which has been denuded by construction activity.

Table 8-1 Characteristics of Oligotrophic, Mesotrophic, and Eutrophic Lakes

Oligotrophic Lake	Mesotrophic Lake	Eutrophic Lake
Poor in nutrients	Intermediate	Rich in nutrients
Deep basin	Intermediate	Shallow basin
Gravel or sandy bottom	Intermediate	Muddy bottom
Clear water	Intermediate	Turbid water
Plankton scarce	Intermediate	Plankton abundant
Rooted vegetation scarce	Intermediate	Rooted vegetation abundant
Cold water	Intermediate	Warm water
Characteristic fish: lake trout, whitefish, ciscoes	Characteristic fish: Northern Pike walleyes, black bass	Characteristic fish: sunfish, yellow perch, carp, bullheads

oxygen, and total biomass are intermediate between those of oligotrophic and eutrophic lakes. These lakes are good for swimming, boating, and fishing. Fish like northern pike and walleyes may be plentiful in more northern lakes; bass may abound in southern lakes. Most of the lakes in the United States were probably mesotrophic at the turn of the century.

As time passes, the nutrient-enrichment process described earlier continues. As a result, a mesotrophic lake is gradually converted into the extremely fertile **eutrophic** lake. Such a lake has many undesirable features, such as a muddy bottom (poor spawning surface for most desirable fish), algal blooms that color the water pea green, and populations of **rough**, or undesirable, fish such as carp. The dense blooms of phytoplankton shade out bottom-dwelling plants, which, in oligotrophic and mesotrophic lakes, release large amounts of oxygen during photosynthesis. Although phytoplankton are also photosynthetic, they usually occupy the upper levels of the lake. Therefore, much of the oxygen they release escapes into the atmosphere. As a result, levels of dissolved oxygen in eutrophic lakes are actually less than in mesotrophic or oligotrophic lakes, despite the much greater abundance of phytoplankton. Carp are often abundant in eutrophic lakes because they are adapted to live in warm, shallow, turbid (cloudy), oxygen-poor waters. When conditions are bad, these fish often rise to the surface to gulp air.

Algal Blooms. When the average concentration of soluble inorganic nitrogen exceeds 0.3 ppm and the soluble inorganic phosphorus content exceeds 0.01 ppm, algal populations may "explode." Occurring usually during the summer, **algal blooms** convert once-clear water into "pea soup" and restrict visibility to 0.3 meter (1 foot) (Figure 8-8).

The effects of such a bloom are many:

1. It destroys the aesthetics of the lake, rendering it repulsive to swimmers and other sports enthusiasts. Canoe paddles, motorboat propellers, water skis, and fishing lines (as well as human arms doing the crawl stroke) become fouled up in the green slime.
2. The bloom impairs water quality by giving it a bad taste and odor. (Figure 8-9). If the lake is a source of drinking water, considerable expense may be involved in improving its quality.
3. As a result of wind and wave action, huge masses of algae (and even rooted plants that have been torn loose from the lake bottom) can pile up along the shore and decompose. Hydrogen sulfide (H_2S) gas is given off. This gas smells like rotten eggs, and in high enough concentrations it is also toxic.
4. Some of the blue-green algae release chemicals that are poisonous to fish and humans.

CULTURAL EUTROPHICATION. Human activities are greatly accelerating the eutrophication process. Scientists estimate, for example, that roughly 80 percent of the nitrogen and 75 percent of the phosphorus entering lakes and streams in the United States come from human activities. As a result, the eutrophication of many lakes is proceeding 100 to 1,000 times faster than it would under natural conditions. An estimated 33,000 medium-sized to large lakes, and about 85 percent of the large lakes located in urban areas in the United States, are undergoing cultural eutrophication. The effects are summarized in Table 8-2.

STREAM EUTROPHICATION. Although eutrophication can occur in streams as well as lakes, the effects are usually not quite so severe. Many rivers are naturally oligotrophic at their headwaters, where the waters flow clear and cold. Such is the case of the small northern streams feeding into the Mississippi. However, by the time the water has neared the stream's mouth, it has received so many nutrients that it becomes turbid, warm, muddy, and weedy, harboring bullheads and carp rather than trout. Stream eutrophication is more

FIGURE 8-8 "Scenic" Lake Tahoe. Boaters try to make headway through an algal mat caused by eutrophication.

easily reversed than lake eutrophication; because the nutrient input is often stopped, the current eventually purges itself.

SOURCES OF NUTRIENTS. There are three major sources of nutrients: (1) agricultural fertilizers, (2) domestic sewage, and (3) livestock wastes (Figure 8-10).

Agricultural Fertilizers. Commercial fertilizers promote crop production because they are rich in nitrates and phosphates. Regrettably, however, as our nation's farmers strive to feed a rapidly growing human population, they inadvertently are promoting a population explosion of aquatic plants. The amount of agricultural fertilizer used in the United States has increased from less than 5 million metric tons in 1950 to about 20 million metric tons in 1985—a fourfold increase. Much of the fertilizer, which is not absorbed by crop roots, is washed by runoff waters into lakes and streams. Scientists estimate that over 0.45 billion kilograms (1 billion pounds) of agriculture-generated phosphorus enters America's aquatic ecosystems yearly.

Domestic Sewage. Domestic sewage containing human wastes and household detergents contributes millions of kilograms of phosphorus to aquatic ecosystems yearly. Most sewage treatment plants remove only about half of the nitrogen and one third of the phosphorus from domestic sewage. The rapid increase of water milfoil, sea lettuce, and algae in the lower Potomac River below Washington, D.C., several years ago was attributed to the 40 metric tons of nitrogen and phosphorus compounds contained in the domestic sewage it received daily.

FIGURE 8-9 Biologist at the Amarillo, Texas, water treatment plant obtains water sample to determine algal population. If algal populations are high water will have a bad taste. Much of Amarillo's drinking water comes from Lake Meredith, 45 miles northeast of town.

Table 8-2 Adverse Effects of Nutrient Pollution on a Lake

Lake aesthetics are destroyed.

The recreational values of a lake are destroyed.

Water quality is impaired by foul tastes and odors.

Gases that emanate from rotting algae have foul odors, tarnish silverware, and discolor painted houses.

Toxins given off by algae result in gastric disturbances if ingested.

Dense algal blooms at the surface reduce penetration of sunlight to the lake bottom.

Decomposing algae at the lake bottom represent a high BOD load.

Pollution contributes to the winter kill of fish in northern lakes.

Rooted weeds interfere with navigation and recreation.

Game fish are replaced with trash fish.

Lake basins are gradually filled in, and the lake becomes extinct.

Animal and Livestock Wastes.   The waste deposited on city lots, sidewalks, and streets by this affluent nation's 100 million pet dogs and cats contributes significantly to eutrophication. In New York City alone, 500,000 dogs produce 18,000 metric tons (20,000 tons) of feces and 4 million liters (1 million gallons) of urine annually. It is not surprising, therefore, that urban runoff may carry up to 5 ppm of both nitrogen and phosphorus. Each of the more than 100 million cattle in the United States produces 10 times as much waste per day as a human being. In other words, our country's cattle alone produce the waste equivalent of

1,000 million people—four times the U.S. population. That does not include the waste produced by other types of livestock, including horses, sheep, pigs, goats, chickens, ducks, and turkeys. If all this animal waste were washed into lakes and streams, its eutrophication potential would be enormous. During the winter, it has long been the farmer's custom in the northern states to spread animal manure on the frozen ground. When spring comes, of course, some of the nitrogen and phosphorus is absorbed by crop root systems. Unfortunately, however, almost half of this manure may be washed by spring runoff into aquatic ecosystems.

The problem has been accentuated by the recent practice of crowding livestock into feedlots, where food is brought to the animals, instead of permitting them to forage for their own food in the open pasture (Figure 8-11). A large portion of our nation's cattle are maintained in feedlots. One large lot, accommodating 10,000 cattle, yields 180 metric tons (200 tons) of manure daily. The total amount of waste generated by our nation's feedlots amounts to 720 million metric tons (800 million tons) annually. Without proper control measures, much of this manure, of course, eventually contributes to the process of accelerated eutrophication. One method of control, involving the catch basin, is shown in Figure 8-11.

CONTROL OF EUTROPHICATION.   Eutrophication may be controlled by both input and output methods.

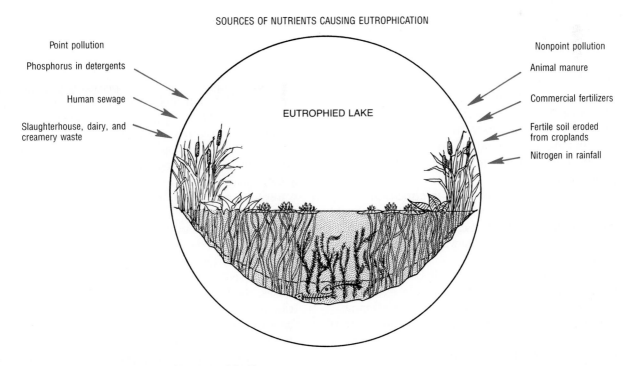

SOURCES OF NUTRIENTS CAUSING EUTROPHICATION

Point pollution

Phosphorus in detergents

Human sewage

Slaughterhouse, dairy, and creamery waste

EUTROPHIED LAKE

Nonpoint pollution

Animal manure

Commercial fertilizers

Fertile soil eroded from croplands

Nitrogen in rainfall

FIGURE 8-10   Sources of nutrients causing eutrophication.

FIGURE 8-11   Control of feedlot runoff at Boystown, Nebraska. This basin "catches" the manure and urine that would ordinarily be washed into a stream or lake after a rainfall. Catch basins, however, can release pollutants into ground-water.

1. *Input Controls in Urban Areas*
   a. Banning the use of phosphate detergents. Such bans have already been imposed by several cities (Akron, Chicago, Miami, and Syracuse) and states (Indiana, Michigan, Minnesota, Wisconsin, New York, Maryland, and Vermont). Several states have limited the phosphorus content in detergents to less than 9 percent.
   b. Imposing an excise tax on lawn and garden fertilizers to reduce sharply the volume of use.
   c. Passing city ordinances that would limit the number of pets per family. The cost of pet licenses could be sharply increased.
2. *Input Controls in Rural Areas*
   a. Minimizing the use of fertilizers.
   b. Injecting liquid fertilizer directly into the soil.
   c. Postponing application of manure in northern states until after the spring melt of ice and snow.
3. *Output Controls*
   a. Upgrading many wastewater treatment plants to the tertiary (advanced) level. These plants would remove a high percentage of the phosphorus and nitrogen before the sewage enters lakes and streams.
   b. Using detention basins on feedlots to collect animal wastes that otherwise would eventually be washed by runoff water into lakes and streams.
   c. Employing weed-cutting machines to remove excess vegetation from aquatic ecosystems. Unfortunately, this would have to be done several times during the year and is rather costly.

   d. Destroying plant growth with herbicides. Great care must be taken to prevent fish kills and the destruction of spawning beds.
   e. Dredging the bottom sediment from lakes to remove the nutrients. This is rather costly. It would be impractical in deep lakes.
   f. Removing undesirable fish (carp) by periodic seining.

THERMAL POLLUTION

Biscayne Bay, Florida, is an unusually productive ecosystem, supporting many species of aquatic organisms, including lobsters, crabs, fish, and wading birds. More than 270,000 kilograms (600,000 pounds) of seafood are harvested annually from the bay. It was thus significant when biologists in the early 1970s found a 30-hectare (75-acre) region that was virtually lifeless—a biological desert caused by the discharge of heated water from a Florida Power and Light Company's power plant.

Thermal pollution is an increase in the temperature of water that adversely affects organisms that live there. Although thermal pollution may result from both natural (excessive heating by the summer sun) and industrial causes, the latter are far more significant. Many industries take water from a lake or stream to cool equipment or products. The electric power, steel, and chemical industries are the most important users of cooling water. Electrical generating plants in the United States use 3.2 billion gallons per day.

Clean Clothes and Dirty Lakes:
The Detergent Story

The Problem

The principal type of detergent used in washing machines throughout the United States did a good job of cleaning clothes. One big advantage over old-fashioned soaps was that it cleaned clothes in hard water (water with a high calcium level) without leaving a curd-like precipitate on the clothes. The detergent worked so well in hard water because of the antiprecipitate or "builder" compound it contained. Unfortunately, this antiprecipitate compound contained phosphorus. This, of course, was bad news for state and federal agencies and environmentalists, in general, who were fighting the battle against eutrophication. By the early 1970s, our nation's detergent industry was producing 5 billion pounds of phosphate annually and accounted for half of the phosphorus load in domestic sewage.

Possible Solutions

There have been three basic approaches to solving the problem caused by phosphorus-containing detergents:

1. *Upgrading sewage plants for phosphorus removal.* The detergent industry, as might be expected, strongly suggests that upgrading sewage plants to remove phosphorus is the most effective method for solving the problem. The big drawback, however, is that the large majority of sewage treatment plants do not have the ability to remove phosphorus. Their upgrading for this purpose would be costly.

2. *Banning phosphorus-containing detergents.* By 1988, a number of communities and states had banned phosphorus-containing detergents. Several other states limited the phosphorus content in detergents to 8.7 percent. The result has been a dramatic improvement in water quality in some regions. Take Lake Onandaga in New York, for example. For

many years, it served as a liquid container for the sewage of Syracuse. The once beautiful lake gradually took on the pea-green color of eutrophication. The outraged city officials passed an ordinance banning the use of phosphorus-containing detergents. In only 1.5 years, the phosphorus level in the lake was reduced by 57 percent, the frequency of algal blooms decreased, and dissolved oxygen levels suitable for game fish were restored.

Unfortunately, that method of control, attractive as it might appear, may have been a mixed blessing. The trouble lies with the substitutes for the phosphate builder. Several substitutes, which at first seemed promising, have certain highly undesirable features. For example, one of them (carboxy methyl cellulose) appears to be nonbiodegradable. A second one (sodium carbonate) causes skin burns. In addition, it would increase the solubility of phosphates that hitherto had been locked up in the mud of lake bottoms. As a result, these phosphates would become available for promoting the growth of weeds and algae. A third proposed substitute (borax) is toxic to aquatic plants even at concentrations as low as 1 ppm.

3. *Using newly developed phosphate-free natural detergents.* Perhaps the ultimate solution to the phosphate detergent problem is the phosphate-free natural soaps and detergents developed recently by the USDA. Because they are made from beef fats, they are to some degree similar to the old-fashioned soaps used before World War II. They perform as well as or better than phosphorus detergents in hot or cold, soft or hard water. Moreover, they are relatively inexpensive, are biodegradable, and, of course, do not cause eutrophication. The natural detergents have already seen wide acceptance in Japan. For some reason, however, American manufacturers have been slow to produce a product that would seem to solve the detergent-caused eutrophication problem once and for all.

Remember the second law of energy? It states that whenever energy is converted from one form to another, a certain amount is lost as heat. There are several energy conversions involved in a power plant fired by fossil fuel. The chemical energy in coal or oil, or the nuclear energy in radioactive fuels, is converted into heat that generates steam to turn the blades of the turbine. That mechanical energy is then converted into electrical energy by the generator. In order

to condense the steam back to water to return it to the boiler, the steam is passed over coils that carry cold water drawn from a stream or lake (Figure 8-12). As a result, the steam is condensed and heat is transferred to the cooling water. The temperature of the cooling water may be raised 20°F. This warmed-up cooling water may then be discharged into a lake or stream. The warmed-up area that results is called a **thermal plume.** Such plumes may extend 1 kilometer

(3,280 feet) or more from the point of discharge (Figure 8-13).

Harmful Effects

Thermal pollution has many adverse effects on aquatic ecosystems. Let us consider some of them.

REDUCTION OF DISSOLVED OXYGEN. When water is warmed, its capacity for dissolving oxygen falls. For example, at 0°C (32°F) water that has been thoroughly mixed with oxygen has an oxygen content of 14.6 ppm, but at 40°C (104°F) it contains only 6.6 ppm. Unfortunately, as water temperature increases, oxygen requirements for fish increase. The lowly carp, for example, requires only 0.5 ppm of oxygen at 0.6°C (33°F), but it needs at least 1.5 ppm at 35°C (95°F) to survive. Cold-water fish such as trout and salmon, which need about 6 ppm to survive, cannot tolerate the warm water that prevails in the thermal plume. If they remain in the plume, they will die from oxygen starvation.

INTERFERENCE WITH REPRODUCTION. Fish are cold-blooded animals whose body temperature (and activity level) vary with that of the external environment. Most fish are extremely sensitive to slight thermal changes. Many kinds of fish are instinctively "tuned" to certain thermal signals that trigger such activities as nest building, spawning, and migration. Changes in temperature can disrupt these activities and may kill eggs.

INCREASED VULNERABILITY TO DISEASE. The ability of some bacteria such as *Chondrococcus* to penetrate the body of a fish is poor at 16°C (60°F), but it gradually increases with rising water temperatures. *Chondrococcus* is believed to be responsible for the massive kills of blueback salmon in the Columbia River in 1946. Thermal pollution of the Columbia was undoubtedly a contributing factor.

DIRECT MORTALITY. The body temperature of a fish is determined by the temperature of the water in which it lives. A lake trout will perish if the water temperature is much higher than 10°C (50°F). Because the discharge of cooling water may raise stream or lake temperatures 11°C (20°F) above normal, cold-water fish caught in the thermal plume die from shock. Such species would have to emigrate to survive.

INVASION OF DESTRUCTIVE ORGANISMS. Thermal pollution may permit the invasion of organisms that

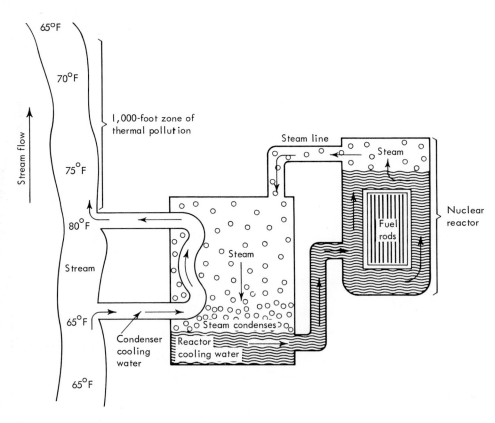

FIGURE 8-12 Nuclear reactor cooling system. Note the 1,000-foot zone of thermal pollution caused by the discharge of cooling water.

FIGURE 8-13 Aerial photo of thermal plume in lake Michigan caused by discharge of warmed-up cooling water from the Point Beach nuclear plant on the Wisconsin shore. Picture was taken with infrared film.

are tolerant to warm water and highly destructive. A good example is the invasion of *shipworms* (highly specialized relatives of clams and oysters) into New Jersey's Oyster Creek. A few years ago, shipworms were absent from Oyster Creek, apparently because they could not tolerate the cold water. (Remember the law of tolerance.) However, thermal discharges from the New Jersey Central Power and Light Company's power plant gradually warmed up the creek. One result was the shipworm invasion. They burrowed into wooden docks and the hulls of ships, wreaking considerable damage.

UNDESIRABLE CHANGES IN ALGAE POPULATIONS. Each of the three major groups of algae—diatoms, green, and blue-green—have distinct tolerance ranges for water temperature (Figures 8-14 to 8-16). Thus, the greatest species diversity for diatoms, green algae, and blue-green algae occurs at 14°C (58°F), 32°C (90°F), and 40°C (104°F), respectively. The most valuable algae, as far as fish and human food chains are concerned, are the diatoms, which prefer cool water. On the other hand, those that prefer warm water—the blue-green algae—are the least desirable as aquatic animal food. Many are too large to be eaten by small crustaceans such as "water fleas." Not only that, they give off toxic substances and cause the multiple problems already discussed under "Nutrient Pollution." Along with nutrients, elevated water temperature is an important factor in promoting blue-green algal blooms. It is

easy to see how aquatic food chains could be disrupted by discharges of heated water effluents. As Richard Wagner, environmentalist at the University of Pennsylvania, states: "A water flea, for example, which might be able to tolerate the thermal extreme of 95°F, would probably starve to death if the diatoms on which it fed were unable to survive at that temperature. In turn, fish feeding on water fleas would be similarly hard pressed to survive, regardless of their tolerance or adaptability to high temperature."

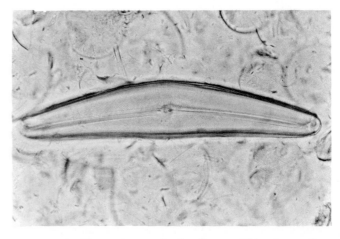

FIGURE 8-14 Photomicrograph of a diatom. This alga prefers a water temperature of about 58 degrees f. It is an important producer link of fish food chains.

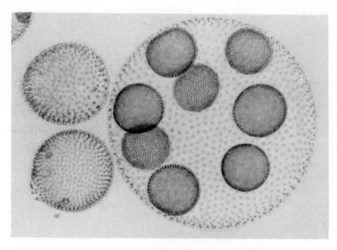

FIGURE 8-15 Photomicrograph of a green alga. This is Volvox. It prefers water temperatures of about 58 degrees C (90 degrees F).

DESTRUCTION OF ORGANISMS IN COOLING WATER.

The volume of water removed from a stream for cooling is enormous, sometimes involving a substantial part of a stream's total flow. Unfortunately, many of the plankton, insect larvae, and small fish that are sucked into the condenser along with the cooling water are destroyed by thermal shock, as well as by water velocity and pressure.

Control

After much prodding by state and federal environmental protection agencies, the power industry has

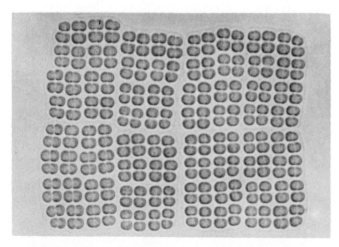

FIGURE 8-16 Photomicrograph of a blue-green alga. This colonial form prefers water temperatures of about 72 degrees C. (104 degrees F.). An abundance of blue-green algae may be a sign of thermal pollution. In general, blue-green algae are not important producer links of fish food chains. Moreover, some species may be toxic to fish and other aquatic animals, as well as to humans.

tried to control the thermal pollution problem with **cooling towers**. These towers transfer heat from the water to the atmosphere. Cooling towers are mammoth structures about 30 stories tall (Figure 8-17). They are large enough at the base to cover a football field. In the *wet* cooling tower illustrated in Figure 8-18, the heated water is piped to the top of the tower and then flows downward over a series of baffle plates. During this time, about 2.5 percent of the water evaporates, a process facilitated by the upward flow of fan-propelled air. The coolant water is then either (1) discharged into the stream, lake, or ocean from which it was drawn, (2) directed into a lagoon for further cooling, or (3) cycled back to the plant's condenser.

Although cooling towers reduce the thermal pollution problem somewhat, they also create some problems. First, when the air temperature is at or below the freezing point, the towers generate a considerable amount of fog; further, if the fog comes in contact with a solid surface, a thin layer of ice is formed. When located near highways, cooling towers can greatly increase traffic hazards. Second, the water that evaporates is consumed. In other words, it is lost to the aquatic ecosystems (rivers and lakes) from which it came. Third, toxic materials, such as chlorine, used to prevent pipe-clogging bacterial slimes, are poisonous to aquatic life and must be removed from the cooling water before it reenters lakes or streams. Fourth, although the towers are remarkable engineering accomplishments, they are 121-meter (400-foot)-tall masses of concrete and steel that dominate the skyline, becoming eyesores. Fifth, the towers are very expensive, costing about $100 million each. Such an expenditure, of course, is eventually passed along from the utility to the consumer in the form of increased electric rates, adding perhaps 1 percent to a customer's annual bills. This cost, say environmentalists, seems reasonable when weighed against the damages caused by thermal pollution.

Beneficial Effects of Heated Water

Artificially heated water is usually harmful to aquatic ecosystems. Nevertheless, under certain circumstances, it may have a beneficial effect. Let's consider some examples.

1. In Eugene, Oregon, heated water from a paper mill was sprayed on fruit trees to prevent frost damage.

2. In Vineyard Haven, Massachusetts, heated cooling water is used by a hatchery to accelerate the growth of lobsters. The time required to produce a marketable lobster has been reduced from 8 to 2 years.

3. Researchers in Georgia have found that thermal pollution of the Savannah River resulted in an in-

FIGURE 8-17 Wet cooling towers in operation. Note water vapor being discharged into air by one of the towers.

creased rate of growth in black bass. The heated water also attracted fish to the area; as a result, fishermen enjoyed huge catches.

4. At Silver Lake in Rochester, Minnesota, heated cooling water from a large power plant prevents the formation of an ice cover in the winter. As a result, thousands of Canada geese overwinter on the lake and form an attraction for bird watchers, camera buffs, and tourists.

5. It has been suggested that cooling water, bearing a thermal load, and domestic sewage effluent, bearing a nutrient load, might be combined in special lagoons. In this scheme, *both the nutrient and thermal pollutants could be put to constructive use.* For example, fast-growing Asiatic milkfish could be stocked in the lagoons. Because they are of tropical origin and adapted to warm waters, the relatively high lagoon temperatures would pose no problems. Moreover, during winter in the northern states, the warm water would prevent ice from forming and permit the milkfish to feed and grow year round. Furthermore, because the fish are plant eaters, not only would the nutrients be efficiently converted into fillets, but the weed problem commonly associated with eutrophic ponds would be under control.

6. The warm coolant water could be used to heat homes. Because pipes required for conducting the heated water are very expensive, however, the power plants and the homes that are to use the water must be designed with this heating scheme in mind.

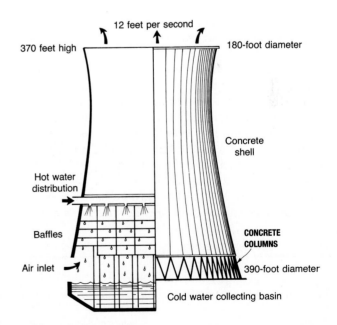

FIGURE 8-18 Operation of a wet cooling tower. Heat from cooling water is removed by evaporation on direct contact with air rising up through the hollow concrete shell. Its large size is necessary to provide sufficient surface area and draft to cool thousands of gallons of water each day. The distinctive shape channels the airflow and provides great structural strength with a minimum of material.

DISEASE-PRODUCING ORGANISMS

Water that is contaminated with infectious organisms is responsible for more cases of human illness worldwide that any other environmental factor. Diseases such as cholera, typhoid fever, dysentery, polio, and infectious hepatitis are all caused by microorganisms that are transmitted by water polluted with human and/or animal wastes. Humans contract the disease when they drink contaminated water. Fortunately, the death rate from these diseases has dropped dramatically in the last century. For example, in the 1880s the death rate from typhoid was 75 to 100 per 100,000 people per year. Today it is a mere 1 per 1 million people. Nevertheless, Americans are not exactly germ free. For example, from 1975 to 1986, water contaminated with harmful bacteria caused illness in 90,000 people in the United States.

Don't be startled, but if you live in a densely populated region, the last glass of water you drank may already have passed through the bodies of eight other people. Our use and reuse of water from streams into which cities dump their sewage is very intensive. Such recycling of precious water supplies will probably become more and more necessary in the future because of our increase in population. It is apparent, however, that such reuse will depend on extremely effective fail-safe water-treatment methods to reduce harmful microorganisms to very low levels. Without such methods, the incidence of infectious, waterborne diseases in our nation will certainly increase.

State and municipal health departments take frequent samples of drinking water supplies to ensure that disease-causing bacteria are held to an absolute minimum. This procedure is both time-consuming and expensive. Because the disease-causing bacteria are so numerous, it is not practical to count each type. Instead, counts are made of the **coliform bacteria**, the relatively harmless organisms that live in the human gut. These bacteria pass from the human intestine in the feces, and therefore occur in sewage-contaminated waters. A low coliform count indicates a low level of harmful bacteria. A high coliform count indicates the presence of a large number of disease-causing bacteria. If water has more than two coliform bacteria per 100 milliliters, it is considered unsafe to drink. The city's water treatment plant then has to increase chlorination to destroy the bacteria. An alternative option might be to shift to another water source, such as a well or lake. When the coliform count of a lake or stream exceeds 200 per 100 milliliters, it is considered unsafe for swimming and the beaches are closed (Table 8-3).

Noncommunity Water

You are at Madison Square Garden in the Big Apple. It is half-time during a basketball game between the Knicks and the Los Angeles Lakers. You leave your seat to get a drink of water. The water at the Garden, and at 150,000 other sources outside the home, such as ball parks, schools, restaurants and buses, is called **noncommunity water**. Such sources serve more than 36 million people in the United States each year. Unfortunately, even though this water may look and taste pretty good, it might be a threat to your health. Why? According to the National Centers for Disease Control in Atlanta, 45 percent of 484 water-transmitted disease epidemics in the United States from 1971 to 1985 were traced to noncommunity water supplies.

Who is to blame? Probably the EPA. This agency's regulation of such water has been extremely lax, so much so that in 1989 the National Wildlife Federation prepared to sue the EPA because of its failure to enforce the Safe Drinking Water Act of 1974. The suit was largely based on a four-state sample survey showing that at least 40 percent of the noncommunity water sources in Pennsylvania and West Virginia in 1986 violated the provisions of the act.

Water Pollution by Toxic Organic Compounds

The key element in **organic compounds** is carbon. Carbon atoms may combine with other carbon atoms, as well as with hydrogen, oxygen, nitrogen, phosphorus, sulphur, chlorine, and others. Organic compounds

Table 8-3 Diseases Transmitted by Water Contaminated with Fecal Matter

Disease	Organism	Symptoms	Comments
Typhoid fever	Bacterium	Vomiting, diarrhea, fever, intestinal ulcers, reddish spots on skin; may be fatal	500 cases in the United States annually
Cholera	Bacterium	Vomiting, diarrhea, water dehydration; may be fatal	Rare in the United States
Traveler's diarrhea	Amoeba	Diarrhea, vomiting	Not uncommon
Amoebic dysentery	Amoeba	Diarrhea, chills, fever, abdominal pain; death may occur	May be gotten by eating infected oysters and clams
Infectious hepatitis	Virus	Headache, fever, loss of appetite, enlarged liver	May be gotten by eating infected oysters and clams
Polio	Virus	Headache, fever, sore throat, weakness, paralysis; may be fatal	Rare in the United States since the use of the polio vaccine

Cooling Cycles

Power plants use two basic methods for condensing steam: open and closed cycles.

Open Cycle

In the open cycle, cold water is withdrawn from a nearby lake, stream, or bay for steam-condensing purposes; then, with its temperature increased about 15°F, the water is discharged back to the lake or stream from which it came. Most of the thermal pollution problems described here were caused by this type of cooling cycle. Open cycles on new plants were banned by the EPA in 1974.

Closed Cycle

In the closed cycle, the warmed-up cooling water is pumped to a **cooling tower** or a **cooling pond**, where the heat is removed. The cooled water is then recirculated through the condenser. This cycle is repeated many times. Unfortunately, despite its name, this system is not completely closed. A small percentage of water is lost by evaporation and a small amount, known as **blow-down water**, is discharged. The water that leaves the system in this way must be made up by an equal volume of intake. All new steam electric plants, with few exceptions, are required by the EPA to use closed-cycle systems. As the older open-cycle power plants are phased out, the thermal pollution problems should gradually be reduced.

---

are important components of all organisms, hence the name **organic**. Typical organic compounds occurring in the human body are carbohydrates, proteins, and fats. Such compounds obviously occur naturally. Our interest here, however, is with toxic organic compounds, which are synthesized in chemical factories and often released into ground and surface water.

During this century, hundreds of thousands of such synthetic organic compounds have been produced. They form the basis of drugs, plastics, solvents, pesticides, and synthetic fibers. Unlike naturally occurring organic compounds, many of the synthetic organics resist decomposition by bacteria, sun, air, or water. As a result, once they are discharged into a body of water, they may persist as pollutants for several years. Good examples of such persistent organics are the pesticide DDT and the industrial chemicals called **polychlorinated biphenyls (PCBs)**.

The toxicity of synthetic organic compounds is largely a result of their ability to disrupt normal enzyme function in living cells. Although these compounds pollute lakes and streams, we shall here consider their role in what is becoming an increasingly serious problem—groundwater contamination.

It is easy to ignore groundwater because we cannot see it. It moves slowly through stone and gravel aquifers far beneath our feet. Yet, within only one-half mile of the earth's surface, this vast water resource has four times the volume of the Great Lakes—about 160 quadrillion liters (40 quadrillion gallons)! More than one-half of the people of the United States depend on this unseen resource for their drinking water, consuming more than 24 trillion liters (6 trillion gallons) yearly. At present, Americans are already pumping 100 billion liters (25 billion gallons) of groundwater each day, and usage is increasing at the rate of 12 percent every 5 years. This underground resource serves as drinking water for 95 percent of our rural households and for 35 of our nation's largest cities.

Unlike a flowing river, groundwater has virtually no natural cleansing or diluting mechanisms. As a result, once it becomes contaminated, it may remain so for thousands of years. It is obvious, therefore, that pollution *prevention* is of the utmost importance in groundwater management.

SOURCES OF GROUNDWATER POLLUTION. The synthetic organic compounds that pollute groundwater come from a variety of sources: municipal and industrial landfills (sites where waste is buried), lagoons holding industrial wastes, agricultural and mining sites, places where sewage sludge is applied to the land, wells that inject industrial waste into the earth, septic tanks in rural and suburban areas, and underground gasoline storage tanks at service stations (Figure 8-19). Because water flows so slowly through most aquifers, it may take decades for a pollutant to move a mile or two from the site of contamination.

1. *Industrial landfills.* For many years, industries contained their liquid wastes in steel drums. These drums were then placed in trenches or pits they covered with soil. Such waste disposal sites are called **landfills**. Unfortunately, much of this waste has been

FIGURE 8-19 Sources of groundwater pollution.

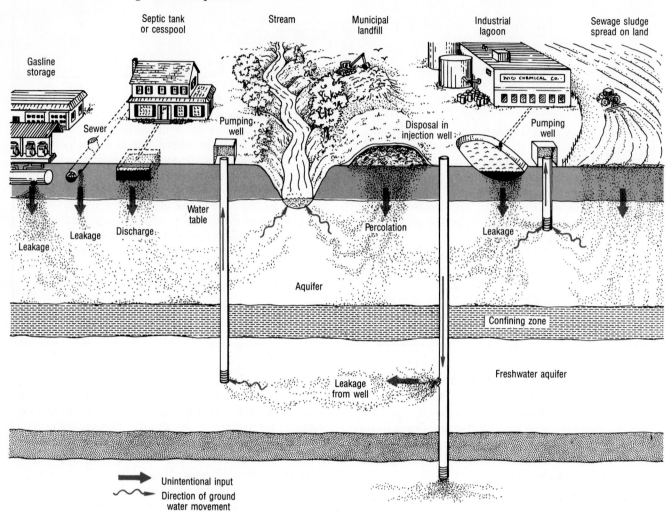

classified as hazardous by the EPA. The Chemical Manufacturing Association estimates that about 250 million metric tons of hazardous waste are generated annually in the United States—over 1 metric ton for each American. Among these hazardous wastes are substantial amounts of toxic organic compounds.

2. *Septic tanks.* In 1987, about 20 million homes relied on septic tanks for waste disposal. These systems discharge more than 1 trillion gallons of waste into the ground annually. Families using septic tanks usually rely on private wells for drinking water. Unfortunately, these wells frequently become contaminated with toxic organics from the septic tank system.

3. *Gasoline storage tanks.* There are about 1.3 million underground gasoline storage tanks in the United States. They are mainly located at service stations, at airports, and on farms. Many have a capacity of several thousand gallons. The older tanks were made of steel and were designed to last for 15 to 20 years. Unfortunately, an estimated 350,000 of

these tanks have become corroded and are leaking gasoline into the surrounding groundwater at the rate of 42 million liters (11 million gallons) a year. A recent EPA survey indicated that an additional 350,000 tanks will start leaking fuel between 1987 and 1992. Such leakage poses an enormous threat to community water supplies.

ADVERSE EFFECTS ON HEALTH. Obviously, groundwater—the source of drinking water for 125 million people in the United States—is not free of impurities. As better instruments for detecting toxic organics become available, more and more are found. The question naturally arises: "If I drink such contaminated water, will I eventually come down with some serious illness?" Unfortunately, the answer is "Maybe." Health officials simply cannot say that if you drink X liters of water contaminated with Y chemical at a concentration of Z ppm over a period of many years, you will develop cancer. At this point, medical knowledge is inadequate (Table 8-4). Of considerable interest in

Table 8-4 Effects of Some Toxic Organic Chemicals on the Health of Occupationally Exposed Workers

Chemical	Exposure	Effects*
Carbon tetrachloride	Inhalation; absorption through skin	Liver and kidney damage Vomiting Abdominal pain Diarrhea Jaundice Red and white blood cells in urine Coma Death
Chloroform	Inhalation	Anesthetic effect Dizziness Mental dullness Kidney damage Liver enlargement Digestive disturbances Coma Death
Vinyl chloride		Chromosome abnormalities Increased spontaneous abortions (in the opinion of exposed workers)
Ethylene dibromide		Decreased fertility
Benzene		Prolonged menstrual bleeding Leukemia (blood cancer)

*All of these chemicals have caused cancer in laboratory rats and mice.
Source: Council on Environmental Quality, *Contamination of Ground Water by Toxic Organic Chemicals.*
Washington, D.C.: U.S. Government Printing Office, 1981.

this regard, however, is a study conducted by a team of Harvard University scientists at Woburn, Massachusetts. Their investigation suggested a strong cause-and-effect relationship between the ingestion of certain industrial solvents (trichloroethylene, benzene, and chloroform) in contaminated drinking water and an abnormally high incidence of stillbirths, sudden infant deaths, and childhood leukemia.

It should be emphasized that polluted well water rarely contains only a single organic contaminant. Usually a given sample contains several. This means that it is possible for two or more organic compounds to interact and cause a **synergistic effect** on the body—an effect that is greater than the sum of the effects of each pollutant acting separately. Medical researchers have found, for example, that the industrial solvent TCE causes greater kidney damage when the individual is simultaneously exposed to PCBs.

Another question that arises is whether the fetus is adversely affected by organic toxins ingested by the mother. The answer is "yes," at least in some cases. For example, PCBs are passed from the mother to the fetus and cause (1) delayed development, (2) reduced size at birth, (3) retarded reflexes, and (4) impaired memory.

In the early 1980s, a rash of illnesses occurred in Hardeman County, Tennessee. Among them were blurred vision, kidney malfunction, and liver damage. Health authorities concluded that the sicknesses resulted from drinking water that was contaminated with at least 15 different chemicals, including the organic solvents carbon tetrachloride and benzene. Further investigation showed conclusively that these toxic materials had leached into the source of drinking water from a "leaky" industrial landfill operated by the Velsicol Chemical Company, one of our nation's biggest chemical manufacturers. Finally, in 1986, after a series of legal skirmishes, the U.S. District Court ordered Velsicol to pay $12.7 million to about 100 people who had become ill from drinking the tainted water.

The Invisible Threat: Toxic Chemicals in the Great Lakes

The massive pollution of the Greak Lakes in the 1960s was quite visible. Symptoms of gross eutrophication abounded: turbid bays, weed-choked shallows, floating mats of algae, rotting fish fouling once attractive beaches. Fortunately, however, those obvious signs of pollution gradually receded, thanks to a $9 billion Canadian–American investment in modern municipal and industrial wastewater treatment systems along the perimeter of these huge lakes. Today, the waters of the lakes once again, for the most part, are clear and sparkling.

Appearances are deceiving, however. An invisible threat is present in these waters—a threat posed by a chemical "broth" of toxic chemicals (Table 8-5). In fact, a joint study by American and Canadian scientists has

Table 8-5   Some Toxic Chemicals in the Great Lakes

Name	Use	Probable Source	Found In	Characteristics/Health Effects
Asbestos in taconite tailings	By-product of iron ore mining.	By-product of iron ore mining. Secured on-land disposal ordered by court, April 1980.	Lake Superior	Airborne effects may include asbestosis, lung cancer; water-borne effects not known, but cancer is implied.
DDT, chlordane, dieldrin, aldrin	Pesticides used widely in Great Lakes region to control insects and rodents. DDT banned in 1971; others now restricted.	Residues from previous widespread use; runoff from agricultural and forested areas, leaching from improper waste disposal sites; and atmospheric deposition.	All five Great Lakes	Bioaccumulation in fish, wildlife, and humans. Persistent in the environment. Long-range effects include reproductive disorders in wildlife; suspected cause of cancer in humans.
Heavy metals (mercury, lead, arsenic, cadmium, copper, chromium, iron, selenium, and zinc)	Wide variety of industrial uses, from anti-knock agent in gasoline to paints, pipes, pesticides, glass and electroplating.	Industrial discharges, medical profession wastes via municipal discharges, agricultural runoff, disposal of waste products; mine tailings; urban nonpoint sources.	Lake Superior, Lake Ontario, Lake Huron, and Lake Erie	Excessive levels of heavy metals bioaccumulate in fish and wildlife. Human consumption of contaminated food may cause a variety of health problems. Mercury can cause brain damage, birth defects. Lead can cause anemia, fatigue, and irreversible brain damage, especially in children. Cadmium can cause kidney damage, metabolic disturbances. Arsenic can cause damage to the liver, kidney, digestive system, bone marrow; suspected cause of cancer in humans. Copper, chromium, iron, selenium, and zinc are toxic to fish.
Mirex	Insecticide used to control fire ants; flame retardant; plasticizer.	Was produced, processed in Great Lakes region until ban in 1975; spills.	Buffalo, Niagara Rivers; Lake Ontario	Bioaccumulation in fish, wildlife and humans. Persistent in the environment. Suspected cause of cancer in humans.
PAHs (polyaromatic hydrocarbons)	Variety of industrial uses.	Industrial oil and grease dischargers; by-product of all types of combustion; urban nonpoint sources; smelting.	All five Great Lakes	Persistent in the environment. Can induce cancer and cause chromosome damage in fish, wildlife, and humans.
PCBs (polychlorinated biphenyls)	Insulation for electrical capacitors, transformers; plasticizer, carbonless copy paper, wide industrial use. Total ban except by special EPA permit in July 1979.	Industrial discharges, municipal sewage treatment plant discharges, harbor sediments, low-temperature incineration of wastes; atmospheric deposition.	All five Great Lakes	Bioaccumulation in fish, wildlife, and humans. Persistent in the environment. Test monkeys developed reproductive failures, skin and gastrointestinal disorders. Probable human carcinogen.
Dioxins	No known technical use.	Microcontaminants in chlorophenols and banned pesticide 2,4,5,-T. Also bleach kraft paper process, and atmospheric deposition.	All five Great Lakes	Bioaccumulation in fish. Probable human carcinogen. Cause of birth defects and reproductive disorders in wildlife.

indicated that the 40 million people living in the Great Lakes region are exposed to more toxic pollutants than any other area on the North American continent.

One of the few obvious symptoms of the pervasive toxic contamination of this 162,500-square-kilometer (65,000-square-mile) expanse of fresh water is the appearance of skin lesions and cancers in fish. For example, liver cancers are frequently found in bullheads taken from Ohio's Cuyahoga River where it flows into Lake Erie. Bottom-feeding fish, like carp, suckers, and

catfish, are showing an increasing frequency of cancer—probably because they are ingesting toxic chemicals released from sediments. In the more contaminated tributaries of the Great Lakes, 9 of every 10 fish may have some form of cancer!

When the bodies of these fish are ground up and analyzed, they are usually found to contain relatively high levels of toxic chemicals; the older and bigger the fish, the higher the concentration of contaminants. As a result, health authorities have issued fish consumption

Rules in Toxic Risk:
Not Just a Toss of the Dice

Any substance can be harmful if exposure to it is too great. Toxics, however, are generally thought of as those that cause harm from relatively small amounts of exposure. They cause problems by touching our skin, being breathed, or being swallowed. When studied enough, a dose–response curve can be developed to show how different amounts affect an average person. Each substance can have a curve of its own and its own set of responses. Some individuals may respond differently if they happen to be more sensitive or more resistant to a given toxicant. Unfortunately, not enough research has been done to develop reliable dose–response curves for all potentially toxic substances.

For noncarcinogenic substances, the dose–response curve eventually drops to a "no effect" level. But not for cancer-causing substances. For these, as the dose gets lower, the risk gets lower, but it never reaches zero. The theory is that even a single molecule of a carcinogen can still combine with one body cell to initiate a malignant growth. Fortunately, this happens rarely or not at all, or we would all be long gone.

Risk Level—The Numbers Game

In order to put risks into some kind of sensible perspective, it is helpful to try and quantify them. The insurance industry has been doing this for as long as they have been in business. They couldn't write policies or set rates if they didn't know the average probability of certain events occurring. For example, figures show that on the average, one out of every 30,000 workers will die in an industrial accident every year—a probability of one in 30,000 in any given year.

Similar probabilities can be generated for toxic risks by studying human health statistics or conducting animal experiments. Health statistics are probably the most reliable, but to date, adequate data to definitively show that a toxicant causes a specific problem exists for only about 25 substances. Examples are lung cancer from smoking and from exposure to vinyl chloride or asbestos.

Human health statistics are generally not accurate enough to detect a risk of less than one in 1,000, and that just isn't good enough. The old philosophy in public health was that there wasn't

a problem until sick and dying people could be counted. The new philosophy, based on better scientific techniques, is that problems can be anticipated and averted before they happen. So for practical reasons, most toxicological data comes from controlled experiments with laboratory animals.

Risk Management Decisions—How to Proceed in the Face of Uncertainty

Science will take us a long way toward making sound risk management decisions, but they are not based on scientific data alone. This is because personal values and social values are also factored in.

Recognizing that many decisions are very complex and won't all be made in exactly the same way, the Department of Natural Resources strives for sound decisions by weighing many factors. Before recommending how much of a chemical is safe in drinking water, air, fish, or wildlife, DNR tries to answer a number of questions:

Do health statistics or animal research suggest that there is a "safe" exposure level?

Can we remove or reduce the risk?

How much will it cost? Who has to pay?

What laws or rules apply?

How concerned are the people who will be affected by the decision?

This process not only considers the best scientific information brought out through the risk assessment process, it also balances this information against economics, existing law, and public concern. The alternative that is finally selected is the one that best satisfies all four components.

The most important factor in making the risk assessment process work is an informed and interested public.

It is critical that everyone know that there are toxic materials out there and that risks are involved—in the air we breathe, the water we drink, the food we eat, the soil where that food grows, and even in our soda pop.

Reprinted excerpts from John M. Cain and Michael D. Witt, "Rules in Toxic Risk: Not Just a Toss of the Dice," *Wisconsin Natural Resources*, 11:1 (January–February 1977), pp. 14–15.

"Get the Lead Out"—of Your Tap Water

"Get the lead out" warns the EPA, toxicologists, and public health officials throughout the nation. They are concerned that levels of toxic lead in the tap water drunk by 40 million Americans are sufficiently high to cause a health risk. What are the risks?

It has long been known that lead poisoning causes mental retardation and stunts growth in youngsters. At present, however, the greatest concern among health authorities is the subtle adverse effect of relatively low concentrations of lead in drinking water on embryonic development and on learning and memory in children. Children under the age of 10 are especially vulnerable. The EPA estimates that the intellectual capacity of 143,500 American children is reduced by up to 5 IQ points annually because of lead-contaminated tap water. Unfortunately, lead in drinking water cannot be seen, smelled, or tasted. Consequently, its presence is not suspected until some time after the first symptoms of poisoning appear.

Where does the lead come from? Contamination occurs when soft (acidic) water leaches the lead from old lead pipes (of pre-1930 vintage) or from the lead solder used to join modern copper pipes together. (The solder is easily identified as a silver-gray band.) As of 1987, the federal lead level standard for drinking water was 50 parts per billion (ppb). Average lead levels in tap water samples tested by the EPA recently ranged from 5 ppb in California to 269 ppb in Vermont. The highest concentration found was 10,000 ppb in a sample from Illinois. In 1988 the EPA standard was tightened from 50 ppb to 5 ppb. The new standard of 5 ppb can be attained, but at a considerable cost—up to $145 million nationally per year. Nevertheless, the $1 billion annual benefit resulting from reduced medical costs would make this attainment highly desirable.

What can you do the get the lead out of your tap water? Several things:

1. Check your kitchen and basement water pipes to see whether the pipes are made of lead (dark gray) or whether lead solder (silver gray) was used to join copper pipes.

2. If lead is present, ask your water district or city health department whether your water is soft (corrosive) or hard (noncorrosive).

3. If your water is corrosive, have it tested for lead by a certified laboratory. Average cost: $30-$50.

4. If the lead level exceeds the 20 ppb recommended by the EPA, purchase a lead filter for your tap water. Cost: $300.

advisories that instruct people to restrict their consumption of salmon, lake trout, and certain other species of Great Lakes fish (Table 8-6). Fetuses as well as young children apparently are especially vulnerable to the toxins.

Two questions naturally arise: What is the origin of these chemicals? and How did they get into the Great Lakes? (Table 8-5). Let's consider the case of toxaphene. This organic pesticide has been found in the tissues of fish taken from a lake on Isle Royale, an island surrounded by Lake Superior. Since toxaphene has never been used on Isle Royale, the only possible mode of entry to the island lake was by "fallout" from the atmosphere. Scientists believe that the toxaphene comes from southern states, like Texas, where it has been used to control the cotton boll weevil. Northward-blowing winds carry the toxaphene to the lake. Other pesticides like DDT and chlordane, as well as PCBs and heavy metals like lead and zinc, apparently also enter the Great Lakes in substantial amounts. Other modes of entry for the more than 450 chemical contaminants of the Great Lakes ecosystem include (1) industrial wastewater discharge, (2) leaching from industrial waste storage lagoons, (3) municipal waste discharge, (4) agricultural runoff, (5) urban runoff, (6) mining site runoff, and (7) release from bottom sediments.

The health effects of many of these toxins, which are ingested in contaminated fish and drinking water, are only beginning to be understood. After all, it is one thing to feed laboratory animals high levels of a given toxic chemical and observe the harmful effects, and quite another to determine precisely what will happen to human beings who ingest a few parts per trillion of a toxin every day for 30 years. And since these contaminants in fish flesh or drinking water are not only invisible, but tasteless and odorless as well, it is extremely difficult for a regulatory agency to convince legistlative bodies and the public that something should be done about them.

In 1909 the United States and Canada formed the International Joint Commission to identify mutually important problems. As the water pollution problem in the Great Lakes became increasingly serious, the two nations entered into a Great Lakes Water Quality Agreement. Under the terms of this agreement, both nations have attempted to monitor the Great Lakes

Table 8-6 Health Advisory: PCB and Pesticide Contamination in Lake Michigan Fish

Group 1	**Group 2**	**Group 3**
These fish pose the lowest health risk	Women and children should not eat these fish	No one should eat these fish
Lake trout up to 20"	Lake trout 20 to 23"	Lake trout over 23"
Coho salmon up to 26"	Coho salmon over 26"	Chinook salmon 32 to 35"
Chinook salmon up to 21"	Chinook salmon 21 to 32"	Chinook salmon over 35"
Brook trout	Brown trout up to 23"	Brown trout over 23"
Pink Salmon		Carp
Smelt		Catfish
Perch		

water under their jurisdictions, to identify Areas of Concern (*hot spots*), and to explore ecologically sound methods to control the pollutants. The United States and Canada have identified about 50 toxic hot spots that need immediate attention. One of them is the Detroit River, a tributary of Lake Erie. This waterway serves as a sewer for both municipal and industrial waste from scores of nearby cities. Even though this waste receives conventional treatment, the river is a diverse mix of toxins, ranging from mercury to phenols, from PCBs to polyaromatic hydrocarbons (PAHs). Hundreds of contaminants are present in the bottom sediments of this stream. Other areas of concern include the harbors of Milwaukee, Gary (Indiana), Muskegon (Michigan), Cleveland, Toronto (Ontario), and Rochester (New York), as well as the mouths of many great rivers.

Under the terms of the Water Quality Agreement, the United States and Canada are using an ecosystem approach to deal with these focal points of contamination. The Remedial Action Plans drawn up so far are based on the premise that problems at a hot spot must be considered in their total ecological context before appropriate solutions can be developed. An important component of a given Remedial Action Plan, for example, is the examination and regulation of the modes of entry for a particular toxin. For example, if pesticide contamination of the Buffalo River originates in agricultural runoff, farmers in the Buffalo River drainage will be urged to reduce their use of chemicals in pest control and to adopt more effective strategies to prevent soil erosion, such as contour farming and conservation tillage.

If the Remedial Action Plans developed by the United States and Canada for the detoxification of the Great Lakes are to succeed, the lifestyles of many people living in this region may have to change. Moreover, great commitment and cooperation will be required from the industrial sector, from environmental agencies, and from government at all levels. Only in this way will the "invisible" chemical threat to the 40 million people of the Great Lakes be really made to disappear.

Oxygen-Demanding Organic Wastes

We are will aware that if the garbage collector fails to make a pickup for several days, the accumulating debris will begin to decay and give off a vile odor. The same would be true of the rabbit remains left by a fox. What is happening? Bacteria are at work, using oxygen from the air to break down (oxidize) the complex, energy-rich compounds in the garbage. The energy that is released during decomposition is then used by the bacteria to sustain life.

Organic matter, however, may also accumulate in aquatic environments as, for example, when an autumn leaf fall almost blankets a woodland stream, when a massive fish kill occurs, or when slaughterhouse debris is discharged.

The process by which such organic material is eventually decomposed by bacterial action may be summarized as follows:

high-energy organic molecules
(fats, carbohydrates, and proteins)
+
oxygen
↓
low-energy carbon dioxide
+
energy (used by bacteria to sustain life)
+
water
+
nitrate ions (NO_3^{2-})
+
phosphate ions (PO_4^{3-})
+
sulfate ions (SO_4^{2-})

The amount of dissolved oxygen (DO) in the *water* is not nearly as great as *atmospheric* oxygen. As a result, the bacteria actively *compete* with other oxygen-demanding aquatic organisms (fish, crustaceans, insect larvae, and so on). If sufficient organic food is available, and if other conditions such as water temperature are favorable, the oxygen-consuming bacteria multiply rapidly. Levels of dissovled oxygen fall as the bacterial population increase. Levels may plummet from 10 ppm to less than 3 ppm, to the detriment of aquatic organisms.

The federal government maintains a network of stream-monitoring sites at which dissolved oxygen levels are systematically checked. Of the thousands of measurements taken in the past few years, fewer than 5 percent were below 5 ppm of dissolved oxygen—the minimal level required for quality fish populations.

Biologists refer to the oxygen used by bacteria in decomposing organic waste in bodies of water as the **biological oxygen demand**, or **BOD**. It is also customary to speak of the BOD of human sewage, of slaughterhouse wastes, and so on, since this material supports bacteria that require or demand oxygen. Every time you flush your toilet, you are making it a bit tougher for scrappy game fish in the stream or lake near your home to survive, for there are about 250 ppm BOD in the wastewater going down the pipe.

Many of the wastes from canneries, cheese factories, dairies, bakeries, and meat-packing plants have BOD levels ranging from 5,000 to 15,000 parts per million. In the late 1960s seven paper and pulp mills in the State of Washington discharged 210 million gallons of mill waste into Puget Sound. In terms of BOD, this was equal to the domestic sewage from a population of 814 million people.

THE BOD TEST. How do water quality experts measure the BOD of organic waste? First, a sample of polluted water whose dissolved oxygen content has been determined is placed in a container from which all air and light are excluded. It is then incubated for 5 days at 20°C. The amount of oxygen consumed by bacteria in the water is then determined by comparing the amounts present before and after incubation. This is the BOD.

THE EFFECT OF A HIGH BOD ON STREAM ANIMALS. Does sewage effluent with a high BOD have a noticeable effect on aquatic animal populations? The answer, of course, is of vital interest to fishermen, nature lovers, stream-side property owners, and resort operators, as well as to biologists. The answer to the question is frequently sought by aquatic biologists working for state environmental protection agencies. They could get the answer simply by determining the kinds and numbers of organisms occurring immediately above and at several sites below the point of sewage discharge. Note that in Figure 8-20, point A, just above the outfall, the river is characteristic of an unpolluted stream. The high levels of dissolved oxygen (8 ppm), and the abundant food in the form of mayfly and caddis fly larvae, make possible the survival of highly prized game fish such as bass and trout. However, at point B, in the Zone of Decline, immediately below the outfall, dissolved oxygen levels drop rapidly because of the high organic component of the waste. In some streams the dissolved oxygen may drop to 3 ppm or less, which is insufficient to support the oxygen requirements of more desirable fish, such as black bass, walleyes, and trout. Instead, only less desirable fish, such as carp and bullheads, which have low oxygen requirements, can survive. The larvae of may flies, stone flies, and caddis flies, which require higher oxygen levels, are virtually absent. The dissolved oxygen concentration is so drastically reduced in the Damage Zone, in fact, that even carp and bullheads cannot survive.

We should emphasize that a *single* decrease of dissolved oxygen down to 1 ppm could destroy every fish in a stretch of stream. For example, the massive discharge of sewage into the Potomac River below Washington D.C., some years ago reduced dissolved oxygen levels to less than 1 ppm. As a result, extensive fish kills occurred each May when several species of fish moved through the oxygen-depleted waters during their spring spawning runs.

The most typical bottom-dwelling animals in the Damage Zone are reddish sludge worms, of which there may be 180,000 per square meter of stream bottom; bloodworms; and the red rat-tailed maggot (Figure 8-20). These animals are sometimes used as **index organisms;** their occurrence indicates that a particular stretch of stream is highly contaminated with organic waste. Unpolluted aquatic ecosystems usually have a much greater species diversity than their polluted counterparts. Rather surprisingly, however, the total **biomass** in severely deoxygenated areas may approach that of unpolluted water. The reason is that the few highly specialized species that *can* survive, such as the sludge worms, develop huge populations.

Beginning at point D in the Recovery Zone, the amount of oxygen removed by the sewage bacteria is more than counterbalanced by the oxygen entering the stream from the atmosphere because of wind action or photosynthesis of stream-swelling plants. As a result, the dissolved oxygen level rises, permitting once again the occurrence of carp and garpike. Finally, still farther downstream at point E, most of the organic material discharged from the sewage plant has been decomposed; the level of dissolved oxygen rises to its original value. Fish and other organisms supported by the stream above the point of discharge can survive in the water below point E.

FIGURE 8-20 Effect of sewage with a high BOD level on the amount of dissolved oxygen and the type of aquatic organisms in the stream.

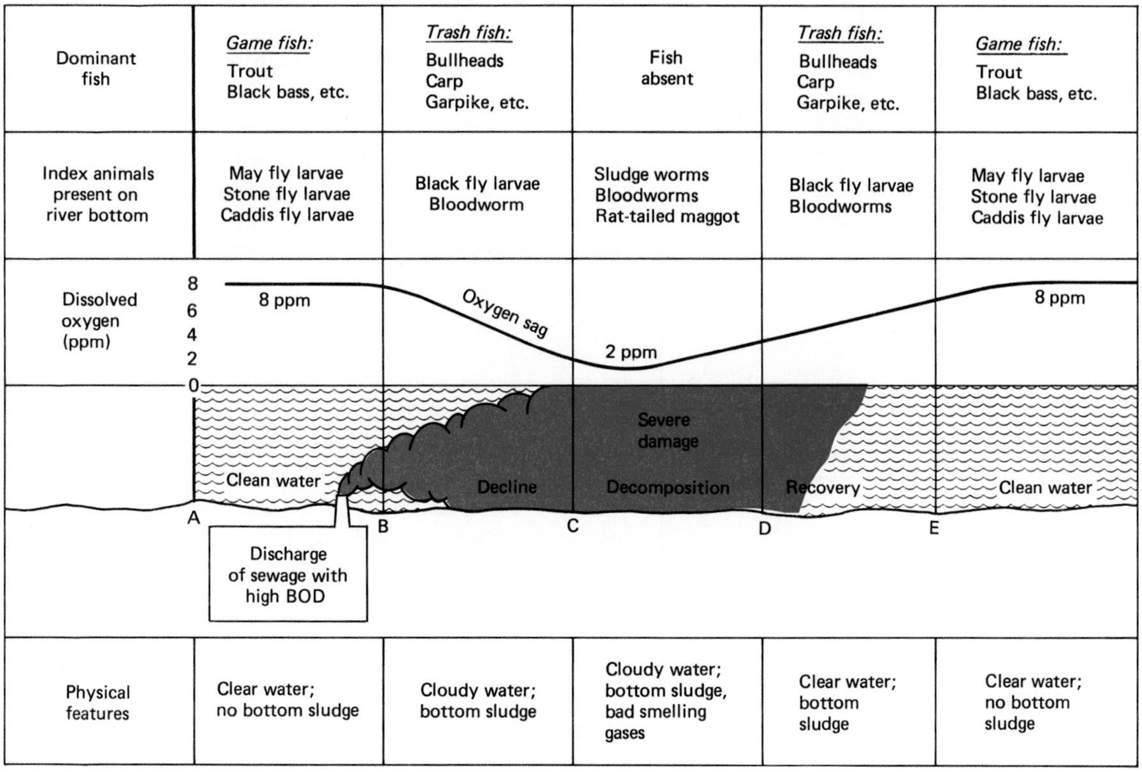
Dominant fish
Game fish:
Trout
Black bass, etc.
Trash fish:
Bullheads
Carp
Garpike, etc.
Fish absent
Trash fish:
Bullheads
Carp
Garpike, etc.
Game fish:
Trout
Black bass, etc.
Index animals present on river bottom
May fly larvae
Stone fly larvae
Caddis fly larvae
Black fly larvae
Bloodworm
Sludge worms
Bloodworms
Rat-tailed maggot
Black fly larvae
Bloodworms
May fly larvae
Stone fly larvae
Caddis fly larvae
Dissolved oxygen (ppm)
8
6
4
2
0
8 ppm
Oxygen sag
2 ppm
8 ppm
Severe damage
Clean water
Decline
Decomposition
Recovery
Clean water
A
B
C
D
E
Discharge of sewage with high BOD
Physical features
Clear water; no bottom sludge
Cloudy water; bottom sludge
Cloudy water; bottom sludge, bad smelling gases
Clear water; bottom sludge
Clear water; no bottom sludge

The characteristic dip of the oxygen curve at points *B* and *C* is known as the **oxygen sag**. The slope of the dissolved oxygen curve, which is highly variable, depends on the amount of BOD in the sewage, the rate at which oxygen enters the stream, the water temperature, and the water velocity. The rate of recovery, of course, depends on the number of discharge pipes on a particular stretch of stream.

HEAVY METAL POLLUTION

The metal pollution of lakes and streams may have many sources. Heavy rains may wash lead, copper, zinc, cadmium, and other metals from abandoned mine sites in the Rockies, as well as from the streets and parking lots of cities. These metals eventually drain into aquatic ecosystems. Point sources include metal-processing plants, dye-making firms, and paper mills. Some of our nation's streams are heavily contaminated with metals. For example, every year, more than 90 tons of lead enter the 150-mile stretch of the Hudson River between New York and Manhattan alone!

A major problem with metals is that, unlike organic pollutants, they are not broken down by bacteria. Consequently, they may persist in the water or bottom sediments for many years and eventually enter human food chains.

Metals are poisonous because they interfere with the normal function of enzymes—the compounds that facilitate many life-sustaining functions of the human body. The intake of metals through contaminated food and water may cause serious illness. Lead poisoning, for example, may result in a broad spectrum of effects, ranging from decreased learning ability and gastric upsets to convulsions, coma, and death. A summary of the effects of four heavy metals on human health is presented in Table 8-7.

For the most part, conventional municipal sewage treatment plants do not efficiently remove metals from the wastes. In fact, some metals may be toxic to the very bacteria the plant relies on to digest organic materials. It is therefore important that the amount of metal contamination in the incoming waste be reduced to a minimum. Local, state, and federal regulations require industries to pretreat their metal-laden waste before sending it on to a municipal sewage treatment plant. Under ideal circumstances, most of the metals are removed and transported to a certified hazardous waste dump. However, in most cases, our nation's industries have a long way to go. For example, in 1987 the Milwaukee Metropolitan Sewerage District reported that 104 of 139 (74.8

Table 8-7 Effects of Four Heavy Metals on Human Health

Mercury	Arsenic
Fatigue	Headache
Headache	Dizziness
Irritability	Fatigue
Loss of coordination	Vomiting
Numbness of hands and feet	Diarrhea
Shortening of attention span	Abdominal pains
Memory loss	Muscular pains
Kidney damage	Blood in urine
Death	Anemia
	General paralysis
Lead	Heart malfunction
Intestinal colic	Coma
Irritability	Death
Reduced resistance to infectious	
diseases	
Anemia	*Cadmium*
Blood in urine	Degenerative bone disease
Brain damage	Severe crippling
Partial paralysis	High blood pressure
Mental retardation	Heart malfunction

percent) industrial waste discharge pipes failed to meet the district's standards.

However, manufacturing plants are not the only source of metal contamination. Agricultural irrigation, rather surprisingly, has also caused this type of pollution. In 1983 officials at the Kesterson Wildlife Refuge in California were mystified by an extensive die-off of fish and waterfowl. In addition, many birds were hatched with deformities, such as crossed bills, which made feeding impossible. Futhermore, an abnormally high number of embryos died before hatching. Chemical analysis of the marsh water revealed very high levels of selenium. The selenium was traced to runoff irrigation water from nearby croplands. Irrigation water leaches selenium from soils that naturally contain high concentrations of the potentially toxic element.

SEWAGE TREATMENT AND DISPOSAL

During the Middle Ages, in some of the densely populated cities of Europe such as London and Paris, human waste was often disposed of simply by opening a window and dumping it into the street below. The stench that assaulted the passers-by along those streets was so vile that refined gentlemen carried sweet-smelling spices as deodorants. Before the advent of indoor plumbing in the United States, human waste was disposed of by means of the backyard outhouse—a method still in use today in some rural areas and in poverty-stricken regions such as Appalachia.

All the types of water contaminants described thus far—sediments, infectious organisms, detergents, human excrement, toxic chemicals, and organic mate-

rial—are components, to a greater or lesser degree, of municipal sewage (Table 8-8). In order to minimize the potentially harmful effects of these pollutants, municipal sewage is usually treated at **sewage treatment plants** before it is discharged into a lake, stream, or ocean.

Sewage treatment plants have traditionally been built by cities to accommodate only wastewater. But sewage and storm water often flow in the same pipes to the treatment facility. After heavy thunderstorms, the volume of storm water runoff to the treatment plant may be 100 times that of the wastewater alone. As a result, the incoming flow overwhelms the plant's capacity and the excess is allowed to overflow into a lake, stream, or bay. Regrettably, this overflow, which is a mixture of sewage and storm water, may pollute the receiving body of water so badly that it cannot be used for recreational activities. So, you ask, "Why don't communities build separate pipelines for storm runoff and sewage?" The answer is that the cost, in many cases amounting to millions of dollars for large cities, is prohibitive.

Sewage Treatment Methods

Since 1880, when our nation's first sewage treatment plant was built in Memphis, Tennessee, more than 13,000 have been constructed. Domestic sewage treatment may be primary (rudimentary but rather inexpensive), secondary (more effective and of moderate cost), or tertiary (most effective but very expensive).

PRIMARY TREATMENT. About 23 percent of our nation's sewage receives only primary treatment (Figure 8-21). It is mainly a physical process, rather than biological or chemical. The major function of primary treatment is to separate the solids from the wastewater, as shown in Figure 8-22. After the screening out of large objects (gravel, garbage, leaves, feces, etc.), the stream of wastewater is pumped to **settling tanks**, often called **clarifiers**, where suspended organic solids settle to the bottom. The fluid that remains is then chlorinated to destroy disease-causing organisms and discharged into a lake or stream. The solids that have accumulated at the bottom of the settling tank are pumped to a sludge digester, where millions of bacteria "feed" on the sludge—break it down in the absence of oxygen. One decomposition product, methane gas, is frequently burned to heat the digester to the temperature required for most effective bacterial action.

Primary treatment removes about 60 percent of the suspended solids and about 33 percent of the oxygen-demanding waste (BOD). Although primary treatment makes sewage look a lot better, it leaves a substantial amount of organic material, nitrates, phosphates, and

Table 8-8 Water Pollution: Sources, Effects, and Control

Contaminant	Source	Effects	Control
Oxygen-demanding waste	Soil erosion Autumn leaf fall Fish kills Human sewage Domestic garbage Remains of plants and animals Runoff from urban areas during storms Industrial wastes (slaughterhouses, canneries, cheese factories, distilleries, creameries, and oil refineries)	Bacteria that decompose the organic matter will deplete the stream of oxygen Game fish are replaced by trash fish. Valuable food for game fish (may flies, etc.) is destroyed Foul odors develop	Reduce runoff from barnyards Reduce BOD of sewage with modern secondary sewage treatment plants Reduce runoff from feedlots with catch basins
Disease-producing organisms	Human and animal wastes Contaminated aquatic foods (clams, oysters)	High incidence of water-borne diseases such as cholera, typhoid fever, dysentery, polio, infectious hepatitis, fever, nausea, and diarrhea	Reduce runoff from barnyards and feedlots More effective sewage treatment Proper disinfection of drinking water
Nutrients	Soil erosion Food-processing industries Runoff from barnyards, feedlots, and farmlands Untreated sewage Industrial wastes Household detergents Exhaust of motor cars	Eutrophication May cause methemoglobinemia in infants Foul odors Decreased recreational and aesthetic values	Tertiary sewage treatment Reduce use of commercial fertilizers Change detergent formula Control soil erosion with strip-cropping, contour plowing, and cover cropping Control feedlot runoff with catch basins
Sediment	Soil erosion from farmland, strip-mined land, logged-off areas, and construction sites (roads, homes, and airports)	Fills in reservoirs Clogs irrigation canals Increases probability of floods Impedes progress of barges Interferes with photosynthesis, reducing DO Destroys freshwater mussels (clams) Fish die from asphyxiation Destroys spawning sites of game fish Necessitates expensive filtration of drinking water	Employ erosion control practices on farms such as contour plowing, cover cropping, and shelter belting Employ erosion-control practices at construction sites: sodding, use of catch basins, etc. Use mulching and jute matting on seeded road banks Establish temporary cover, such as rye and millet, at construction sites
Heat	Midsummer heating of shallow water by the sun Discharge of warm water from electrical power, steel, and chemical plants	Disrupts structure of aquatic ecosystems Causes shift from desirable to undesirable species of algae and fish Kills cold-water fish such as salmon and trout Blocks spawning migrations of salmon Interferes with fish reproduction Increases susceptibility of fish to diseases and to the toxic effects of heavy metals such as zinc and copper	Reduce the nation's energy demands for electricity Use closed cooling systems exclusively Instead of discharging heated water to streams, use it to heat homes, extend growing seasons on cropland, increase growth rate of food fish and lobsters, and prevent frost damage to orchards

bacteria, some of which may cause human disease. Fortunately, with the aid of cost-sharing grants from the federal government during the past two decades, thousands of American cities have been able to replace their primary plants with secondary plants.

SECONDARY TREATMENT. About 72 percent of the municipal sewage in the United States receives *secondary treatment* (Figure 8-23). Primarily biological in nature, it uses bacteria and other decomposers to break

down organic materials and remove nitrates and other substances. Two major methods available for secondary treatment are (1) the **activated sludge process** and (2) the **trickling filter** (Figure 8-24).

Activated Sludge Process. Fluid from the first settling tank (clarifier) is piped to an **aeration tank** in which air is bubbled to provide a maximal supply of oxygen. This enables the aerobic (oxygen-using) bacteria to decompose the organic compounds at a maximum rate. The greater the amount of atmospheric

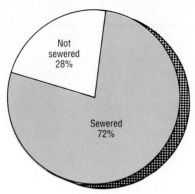

Total U.S. Population

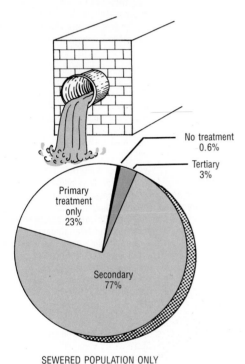

SEWERED POPULATION ONLY

FIGURE 8-21 Types of sewage treatment available to the American population.

oxygen used by bacteria to oxidize this material, the smaller the demands on the limited supply of dissolved oxygen in the stream or lake into which the treated waste water will be discharged. (In other words, the BOD of the sewage is being greatly reduced.) The liquid that accumulates at the top of the second sedimentation tank is then chlorinated and discharged. However, the sludge that settles to the bottom of the second tank is then called **activated sludge** because it contains a large number of bacteria. A portion of the activated sludge is piped to the sludge digester, where bacteria break down organic material in the absence of oxygen. The remainder is recycled back to the aeration tank and the second settling tank (clarifier), where in turn, it provides a "seed" population of bacteria to act on the incoming

waste. Secondary treatment removes 90 percent of the BOD and 90 percent of the suspended solids. However, 50 percent of the nitrogen compounds and 70 percent of the phosphorus compounds (the chemical culprits responsible for eutrophication) still remain.

Trickling Filter. In the **trickling filter process** the sewage is sprayed by the arms of a slowly rotating sprinkler onto a filter bed made up of stones (Figure 8-24). The filter bed may be about 2 meters (6 feet) thick and up to 60 meters (200 feet) in diameter. The stones are coated with a slime of bacteria that has accumulated during the operation of the filter. The sewage, containing a load of dissolved organic compounds, trickles down through the stones, and the organics are fed on by the bacteria. Leftover solids are piped to a settling tank and later transferred to a sludge digester. About 80–85 percent of the dissolved organic compounds are removed by the trickling filter system. However, the wastewater still contains a high level of nutrients, such as phosphates, ammonia (NH_3), and nitrates, which could eutrophy the lakes and streams into which they are discharged. The removal of these materials depends on still another process: tertiary treatment.

TERTIARY TREATMENT. This is the most advanced phase of sewage treatment. The water quality of our streams and lakes would be considerably better if all sewage were given tertiary treatment. Unfortunately, these plants are twice as expensive to build as secondary sewage plants and four times as expensive to operate. As a result, tertiary treatment is not used unless it is necessary to maintain a high level of purity in the receiving body of water. Only about 5 percent of the sewage is treated in this way in the United States.

The effects of primary, secondary, and tertiary treatment of sewage are summarized in Figure 8-25.

Septic Tanks

Many rural and suburban families, forming a population of about 50 million, have backyard **septic tank** systems that process their wastes (Figure 8-26). Septic tanks are underground sewage containers made of concrete or steel into which all household wastewater flows. Solids settle to the bottom of the tank and form sludge. The fluids flow from the tank into a system of perforated pipes buried underground in a **drain field**. The waste stream then passes through the holes in the pipes and slowly percolates through the soil. The soil acts as a natural filter, removing bacteria, some viruses, and suspended materials. Phosphate binds chemically to the soil particles and hence is removed from the effluent. Organic material is decomposed by soil bacteria. The sludge that accumulates at the bottom of the septic tank also undergoes bacterial decay.

Oil Spill on the Monongahela

"It was a terrible noise. I couldn't believe my eyes. The tank just disintegrated. It was a twisted mess. I was so scared I almost forgot my name." The words tumbled out as an excited Alva Rogerson described the sudden collapse of a huge oil tank near Pittsburgh, Pennsylvania, on January 2, 1988. She was in the process of taking down Christmas decorations when she observed the most infamous inland oil spill in our nation's history. It was all over in a matter of seconds. The tank burst with a deafening rumble, releasing 760,000 gallons of diesel fuel. The tidal wave of oil surged onto Route 827, gurgled through a culvert into the Monongahela River, and then began a rapid journey downstream to the Pittsburgh area, only 23 miles distant.

The tank belonged to the Ashland Oil Company, producers of Valvoline Motor Oil. Originally used in Cleveland, the tank had been disassembled and then moved to its Pennsylvania site and reconstructed. It had just been filled for the first time. Critics have offered several possible reasons for the tank's collapse: (1) the reused metal was defective; (2) the metal became brittle because of the intense cold; (3) the Ashland Oil Company did not test the tank by filling it first with water—a routine procedure; (4) the tank's foundation was unable to support a combined metal and oil weight of more than 22,000 metric tons.

Within 9 hours of the accident, the U.S. Coast Guard had placed several booms on the Monongahela. The booms are sausage-like floats with oil-trapping aprons that extend down into the water (Figure 1). However, only about 160,000 gallons, about one-seventh of the oil, could be removed by the booms. The Pittsburgh Fire Department's trucks rushed to the pollution site with sirens wailing and promptly set up a fire hose "blockade" across the path of the slick, but with little success.

As the 14-mile-long slick moved downstream, more than 70 communities along the Monongahela, and later the Ohio River, were forced to stop drawing river water for municipal use. Only 1 day after the accident, 23,000 residents in the Pittsburgh area found themselves without water. For another 750,000 residents, unpolluted water was so scarce that it had to be rationed. Harried residents tried to build up water reserves by filling jugs, bottles, bath tubs, and swimming pools. Pennsylvania's Governor Robert Casey decreed that every person in the area affected by the spill had to conserve water. Failure to do so would result in a $200 fine. More than 1,000 workers found themselves jobless because of factory shutdowns. Distress, frustration, and anxiety were commonplace. But 20,000 students had cause for joy—they were excused from classes.

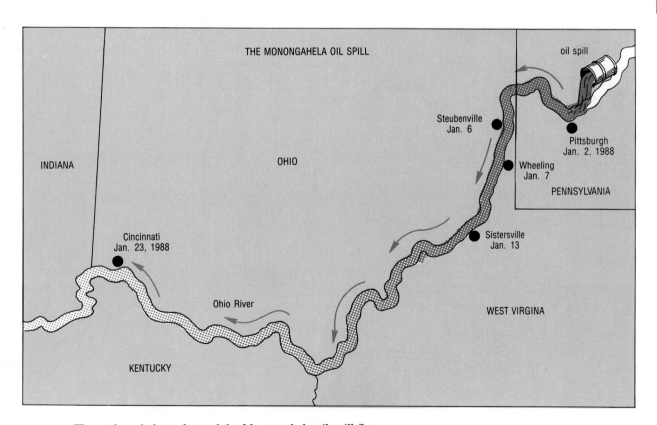

The path and chronology of the Monongahela oil spill flow.

In North Fayette, Pennsylvania, 17 miles downstream from Pittsburgh, dirty laundry piled up and people ate from paper plates. Bottled water was hauled to the sick and elderly by funeral director Tom Somma's hearse. Stream-side communities from West Elizabeth, Pennsylvania, to Wheeling, West Virginia, saved precious water by taking sponge baths and flushing their toilets with melted snow.

The diesel fuel gradually became diluted because of the turbulent action of the river. Moreover, some of the oil volatilized and dispersed into the atmosphere. In addition, some was gradually decomposed by bacterial action. As the oil moved downstream, first Stebenville, Ohio, and later Wheeling, West Virgina, issued water crisis alerts. But the contamination problem gradually lessened.

What was the attitude of Ashland Oil in this pollution crisis? Apologetic and cooperative. Shortly after becoming aware of the scope of the disaster, John Hall, Ashland's chairman, assured the EPA that his company would pay the millions of dollars of cleanup costs. However, this was only part of the company's money woes. It also had to face dozens of lawsuits filed by outraged citizens and industries adversely affected by the spill.

The oil slick gradually diminished in size as it moved downstream. On January 23, 3 weeks after the accident, it reached Cincinnatti, Ohio. However, by that time, the concentration of the fuel had been reduced to only 4 ppm. A few days later, the great Monongahela oil spill was history.

PROBLEMS. Septic tank systems, however, do have drawbacks:

1. They cannot be used if the water table is too high or if the soil is relatively impermeable.
2. If the system is overtaxed, the drain field may become clogged with organic material. As a result, the partially decomposed waste may rise to the surface, causing visual pollution and generating foul odors.
3. The septic tank must be pumped out regularly at substantial cost to the home owner. The sludge is then hauled to a sewage treatment plant.
4. Septic tank systems are the most frequent cause of bacterial contamination of groundwater, especially in areas where the population density is high.
5. The average life expectancy of the drain field portion of the system is only 10 years.
6. Sewage from lake-shore homes is frequently treated by septic tank systems. Unfortunately, however, if

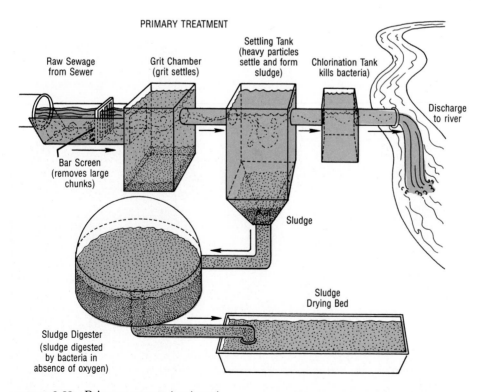

FIGURE 8-22 Primary sewage treatment.

FIGURE 8-23 Secondary sewage treatment.

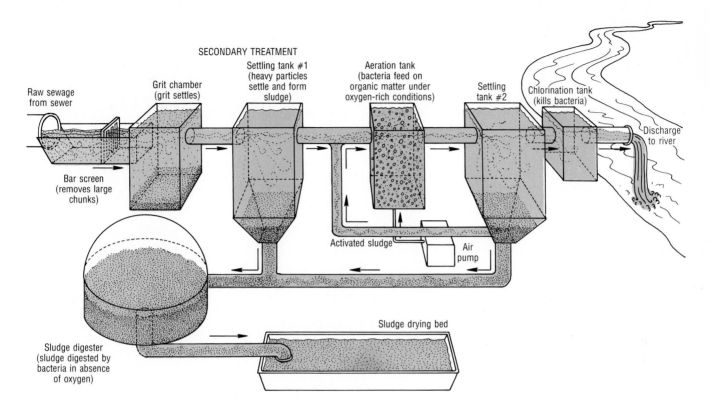

SECONDARY TREATMENT

Raw sewage from sewer

Bar screen (removes large chunks)

Grit chamber (grit settles)

Settling tank #1 (heavy particles settle and form sludge)

Aeration tank (bacteria feed on organic matter under oxygen-rich conditions)

Settling tank #2

Chlorination tank (kills bacteria)

Discharge to river

Activated sludge

Air pump

Sludge digester (sludge digested by bacteria in absence of oxygen)

Sludge drying bed

FIGURE 8-24 Secondary sewage treatment. This rotary trickling filter device handles four million gallons of wastewater from Sacramento, California daily. After chlorination the effluent is discharged into the American River.

FIGURE 8-25 Relative effects of treatment on the removal of pollutants from sewage.

RELATIVE EFFECTS OF SEWAGE TREATMENT
ON POLLUTANT REMOVAL

Pollutant	Treatment		
	Primary	Secondary	Tertiary
Solids	Solids removed	Little removed	Little removed
Harmful bacteria	Bacteria removed	Little removed	Little removed
Dissolved organics	Little removed	Dissolved organics removed	Little removed
Harmful viruses	Little removed	Viruses removed	Little removed
Phosphorus	Little removed	Little removed	Phosphorus removed
Nitrogen	Little removed	Little removed	Nitrogen removed

the population density is high, the nutrients resulting from bacterial decay of organic wastes may leach into the lake in sufficiently large amounts to trigger algal blooms and accelerate eutrophication.

Alternative Sewage Treatment Methods

HOLDING PONDS. Once sewage has undergone secondary treatment, as indicated in the box on "Sewage Treatment Methods," the major contaminants remaining in the sewage are nutrients, dissolved organics, and heavy metals. These contaminants can be removed by tertiary treatment, which involves sophisticated (and expensive) chemical methods such as air stripping of ammonia, precipitation of phosphates by the addition of lime, and absorption of organic solvents on carbon. Unfortunately, tertiary treatment is prohibitively expensive for most communities.

A less expensive further treatment would involve pumping the sewage into holding ponds. In a short time, various species of aquatic plants such as algae, coontail, water lilies, water hyacinths, and duckweed will become established. The tiny duckweed is a floating plant smaller than your little finger nail. In some ponds,

they grow profusely enough to form a solid green "living blanket" over the water. All these plants, of course, grow rapidly because they have access to the abundant supply of sewage nutrients. Duckweed plants not only absorb dissolved organics directly from the water, but, along with the other vegetation, can be harvested and fed to livestock or even used as human food. In Thailand and Burma, the natives have long consumed duckweed, a highly nutritious plant that has six times the protein content of a soybean field of equal area! (The vegetation should be analyzed for the presence of metals before being eaten.) Such sewage holding ponds may even serve as wildlife habitats.

LAND APPLICATION. Treated wastewater may be sprayed directly on land by means of tank trucks or conventional irrigation systems. In Lubbock, Texas, and Muskegon County, Michigan, this method is used extensively. Phosphates and nitrates are absorbed by crop roots and enhance yields. Any disease-causing microorganisms in the wastewater could be destroyed by preheating the waste before disposal. The organic material in the wastewater improves soil structure and increases its ability to absorb moisture and resist erosion.

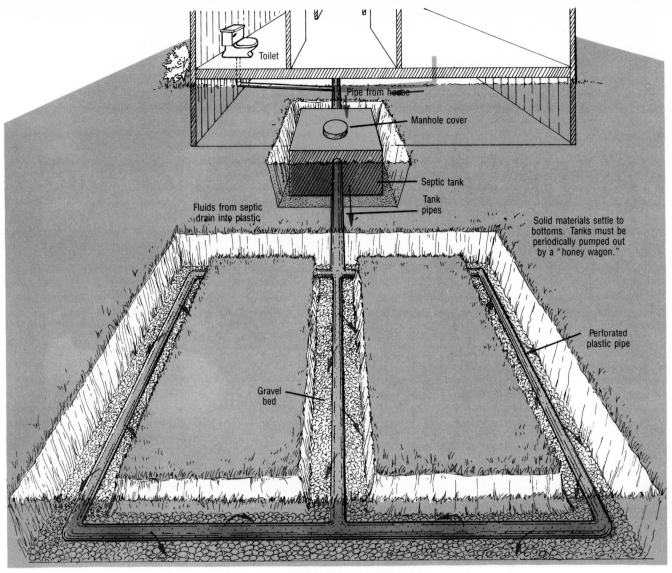

Toilet

Pipe from house

Manhole cover

Septic tank

Tank pipes

Fluids from septic drain into plastic

Solid materials settle to bottoms. Tanks must be periodically pumped out by a "honey wagon."

Perforated plastic pipe

Gravel bed

A. Septic Tank and Drain Field

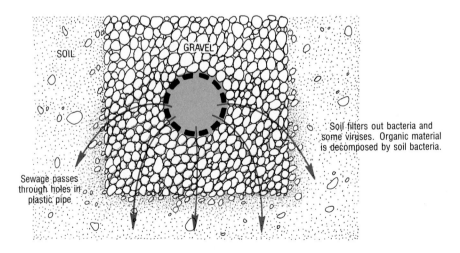

SOIL

GRAVEL

Soil filters out bacteria and some viruses. Organic material is decomposed by soil bacteria.

Sewage passes through holes in plastic pipe

B. Cross Section of Drain Pipe

FIGURE 8-26 The septic tank and drain field system of sewage disposal.

For many years, Nassau County, Long Island, New York, dumped its sewage In the Atlantic Ocean. This practice has recently become illegal. As a result, the county, as of 1989, is planning to spray its treated sewage on land that overlies a severely depleted sandstone-limestone aquifer. As the wastewater percolates down through the soil, the impurities will gradually be removed and the aquifer will be recharged. In the not too distant future, the good citizens of Nassau County will be taking showers and brewing their breakfast coffee with water that once suspended human waste—a remarkable example of the recycling of a precious resource.

SEWAGE SLUDGE: A RESOURCE IN DISGUISE?

The black, partly watery, partly solid material that remains after sewage treatment in a municipal plant is known as **sludge**. For many years, it has been buried in landfills or burned in order to get rid of it. Recently, however, many people have begun to regard sludge as a resource rather than a waste. There is good reason, since sludge has potential value as fuel, livestock feed supplement (Figure 8-27), soil conditioner, fertilizer, and building materials.

1. *Fuel.* As you recall, during primary treatment of municipal sewage, much of the organic material in sewage is sent to a digester, where it is decomposed by bacteria in the absence of oxygen. During this process, a fuel called **biogas** is released that is mainly methane, the principal component of natural gas, a common household and industrial fuel. This biogas may be used at the sewage plant itself to heat the digester to the temperature required for proper operation and to power generators that provide electricity needed to run the plant. Even after removal from the digester, the treated sludge still has some fuel value left. If dried, it can be burned in an incinerator. The heat can then be recovered and used in industrial processes or to warm buildings.

2. *Livestock feed.* Since appropriately treated sludge has a fair content of nutritional proteins and fats, it has value as a feed supplement for cattle, pigs, and chickens.

3. *Soil conditioner.* Sludge has considerable value as a soil conditioner. It improves the ability of soil to retain nutrients, reduces erodibility, and promotes the ability of the soil to hold oxygen and moisture. The Metropolitan Sewage District of Milwaukee packages much of its sludge and markets it under the name Milorganite (Figure 8-27). Much of it is bought for use on lawns and gardens. At least 500 farms in the Milwaukee area regu-

FIGURE 8-27 Sludge as a resource. The Milwaukee Sewerage District produces a commercial fertilizer, known as Minorganite, from processed sewage sludge. It is widely used on golf green, gardens and lawns.

larly receive applications of Milwaukee sewage plant sludge.

4. *Fertilizer.* Since sludge contains a fair amount of nitrogen and phosphorus, it has some value as fertilizer (Figure 8-28). However, the fertilizer value per pound is small compared to that of commercial fertilizers. Nevertheless, Milwaukee area farmers who treat their land with sludge save almost $185 per hectare ($75 per acre) in fertilizer costs. About 25 percent of all municipal sludge in the United States is now returned to the land as fertilizer.

5. *Building materials.* In Washington, D.C., stands one of the world's most unique buildings; it is made in part of sewage sludge!   The existence of this construction marvel is based upon a technique recently developed by scientists at the University of Maryland. They succeeded in producing bricks from a mixture of sludge, clay, and slate. These so-called biobricks have no odors and look like ordinary bricks. The 750-square-meter (8,300-

FIGURE 8-28 Application of sludge fertilizer into the soil of a Wisconsin farm.

square-foot) sludge building was constructed by Washington's Suburban Sanitary Commission out of 20,000 biobricks. These sludge bricks must be doing their job; as of 1989, the building is still standing strong and tall. The widespread use of biobricks could have multiple environmental benefits, such as (1) reducing the cost of sewage disposal, (2) slowing the rate at which landfills are filling up, (3) reducing ocean contamination by sludge dumping, and (4) reducing both the soil erosion and visual pollution caused by the mining of clay.

INDUSTRIAL WASTE AND ITS DISPOSAL

Industry's water use is increasing daily. It is estimated that the 5 billion gallons per day used in 1980 will increase 100 percent by the year 2000. Water is one of industry's most important raw materials. It is used as a solvent, as a cleansing agent, as a mineral extractant, as a coolant, and as a waste-removal agent.

In the early 1970s, industrial pollution of water was much in evidence. Dyes from a factory stained a Mississippi tributary green. Oily scums spread over the Rouge River near Dearborn, Michigan. The Merrimack River in Connecticut bubbled with nauseating gases. Water from a Minnesota iron mine stained a trout stream reddish-brown. Partly because of industrial pollution, Niagara Falls emanated foul odors. Parts of the Missouri ran red with slaughterhouse blood. Because thousands of industrial plants were using the Mississippi River as an open sewer, conservationists renamed it the "colon of mid-America." There was certainly little resemblance between its clear, sparkling headwaters at Lake Itasca in Minnesota and the foul-smelling broth of domestic and industrial waste that spewed into the Gulf of Mexico at New Orleans.

The effective treatment of industrial wastes, in particular those from chemical industries, is exceedingly complex. In many cases, effective methods of treatment are unknown.

Some of the waste disposal schemes employed by industry have not been well conceived. Consider **injection wells**, for example. Certain wastes, such as arsenic compounds, cyanides, and radioactive materials, are potentially so harmful to humans that to discharge them directly into lakes and streams would be unthinkable. Furthermore, these wastes cannot be properly treated by conventional waste disposal plants. Instead, many industries have injected them into wells from 100 meters (300 feet) to over 3.3 kilometers (2 miles) deep. For example, in order to dispose of the strong acid wastes that resulted from a steel-cleaning process, one company drilled a well 1.3 kilometers (0.80 mile) deep into a 540-meter (1,800-foot)-thick layer of porous sandstone. In theory, the wastes would then "stay put" because the waste-holding sandstone was completely walled off by impervious rock. However, if there were earthquakes, the wastes might be released from their sandstone "prison," move laterally, and eventually contaminate an aquifer used by a community as a source of drinking water.

There is good evidence to suggest that the deep well injection technique may actually cause earthquakes. Scientists have demonstrated a well-defined correlation between the volume of waste injected by the U.S. Army's chemical plant near Denver, Colorado, and the frequency of earthquakes in the immediate region. Certainly, the injection well technique is similar to "sweeping pollution under the rug." It may be a stopgap answer for our generation, but the final effective solution is simply being postponed for our descendants, who may have a dire need for these aquifers in the next century.

LEGISLATING WATER POLLUTION CONTROL

The Federal Water Pollution Control Act of 1972 is one of the most important environmental laws passed by Congress. Under the terms of the act, (1) minimal water quality standards were set, (2) deadlines were established for industries and cities to clean up their wastes, (3) pollutant discharges from point sources were banned without EPA-approved permits, (4) cities were required to provide at least secondary sewage treatment, (5) our nation's waters should be fishable and swimmable, and (6) repeated violations of the act would result in fines of up to $50,000 per day and jail sentences of up to 2 years.

In 1977 the Federal Water Pollution Control Act was amended under the name of the Clean Water Act.

Amendments were also passed in 1981 and 1987. The 1987 amendments required all municipalities to have secondary sewage treatment plants in operation by July 1, 1988. The construction, operation, and maintenance of such plants were supported with $45 billion in federal funding and $15 billion in state and local funding during the period 1972–1986. Although an expenditure of $18 billion in additional federal funds was authorized by the 1987 amendments for the period 1987–1996, this represents a considerable reduction in the level of federal funding compared with the 1970s. As of 1987, only about 70 percent of our nation's municipalities had constructed secondary sewage treatment plants. The inability of many towns to meet the July 1, 1988, deadline can be largely attributed to the Reagan administration's 35 percent cut in federal spending for water pollution control. The adverse effect of such budget cuts on the water quality of our lakes and streams is considerable. After all, 172 million Americans discharge 27.6 billion gallons of sewage to treatment plants every day.

TRENDS IN WATER QUALITY

The Clean Water Act classifies our surface waters according to their "designated use": (1) drinking water; (2) swimming and fishing; and (3) transportation and agriculture. Most of our surface waters are in the swimming and fishing category, and pollution control of these waters is meant to make such use possible. On the other hand, 120,000 miles of streams must have better quality because they must serve as a source of potable water. The designated use of 32,000 miles of streams is for transportation and/or agriculture. The quality of these waters can be somewhat less than those in the swimming and fishing category.

In 1986 the General Accounting Office (GAO), a federal watchdog agency, reported that we have surprisingly scant information on the quality of our nation's waters or on the changes in quality and what causes them. We do not even know precisely what effect the multi-billion-dollar wastewater treatment plant program has had on water quality in the United States. According to the GAO, many conclusions concerning water quality are based on the subjective opinion of pollution control experts. Instead, they should be based on precise data resulting from intensive and comprehensive monitoring programs in which pollutant levels are measured.

The most inclusive information on water quality in the United States to date has been provided by the monitoring program of the U.S. Geological Survey. It is called the **National Ambient Stream Qualtiy Accounting Network (NASQAN)**. It includes 501 monitoring stations located on streams distributed throughout the country. The latest NASQAN report covers the period 1974–1981. It showed that some streams improved during this period, while others degraded. Twenty-three percent of the streams monitored showed a reduction of lead levels, 17 percent a lowering of BOD, and 16 percent a drop in the number of fecal coliform bacteria.

A WORLD VIEW OF WATER POLLUTION

Water pollution cleanup *in the more developed countries* has been moderate and, in many nations, is probably on a par with progress in the United States. In the late 1980s, for example, wastewater treatment plants were serving more than 50 percent of the aggregate population of 21 countries. The percentage of the population served ranges from 0.5 percent in Greece to 100 percent in Sweden. However, there are a number of trouble spots. For example, in the Soviet Union, water pollution control is just beginning. The stretch of Poland's Vistula River that flows through Krakow is said to be devoid of life. The canals of Venice reek with the stench of untreated human and industrial sewage.

The water pollution problems *in the less developed countries* in general are much worse than those of the United States. There are several reasons for this: (1) lack of properly educated and technically trained personnel; (2) lack of funding for construction of waste treatment plants; (3) lack of tough pollution control legislation; and (4) lack of enforcement of such laws, if indeed they do exist. South American countries, for the most part, have relatively safe drinking water. However, many streams are seriously polluted with runoff from lead, zinc, and silver mines. As deforestation intensifies on this continent, river contamination with pesticides, fertilizer, and sediment is expected to increase accordingly. In Mexico, the drinking water has such high counts of infectious bacteria that American college students studying there have been advised to boil the water before drinking it lest they come down with diarrhea, fever, chills, and nausea, a complex of symptoms facetiously dubbed **Montezuma's revenge**. The scarcity of safe drinking water is probably even greater in Africa. For example, in rural Guinea, only 1 of every 50 people has access to it! Less than 10 percent of the rural populations of Madagascar, Mali, Sierra Leone, and Zaire have good drinking water available. In Pakistan, most of the human diseases, such as typhoid, diarrhea, dysentery, and infectious hepatitis, are caused by microorganisms that have contaminated public water supplies. In India, the Yamuna River receives 200 million liters (54 million gallons) of untreated sewage from New Delhi every day. As a result, the coliform count in this stream is an almost unbelievable 24 million per 100 milliliters. (Recall that 200 per 100 milliliters is the standard for swimmable waters in the United States.) In Malaysia, 42 major rivers have been declared "ecological disasters" since they are virtually unable to support desirable aquatic life. Seventy percent of some stretches of Manila's Pasig River consist of untreated sewage.

In 1980 the United Nations launched the International Drinking Water and Sanitation Decade (1981–1990). The major objective of this program was to make all nations, especially the LDCs, acutely aware of the importance of safe drinking water in the fight against disease. The ambitious goal of the International Decade is to supply an additional 500,000 people with drinkable water *every day* of the decade! Unfortunately, this goal now appears unattainable.

RAPID REVIEW

1. Water pollution can be defined as any contamination of water that lessens its value to humans and nature.

2. Two broad classes of water pollution are point and nonpoint.

3. Point pollution has its origin in specific, well-defined sources such as the discharge pipes of sewage treatment plants; nonpoint pollution stems from widespread sources such as the runoff from agricultural lands or urban areas.

4. Sediment pollution has many adverse effects. It (a) silts in reservoirs, (b) damages hydroelectric plants, (c) clogs irrigation canals, (d) interferes with barge traffic along the Mississippi River, (e) destroys fish spawning grounds, (f) reduces the photosynthetic activity of aquatic plants, and (g) makes necessary the costly filtration of water.

5. Natural eutrophication is a slow process of nutrient buildup that takes thousands of years.

6. Cultural eutrophication is caused by human activities and may age a lake 25,000 years in only 25 years.

7. Oxygen-demanding organic wastes come from (a) fruit and vegetable processing industries, (b) cheese factories, (c) creameries, (d) distilleries, (e) pulp and paper plants, (f) slaughterhouses, and (g) bakeries.

8. The discharge of organic waste with a high BOD into a stream reduces the dissolved oxygen in the stream and is lethal to many species of fish.

9. Thermal pollution has multiple adverse effects: (a) fish mortality resulting from the reduction of dissolved oxygen, (b) direct mortality of fish because of the heat, (c) replacement of beneficial diatoms with undesirable blue-green algae, (d) acceleration of the process of eutrophication, and (e) destruction of plankton in the cooling waters of power plants.

10. Thermally polluted (enriched?) water may be beneficial in several ways: (a) it provides ice-fee areas for waterfowl during the winter, (b) it prolongs the crop-growing season, (c) it prevents frost damage to fruit trees, (d) it increases the growth rates of game fish and lobsters, and (e) it can be used to heat homes.

11. A high coliform bacteria count indicates that the water sample may contain high levels of microorganisms capable of causing disease.

12. The key element in all organic compounds is carbon. It reacts readily with hydrogen, oxygen, nitrogen, phosphorus, sulfur, and chlorine. This reactivity makes possible the synthesis of hundreds of thousands of organic compounds, many of which have proven toxic to humans when ingested in contaminated water.

13. Our nation's groundwater amounts to 150 quadrillion liters—equal to the volume of the Great Lakes.

14. More than 50 percent of the people in the United States depend on groundwater for drinking purposes and household uses.

15. The groundwater contamination of drinking water wells is severe in many regions of the United States. Sources of groundwater pollution from toxic organic compounds are (a) industrial landfills and lagoons, (b) municipal landfills, (c) septic tanks, and (d) underground storage tanks for gasoline and other chemicals.

16. The chlorine used to disinfect drinking water has been found to react with organic compounds to form chlororganics such as chloroform and carbon tetrachloride; both of these compounds cause cancer in laboratory animals.

17. The level of chlororganics in drinking water can be greatly reduced with activated carbon treatment—an expensive method that will cost American taxpayers about $1 billion yearly.

18. People who have been occupationally exposed to toxic organic compounds in groundwater have experienced a variety of symptoms, including dizziness, fatigue, vomiting, kidney and liver damage, reduced fertility, and spontaneous abortions.

19. Health effects of toxic compounds include skin and eye irritations; brain and spinal cord damage; interference with normal kidney, liver, and lung function; cancer; and gene mutations.

20. Canada and the United States have identified about 50 toxic hot spots, or Areas of Concern, in the Great Lakes ecosystem.

21. In the more contaminated tributaries of the Great Lakes, 9 of every 10 fish have cancer.

22. The EPA estimates that the IQ of more than 140,000 American children has been reduced by 5 points because of lead in their drinking water.

23. The toxicity of many heavy metals is based upon their ability to interfere with normal enzyme function.

24. Primary treatment is mainly a physical process in which solids are removed by sedimentation.

25. Secondary treatment is primarily a biological process in which organic wastes are decomposed by bacterial action.

26. The bacterial decomposition of organic waste during secondary treatment can be accomplished either by the activated sludge process or by trickling filters.

27. Tertiary sewage treatment, which is rather expensive, removes much of the nitrogen and phosphorus from the waste.

28. Some industries have curbed water pollution by converting their waste into commercially valuable by-products.

29. The level of federal funding for municipal treatment plants dropped sharply during the 1980s. As a result, many cities were unable to meet the 1988 deadline for secondary treatment set by the EPA.

30. Important federal water pollution control laws include the Federal Water Pollution Control Act of 1972 (now called the Clean Water Act) and its amendments (1977, 1981, 1987).

KEY WORDS AND PHRASES

Activated carbon process
Activated sludge process
Algal bloom
Amebic dysentery
Areas of Concern
Atmospheric deposition
Biodegradable
Biological oxygen demand (BOD)
Biomass
Blue-green algae
Caddis flies
Catch basin
Chlorination
Clean Water Act
Closed-cycle cooling system
Cold-blooded animal
Cooling tower
Cultural eutrophication
Cuyahoga River
Detergent
Dry cooling tower
Eutrophication
Eutrophic lake
Feedlot
Great Lakes Water Quality Agreement
Groundwater
Heavy metals
Holding ponds
Hydroseeder
Industrial sewage
Infectious hepatitis
Injection well
International Joint Commission
Land application of sewage
Landfill
Laws of energy
Lead poisoning
Limiting factor
May flies
Mercury poisoning
Mesotrophic lake
Milkfish
Milorganite
National Ambient Stream Quality Accounting Network (NASQAN)
Natural eutrophication
Nonpoint pollution
Oligotrophic lakes
Open-cycle cooling system
Oxygen sag curve
Parts per billion (ppb)
Parts per million (ppm)
Point pollution
Primary sewage treatment
Remedial Action Plan
Rough fish
San Gabriel Valley, California
Secondary sewage treatment
Sediment pollution
Septic tank
Settling tank
Sludge
Sludge digester
Sludge worms
Soil conditioner
Species diversity
Stone flies
Synergism
Tertiary sewage treatment
Thermal enrichment
Thermal pollution
Toxaphene
Toxic organic chemicals
Toxic Substances Control Act
Trickling filter
Water Pollution Control Act
Wet cooling tower

QUESTIONS AND TOPICS FOR DISCUSSION

1. Define water pollution.

2. List the seven basic types of water pollution.

3. List eight differences between oligotrophic and eutrophic lakes.

4. Distinguish between natural and cultural eutrophication.

5. Because photosynthetic levels are high in eutrophic lakes, you might suppose that the water would contain a relatively large amount of dissolved oxygen. Does it? If not, why not? Discuss your answer.

6. List five adverse effects of algal blooms.

7. Describe the effects of a high level of BOD waste on the aquatic life of a stream.

8. Roughly what levels of dissolved oxygen does a particular stretch of stream have if one of the dominant organisms found in it is (a) a carp, (b) a trout, (c) a sludge worm, (d) a may fly larva?

9. What does the term *biological oxygen demand (BOD)* mean?

10. Some manufacturers feel that thermal pollution should really be called *thermal enrichment*. Do they have a case for such a change in terminology? Discuss.

11. What is the importance of coliform bacteria to human health?

12. Describe four important methods for controlling sediment pollution.

13. Summarize the main benefits derived from (a) primary sewage treatment, (b) secondary sewage treatment, and (c) tertiary sewage treatment.

14. Why is groundwater contamination more serious than that of surface waters?

15. Describe a dose–response curve for a hypothetical toxic chemical.

16. How is it possible for toxaphene, a pesticide never used in the Great Lakes region, to occur in the water of a lake on an island surrounded by the waters of Lake Superior?

17. Name six heavy metals that are toxic to humans when ingested.

18. What is a possible source of lead in drinking water in a modern home?

19. Several years ago, a book was published with the title *The Grass Is Greener over the Septic Tank*. Discuss the title's validity.

20. Discuss the status of water quality in the LDC's.

SUGGESTED READINGS

Baker, B. J. "Toxic Shock." *Wisconsin Natural Resources* 11(1):23–24, 1987. Excellent, highly readable overview of the sources, effects, and modes of entry of major toxic contaminants of Lake Michigan and other Great Lakes.

Council on Environmental Quality. *Annaul Reports*. Washington, D.C.: Council on Environmental Quality, 1970–present. This is excellent material written in nontechnical language and well illustrated. There is a sharp focus on the groundwater contamination problem in recent issues.

Speth, J. G. *Our Polluted Environment: A Long Term Perspective*. New York: Basic Books, 1988. An authority examines long-term pollution trends in the United States and the world. He describes several social and technological changes needed to reduce pollutants at their source.

Cobb, C. E. "The Great Lakes' Troubled Waters." *National Geographic* 172(1):2–31, 1987. Highly readable treatment of the problems posed by toxic contaminants in the Great Lakes ecosystem.

World Resources Institute. *World Resources—1988–1989*. New York: Basic Books, 1988. One section of this book contains a comprehensive view of water pollution in the United States and abroad.

9

Fisheries Management

Early in 1989, President George Bush appeared on television before millions of Americans watching the evening news. But the setting was not the White House or even the Capitol. Instead, it was one of the president's favorite fishing haunts, where he was filmed wetting a line in quest of a "big one." Angling is not reserved for holders of high office. In fact, more than 40 million nonpresidents go fishing every year in the United States. They spend more than $15 billion and travel more than 30 billion miles in pursuit of their favorite sport every year.

THE LAKE ECOSYSTEM

The fish sought by our nation's sports enthusiasts occur in a great variety of freshwater habitats, from rushing mountain streams to slowly flowing rivers, from tiny farm ponds to the Great Lakes. So that you can better understand aquatic habitats and their relation to fish management, we shall first discuss the major zones of lake ecosystems: the littoral, limnetic, and profundal.

The Littoral Zone

The **littoral** zone is the shallow margin of lake. It is characterized by rooted vegetation (Figure 9-1). The rooted plants usually are arranged in a well-ordered sequence, from shore toward open water, as emergent, floating, and submergent. Typical **emergent plants**, that is, those that extend above the water, include cattails and bulrushes. Characteristic floating plants are water lilies and duckweed. Plants that are completely underwater, such as pondweed and milfoil, are called **submergents**.

Because sunlight penetrates to the lake bottom in the littoral zone, it sustains a high level of photosynthetic activity. In this zone, floating microorganisms, known as **plankton**, frequently give the water a faint greenish-brown color. Plankton are largely incapable of independent movements and therefore are passively transported by water currents and wave action. Plankton consist of two groups: plants (chiefly algae), known as **phytoplankton**, and animals (primarily crustaceans and protozoa), known as **zooplankton**.

The Limnetic Zone

The **limnetic** zone is the region of open water beyond the littoral zone. It extends from the surface to the maximum depth at which there is sufficient sunlight for photosynthesis (Figure 9-1). At this depth, photosythesis balances respiration. It is known as the **compensation depth**. The light intensity here is only 1 percent of that of full sunlight. Although rooted plants are absent, this zone frequently contains numerous phytoplankton, mostly algae. In large lakes, the phytoplankton may actually produce more total biomass than the much larger rooted plants of the littoral zone. In spring, when nutrients and light are optimal, phytoplankton populations can "explode" to form **blooms**.

The limnetic zone derives its oxygen from the photosynthetic activity of phytoplankton and from the atmosphere immediately over the lake's surface. The atmosphere becomes a significant source of oxygen primarily when the water's surface is disturbed by wind and waves. Suspended among the phytoplankton are the zooplankton (animal plankton), primarily tiny crustaceans that form a trophic link between the phyto-

FIGURE **9-1** The principal zones of the lake ecosystem.

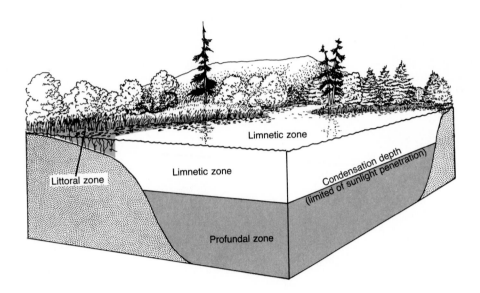

plankton food base and larger aquatic animals like fish (Figure 9-2).

The Profundal Zone

The **profundal** zone lies beneath the limnetic zone and extends to the bottom of the lake (Figure 9-1). Because of the limited penetration of sunlight, green plants are absent. In north-temperate latitudes, where winters are severe, this zone has the warmest water in winter and the coldest water in summer. Large numbers of bacteria and fungi occur in the bottom ooze, sometimes up to 1 billion per gram. These bacteria constantly decompose the organic matter (plant and animal remains and wastes) that accumulates on the bottom. Nitrogen and phosphorus are released during decomposition and are put back into circulation as soluble salts. In winter, the metabolism of aquatic life is reduced and the colder water has greater oxygen-dissolving capacity. At this time, therefore, oxygen usually is not an important limiting factor for fish if the ice cover remains clear of snow. In midsummer, however, when the metabolic rates of aquatic organisms are high, the oxygen-dissolving capability of the warm water is relatively low, and the oxygen-demanding processes of bacterial decay proceed at high levels. Under these conditions, oxygen depletion, or stagnation, of the profundal waters may cause extensive fish mortality.

Thermal Stratification

In temperate latitudes lakes show marked seasonal temperature changes.

WINTER. As temperatures drop below freezing, ice forms. Since ice is less dense than the water, it floats on the surface. The water at increasing depth below the ice is progressively warmer than the surface layer. The heaviest water, at the bottom of the lake, has a winter temperature of 4°C (39°F). All winter the water remains relatively stable (Figure 9-3).

SPRING. Following the ice melt, the surface water gradually warms to 4°C (39°F). At this point, all the water is of uniform temperature and density from the surface to the bottom (Figure 9-4). Strong spring winds stir the water causing a complete mixing of water, dissolved oxygen, and nutrients from the lake surface to the lake bottom. This mixing is called the **spring overturn**. As spring progresses, however, the surface water becomes warmer and lighter than the water at lower levels. As a result, the lake becomes thermally stratified again. The upper stratum usually has the highest oxygen concentration and is characterized by a temperature gradient of less than 1°C per meter of depth. It is called the **epilimnion** (upper lake). The middle layer of the lake, typified by a temperature gradient of more than 1°C per meter is the **thermocline**. The bottom layer of water, the **hypolimnion** (bottom lake), has a temperature gradient of less than 1°C per meter.

SUMMER. In summer the hypolimnion of many lakes becomes depleted of oxygen. This is caused by the biological oxygen demand (BOD) of bacterial decomposers, the lack of photosynthetic activity due to the absence of sunlight, and the minimal mixing with upper waters as a result of density differences (Figure 9-5).

AUTUMN. The surface waters gradually cool in the fall. Eventually a point is reached where the lake temperature is uniform from top to bottom. Because the water is now also of uniform density, it becomes well mixed by wind and wave action during the **fall overturn** (Figure 9-4). Nutrients, dissolved oxygen, and plankton become uniformly distributed.

FIGURE 9-2 Characteristic plants and animals of the lake ecosystem. 1. reed 2. cattail 3. yellow flag 4. adult caddis fly 5. moth 6. warbler 7. damsel fly 8. coot 9. dragon fly 10. mallard 11. mayfly 12. heron 13. frog 14. phytoplankton 15. water lilly 16. minnow 17. duckweed 18. snail 19. snail 20. hydra 21. may fly (immature) 22. water boatman 23. diving beetle 24. leech 25. stickleback 26. black bass 27. tadpoles 28. water strider 29. diving beetle larvae 30. gnat larvae 31. crayfish 32. fresh water shrimp 33. caddisfly larva

FIGURE 9-3 The lake ecosystem in the northern states in winter. Because water becomes less dense as its temperature drops below 4°C. (39°F.), the ice which forms at 0°C. (32°F.) is relatively light and floats at the surface. Note that the concentration of dissolved oxygen drops off sharply in the deeper part of the lake from about 10 ppm to only 1 ppm. Fish remain where the level of dissolved oxygen is high.

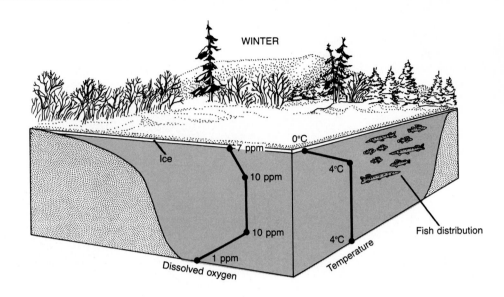

WINTER. As winter approaches, the lake gets colder until the water reaches a uniform temperature of 4°C (39°F), at which it has maximal density. As the surface cools, it becomes lighter. Eventually the surface water freezes. During the winter season, in ice-bound lakes there exists an inverted temperature stratification, with the coldest water (ice) at the surface and the warmest water (4°C, 39°F) on the bottom (Figure 9-3).

THE STREAM ECOSYSTEM

Although lakes and streams are both aquatic habitats and have many characteristics in common, they are, nevertheless, different in many aspects. Therefore, the problems facing the fisheries biologist in a lake may be quite different from those in a stream. Let us examine a few of the basic characteristics of streams.

Current

Water flow is the most important factor determining the kinds of organisms in the stream. Current velocity is determined by the stream gradient. Fish distribution is frequently correlated with gradient flow. For example, black bass are virtually absent from Ohio streams where the gradient is below 0.5 meters or above 4.8 meters per kilometer (or below 3 or above 25 feet per mile). The highest bass populations occur in sections where the gradient ranges from 1.3 meters to 3.7 meters per kilometer (7 to 20 feet per mile).

Land–Water Interchange

The amount of shoreline per unit volume of water is much greater in streams than in lakes. Therefore, streams are rather open ecosystems. Materials are con-

FIGURE 9-4 The lake ecosystem in spring and autumn. Note the uniform distribution of temperature and dissolved oxygen from top to bottom due to the "turnover" or thorough mixing of the water. Fish are also uniformly distributed in the vertical dimension.

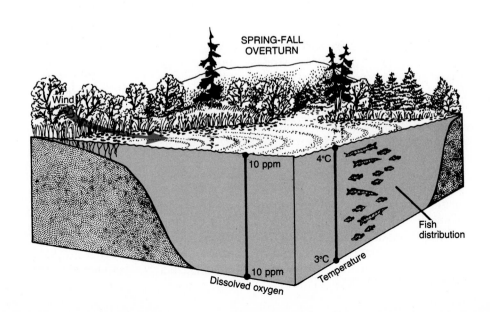

FIGURE 9-5 The lake ecosystem in summer. Cross-sectional view showing thermal stratification and the vertical distribution of dissolved oxygen.

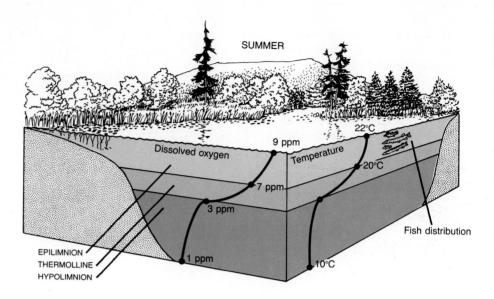

stantly being received from the terrestrial ecosystems that border it. Stream food chains, for example, receive a considerable portion of their basic energy supply from materials originating on land—leaves that fall into the water in autumn or organic debris (stems, nuts, twigs, seeds, dead weeds, cow manure, and the bodies of insects, worms, and mice) that is washed into the stream during the spring runoff. In fact, many of the primary consumers in a stream consume **detritus** (decomposing organic material) rather than living aquatic vegetation. Streams do have their own producers in the form of specialized **diatoms** that form a crust on rocks and plants and **water moss**, which sometimes forms a bright green, slippery covering on a stream bottom. However, these producers typically supply only a fraction of the energy required by stream life.

Dissolved Oxygen

Streams are usually very well aerated. Flowing water, the relative shallowness of the stream, and the large surface area exposed to the atmosphere all contribute to oxygenation. All things being equal, the waters of shallow, fast-moving streams have much higher oxygen levels than those of deep, sluggish streams. The photosynthetic production of oxygen is not nearly as important as it is in a pond or lake. Because of the thorough mixing of stream water, oxygen depletion occurs less frequently than in lakes. However, stream fish are very sensitive to even slight reductions of oxygen levels. Therefore, if a stream becomes polluted with oxygen-demanding organic material, such as human sewage or the waste from slaughterhouses, pulp mills, and canneries, the oxygen reduction that results may trigger a massive fish kill (Chapter 8).

Longitudinal Zonation

Fish populations frequently reflect the changing physical (chemical, thermal, and so on) character of the stream. Several years ago, a study was made of the fish distribution in Little Stony Creek near Mountain Lake, Virginia. It showed that the distribution was correlated with changes in pH, water temperature, and velocity of the current (Figure 9-6). Thus, the colder, more acidic upper stretches of the creek supported brook trout. In the warmer, alkaline lower stretches, the book trout were missing, but seven other species were present, including the rainbow trout, several kinds of minnows, and the common sucker.

THE REPRODUCTIVE POTENTIAL OF FISH

Like most organisms, freshwater fish have great ability to reproduce. For example, a 16-kilogram (35-pound) female muskellunge may produce 225,000 eggs during a single breeding season. Some bass nests in Michigan contain more than 4,000 young per nest. In some species, like the bluegill, nests are built very close together. Such gregarious breeding behavior promotes reproductive success because an optimal spawning habitat can be shared by a large number of individuals. The reproductive characteristics of some species of fish are summarized in Table 9-1.

ENVIRONMENTAL RESISTANCE ENCOUNTERED BY FISH

Were it not for the extensive mortality caused by environmental resistance, the lake basins and river channels would be choked with fish. Tagging studies have

FIGURE 9-6   Longitudinal differences in temperature and pH along a 14-mile stretch of Little Stony Creek, Virginia.

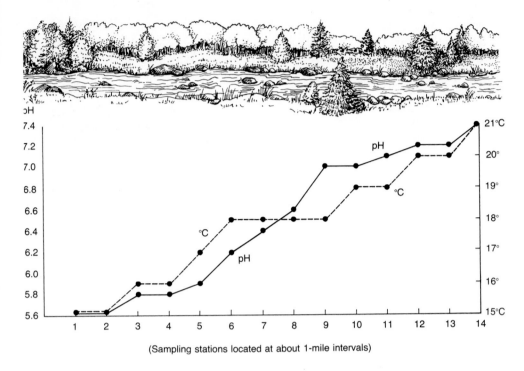

(Sampling stations located at about 1-mile intervals)

revealed that roughly 70 percent of a given fish population dies each year. Thus, if 1 million young of a given species hatch, 300,000 will be alive at the end of the first year, 90,000 by the end of the second, but only 6 by the end of the tenth. Let us now examine some of the major environmental factors that cause mortality in fish populations.

Water Pollution

More than 30 million fish are killed by water pollution in the United States each year. In the previous chapter, we described fish kills caused by industrial and municipal pollutants. Here we shall describe mortality caused by eutrophication, sedimentation, and acid deposition.

Table 9-1   Reproductive Characteristics of Major Species of Fish

Common Name	Reproductive Age (or Length)	Spawning Time	Number of Eggs	Type of Reproduction
Bass, largemouth	2 years	Spring	2,000–100,000	Nest
Bass, smallmouth	2 years	Spring	2,000–20,800	Nest
Bluegill	1 year	May–August	2,300–67,000	Community nest
Carp	12 inches	Spring	790,000–2,000,000	Eggs, scattered
Channel catfish	12 inches	Spring	2,500–70,000	Nests
Muskellunge	3–4 years	Spring	10,000–265,000	Eggs, scattered
Northern Pike	2–3 years	Spring	2,000–600,000	Eggs, scattered in marsh
Salmon, chinook	4–5 years	Fall	3,000–4,000	Eggs buried in gravel
Salmon, coho	3–4 years	Fall	3,000–4,000	Eggs buried in gravel
Trout, brook	2 years	Fall	25–5,600	Eggs buried in gravel
Trout, brown	3 years	Fall	200–6,000	Eggs buried in gravel
Trout, rainbow	3 years	Spring	500–9,000	Eggs buried in gravel
Trout, lake	5–7 years	Winter	6,000	Eggs scattered over gravel
Walleye	3 years	Spring	35,300–615,000	Eggs scattered

Source: What Fish is This, Illinois Dept. of Conservation, June, 1986.

EUTROPHICATION. As you recall, the enrichment of a body of water with nutrients that promotes the excessive growth of aquatic vegetation is known as **eutrophication**. Dense algal blooms form near the surface, preventing sunlight from reaching the billions of algae at lower depths. As a result, algae and submerged vegetation sink to the lake bottom, and form a dense organic ooze. Billions of bacteria in the bottom sediment decompose this material, consuming the oxygen dissolved in the surrounding water. As a result, the oxygen concentration in the deep water (hypolimnion) may fall rapidly from 7 to 2 ppm or less. If the oxygen levels fall below a fish's range of tolerance and there is no place to go, fish die in large numbers. Eventually the dead fish float to shore, decompose, begin to smell, and attract flies.

SEDIMENTATION. Many tons of soil are washed into nearby lakes and streams by runoff waters as a result of abusive land practices, whether on a farm, a mine, or an urban construction site. Sediment depresses the photosynthetic activity of aquatic plants because it reduces sunlight penetration of the water. This, in turn, causes levels of dissolved oxygen to drop sharply. This is especially stressful to fish like trout and salmon which require a minimum of 5 ppm of dissolved oxygen. Although fish may tolerate turbidities of up to 100,000 ppm for brief periods, concentrations of 100–200 ppm are harmful if they persist for any length of time.

Thousands of fish die annually in American lakes and streams from asphyxiation caused by silt-clogged gills (Figure 9-7). Suspended sediment also interferes with the reproductive behavior of fish, which depend on visual cues provided by the gravel and sand of the stream of lake bed, as well as on the color, shape, and behavior of the sex partner. Vast beds of inshore aquatic

FIGURE 9-7 Fish kill caused by sediment. These fish were choked to death when sediment clogged their gills during a flooding of the Iowa River in New Mexico.

vegetation that were once important spawning beds for Great Lakes fish have been smothered by sediment. Mud may also cover fertilized eggs and reduce hatching success. A study of trout reproduction in Bluewater Creek, Montana, for instance, showed that egg hatching success was highest (up to 97 percent) where siltation was minimal (Figure 9-8). The larvae of aquatic insects, such as may flies and stone flies, which are favored fish foods, may also be destroyed by silt. Finally, mud sharply reduces the visual range of predatory fish,

FIGURE 9-8 Effect of sediment from irrigation runoff on a Montana trout stream.

EFFECT OF SEDIMENT FROM IRRIGATION RUNOFF IN MONTANA TROUT STREAM

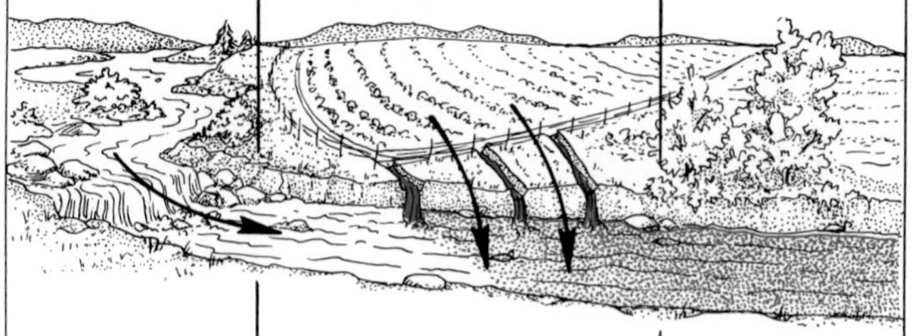

Upstream		Irrigation runoff		Downstream
18		Sediment concentration (ppm)		319
1.2		Average number of trout per mile		2,700
216		Maximum daily sediment load (tons per day)		6
7		Average number of rough fish per mile		378

like bass, pike, and muskellunge, in their search for the smaller fish on which they feed.

ACID DEPOSITION. Can the burning of coal in an Ohio steel plant cause the death of trout high in the Adirondack Mountains of New York? Although it seems highly improbable, the answer is "yes." The sulfur dioxide gas that is released from the smokestacks undergoes chemical reactions with oxygen to form sulfuric acid and water. Prevailing winds carry the acid droplets northeastward in clouds to a point high over the Adirondacks. Rain (or snow) then washes the acid into the lakes.

Normal, unpolluted rain has a pH of 5.6—slightly acid because carbon dioxide is dissolved in it to form carbonic acid. (The chemistry of pH is discussed in Chapter 18.) However, much of the **acid rain** in the eastern states has a pH below 4—about 100 times as acid as normal rain.

The effects of acid rain were not fully appreciated until the 1970s. Biologists have found that when the pH of lake water falls as low as 5, fish begin to die. The pH of many Adirondack lakes is below 5. Under such conditions, lake trout become deformed and embryos suffer high mortality.

The acidic water from rain and snowmelt also affects the chemical composition of the water. As the water drains off the land, the acids dissolve toxic metals from the soil and carry them into lakes and streams. Aluminum, leached from the soil, for example, causes mucus to build up on the gills of fish. As a result, the fish suffocate. Aluminum is especially troublesome in the spring when the snows begin to melt, sending torrents of acidic water across the soil and eventually into lakes and streams.

A recent survey conducted by the New York State Bureau of Fisheries revealed that many of the 2,877 Adirondack lakes above 2,000 feet in elevation were devoid of fish. Lakes like Avalanch and Coldman were once famous for their brook trout. Today not one trout swims in their waters. The Adirondack lakes are not exceptional. Many lakes in the northern parts of Minnesota, Wisconsin, and Michigan are also threatened.

The elimination of a species of fish from a lake may not occur suddenly. Instead it may develop gradually over a period of years due to the inability of fish to spawn successfully. The effects of increasing acidity on fish populations in George Lake, Ontario, are shown in Figure 9-9. If present trends continue, scientists believe that acid rain will eliminate all fish from 40,000 Canadian lakes by the year 2000. (For more on acid deposition, see Chapter 18.)

Winterkill

Another environmental factor that controls fish populations is winterkill. During the long winters of the northern states, an icy barrier seals lakes off from atmospheric oxygen. However, as long as the ice remains clear of snow, sufficient sunlight may penetrate the ice to sustain photosynthesis (Figure 9-10). As a result, oxygen levels remain adequate. Snow, however, forms an opaque barrier that prevents sunlight penetration. If photosynthesis falls, so do oxygen levels, often resulting in heavy fish kills, especially if the lake is fertile and shallow. The decay of dead vegetation worsens the problem. As winter progresses, oxygen levels may drop to 5 ppm, at which point many of the more sensitive fish die; the more resistant fish, such as carp and bullheads, may die later if levels drop to about 2 to 3 ppm.

A classic example of winterkill occurred several years ago in a shallow southern Minnesota lake that had a dense population of bullheads. Although the ice cover that formed in November ultimately became 50 cen-

FIGURE 9-9 Effect of increasing acidity (decreasing pH) of water on fish populations of George Lake, Ontario.

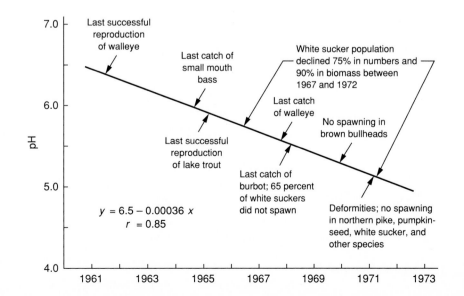

Case Study:
Salmon Migration—The Swim for Survival

The salmon is an **anadromous** fish—it spends most of its growing years in the ocean and, after attaining sexual maturity, ascends freshwater streams to spawn. The chinook, or king salmon, is a handsome Pacific species that may attain a weight of up to 45 kilograms (100 pounds). On the breeding grounds, the female excavates a shallow trough, the **redd**, in the sandy or gravelly bed of a swiftly flowing stream emptying into the Pacific Ocean in California, in British Columbia, or in Oregon and Washington (Figure 1). The female may deposit several thousand eggs in the redd. After the male has fertilized them, the female covers them with a protective layer of gravel. Following a 2 month incubation period, the eggs hatch and the young gradually move downstream. They suffer heavy losses from predation by fish, birds, and mammals. In some streams, such as the Columbia,

many young salmon are killed by **nitrogen intoxication**, resulting from the high levels of nitrogen in the turbulent waters immediately below dams. Only 10 percent of the salmon fry ultimately reach the ocean.

Many salmon move a long way from the mouth of their native stream. For example, adult salmon tagged off Baranof Island, Alaska, were recovered in the Columbia River of Washington, 3200 kilometers (2,000 miles) away. Salmon remain in the Pacific Ocean for 4 to 7 years, feeding intensively on small fishes such as herring and anchovies, floating in ocean currents.

When they become sexually mature, the salmon swim to the Pacific Coast and then ascend their native streams, apparently recognizing them by their distinctive smell. The hatching fish apparently learn how their native stream smells and remember it for the rest of their lives. The adult salmon gradually make their

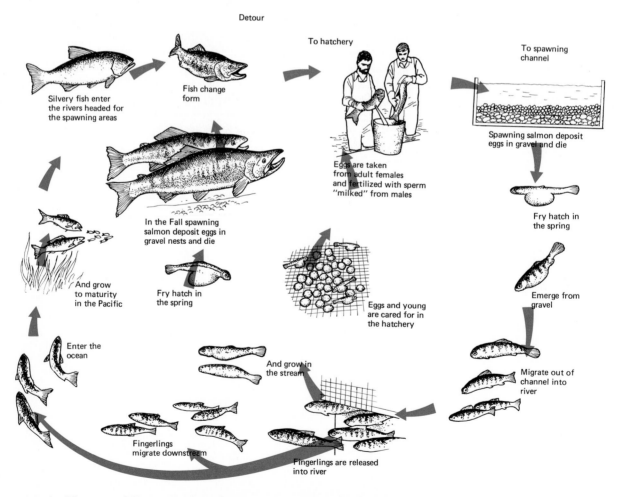

FIGURE 1   The natural live cycle of the Pacific salmon (left). Fisheries biologists at the Feather River hatchery in California have modified this natural cycle as indicated.

way to the shallow headwaters near the site of their hatching. This is accomplished only after they have negotiated all sorts of obstacles, including waterfalls, predators (gulls, ospreys, and bears), anglers, pollution, the nets of research biologists, and dams (Figure 2). Once they arrive at the headwater, they immediately spawn and die, thus completing their life cycle.

Human activities can seriously alter the salmon cycles. Some years ago, railroad builders accidentally set off an avalanche of rock and rubble that clogged up the narrow channel of the Fraser River at Hell's Gate, British Columbia. As a result, the sockeye salmon run was hopelessly blocked, and thousands of fish, loaded with eggs and sperm, died below the rock slide, unable to press on to their spawning grounds.

The erection of dozens of power dams (such as the 166-meter [550 foot]-tall Grand Coulee on the Columbia) across the migration path of the Pacific salmon has cut off considerable numbers from their spawning areas. In other rivers, fish ladders have been constructed to enable the fish to reach their spawning grounds, but even so salmon have never fully recovered (Figure 2). High water temperatures may be just as effective a barrier as a dam. Water temperatures of 20°C (70°F) or above blocks the upstream movement of sockeye salmon from the Columbia River into the Okanogan River. When temperatures drop below 20°C (70°F), however, the migration is quickly resumed. In recent years, there has been a marked decline in the once abundant Columbia River salmon harvest. Where once there were 10 to 15 million salmon, today there are only about 2.5 million. Thermal and concrete barriers to migration, together with pollution and overfishing, have been important factors in the decline.

FIGURE 2 King (chinook) salmon leaps up the top step of a fish ladder at the Red Bluff Diversion Dam during a late spring spawning run. This fish ladder enables salmon to move upstream beyond the dam and eventually spawn in California's Sacramento River.

Case Study:
The Sea Lamprey—Scourge of the Great Lakes

Imagine a predator so efficient that it could destroy 97 percent of the lake trout population of the Great Lakes in only 21 years! That predator is the sea lamprey—an olive-gray, blood sucking killer, which completed its invasion of the Great Lakes in the 1950s. The lamprey is a primitive, jawless vertebrate with a slender, eel-like body. The muscular funnel around its circular mouth enables it to attach firmly to its prey (Figures 1 and 2). It moves its piston-like tongue, armed with numerous hard, rasping teeth, back and forth through the lake trout's tissues, tearing flesh and blood vessels and causing severe bleeding. An anticoagulant prevents the blood from clotting. After gorging itself on a meal of blood and body fluid, the predator may

drop off its host and permit it to swim weakly away. The trout may die from the direct predatory attack, or it may eventually succumb to bacterial and fungal infections that become established in the open wounds. During its short adult life of about 15 months, the average lamprey kills about 40 pounds of trout, salmon, and other Great Lakes fish. Even if a lake trout survives, the ugly scar left on its body would scarcely be admired by the grocery-buying homemaker.

The Great Lakes lampreys spend their entire life cycle in fresh water. When sexually mature, the adults swim up tributary streams to mate, spawn, and die. After hatching from the eggs, the larval lampreys are needle-thin and about 3 millimeters (one-eighth

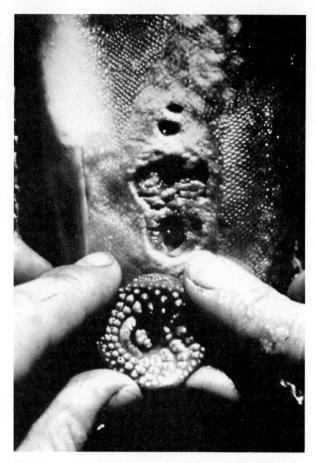

FIGURE 1 Close-up of the muscular funnel, mouth and rasping "tongue" of the sea lamprey. The end of the piston-like tongue is visible inside the circular mouth in the center of the funnel. Note the wounds caused by the lamprey on the lake trout.

FIGURE 2 Lamprey adheres to netted lake trout.

inch) long. They drift downstream until they come to a muddy bottom. They then burrow tail first into the mud, allowing only their heads to remain exposed to the current. During this time they feed on small algae, insects, worms, and crustaceans. Several years later, when they have grown to the size of a pencil, they acquire the muscular funnel and rasping tongue of the adult, emerge from their burrows, and swim into the open waters of the lake to prey on fish (Figure 3).

The lamprey originally occurred in the shallow waters off the Atlantic seaboard from Florida to Labrador, in the waters of the St. Lawrence River, and in Lake Ontario at the eastern end of the Great Lakes chain. For many centuries, the westward extension of the lamprey's range into Lake Erie was blocked by Niagara Falls. However, in 1833 the Welland Canal was constructed to promote commercial shipping. Unfortunately, however, the canal also provided the lamprey with an invasion channel to Lake Erie (Figure 4).

The lamprey's colonization of Lake Erie was a

slow process, probably because of a lack of suitable tributary spawning streams. However, once it invaded Lake Huron, it spread rapidly into Lake Michigan and Lake Superior. By 1950 the lamprey was found in the western end of Lake Superior and had completed its Great Lakes invasion (Figure 4). Its predatory activity soon threatened the multi-million-dollar Great Lakes trout fishing industry with total collapse. The annual catch declined form 4,544 metric tons (10 million pounds) in 1940 to 151 metric tons (one-third of a million pounds) in 1961, a 97 percent reduction in only 21 years! Idle nets rotted along the waterfront. Veteran fishermen, too old to acquire new skills, went on relief. Many of the younger men moved to Minneapolis, Milwaukee, Chicago, and Detroit in search of work.

In 1955 the Great Lakes Fishery Commission was formed by treaty between the United States and Canada to control the sea lamprey. Members of the commission included all the Great Lakes states and the province of Ontario. A variety of control strategies were tried. Adult lampreys were netted and seined. They were even shocked with "electric fences" as they tried to move up their spawning

FIGURE 3 Life cycle of the sea lamprey.

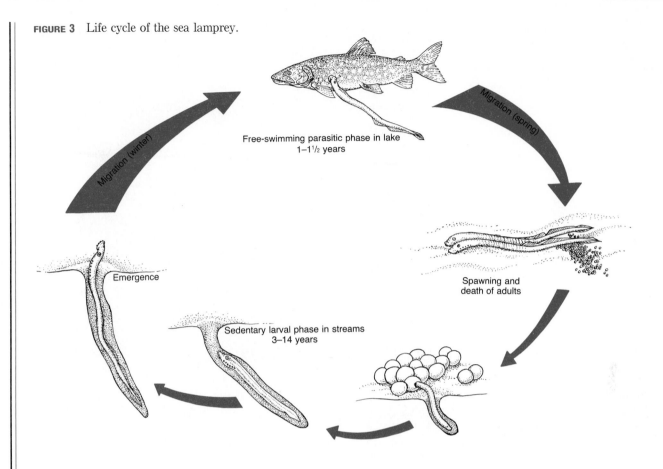

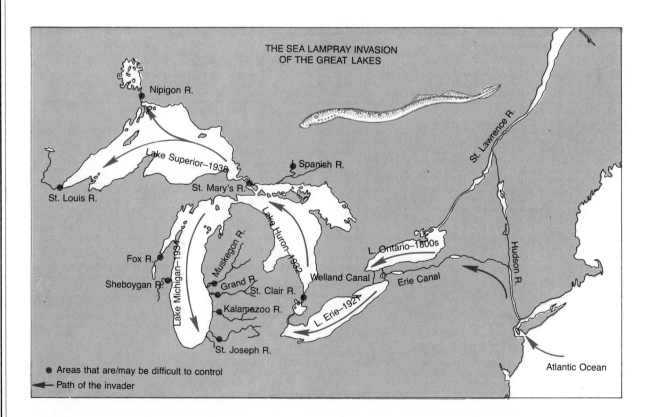

FIGURE 4 Sea lamprey invasion of the Great Lakes.

FIGURE 5 Electric "fence" placed across Michigan stream near its entrance to Lake Michigan. As the lampreys swim through the "fence" they are stunned by an electric charge, float to the surface, and are easily removed.

streams (Figure 5). These methods, however, had only limited success. It was decided, therefore, to try chemical control—to use a **lampricide**. From 1951 to 1959, therefore, more than 6,000 compounds were tested as potential lamprey killers. Eventually an obscure poison, known as TFM, was selected. TFM was essentially nontoxic to humans, as well as to game fish and their food organisms, such as minnows and aquatic insects. But it was lethal to lampreys. Larvae treated with low levels of TFM popped out of their burrows and quickly died from hemorrhage.

By 1960 the Great Lakes Commission had treated all of the lamprey-infested tributaries of Lake Superior with TFM. Only two years later, this chemical had reduced the number of spawning lampreys in these streams by 85 percent.

In the ensuing years, the lampricide was also used on tributary streams of Lake Michigan (1963), Lake Huron (1970), and Lake Ontario (1972)—with equally effective results. Ohio began chemical control of the lamprey on Conneaut Creek (Ashtabula County), a stream that flows into Lake Erie, in 1986.

timeters (20 inches) thick, oxygen levels initially were adequate. During the second week of January, however, a storm covered the ice with a 6 inch layer of snow. Two days later, oxygen levels fell sharply. After the ice melted in spring, thousands of dead bullheads littered the shore. Not one fish survived.

Predation by Native Animals

Fish are subjected to intense predatory pressure from other fish and from reptiles, birds, and mammals. A 6-inch muskellunge will consume 15 minnows a day! Three thousand fish are eaten by a walleye by the time it is 3 years old. When other food is scarce, many fish resort to cannibalism. Smaller species may eat the eggs of larger species, which as adults regularly feed on the smaller forms.

Wading birds and other water fowl, such as egrets, herons, and ducks, consume large numbers of fish. A single merganser (a diving duck) may eat more than

35,000 fish annually! Bear, otter, fisher, and mink prey extensively on fish, especially during droughts, when water levels are low, and the fish are easily caught. The Alaskan brown bear can easily eat 15 large salmon per day.

Predation by Exotics: The River Ruff

A number of exotic species of fish have been willfully and accidentally introduced into our nation's lakes and streams. Several have adversely affected the reproduction, growth, and survival of some of our most highly prized native fishes. One of the most recent is the **river ruff**, an import from Europe.

The river ruff may have been accidentally introduced into Lake Superior in 1987 from a cargo slick that docked at Duluth, Minnesota. The ruff is a potential threat to the multi-million-dollar commercial fishery of the Great Lakes because it is a ravenous consumer of the eggs of the whitefish and other species. Since the

FIGURE 9-10   Winter kill of fish.

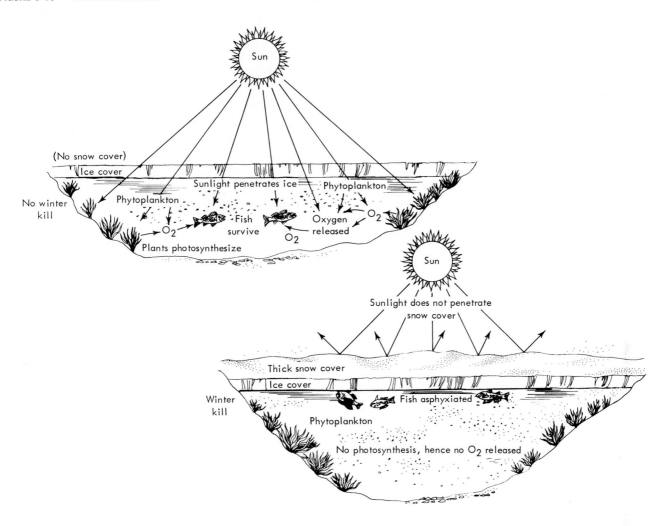

ruff becomes sexually mature when only 1–year old, it has a reproductive edge on most species of native fish. In 1989, only 2 years after its introduction, the ruff's population had increased sharply in the harbor of Duluth. To control this problem, fisheries biologists planned to reduce the number of muskies and pike that anglers can take in Duluth harbor. They hope that these fish will prey on the ruff.

Predation by Humans

Fishing has been a major factor in the decline of many of our freshwater commercial and game fishes. The classic example of extreme fishing pressure is offered by anglers on the opening weekend of the trout season. During their enthusiastic quest for the king of American game fish, they frequently stand shoulder to shoulder along stream margins.

Fishing pressure is increasing. The number of licensed anglers has risen from 10 to 40 million within the last three decades. One of every six Americans tries his or her luck with a hook and line each year. And with the nation's growing population, the increase in leisure hours and mobility, and the desperate need for a release from urban tension, the impact of the human predator on fish populations is bound to intensify.

FISHERIES MANAGEMENT
The Job of the Fish Manager

So you finally landed that scrappy 2.2-kilogram (5-pound) bass! It was quite a thrill, wasn't it? Maybe the fight lasted for only 3 minutes. Nevertheless, behind that fight were probably thousands of hours of research and management on the part of university biologists or state and federal conservation staffs who made possible the population of large bass from which your catch was taken. Many of these professional people have Ph.D.s in fisheries management of related areas. The fisheries manager is knowledgeable about chemistry, botany, zoology, ecology, and statistics—and, perhaps most important, the art of getting along with people.

The fishery manager has a challenging job—to protect and upgrade fisheries in the face of rising angling pressure, which is expected to increase 35 percent by the year 2000. One reason the manager's job is so demanding is that each fishery, whether in a lake, stream, or impoundment, is a unique system and should be managed according to its particular needs. Another reason the manager's job is taxing is that the successful production of just a single species, depends on the interaction of a whole series of chemical, physical, and biological factors. Among these are lake (or stream) size, bottom, and depth; water currents; water temperature; dissolved oxygen; water acidity or alkalinity; water pollution; water fertility (dissolved nutrients); shelter (cover); food availability; predator–prey relationships; reproductive potential; mortality rates; fishing pressure; fishing regulations; species composition; population size; population age structure; and growth rates. In the next section, we shall see how the fisheries manager acquires information on some of the factors that determine successful fish production.

Getting Information on Fish Populations

NUMBERS AND KINDS OF FISH. Before a fish population of a lake or stream can be effectively managed, the fisheries biologist must know which species are present and the size of their populations. Knowledge of the total fish biomass in kilograms per hectare (pounds per acre) or in lake or mile of stream is also essential. On the basis of such data, the fish manager can determine (1) whether or not the body of water should be stocked, and if so, with what species, (2) whether or not undesirable species, such as carp, should be eliminated, (3) whether the fish habitat should be upgraded, and (4) whether fishing regulations, such as size limits and number of fish taken per day, should be revised.

Roughly 90 percent of such information is derived by **shocking fish** (Figure 9-11). Power is supplied by gasoline or a battery. Electrodes on a boom shocker are suspended from a boom mounted on the front of the boat. The electrodes pass through the water as the boat moves. The fish that are stunned by the electrical current float to the surface and are scooped up with nets. These fish are counted and then released unharmed.

Fish ladders have been constructed on some salmon streams, particularly in the West, to permit fish to swim past dams and move upstream to spawn. Observation windows have been placed at the upper end of such ladders to permit researchers to identify and count the fish.

The **echo sounder** generates sound waves that are reflected from the lake or river bottom, from plankton, and from the bodies of fish. The sound echoes are recorded on charts or tapes. A computer then integrates and interprets the data. Echo-sounding equipment are

FIGURE 9-11 Electro-shocking. These men are gathering information on the fish population of a Michigan stream. This boom-shocker generates a weak electrical current which stuns fish swimming nearby. The fishery biologists are poised with nets, ready to scoop up the shocked fish.

used intensively in the Great Lakes by fisheries biologists, who make soundings along predetermined grid lines. The information obtained is then used to make three-dimensional "pictures" of fish densities, as shown in Figure 9-12.

AGE DETERMINATION. Information on age can be obtained by counting the "year markers" on ear bones, vertebrae, and scales. Figure 9-13 shows a highly enlarged scale taken from a 40-centimeter (16-inch) largemouth bass. Notice the concentric growth rings. During a growth spurt, such as occurs in summer, the rings are spaced far apart. In winter, when growth virtually stops, the rings are very close together. Each dark band in the scale in Figure 9-13 represents a winter season or the end of one year's growth.

If such "scale reading" shows that a given fish population is dominated by older fish, the manager knows that the population is shrinking. This may be the result of siltation of spawning beds or some other form of environmental resistance. On the other hand, if young fish are most numerous, the population is expanding. Based on this information, fishing pressure can be adjusted to meet specific objectives of the fishery.

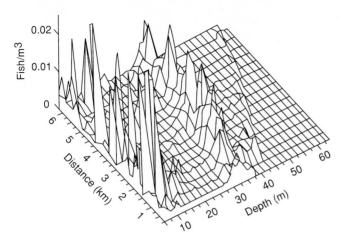

FIGURE 9-12 Three dimensional "picture" of fish population densities in the Great Lakes made with the aid of computer and sonar. Note that the populations showed a two-layered phenomenon, being relatively high at water depths of about 10 meters (33 feet) and 40 meters (132 feet), but relatively low at intervening depths.

GROWTH RATE DETERMINATION. The rate of fish growth is determined by three major factors: (1) the species present, (2) the length of the growing season, and (3) the amount of food available.

Species. Each species has a basic rate of growth that is inherited. For example, a spotted bass grows faster than a smallmouth bass, but a largemouth bass grows even faster.

Growing Season. The growing season is the period during which the water temperature is at least 18°C (65°F). The farther north the fish lives, the shorter its season of growth; the farther south it lives, the longer the growing season. For example, in California's Big Sage Reservoir, near the Oregon border, bass average 17.5 centimeters (7 inches) when 3 years old. However, in Clear Lake (Lake County), roughly 400 kilometers (250 miles) to the south, bass that age are twice as long.

Food. The food available to a fish is, in part, dependent upon the fertility of the water. A rainbow trout living in a nutrient-poor mountain stream in California may be only 5 inches long when 2 years old. However, a rainbow trout of the same age from fertile Lake Almanor, north of Sacramento, may be three times that size.

The fish manager, of course, can easily determine growth rates by measuring (and/or weighing) a fish and reading its scales to determine its age. Suppose, for example that the bass population in a given lake is growing too slowly, and only "runts" are being caught by the angler. What can be done?

1. A strain of bass that grow more rapidly might be introduced. For example, a fast-growing strain of Florida largemouth bass has been introduced into California waters with great success.

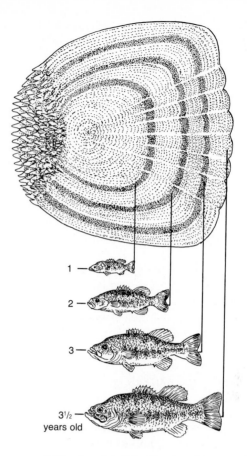

FIGURE 9-13 Age determination in a large mouth bass. A scale from a 16-inch largemouth bass was removed and examined under the microscope. Each dark band, known as an annular ring, represents the end of one year of growth. This bass was about 3¹/₂ years old.

2. More food can be introduced. For example, young bluegills might be introduced to serve as food for game fish.

3. On the other hand, there may be plenty of prey fish, but the bass simply cannot find them because the dense growth of aquatic weeds (thanks to the eutrophication process) provides the bluegill with so many hiding places. In that event, the fisheries manager might thin out the weeds by anchoring sheets of plastic on the lake bottom in the littoral zone or could find ways to reduce nutrient pollution.

Protective Laws

Fish populations can also be controlled by regulations that limit the take—the size and number of fish an angler can take home. Closed seasons are also used to protect species at critical times. Fisheries biologists have long recognized that when female bass or walleye are taken when swollen with eggs, anglers are removing much more than a single adult. They are also removing hundreds of future young fish. Over the years, certain fishing techniques have also been outlawed, such

FIGURE 9-14 Size limits on northern pike have very little, if any effect on the number of northerns that die during a given year. Even if no fishing at all is permitted, the morality of a given northern pike population will be the same.

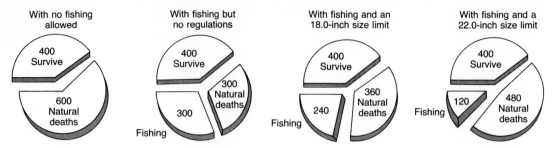

as seining, poisoning, dynamiting, spearing, and using multiple-hook lines.

In recent years, fisheries biologists have been experimenting with more liberalized regulations on many species of warm-water fish. In many states, size limits on panfish (sunfish, bluegills, rock bass, and crappies) have been lifted, permitting fish of any size, from runts to giants, to be taken. On the other hand, minimum-size limits have been placed on predatory species such as bass, pike, walleyes, and muskies. The main objective of these regulations is to ensure the presence of large predators that can control populations of panfish. Such regulations provide more opportunities for anglers to land a lunker bass or pike. However, researchers have shown that size limit regulations do not affect the survival rate of northern pike (Figure 9-14). The effects of creel limits, varying fish methods and gear, open and closed seasons, and winter fishing on fish populations are continually being evaluated (Table 9-2).

The most ecologically sound and hence most effective, regulations are those that are tailored to a given body of water. Such regulations are formulated on a lake-by-lake or stream-by-stream basis. Unfortunately, however, their administration and enforcement are often difficult.

Artificial Propagation and Stocking

In the early history of fish management, it seemed logical to biologists and anglers alike that if human beings could supplement the natural reproduction of a given fish species by artificial methods and introduce those artificially propagated fish into lakes and rivers, fish populations would be augmented and the angling success of fishermen virtually assured. In 1937 Wisconsin set a national record by stocking more than 1 billion fish. Unfortunately, however, after intensive studies of population dynamics, it has become apparent that this technique is often a dismal failure, especially if the objective is to increase the size of an already well-established species. Moreover, the cost of artificial propagation in terms of facilities, maintenance, staff, rearing, and eventual distribution of the young fish is almost prohibitive. (It costs $2 to stock one 25-centimeter (10-inch) muskie. Salmon may cost $6 apiece.) For these reasons, artificial propagation is not well regarded by some fisheries biologists.

Fish stocking can be valuable in some cases. It may be used to reestablish fish populations that have been destroyed by predators, drought, pollution, disease, or some other environmental factor. Fisheries biolo-

Table 9-2 Typical Fishing Regulations for a Northeastern State

Species	Season	Daily Limit	Minimum Size
Largemouth bass	May 7–March 1	5	None
Bluegill, sunfish, crappie, perch	Open all year	50 in all	None
Catfish	Open all year	10	None
Muskellunge	May 28–Nov. 30	1	32 inches
Northern pike	May 7–March 1	5	None
Wallaye	May 7–March 1	5	None
Lake trout	Jan. 2–Sept. 30	2	17 inches
Trout (other than lake trout)	May 7–Sept. 30	3 in all	Brook trout—10 inches Brown trout—13 inches Rainbow trout—6 inches

gists may stock southern farm ponds with tilapia to get rid of excess aquatic vegetation. They may stock reservoirs with predatory species to reduce the number of bluegill. Reservoirs may be stocked with rainbow, brook, or brown trout if the water temperature is suitable. Largemouth bass may be stocked in reservoirs and farm ponds where water gets too warm for trout.

The U.S. Fish and Wildlife Service maintains a number of salmon hatcheries along the Columbia and Sacramento rivers. Their performance in many instances has been poor. Hatchery-raised fish can spread disease to native fish and often are less well suited to streams they are released into. Without the artificial propagation of trout, the thrill of hooking one of those scrappy fish would soon be nothing but a memory for most anglers. For instance, in Virginia, about 850,000 catchable trout are stocked annually in 185 streams and 20 lakes. Currently, both federal and state fish hatcheries rear brook, brown, cutthroat, rainbow, and lake trout. In mountainous areas of Wyoming and Colorado, trout fingerlings may be stocked by means of aerial drops. In Colorado nearly all of the trout stocked in its rivers are caught in just a few months!

The official policy of federal hatcheries is to propagate trout to fill the following needs: (1) to stock trout in suitable waters in which they do not occur; such waters may be newly created reservoirs or may be water from which competitive rough fish have been removed; (2) to stock trout in waters where conditions for growth are good but where natural spawning sites are inadequate; growth usually is rapid, but nevertheless, such streams must be restocked at intervals of 1 to 3 years; (3) to stock trout in waters where fishing pressure is heavy but there is no natural production. This is sometimes known as **put-and-take-stocking**. The trout planted are of catchable size. Most of them are caught the same season they are planted. Put-and-take-stocking is common in urban areas. For instance, thousands of legal-sized rainbow trout are planted annually in lakes in the metropolitan area of Denver, Colorado. Several of our nation's sportsmen presidents, such as Dwight Eisenhower and Lyndon Johnson, have waxed eloquent about the fishing potential of a particular trout stream on the basis of the lunkers they hooked only minutes after strategic stocking by publicity-sensitive conservation officials!

Local sportsmen's groups can greatly increase trout populations in their favorite streams by using a simple but ingenious device called a **Vibert box** (Figure 9-15). This is a plastic box with slots on all sides to permit the free flow of stream water. About 100 trout eggs are placed in the box, which is then planted in the gravel bed of the stream. The Vibert box: (1) permits the eggs to develop under natural conditions, (2) protects the eggs from predation, and (3) is inexpensive. (One trout fishermen's club planted 50,000 brown trout eggs by this method at a cost of only $300. Hatchery production methods would have been 10 times as expensive.) Ninety percent of the eggs in a Vibert box actually hatch compared to a natural hatching success of only 15 percent. The newly hatched fish (fry) are immediately conditioned to their environment of dissolved oxygen, water temperature, water chemistry, and stream flow. They therefore have greater ability to resist environmental stress than hatchery-reared stock.

Introductions

An **introduction** is the stocking of a fish in a new region. It is widely practiced in the United States. Thirteen of the 189 species of fish occurring in Illinois have been introduced. The introduced species may not always be native to this country.

NATIVE INTRODUCTIONS. Coho salmon and chinook salmon have been successfully introduced into the Great Lakes from the Pacific Coast. Many lakes in Minnesota, Michigan, New York, and other states that had no walleye or muskie fishing now produce trophy-sized specimens, thanks to introductions from other waters in this country. New reservoirs are frequently stocked with species that were not originally found at the site. The great success of warm-water sport fishing in California has been possible largely because of native introductions. Twenty-one of 24 warm-water species in California were introduced from states east of the Rocky Mountains, mostly in the late 1800's (Table 9-3).

INTRODUCTION OF EXOTICS: FOR BETTER OR FOR WORSE? The U.S. Fish and Wildlife Service is increasingly concerned with the "biological pollution" of native fish populations with **exotic** (nonnative) species. Some of the foreign fish were deliberately introduced by fisheries biologists to provide a desirable game or food fish or to aid in controlling an environmental problem. On the other hand, many exotics have been accidentally introduced. In either case, a number of the introductions have been highly destructive. Thirty-nine of the 84 exotic species of fish in our lakes and streams reproduce successfully. Even more significant, six of those exotics are rapidly expanding their ranges.

Beneficial Introduction: The Brown Trout. The introduction of the European brown trout roughly 100 years ago was highly successful. This species has established itself in waters either too warm or too badly polluted for native trout. As a result, it has provided angling thrills for the anglers even in urban areas. The brown trout is able to survive in the relatively warm, somewhat muddy waters of Lowes Creek, for example, which is only a stone's throw from the city limits of Eau Claire, Wisconsin, a bustling city of 50,000.

FIGURE 9-15 Stream-planted Vibert box. View of section through gravel on stream bottom. All stages of fry development are shown.

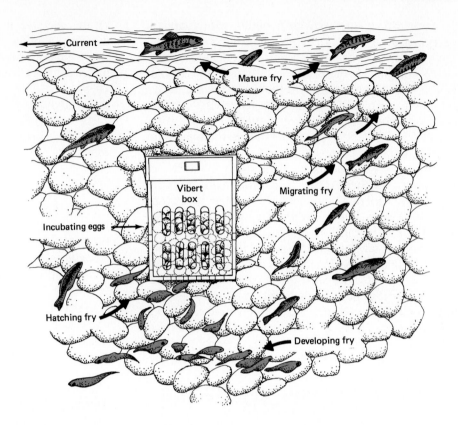

Harmful Introduction: The European Carp. The European carp is the most destructive exotic fish ever brought to the United States (Figure 9-16). It was originally introduced to California (1872), the Great Lakes (1873), and Washington, D.C. (1877). Hundreds of requests from all over the nation came to the U.S. Bureau of Fisheries to stock this so-called wonder fish in order to provide Americans with a valuable source of food.

The carp proved to be an extraordinarily adaptable fish. The introduced populations grew rapidly, following the characteristic S-shaped growth curve. Only 20 years after the introduction of European carp to Lake Erie, fishermen were able to harvest 1.6 million kilograms (3.6 million pounds) in a single year. Soon, however, the carp were affecting aquatic ecosystems in ways that had not been predicted. They uprooted aquatic vegetation during bottom-feeding. The results have been exceedingly harmful to game fish populations because (1) their spawning grounds were destroyed, (2) their food supplies were diminished, and (3) levels of dissolved oxygen were reduced as a result of the interference with photosynthesis caused by the muddying of the waters.

Table 9-3 Some Native Fish Introductions to California's Inland Waters

Species	Year	Source	Introduction Site
Smallmouth bass	1874	Lake Champlain, Vt.	Napa River
Channel catfish	1874	Mississippi River	San Joaquin River
Largemouth bass	1879	Eastern United States	Crystal Spring Reservoir (San Mateo County)
Yellow perch	1891	Illinois	Feather River (Butte County)
Lake trout	1894	Michigan	Lake Tahoe
Bluegill	1908	Illinois	(Placer and Orange Counties)
White bass	1965	Nebraska	Lake Nacimiento (San Luis Obispo County)
Blue catfish	1969	Arkansas	Lake Jennings (San Diego County)

FIGURE 9-16 The carp, an exotic introduced into American waters from Europe during the late nineteenth century. Note the mouth, specialized for bottom feeding. This feeding habit causes this species to muddy waters and spoil habitat for game fish.

SALMON FEVER IN THE GREAT LAKES

The Great Lakes' fishery was almost destroyed 25 years ago because of overfishing, pollution, and the invasion of the predatory sea lamprey. Since then, however, the fishery has changed dramatically. Today, for example, the Great Lakes boast some of the best salmon fishing on this planet. Sport fishing attracts more than 5 million anglers annually and is worth more than $4 billion to the Great Lakes region. A key species that has made the salmon boom possible is the alewife.

The Alewife Invasion

A silvery, sardine-like fish, the alewife invaded the upper lakes from Lake Ontario. It first appeared in Lake Michigan in 1949. Lake trout fed on it ravenously, keeping its population down to moderate levels. However, a dramatic decline in lake trout stocks occurred soon thereafter, due to heavy predation by the sea lamprey and overfishing. In the 1950s, the alewife population exploded, probably due, in part, to the plummeting population of lake trout, its principal predator. By the 1960s the alewives formed 80 percent of the fish in Lake Michigan and over 50 percent of the lake's fish biomass.

During the spring of 1967, the alewives suddenly experienced a massive dieoff in Lake Michigan due to unusually cold weather and starvation. The carcasses of millions of these small fish washed up on shore, littering swimming beaches, decaying, releasing vile odors, and attracting flies. This was an unpleasant signal to fisheries biologists that the Great Lakes ecosystem was in trouble.

Salmon Stocking

In 1964, Michigan's Department of Natural Resources obtained 1 million coho salmon eggs from fish taken in the Columbia River on the Washington–Oregon border. This momentous event signalled the beginning of one of the great experiments in the history of American fisheries. In 1966, the 2-year-old salmon were planted in Lake Michigan and Lake Superior. By 1967, a few of the sexually mature coho, now 3 years old, began to make spawning runs up tributary streams. These sleek, muscular, heavy-bodied fish caused "coho fever" to rage among Michigan anglers. During the fall of 1967, more than 150,000 of them swarmed to the shores of Lake Michigan near Frankfort and Manistee. In their frenzied excitement, seven coho-crazy anglers ignored storm warnings and drowned when their boats sank in rough waters.

In 1968, coho were planted into the other Great Lakes. The success of these programs prompted the stocking of another Pacific salmon—the chinook. This species is often called the **king salmon** because of its unsurpassed fighting qualities and huge size.

Salmon stocking rates increased year by year. By 1983, 84 million coho and 108 million chinook had been stocked in the Great Lakes. These predators from the Pacific fattened up on their alewife prey. And the ultimate predators, the anglers, with their varied array of strategies and lures, were just as successful in catching the salmon. They landed 610,000 coho in a single year.

PROBLEMS. The great Great Lakes salmon-stocking experiment, however, has not been without its problems. First, for some unexplained reason, the coho has not been able to spawn successfully except in the tributary streams of Lake Superior. Second, there is some concern that the coho of Lake Superior will interfere with the spawning activities of the long-established brown and rainbow trout—highly prized game fish in their own right. The most serious problem, however, has been the *86 percent reduction in the population of the alewife*. Since 75 percent salmon diet consists of alewives, fisheries biologists have become rightly concerned that salmon growth and reproduction might be sharply diminished resulting in a disastrous collapse of the billion-dollar Great Lakes sport fishery.

Two strategies to prevent this problem have been considered. One is to reduce the tonnage of alewives

FIGURE 9-17   Stream habitat improvement for trout.

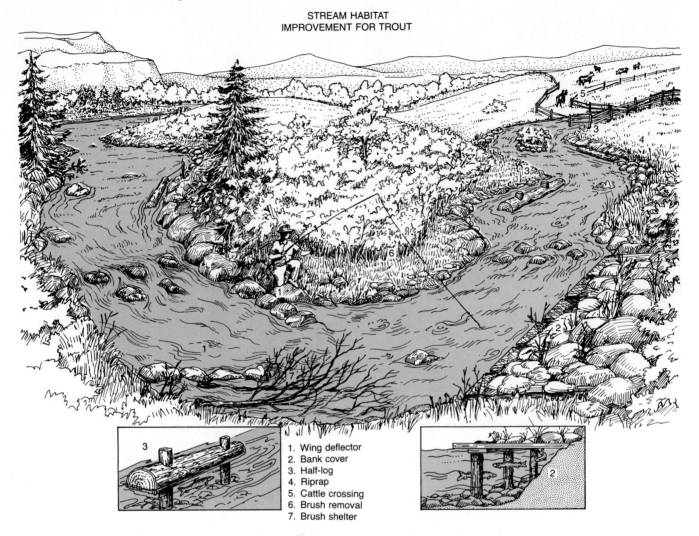

1. Wing deflector
2. Bank cover
3. Half-log
4. Riprap
5. Cattle crossing
6. Brush removal
7. Brush shelter

that can be taken by commercial fisherman. In Lake Michigan alone in the mid-1980s, the annual commercial harvest of alewives, used as fertilizer and pet food, amounted to about 18 million metric tons. The second strategy is to cut back on the salmon-stocking program. Wisconsin reduced its stocking rate by 10 percent in 1986.

What does the future hold? Conservation agencies of the Great Lakes states, as well as the U.S. Fish and Wildlife Service, are cautiously optimistic. Guided by computer models of predator–prey interactions, biologists hope to stabilize both the salmon and alewife stocks.

Improving Habitat for Trout

Wild trout populations may increase considerably when the carrying capacity of their environment is raised. Various methods can be used to improve the stream habitat for trout. The components of the habitat that can be effectively managed are (1) water flow, (2) space, (3) cover, and (4) food. Some methods of stream improvement are shown in Figure 9-17.

Each management method will have a positive effect that, in turn, may result in other positive effects. For example, suppose that cover is increased by the introduction of brush shelter (Figure 9-17). The cover protects the trout from predation by mink, otters, bear, fish hawks, and herons. As a result, trout become more numerous. Shelter have an additional positive effect. As shown in Figure 9-18, the twigs and branches of the shelter serve as attachment sites for insect larvae, snails, and crustaceans. Those organisms provide food for the growing trout populations. As a consequence, the growth rates of trout increase, resulting in bigger fish. Such shelters also provide shade where fish may retreat during the

Table 9-4 Fish Kills Caused by Water Pollution in Ohio, 1984

Date	County	Name of Water	Number Killed	Suspected Pollutant
9/2	Montgomery	Great Miami River	158,234	Sewage and corn syrup
7/17	Daske	Greenville Creek	122,057	Hog manure
6/15	Fulton	Brush Creek	79,110	Ammonium nitrate
4/16	Crawford	Broken Sword Creek	57,237	Nitrogen fertilizer
9/1	Butler	Four-Mile Creek	41,335	Sewage
3/26	Columbiana	Beaver Creek	26,986	Gasoline
9/10	Coshocton	White Eye Creek	13,170	Cow manure
6/27	Morgan	Bell Creek	3,274	Cleaning chemicals
5/3	Marion	Riffle Creek	2,905	Herbicides

Source: Water Pollution, Fish Kill and Stream Litter Investigation—1984. Ohio Department of Natural Resources, Columbus, 1985.

heat of the day. The cooling effect on the water enables it to dissolve more oxygen. The increased levels of oxygen enable the trout to swim faster. Figure 9-18 shows the pathways of effect for several other stream management methods such as cover, the increase of water flow, and the improvement of water fertility.

A series of brush shelters may be anchored along the inner margin of a lake's littoral zone with great effectiveness. In the winter season, brush piles can be set up on the ice cover in strategic areas and weighted with bags of stones; they will gradually sink to their proper place on the lake bottom as soon as the ice melts in spring.

Cattle graze heavily on stream-side vegetation, if available, due to its succulence and variety. Unfortunately, however after several years the heavy grazing pressure can eliminate plant cover, trigger erosion, and result in many harmful effects on the carrying capacity of the stream for trout. A study of a Montana stream showed that the portions with ungrazed banks had 27 percent more fish over 15 centimeters (6 inches) long than grazed sections. Fortunately, U.S. Forest Service research has shown that if the sides of a severely grazed stream are fenced off from cattle for 5 to 10 years, its original ability to support large trout populations will be restored, as shown in Figure 9-19.

Development of Spawning Sites

The fish production of a body of water may be increased by improving natural spawning sites and by providing artificial spawning surfaces where suitable natural ones are lacking.

1. *Sites for bass.* Sand or small gravel can be spread on the muddy bottoms of lakes and streams to provide spawning sites for bass. Nylon mats can be used as an artificial spawning surface for largemouth bass. In one experiment, 90 mats were tested in several ponds. Over a 2-year period, the bass spawned on nearly 75 percent of the mats.

2. *Sites for northern pike.* Intensive study of the breeding behavior of the northern pike has shown that the shallow, marshy fringes of the littoral zone are the preferred spawning habitat. Regrettably, in recent years, suitable spawning sites for this species have been greatly reduced as a result of real estate development, marina construction, and industrial expansion. State fish and game departments are attempting to rectify the situation. Wisconsin, Iowa, and Minnesota, for instance, have acquired thousands of acres of marshes to provide suitable pike breeding habitats.

3. *Sites for lake trout.* Hatchery-reared lake trout have been stocked in the Great Lakes for several decades. However, only a small percentage of the trout successfully spawn. Ross Horrall, a researcher from the University of Wisconsin–Madison, has recently located traditional lake trout spawning reefs (mounds of submerged rocks) that were successfully used long before the sea lamprey decimated this species. One of these reefs is located near the Apostle Islands in Lake Superior. The Horrall research team placed 273,000 fertilized lake trout eggs in huge Astroturf "sandwiches" (Astroturf is the plastic "grass" used on football fields). The sandwiches stabilize the eggs, protect them from sediment and predators, and make easy retrieval possible (Figure 9-20). After a 7-month incubation period, the Horrall team found that 88 percent of the eggs had hatched. The researchers hope that the young trout will remember the spawning reef and will return to breed when sexually mature.

Controlling Predators

Just as many deer hunters feel that any deer-eating wolf should be shot on sight, so the angler becomes

FIGURE 9-18 "Chain responses" resulting from the application of various habitat-improvement methods to trout streams. The methods are shown in boxes.

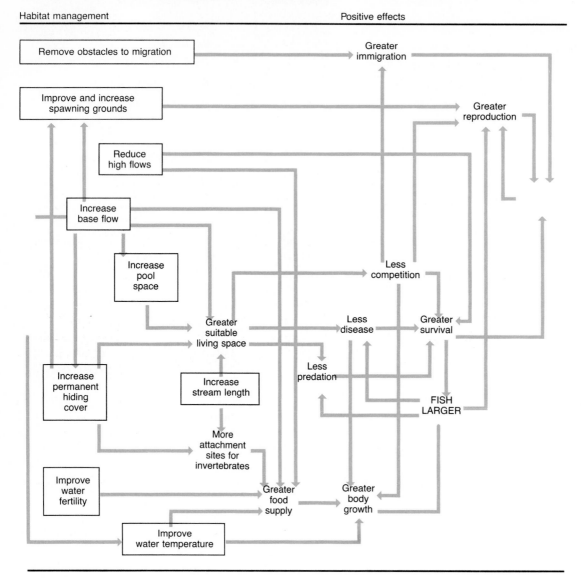

Table 9-5 Stream Habitat Improvements

Problem	Habitat Improvement	Result
Not enough shelter or living space	Wing deflector (1) Bank cover (2) Half-logs (3)	Channel deepens, pools form Cover increases, predation and competition decrease
Stream overgrown with trees and shrubs	Brush removal (6)	Sunlight reaches stream, more food produced
Erosion of stream banks	Rifraf (4) Cattle crossing (5) Fencing (7)	Banks stabilize; water clears, channel deepens
Poor spawning success	Wing deflection (1)	Silt scoured from gravel beds
Water too warm	Narrow and deepen channel	Colder water
Too much predation Lack of food	Brush shelters (8)	Provides cover from predators, as well as habitat for food organisms

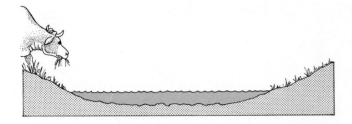

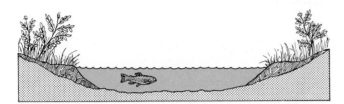

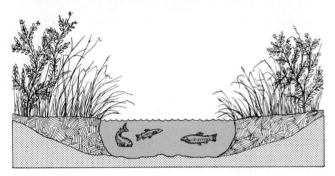

FIGURE 9-19 Schematic representation of stream conditions subject to heavy grazing (upper). Banks are grazed and trampled, leading to increased stream width, shallow water, and poor habitat for trout. Shallow water may be warmed enough by direct sunlight to limit a trout fishery. After two to three years without grazing, vegetation begins recovering as stream banks again develop their structure (middle). The habitat is improving for trout as food, cover and spawning conditions become more favorable. Conditions after five to ten years without grazing offer excellent trout habitat (lower). Overhanging banks and deeper water have been restored as the vegetation recovered. Sedimentation also is reduced significantly.

equally upset over the fish-eating activities of herons, mergansers, loons, mink, otter, and bear. A few predators, such as the sea lamprey, can severely reduce fish populations (the case study on "The sea lamprey—scourge of the Great Lakes"). However, for the most part, fish-eating animals perform important functions: they minimize the number of stunted fish caused by food shortages and they reduce the incidence of infectious diseases. The absence of predatory pressure leaves more fish for the angler, but many are so small as to be hardly worth catching. In any case, when food-analysis studies are made, the accusations of sportsmen frequently appear unfounded. Thus, a study of the digestive tracts of otters from Wisconsin, Michigan, and

FIGURE 9-20 Astro-turf egg sandwich! Ross Horall, a fisheries biologist at the University of Wisconsin-Eau Claire, displays an astroturf "dandwich", a recently developed device which holds and protects lake trout eggs during incubation.

Minnesota revealed that although fish were indeed the otter's main prey, game fish were seldom taken.

Removing Undesirable Fish

Because of their destructiveness to game fish, fish such as carp, bowfins, and gar are frequently the focus of intensive eradication projects. Even gizzard shad and panfish, ordinarily valuable as forage for game fish, may require control if they become abundant. However, eradication of any of these species from any body of water is an enormously difficult task.

Various control methods under study involve chemicals, seining, commercial fishing, manipulation of water levels, and fish-spawning control. Before state of federal biologists use a specific chemical, it must first be registered with the USDA and approved by state health and pollution agencies and by the Federal Committee on Pest Control.

Rotenone, a chemical derived from the roots of an Asiatic legume, kills fish at a concentration of only 1 ppm within minutes at a water temperature of 21°C (70°F). Unfortunately, poisoning with rotenone is unselective, resulting in the indiscriminate death of many species (Figure 9-21).

FIGURE 9-21 Chemical control of undesirable fish. Dead fish by the thousands float belly-up in a small bay of Clear Lake near Watkins, Minnesota. The lake's entire population of undesirable (rough) fish, including carp and bullheads, was destroyed after the lake was treated with rotenone, a chemical lethal only to fish and other gill-breathers. This lake was later stocked with valuable species of gamer fish.

The chemical control agent **antimycin** kills carp more readily than it does most other fish and does not appear to be deleterious to invertebrates. Several years ago, the Wisconsin Department of Natural Resources made extensive use of antimycin in an attempt to reduce the carp population in the Rock River drainage system of southeastern Wisconsin. The project triggered a storm of controversy. Opponents of the program believed that irreparable damage would be inflicted on the ecosystem and that certain rare species of fish might be eliminated as well. Moreover, suppose that some fishermen came along later and dumped their surplus carp-bait minnows into a stream that had just been "decarped." Due to their tremendous reproductive capacity, the carp would soon be just as numerous as before. The opponents of the project argue that it would have been more acceptable to keep the carp population down to reasonable levels either by trapping them on their spawning grounds or by periodic seining.

Controlling Oxygen Depletion in Winter

Various methods are available to reduce winterkill of fish caused by oxygen depletion. (1) If the lake is small, the opaque snow blanket may be removed with plows. This will permit sunlight to penetrate to aquatic vegetation so that photosynthesis can occur and the water can be oxygenated. (2) Dynamite may be used to blast holes in the frozen lake to expose surface waters to atmospheric oxygen. (3) Oxygen can be introduced through ice borings by motorized aerators.

Selectively Breeding Superior Fish

Larger and higher-quality fish are being developed at the Federal Fish Farming Station at Stuttgart, Arkansas.

A rapidly growing hybrid catfish, for instance, has been produced by crossing a channel catfish with a blue catfish. When 2 years old, the hybrids weigh 32 percent more than a similarly aged blue catfish and 41 percent more than a channel catfish of the same age.

Fisheries biologists in Wisconsin have crossed northern pike with muskellunge to develop a hybrid known as a tiger muskie. The tiger muskie has been successfully stocked in reservoirs. In these artificial lakes, they fare much better than either of the parental species.

Geneticists in New York have successfully developed strains of trout that can survive in highly acid waters. It is hoped that they can be used to stock certain Adirondack lakes in New York where fish have been eliminated by acid rain.

With the **gene-splicing** techniques now available to geneticists, new strains of fish may be developed that grow faster and fight harder than present-day sport fish; are more resistant to pesticides, heat, and sediment; have greater reproductive potential; use a greater variety of spawning habitats; perhaps respond more readily to artificial lures; and even form tastier meals.

Reservoirs: A Special Challenge to Fisheries Management

Very few states are blessed with the number of natural lakes found in Minnesota (22,000) or Wisconsin (8,000). However, damming rivers for hydropower production, flood control, and recreation has resulted in the formation of thousands of artificial lakes, or **reservoirs**, throughout the United States, especially in the South and West. Today they account for more than 25 percent of all freshwater fishing.

The temperature, chemistry, and biology of a reser-

FIGURE 9-22   Reservoir drawdown and the nutrient flush cycle.

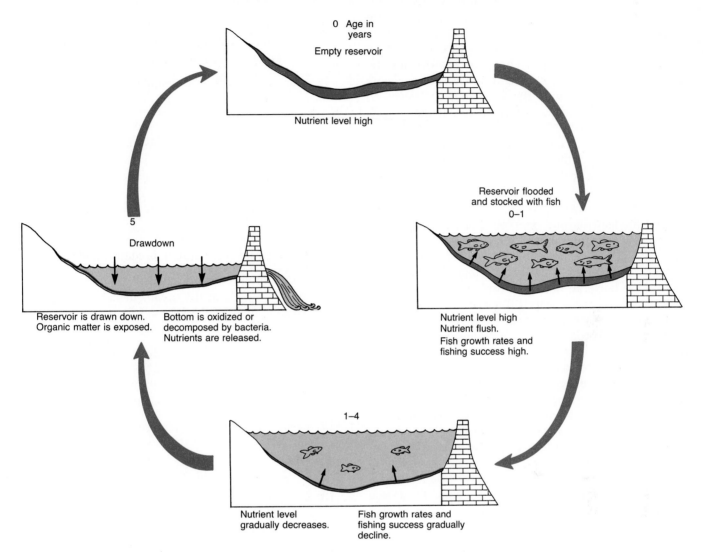

THE RESEVOIR DRAWDOWN AND THE NUTRIENT FLASH CYCLE

0 Age in
years

Empty reservoir

Nutrient level high

Reservoir flooded
and stocked with fish
0–1

Nutrient level high
Nutrient flush.
Fish growth rates and
fishing success high.

5

Drawdown

Reservoir is drawn down.   Bottom is oxidized or
Organic matter is exposed.   decomposed by bacteria.
                             Nutrients are released.

1–4

Nutrient level   Fish growth rates and
gradually decreases.   fishing success gradually
                        decline.

voir are quite different from those of the portion of the river above the dam. Of great significance to fish management is that the waters of the newly created reservoir dissolve nutrients from the newly submerged soil. The sudden increase in water fertility that results is called a **nutrient flush**. The water-killed organisms (grass, shrubs, insects, worms, mice, etc.) will eventually decompose and release nutrients as well. These nutrients are then channeled upward through the aquatic food chain. As a result, fish growth and reproduction are usually excellent. In one impoundment in Kentucky, anglers caught twice as many fish as they had at the same location prior to the construction of the reservoir. Regardless, dams can be costly and can compromise other uses, such as rafting and canoeing.

STOCKING RESERVOIRS. Fishing success may improve dramatically if reservoirs are stocked. For example, as a result of stocking in Virginia's Smith Mountain Lake, it is now possible to catch trophy-sized muskies there. Fish stocking is most effective (1) in newly formed impounds, (2) when introducing predators (bass) to control an overpopulation of stunted prey (bluegill), (3) when compensating for the severe reproductive failure of a game species, and (4) when stocking a forage fish (bluegill, threadfin shad) to provide food for desirable predatory species (spotted bass, northern pike). If the reservoir is sufficiently deep, it becomes thermally stratified during the summer, complete with epilimnion, thermocline, and hypolimnion. Such an impoundment is referred to as a **two-story reservoir**. At least 30 states stock their two-story reservoirs with both warm and cold-water species: bass, catfish, and bluegill for the warm epilimnion and rainbow, brown, and lake trout for the cold hypolimnion.

HARMFUL DRAWDOWNS. If used for flood control or hydropower, a reservoir can be purposely lowered or raised by the dam operator. Unfortunately, the fluctuating water level may seriously affect the fish (Figure 9-22). For example, a drawdown of just a few meters shortly after the lake trout have spawned could leave their eggs "high and dry." The entire spawn could be destroyed. On the other hand, if a drawdown occurs shortly before spawning, the lake trout are forced to spawn in an area where many of the eggs might be consumed by other fish, such as bullheads. Thus, the fish manager needs the cooperation of the owner and operator of the dam if the fish production potential of the reservoir is to be realized.

BENEFICIAL DRAWDOWNS. Drawdowns can also benefit the fisheries of a reservoir. For example, in late summer, fish managers may request dam operators to draw down 10 to 80 percent of the water. The objectives include (1) aeration of the bottom muck, (2) acceleration of the bacterial decomposition of organic material and the release of nutrients, (3) restriction of forage fish to a small area where they can be more easily caught and eaten by predatory game fish, and (4) facilitation of rough fish removal.

Some time after drawdown, the reservoir is refilled and restocked with game species. Due to the **nutrient flush** effect, a large quantity of food (diatoms, crustaceans, insects, minnows, and so on) become available to the fish of this artificial ecosystem. As a result, both growth and reproduction are enhanced. For example, in the 11,200-hectare (28,000-acre) reservoir in Beaver Creek, Arkansas, the average weight of pike increased 2 kilograms (4.4 pounds) annually during the first 3 years after drawdown. In an impoundment on the Rough River in Kentucky, the average weight of catfish progressively increased through the fourth postdrawdown year, at which time it was 473 percent greater than during preimpoundment years! Unfortunately, however, in most reservoirs, the positive effects of the nutrient flush diminish by the third or fourth year. At this time, therefore, another drawdown is required.

RAPID REVIEW

1. Ecologists recognize three major lake zones: littoral, limnetic, and profundal.

2. The littoral zone is the shallow marginal region of a lake that is characterized by rooted vegetation.

3. The suspended, floating microorganisms in a lake are known as *plankton*.

4. The limnetic zone is the region of open water beyond the littoral zone down to the maximum depth at which there is sufficient sunlight for photosynthesis. The profundal zone lies beneath the limnetic zone.

5. In spring and autumn the lakes in the temperate zone undergo a thorough mixing that is known as the *spring* and *fall overturn*.

6. The *current* is the most important factor in determining the kinds of organisms present in streams.

7. A stream receives a considerable portion of its energy supply from materials like leaves and twigs that originate on land.

8. The distribution of the kinds of fish in a stream is correlated with changes in pH, temperature, and the velocity of current.

9. Roughly 70 percent of a given fish population dies each year due to pollution, predation and winterkill.

10. The salmon is an andromous fish—one that spends most of its life in the ocean; then, after becoming sexually mature, it swims up its native freshwater stream to spawn.

11. Some Columbia River salmon must negotiate a number of hazards, such as rushing cataracts, predators, fishermen, pollution (silt, heated water, radioactive materials, and chemicals) and big dams.

12. Predation by the sea lamprey caused the annual lake-trout harvest in the Great Lakes to drop from 10 million pounds in 1940 to .33 million pounds in 1961—a 97 percent reduction in only 21 years.

13. Lamprey populations in the Great Lakes have been controlled by treating their spawning streams with the chemical TFM.

14. Severe winterkills of fish caused by oxygen starvation occur in shallow lakes when snow cover prevents aquatic plants from getting sufficient sunlight for photosynthesis.

15. Fisheries management is the manipulation of fish populations and their environment to increase both sport and commercial fish harvest.

16. Techniques of fisheries management include restrictive laws, artificial propagation, introductions of both native and exotic species, habitat improvement (artificial spawning-site development, fertilization, predator control, removal of trash fish, control of oxygen depletion, and farm pond and reservoir construction), and the selective breeding of superior fish.

17. Carp populations have been brought under partial control, in some regions, by periodic seining and the use of selective chemicals such as antimycin.

18. Levels of dissolved oxygen in snow-covered northern lakes can be increased by snow removal, opening the ice cover with dynamite, and using motorized aerators.

19. Selective breeding has resulted in the development of superior strains of fish that have better sporting qualities and are more resistant to disease and pollution.

20. The Great Lakes Fishery Commission, composed of the Great Lakes states and Ontario, was formed in 1955 to coordinate fisheries management, especially in regard to sea lamprey control.

21. The freshwater fishery manager has a challenging job—the upgrading of a fishery in the face of angling pressure, which is expected to increase 35 percent by the year 2000.

22. More than 80 percent of the species of warm-water game fish in California were introduced from states east of the Rocky Mountains.

23. Two-story reservoirs are stocked with warm-water species in the epilimnion and cold-water species in the hypolimnion.

24. The water of a newly created reservoir receives a nutrient flush that greatly increases the abundance of fish food.

KEY WORDS AND PHRASES

Acid rain
Aeration
Algal bloom
Anadromous fish
Antimycin
Artificial propagation
Astroturf sandwich
Biological oxygen demand
  (BOD)
Biotic potential
Brown trout
Carp
Carrying capacity
Catadromous fish
Coho salmon
Detritus
Drawdown
Echo sounder
Emergent vegetation
Environmental resistance
Epilimnion
Eutrophication
Exotic species
Fisheries management
Restrictive laws

Fishing pressure
Forage fish
Habitat improvement
Hypolimnion
Introduction
Lake trout
Lampricide
Limnetic zone
Littoral zone
Longitudinal zonation
  (streams)
May fly
Native species
Natural selection
Nitrogen intoxication
Nutrient flush
Oxygen depletion
Phytoplankton
Plankton
Predator control
Profundal zone
Put-and-take stocking
Redd
Reservoir
TFM

Riprap
Rotenone
Rough fish
Salmon migration
Sea lamprey
Sonar
Spring overturn
Stagnation
Submergent vegetation
Sustained yield

Thermal stratification
Thermocline
Threadfin shad
Tilapia
Two-story reservoir
Vibert box
Welland Canal
White amur
Winterkill
Zooplankton

QUESTIONS AND TOPICS FOR DISCUSSION

1. Describe the characteristic distribution of rooted plants in the littoral zone.

2. Identify three insects, three fish, and three birds that are characteristic of the littoral zone.

3. Suppose that the light intensity on the bottom of a lake is 10 percent of that at the compensation depth. What percentage of full sunlight would that be?

4. Identify two sources of the dissolved oxygen present in the lake.

5. Give three reasons why oxygen might be a limiting factor for fish in northern states during the winter season.

6. Describe the vertical temperature pattern of a northern lake in summer, fall, winter, and spring.

7. What causes the fall turnover? What causes the spring turnover?

8. Do the fall and spring turnovers have any significance for the survival of aquatic organisms? Explain your answer.

9. Suppose that a given lake has 100 black bass. If no reproduction occurred, how many bass would you expect the lake to have 1 year later?

10. What is the source of acid rain? What is its effect on fish?

11. What causes the winterkill of fish in northern lakes? How can it be prevented?

12. Describe three activities of carp that are harmful to game fish populations.

13. Describe the life cycle of the Pacific salmon.

14. List six adverse environmental factors that may be encountered by Pacific salmon as they swim to their spawning grounds.

15. Discuss the pros and cons of artificial propagation.

16. Name three native fish that have been successfully introduced into new bodies of water in the United States.

17. How can the stream habitat be improved for fish?

18. Discuss the statement "Predator control is an effective method for increasing game fish populations in the United States." Is it valid? Why or why not?

19. Describe the life cycle of the sea lamprey.

20. Human activities frequently have harmful effects on wildlife. Was this true in the case of the sea lamprey? Discuss your answer.

21. Describe efforts to control the sea lamprey in the Great Lakes.

22. Discuss four methods that might be used to prevent winterkills of fish in northern lakes.

23. Describe three methods the fish manager could use to determine the population density of a particular body of water.

24. Briefly list four benefits that may be derived from the drawdown of reservoirs.

25. Discuss the role of alewives in the salmon boom on the Great Lakes.

SUGGESTED READINGS

California Department of Fish and Game. *Warmwater Game Fishes of California*. Sacramento, Calif.: Department of Fish and Game, 1981. Well-written, interesting treatment on the distribution, life history, and management of 27 important species.

Mulhern, R. "Computer-Modeled Fish: A Printout for the Future." *Wisconsin Natural Resources* 11:40–43, 1987. Discusses the use of computer modeling in modern fish research.

Robinson, W. L., and Bolen, E. G., *Wildlife Ecology and Management*. New York: Macmillan, 1983. Chapter Eight, "Wildlife and Water," has excellent material on the management of reservoir fisheries.

The Fisheries of the Great Lakes. Madison: University of Wisconsin Sea Grant Institute, 1986. A topnotch overview covering the early history, the sea lamprey invasion, and the establishment of the successful salmon fishery.

Cobb, C. E., "The Great Lakes Troubled Waters." *National Geographic* 172(1):3-21, 1987. Describes the effect of toxic pollutants on the survival of Great Lakes fish.

10

Coastlands, Estuaries, and Oceans

The ocean shores are biologically rich and aesthetically stunning. However, they are also highly sensitive to human impact (Figure 10-1) This poses a serious dilemma, for today nearly one of every two Americans is living within 80 kilometers (50 miles) in this delightful region where the land meets the sea. Shortly after World War II, our coastlands were invaded by enterprising developers, who soon launched a multibillion-dollar building boom. Many expensive beachfront homes, condominiums, hotels, and resorts were constructed. Ample federal subsidies were given for water supply systems, sewers, roads, bridges, and shoreline stabilization, spurring the feverish spate of construction.

Off the Atlantic and Gulf coasts are 295 narrow strips of sand, grass, marsh, and smatterings of pine and oak, known as **barrier islands** (Figure 10-2). The maximum width of these islands is 5 kilometers (3 miles); the maximum length is 100 kilometers (62 miles). Only 10 percent of these barrier islands were developed before World War II. Today at least 25 percent are choked with construction. Typical examples are Coney Island (New York), Miami Beach (Florida), Ocean City (Maryland), and Atlantic City (New Jersey). The urbanization of barrier islands progressed rapidly from 1946 to 1980. By the early 1980s, more than 100,000 hectares (230,000 acres) were under development. Unfortunately, much of this construction was probably not very wise

FIGURE 10-1 Humans invade the beaches of Padre Island—a barrier island which stretches for 100 miles (160 kilometers) along the Texas coast.

FIGURE 10-2 Major barrier islands along the Atlantic and Gulf coasts of the United States. These islands were built up from sediments by the action of the sea.

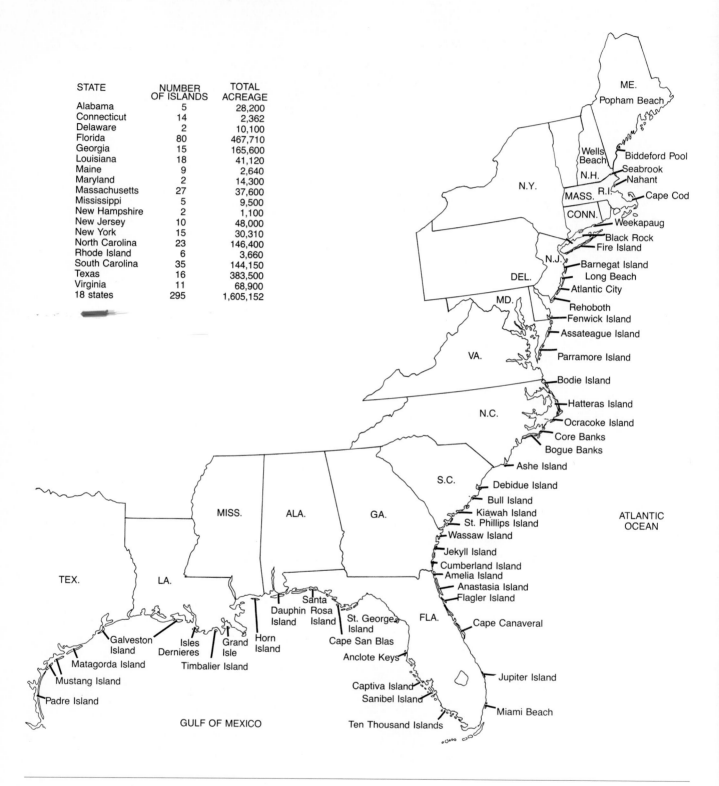

STATE	NUMBER OF ISLANDS	TOTAL ACREAGE
Alabama	5	28,200
Connecticut	14	2,362
Delaware	2	10,100
Florida	80	467,710
Georgia	15	165,600
Louisiana	18	41,120
Maine	9	2,640
Maryland	2	14,300
Massachusetts	27	37,600
Mississippi	5	9,500
New Hampshire	2	1,100
New Jersey	10	48,000
New York	15	30,310
North Carolina	23	146,400
Rhode Island	6	3,660
South Carolina	35	144,150
Texas	16	383,500
Virginia	11	68,900
18 states	295	1,605,152

FIGURE 10-3 This beach house, located on the North Carolina coast, is much too close to the sea. It is very vulnerable to flooding and beach erosion.

(Figure 10-3). After all, the barrier islands are constantly changing shape and size because of the erosion caused by wind, waves, and offshore currents.

PROPERTY DAMAGE AND LOSS OF LIFE FROM STORMS

Because of the mushrooming development on the coastlands and the barrier islands, both property and human life have become extremely vulnerable to hurricanes and other ocean storms. Some examples follow:

1926. Storm waters drowned 243 people when 13-foot waves surged into Miami Beach shortly after it had been converted into a resort community.

1938. The most damaging hurricane of the first half of the century in the Northeast caused $3.2 billion in property loss (1987 dollars) and took the lives of 600 people.

1969. Louisiana and Mississippi suffered $1 billion in damage from hurricane Camille when a surge of water 25 feet high crumbled 2,822 homes and damaged 40,000 more.

1989. Hurricane Hugo struck the east coast, killing 32 people and causing property damage of well over $4 billion. Fifty thousand people were left homeless in Charleston, S.C.

Hurricanes can devastate human settlement in coastal regions. Coastal development also causes permanent degradation of the scenic shoreline, accelerates beach erosion, destroys the potential for public recreation, and ruins fish and wildlife habitats, especially coastal wetlands and estuaries. To preserve the aesthetic and environmental values of their coastal regions, many states have enacted legislation to protect these vulnerable ecosystems. In Delaware, for instance, state law forbids the construction of any industrial plants within 3 kilometers (2 miles) of the seashore. New Jersey's Waterfront Development Act (1988) empowers the Department of Environmental Protection to fine waterfront owners $1,000 if they illegally place structures too close to the shoreline and to impose a $100-a-day fine for each day the violation continues.

California and North Carolina have perhaps the strongest and most comprehensive coast-protecting legislation. For instance, the California law (1) protects estuaries, (2) preserves coastal farmlands, (3) ensures that recreationists (swimmers, hikers, bird watchers) have access to the ocean shore, (4) mandates that the public as a whole be served by future development, and (5) requires that strict environmental safeguards be included in any energy development, such as oil well drilling or nuclear power plant construction.

The National Coastal Zone Management Act (1972 and 1980) has provided financial assistance to 30 ocean-bordering states. Funding facilitates the development of ecologically and economically sound strategies for the development and protection of their coastlands and barrier islands. By the end of 1986, more than 90 percent of the coastal areas in 24 states had developed coastal management plans that gained the federal government's stamp of approval.

COASTAL EROSION PROBLEM

Our nation's ocean shores are eroding rapidly. Billions of dollars of coastal development, such as homes, resorts, and hotels, could be destroyed by the end of this century. Hundreds, maybe thousands, of human lives could be in jeopardy. The delicate balance of unique ecosystems such as wetlands may be severely disrupted. What has caused this accelerated erosion? The answer is complex, for there are a number of contributing factors. Some of them are natural and others are of human origin.

1. *Rise of the oceans.* Ocean levels have been rising since the end of the last Ice Age about 11,000 years ago. However, in the last century or so, the rate has quickened. Why? The primary cause is the greenhouse effect resulting from the increasing levels of

FIGURE 10-4   Structural control of beach erosion with cord grass plantings.

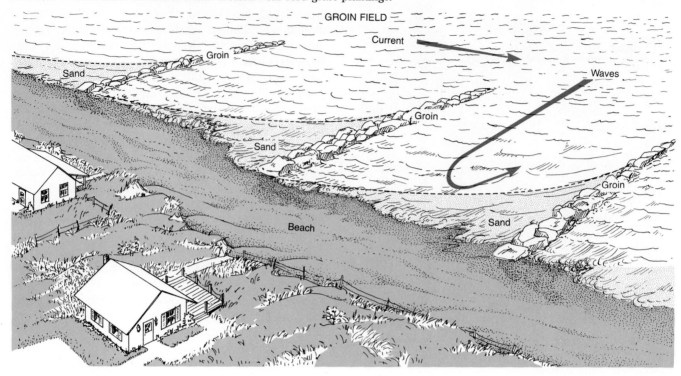

carbon dioxide in the atmosphere. (See Chapter 18 for more details.) This increase has resulted from the burning of fossil fuels (coal, oil, and natural gas). Carbon dioxide has a warming influence on the atmosphere. The slight increase in temperature has caused the melting of some glaciers and ice caps. As a result, the sea level has risen. Within the next century, carbon dioxide levels should double. As a result, ocean waves might surge inland hundreds of meters in low-lying coastal regions, washing away beaches, causing serious property damage, and inflicting considerable mortality on both wildlife and humans.

2. *Dam construction.* Numerous upstream dams have been constructed to generate hydroelectric power or to provide irrigation water for agriculture. These dams have blocked the flow of water that formerly carried millions of tons of sediment to river mouths to form deltas. Many deltas and beaches, therefore, are no longer replenished. This factor, combined with rising ocean levels, has resulted in a rapid reduction of deltas and seashores.

3. *Land subsidence.* The extraction of oil in coastal regions and the mining of water from coastal aquifers in Louisiana, Texas, and California have caused the surface of the land, which already was roughly at sea level, to sink or subside. This permits ocean waves to surge inland and wash soils away. In Louisiana the land has subsided 1 meter (3 feet) in the past 100 years.

Examples of Erosion

Long Island. Aerial photographs show that Long Island's shoreline has retreated 30 meters (100 feet) in the past half-century.

Louisiana. Since 1970 more than 762 square kilometers (300 square miles) of coastal areas have been flooded by waters of the Gulf of Mexico, washing away once useful soil.

North Carolina. The Cape Hatteras lighthouse may be surrounded by the sea in the near future.

California. More than 86 percent of California's 1,771 kilometers (1,100 miles) of exposed Pacific shoreline is receding at an average rate of 15 centimeters (6 inches) to 60 centimeters (2 feet) per year. Monterey Bay, south of San Francisco, loses 152 centimeters (5 feet) to 300 centimeters (10 feet) annually.

Washington. Cape Shoalwater, on Washington's Olympic Penninsula, has eroded 30 meters (100 feet) per year since the turn of the century. Its sparsely settled sand dunes have retreated more than 3.2 kilometers (2 miles) since 1910.

Control of Erosion

What strategies can be used to eliminate or lessen the problems just described?

1. *Erosion control structures.* A **riprap** is a pile of rock and boulders placed along the shoreline to intercept

FIGURE 10-5   Wetland along the North Carolina coast protects the coastline from erosion.

FIGURE 10-6   Estuary of the San Joaquin River, California. Note the wetlands associated with the estuary.

waves. Coastal residents in California pay up to $700 per foot for riprap.

Groins are piers of stone spaced about 30 meters (100 feet) apart that extend into the sea at right angles to the shoreline (Figure 10-4). They trap sand washed against them by currents that move parallel to the shore. However, they deprive shores that are immediately down current of beach-replenishing sand. So, in a sense, the groins "rob Peter to pay Paul." The construction of 15 groins by the U.S. Army Corps of Engineers in Suffolk County (Long Island) trapped large quantities of sand, but in doing so accelerated erosion down current in the Westhampton (New York) area. Suffolk County was sued for $70 million by Westhampton residents.

2. *Beach nourishment.* Sand may be trucked in to eroded beaches to replenish material lost during storms or as a result of normal beach erosion. In 1976 New York City began a beach replenishment project for Rockaway Beach. The proposed year of completion was 1988. This ambitious program, funded by more than $50 million from city, state, and federal coffers, involved the transport of 11.5 million cubic years of beach-replenishing sand.

However, the benefits of beach nourishment are only temporary. For example, a $2 million nourishment project at Ocean City, Maryland, lost 60 percent of its sand to furious storms only 2 weeks after it was completed!

3. *Vegetative control of erosion.* Patches of salt-tolerant ordgrass are being planted by Texas conservation workers in the shallow waters near the coastline of Galveston Bay. This grass will serve as a living buffer against the sand-washing waves of the Gulf (Figure 10-5).

4. *Restriction of coastal development.* A number of coastal states have adopted legislation to control erosion-inducing construction on their respective shorelines. In North Carolina, for example, new buildings must be located at least 40 meters (120 feet) inland from the first line of dunes.

ESTUARIES

The Estuarine Ecosystem

Estuaries are transitional zones between coastal rivers and the sea (Figure 10-6). In one sense they represent a river–ocean hydrid, possessing some of the characteristics of each ecosystem. Nevertheless, the estuary has some distinctive properties and therefore must be considered a unique ecosystem.

Major Characteristics

1. The water in the estuary is a mixture of fresh water from the stream and salt water from the ocean. The

FIGURE 10-7   The major food chains (and webs) of the estuary are based on detritus—the decomposed bodies of plants and animals.

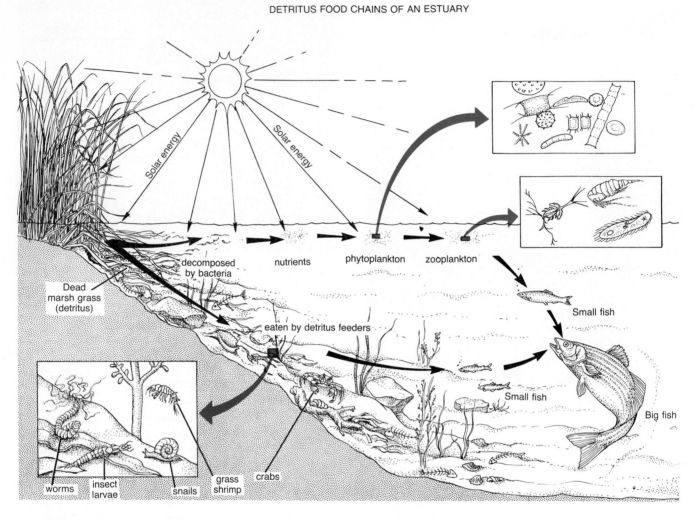

DETRITUS FOOD CHAINS OF AN ESTUARY

salinity of estuarine water is highly variable, changing by a factor of 10 within a 24-hour period; it is higher when the tide comes in and lower when the tide moves out.

2. The water level rises and falls with the tides.

3. The concentration of dissolved oxygen is relatively high because estuaries are shallow and the water is generally quite turbulent.

4. The turbidity is characteristically high because of the stirring action of the tides. Phytoplankton populations, therefore, are limited because of the reduced penetration of sunlight.

5. The nutrient levels are high. Nutrients carried down to the estuary by stream flow and those carried up by the incoming tides are concentrated in the estuaries.

Two food chains operate in the estuary. The first is the grazer food chain where dissolved nutrients may be absorbed directly by phytoplankton and rooted plants, then pass into consumers. The second is the decomposer food chain where inert organic material (decayed bodies of marsh grasses, crustaceans, worms, fishes, bacteria, and algae), known as **detritus**, is consumed directly by detritus feeders, such as clams, oysters, lobsters, and crabs (Figure 10-7).

Because of the abundant supply of nutrients and the high oxygen levels, the estuarine habitat produces more organisms than any other ecosystem except the coral reef.

Values of Estuaries and Coastal Marshes

Estuaries and coastal marshes have many values (Figures 10-8 and 10-9);

1. They are indispensable to a marine fishing industry worth $15 billion annually. Sixty percent of the

FIGURE 10-8   Coastal wetlands provide valuable wildlife habitat. Great egrets feeding in marshes along the New Jersey coast.

marine fish harvested by American commercial fishing interests spend part of their life cycle in estuaries.

Of every 100 fish taken in the Gulf of Mexico, 98 are estuary and salt marsh dependent. Many marine species use the estuary as a "nursery" in which they spend their larval period immediately after hatching from the egg. Other species, such as the Pacific salmon, pass through estuaries twice during their stream–ocean–stream migration.

2. They provide food, shelter, and breeding sites for millions of waterfowl and fur-bearing animals, such as muskrat.

3. Coastal wetlands play an important role in flood control. They absorb the shock of storm-driven waves before they rush inland and cause destruction of property and human life in heavily populated areas.

4. Estuaries and coastal wetlands are also natural pollution-filtering systems. They cleanse the water of industrial and domestic sewage delivered to the estuaries by rivers. Only 5.6 hectares (14 acres) of estuary have the same pollution-reducing effect as a $1 million waste treatment plant!

Destruction of Estuarine Habitat and Coastal Wetlands

According to the U.S. Fish and Wildlife Service, dredging to deepen channels for navigation and filling to form solid land for construction sites destroyed 260,000 hectares (640,000 acres) between 1950 and 1969. This represented 4 percent of our estuarine habitat. More than 180,000 hectares (450,000 acres) of our nation's wetland acres (much of it in estuaries) were destroyed annually in the early 1980s, much of them in California, Florida, Louisiana, New Jersey, and Texas. Louisiana alone is losing 25,000 acres per year. Freshwater fisheries in the estuaries were severely damaged by dams that block the inflow of fresh water. This results in salt water intrusion from the ocean. Wave action produced by ship and boat traffic has caused substantial erosion of estuarine margins. The National Marine Fisheries Service estimates that estuarine destruction has cost the U.S. fishing industry $200 million per year since 1954.

Estuarine and Coastal Wetland Restoration

In 1988 the U.S. Army Corps of Engineers planned to launch a $25 million project to divert fresh water from the Mississippi River into Louisiana wetlands and estuaries to check salt water intrusion. Gulf Coast wetlands are also now being created from scratch. For example, the U.S. Army Corps of Engineers is now using sediment dredged from river channels to create new marshes. They have already created 1,200 hectares (3,000 acres) of new marshes in the coastal region of the Gulf. Important as these gains are, they

The Chesapeake Bay:
Case Study of an Estuary

The Chesapeake Bay, North America's largest estuary, is a long, narrow arm of the Atlantic Ocean that extends northward into Maryland and cuts the state into two parts. It includes two major ports: Baltimore to the north and Norfolk (Virginia) to the south. Other major cities included in its drainage basin are Washington, D.C., Annapolis, Maryland, and Richmond, Virginia. It has a shoreline of more than 12,800 kilometers (8,000 miles). It is fed by over 150 rivers (Figure 1). The bay has supplied abundant protein, as well as providing shipping and recreational resources for Americans for almost two centuries. Stresses on

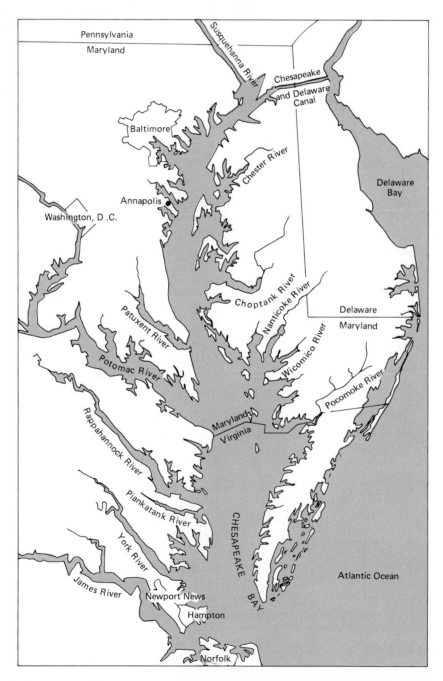

FIGURE 1   The Chesapeake Bay and Tributaries.

this vast ecosystem are already formidable and will intensify in the near future.

The population living near the bay has grown rapidly, from 3.7 million in 1940 to 14 million in 1988. The bay will grow by an additional 1.6 million people by the end of this century. By the year 2020, the bay area population will be 40 percent greater, cargo transport will have doubled, recreational boating will have increased threefold, and fishing pressure on the bay will have risen sharply.

The bay is the largest producer of blue crabs in the world. It yields more oysters and soft-shelled clams than any other region in the United States. It provides wintering grounds for more than 500,000 Canada geese. Important food fishes, such as striped bass, white perch, and shad, spawn in its tributaries. The bay's annual fish harvest is worth more than $100 million—a vaild reason for calling the bay "one vast outdoor protein factory."

Within the past few decades, the ecological stability of Chesapeake Bay has been threatened by pollutants from both point and nonpoint sources.

From 1976 to 1983, the EPA conducted a $27 million study of the bay. It concluded that immediate and intensive efforts at pollution control would be necessary to restore its health. In response to this warning, in 1983 the federal government and the states along the bay signed the Chesapeake Bay Agreement, pledging to correct the problems. This is a formidable task. More than 2,640 facilities hold permits to use the bay as a cesspool for their pollutants.

Eutrophication

One serious pollution problem in the bay is eutrophication. The nutrients responsible for this pollution come from a large number of sources, such as sewage treatment plants, food-processing facilities, and farm runoff. Still another source is erosion caused by shoreline development. Jerome Williams, professor of oceanography at the U.S. Naval Academy, comments on this source: "Mud goes into the Bay every time it rains. Fewer trees, more construction, more parking lots, more runoff—just about everything man does stirs up the water."

The increased fertility of the water has caused the formation of dense blankets of floating algae. These algal blooms, in turn, have shaded out much submerged aquatic vegetation (SAV). As a result, the SAV population has declined dramatically. For instance, a 241-hectare (600-acre) area that had been densely populated with these plants in 1953 is now completely bare! Today the amount of SAV in the bay is about 80 percent less than it was in the late 1960s. This drastic decrease in SAV, in turn, has caused a sharp reduction in the number of diving ducks that fed on the molluscs and crustaceans associated with the SAV. Moreover, populations of fish (shad, herring, striped bass) that use the SAV as favored spawning habitat have also declined.

Fortunately, eutrophication can be controlled by reducing nutrient input. To this end, more than $700 million of state and federal money has been spent to upgrade sewage treatment plants. The ultimate cleanup costs may well exceed several billion dollars. In addition, Maryland has banned the use of phosphate detergents. All six states in the bay's drainage basin should follow Maryland's lead. Bay region farmers have been strongly encouraged to control manure and fertilizer runoff and to practice conservation tillage to reduce soil erosion. Furthermore, under the Critical Area Act, Maryland has recently established certain "critical areas" along the bay shores where erosion-inducing development would be greatly restricted. These strategies to control eutrophication are beginning to pay off. For example, within 3 years, the amount of phosphorous discharged into the bay fell from 23.8 million kilograms (10.8 million pounds) to 19.3 million kilograms (8.8 million pounds) annually.

Contamination of the Bay Food Web with Toxic Substances

Poisonous chemicals that adversely affect the Chesapeake food web are entering the bay from multiple sources. Point sources include industrial discharges and accidental oil spills. Nonpoint sources include agricultural runoff, urban runoff, atmospheric fallout, and rainfall.

One factor that complicates the problem is the bay's low flushing rate. Only 1 percent of the settleable waste that enters the bay eventually is flushed to the ocean. The remainder settles in the water to form bottom sediment. Among the toxic substances polluting the bay's waters are metals such as cadmium, chromium, copper, lead, nickel, and zinc. Most of the toxic substances persist in the environment for many years. As they feed, burrowing clams nose their way through the bottom muds, where they ingest considerable amounts of toxic materials. A mechanism is thus provided by which toxic chemicals enter human food chains. The contaminated clams may be eaten directly by humans, or by the ducks and fish that are in turn eaten by humans. The massive release of the toxic pesticide Kepone into the James River at Hopewell, Virginia, in 1975 was one of the most serious toxic insults ever suffered by the bay ecosystem.

Toxic chemicals may be the cause of the drastic population decline of the striped bass in the bay. The harvest of this fish dropped dramatically from 2,608 metric tons in 1970 to only 272 metric tons in 1983—an 89 percent reduction. U.S. Fish and Wildlife scientists have found high levels of lead, zinc, arsenic, and selenium in young fish taken from the Potomac River. Moreover, the backbones of these fish were 20 percent weaker than normal. A weakened backbone reduces the ability of striped bass to compete for food, avoid predators, or endure the stresses of migration and reproduction. Fish and Wildlife Service biologists believe that the toxic chemicals cause abnormal development of the backbone even before the fish are 3 months old. At present, the eggs and young of this fish, as well as bottom sediments in six tributaries of the bay, are being intensely monitored to determine the kinds and concentrations of the toxic chemicals present.

Until recently, the EPA and state environmental agencies permitted old industrial plants to discharge large amounts of pollutants into the bay. For example, a Baltimore steel plant could legally discharge 38 million tons of cyanide every year. Fortunately, the rules are now being tightened. Stricter discharge permits forced Bethlehem Steel to reduce its toxic emissions by 95 percent by 1987. To accomplish this, Bethle-

hem spent $25 million to upgrade its waste treatment facility.

Unfortunately, it will take much more than money to nurse the bay back to ecological health. It will require the dedicated and highly integrated effort of the six states in the drainage system of the bay. It will demand a much greater sense of environmental responsibility on the part of municipal and industrial dischargers. And the control of nonpoint pollution will require the coordinated actions of thousands of bay area cities, as well as millions of farmers and citizens on a scale unprecedented in the history of estuary cleanups. The challenge is enormous!

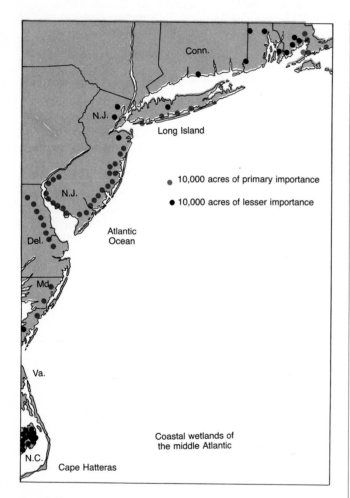

FIGURE 10-9 Coastal wetlands of the Mid-Atlantic.

are minuscule compared to the current rate of destruction.

THE OCEAN

From the Stone Age to the Space Age, the ocean has served human needs in a great variety of ways: (1)

Its 32 million-cubic-mile volume is a virtually limitless water supply for all organisms on this planet, including humans. (2) Trillions of tiny algae in its sunlit waters have aided in replenishing the oxygen supply of the earth's atmosphere, upon which the survival of all life depends. (3) It has served as a highway for international transport. (4) Ever since primitive human beings scooped fish from its tidal pools with their bare hands, the ocean has provided humans with abundant supplies of essential protein.

Major Features of the Marine Ecosystem

Some of the major ecological features of the oceanic environment are as follows:

1. It covers 70 percent of the earth's surface.
2. It extends to a depth of up to 11 kilometers (6.5 miles) (Mariana Trench) and hence has a much greater vertical dimension, or "thickness," than the terrestrial or freshwater environment.
3. The ocean is about 70 times as salty as a lake or stream.
4. The ocean is continuously circulating (Figure 10-10). The Alaskan Current brings cold water down the Pacific coast; the Gulf Stream brings water upward along the Atlantic Coast. These currents modify the temperatures of nearby coastal regions. (As a result, New York City has a relatively moderate climate, even in winter, whereas summer evenings in San Francisco may be quite chilly.) Vertically moving currents, or upwellings, bring nutrient-rich cold water from the ocean bottom to the surface (Figure 10-11).
5. The sea is relatively infertile compared to fresh water. Nitrates and phosphates are extremely scarce. Two exceptions to this are the areas of upwelling and estuaries where streams discharge massive loads of sediment.

FIGURE 10-10 Major ocean current. The closer the flow lines are together, the stronger the current.

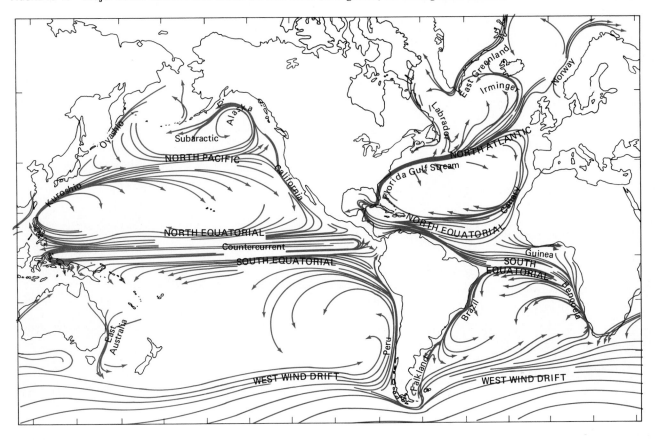

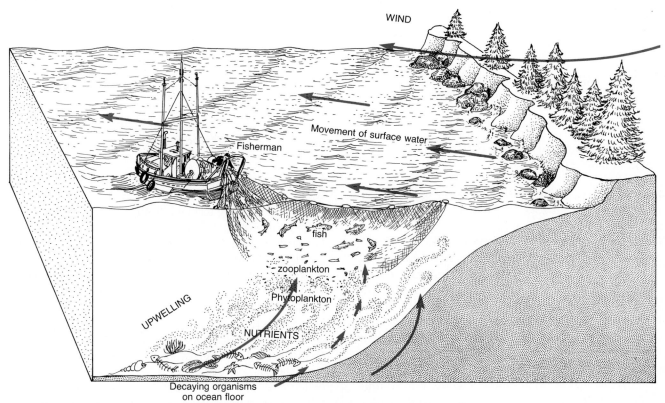

FIGURE 10-11 The upwelling phenomenon. Wind moves the surface water outward. As a result cold water from the ocean bottom moves upward and shoreward carrying dissolved nutrients with it. Consequently the area of upwelling is biologically productive.

FIGURE 10-12 Life zones of the ocean and their characteristics.

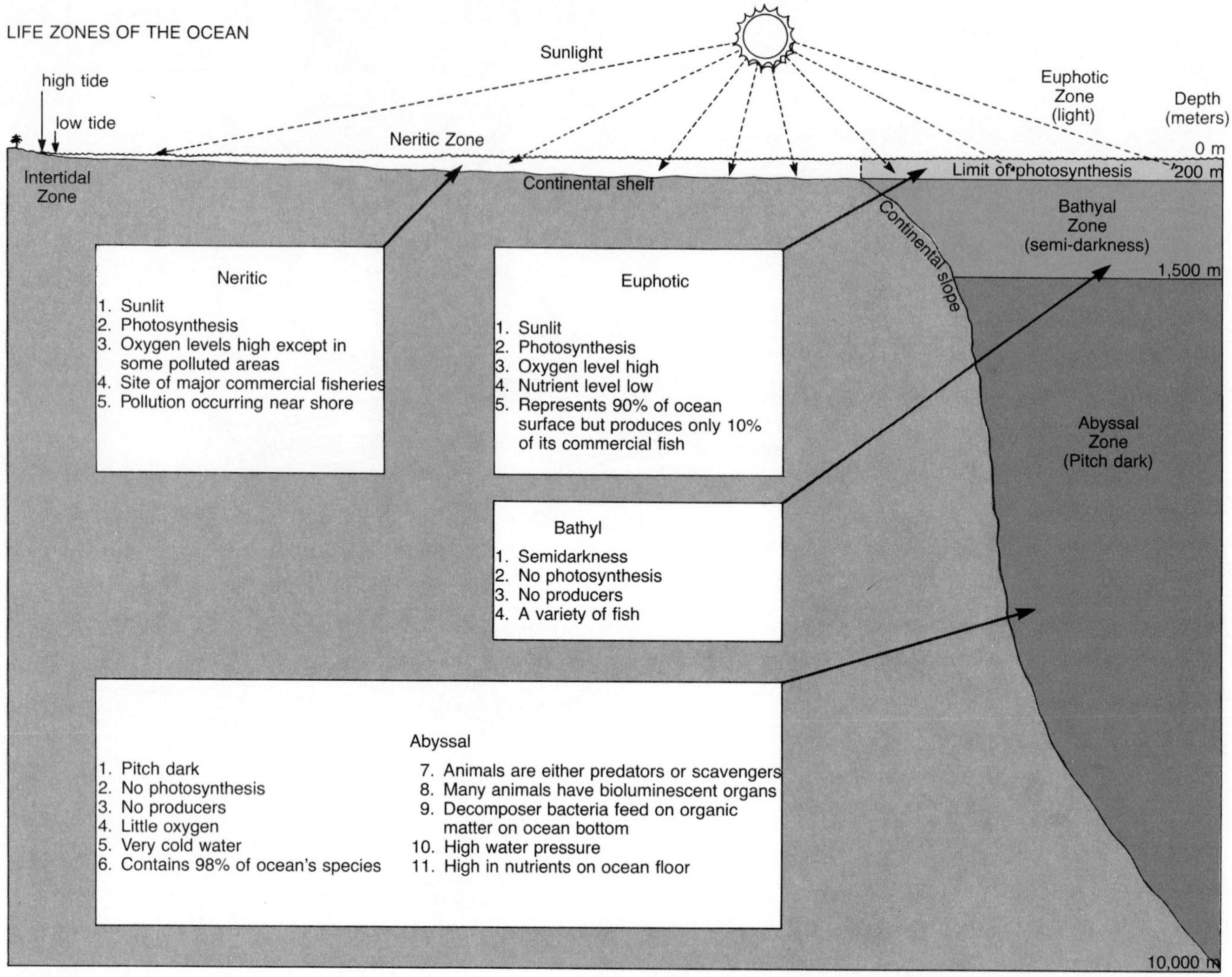
LIFE ZONES OF THE OCEAN
Sunlight
high tide
low tide
Euphotic Zone (light)
Depth (meters)
Neritic Zone
0 m
Intertidal Zone
Continental shelf
Limit of photosynthesis
200 m
Continental slope
Bathyal Zone (semi-darkness)
1,500 m
Neritic
1. Sunlit
2. Photosynthesis
3. Oxygen levels high except in some polluted areas
4. Site of major commercial fisheries
5. Pollution occurring near shore
Euphotic
1. Sunlit
2. Photosynthesis
3. Oxygen level high
4. Nutrient level low
5. Represents 90% of ocean surface but produces only 10% of its commercial fish
Abyssal Zone (Pitch dark)
Bathyl
1. Semidarkness
2. No photosynthesis
3. No producers
4. A variety of fish
Abyssal
1. Pitch dark
2. No photosynthesis
3. No producers
4. Little oxygen
5. Very cold water
6. Contains 98% of ocean's species
7. Animals are either predators or scavengers
8. Many animals have bioluminescent organs
9. Decomposer bacteria feed on organic matter on ocean bottom
10. High water pressure
11. High in nutrients on ocean floor
10,000 m

Zonation of the Ocean

The ocean consists of several ecological regions, as shown in Figure 10-12.

Neritic Zone. The neritic zone is the marine counterpart of the littoral zone of the lake. It is a relatively warm, nutrient-rich, shallow region. It overlies the continental shelf, a submerged extension of the continent. Occurring along our Atlantic, Pacific, and Gulf coasts, it is 16 to 320 kilometers (10 to 200 miles) wide and up to 60 to 180 meters (200 to 600 feet) deep. The neritic zone ends where the continental shelf abruptly terminates and the ocean bottom plunges to great depths. The nutrients of the neritic zone are supplied primarily by upwelling and the sedimentary discharge of streams. Sunlight normally penetrates to the ocean bottom, permitting considerable photosynthetic activity in a large population of floating and rooted plants. Animal populations are rich and varied (Figure 10-13). Oxygen depletion is not a problem because of photosynthesis and wave action. The total amount of biomass in the neritic zone is greater per unit volume of water than in any other part of the ocean.

Euphotic Zone. The euphotic zone is the open-water zone of the ocean that corresponds to the limnetic zone of a lake. The term **euphotic**, which literally means "abundance of light," is appropriate to this zone, for it has sufficient sunlight to support photosynthesis and a considerable population of phytoplankton. In turn, the phytoplankton support a host of tiny "grazing" herbivores such as the small crustaceans. The total energy available to animal food chains by euphotic phytoplankton is much greater than that produced by plants of the neritic zone; this is largely because of the vast area of the euphotic zone, which extends for thousands of miles across the open sea. The degree to which light penetrates, of course, depends on the transparency of the surface waters. Because sunlight cannot penetrate deeper than 200 meters (650 feet) in most marine habitats, this is frequently considered the lower limit of the euphotic zone.

FIGURE 10-13 Communities occupying the neritic zone. Seaweeds and algae are the producers. They form the base of the food chains and webs. Tiny zooplankton feed on the producers and in turn are consumed by fish, lobsters, crabs and whales. The top consumers are the sea birds, tuna, swordfish and humans. The bottom dwellers which cling to rocks or are buried in the mud, include clams, snails, crabs and bacteria. They feed on detritus. The arrows on the left indicate upwelling of nutrients from the ocean bottom.

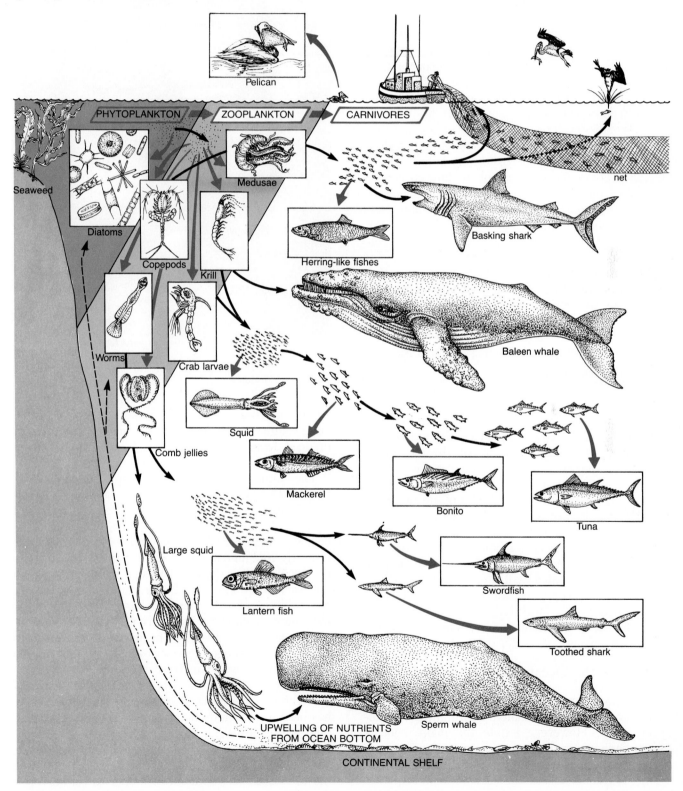

BATHYAL ZONE. Beneath the euphotic zone is the **bathyal zone**. It is a region of semidarkness. Photosynthesis cannot occur here and so no producer organisms can survive.

ABYSSAL ZONE. Beneath the bathyl zone is the abyssal zone. The abyssal zone is the cold, dark-water zone of the ocean depths that roughly corresponds to the profundal zone of the lake habitat. It lies immediately above the ocean floor. Animal life is rather sparse there. Any animal living in the abyssal zone must be adapted to low light, to intense cold (because the abyssal water frequently approaches the freezing point), to extremely low levels of dissolved oxygen (because no photosynthesis can occur here), to water pressures of thousands of pounds per square inch, and to scarcity of food.

In many areas, the sediment of the abyssal zone is rich in nutrients. These nutrients come from the decaying bodies of organisms from the sulit waters above and from excretions of living animals. For example, in certain regions of the western Atlantic, the phosphate concentration at a depth of 900 meters (3,000 feet) may be 10 times greater than the concentration at 90 meters (300 feet). Because neither phytoplankton nor herbivorous animals can exist in the abyssal zone, most consumers are either predators or detrivores. A number of the deep-sea fish of the abyss have evolved luminescent organs that may aid them in finding food and mates.

Marine Food Chains

Because the ocean covers 70 percent of the earth's surface, it receives 70 percent of the earth's solar energy. Except for the anchored green plants of the neritic zone, this solar energy is trapped primarily by the phytoplankton (producers) in the open water of the oceans. Scientists estimate that 18 billion metric tons of living plant matter (mostly phytoplankton) are produced annually. This, in turn, supports 4.5 billion metric tons of zooplankton. Marine zooplankton may be consumed by a variety of filter feeders, including shrimp, herring, anchovies, and whales. The terminal link of the marine food chain is represented by fish-eating predators such as the shark, barracuda, cod, salmon, cormorants, pelicans, and humans. As in the terrestrial food chains, the shorter the chain, the more biomass is available to the top-level organisms.

Pollution of the Oceans

In a very real sense, the ocean is our last frontier—the last reasonably uncontaminated environment remaining on earth. However, despite the many benefits humans derive from the ocean, we treat it as if it were expendable. We use it as the world's largest sewer.

OCEAN DUMPING OF SEWAGE. For decades the neritic zone bordering our Atlantic, Gulf, and Pacific

FIGURE 10-14 Barge hauling refuse from New York City to dumping grounds.

coasts has been used as a dumping ground for a large volume and variety of wastes, including sediments dredged from harbors and rivers, municipal sewage sludge, industrial wastes, and even household garbage.

The National Oceanic and Atmospheric Administration (NOAA) today monitors the levels of toxic pollutants in oysters and bottom-dwelling fish at 150 coastal stations. This so-called Oyster Watch, which scientists believe is highly reliable, has pinpointed the five most seriously contaminated sites along our coasts. They are (1) the New York Bight, (2) Boston Harbor, (3) Salem (Massachusetts) Harbor, (4) Raritan Bay (New Jersey), and (5) the coastal waters off San Diego, California. Let's now examine the most seriously polluted site.

The New York Bight. The harmful effects of the dumping of sewage and sewage sludge on marine ecosystems are well illustrated by the problems at the New York Bight. The bight is a relatively shallow area over the continental shelf opposite New York Bay. It has been used as a dumping ground for sewage sludge (and other wastes) for more than 60 years (Figure 10-14). In the early 1870s, for example, more than 7 billion liters (1.8 billion gallons) of sewage sludge from the New York metropolitan area spewed through 130 discharge pipes directly into the bight each year. More than 16 percent of this sewage had received no treatment whatsoever. In addition, raw sewage from 23 New Jersey towns entered the bight. As a result, the bottom of the bight is blanketed with a layer of black sludge that is 105 square kilometers (40 square miles) in area. This "blanket" is contaminated with a large variety of pollutants ranging from toxic metals and organic compounds (PCBs) to viruses and bacteria that can cause human disease.

The long-continued dumping of sludge and raw sewage in the New York Bight has had many adverse effects on the marine ecosystem:

1. Because of the high BOD of much of the waste, the concentration of dissolved oxygen in the region was often less than 2 ppm. Populations of microscopic algae and crustaceans fell sharply or disappeared altogether. This alteration, in turn, caused a decline in many commercially valuable species of plankton-eating fish.

2. The stomachs of bottom-dwelling fish like flounders, which were caught near the dump site, contained a number of abnormal items, like bandages, cigarette filters, and hair.

3. Some fish suffered from black gill disease, characterized by abnormally dark gill membranes and reduced respiratory function.

4. Toxic metals such as nickel, chromium, and lead reached unusually high levels in some fish.

5. A considerable number of harmful mutations resulting from chromosome damage were observed in young mackerel. Moreover, clam and oyster beds were so highly contaminated with disease-causing microorganisms that these crustaceans were unfit for human consumption. Apparently the bacteria and viruses were transported from the waste to the clam and oyster beds by shoreward-moving currents.

In 1985 the EPA directed New York City to dump its sewage sludge at a newly designated site at the edge of the continental shelf 170 kilometers (106 miles) from the coast. The city began dumping its sludge at the new site in 1987. But, in 1988, the U.S. Congress agreed to ban all ocean dumping as of January 1, 1992. Severe fines will be imposed on any community in violation of the ban. This action should finally put an end to sludge dumping by cities in New York and New Jersey, which has amounted to 7 million metric tons per year.

DREDGE SPOILS. Eighty percent of the waste that has been dumped into our coastal waters is **dredge spoil**. This is sediment (sand, silt, clay, and gravel) that has been scooped from harbor and river bottoms to deepen channels for navigation. About 40 million cubic meters (52 million cubic yards) are dredged annually—about 1 cubic meter for every six people in the United States. This waste poses an enormous waste disposal problem.

The urgently needed dredging of Baltimore Harbor was postponed for 15 years because no agreement could be reached on where to dump the spoil. Because land dumping is unfeasible due to the lack of suitable sites and the high cost, much of the spoil generated in the mid-1980s was dumped in 70 different ocean sites designated for that purpose.

Unfortunately, about 1 of every 3 tons of dredge spoils is contaminated with both urban and industrial waste, as well as with pollutants resulting from urban and agricultural runoff. These contaminants (PCBs, heavy metals, and so on) could eventually enter marine food webs and harm not only ocean life but humans as well. Under the terms of the Marine Protection, Research, and Sanctuary Act, the U.S. Army Corps of Engineers, which does most of the dredging, was charged with finding suitable disposal sites beyond the continental shelf. At such sites, the water is so deep that most of the pollutants would be greatly diluted, so that their adverse effects on the marine ecosystem would be minimized.

PLASTIC POLLUTION. The world's oceans are seriously polluted with plastic (Figure 10-15). The enormous volume of plastic debris riding the waves is not appreciated until one hikes along a beach. During a recent 3-hour cleanup of a 260-kilometer (157-mile) stretch of the Texas coast, the following plastic objects were removed: 31,800 bags, 30,000 bottles, 29,000 lids, 7,500 milk jugs, 15,600 six-pack rings, 2,000 disposable diapers, and 1,000 tampon applicators. Although seemingly harmless, such materials kill at least 1 million sea birds and more than 100,000 whales, porpoises, and seals every year (Figure 10-16). The gut of a sea turtle found dead in Hawaii was jammed with a variety of lethal objects, ranging from golf tees and bottle caps to bags and imitation flowers. Furthermore, hundreds of sea birds, salmon and marine mammals die when they become entangled in discarded fish nets.

Plastic causes wildlife mortality in several ways: (1) After being swallowed, it can neither be digested nor voided. Death is caused by blockage of the digestive tract. (2) Plastic entanglement may cause death by drowning. (3) Plastic entanglement may cause starvation because it prevents marine birds and mammals from searching for food.

The sources of these lethal plastic pollutants are many. Every industrialized society lives in a plastic world. Manufacturers in the United States alone annually produce 6 million metric tons of plastic. Much of it is discarded into streams by litterers and then carried downstream to the ocean or dumped directly into the ocean from fishing boats and steamers or from garbage barges. The National Academy of Sciences reports that more than 5 million plastic containers are tossed overboard from ocean-going vessels every day. Over a 3-year period, that would be one container for

FIGURE 10-15 This "plastic mountain" represents only one week's accumulation of plastic and styrofoam waste by an American middle class family. The following items are included: 6 pieces of foam cushioning, 5 kitchen garbage bags, 5 sandwich bags, 2 toothbrush holders, 2 egg cartons, 1 waste basket, 2 motor oil bottles, 1 soap tray, 1 mixing spoon, 1 fork, 1 ice cream bucket, 1 waste basket, 1 milk jug, 1 motor coolant jug, 1 plant food container, 1 cook's mixing bowl, and 1 bag for dry-cleaned clothes! Many plastic throw-aways are also accumulated at sea by fishermen, ship's crews and passengers and are dumped overboard.

each person on earth. In some regions of the Atlantic and Pacific oceans, polyethylene packing pellets reaching a density of 2,500 to 10,000 per hectare (1,000 to 4,000 per acre) have been found floating on the surface. Part of the problem lies in the fact that plastic cannot be broken down by bacteria; in other words, it is nonbiodegradable. Another problem is that most plastic items are quite buoyant. This makes it possible for a golf tee from a Seattle golf course eventually to serve as "food" for a sea bird in the South Pacific.

The amount of plastic floating and bobbing on the global seas will certainly increase. After all, world production of plastic is expected to double by the year 2000. Commercial fishers lose more than 136,000 metric tons of plastic lines and nets annually. In the North Pacific alone, more than 32,000 kilometers (20,000 miles) of plastic nets are set out by fishermen nightly. Within a year, more than 4,800 kilometers (3,000

FIGURE 10-16 Plastic six-pack frame threatens Western Gull on California beach with death by strangulation.

miles) of netting is lost, forming a considerable threat to marine life. It is ironic that 10 times as many fur seals die from fish net entanglement as are killed by the Pribilof Island (Alaska) hunters, who have been sharply criticized for their fur seal "butchery."

Control of Plastic Pollution. How can plastic pollution be controlled? At present, the dumping in the ocean is regulated by the London Dumping Convention (1972), which has been ratified by 58 nations. It regulated disposal from all *trash-hauling ships.* In the United States this convention was implemented by the Ocean Dumping Act, already discussed with reference to sludge disposal. Another international law that controls plastic pollution is the 1973 Marine Pollution Convention, or MARPOL Act. Annex V of the act regulates the dumping of plastic by all ships *other* than trash ships. After several years of deliberation, Annex V was eventually ratified when both the United States and Great Britain signed the act in 1987. As a result, beginning December 31, 1988, it was illegal for the ships of the 15 signatory nations and for the ships of *any* nation plying their waters to dump plastic at sea. Since the 15 signatory nations represent over 50 percent of the gross tonnage of the world's commercial ships, this agreement should help reduce plastic pollution. The Coast Guard will enforce Annex V for the United States.

Another way to reduce this problem would be to recycle more plastic materials. Some progress is being made. For example, in the United States, about 20 percent of all plastic soft drink bottles are reprocessed into paint brushes, stuffing, and industrial straps. Some discarded plastic is recycled into "lumber" used in the construction industry.

Perhaps the ultimate solution to plastic pollution is at the source of the plastic—the manufacturing process. Some manufacturers, for example, have recently developed a type of plastic that is photodegradable; it will disintegrate when exposed to ultraviolet light from the sun. At least 11 U.S. states have laws that require photodegradable plastic in some products, such as the "rings" for soft drink and beer six-packs. A few manufacturers in the United States, Canada, and Italy are now producing biodegradable plastic bags. When photo- or biodegradable plastics come into mass production, this curious but potent threat to marine life may gradually disappear, so long as the breakdown products are not harmful.

OIL POLLUTION

Sources of Oil Pollution.   Oil has always polluted the sea. About half of the oil in the seas has seeped through cracks in the ocean floor. This naturally occurring oil, however, is of little concern because the sources are widely distributed. It is the oil from human activities that concerns most conservationists (Figure 10-17).

Even though it only accounts for the other 50 percent of the oil in the ocean, it is generally spilled in localized regions where it can do considerable damage (Figure 10-17). The spill off the coast of Alaska in March of 1989 is a good example.

Although *oil-tanker accidents* are the most dramatic source, they account for only 5 percent of the oil that enters the ocean. Tanker accidents are widely publicized by the press, radio, and TV (Figures 10-18 and 10-19). In fact, it was the breakup of the *Torrey Canyon* off the British coast in 1968, during which over 136 million liters (36 million gallons) of oil were lost, that first alerted the general public to the problem. In 1976 the *Argo Merchant* broke apart on the Nantucket Shoals, 24 miles off the Massachusetts coast and polluted the seas with 29 million liters (7.7 million gallons) of heavy fuel oil. On March 17, 1978, one of the world's most serious tanker spills occurred. The Council on Environmental Quality describes the episode: "The oil tanker *Amoco Cadiz* went aground 2 kilometers (1.2 miles) off Portsall on the coast of France. Efforts to stop the spill or contain it were unsuccessful." The ship broke apart, and big winds and seas made it impossible to transfer oil to other tankers. As a result, the entire cargo of 228 million liters (60 million gallons) of crude oil was spilled, polluting the waters and shoreline along 198 kilometers (124 miles) of coast and 61 kilometers (38 miles) out to sea. Not only was there severe destruction of fish and seabirds, but the heavy oil ruined the beauty of the coastal area and had an economic impact on the shore-based villages. A number of citizen's lawsuits were filed against the Amoco Oil Company, owners of the tanker.

FIGURE 10-17 Sources of oil pollution in the ocean. Most of the oil comes from river-runoff, tankers and other transportation, and municipal and industrial sources.

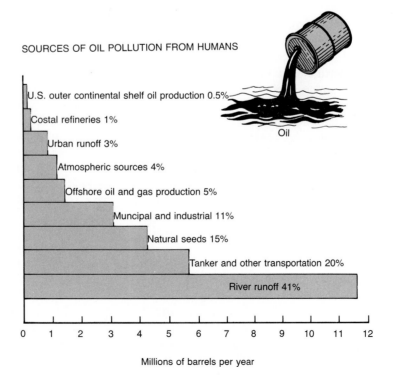

SOURCES OF OIL POLLUTION FROM HUMANS

Oil

U.S. outer continental shelf oil production 0.5%

Costal refineries 1%

Urban runoff 3%

Atmospheric sources 4%

Offshore oil and gas production 5%

Muncipal and industrial 11%

Natural seeds 15%

Tanker and other transportation 20%

River runoff 41%

0 1 2 3 4 5 6 7 8 9 10 11 12

Millions of barrels per year

FIGURE 10-18 Aerial view of the ill-fated oil tanker Argo Merchant, which broke in two off Nantucket Island near Massachusetts on December 16, 1976. As a result of the accident, 29.2 million liters (7.7 million gallons) of oil were released, more than half of the oil spilled in U. S. waters in 1976–77. This one spill released more oil than 10,553 lesser incidents during 1976.

In 1988, almost 10 years after the spill, the company was ordered by the courts to pay out millions of dollars in compensation.

On March 24, 1989, Americans were horrified by news of a 40-million-liter (11-million-gallon) oil spill in Alaska's Prince William Sound near the port of Valdez. Exxon's supertanker ran aground on a reef in the sound, releasing much of its oil into the pristine, biologically rich waters. The oil slick spread quickly and by the end of the summer had polluted 2300 kilometers (1400 miles) of shoreline. Thousands of seabirds and otters perished in the oil, which formed a layer a meter thick in some places (Figure 10-20). Making matters worse, the spill occurred only two weeks before migrating flocks of waterfowl arrived. Many birds spend the summer in the waters of Prince William Sound; others merely stop there to feed and rest on their way to the Arctic tundra where they breed.

The Valdez spill was not the largest in history, but probably will go down as one of the most costly, economically and environmentally. The damage can be attributed to four key factors. First, the spill occurred in the relatively protected waters close to land. Second, cleanup was delayed for several crucial days. The special cleanup force stationed at Valdez had been all but abandoned by the oil companies operating there. There was an insufficient number of oil skimmers close at hand. Third, the waters off the sound are cold. Biological degradation of the oil could be retarded. Fourth, the waters were extraordinarily rich in sea life.

For many years, the ecosystems of Antarctica were considered to be pristine—virtually unaffected by human activity. Unfortunately, on January 28, 1989 the *Bahia Paraiw*, an Argentine tanker, struck a reef off the northern coast, ripped a 30-foot gash in its hull, and began releasing kerosene into the frigid water at the rate of 800 liters (3000 gallons) per day. The spreading oil destroyed large numbers of crustaceans (krill) used as food by fish, sea birds, and whales. Many penguins were soaked with kerosene and threatened with death. Nearly all the chicks of the skua, a huge gull-like bird, were destroyed. As a top scientist who had rushed to the scene to oversee the spill lamented: "This is the worst ecological disaster for Antarctica, period!"

Offshore Oil-Well Accidents. In 1969 a major oil well off the coast of Santa Barbara, California, accidentally released thousands of gallons of oil because of a faulty drilling technique (Figure 10-21). However, the spill was a mere grease spot compared to the oil well blowout that occurred in the Bay of Campeche off Mexico's east

MAJOR OIL SPILLS

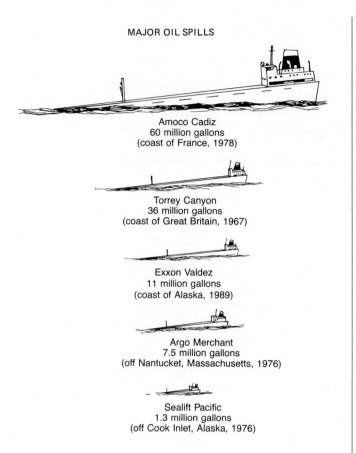

Amoco Cadiz
60 million gallons
(coast of France, 1978)

Torrey Canyon
36 million gallons
(coast of Great Britain, 1967)

Exxon Valdez
11 million gallons
(coast of Alaska, 1989)

Argo Merchant
7.5 million gallons
(off Nantucket, Massachusetts, 1976)

Sealift Pacific
1.3 million gallons
(off Cook Inlet, Alaska, 1976)

FIGURE 10-19 Major tanker oil spills.

FIGURE 10-20 An oil-soaked cormorant registers its protest to the atrocious oil spill off Alaska's coast in the once-pristine waters of Prince William Sound. Thousands of birds and mammals died. Volunteers cleaned many birds and mammals that were caught in the oil and survived, but the animals prospects for survival were still often dim.

coast in 1979. Oil escaped from the well for several months, threatening marine life along the Texas shore, several hundred kilometers to the north.

Without tighter controls, oil well accidents could increase dramatically in the future. For example, American oil companies alone drill about 1,300 offshore oil wells a year (Figure 10-22). Four thousand new offshore wells are drilled worldwide each year.

Inland Sources of Oil Pollution. You might be surprised to know that about 30 percent of the oil in the ocean comes from inland sources far from the ocean shore. The major sources are service stations, motor vehicles, and factories.

1. *Waste oil from service stations.* Remember the last time you drove up to a service station and asked for an oil change? Did you ever wonder what happened to the old oil? Until quite recently, it was probably discharged into sewers that drain into rivers and eventually flowed to the sea. Two or three quarts of oil doesn't seem important. But how about billions of quarts? In fact, millions of motorists throughout the world are indirectly responsible for a much greater volume of oil pollution of the oceans than is caused by tanker breakups and oil well blowouts.

2. *Airborne hydrocarbons from factories, service stations, and vehicles.* Maybe you fill up at a self-service

pump. If so, you are well aware of the pungent odor of evaporating gasoline. Obviously, not all of the gasoline went into your tank. Some of it escapes into the air. Some unburned gas also escapes from your exhaust pipe and becomes airborne. Evaporation of petroleum also occurs at thousands of industrial plants throughout the world. These pollutants wash from the sky polluting the oceans with at least 20 million metric tons of airborne petroleum hydrocarbons annually.

Adverse Effects of Oil Pollution. Precisely how a given oil spill will affect marine life is difficult to predict. Why? Because the effects depend on a number of highly variable factors, such as the amount and type of oil (crude or refined), proximity to organisms, season of the year, weather, ocean currents, and wind velocity.

1. *Reduction of photosynthetic rates.* Because a heavy oil slick is opaque, it blocks sunlight. Photosynthetic activity of the marine algae below the oil barrier is sharply reduced, if not arrested completely. Such diminished rates of food production restrict the growth and reproduction of all organisms directly or indirectly dependent on marine algae for food.

2. *Concentration of chlorinated hydrocarbons.* An oil spill may greatly increase the concentration of chlorinated hydrocarbons, such as the pesticides DDT, dieldrin, toxaphene, and the PCBs. These com-

FIGURE 10-21 Beach clean-up after the Santa Barbara oil spill. The straw in the foreground was used to soak up the oil.

FIGURE 10-22 Offshore oil platform.

pounds are highly soluble in oil and tend to be concentrated in the oil from surrounding waters. Their concentration in the oil slick may be many times that in the surrounding water. As a result, marine organisms such as phytoplankton, as well as animals such as crustaceans and larval fishes, which migrate to the sea surface at night, are adversely affected. Even if those organisms are not killed directly, their physiology, growth, reproduction, and behavior may be impaired.

3. *Mortality of marine animals.* The heaviest influx of oil occurs in the neritic zone near the continental margins—the zone where virtually all of our shellfish (oysters, lobsters, and shrimp) and over half of our commercial fish crop are produced (Figure 10-23). (The *Amoco Cadiz* spill caused $25 million in damage to the French oyster industry alone.) The number of sea birds killed annually worldwide is enormous. In a single winter, more than 250,000 murres, eiders, and puffins were destroyed by oil pollution. In 1988, thousands of these birds were destroyed by oil spills in the North Sea.

4. *Food chain contamination with carcinogens.* Crude oil is not just a single compound but a complex mixture of dozens of different hydrocarbons such as benzopyrene, an acknowledged cancer-inducing

FIGURE 10-23   Distribution of world fisheries. Coastal areas and upwelling areas together supply over 99 percent of world fish production. The deep ocean (white in above figure) forms 90 percent of the ocean area but accounts for only 1 percent of the fish catch, if upwelling areas are excluded.

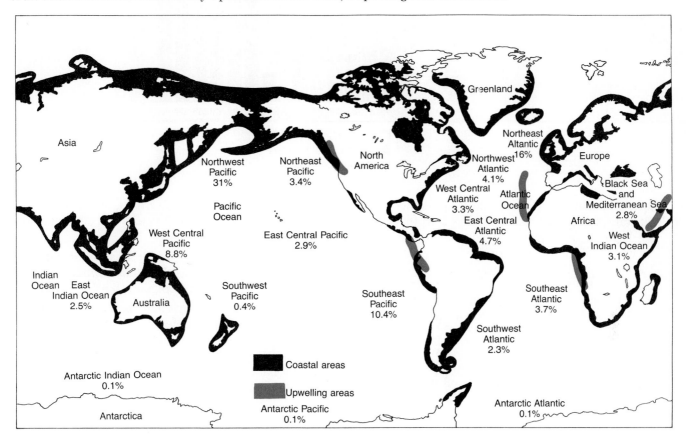

chemical, or carcinogen. These carcinogens may be concentrated in marine organisms such as shrimp, lobsters, and fish, and may eventually be consumed by humans.

5. *Distruption of chemical communication in marine mammals.* Several of the hydrocarbons in crude oil mimic chemicals used by marine animals to guide them during mating, feeding, homing, and migrating. Flooding the ocean with psuedosignals from oil spills might derange the behavior of marine animals, causing them to expend valuable energy in nonadaptive pursuits. The eventual decline in vitality and numbers of the species would seem assured.

Control of Oil Pollution.   Upgrading tankers, inspection systems, and international cooperation have reduced the number of oil spills from tankers. But tighter controls are still needed. Let's examine some strategies for oil pollution control after a spill has occurred.

1. *Fingerprinting.* The EPA's research laboratory at Athens, Georgia, is perfecting techniques by which a given oil sample can be indentified by its "finger-prints." The distinctive fingerprints are recorded by a sophisticated instrument known as a **gas-liquid chromatograph**. By this technique, investigators trying to locate the source of an oil slick can determine with certainty whether the oil comes from a natural oil seep, a particular pipeline, a certain offshore oil well, or a tanker transporting oil from, say, Kuwait or Alaska. Once the source is identified, appropriate legal action can be taken against the parties responsible for the spill.

2. *Physical cleanup*. Oil that washes ashore may be cleaned up manually or with machines. In the Valdez spill, for example, workers sopped up oil with absorbent pads. Other workers scoured the beaches with hot water, washing the oil back into the sound where it was picked up by oil skimmers, vacuum type devices that skim the oil off the surface and empty it into barges. Early in the spill, planes dropped absorbent material on slicks, which were later picked up by boats. In many spills, straw has been used to sop up oil washing ashore.

   All these methods are time consuming and costly. Many of them are fairly ineffective. Oil washed off the beaches near Valdez, for example, was spread

FIGURE **10-24** The quantity and value of the U.S. fish harvest—1970–1985. The harvest has been quite constant since 1980.

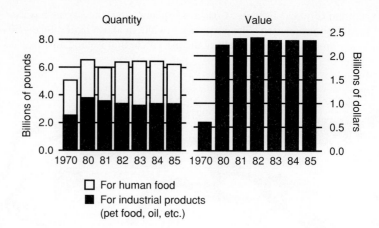

□ For human food
■ For industrial products
(pet food, oil, etc.)

back on by the rising tides. Clean up methods also generate substantial amounts of waste that must be disposed of safely to avoid creating problems elsewhere. Given the shortcomings of these methods, it is clear that they are no substitute for prevention. To remind the public of the need for prevention, one environmental group sold T-shirts with the motto "An ounce of prevention is worth 11 million gallons of cure."

3. *Decomposition of oil by bacteria.* Two Israeli scientists developed a technique that uses bacteria to break down oil. Theoretically, an oil slick could be "seeded" by helicopter with the bacterial powder, accelerating the rate of decomposition and ultimate oil-slick breakup. In the process of breaking down the oil, the bacterial population multiplies rapidly to the point where it can be used as protein feed for livestock. The Israeli scientists estimate that hundreds of tons of animal food could be obtained from a spill. In the Valdez spill, Exxon applied oil-degrading bacteria to somes beaches and found they accelerated the destruction of oil.

THE U.S. MARINE FISHERY INDUSTRY

There are more than 20,000 species of fish swimming in the global seas. However, annual harvests of more than 100,000 metric tons consist of only 22 (0.1 percent) of these species. In 1985 the catch of our nation's commercial fleet was worth $2.3 billion (Figure 10-24). The most valuable species catches were salmon ($439 million), flounder ($129 million), and menhaden ($100 million). The U.S. commercial fishing industry ranks third in the value of its annual catch, behind Japan and the Soviet Union.

Methods of Locating Fish

In recent years, some highly sophisticated methods have been developed for locating commercial stocks of marine fish.

1. *Sonar or echo-sounding systems*, which use sound waves, help to locate fish schools and determine their relative abundance.

2. *Moored buoys*, equipped with sonar or other devices, detect the presence of fish schools swimming nearby and then radio the information to fishing vessels.

3. *Color enhancement* by either photographic or electronic means, can detect color differences in the ocean environment that are undetectable with the unaided eye. Such color-enhanced images provide information on the location of fish and on marine plant life and pollutants.

4. *Infrared sensors*, borne by airplanes or spacecraft, sense the ocean's temperature and detect fish movement. Temperature detection is valuable because some species of commercially valuable fish, such as tuna, have highly specific water temperature preferences.

5. *Ultraviolet sensors* can detect the presence on the ocean surface of oils given off by fish as they swim through the water. Since the oil rapidly dissipates when exposed to air, its occurrence indicates the relatively recent presence of a fish.

6. *Airborne electronic image intensifiers* can detect the flashes of light (bioluminescence) given off at night by microscopic marine organisms when disturbed by passing fish. The faint light is intensified 55,000 times and then projected on a television monitor.

Methods of Harvesting Fish

Commercial fishing fleets use three types of nets: purse seines, gill nets, and trawl nets.

1. *Purse seine.* More fish are caught by purse seines than by any other type (Figure 10-25). The net is played out in a circle around schools of fish. When the school is completely encircled, the bottom of the net is drawn in to prevent fish from escaping. The purse line at the net bottom works like the drawstring on an old-fashioned purse. A large purse seine

FIGURE 10-25 Purse-seining for salmon—equipment and techniques.

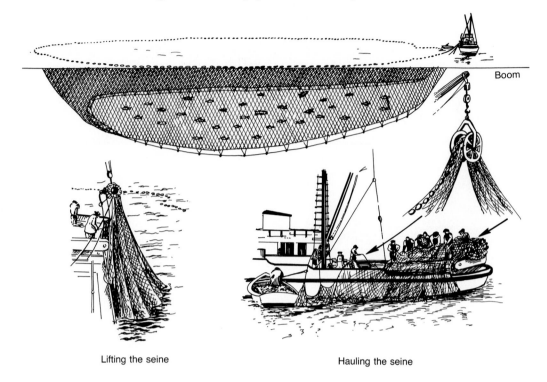

Boom

Lifting the seine

Hauling the seine

may be almost 1.6 kilometers (1 mile) long, have 16,000 floats, and weigh 15 tons.

2. *Gill net.* The fishing vessel bearing a gill net moves into a promising area shortly before nightfall. Up to 4.8 kilometers (3 miles) of net may be laid at right angles to the incoming or outgoing tide. The net is buoyed up by floats at the top and is weighted at the bottom with lead sinkers, thus forming a wall across the path of targeted fish stocks (Figure 10-26). The boat and net may drift all night. As schooling species try to pass through the net on the way to their fishing grounds, their gills become entangled in the net and the fish die. The mesh is designed so that only fish above a minimum size are caught. The catch is hauled into the boat at dawn.

3. *Trawl net.* The trawl is a bag-like net that is pulled by the fishing vessel. Most trawls are drawn over the ocean bottom and are used to harvest such fish as cod, flounder, haddock, and ocean perch.

Fisheries Decline from Overfishing

PACIFIC SARDINE FISHERY. The sea is the world's biggest commons—a public area over which no single nation has sovereignty. The tragedy of such a commons, however, as pointed out by Garrett Hardin of the University of California–Santa Barbara, is that its resources are ruthlessly plundered. After all, with no restriction on the take, it would seem foolish for a country bordering the ocean not to get what it can as long as

possible. This attitude has dominated the fishing industries of seaboard nations for years. As a result, many fishing stocks have been severely depleted. Others are now threatened by human short-sightedness.

A classic example of the collapse of a once major fishery caused by intense human predation is that of the Pacific sardine. In 1936–1937 the Pacific coast sardine industry reached its peak. More than 800,000 tons were netted. The industry ranked first in the nation in pounds harvested and third in value of catch. It grossed $10 million annually. The fish were used in many ways, from canned sardines to fish bait, from pet food to fertilizer. Unfortunately, the industry's prosperity depended on overexploitation. The fishing fleet was enlarged to make up for decreases in the harvest per boat. The industry rejected regulations based on the advice of fisheries scientists. The Washington–Oregon fishery collapsed in 1947–1948. In 1951 the San Francisco fleet returned with only 80 tons, less than 1 percent of its take only a decade earlier, and the fishery closed down for good (Figure 10-27).

COLLAPSE OF OTHER FISHERIES. Unfortunately, the sardine fishery is only one among many that have been going downhill in the past few years (Figure 10-28). For example, in the 1980s, the Food and Agricultural Organization (FAO) of the United Nations estimated that 11 major ocean fisheries were badly overharvested. Annual catches have dropped far below their potential. Among the depleted fisheries are (1) cod

FIGURE 10-26 Gill nets being used on ocean bottom. These nets may also be suspended from the surface by floats. Fish become entangled in the net as they try to swim through it.

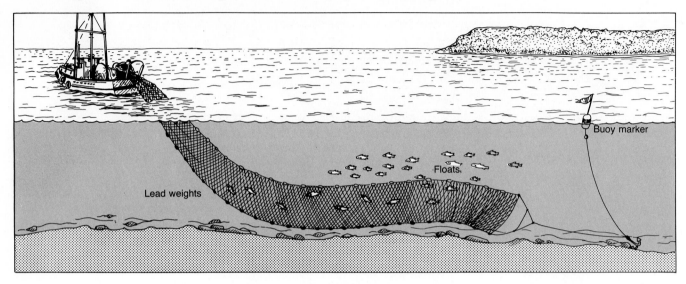

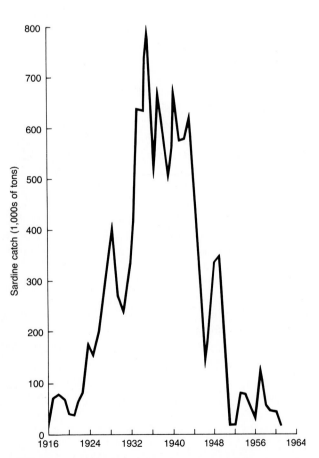

FIGURE 10-27 Pacific sardine catch 1916–1963.

and herring in the northwestern Atlantic, (2) king crab and halibut in the northeastern Pacific, (3) salmon in the northwestern Pacific, and (4) anchovy in the southeastern Pacific. The total loss in the catch due to the mismanagement of these fisheries was estimated to be 11 million metric tons annually. This is equal to 16 percent of the total global harvest in the late 1980s of about 80 million metric tons. Unfortunately, the stocks of 10 species of fish that are highly favored by the American consumer (and hence the U.S. fishing fleet) continue to be overfished. They form 75 percent of the annual catch of our nation's fleets.

Marine Fisheries Management

CONSTRUCTION OF ARTIFICIAL REEFS. Marine fisheries biologists are currently exploring the potential of artificial reefs to provide food and cover for both game and commercial species. Artificial reefs are especially helpful in raising the carrying capacity of flat, sandy coastal plains.

Marine scientists at the State University of New York at Stony Brook have constructed a reef from blocks of compacted sludge and fly ash—materials that create major disposal problems. These researchers have formed a 500-ton reef by dumping 18,000 blocks in the Atlantic Ocean 4 kilometers (2.5 miles) south of Saltaire, Long Island. It is hoped that such reefs will enhance sport and commercial fishing in an area of high human population density and will not release toxins that contaminate the very fish they support. It could help solve an increasingly serious waste-disposal problem for operators of coal-fueled power plants.

FIGURE 10-28 Exhausted fish stocks in the North Atlantic. The depletion of the plaice fishery in the North Sea became obvious in 1880. Since that time many other fisheries have declined sharply. Note the depletion of the cod, ocean perch and haddock fisheries off Labrador and Newfoundland.

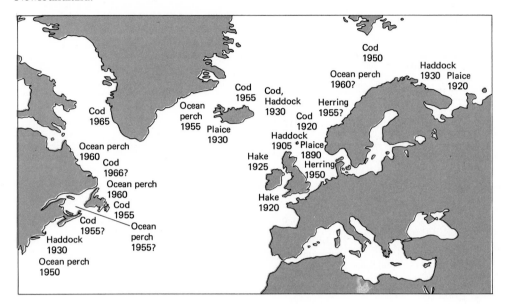

A series of reefs have been constructed along the New Jersey coast from Sandy Hook to Cape May by the New Jersey Department of Environmental Protection. Construction materials range from discarded tires and stainless steel drums to concrete bridge rubble and purposely sunken barges. More than 36,000 baled tires were placed on the Garden State reef in one year alone (Figure 10-29). The reefs provide excellent recreational and commercial fishing for such highly regarded species as sea bass, cod, bluefish, mackerel, and tuna.

REGULATIONS TO ENSURE MAXIMUM SUSTAINED YIELD. In 1976 Congress passed the Fishery Conservation and Management Act to rebuild and sustain our dwindling fish stocks. The act calls for quotas that are appropriate for each species on the basis of maximum sustained yield (MSY). The MSY of a fish stock during a given year can be expressed as an equation: $SE = SB + R + G - (FM + M)$.

SE (stock ending) is the harvestable stock that remains at the end of the fishing year. SB (stock beginning) is the harvestable stock at the beginning of the fishing year. In commercial fisheries, it represents the fish large enough to be taken. R (recruitment) is the number of young fish that are added to the harvestable stock by growth during the year. G (growth) represents the biomass increase during the year due to the growth of R after entering the harvestable stock, plus the growth of SB. FM (fish mortality) is the total weight of fish harvested during the year. M (nonfishing mortality) represents the catchable stock that died from all causes except fishing.

FIGURE 10-29 Artificial reef being formed off the New Jersey coast from tires which have been baled together and dumped overboard.

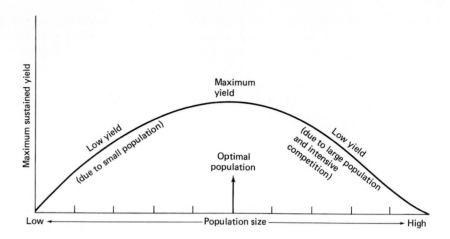

FIGURE 10-30 The dynamics of maximum sustained yield of marine fish stocks.

R (recruitment) depends to some degree upon food conditions, spawning success, and population density. *G* (growth) depends on the abundance of food and water temperatures. FM is variable, depending on fishing pressure and the nature of fishing regulations. *M* is based on environmental resistance—parasites, disease organisms, competitors, pollution, oxygen depletion, adverse winds, and thermal changes.

In determining allow catches, an important point to remember is that young fish convert food to biomass more efficiently than older fish. Fishing pressure on an old, slowly growing population may be beneficial up to a critical point—for it permits younger age classes to become established. The optimal population size for maximum sustained yield is shown in Figure 10-30.

For optimal sustained harvest, fisheries biologists must establish regulations to ensure the most effective fishing rates. To this end, the following kinds of regulations may be established:

1. Minimum size limits on fish that may be harvested.
2. Limits on the number (or poundage) of a given species of fish that may be taken.
3. Fishing prohibitions on the spawning grounds of a given species.
4. Fishing prohibitions during a given season or year.
5. Restrictions on the number of times a particular vessel can fish.
6. Restrictions on the number of boats that can fish in a particular region.
7. Limits on the number of fishing vessels that may be built during a given year.

Many of these regulations could be used to control fishing in international waters. All nations exploiting fish stocks in international waters would have to comply with mutually accepted restrictions to ensure a continued MSY year after year. Unfortunately, agreements on harvesting fish in a commons are usually difficult, if not impossible, to attain.

Management of Large Marine Ecosystems

In 1988 the World Resource Institute reported on a new approach to fisheries management in which large marine ecosystems (LMEs) were the units of focus. This concept was first developed by Kenneth Sherman of the National Marine Fisheries Service. In this approach, a large region of the ocean, often more than 200,000 square kilometers (80,000 square miles), with well-defined physical features, such as water currents, water temperature, dissolved nutrients, dissolved oxygen, is managed as an ecolgical unit.

In this management concept, *all* species of fish (and other organisms) are the focus of attention, rather than merely one or two commercially valuable species. An effort is made to understand how the fish (and other organisms) interact with each other and with the physical features of the LME. Obviously, the LME approach to marine fisheries management is both highly complex and challenging.

In the past, fisheries managers have often been frustrated by their inability to predict accurately the tonnage of a commercially valuable species that could be taken in the year ahead without exceeding the MSY. In Kenneth Sherman's view, such information can be adequately obtained only by an intensive study of the LME to which the species belong.

Sherman has identified 20 LMEs in the global oceans to date. He recognizes two basic types of LMEs. In one type, the *environment* (pollution, dissolved nutrients, and so on) is the dominant factor regulating the populations of commercially valuable species of fish. A good example of such an LME is the California Current Ecosystem off the Pacific Coast of the United States. In the environmentally dominated LME, restrictions on the catch of a species whose populations are in decline would not necessarily result in the future recovery of that species, but could certainly help.

A second major type of LME is one in which *predation* is the dominant factor regulating commercially important species of fish. (Fishing itself is a predatory act.) The Northeastern Continental Shelf off our Atlantic Coast exemplifies this type of LME.

Several years ago, this LME experienced a **biomass flip** in which the originally dominant herring, a commercially valuable species, was replaced by a commercially worthless species, the sand eel. Intensive studies of the LME of the Northeastern Continental Shelf revealed that sand eels are the favorite prey of herring. When the herring population declined from overfishing (excessive human predation), the sand eel population increased. However, now that restrictions have been placed on the herring harvest, the herring population should gradually recover. Sand eel populations should gradually decline due to the increased predatory pressure by the herring.

The Exclusive Economic Zone

One important result of the recent United Nations Conference on the Law of the Sea was the agreement that each nation would have economic jurisdiction over a 330-kilometer (200-mile) belt of sea space bordering its coasts. Each such area has been termed an **Exclusive Economic Zone (EEZ)**. Scientists estimate that 95 percent of the world's living marine resources are contained within these EEZs. Maritime nations throughout the world now have a much stronger incentive to manage their marine resources on a long-term, sustained-yield basis. The establishment of the EEZ zone should be expecially welcome to an LDC like Indonesia, which derives more than 70 percent of its animal protein from its coastal waters.

In the EEZ of the United States, fishing by both American and foreign fleets is regulated by the U.S. Fishery Conservation and Management Act. Under the terms of this act, foreign fishing interest may not operate in the American EEZ without special permits. Currently, 96 percent of all foreign fishing in the American EEZ takes place off the Alaskan coast.

Before the formation of the EEZs, the far-flung fishing fleets of foreign nations, such as Japan and the USSR, agressively competed with American ships for limited stocks of salmon, haddock, and cod only 12 miles or so from the U.S. coast.

America's commercial fishing interests have greeted the new law with jubilation. From the Gulf of Alaska to New England's George's Bank, they are catching more fish off their own shores than foreigners—something that has not happened for a long time.

OCEAN HARVESTS AND GLOBAL FOOD NEEDS

Many authorities regard the ocean as an abundant future source of animal protein that could help fore-

stall global hunger. There seems to be some basis for this hope: First, the oceans cover 70 percent of the earth's surface and, hence, receive the same percentage of the earth's incident solar energy. Second, the marine phytoplankton are efficient photosynthesizers. Third, the ocean environment is still relatively uncontaminated with pollutants, although oil, pesticides, sewage, and industrial chemicals are of increasing concern in the neritic zone.

Annual global fish harvests increased from 20 million metric tons in 1950 to about 80 million metric tons in the late 1980s. These gains were achieved under extremely heavy fishing pressure and the use of sophisticated techniques such as sonar and aerial surveillance. Since 1984, however, the growth rate of fish catches has slowed dramatically.

Some experts believe that the MSY for our global fisheries is about 100 million metric tons annually. Others argue that this estimate is much too high. But even if global fish harvests can be substantially increased, would that mean that the poor people on this planet would no longer suffer from protein deficiencies? Not at all. Remember that the global population is still riding the J-curve. And even if we could increase our global fish catch to 200 million tons by the year 2030, the amount of fish protein available per person would actually be *less* than it is today.

It may be possible to increase our fish harvest somewhat by shifting attention from traditional fishing areas like the North Sea, the Grand Banks of Newfoundland, and the Pacific coast of California, which are already overfished, to virtually unexploited fisheries in the Indian Ocean and the southwestern Atlantic being careful not to overfish them as well. Although stocks of cod, tuna, haddock, and salmon are largely overfished, there are still a few species that could withstand a more intensive fishing effort. Good examples are anchovies off the coast of West Africa and squid in the eastern Pacific. Another strategy that might improve the amount of fish protein available to humans simply involves a shift in food preferences. For example, more than 20 million tons of trash fish, which are high in protein value, are caught, almost accidentally, every year. There is no reason why they, with some culinary tricks, cannot be made reasonably acceptable to the human palate.

Millions of malnourished people in the less developed countries of South America, Africa, and Asia are suffering from a protein-deficiency disease called **kwashiorkor**. It causes irreversible mental retardation in young children, along with a host of other afflictions. The average adult requires a mimimum of 36 grams of animal protein daily. But most animal protein, when derived from land animals such as cattle, sheep, or swine, is very expensive. In contrast, fish protein from the sea is relatively cheap. Thus, we might expect that at least the poor people living close to the ocean would receive an adequate supply. Regrettably, this is not the case. For example, for several years the Peruvian anchovy fishery yielded more than 12 million metric tons annually. Most of the fish were shipped to the already overfed countries of Western Europe and the United States, not to be used as human food, but to be processed into food pellets for cattle, swine, cats, and dogs. Perhaps the next time you savor that pork chop or watch Fido devouring his chow, you might reflect on the inequalities of human existence.

Farming the Seas

For thousands of years, human beings obtained their food by hunting animals and gathering eggs, fruits, berries, nuts, and seeds—a rather inefficient process that was unable to support more than a few million people the world over. Eventually, humans invented agriculture—the controlled rearing of plants and animals—a process that has been able to feed many more people. In a similar fashion, humans have for many years harvested fish from the sea by a relatively inefficient hunting-and-gathering technique: Fishing vessels move to fishing grounds where the harvest is unpredictable and then transport the catch back to market. The controlled culturing of fish and other aquatic food organisms is potentially a much more efficient process. When this technique is practiced in ponds, it is called **aquaculture**; when practiced in shallow bays or estuaries, it is called **mariculture** (Figure 10-31).

Proponents believe that aquaculture holds considerable promise for boosting the meat protein in the oth-

erwise starch-heavy diets of millions of malnourished poor in the less developed nations of the world.

BASIC PRINCIPLES OF MARICULTURE. The basic prinicples of mariculture are the following:

1. Cultivate a species that is low on the food chain, such as a **producer** (algae) or a **detritus feeder** (shrimp, crayfish). Humans could consume the producers directly, thus minimizing the energy losses that occur between successive food chain links. The next best strategy would be for humans to culture herbivores (carp, milkfish), somewhat analogous to our raising of herbivorous livestock such as cattle, sheep, and goats in land-based agriculture.

2. Increase productivity of the water by providing nitrogen and phosphorus nutrients from plant, animal, and human waste (Figure 10-31).

3. Use a technique known as **polyculture**. This involves the culture of several species of marine organisms, each with *different* food and habitat preferences, *simultaneously*. For example, if the food base consists of algae and detritus, two fish species could be cultured, one adapted to feed on algae and the other specialized to feed on detritus. The two species probably would stratify themselves in the water column, the algae eater feeding normally at a higher level than the detritus feeder.

4. Locate the site of mariculture as close as possible to the potential consumers of the organisms being

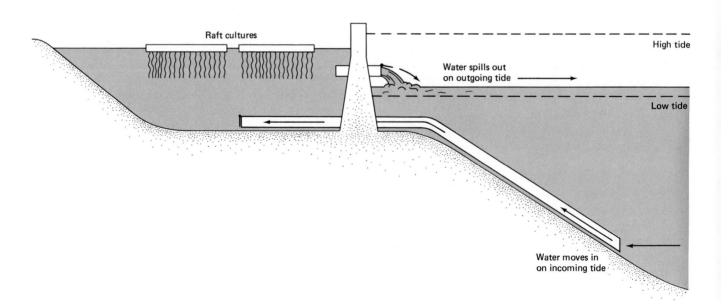

FIGURE 10-31 Oyster culture. The productivity of in-shore culturing areas could be increased in the number of ways. Here deep nutrient-rich water enhances the growth of algae. Because the oysters either feed on the algae directly or on crustaceans that feed on the algae, oyster production on inshore rafts is increased significantly.

raised—in other words, near big cities—to minimize costly transportation.

Whales and Porpoises

For thousands of years, whales and porpoises have evoked human curiosity, wonder, and admiration—as in October 1988, when three gray whales, 25 to 35 feet long, were trapped in Arctic ice off Point Barrow, Alaska. Hundreds of millions of people throughout the world watched with fascination as the animals' life-and-death struggle unfolded on the evening news.

Unlike fish, whales are warm-blooded, air-breathing creatures that have hair and give birth to their young. Throughout the centuries, they have provided many valuable materials—food and furs, bones, and tusks for tools and ornaments, oils for illumination, and ingredients for perfume.

METHODS OF FEEDING. Whales are divided into two major groups on the basis of feeding methods: the **toothed** whale and the **baleen** whale.

Toothed Whales. The toothed whales include the porpoises and the killer and sperm whales. They feed primarily on octopi, squid, fish, and marine mammals. The killer whales hunt in packs and may pursue sharks, seals or large baleen whales, much as wolves chase deer. Aquatic birds and small seals may be swallowed whole.

Baleen Whales. The baleen whales include the blue, gray, and humpback whales—among the largest animals known to science. The upper jaw has 200–300 plates composed of a horny material called **baleen** or **whale bone**. The plates are used to strain small organisms from the water. Many baleen whales, such as the blue, feed almost exclusively on tiny shrimp-like crustaceans called **krill**. Krill frequently occur in schools 2.5 square kilometers (1 square mile) in area and up to 10 meters (30 feet) thick. When on the edge of such a school, the whale opens its mouth wide and swims into its meal. It then closes its mouth and forces the water through the baleen plates with its tongue. Almost a ton of krill has been found in a single whale's stomach.

Many people are concerned about the protein-deficiency diseases in many of the less developed countries. To help cope with this problem, marine biologists have suggested harvesting the protein-rich krill. During the mid 1980s, 500,000 metric tons were harvested annually. Unfortunately, the intensive harvesting of krill places humans and the whales in direct competition for a common food supply. The eventual result would be the accelerated decline of the blue whale, which is already an endangered species.

PORPOISE POPULATION DECLINE. In the past few years, the porpoise populations off both the Pacific and Atlantic coasts of the United States have declined. The mortality has been caused by both human and nonhuman (natural) factors.

A Human Cause of Mortality: Commercial Fishing. Porpoise and tuna populations frequently occur close together in the eastern Pacific Ocean. The tuna swim directly below the porpoises. The significance of this curious relationship is unknown. However, tuna fishermen have long taken advantage of it. When they spot a school of porpoise, they lower their nets in the hope of making a haul of tuna. In the process, though, they caught and killed hundreds of thousands of porpoises annually during the 1960s and early 1970s.

In 1972, Congress passed the Marine Mammal Protection Act. A major goal of the act was to reduce sharply such accidental porpoise killing. The following measures were taken: (1) tuna netting techniques were made more selective, (2) federal inspectors were required on tuna boats, and (3) an annual limit of 20,000 porpoise deaths was placed on the American tuna industry (Figure 10-32). As a result of these measures, the average number of porpoise deaths for the 8-year period 1978–1985 was only 17,577—far below the 368,600 accidentally killed in 1972.

A Natural Cause of Mortality: Red Tide Organisms. Under certain conditions of water temperature and salinity, some species of reddish-brown marine protozoa and algae grow so abundant that the water becomes a "red sea" or "red tide." Toxic chemicals released by these microorganisms have caused spectacular fish kills along the California, Florida, and New Jersey coasts.

In 1987–1988, hundreds of dead and dying porpoises washed ashore from Florida north to New Jersey. The massive die-off spurred an investigation. In 1989, 18 months and more than 1,000 laboratory tests later, scientists found the chemical culprit responsible for the porpoise die-off. It was brevertoxin, a powerful poison produced by red tide organisms.

Apparently, the porpoise received lethal doses of brevertoxin after consuming contaminated fish. During the period of die-off, the count of red tide algae off North Carolina reached 20 million per liter of ocean water. (This density is 4,000 times greater than the maximum under which oysters can be safely harvested and eaten by humans.) A federal fisheries expert estimated that up to 50 percent of the porpoise population off the Atlantic Coast had been destroyed. Because of their low reproductive rate, it may take 100 years for the population to be restored.

WHALE POPULATION DECLINE. Biologists estimate that in 1900 about 4.4 million whales lived in the oceans. Unfortunately, however, because of commercial whaling, their number has been reduced to about 1 million. The world population of the magnificent blue whale, the largest animal that has ever lived, is now

FIGURE 10-32 (A) Tuna fishers accidentally net porpoises along with tuna. This happens rather frequently because the porpoises swim underneath the tuna schools. Fishers are now legally committed to rescue as many porpoises as possible. (B) To permit the escape of the porpoises, the fishers first draw their net into an elongated shape. Then men on rafts help "spill" the porpoises over the end of the net into the open sea.

about 16,000, only 16% of the 180,000 alive in 1900. For many years after 1956, there was a steady decline in the number of whales taken by whaling fleets despite the most sophisticated methods of locating and killing them.

The International Whaling Commission (IWC), which attempts to regulate commercial whaling, was organized in 1946. It has one representative from each of the 41 nations that have at one time or another had whaling fleets. For many years, the IWC established quotas for particular species and placed seasonal and geographical limits on commercial whaling. Unfortunately, these quotas were probably too high. Moreover, the IWC had no enforcement power, and

therefore many of the whaling nations (Japan, the Soviet Union, Norway, South Korea, and so on) simply ignored its regulations. Most whaling nations were more interested in short-term profits than in harvesting whales on a long-term, sustained-yield basis. (Such exploitation seems to be a recurring theme in the history of resource use, whether it involves soil, forests, fisheries, or whales.)

By the 1960s, it had become obvious that the Antarctic stock of the blue whale was on the verge of extinction. Eight of the nine species of large whales, including the blue, gray, and sperm whales, were officially designated as endangered species (as defined by the U.S. Endangered Species Act). First marine biologists and conservationists and then grass-roots environmental groups, became aroused over the senseless whale butchery. "Save the Whale" campaigns were organized nationwide and gained mass-media publicity. Hundreds of antiwhaling articles appeared in periodicals like *Science*, *Audubon*, and *National Wildlife*. Harvard University scientists even canceled an order for an electron microscope from Japan in protest of that nation's role in whale overkill. Finally, with whale populations continuing to plummet, the IWC called for a moratorium on all whaling beginning in 1986.

Unfortunately, there is a loophole in the IWC moratorium that permits whaling for scientific purposes. Under the guise of conducting research, Japan, South Korea, Iceland, and Norway slaughtered more than 6,000 of these magnificent animals in 1986. These nations have insisted on conducting their research at least until 1990 and perhaps longer.

Ironically, the IWC itself has no power to enforce the moratorium; its regulations are only morally and psychologically binding. However, recent laws make it possible for the United States to impose sanctions on nations that violate the moratorium. For instance, the United States may refuse to import fish from a violator or it may reduce the amount of fish a violator can harvest in our EEZ by 50 percent or more. In effect, therefore, the United States is the only IWC nation that can enforce the moratorium on commercial whaling. The economic interests of a whaling nation would probably be best served if it respected the moratorium.

Faced with the threat of such sanctions, the whaling nations of Japan, the Soviet Union, and Norway, all fiercely opposed to the moratorium, reluctantly agreed to end commercial whaling in 1988.

What is all the fuss about? Are whales really worth the struggle? To some people, a whale is more than a few thousand pounds of bone, blood, and blubber. What whales really mean to them is eloquently expressed by marine biologist Victor Scheffer: "Whales have become symbolic of life itself. . . . They live in families. They play in the moonlight. They talk to one another. And they care for one another in distress. They are awesome and mysterious. They deserve to be saved, not as potential meatballs, but as a source of inspiration for mankind."

RAPID REVIEW

1. Because of the rapid development of the coastlands and barrier islands, human life and valuable property have become threatened by hurricanes and other oceanic storms.

2. Some of this development has (a) degraded scenic beauty, (b) accelerated beach erosion, (c) destroyed recreational opportunities, and (d) ruined fish and wildlife habitats.

3. The National Coastal Zone Management Act (1972 and 1988) has provided financial assistance to 30 coastal states to help them develop sound strategies to protect their coasts and barrier islands.

4. Among the factors contributing to coastal erosion problems are (a) the rising ocean level, (b) the reduction of sediment discharge into the ocean due to dam construction, and (c) subsidence.

5. Among the methods that have been used to control coastal erosion are (a) structures such as riprap and groin fields, (b) beach nourishment projects, (c) vegetative control, and (d) restriction of coastal development.

6. A typical estuary is characterized by: (a) brackish water, (b) water levels that rise and fall with the tides, (c) high levels of dissolved oxygen, (d) high turbidity, and (e) high nutrient levels.

7. Chesapeake Bay is fed by more than 150 rivers and has over 8,000 miles of shoreline. In 1988 more than 40 million people lived in the Chesapeake Bay region.

8. The bay has many values: (a) it is the largest producer of blue crabs in the world, (b) it yields more oysters than any other region in the United States, (c) it is the base of an annual $100 million fish harvest, and (d) it provides food, cover, and nesting sites for multitudes of waterfowl.

9. The most serious environmental problem facing the bay is water pollution. This pollution has resulted in (a) a drastic decline in submerged aquatic vegetation, (b) eutrophication, and (c) contamination of the bay's food web with toxic metals.

10. The amount of phosphorus discharged into Chesapeake Bay has decreased substantially due to (a) bans on phosphate detergents in Maryland, (b) control of fertilizer and manure runoff, and (c) upgrading of sewage treatment plants.

11. The ocean (a) covers 70 percent of the earth's surface, (b) contains vertical and horizontal currents, (c) is about 70 times as salty as a lake or stream, and (d) is relatively infertile.

12. The three major zones of the ocean are (a) neritic, (b) euphotic, and (c) abyssal.

13. The neritic zone is a relatively warm, shallow, nutrient-rich region adjoining coasts.

14. The euphotic zone is a region in the open ocean that extends from the surface to the deepest area where there is sufficient sunlight for photosynthesis.

15. Beneath the euphotic zone is the bathyal zone, a region of semidarkness.

16. The abyssal zone lies immediately above the ocean floor. It is characterized by (a) darkness, (b) intense cold, (c) low levels of dissolved oxygen, and (d) a scarcity of food.

17. In areas of upwelling, fish production is highly efficient because many of the food chains have only two links: the producer phytoplankton and the consumer fish. In the deep waters of the open sea, however, fish production is much less efficient because the food chains may have as many as six links.

18. For decades the neritic zone bordering our nation's coasts has served as a dumping ground for raw domestic sewage and sewage sludge, industrial wastes, and dredge spoils.

19. The most seriously contaminated coastal regions are (a) the New York Bight, (b) Boston harbor, (c) Salem (Massachusetts) harbor, (d) Raritan Bay (New Jersey), and (e) San Diego harbor.

20. Waste dumping at the New York Bight has caused (a) reduced levels of dissolved oxygen, (b) declines in plankton and plankton-dependent fish, (c) fish disease epidemics, (d) fish contamination with toxic metals, and (e) high rates of harmful mutations in fish.

21. Plastic pollution causes wildlife mortality by (a) blocking digestive tracts, (b) entangling-induced drowning, and (c) entangling-induced starvation.

22. A U.S. law that helps control plastic pollution is the Ocean Dumping Act, which bans plastic dumping from trash ships.

23. The main sources of oil in the marine environment are (a) natural seeps, (b) oil well blowouts, (c) pipeline breaks, (d) tanker spills, and (e) inland disposal.

24. Oil pollution adversely effects the marine ecosystem, by (a) reducing photosynthetic rates in marine algae, (b) concentrating chlorinated hydrocarbons such as pesticides, (c) contaminating human food chains with carcinogens such as benzopyrene, (d) disrupting chemical communication in marine organisms that adversely affects such activities as feeding, reproduction, and escape from predators, (e) killing animals, as in the case of an estimated million seabirds each year, and (f) causing long-term effects such as liver cancers resulting from chronic exposure to low levels of oil.

25. The input control of oil pollution includes (a) the upgrading of tanker and offshore oil wells to mini-mize accidents and (b) more thorough inspection of tankers and offshore wells.

26. The output control of oil pollution includes (a) use of finger-printing to determine the source of the spilled oil, (b) soaking up oil with straw and absorbent material, (c) decomposing oil with bacteria, and (d) using oil skimmers.

27. Among the techniques and instruments employed by commercial fishermen to locate marine fish are (a) sonar or echo-sounding systems, (b) moored buoys, (c) color enhancement of aerial photos, (d) infrared sensors, (e) ultraviolet sensors, and (f) electronic image intensifiers.

28. Fish are harvested with a variety of nets, including (a) purse seines, (b) gill nets, and (c) trawl nets.

29. Among the fisheries that have been depleted due to overfishing are the (a) Pacific sardine fishery, (b) northwestern Atlantic cod and herring fisheries, (c) northwestern Pacific salmon fishery, and (d) southeastern Pacific anchovy fishery.

30. Management methods employed to increase the production of marine fish include (a) construction of artificial reefs and (b) regulation of the harvest.

31. Managing large regions of the ocean, called large marine ecosystems, may prove helpful in ensuring sustainable yields of fish and other commercially important species. In this management strategy, all aquatic species are considered, rather than one or two commerically important ones.

32. The establishment of exclusive economic zones is helping nations regulate fishing off their shores. The United States, for instance, can determine who, if anyone, it allows to fish within 330 kilometers (200 miles) of its coastline.

33. The ocean is a rich source of food, but has been so heavily fished over the years that catches have fallen drastically in many once productive areas. One way to help feed the world's people is to increase the amount of fish taken from the sea. That can be done by harvesting other types of fish, increasing fishing in areas now "underfished," and by growing fish in harbors. Increasing the annual catch will have little effect on human hunger in the Third World unless the rapid growth of population in many nations is curbed. Increasing the annual catch can also be a license for disaster if fish populations are harvested on an unsustainable basis.

34. There are two major groups of whales, based on feeding habits: toothed whales and baleen whales. The toothed whales (porpoises, killer whales, sperm

whales) feed primarily on fish, sharks, and seals. Baleen whales strain out small organisms such as crustaceans (krill) from the water through a series of plates suspended from the upper jaw. The baleen group includes the blue whales, the largest animals known to science.

35. During the 1960s and early 1970s, hundreds of thousands of porpoises were accidentally destroyed by tuna fishermen yearly. In the 1980s about half of the Atlantic dolphins perished from red tide.

36. Eight of the nine species of large whales, including the blue, gray, and sperm whales, are officially designated as endangered, as defined by the U.S. Endangered Species Act.

37. The International Whaling Commission called for a moratorium on all whaling beginning in 1986 so that the declining populations of the endangered species could recover.

KEY WORDS AND PHRASES

Abyssal zone
Alaskan current
Amoco Cadiz
Argo Merchant
Artificial reef
Baleen whale
Barrier islands
Beach nourishment
Benzopyrene
Biological magnification
Bioluminescence
Brevertoxin
Chemical communication
Chesapeake Bay
Coastal erosion
Color enhancement
Critical Area Act
Detritus feeder
Dogfish shark
Dredge spoil
Echo-sounding system
Electronic image
  intensifier
Estuary
Euphotic zone
Exclusive Economic Zone
  (EEZ)
Factory ship
Fingerprinting
Gill net
Groin fields
Gulf Stream
International Whaling
  Commission (IWC)
Krill
Land sinking (subsidence)
Large marine ecosystems
  (LMEs)
London Dumping
  Convention
Mariculture
MARPOL Act
Maximum sustained yield
  (MSY)
National Coastal Zone
  Management Act
Neritic zone
New York Bight
Ocean dumping
Ocean Sanctuary Act
Oyster culture
Oyster Watch
Plastic pollution
Porpoise mortality
Purse seine
Recruitment
Red tide
Riprap
Santa Barbara oil spill
Seaweed culture
Sonar
Submerged aquatic
  vegetation (SAV)
Toothed whale
Torrey Canyon
Trawl net
Ultraviolet sensor
Upwelling

QUESTIONS AND TOPICS FOR DISCUSSION

1. Define the key words and phrases in the list of key words and phrases.
2. Discuss the factors that have caused the massive erosion and flooding of our coastal regions.
3. In what ways does an estuary differ from an ocean? From a river? Why are estuaries so productive?
4. Briefly list three major environmental problems in the Chesapeake Bay.
5. Why is the decline of submerged aquatic vegetation in the Chesapeake Bay of such serious concern to EPA scientists? What is being done to correct the problem?
6. Characterize the neritic, euphotic, and abyssal zones of the ocean.
7. Discuss the effect of plastic pollution on marine life.
8. Briefly list five sources of the oil that pollutes the oceans.
9. Discuss five adverse effects that oil has on marine organisms.
10. Discuss input methods of controlling oil pollution. Discuss three output methods.
11. Discuss the relationship between the current "pet explosion" in the United States and the incidence of kwashiorkor in the LDCs.
12. Discuss the importance of the recently established Exclusive Economic Zones (EEZs) to coastal nations.
13. Briefly describe four methods used by commercial fishers to locate fish schools.
14. Describe the basic principles of polyculture.
15. Compare the feeding habits of toothed and baleen whales.
16. Discuss the pros and cons of the moratorium on commercial whaling that began in 1986.

SUGGESTED READINGS

Cobb, C. E., Jr. "North Carolina's Outer Banks." *National Geographic* 172(4):484–513, 1987. Highly readable account of the coastal erosion problem.

Jackson, J. B. C., et al. "Ecological Effects of a Major Oil Spill on Panamanian Coastal Marine Communities", *Science* 243:37–41, 1989. Discusses the effects of an 8-million-liter oil spill in 1986 on seagrass and coral reef ecosystems along the east coast of Panama.

Millemann, B. "Wretched Refuse Off Our Shores." *Sierra* 74:26–28, 1989. Nontechnical, interesting account of the effects of ocean dumping and regulations for its control.

Powers, A. "Protecting the Chesapeake Bay: Maryland's Critical Area Program." *Environment* 28:5, 44–45, 1986. Discusses novel state legislation that establishes a protective corridor along the shores of Chesapeake Bay in an attempt to halt destruction of the estuary.

Walsh, J. "Research Whaling on the Table." *Science* 237:481, 1987. Discusses the IWC's moratorium on commercial whaling and Iceland's temporary agreement to halt whaling for "scientific" purposes.

Weisskopf, M. "In the Sea, Slow Death by Plastic." *Smithsonian* 18(12):58–67, 1988. Nontechnical but authoritative overview of the plastic pollution problem with dramatic illustrations.

11

Rangeland Management

It happened several years ago during the height of a nationwide meat shortage. The customer entered a midwestern supermarket, strode briskly to the meat counter, and stared in disbelief. The rows of sterile, gleaming meat trays were empty, except for one scrawny chicken that was selling at a preposterous $3.05 per kilogram ($1.39 per pound). Gone were the sirloins, the T-bones, the lamb chops.

These were the days when the lowly hamburger and hot dog suddenly enjoyed luxury status, the days when homemakers throughout the nation acquired the beans, pancakes, and spaghetti routine, much to the distress of their families. It wasn't much gastronomic fun to move down to the second link of the food chain, the ecological position occupied by most of the world's people.

These were the days when hitherto law-abiding citizens began poaching deer and grouse; when cattle rustlers, long relegated to TV westerns, were suddenly being recorded "live" on ranches throughout the nation. Regrettably, only during periods of acute shortage such as this do Americans appreciate their enviable lifestyle and their abundant resources. And only at times like this do they begin to appreciate the value of the livestock industry and our rangelands, upon which the industry depends. This chapter is concerned with rangelands—their value and the ways they are abused. It concludes with a look at ways to manage these important lands more successfully.

THE GROWTH CHARACTERISTICS OF RANGE GRASSES

Dozens of native grasses capture energy from sunlight and use it to produce organic foodstuffs used by

FIGURE 11-1 Herefords ("white face") and Black Angus graze on open range near Choteau, Montana. (Rocky Mountains in background.)

animals. Grazing herbivores, such as cattle, sheep, and goats, obtain this energy directly by chewing and digesting the grasses (Figure 11-1). Carnivorous humans acquire this energy in the form of veal, beef, mutton, or lamb. In a very real sense, therefore, the biblical statement "All flesh is grass," is true.

A leaftip of rangeland grass can be nibbled off without affecting growth as long as the **basal zone** (the lowermost portion of the leaf) remains intact. In a short time, the leaf can grow to its original length. In fact, the grass leaf can be grazed again and again without adverse effects, thus providing a continuous food reservoir for the grazing animal.

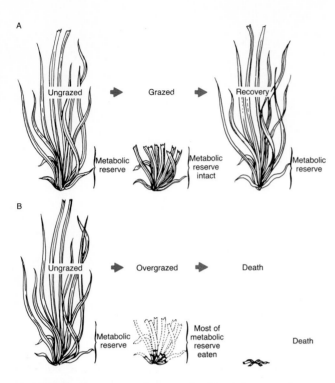

FIGURE 11-2 Grasses can be grazed without harm as long as the metabolic reserve is left intact. Without it the plant dies.

Range ecologists generally regard the upper 50 percent of the grass shoot (stem and leaves) as a "surplus" that can be safely eaten by livestock or wild herbivores (deer, antelope, elk, and so on) without damaging the plant. The lower 50 percent, known as the **metabolic reserve**, is necessary for grass survival (Figure 11-2). This provides the minimum amount of photosynthesis needed to manufacture foods for the roots. Many root systems extend to a depth of 2 meters (6 feet) or more. Large amounts of nutrients are stored in them. This nutrient reserve enables range grasses to survive drought as well as *brief* periods of overgrazing. When a range is overgrazed, the herbivorres bite into the metabolic reserve, frequently clipping the grass to the ground, starving and killing the root system, and leaving the site vulnerable to erosion.

RANGELAND ABUSE

The cattle industry's phenomenal expansion during the 1800s was responsible for much of the settlement of the West. For this we can thank thousands of courageous, hard-working ranchers and farmers. However, in their zeal, many abused our once bountiful grassland and caused widespread destruction that is still evident today.

Cattlemen allowed their cattle to overgraze the ranges in many areas. Where a given pasture could support

25 cattle, many grazed 100. Big bluestem, bluegrass, and buffalo grass were chewed off at the roots. Once the grass plant's metabolic reserve had been eliminated, the root system withered and died. Many of these stockmen were so engrossed with large numbers of range animals that they ignored the fact that four head of livestock, sick and scrawny from undernourishment, would sell for less than one head in prime condition after grazing on good forage.

Finally, in 1932, the seriousness of the range problem prompted Congress to request the U.S. Forest Service to survey the range condition. The survey showed that rangeland productivity in the United States had been reduced by 50 percent. On some Utah ranges, rice grass (a valuable winter forage species when most rangeland is covered with snow) had been reduced by 90 percent by intense grazing (Figure 11-3). The survey further revealed that the extensive removal of grass cover had resulted in erosion on 80 percent of the range.

Taylor Grazing Control Act

In 1934, as a direct consequence of the Forest Service report, Congress enacted the Taylor Grazing Control Act. This was the successful culmination of a long struggle on the part of conservationists to place our ailing public rangelands under federal control. This act had three major objectives: (1) to halt deterioration, (2) to improve and maintain ranges, and (3) to stabilize the rangeland economy. Although much grazing land was under private ownership, the major focus of the Taylor Grazing Control Act was on rangeland owned by the public, which had been seriously abused by western ranchers. Since the end of World War II, these public grazing lands have been under the supervision of the

FIGURE 11-3 A severely overgrazed range. Note the denuded land and the scrawny cattle.

Bureau of Land Management (BLM) in the Department of the Interior.

Under the provisions of the Taylor Grazing Control Act, the public range was divided into operational units called **grazing districts**, which are roughly analogous to the soil conservation districts discussed in an earlier chapter. Each grazing district is run by a local committee of ranchers and representatives of the BLM. Each rancher is required to purchase **grazing permits** before he or she can graze livestock on public lands in a grazing district. By this scheme, at least in theory, grazing pressures and rangeland abuse can be controlled. Unfortunately, most conservationists would say that, in practice, this permit system does not really work very well. Ranchers typically fight restrictions on the number of animals they can graze on public lands.

The Grazing Permit Controversy

In the mid-1980s, ranchers bought permits to graze 2 million cattle and 2.3 million sheep annually. The cost of a grazing permit for cattle in 1986 was $1.35 per head per month. This fee is only about one-fifth that charged by private landowners. U.S. taxpayers, who own the public grazing lands, are therefore subsidizing those ranchers who hold federal grazing permits. In 1986 this subsidy amounted to more than $30 million. (This is akin to the huge subsidies western farmers get on the purchase of water from federal irrigation systems.)

Despite 50 years of management by the BLM, a recent survey showed that 44 percent of the public rangelands were in only "fair" condition and 20 percent were rated "poor." Even though the range quality is inferior, however, ranchers are eager to graze their livestock on it because federal grazing permits are so cheap. In fact, ranchers continuously pressure the BLM to grant more permits. From the ranchers' viewpoint, the extremely low price of the grazing permits is justified because the public range is of such poor quality. On the other hand, range scientists and environmentalists argue that it is of such inferior quality because of the severe overgrazing. Nevertheless, it is unlikely that the price of federal grazing permits will be raised because the profit margin for most ranchers using public rangelands is razor thin.

Effect of Drought on Range Forage

Drought is one of the greatest environmental problems for ranchers. They can, to some degree, control rodents, poisonous plants, brush and weeds, predators, insects, and unfavorable soil chemistry, but there is absolutely nothing they can do to control drought. They can adjust to it, but that is all. Moreover drought is unpredictable.

A severe drought results in a drastic deterioration of the rangeland plant community, even when grazing is light. In the Snake River region of southern Idaho dur-

ing the height of the Dust Bowl era in 1934, extended drought caused an 84 percent reduction in plant cover in ungrazed areas.

Once a dry spell has ended, range recovery may be fast or slow, depending upon the amount of precipitation. Thus, a lightly grazed Montana pasture required 8 years to return to good condition after a severe drought because of limited rainfall. On the other hand, a Kansas range recovered very rapidly when rainfall was adequate (Figure 11-4).

RANGE CONDITION

The term **range condition** may be defined as the current condition of the range site in relation to its theoretical potential. It refers to the health or productivity of the range.

Classification Criteria

Various criteria are used to establish categories of range condition. Among them are (1) the species composition of the plant community, (2) the vigor of the plants, (3) the amount of plant residue (mulch) on the ground, (4) the condition of the soil, and (5) the number of animals that can be supported per hectare (acre).

Five range-condition classes are recognized: *excellent, good, fair, poor* and *very poor* (Table 11-1). It must be emphasized that in comparing range conditions, one must always deal with ranges belonging to identical or very similar range sites. It is apparent that a range in the arid sagebrush region of Wyoming may be in excellent condition and still be much less productive than a good range in the semiarid short-grass region of Nebraska.

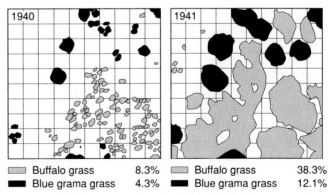

▨ Buffalo grass	8.3%	▨ Buffalo grass	38.3%
■ Blue grama grass	4.3%	■ Blue grama grass	12.1%

Total coverage of quadrat 12.6% and 50.4%

FIGURE 11-4 Recovery of range from drought following a period of adequate rainfall. Basal cover of range vegetation near Ness City, Kansas, had been reduced to only 12.6 percent of the area of a sample square meter by autumn of a drought year. Overgrazing had contributed to the deterioration. However, within one year after the return of adequate rainfall, range grasses responded sufficiently to cover 50.4 percent of the sample plot.

Table 11-1　A Range Condition Score Sheet

Factors Evaluated	Excellent	Good	Fair	Poor	Very Poor
1.　Relative potential forage yield (in percent)	90–100	75–90	50–75	25–50	0–25
2.　Important desirable forage plants (percentage of ground surface covered by each species): 　　Wild oats, *Avena* spp. 　　Soft chess, *Bromus mollis* 　　Calif. bunchgrass, *Stipa pulchra* 　　Cutleaf filaree, *Erodium cicutarium* 　　Bur clover, *Medicago hispida*, etc.	85–100	65–85	35–65 Decreasers	10–35	0–10
3.　Less desirable forage plants (percentage of ground covered): 　　Ripgut brome, *Bromus rigidus* 　　Annual fescue, *Festuca megalura* 　　Foxtail, *Hordeum murinum* 　　Yarrow, *Achillea millefolium* 　　Blue dicks, *Brodiaea capitata*, etc.	0–15	10–30	15–50 Increasers	25–65	40–90
4.　Undesirable forage plants: 　　Medusahead grass, *Elymus caput-medusae* 　　Nitgrass, *Gastridium ventricosum* 　　Star thistle, *Centaurea melitensis* 　　Dwarf plantain, *Plantago erecta* 　　Tarweed, *Hemizonia* spp., etc.	0–15	5–20	10–40 Invaders	25–75	40–100
5.　Plant residue or litter per acre	Abundant	Adequate	Moderate	Scarce	Very Scarce
6.　Erosion	None	None to slight	Slight to moderate	Moderate to severe	Severe
7.　Acres per animal unit month	0.75–1	1–2	2–3	3–5	5 plus

Source: For California Annual Grass Range in North-Central California. Adapted from Grover (1945).

We shall now describe the range condition in terms of the preceding criteria.

COMPOSITION OF THE PLANT COMMUNITY. Ranchers frequently classify the various range plants into three categories with respect to the dynamics of plant succession: decreasers, increasers, and invaders.

Decreasers are highly nutritious, extremely palatable members of the climax community that generally decrease under heavy grazing pressure (Figure 11-5). Representative decreaser species are big bluestem, little bluestem, blue grama, wheat grass, and buffalo grass.

Increasers, on the other hand, are generally less palatable but are still highly nutritious climax species that tend to increase (at least temporarily) when a range is heavily grazed (Figure 11-6). Apparently this increase is the result of reduced competition with the decreasers. When severe grazing pressure continues over a long period, even the increasers begin to decrease, apparently unable to withstand trampling by hoofs of grazing animals. They are replaced by invaders.

The **invaders**, such as ragweed, cactus, and thistle, may be considered undesirable weed species, are low in nutritional value, and are not very desirable for grazing animals (Figure 11-7). Some may be poisonous. An invader like downychess has sharp seeds that can harm animals by lodging in their throats or by piercing their skin. Invaders frequently are annual plants that thrive best under sunlight intensities much higher than the 1–2 percent of full sunlight occurring in a dense stand of climax grasses. Because their roots are taproots instead of the dense fibrous roots of a typical grass, these invaders are not very effective in binding the soil.

A range in excellent condition has a high percentage of decreasers and no invaders. Conversely, a range in poor condition has a low percentage of high-forage-value decreasers and a large percentage of low-forage-value invaders (Table 11-2).

PLANT VIGOR. Plant vigor, or vitality, is the second criterion used to assess range condition. The vigor of plants usually falls before there is a change in the

FIGURE 11-5 Decreasers. These plants are components of the climax community. They are highly nutritious and palatable. They decrease under heavy grazing pressure.

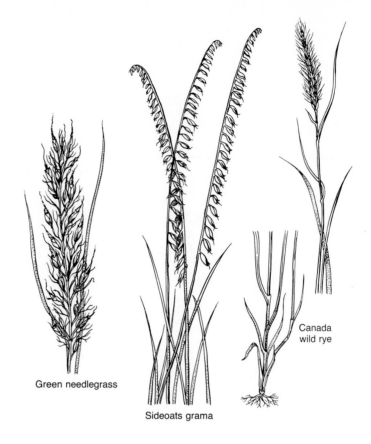

Green needlegrass

Sideoats grama

Canada wild rye

FIGURE 11-6 Increasers. These plants increase in number under grazing pressure and replace the decreasers. Although they are fairly nutritious, they are less palatable and less preferred by cattle.

Blue grama

Needle-and-thread

Nebraska sedge

FIGURE 11-7 Invaders. These weeds replace the increasers if the range continues to be grazed heavily. some of the invaders like military grass (downy chess) have sharp seeds which can harm livestock by lodging in their throat or piercing their skill. Thistles, of course, have sharp spines which make them useless as forage.

Canada thistle   Salsify   Curly cup gumweed   Chess

species in the plant community. Thus, if decreased vitality of forage species can be detected quickly enough, a rancher can reduce the size of his or her herd to allow the range to regain its original vigor naturally. Recognition of reduced vitality is based upon plant color (dark green or yellow), number of leaves, seed production, and plant size and weight.

PLANT RESIDUE OR MULCH. **Mulch** is the dead plant material that accumulates on the ground (Figure 11-8). It is a reliable indicator of range condition. Mulch represents a link between the forage plants and the organic content of the soil. When the amount of mulch decreases, soil fertility ultimately declines and the range deteriorates. Mulch increases the porosity (and hence the drainage and aeration) of the soil.

The amount of mulch on the range varies with the temperature, moisture, kinds of plants, grazing pres-

sure, and other conditions. A study of a California range dominated by wild barley showed 1,700 kilograms of mulch per hectare (1,500 pounds per acre) where forage was in excellent condition compared with 450 kilograms per hectare (400 pounds per acre) on range in poor condition. In humid regions, the weight of mulch on excellent range may reach 1,100 kilograms per hectare (1,000 pounds per acre) and may equal the current annual forage production.

CONDITION OF THE SOIL. As might be expected, an excellent range has a relatively thick layer of fertile, spongy, erosion-resistant soil. Runoff is clear and minimal. The soil of a poor range, on the other hand, is shallow and infertile. Moreover, because of the considerable area of bare ground, and because the taproots of the annual weeds that invade the poor range are inadequate soil binders, the land is highly sus-

Table 11-2 Successional Changes with Grazing and Protection on the North American Prairie

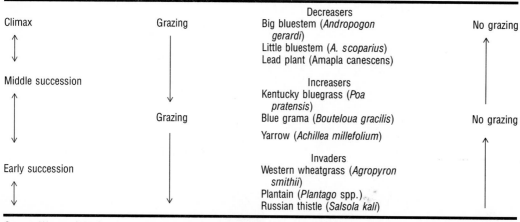

Climax	Grazing	**Decreasers** Big bluestem (*Andropogon gerardi*) Little bluestem (*A. scoparius*) Lead plant (*Amapla canescens*)	No grazing
Middle succession	Grazing	**Increasers** Kentucky bluegrass (*Poa pratensis*) Blue grama (*Bouteloua gracilis*) Yarrow (*Achillea millefolium*)	No grazing
Early succession		**Invaders** Western wheatgrass (*Agropyron smithii*) Plantain (*Plantago* spp.) Russian thistle (*Salsola kali*)	

Source: Weaver (1954).

FIGURE 11-8 **FIGURE 11-8**   This range near Miles City, Montana, is in good condition.

ceptible to erosion. Frequently the range is dissected with gullies. Runoff water is brown with silt and is excessive.

ANIMAL UNITS. The forage potential of a given range is usually described in terms of **Animal Unit Months** (AUMS). For example, one AUM is the amount of forage necessary to keep one head of cattle well fed for 1 month. When a range is in excellent condition, 0.4 hectare (1 acre) may equal one AUM. However, on poor range, it may require 2 hectares (five acres) to equal one AUM.

PRODUCTION OF LOW-CHOLESTEROL BEEF

In the past few years, America's rangelands have supplied only about 16 percent of the total amount of the forage that cattle consume prior to slaughter. The remaining 84 percent is provided by crops such as alfalfa, which are grown on fertilized pastures. This surprising statistic is explained by the fact that most cattle graze on the range only until they are mature. They are then shipped to feedlots (enclosed pens), where they are crowded together and fed with grain (largely grown on irrigated farms on the Great Plains) and special feeds to fatten them up for slaughter (Figure 11-9). Some feedlots in Nebraska hold as many as 10,000 cattle at a time.

The overriding importance of feedlots and the relatively minor role of rangelands in livestock nutrition is being modified somewhat because of America's aware-

ness of the role that high-fat, high-cholesterol meat plays in heart disease and stroke. These health concerns have resulted in a dramatic decrease in per capita beef consumption from 42 kilograms (92 pounds) in 1977 to only 34 kilograms (75 pounds) in the mid-1980s. It so happens that the longer cattle are grazed on rangelands, the lower the fat content of their meat. Ever sensitive to consumer demands, the livestock industry is now keeping cattle on the range until they weigh 300 kilograms (660 pounds) — twice the weight at which they were once shipped to feedlots.

A few farsighted ranchers are replacing some of the traditional strains of cattle, such as the shorthorn and Hereford, with the leaner-meated longhorn — a favorite of the young livestock industry in the nineteenth century. Even more interesting, scientists in Florida are considering introducing the water buffalo, an ox-like animal from Southeast Asia, to the warmer rangelands of the United States. Water buffalo steaks are both tasty and lean, and should satisfy cholesterol-conscious Americans.

RANGE MANAGEMENT

With this background material in mind, let us now examine methods by which the range manager can bring the range into excellent condition and keep it that way.

The ability of a particular range to support a given number of cattle or sheep on a sustained basis is known as its **carrying capacity**. Obviously, a range in poor condition has low carrying capacity; one in excellent

condition has high carrying capacity. The carrying capacity is dependent in part on the volume, nutrient content, palatability, and availability of forage plants. However, when other rangeland species like grasshoppers and jackrabbits compete with livestock for forage they can effectively decrease carrying capacity. Predators such as coyotes can also play a role in determining the carrying capacity of a range. Several range management options are available to increase carrying capacity. They are: stock manipulation, controlled burning, artificial seeding, and the control of plant and animal pests.

Stock Manipulation

DISTRIBUTION OF WATER AND SALT. Ranchers must make sure that livestock will graze their land uniformly. Because cattle tend to concentrate in wet meadows and along stream margins and to avoid ridges and slopes, part of a range may be severely overgrazed while another part may be ignored. Grazing can be directly controlled by barbed wire fencing and herding, both of which are rather costly methods. Ranchers can also use indirect methods that are much less expensive but highly effective. For instance, they can strategically locate water holes and salt blocks. Because cattle and sheep normally congregate around water sources, the salt blocks should be placed roughly 0.8 kilometer (0.5 mile) from the nearest water source, preferably on ridges, gentle slopes, or openings in brush or forest, to induce livestock to frequent areas they would normally avoid.

Salt is essential to the vigorous health of range animals. Within 3 weeks after having been deprived of salt, cattle develop an unusual craving for it. When salt deprivation continues, the animals lose their appetite, become emaciated and weak, and may collapse. On the same ranges where the soil is naturally high in phosphate and sulfate salts, livestock may partially satisfy their salt requirements by grazing on salt-absorbing vegetation.

DEFERRED GRAZING SYSTEM. When livestock are allowed to graze in a pasture continuously throughout the grazing season, the more palatable (and usually more nutritious) range plants frequently are so seriously overgrazed that they lose vitality and nutritional value. To remedy this, several range management experts advise **deferred grazing**, temporarily withdrawing fields from use.

The main features of this system are presented in Figure 11-10. Note that the ranch is divided into three pastures, *A*, *B*, and *C*, and that each of them is deferred for 2 successive years within a 6-year period. During years 1 and 2, forage plants in pasture *A* are allowed to reach maturity and drop their seeds before livestock are permitted to graze on them late in the season (Figure 11-10). Even though the grasses become rather dry at this time, they still are highly nutritious. A certain amount of grazing after the seeds have been produced may be advantageous to the pasture, because foraging cattle scatter the seeds and trample them underfoot, forcing the seeds into the ground and enhancing germination. Deferred grazing increases the size, density, weight, vitality, reproductive capacity, and nutritional value of forage species. Note that in Figure 11-10 pasture *A* is deferred the first and sec-

FIGURE 11-10 Deferred Grazing.

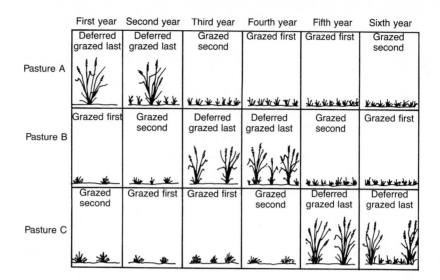

	First year	Second year	Third year	Fourth year	Fifth year	Sixth year
Pasture A	Deferred grazed last	Deferred grazed last	Grazed second	Grazed first	Grazed first	Grazed second
Pasture B	Grazed first	Grazed second	Deferred grazed last	Deferred grazed last	Grazed second	Grazed first
Pasture C	Grazed second	Grazed first	Grazed first	Grazed second	Deferred grazed last	Deferred grazed last

ond years, pasture *B* the third and fourth years, and pasture *C* the fifth and sixth years. Thus, for this hypothetical ranch, all three pastures, within a 6-year rotation plan, are temporarily removed from grazing pressure.

Controlled Burns

Carefully burning rangeland according to a prearranged plan is known as **prescription** or **controlled burning** (Figure 11-11). The use of this range management technique has increased dramatically in the past few years, especially in the Southwest. In 1987 Harvey A. Wright, professor of range management at Texas Tech University in Lubbock, described some of the benefits derived from the prescription burning of rangelands in Texas, New Mexico, and Oregon:

1. It destroys undesirable woody shrubs, like mesquite and juniper, which compete with range grasses for space and sunlight, as well as soil moisture and nutrients.
2. It can reduce a pest like prickly pear cactus by 98 percent if the burn is used after the aerial application of a herbicide (picloram). Control of prickly pear is highly desirable, since cattle suffer mouth injuries from the sharp spines. Moreover, when the seeds of this cactus are eaten by sheep and goats, they may plug up the digestive tract, causing serious illness.
3. It results in increased yields of valuable forage plants such as grama, bluestem, and buffalo grasses.
4. Cattle "beef up" much more readily on control-burned ranges compared to unburned ranges. This rapid weight gain is due not only to the increase in the protein, phosphorus, and moisture content of the

forage plants after a burn, but to their enhanced palability and digestibility as well.
5. It can result in a more uniform distribution of grazing livestock.
6. It can destroy the disease-causing fungi that may infect range grasses.

Artificial Seeding

Ranchers can improve their rangelands by periodic seeding. Seeds may be broadcast by hand or airplane. However, unless some provision is made for covering them, seeding will probably fail. Uncovered seeds may be blown away by strong winds, killed by severe winter cold, eaten by birds and rodents, or washed away during heavy rainstorms. Ranchers can drive a herd of cattle over the area to trample the seeds into the ground.

FIGURE 11-11 Controlled burning of Montana range.

Case Study: San Joaquin Basin in California

The San Joaquin Basin comprises the southern half of the Central Valley of California. When irrigated, it is one of the most productive agricultural regions in the world. In an average year, the eight counties of the San Joaquin Basin produce about $5 billion worth of farm products, more than any state except Iowa, Texas, and Illinois. The area produces cotton, grapes, tomatoes, alfalfa, sugar beets, almonds, and apricots. It also has a sizable livestock industry.

In the San Joaquin Basin, all the major causes of desertification are involved (Figure 1):

1. Overgrazing. Eighty percent of the 1.6 million hectares (4 million acres) of rangeland in the basin is seriously overgrazed. As a result, the palatable species of grasses preferred by cattle are being replaced by woody vegetation of minimal food value. The resultant forage loss is estimated at $1.2 million.

2. Poor drainage of irrigated land. Today about 160,000 hectares (400,000 acres) of irrigated land in San Joaquin are now undergoing severe waterlogging and salinization. At the present rate, the amount of such degraded land will increase to 280,000 hectares (700,000 acres) by 2000, and annual crop losses will reach $320 million.

3. Groundwater depletion. Thirty percent of the irrigation water used in the basin is pumped from aquifers. These supplies are being depleted at the rate

FIGURE 1   The San Joaquin Basin—a region of serious desertification.

of 180,000 hectare-meters (1.5 million acre-feet) per year.

4. Abuse from off-road vehicles. More than 0.2 million hectares (0.5 million acres) of rangeland have deteriorated due to intensive abuse by off-road vehicles. The use of such vehicles has become very popular during the past decade. The result has been massive devegetation and soil erosion.

If seeding is done in recently burned-over timberland, the loose covering of ashes may ensure the success of reseeding. Similarly, if reseeding is synchronized with autumn leaf fall, the leaf litter may provide sufficient seed cover for successful germination.

Aerial broadcasting is the only feasible method in rugged mountainous regions. It can be highly effective. For example, several years ago, a burn in a fir and pine stand in the Cabinet National Forest of Montana was seeded by plane. Only 2 years later, the area was cloaked with a dense stand of timothy grass and Kentucky bluegrass. This vegetation provided not only excellent protection from erosion but also 2,100 kilograms of food per hectare (1,900 pounds per acre) for grazing animals.

In general, ranges that have been properly reseeded support a greater number of livestock in better condition over a longer period than equivalent ranges that have not been reseeded. Many plantings in the West,

for example, have been grazed for 15 successive years and still produce 3 to 20 times as much forage as they did before seeding. A classic example of how artificial reseeding can improve rangeland is provided by a 200-hectare (500-acre) plot in the Fish Lake National Forest in Utah. Before seeding, this area supported a vigorous cover of sagebrush and rabbit brush, which provided forage for only eight head of cattle. However, only 3 years after it was seeded to wheatgrasses and bromes, it was able to sustain 100 head (Figure 11-12).

Control of Rangeland Pests

Another important aspect of rangeland management is the control of plants, such as mesquite, which compete with range grasses as well as the control of herbivores (grasshoppers, rodents, rabbits), which compete with livestock for food.

FIGURE 11-12   Crested wheatgrass. This is an exotic bunch grass which was introduced from Russia. It thrives in the northern Plains States where summers are cool.

CONTROL OF PLANT PESTS. Ranchers are periodically confronted with invasion of their grazing land by woody, low-value shrubs, such as mesquite, sagebrush, and juniper, which compete with range grasses for soil moisture, nutrients, and sunlight (Figure 11-13). Invasion of these shrubs is especially likely if the land is overgrazed. Unless effective control methods are established, the aggressive spread of these species may seriously lower the livestock-carrying capacity of the range. Consider the mesquite.

The mesquite is a thorny desert shrub with small leathery leaves. Like all members of the pea family, it produces large pulpy seed pods. The extensive root system may extend to a depth of 15 meters (50 feet).

Of all the woody plant invaders of southwestern grasslands, mesquite ranks first in distribution, abundance, and aggressive encroachment of rangeland. Plant ecologists believe that, for millennia, mesquite invasion was prevented by periodic fires that were ignited by lightning strikes or by Plains Indians (as an aid to hunting). Grasses were consumed in the fires along with mesquite. Many grass species, however, can mature and produce seeds in 2 years, whereas mesquite requires a

longer period. For this reason, recurrent fires can control mesquite growth.

Ecologists believe that climax vegetation of the grassland biome, with the aid of deep, fibrous root systems, can compete successfully with mesquite for sunlight and limited soil moisture. However, when the white settlers drove off the Indians, introduced cattle and sheep by the millions, and instituted new methods to control fire, the main factor responsible for confining mesquite vanished. Ranchers frequently overstocked range herds caused the deeply and extensively rooted climax species (decreasers) to decline. They, in turn, were replaced by increasers, which were replaced by invaders. The shallow taproots of the first invaders were competitively inferior to mesquite, which gradually took over. The mesquite invasion was further facilitated by cattle. The late-summer-maturing mesquite pods, some up to 20 centimeters (8 inches) long, provide cattle with nutritious food. After digesting the pulp, cattle eventually void the seeds with their waste, frequently at a considerable distance from the parent plant. The seeds, still viable and well fertilized, show a surprisingly high germination rate.

Dense, mature mesquite stands can be controlled with flame torches. In this way, the rancher can duplicate the natural control by fire that operated thousands of years before the coming of the white settlers. Grubbing the mesquite plants out of the ground or plowing them up are effective but very costly. In the case of plowing, the whole area would have to be carefully reseeded with nutritious forage grasses. The control of extensive

FIGURE 11-13   Woody shrubs like sage brush (pictured here), rabbitbrush and greasewood provide forage and cover for wild browsing animals like mujle deer. Many of these shrubs invade rangeland that is overgrazed, and are "indicators" of range in poor condition.

FIGURE 11-14 Grasshopper outbreak. An insect specialist examines grasshoppers in his sweep net. By sweeping the range grasses a few times with his net he can determine the severity of the outbreak. Appropriate control measures can then be applied.

acreages of mesquite can best be accomplished by the aerial spraying of herbicides. Great care must be taken, however, so that the chemicals have no harmful effect on valuable plants and animals of the rangeland ecosystem.

CONTROL OF HERBIVORES

Grasshoppers. Of the 142 species of grasshoppers collected in western range vegetation, the most destructive and widely distributed are the lesser migratory grasshoppers (Figure 11-14). During periods of peak abundance, they may gather in swarms and migrate several hundred kilometers.

When the weather is wet, grasshopper populations remain small. The rancher may not even be aware of their presence. Then, however, may come a severe drought, with only 12.5 centimeters (5 inches) rather than the usual 37.5 centimeters (15 inches) of rainfall. With environmental factors now optimal for the grasshoppers' tolerance range, the populations rapidly increase until it is almost impossible to take a single step through a grama grass pasture without flushing several of them. During a peak year, grasshoppers may so deplete forage that livestock must move to other pastures or starve. During a severe drought, grasshopper density may reach 25 per square meter; the insects may consume 67 percent of the forage and inflict a $100 million annual loss on our nation's livestock industry.

One interesting facet of the grasshopper–rangeland relationship is that these insects are much more numerous in overgrazed ranges than in moderately grazed

fields. A study in southern Arizona revealed that the grasshopper population was 450,000 per hectare (180,000 per acre) on overgrazed lands compared with only 50,000 per hectare (20,000 per acre) on range in average condition—a 9:1 differential. It may be, therefore, that an effective method of controlling grasshopper plagues is to ensure that the range is not being subjected to excessive grazing pressure.

Jackrabbits. During a drought, jackrabbits compete aggressively with cattle and sheep for high-quality forage (Figure 11-15). Seventy jackrabbits consume as much forage as one cow, and 15 eat as much as one sheep. During severe droughts, jackrabbit populations on western rangeland may reach a density of one per 3 hectares (7 acres). The total weight of the jackrabbits may be 7 percent of the weight of the cattle with which they compete. A dense jackrabbit population, therefore, exerts heavy grazing pressure. This prevents the reestablishment of highly nutritious decreasers and favors the intrusion of lower-value increasers, as well as invaders like catcus and thistle.

Control of Herbivorous Pests by Proper Stocking. The rangeland pest, whether grasshopper, jack rabbit, prairie dog, or kangaroo rat, becomes a serious problem only during population peaks, and these peaks usually coincide with rangeland deterioration. It should be emphasized that these pests do not *cause* the initial depletion of the pasture. They are a *symptom* rather than a *cause* of range deterioration. We can compare range abuse to a wound. The "wound" was initially inflicted by excessive stocking, and the ensuing pest buildup merely irritated the wound and prevented it

FIGURE 11-15 The jackrabbit competes with livestock for forage. However, it becomes a serious pest only when the range has been overgrazed, as is obviously the case in this photo of the Santa Rita Experimental Range, Arizona.

from healing properly. Just why a range in good condition (well stocked with climax plants) should be an unsuitable habitat for certain rabbits and rodents has never been fully explained. It may be that the tall vegetation obstructs the vision of these relatively defenseless animals and makes them more vulnerable to predators. In any event, most rangeland experts agree that shooting, trapping, and poisoning campaigns are only stop-gap procedures; the best long-term solution to the pest problem seems to be simply a four-strand barbed-wire fence to keep excess cattle off the deteriorating range.

CONTROL OF PREDATORS: THE COYOTE. Of all rangeland predators, the coyote poses the most serious problem to sheepherders. The wily "brush wolf" has become a romantic symbol of the western plains. At the same time, however, it has become a thorn in the side of sheep ranchers, inflicting on them an estimated annual $20 million loss.

When a rancher destroys a coyote that has been killing, say, 10 sheep per year, simple arithmetic might suggest that this rancher will be 10 sheep richer each year thereafter. However, things are not quite that simple and straightforward in nature. For one thing, the coyote feeds on animals other than sheep. Fifty percent of its diet is composed of range grass–consuming jackrabbits and rodents. Therefore, the value of the few sheep saved by destroying a coyote may be less than the value of the forage consumed by the hundreds of rodents

and rabbits that the coyote would have removed from the rangeland community had it been allowed to live. Nevertheless, our nation's livestock industry appears irrevocably committed to predator control as a range management tool. In fact, where coyotes have become numerous, sheep ranchers have waged all-out extermination campaigns—poisoning, trapping, shooting, and even pursuing them to their dens (Figure 11-16).

The control of predators on grazing lands became a federal government responsibility by an act of Congress in 1931. Under the federal Animal Damage Control Program, 70,000–85,000 coyotes are destroyed annually in 13 western states. The annual kill represents 18 to 29 percent of the coyote population in this region. However, in light of the latest predation data, it should be emphasized that coyote control should focus on those relatively few ranches where sheep kills have actually occurred. A widespread, nonselective campaign to destroy all coyotes would be expensive, time-consuming, and highly unwarranted.

Methods of Coyote Control

Use of Guard Dogs. For several centuries, European sheepherders successfully used guard dogs to protect sheep from predatory coyotes (Figure 11-17). Dogs with superior guarding instincts have been selectively bred at the Hampshire College Farm Center in Amherst, Massachusetts. Since 1978, sheep ranchers in 31 states have been using these dogs to protect their flocks. When placed in sheep flocks when still pups, the dogs soon consider themselves as a natural part of the flock. When a coyote approaches a sheep, the guard dogs react quickly, rushing fiercely at the intruder and causing it to flee.

The guard dog system is highly effective and can be a financial boon to the sheep rancher. For instance, a 1984 survey showed that one of every three ranchers who had experienced heavy sheep losses from marauding coyotes reported not a single attack once guard dogs were used. Environmentalists firmly support the guard dog system. Nevertheless, many ranchers do not use guard dogs because (1) they are unwilling to try a new approach to coyote control or (2) they mistakenly believe that the dogs themselves will kill some sheep.

Use of Guard Cattle. A recently developed predator control strategy involves the intermingling of lambs and young cows in pens for 1 month. During this period, the animals develop a strong attachment for each other. When released on the open range, the cattle protect the sheep from predators by kicking and butting them. According to a 1986 report by the USDA, sheep kills by coyotes can be sharply reduced by this method.

Birth Control Chemicals. Carcasses of livestock are laced with birth control chemicals that reduce the reproductive ability of coyotes that consume the meat. Theoretically, coyote populations should then decline. Unfortunately, however, such a decline would probably be only temporary. The reason? Like many other species of wildlife, coyotes have tremendous reproductive resilience. When a population declines in a given year, the number of young the next year generally increases. The coyote is so resistant that, to eradicate it completely, 75 percent of the population would have to be destroyed year after year for half a century!

Chemical Repellants. This method, still in the experimental stage, involves the injection of a bad-tasting, nausea-inducing chemical, lithium chloride, into the carcasses of dead sheep. The carcasses are then left out for coyotes to feed on. When a coyote eats the tainted flesh, it becomes very sick, and hopefully will avoid live sheep thereafter.

Lethal Poison: Compound 1080. The use of sodium monofluoroacetate, popularly known as Compound 1080, for coyote control has been highly controversial. The general public, environmentalists, organizations like the Defenders of Wildlife, the National Audubon Society, and the National Wildlife Federation, have strongly opposed its use. For one thing, it is extremely toxic; 28 grams (1 ounce) is sufficient to kill 20,000 coyotes.

In 1972, the use of Compound 1080 on all federal lands and by federal agencies anywhere was banned by an executive order of President Richard Nixon. A short time later, the EPA banned its use by state agencies and private individuals as well.

One major complaint concerning its use has been the accidental but fatal poisoning of nontarget species like golden eagles and bobcats, which had eaten Compound 1080-laced bait intended for coyotes or even the carcasses of poisoned coyotes. Some wildlife biologists esti-

FIGURE 11-16 The coyote—a stealthy rangeland predator which has been accused, justly or unjustly, of killing many thousands of sheep annually.

mate that before the ban on Compound 1080, about 9,000 bobcats were accidentally poisoned per year.

Nevertheless, sheep ranchers complained bitterly to their congressional representatives, saying that the ban on Compound 1080 deprived them of the most effective weapon in their coyote control arsenal. In 1985, the EPA yielded to pressure from the Reagan administration and approved the use of the poison in special collars that are worn around the necks of sheep. Since coyotes frequently lunge for the neck of their prey, Compound 1080-containing collars would seem to be an effective way to control these predators.

Is the political struggle to use Compound 1080 really worth the effort? The answer, ironically, is "no." In one

FIGURE 11-17 Sheepherder tending sheep on National Forest land. The sheepherder, of course, can protect the sheep from predation by coyotes.

FIGURE 11-18 Extent of serious desertification of North America.

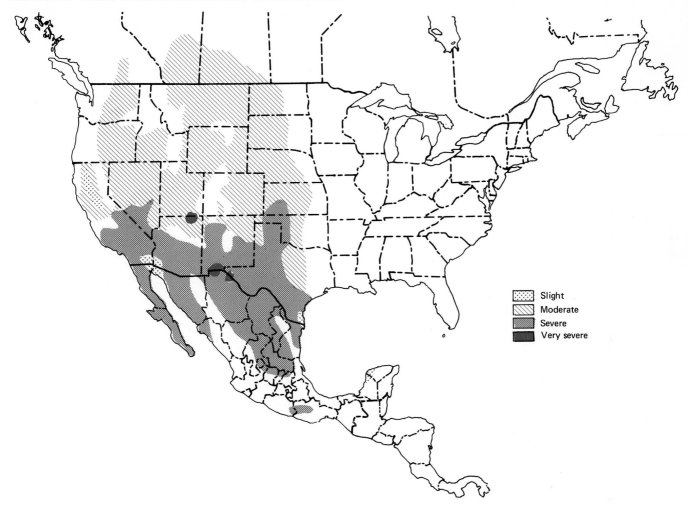

Slight
Moderate
Severe
Very severe

highly regarded study, sheep losses from predators and other causes prior to its use (1940–1949) were compared to losses from 1950 to 1970, when it was widely used. The surprising finding? No detectable difference is sheep losses from predation. It appears that the claims of the livestock industry regarding the effectiveness of Compound 1080 are grossly exaggerated.

DESERTIFICATION

Desertification is the conversion of rangeland or irrigated cropland to desert-like conditions in which agricultural productivity is reduced by at least 10 percent. It is characterized by (1) devegetation, (2) brush invasion, (3) depletion of groundwater, (4) salinization, and (5) severe erosion.

Desertification is not the literal invasion of a desert into a nondesert area. It includes the impoverishment of ecosystems *within* as well as outside of natural deserts. For example, the Sonoran and Chihuahuan deserts of the Southwest are perhaps a million years old, yet

they have become even more barren during the last 100 years. Their animal populations have diminished. Valuable grasses have declined. Invader species such as Russian thistle have multiplied. The original flood plain vegetation has changed beyond recognition in the Santa Cruz River Valley of Arizona.

Extent in North America

Thirty-seven percent of our continent's arid lands, or 2.8 million square kilometers (1.1 million square miles), have undergone *severe* desertification in which agricultural productivity has been reduced by 25–50 percent. On 27,631 square kilometers (10,500 square miles) of North America, desertification is *very severe*, causing more than a 50 percent reduction in productivity. This land is characterized by gullies and sand dunes as a result of the erosion triggered by overgrazing. This land also has salt crusts that formed because of irrigation on soil that was nearly impermeable. About 10 percent of the United States has undergone severe or very severe desertification (Figure 11-18).

A Range Improvement Project

The best strategy in range management is to prevent the range from deteriorating in the first place. However, since roughly 60 percent of our nation's grazing land already has deteriorated to fair or poor condition, we might well ask: "Is it possible to bring the range back to a good or even excellent condition?" Fortunately, the answer is "yes."

One basis for optimism is the result of a classic range rehabilitation project conducted by the Vale Grazing District covering 2.6 million hectares (1.05 million acres) in southeastern Oregon. The $10 million experiment was conducted from 1963 to 1974 by BLM scientists. Researchers applied a number of the management techniques we have been discussing: (1) they developed new water supplies and located them strategically so as to spread out grazing, (2) they used the deferred grazing system to lessen the intensity of grazing, (3) they cut the size of the cattle herds, (4) they used innovative methods of reseeding the deteriorated rangeland, and (5) they controlled brush. Intensive efforts were made so that the recreational and wildlife potential of the district would be realized as well. An examination of the Vale Grazing District by BLM researchers in 1986 showed conclusively that their range improvement project has been a long-term success.

Economic Effects

The United States has already suffered severe economic losses because of desertification. Future losses of far greater magnitude are possible. They will be in the form of (1) lower agricultural yields, (2) increased costs of production, (3) increased costs of conservation programs, or (4) ripple effects of cost increases on local, state, and national economic systems. Methods for controlling desertification may add substantial short-term costs to dry-land economies.

The World View

Desertification is a problem not only in the southwestern United States, but in the arid and semiarid regions

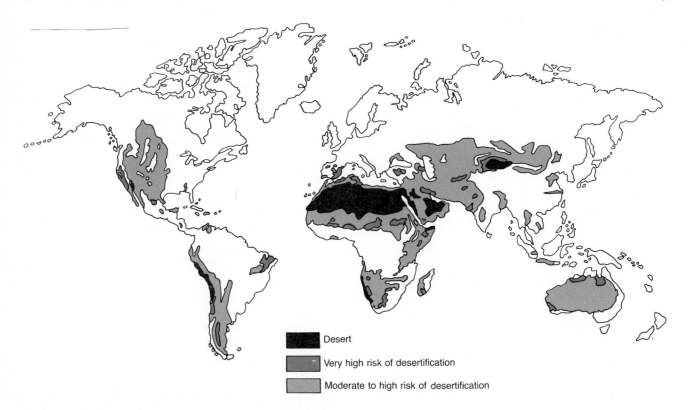

Desert

Very high risk of desertification

Moderate to high risk of desertification

FIGURE 11-19   Areas throughout the world that either have already been desertified or are at risk of becoming desertified due to deforestation or severe overgrazing.

of South America, Africa, Asia, and Australia as well (Figure 11-19). During the last half-century, about 900 million hectares (2 billion acres) have been desertified throughout the world. The ability of almost 0.5 billion of the world's people to produce food has been lessened. This problem is especially severe in the Sahel region, just south of the Sahara in Africa. By 2010, desertification will have occurred on the land now occupied by 20 percent of humankind if it continues at the present rate. Agricultural scientists firmly believe that this process can be stopped, and desertified regions rehabilitated, simply by making intensive use of appropriate soil, water, rangeland, and forest management strategies already developed, many of which have been described in this book (Chapters 5, 6, 10, and 11). The United Nationals Environmental Programme estimates that the global cost would be close to $150 billion. However, the enormous expense of the rehabilitation effort would be more than balanced by income from the increased agricultural productivity that would result.

RAPID REVIEW

1. The upper 50 percent of the grass shoot is a surplus that can be safely eaten by livestock; the lower 50 percent, known as the *metabolic reserve*, is necessary for the plant's survival.

2. The major objective of the Taylor Grazing Control Act of 1934 was to improve the quality of our nation's rangelands.

3. Under the provisions of the Taylor Grazing Control Act, rangeland was divided into grazing districts, each run by a local committee of ranchers and Bureau of Land Management (BLM) personnel.

4. In the mid-1980s, ranchers bought permits to graze 2 million cattle and 2.3 million sheep annually.

5. Extended drought may cause an 84 percent reduction in plant cover on ungrazed rangeland.

6. Rangelands are classified by a number of criteria such as (a) plant composition, (b) plant vigor, (c) amount of mulch, (d) condition of the soil, and (e) number of animals that can be supported per hectare (acre).

7. Only about 16 percent of the roughage (leaves, stems, etc.) consumed by cattle prior to slaughter is derived from rangelands. Roughly 84 percent of the roughage, such as alfalfa, is obtained from cropland pastures.

8. Due to the knowledge that fatty meat and cholesterol in the diet may contribute to heart disease, the consumption of beef by American consumers has sharply decreased since 1975.

9. Scientists are studying the feasibility of introducing the Asiatic water buffalo to the warmer rangelands of the United States.

10. Livestock may be better distributed to prevent overgrazing by (a) the strategic distribution of salt and water and (b) the use of a deferred grazing system.

11. In the deferred grazing system, cattle are successively grazed on several different pastures in order to provide each pasture with a resting period during which the grass can grow to maturity and produce seed.

12. Rangelands in poor condition may benefit from reseeding. For example, the reseeding of a Utah range increased its carrying capacity from 8 to 100 head of cattle in only 3 years.

13. A range rehabilitation project was conducted in southeastern Oregon from 1963 to 1974, involving the use of management techniques such as (a) the strategic distribution of water supplies, (b) deferred grazing, (c) reduction of herd size, (d) reseeding, and (e) brush control. A 1986 evaluation showed that the project was a long-term success.

14. During a severe drought, the total weight of jackrabbits on the range may reach 7 percent of the weight of the cattle with which they compete for forage.

15. Rangeland pests like grasshoppers and jackrabbits become serious problems only when the range is severely overgrazed.

16. Various methods have been used to control coyote predation of sheep, including (a) guard dogs, (b) guard cattle, (c) birth control chemicals, (d) chemical repellants, and (e) lethal poisons like Compound 1080.

17. A highly regarded study showed that the use of the toxic Compound 1080 has no value in reducing sheep losses caused by predation.

18. Desertification is the conversion of rangeland or irrigated cropland to desert-like conditions in which agricultural productivity is reduced at least 10 percent.

KEY WORDS AND PHRASES

Animal Unit Month (AUM)	Basal zone
	Birth control chemicals
Artificial seeding	Broadcasting seeds

Bureau of Land
  Management (BLM)
Carrying capacity
Chemical repellants
Compound 1080
Controlled burn
Decreasers
Deferred grazing system
Desertification
Feedlots
Grazing district
Grazing permit
Increasers

Invaders
Mesquite
Metabolic reserve
Mulch
Predator control
Range condition
Rangeland classification
Stock manipulation
Taylor Grazing Control
  Act
Vale Grazing District
  Project
Water buffalo

QUESTIONS AND TOPICS FOR DISCUSSION

1. Intepret the biblical statement "All flesh is grass" in terms of basic ecological principles.

2. Briefly list three major objectives of the Taylor Grazing Control Act of 1934.

3. What is unique about the growth characteristics of grasses that enable them to survive despite moderate grazing pressure?

4. Name the two federal agencies that administer the public rangelands.

5. What is the function of the feedlot? Is its role becoming more or less important? Why?

6. Describe the deferred grazing system.

7. Briefly describe four negative effects of rangeland burning.

8. What precautions must be taken when reseeding a range by broadcasting?

9. What would be an effective strategy for controlling grasshoppers on rangeland?

10. Why has mesquite become such a serious rangeland pest?

11. Describe one beneficial effect that coyotes have on the rangeland economy.

12. Describe three lethal and three nonlethal methods of coyote control.

13. Discuss the Compound 1080 controversy. Do you favor the position of the ranchers or the environmentalists? Why?

14. List five characteristics of desertification.

15. How can deserted land be reclaimed?

SUGGESTED READINGS

Bernardo, B. J., Engle, D. M., and McCollum, E. T. "An Economic Assessment of Risk and Return from Prescribed Burning on Tall Grass Prairie." *Journal of Range Management* 41(2):78–183, 1988. Excellent but technical review.

Cook, C. W., and Stubbendieck, J. *Range Research: Basic Problems and Techniques*. Denver: Society for Range Management, 1988. Authoritative treatment of the latest range management methods.

Goodall, D. W. (Ed.) *Ecosystems of the World: Managed Grasslands*. New York: Elsevier, 1987. Good reference.

Lambert, D. K. "Ranch Values and the Federal Grazing Fee." *Journal of Range Management* 40(5):397–400, 1987. Good description of grazing fees.

Stubbendieck, J. L., Hatch, S. L., and Kjar, K. J. *North American Range Plants*. Lincoln: University of Nebraska Press, 1982. Comprehensive treatment of the habitats and forage values of American range grasses, with excellent drawings of each species.

Wright, H. A., and Bailey, A. W. *Fire Ecology: United States and Southern Canada*. New York: Wiley, 1982. A state-of-the-art progress report on applied fire ecology in the United States and southern Canada. Includes practical recommendations for its use.

12

Forest Management

Our nation's forests range from the virgin stands of hemlock and Douglas fir in Alaska and the Pacific Northwest, to second-growth oak and hickory in the East, to plantations of pine and black walnut in the South. As shown in Figure 12-1, six major forest regions exist in the United States. The occurrence of a particular forest region is the geological expression of the prevailing environmental conditions, including rainfall, temperature, and soil.

Forest Ownership

Our nation has about 262 million hectares (655 million acres) of forests, covering 29 percent of the total land area of the United States. About two-thirds of this forested area is classified by the U.S. Forest Service as commercial timberland—of high enough quality to be used by the timber industry. Private owners, other than the timber industry, such as farmers and owners of estates, own 58 percent of this commercial timberland. The forest industry owners 14 percent. Eighteen percent is located in the National Forest System (Figure 12-2). Other federal agencies, such as the National Park Services, own 10 percent.

The U.S. Forest Service

Four federal bureaus are charged with administering and managing our nation's forests: the Soil Conservation Service, which is concerned with farm management–associated forests; the Tennessee Valley Authority, which is charged with timberland management near numerous reservoirs along the Tennessee River and its tributaries; and the Fish and Wildlife Service, which is interested in improving the forest habitat for wildlife and fish. However, the U.S. Forest Service, a bureau of the USDA, has the primary responsibility for managing our nation's forests to promote the greatest good for the most people over the long run.

The U.S. Forest Service was established in 1905. President Theodore Roosevelt appointed Gifford Pinchot to be its first chief forester (Figure 12-3). As a forestry professor at Yale University, Pinchot promoted the use of several forest management methods he had learned in Europe. Pinchot was a zealous crusader for conservation, which he defined as the wise *use* of natural resources.

The Forest Service divides its attention among three major areas: (1) administering and protecting the national forests; (2) researching forest, watershed, range, recreation management, wildlife habitat improvement, forest product development, and fire and pest control; and (3) cooperating with the state and private forest owners in the 50 states, Puerto Rico, and the Virgin Islands to promote sound forest management.

The Forest Service protects and manages 155 national forests and grasslands, embracing 77 million hectares (191 million acres). Included under its supervision are the grazing lands of 6 million head of livestock and habitat for one-third of America's big-game animals. In a single year, the Forest Service extinguishes almost 10,000 fires.

FOREST MANAGEMENT

Multiple Uses

A primary objective of the Forest Service is to make the greatest number of forest resources available to the

FIGURE 12-1 Distribution of major forest types in the United States (prior to settlement). Since settlement, of course, much of the forested land has been "opened up" for farming, establishment of towns, construction of roads, and so on.

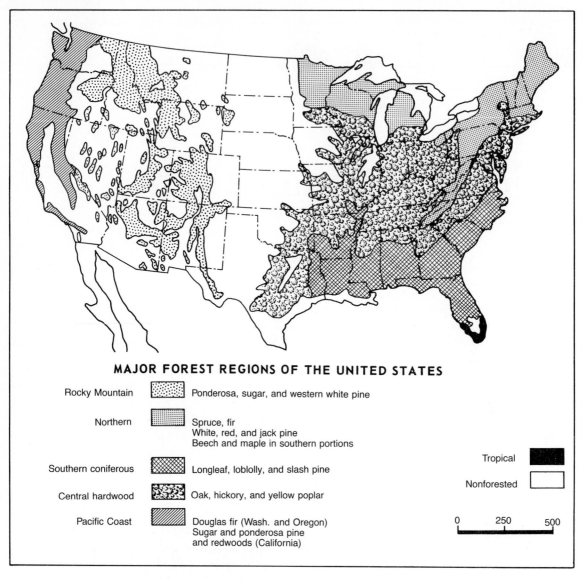

MAJOR FOREST REGIONS OF THE UNITED STATES

Rocky Mountain		Ponderosa, sugar, and western white pine
Northern		Spruce, fir White, red, and jack pine Beech and maple in southern portions
Southern coniferous		Longleaf, loblolly, and slash pine
Central hardwood		Oak, hickory, and yellow poplar
Pacific Coast		Douglas fir (Wash. and Oregon) Sugar and ponderosa pine and redwoods (California)

Tropical

Nonforested

0   250   500

greatest number of Americans, a goal mandated by the **Multiple Use–Sustained Yield Act** of 1960 (Figure 12-4).

The multiple-use management of forests looks simple on paper. In operation, however, it is an extremely complex ecological problem. For example, the Forest Service is frequently forced to use a given forest primarily for one purpose, thus sacrificing its potential use for others. A forest cannot be all things to all people. If a stand of Douglas fir, for example, is developed for high-quality timber, clearcutting may be the best way to harvest it. However, the wholesale removal of timber may impair natural flood and erosion control, and may eliminate wildlife and recreation opportunities.

Sound multiple-use management must weigh the needs of many people, and these needs vary. Thus, tim-

ber production may have top priority in the Douglas fir and Western hemlock stands of Washington and Oregon, but in the low-value second-growth forests of populous New York, where many city dwellers go for a dose of "wilderness tonic," recreational values have high priority.

FORESTS AS A SOURCE OF WOOD PRODUCTS. From early colonial days, when the straight, sturdy trunks of New England spruce and pine were fashioned into masts for the Royal Navy, until today, three centuries later, our forests have been the source of a variety of valuable products. Today our commercial forests provide the raw materials for more than 10,000 products worth about $30 billion annually. They support an industry that employs over 1.5 million people.

FIGURE 12-2   Location of the National Forests of the United States.

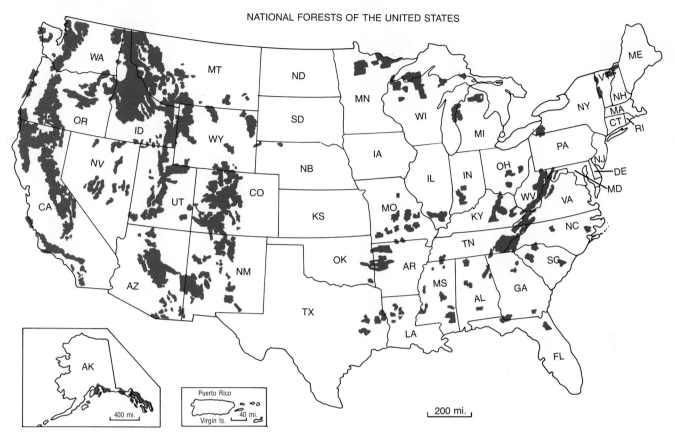

NATIONAL FORESTS OF THE UNITED STATES

FIGURE 12-3 Theodore Roosevelt and Gifford Pinchot (to left of Roosevelt) standing at the base of a giant redwood called "Old Grizzly." Pinchot was the first chief of the U. S. Forest Service.

FIGURE 12-4 Use of the forest as an "outdoor laboratory." Scientist with the Audubon Environmental Education Project explains the ecological aspects of the forest to a nature class.

FIGURE 12-5 Use of forests as a source of fuel. This birch wood which has been gathered in the nearby woods will be burned in an indoor fireplace.

To maintain the world's highest standard of living, the United States uses more wood per capita than any nation on earth—about 204 board feet of lumber per person per year. (A considerable amount is imported from Canada and Scandinavia.) In a typical year, our nation uses about 40 billion board feet, enough to build 3.5 million six-room cottages or a 4-foot-wide boardwalk 70 times longer than the distance of the moon. Americans eat, sleep, work, and play in a world of wood. Whether it is toothpicks, telephone poles, photographic film, maple syrup, acetic acid, or cellophane, we depend heavily on wood and wood-derived products (Figure 12-5).

The types of forest products used have changed dramatically in the past few decades. The harvest of pulpwood, as a source of paper, has increased threefold since 1950. In the 1980s about 50 percent of all the wood harvested in the United States was used as fuel—most of it by the forest products industry itself in its manufacturing processes.

FORESTS IN FLOOD AND EROSION CONTROL. Forest vegetation reduces flooding and soil erosion. This was demonstrated recently in Davis County, Utah, on the eastern edge of the Great Salt Lake, a region fre-

quently plagued by flash floods. Forest Service investigators discovered that much of a flood-triggering runoff originated from areas that had been depleted of vegetation. These denuded parts of the watershed had either been burned, overgrazed, or plowed up and converted into marginal croplands. In some areas, the runoff waters carved gullies 21 meters (70 feet) deep. During one rainy period, runoff was 160 times greater on an abused plot than a nearby undisturbed one. With the aid of bulldozers, the gullies were filled in, slopes were contoured, and the bare soil was carefully prepared as a seedbed and planted with rapidly growing shrubs and trees. Only 11 years later, severe August rainstorms put the rehabilitated watershed to the test. An investigation revealed that fully 94 percent of the rainfall was retained by the newly forested area. Moreover, soil erosion was reduced from the pretreatment figure of 60 cubic meters per hectare (268 cubic feet per acre) to a mere trace.

FORESTS AS RANGELANDS. In addition to timber, U.S. forests frequently include considerable areas of high-quality livestock forage. Thus, of the 191 million acres of national forests and national grasslands, 100 million acres provide forage for 6 million cattle and sheep belonging to 19,000 farmers and ranchers. (Most of this is in the West. In the lake and central states, most forest grazing occurs on farm woodlots.) Ranchers pay fees for the privilege of grazing their livestock in national forests. In a typical year, grazing-fee receipts amount to $4 million, of which 25 percent is returned to the state coffers for improving highways and schools in the counties where the fees were levied.

FORESTS AS WILDLIFE HABITAT. The U.S. national forests, as well as many private woodlands, offer excellent wildlife habitat. More than 60 percent of the elk in the Rocky Mountain region find food, cover, and shelter in national forests.

The Forest Service tries to manage the national forests to provide the best possible wildlife habitat. Sometimes the best management involves increasing the amount of forest edge. Such habitat occurs between the forest and adjoining fields, meadows, and marshes. It frequently includes a considerable number of shrubs that provide food and cover for wildlife. Development of such habitat can be integrated with timber harvesting and the construction of fire breaks and logging roads. Because food and cover for elk and deer are more abundant in early stages of the succession than in climax stages, setting back the succession by periodic controlled burns may be very beneficial to wildlife. About 18,000 hectares (45,000 acres) are burned to improve the habitat of our national forests every year. Some species have shown dramatic increases in recent years. As a result of careful management, for example, the elk population in our national forests now numbers 400,000— an eightfold increase from the 50,000 in 1920.

FORESTS AS WILDERNESS, RECREATIONAL, AND SCIENTIFIC AREAS. In 1964 Congress passed the **Wilderness Act,** which established the **National Wilderness Preservation System.** The act defines **wilderness** as an area "where the earth and its community of life are untrammelled by man, where man himself is a visitor and does not remain." As of 1988, the Wilderness System consisted of about 275 roadless areas. The Forest Service manages 13 million hectares (32.6 million acres), or 31 percent, of the wilderness in the Wilderness System. (The National Park Service manages 14.7 million hectares (36.8 million acres), or 35 percent, of the Wilderness System. Lesser amounts are managed by the Fish and Wildlife Service and the Bureau of Land Management.)

Why is our Wilderness System important? In this polluted age, when urban dwellers from Seattle to Miami and from San Diego to Boston are being crowded together shoulder to shoulder, when air is polluted with industrial gases and automobile fumes, when drinking water tastes of chlorine, and when noise assaults

the ears from all compass points, it is reassuring to know that somewhere in the great forests of America is wilderness. And once you get there, you can hike or canoe for miles, free of modern civilization.

Of the 77 million hectares (191 million acres) of national forest in the United States, about 40 million hectares (51.5 percent) are roadless. About 13 million hectares of the roadless forests have been included in the National Wilderness Preservation System. However, an ongoing controversy has been raging concerning the designation of the remaining 27 million roadless hectares.

In the name of progress, wilderness country has gradually receded under the onslaught of timber and mining interests, highway engineers, and land developers. Environmentalists, led by organizations such as the Sierra Club, the National Audubon Society, and The Wilderness Society, would like most or all of the roadless acreage to be included under the National Wilderness Preservation System.

Under the terms of the Wilderness Act, obtrusive activities such as logging, mining, and the use of automobiles, motorboats, and snowmobiles are prohibited in designated wilderness. In some areas, even aircraft are not permitted to descend below a designated altitude. In the officially designated wilderness area, every attempt is made to permit the forest ecosystem to operate without human interference. If an overly mature pine riddled with bark beetle galleries blows down during a windstorm, it remains where it falls. Barring a major catastrophe, such as crown fire, the official policy is to let nature takes its course. As a result, these areas have considerable scientific as well as recreational value. In such an area, university researchers can make observations, collect data, and formulate hypotheses, and college students can acquire valuable field experiences in geology, entomology, mammalogy, ornithology, ecology, field natural history, and game management, as well as forestry.

FORESTS AS A SOURCE OF FUEL. The supply of fossil fuels (other than coal) is rapidly falling (Chapter 20). As a result, alternative sources of energy are being explored. One such source is the biomass of trees. At present, our commercial forests produce 310 million metric tons of biomass annually—in addition to that used for forest products. Part of this biomass could be used as a source of energy. Of course, the great advantage of wood is that, unlike fossil fuels, it is **renewable.**

At present, wood and wood products provide 1.3 quads,* or 1.5 percent, of the 80 quads of energy con-

---

*One quad equals 1 quadrillion, which equals 1×10^{15}, which equals 1,000,000,000,000,000 BTUs (British thermal units). One BTU equals the quantity of heat required to raise the temperature of 1 pound of water 1°F at 39.2°F.

FIGURE 12-6   A forty-year rotation harvest in a 40 hectare (100 acre) forest.

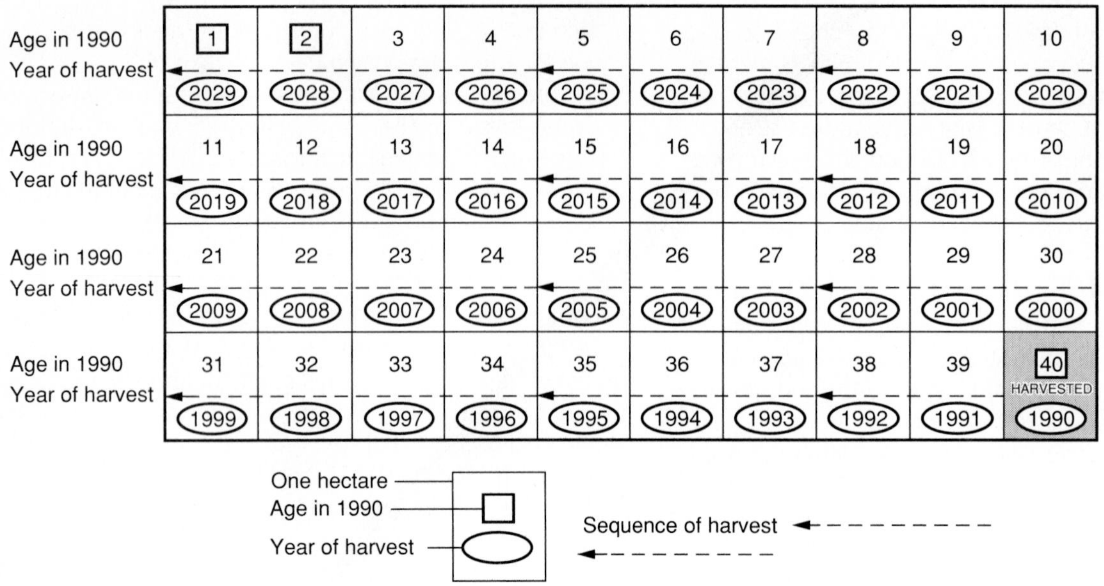

Age in 1990	1	2	3	4	5	6	7	8	9	10
Year of harvest	2029	2028	2027	2026	2025	2024	2023	2022	2021	2020
Age in 1990	11	12	13	14	15	16	17	18	19	20
Year of harvest	2019	2018	2017	2016	2015	2014	2013	2012	2011	2010
Age in 1990	21	22	23	24	25	26	27	28	29	30
Year of harvest	2009	2008	2007	2006	2005	2004	2003	2002	2001	2000
Age in 1990	31	32	33	34	35	36	37	38	39	40 HARVESTED
Year of harvest	1999	1998	1997	1996	1995	1994	1993	1992	1991	1990

One hectare — Age in 1990 — Year of harvest. Sequence of harvest ◄ — — — — — —

sumed in the United States each year. However, in its National Energy Program for Forestry, the Forest Service hopes to increase the amount of wood-derived energy (Figure 12-5).

Unfortunately, wood burning in the home releases a variety of gaseous pollutants, such as carbon dioxide, carbon monoxide, hydrocarbons, and particulates. As a result, the concentration of atmospheric pollutants is often higher inside than outside the home. In some cities and towns, wood burning is a major source of air pollution.

Sustained Yield

Today's many lumbermen are a different breed from the "cut-out- and-get-out" loggers of the late nineteenth and early twentieth centuries. After studying German silvicultural techniques, American foresters learned that a forest can be managed in such a way that a modest timber crop can be harvested indefinitely, year after year, if annual decrements are counterbalanced by annual growth. This is the **sustained-yield** concept. Under terms of the **Multiple Use–Sustained Yield Act** of 1960, foresters have a mandate from Congress to employ the principle of sustained yield in their operations in our national forests.

Nevertheless, despite this mandate, in some regions the harvest exceeds forest growth. In the Pacific Northwest region, for example, because of cutting a large proportion of mature trees, which grow very slowly, the harvest rate has exceeded the growth rate for the past 30 years.

If a forest is managed for sustained yield, the wood produced in a given year should equal the volume removed. Let us see how this might work with clearcutting, a harvest method in which all the trees in a given area are

cut. Suppose that a Georgia farmer owns 40 hectares of pine woods and that the trees are harvested when they are 40 years old. If this pine stand has a "normal distribution," as foresters say, this stand would have 40 age classes, age 1 to 40, each 1 hectare (Figure 12-6). If this forest produces 2 cords* of wood per hectare per year, 80 cords could be clearcut annually from the hectare containing the 40-year-old trees. This operation could be carried out indefinitely as long as the clearcut hectare is properly reseeded or replanted.

The length of the cutting cycle, or rotation, depends on the species of tree and on its intended commercial use. For aspen and birch to be used as pulpwood, it varies from 10 to 30 years; for pine pulpwood it is 40 years. On the other hand, the rotation for Douglas fir to be used as lumber may be up to 100 years.

HARVEST METHODS

Several harvest methods are available to timber companies. The choice of a particular harvest method depends on many factors, both biological and economic. This chapter examines the following methods: clearcutting, stripcutting, selective cutting, and shelter wood cutting.

Clearcutting

The **clearcutting** method of timber harvesting, which is the standard logging practice in the Northwest and other areas in both private and public forests, is employed on even-aged stands composed of one or two species and is applicable only to trees whose

*A stack of wood 8 feet long, 4 feet wide, and 4 feet high.

Controversy: Timber Cuts in the Tongass

The Tongass National Forest of southeastern Alaska is the largest of our nation's national forests. It embraces 6.8 million hectares (17 million acres) of temperate rain forest—much of a wilderness (Figure 1). Gigantic spruce that were 600 years old when the Declaration of Independence was signed soar for more than 200 feet.

The Forest Service has exerted strenuous and costly efforts to stimulate the economy of the timber industry near the Tongass. It considers such a program a mandate under the terms of the **Alaska Native Claims Act** of 1980. In the view of the Forest Service, it is much better to harvest the trees to generate jobs than to let the wood rot. Indeed, according to a plan formed by the service in 1986, 20 billion board feet would be harvested from the Tongass by 2030.

The Forest Service plan has been heavily criticized by many environmental groups, such as the Audubon Society, the Sierra Club, and the Wilderness Society, as well as by many members of Congress. In their view, the Tongass Program

1. Destroys magnificent old-growth forests that cannot be renewed for another eight centuries.
2. Disrupts habitat that now supports the largest concentration of grizzles and bald eagles in the world.
3. Increases sedimentation in high-quality trout and salmon streams.
4. Uses environmentally unsound logging practices.
5. Systematically destroys a vast "scientific laboratory"—the only reasonably intact temperate zone rain forest on this planet.
6. Wastes tax dollars. (In fact, the Forest Service spends $150,000 for a single mile of logging road. Taxpayers pay $36,000 for every logging job created by the Service's Tongass Program—a spendthrift enterprise that has been branded a financial boondoggle.
7. Grossly underprices wood havested by private industry. Loggers in the Tongass pay the Forest Service only $4 per 1,000 board feet of hemlock and spruce, only 2 percent of the going price in the national forests of the Northwest.

Despite these criticisms, however, the Forest Service is undaunted. At hearings before congress, Service Chief R. Max Peterson characterized much of this negative sentiment as unfounded. In his view, the Forest Service has struck a judicious compromise between commercial interests on the one hand and environmental concerns on the other. A number of resource specialists, including Eric Fritzell of the University of Missouri's School of Forestry, believe that the Service, as a whole, is doing a good job of discharging its multiple-use mandate, not only in the Tongass but in our other national forests as well.

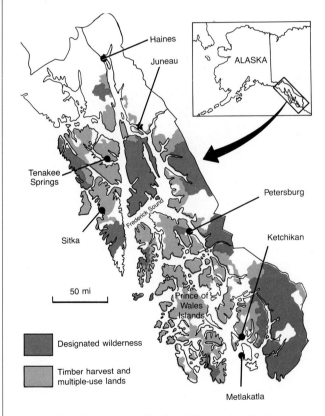

FIGURE 1   The Tongass National Forest in Alaska.

seedlings thrive in full sunlight. The Douglas fir on the Pacific Coast is harvested by this method. Perhaps the most valuable timber species in the world, it has been exported to Europe, where it has proved superior to native species. Some Douglas fir trees in Washington and Oregon are more than 60 meters (200 feet) high and are over 1,000 years old.

A Douglas fir, unlike a beech or maple, is not a climax tree and is not shade tolerant as a seedling. Its seeds do not germinate in the shade of the forest floor. Therefore, the species is not amenable to selective cutting. If it were, its place in the forest would rapidly be appropriated by shade-tolerant species. In addition, a 30-meter (100-foot) Douglas fir weighing several tons could not be removed without badly bruising and killing younger growth.

FIGURE 12-7 Clearcutting of old-growth Douglas fir in the Gifford Pinchot National Forest, Washington. Mt. St. Helens is in the background.

With the clearcutting technique, an entire patch of evenly aged mature trees, 16 to 80 hectares (40 to 100 acres) in area, is removed, leaving an unsightly rectangular scar in the midst of the forest. (In national forests, the maximal size of a cut is 16 hectares [40 acres]). Because a large number of such blocks may be removed, a clearcut forest resembles a giant green and brown checkerboard when viewed from the air (Figure 12-7). In addition to its use on Douglas fir in Oregon and Washington, the clearcutting method has been used effectively in harvesting even-aged stands of southern pine; aspen forests in northern Minnesota, Wisconsin, and Michigan; and coniferous forests in the West.

Clearcutting is done on a rotation basis. If saw timber is wanted, the rotation may be 100 years. The reason for this relatively long rotation is that the trees must be quite mature before the wood has the desirable density and durability. On the other hand, if pulpwood is desired, a rotation of only 30 years is satisfactory, since at that age pulpwood species such as pine, aspen, and birch have optimal characteristics. Moreover, if birch and aspen get much older, they become highly susceptible to diseases and insect attacks. Rotations of 100 years for saw timber and 30 years for pulpwood are the most efficient from the standpoint of harvest volume. In

other words, the trees are harvested before their growth rates sharply decline.

THE CLEARCUTTING CONTROVERSY. The clearcutting practices of the Forest Service became a storm center of controversy in 1971. Much of the criticism focused on the ponderosa pine logging in the Bitterroot National Forest of Montana.

The clearcutting practices of private industry have also been the subject of criticism. Consider the Pacific Lumber Company of California, for example. In 1988 it began to clearcut magnificent, centuries-old redwoods near Eureka, California, at an accelerated pace, allegedly to pay off junk bonds (bonds issued with little or no collateral) that paid for the takeover of a company with a long track record of sustainable harvest. Since one 500-year-old redwood has a market value of more than $50,000 dollars, the accelerated clearcut made financial sense to Pacific Lumber (Figure 12-8). But it did not make aesthetic or ecological sense to an environmentalist group called the Coalition to Save the Redwoods. They protested the clearcut vigorously, even to the point of staging a sit-in on pulley-suspended platforms high up in the doomed trees.

The opponents of clearcutting have listed the following arguments:

FIGURE 12-8 These large redwoods occur in the Pacific forest region. They are located in Del Norte State Park, California. At an age of more than three thousand years, some redwoods are among the oldest organisms on earth.

1. Clearcutting accelerates surface runoff.
2. It increases erosion on sloping land because the trees that protected the soil from rain and wind are removed.
3. It promotes the **blow-down** of trees. In a solid stand, most of the trees are protected from a windstorm. However, when a forest is clearcut, the trees bordering the open areas are left unprotected.
4. It greatly diminishes the carrying capacity (for some species) of an area, at least temporarily. How many grouse or deer can be supported by a bare patch of ground?
5. Clearcutting destroys the scenic beauty of a region, converting it into ugly, desolate scars.
6. It creates a fire hazard. A large amount of debris (loose bark, branches, sawdust, broken logs) is left behind after a forest is clearcut. Such slash could easily be ignited by lighting and start a wildfire.

On the other hand, clearcutting also has advantages:

1. It is the quickest and simplest method of harvesting.
2. A few years after the area has been clearcut, sunloving shrubs and saplings usually become established on the logged-off site, providing cover, food, and breeding sites for a great variety of wildlife such as rabbits, grouse, and deer, as well as many song birds.
3. It is the only way by which forests of highly desirable species, such as Douglas fir, can be regenerated.
4. It is the only effective method for controlling some disease and insect outbreaks. To save the "life" of an infected stand, the forester uses the "surgery" of clearcutting, just as a surgeon amputates infected limbs to save the life of the patient.

Stripcutting

The **stripcutting** method of harvesting timber has been used effectively in the forests of the northeastern United States. In our discussion of erosion control on farmland (Chapter 5), strip cropping on the contour was mentioned as a highly desirable technique. Stripcutting is somewhat similar. It is usually used in hilly terrain where clearcutting might result in massive pollution of streams just below the logging site.

During stripcutting, loggers remove narrow strips of forest. Stripcutting has been successfully used in southern pines. A typical technique involves cutting a

FIGURE 12-9   Typical stripcutting pattern. Residual forested strips are left so that natural reseeding can occur in the harvested strips.

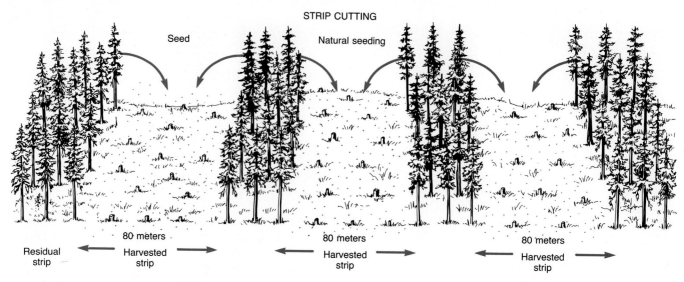

strip 80 meters (250 feet) wide. Residual forested strips are left between the cut strips to serve as seed sources, as shown in Figure 12-9.

Stripcutting has several advantages over clearcutting: (1) it minimizes the loss of soil nutrients from the forest; (2) it curbs the pollution of mountain streams with sediment (thus preventing the destruction of spawning sites for trout and other species); (3) it minimizes the ugliness associated with much larger clearcut areas; and (4) permits more effective reforestation by natural mechanisms.

Selective Cutting

Clearcutting will not work in timber stands composed of unevenly aged trees or in mixed stands composed in part of valuable timber species and in part of commercially unattractive species. Under such conditions, trees are harvested by **selective cutting,** a hunt-and-pick method in which mature trees of quality species are harvested after being marked in advance with spray paint

or some other method. Deformed trees and trash species are removed to upgrade the stand.

The selective-cutting method can be used to harvest single species such as maple, beech, and hemlock, whose seedlings can germinate in the shade of the forest floor. Selective cutting has been used extensively in mixed coniferous–hardwood stands and in deciduous forests (oak, hickory, butternut, and walnut) (Figure 12-10). It is more costly and time-consuming than clearcutting but has many advantages over the latter method. These advantages include the following:

1. It minimizes environmental abuses such as land scarring, accelerated runoff, soil erosion, and wildlife habitat destruction.
2. It reduces blow-down.
3. It decreases the fire hazard because the volume of slash left after the harvest is reduced.
4. It results in a high rate of natural reproduction.

FIGURE 12-10   Selective cutting of an unevenly-aged northern hardwood-hemlock stand. Top: before selective cutting. Trees to be felled are those with a line drawn through the trunk. Bottom: Same stand ten years after selective cutting.

Selective cutting on a given stand is often done on a 10-year rotation. Sustained-yield management is practiced—the volume of wood harvested during a given year being equal to the volume grown since the previous cutting. A small number of trees are removed per acre. They are eventually replaced by natural reproduction.

REFORESTATION

Whenever timber is removed, either by clearcutting or by selective cutting, the denuded area must be reforested to ensure a sustained yield. This may be done by natural or artificial methods. Similarly, any forested land that has been destroyed by fire, insects, disease, hurricanes, or strip-mining also should be reforested, even though timber may not be its ultimate primary use.

About 1 million hectares (2.5 million acres) are reforested annually in the United States. Nevertheless, a backlog of reforestation needs is building up. This is due in part to the extremely rapid increase in the use of woodlands as a source of firewood. Such use, which frequently involves undesirable cutting practices, is expected to increase threefold by the year 2020, especially on farmer-owned woodlots.

Natural Reseeding

After clearcutting, a few mature, wind-firm trees may be left intact as a seed source within the otherwise logged-off site. Scattered by wind and, to a lesser degree, by birds, rodents, and runoff water, the seeds are eventually dispersed throughout the denuded area. Natural reseeding, however, is usually not completely adequate. One reason is that some tree species, such as loblolly pine, may have only one good seed-producing year every 2 to 5 years. (In a good year, seed production may be 10 times that of a poor year.) Another reason

is that the dispersed seeds must reach bare ground to develop properly so that the seedlings can absorb moisture and nutrients from the soil. If they fall on bark, logs, or stones, survival is greatly reduced. Because of these drawbacks, natural reseeding is usually supplemented by aerial, hand, or machine seeding (Figure 12-11).

Seeding by Foresters

In rugged terrain, aerial seeding is the best method. Seed are sown from planes flying slowly just above the treetops. A helicopter can seed 1000 hectares (2,500 acres) per day. Unfortunately, many of these seeds fall on infertile soil or are consumed by birds, mice, and squirrels. To minimize losses to animals, the seeds are frequently coated with a toxic deterrent. Except in the case of unusually small seeded trees, such as hemlock and spruce, rodent eradication is virtually a prerequisite to successful seeding.

If a logged-off site is flat, power-driven seeding machines may be used, as has been done in the cutover land of Wisconsin and Michigan. These machines plant up to 3.3 hectares (8 acres) per day, simultaneously fertilize the soil and apply an herbicide to prevent weed encroachment.

Planting

In addition to bird and rodent problems, a major disadvantage of seeding is the high number of first-year seedlings killed by frost, drought, hot weather, insects, and autumn leaf fall. As a result, seeding, even by artificial methods, is less successful than planting young trees from plantation stock. Moreover, no rodent control is needed. In the South and in the Great Lakes states, trees can be planted at a rate of 150 per worker-hour. On flatland, three workers, a tractor, and a planting machine can set 1,000 to 2,000 trees per hour.

FIGURE 12-11 Forest areas in the United States which have been reforested by planting or seeding. 1950–1985.

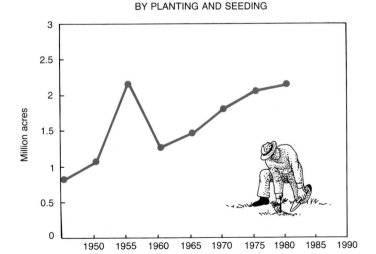

FOREST ACRES REFORESTED
BY PLANTING AND SEEDING

THE MONOCULTURE CONTROVERSY

Monoculture is the practice of growing trees, much as the farmer grows a crop of corn or oats. It involves planting and raising a single-species stand of trees, with all individuals in the stand being of the same age and size (Figure 12-12). Monoculture is advocated by some forest managers and forest-products corporations and economists, but it has been criticized by professional foresters and ecologists. In heated controversies such as this, it is instructive to list the major points both for and against monoculture.

Arguments for Monoculture

1. It is an efficient method of growing and harvesting a large volume of timber.
2. Because growth is rapid, harvesting (by clearcutting) can be done on a relatively short rotation.
3. It is amenable to the intensive application (frequently by air) of fertilizers, herbicides, fungicides, and insecticides.
4. It makes possible maximal use of such recent technological developments as machine seeders, tree-planting machines, the "tree monkey" (which climbs and prunes trees simultaneously), the chip harvester, the one-man logger, and the crusher (which can clear 240 hectares [600 acres] of forested land in 1 month).
5. It makes possible the establishment of sun-loving (shade-intolerant) seedlings of such valuable species as Douglas fir, redwood, longleaf pines, ponderosa pine, yellow poplar, red oak, cherry, and black walnut.
6. It can help increase wood production to meet growing demands.

Arguments Against Monoculture

1. A forest under monoculture is an artificial, simplified ecosystem. As such, it lacks the built-in balancing mechanisms found in the more complex natural ecosystem represented by the multiage, multispecies forest.
2. Although monoculture admittedly grows wood faster, the wood is inferior to the more slowly growing wood in a natural forest.
3. The intensive use of fertilizers results in nutrient runoff, which may contribute to the eutrophication of lakes and streams.
4. The intensive use of insecticides can pollute aquatic ecosystems and the atmosphere. Pesticide contamination of food chains may have adverse effects on wildlife and humans (see Chapter 15). Continuous use of insecticides can result in the development of insecticide-resistant strains of forest insects.
5. This practice depends on intensive use of energy derived from fossil fuels. This energy may be used directly—as in the consumption of gasoline by tree planters, pruners, chain saws, helicopters, and airplanes (used in seeding and in applying fertilizers and insecticides)—or indirectly—in the manufacture of the heavy forest-planting and harvesting machinery or in the production of fertilizers and pesticides.
6. The single-species, single-age forest primarily serves one function: wood production. But other functions, such as erosion and flood control, wildlife habitat, scenic beauty, and recreational opportunities, are much better served by the naturally developed multispecies, multiage forest.
7. Because of the relative scarcity of moisture-absorbing organic material on the floor of the monoculture forest, the forest floor tends to be drier and warmer than that of the natural forest. As a result, the monoculture forest is more susceptible to fire.
8. A forest monotype is very vulnerable to destructive outbreaks of insects and disease organisms.
9. Eventually, of course, the monoculture forest will be clearcut—a harvesting method that results in a whole complex of environmental problems.

FIGURE 12-12 This pine plantation occurs in the Southern coniferous forest region. It is located in the Tennessee River valley. These trees will be used as a source of pulpwood for the paper industry.

Genetic Engineering: The Key to Tomorrow's Superforests

The rapidly developing field of genetic engineering, described briefly in Chapter 6, holds promise for dramatic improvements in our nation's forests. Hereditary traits are determined by genes. These genes, in turn, are present in the DNA molecules of the chromosomes. In one techmique, known as *direct DNA transfer*, the gene responsible for a given trait, such as rapid growth, can be transferred directly to the DNA of single, isolated tree cells. Each of these cells may then develop into a tree with the ability to grow at an accelerated rate.

What does the future hold? On the basis of recent research in the United States, the following may be attainable by 1995:

1. Trees that will be distasteful to protentially destructive browsing herbivores, such as deer.
2. Spruce and hardwood (oak, maple) planting stock

with a whole series of genetically engineered traits such as accelerated growth, reduced need for fertilizer, improved ability to compete with weeds, and higher survival rates.

By 2000, even more exciting results may be realized:

1. Pulpwood species (spruce, aspen, birch) with traits that make them much more valuable to the paper industry.
2. Trees that will actually produce their own "insecticides" to ward off insects, as well as their own "herbicides" to reduce or eliminate weeds that compete with them for soil moisture and nutrients.

If researchers are successful, forestry costs should be lessened substantially.

Tree Farms

A **tree farm** is a private land area used to grow timber for profit. The tree farming movement was started by the Weyerhaeuser Company in Washington in 1941. It is currently sponsored by the American Forest Products Industries (AFPI), which is composed of the timber, paper, pulp, and plywood industries and private owners of forest lands.

In applying for certification by the AFPI, the owner must demonstrate to an inspecting forester that he or she is employing sound forest-management practices, such as sustained yield and effective pest and fire control. When a tree-farm certification committee has approved the forester's report, the tree-farm owner is awarded the official roadside tree-farm sign as recognition of achievement. This movement has grown from 8,000 tree farms on 15.6 million hectares (39 million acres) in 1956 to 35,000 farms covering 75 million acres in the early 1980s.

DEVELOPING GENETICALLY SUPERIOR TREES

In addition to reforestation, another important forest management method is the development of genetically superior trees. Crossing two species of trees, known as **hybridization,** may result in offspring that combine the best traits of the parents. For example, in northern California, plantations of Jeffrey pine were formerly very vulnerable to the attacks of the pine weevil. Economic

damage was severe. The problem has been somewhat reduced, however, by crossing the cold-resistant Jeffrey pine with the weevil-resistant Coulter's pine. The resultant hybrids were resistant to both cold and the pine weevil.

Research shows that in southern pine stands, selective breeding techniques may increase wood volume by 10 percent, straightness of the trunk by 9 percent, wood density by 5 percent, and rust (a fungal disease) resistance by 4 percent. The economic gains resulting from selective breeding may be considerable. A forest breeding program in California, for example, resulted in an increased return of $68 per hectare ($27 per acre).

Seed Orchards

Another way to produce better trees is through **seed orchards**, which produce large quantities of high-quality seeds. Rootstocks are formed by removing the tops of young trees with superior traits. Small branches are then cut from other trees of high quality and grafted onto the rootstocks. The tree that develops from this graft is then crossed with still other trees that are commercially valuable. The seeds from this cross may then be saved for planting in commercial forests.

Tissue Culture

In the tissue culture technique, seeds are collected from superior trees and grown into seedlings. Tiny shoots from these seedlings are then cut off, chopped up, then placed in nutritive solutions. The cells grow into "baby" trees complete with roots, shoots, and leaf buds. Since all these individuals are derived from parts of the same parent tree, they have identical hereditary material and are called **clones.** Few tissue culture programs are now operating in the United States. However, the Weyerhaeuser Corporation is planning to produce 100,000 tissue-cultured clones of the Douglas fir annually for planting in forests of the Northwest.

THE LOGGING PLAN

The forestry management methods we have discussed, such as seeding, planting, hybridization, tissue culture, and selective breeding, are all important in producing a high-quality forest. Once that forest matures, it must be harvested as efficiently as possible. To this end, a detailed **logging plan** is prepared by the forest manager.

In some states, such as California and Massachusetts, the plan must be submitted to a state board for approval. A typical plan might include the following items:

1. A map showing the stand to be logged.
2. A map that shows the location, distribution, age, and volume of the species to be logged. The distribution of species is shown on areas that are to be selectively cut.
3. Harvesting method (clearcutting, stripcutting, shelterwood cutting, or selective cutting) to be employed.
4. The most suitable access roads.
5. An estimate of the amount of time required to complete the logging operation.
6. The cost of the operation and the probable gross income from the sale of the saw timber and/or pulpwood.

THE LOGGING OPERATION

The logging operation includes felling the trees, removing the limbs, and cutting the trunks into logs. The logs are dragged across the forest floor to a central point where they are loaded onto trucks or train cars. The wood is then transported to a pulp or sawmill.

Using a chain saw, a logger can cut about 6,000 board feet of saw timber or seven cords of pulpwood per day. Large companies frequently use **hydraulic shears** and **whole tree chippers.**

The hydraulic shears resemble gigantic pincers. This machine grabs a tree near the base of the trunk and shears it off, cuts the trunk into logs, and loads the logs on a truck or on a flatbed.

A whole tree chipper, used by the pulpwood companies, can "chew up" an entire 50-centimeter (20-inch)-diameter pine trunk, branches and all, into thousands of small wood chips in less than a minute (Figure 12-13). The chips are then blown into a waiting van and hauled to a paper mill.

The chipper has several advantages: (1) it enables the forester to utilize much more of the tree's biomass than the 60 percent harvested by conventional methods; (2) it leaves the forest floor relatively clean, facilitating the growth of new trees, reducing the fire hazard posed by logging-accumulated slash.

CONTROL OF FOREST PESTS

The most serious agents of forest destruction are disease and insect pests (Figure 12-14 and Table 12-1). Under the authority of the **Forest Pest Control Act** of 1947, surveys are conducted annually in both private and public forests to detect pest population buildups so that they can be arrested before they reach disastrous levels.

FIGURE **12-13** A single man here operates equipment that cuts and removes pulpwood trees and transfers them to a chipping machine. The chips can then be trucked to a plant and converted into paper pulp or chipboard.

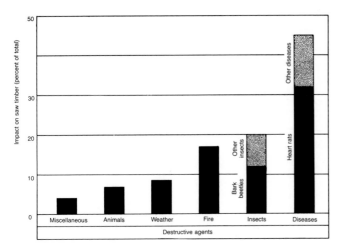

FIGURE 12-14 Impact of destructive agents on sawtimber.

In a typical year, Congress appropriates $10 million for pest control and an additional $3 million for research.

Diseases

One of the natural causes of mortality in trees is disease. Diseases cause 45 percent of the total saw-timber destruction. Heart-rot fungus alone is responsible for about 33 percent of the total forest damage. (This fungus, however, is beneficial as an important agent in the decay of fallen logs, dead stubs, and slash, recycling elements and removing flammable debris.) The remaining disease damage can be attributed primarily to white-pine blister rust, dwarf mistletoe, and Dutch elm disease. The most injurious diseases are exotics, accidentally introduced into the United States, that have suddenly been released from environmental

factors that ordinarily kept them in check in their native habitat (Table 12-2 and Figure 12-16).

Insects

In 1985, more than 7 million hectares (18 million acres) of valuable timber were destroyed by the spruce budworm. Insects account for 20 percent of all timber destroyed, ranking second to diseases as agents of forest damage. Each year they ruin 5 billion board feet of timber, equal to about 10 percent of our total annual harvest.

Each species of tree has its own unique assemblage of insect pests. An oak tree may be eaten by more than 100 species. No part of a tree is spared (Table 12-1). A healthy tree can withstand the nibbling of insects, but if trees are stressed because of drought, crowding or pollution or combinations of the three, they may be damaged by insects. Outbreaks of insects can also be harmful, killing healthy trees.

BARK BEETLES. Almost 90 percent of insect-inflicted timber mortality is caused by bark beetles. They destroy roughly 4.5 billion board feet annually. Adult beetles attack a tree by boring through the bark and then tunneling out egg chambers and galleries with their powerful jaws. The tiny grubs that hatch from the eggs consume the soft inner bark, and, if sufficiently numerous (1,000 per large tree), may actually girdle the tree and kill it within a month. The bark beetle group includes a large number of destructive species.

Pine beetles kill trees by transmitting a fungus that develops inside the tree. The fungus plugs up the vessels that transport water to the leaves, branches, trunk, and roots. The Western pine beetle killed 25 billion board

Table 12-1 Common Insect Pests of Forests: Damage and Control

Name	Principal Species Affected	Type of Damage	Control Method		
			Prevention	Direct Control	Control Season
Bark beetles	Pines	Girdles tree by killing cambium layer under bark	Salvage green, blown-down timber	Fell, peel, and burn bark; salvage infested logs; burn slabs	Spring, summer, fall
Gypsy moth	Oaks, birch, aspen	Defoliation		Spraying insecticide	May–June
Sawflies	Eastern and southern pines and tamarack	Reduces growth by defoliation; epidemics kill stands	Cut mature and over-mature stands	Aerial insecticide spray	Early summer at period of greatest activity
Spruce budworm	True firs, Douglas fir	Reduces growth by defoliation; kills older trees extensively	Cut mature and over-mature stands	Aerial insecticide spray	Early summer as insects emerge
White pine weevil	Eastern white pine, Norway spruce	Kills leaders, causes forked and crooked boles	Maintain shade where possible to 20 ft	Hand spray upper stem and new growth with sodium arsenate or cut and burn infected tip; leave only best side branch on first lower whorl	Early summer as insects emerge

Table 12-2   Common Fungus Diseases of Forest Trees: Damage and Control

Common Name	Host	Symptoms	Control
Root and butt rot	Species of pine, mature stands, and plantations 15–25 years old	Decline in vigor, needles short, becoming yellow and then dying; cones appear prematurely; fruiting bodies at base of tree or one ground surface arising from roots	Avoid planting white or red pine on poorly drained or high-pH soils
Western red rot	Ponderosa pine	None, except presence of decay and red discoloration in heartwood	Periodic pruning of dead branches on crop trees
Brown spot	Longleaf pine	Small spots on needles causing needle dieback; retards growth of seedlings	Controlled burning in third year of seedling's life or spray with prescribed chemicals
Oak wilt	Oak species, particularly those of the black oak group	Leaves crinkle and become pale green, later turning brown or bronze; mature leaves shed at any symptom stage; lower branches affected last; trees usually die after the summer symptoms appear	Some promise of control has been obtained by cutting or poisoning healthy oaks for 50–100 ft. around spot infections. Mechanical or chemical root barriers
Dutch elm disease, associated with attacks by scolytid beetles	American elm	Progressive dwarfing and yellowing of leaves, accompanied by various degrees of defoliation; followed by death of branches or entire tree	Mainly through destruction of infected trees and protection against bark beetles by insecticidal sprays and maintenance of tree vigor by appropriate pruning and feeding practices Lignasan injection

FIGURE 12-15   A young western white pine stand in the St. Joe National Forest in Idaho is being sprayed with phytoactin, a blister rust-killing chemical.

Controlling Insect Outbreaks with Heterotypes

Insect pest populations sometimes build up to impressive numbers. Charles Kendeigh, an ecologist at the University of Illinois, studied a severe spruce budworm outbreak in Ontario. The larvae, which were feeding on coniferous foliage, occurred in such vast numbers that their excreta sounded like drizzling rain as it fell on the forest floor. More recently, an explosion of forest tent caterpillars virtually destroyed 11,000 hectares (26,850 acres) of water tupelo in the region of Mobile Bay, Alabama. Aerial photographs revealed almost complete defoliation of extensive stands of once healthy trees.

Is it possible to control such outbreaks without using expensive insecticides that may have adverse effects on the forest ecosystem? One possible alternative method is to establish forest **heterotypes**, as suggested by Kenneth Watt, an ecologist at the University of California–Davis. When monoculture is practiced in a large area, populations of forest pests tend to fluctutate widely. Over an evolutionary period of millions of years, certain species of insects have specialized to feed on a *particular species* of tree (spruce budworm on balsam fir, larch sawfly on larch, gypsy moth on oak, pine-back beetle on pine, and so on). Many also feed on a particular kind of tree at a *particular stage* (seed, seedling, sapling, or mature tree) in its life cycle. In natural forest ecosystems, the particular food tree to which a species of insect has become adapted may be widely dispersed. An insect, such as a pine-bark beetle, for example, might have to creep, crawl, or fly a considerable distance from one food tree to another. In the process, of course, such an insect becomes vulnerable to predation, windstorms and rainstorms, fire, and other mortality factors. Even if it survives, it may eventually starve to death before it is able to find another food tree. Conversely, in an artificial forest ecosystem, as represented by a monotype, the pine-bark beetle is not only surrounded by the right species of food tree, of the precise age that the beetles prefer. The severity of forest insect outbreaks can be substantially reduced simply by breaking up the large contiguous stands of single-age, single-species trees into small, isolated stands interspersed with trees of different kinds and ages.

---

feet of ponderosa pine along the Pacific Coast between 1917 and 1943. The mountain pine beetle has killed 20 billion board feet of sugar pine, western white pine, and lodgepole pine in California alone.

Overharvesting of trees can result in thick regrowth. These trees are less able to ward off insects like bark beetles. Thinning trees, therefore, effectively controls the beetles.

On a long-term basis, perhaps the best method of control is to prevent infestations from occurring in the first place. This may be done by using **sanitation techniques:** burning all potential bark-beetle breeding sites, such as senile and windblown trees, and logging accumulated slash and debris and the broken-off trunks of lightning- and fire-killed trees. (In removing those trunks, however, the forester is also removing the potential nesting cavities of beetle-eating woodpeckers and is removing nutrients that would be returned to the forest floor, so a cost-benefit analysis would have to be made.) Insecticides can be applied by planes that fly low over the infected area.

INTEGRATED PEST MANAGEMENT. In the late 1970s, certain environmental groups became concerned with the large amounts of chemical pesticides used by the Forest Service to control insect outbreaks. This criticism reached its peak when the Forest Service used DDT (banned except for emergencies) to control an explosion of tussock moths in conifer stands of the Northwest. Ecologists considered this strategy particularly questionable because ordinarily the tussock moth population is held in check by a death-causing virus. Eventually, the Forest Service, stung by criticism from many quarters, decided to adopt the **integrated pest management (IPM)** policy, a concept described more fully in Chapter 15.

Among the IPM strategies now used by the Forest Service are the following:

1. Biological control agents, such as natural predators and parasites, are used.
2. Selective cutting methods are sometimes used in preference to clearcutting methods (since even-aged trees are highly vulnerable to insect attacks).
3. Bark-damaged trees are removed because they serve as focal points of insect infestation.
4. Heterotypes are favored over monotypes whenever feasible.

FIRE CONTROL
Wildfires

Every 3 minutes, a forest fire starts somewhere in the United States (Table 12-3). In the early part of this

Table 12-3   Causes of Wildfires in Protected Areas, 1903

	Thousands of Fires	Percent of Fires
Incendiary (arson)	26.1	27.0
Debris burning	22.7	23.8
Lightning	8.2	8.6
Children	7.0	7.3
Smoking	6.7	7.0
Equipment use	5.9	6.1
Railroads	3.2	3.3
Campfires	2.7	2.7
Miscellaneous	12.6	13.2
Total	95.2	100.0

century, there were more than 100,000 forest wildfires in the United States in a single year (Figure 12-16). They burned more than 27,500 square kilometers (10,450 square miles) of forest, an area the size of Maryland. Even today, fire is responsible for about 17 percent of saw-timber destruction annually. However, because of better fire control techniques, the total acreage of destroyed timber has been sharply reduced in recent years. Nevertheless, occasional serious wildfire outbreaks do occur, especially during periods of extended drought. Consider 1988, for example. In that year, the most severe drought in half a century transformed much of our nation's timber into kindling wood. Lightning strikes set the kindling ablaze. By midsummer, scores of forest fires were raging in Alaska, Idaho, California, Oregon, Colorado, Utah, Wyoming, and Wisconsin. The Forest Service called the summer of 1988 the worst fire season in 30 years. The fires charred at least 3.65 million acres—an area larger than Connecticut. The largest burn in Colorado's history destroyed more than 7,300 hectares (18,000 acres) of prime habitat for elk and deer. The Black Hills' blaze in South Dakota scorched 7,000 hectares (16,500 acres), forced the evacuation of 1,000 campers, and smoke-shrouded the presidential shrine at Mt. Rushmore.

Most of the public's attention, however, was focused on the devastation in Yellowstone National Park. The flames seared more than 161,000 hectares (400,000 acres) and threatened thousands of tourists who had

FIGURE 12-16   Wildfire in the Ochoco National Forest, Oregon.

gathered to witness Old Faithful. Fire boss Fred Roach, who had battled such blazes for two decades, told reporters that he "never saw anything as awesome as this!" Twenty-five hundred army personnel were flown to the scene to help contain the fire. President Ronald Reagan became so concerned that he sent Agriculture Secretary Richard Lyng, Interior Secretary Donald Hodel, and Deputy Defense Secretary William O. Taft to Yellowstone to assess the destruction. Eventually, in early September, due to cooler weather, snow, reduced wind velocities, and the heroic efforts of thousands of fire fighters, the fires went out.

CAUSES. One of 10 of our nation's forest fires are caused by lightning (Table 12-3). The rest are caused by *people*. As John D. Guthrie, a former fire inspector for the Forest Service, has written: "To stage a forest fire you need only a few things—a forest with right atmospheric conditions, and a spark either from a lightning bolt or a match in the hands of a fool or a knave. The formula is simple . . . the larger the forest, the drier the air, the bigger the fire you will have."

Sad to say, roughly 30 percent of our nation's wildfires are started *deliberately*. Sometimes they are started "just for fun," and sometimes to "get even with someone," possibly a big timber company that would not permit a neighboring farmer to graze his cattle on company land. In recent years, intentional fires have burned more than 2,500 square kilometers (1,000 square miles) yearly in the United States—an area the size of Rhode Island.

FIREFIGHTING. The actual suppression or attack pattern used by fighters varies greatly, depending on the size of the fire, terrain, type of fire, wind direction, location of roads, availability of water, and relative humidity. A variety of fire suppression methods are used, including fire breaks, back fires, fire-retarding chemicals, and infrared systems (Figure 12-17).

INFRARED SYSTEM. The components of the infrared system include computers, satellites, satellite dishes, and video cameras. This system can pinpoint the location of a wildfire with considerable accuracy. Moreover, it can track the movements of a windblown fire. Since such movement can be highly erratic and could trap unsuspecting firefighters, the infrared systems have the potential to save lives.

USE OF SMOKE JUMPERS. In rugged mountainous country, smoke jumpers may parachute into the burn area. The national forests of mountainous regions in Washington, Oregon, California, Montana, Idaho, and New Mexico are protected by a corps of 350 Forest Service smoke jumpers. With their help, many remote blazes that in 1930 might have burned out of control may now be extinguished within hours.

FIGURE 12-17 A U. S. Forest Service plane releases a fire-suppressing chemical on a wildfire in the Ozark National Forest, Arkansas.

USE OF CONTROLLED FIRES

Since the 1930s, the Forest Service has used the symbol of Smokey the Bear to alert the American public to the highly destructive effects of wild forest fires. In recent years, however, the Service has come to realize that some wildfires are ecologically beneficial. In fact, it is now believed that fire plays an important role in maintaining many economically important timber stands. Examples include the old-growth, even-aged stands of Douglas fir in the Northwest, red pine in Minnesota, and white pine in Pennsylvania and New Hampshire. Certain less valuable species, such as pitch pine on sandy soils near the mid-Atlantic Coast and jack pine in the lake states, are also considered to be **fire types** or **fire climaxes.**

Today foresters use controlled burns to improve the quality of timber, livestock forage, and wildlife habitat (Figure 12-18).

A **controlled burn** is a fire that is purposely ignited by highly trained foresters for specific purposes. It has a low flame and moves slowly along the forest floor. Forest managers must be extremely cautious when performing controlled burns. They must be certain that the wood is not too dry and that the wind is neither too strong nor headed in the wrong direction.

About .8 million hectares (2 million acres) of pine stands in the South are control-burned annually. At the Alpha Experimental Range in Georgia, controlled burning is conducted only in the afternoon under damp conditions, and the relatively cool, creeping fire is usually extinguished by nightfall. Any pine stand 2-4 meters

FIGURE 12-18   A controlled burn of a 28-year old stand of slash pine in Marion County, South Carolina. Note the low flame.

(8 to 15 feet) high can be control-burned because trees of this size are protected from flames by their cork-like bark.   The highly-resistant longleaf pine (whose terminal bud is protected by a group of long needles) can be burned without ill effect when the seedlings are only 15 centimeters (6 inches) high.

In the longleaf slash-pine stands of the South, controlled burning (1) reduces the crown-fire hazard by removing highly combustible litter, (2) prepares the forest soil as a seedbed, (3) increases the growth and quality of livestock forage, (4) retards a forest succession leading to a low-value scrub-oak climax and maintains the high-timber-value pine subclimax, (5) promotes legume establishment and resultant solid enrichment, (6) increases the amount of soluble mineral ash (phosphorus and potassium) available to the forest plants, (7) stimulates the activity of soil bacteria, (8) controls the brown-spot needle blight, a fungus that is highly destructive to longleaf pine seedlings, and (9) improves food and cover for wildlife and quail.

The "Let-It-Burn" Policy

In 1972 the National Park Service established a policy that utilizes wildfires in 17 national parks, including Grand Teton (Wyoming), Rocky Mountain (Colorado), Sequoia (California), Yosemite (California), and Yellowstone (Wyoming). Under this policy, wildfires are permitted to burn under careful surveillance. This "let it burn" policy is also pursued by the Forest Service in the wilderness areas of our national forests. This policy is quite a turnabout from that of only 25 years ago, when a wildfire was considered the forest's prime evil.

The massive Yellowstone fires in 1988, the most severe in the park's 112-year history—has forced the National Park Service and Forest Service to reevaluate their let-it-burn policies. They admit, for example, that when the present fire management plans were established in the early 1970s, no provision was made for a "fire storm" of the 1988 variety. After all, data from fire-scarred trunks that are centuries old indicate that a configuration on such a scale would occur only once in 150–200 years! In the aftermath of the Yellowstone fires, Interior Secretary Donald Hodel suggested that the let-it-burn policy be scrapped. However, after some cool-headed reappraisal, it was decided that the policy will be retained, except under conditions of extreme drought like that of 1988.

FOREST CONSERVATION BY EFFICIENT UTILIZATION

During the cut-out-and-get-out logging operations of the 1890s, lumbermen were interested only in logs. The rest of the tree—the stump, limbs, branches, and foliage—was left in the forest, where it frequently served as tinder for a catastrophic fire. (Of course, much of this biomass decomposed, and the nutrients were released into the soil for new growth.) Further "waste" occurred at the sawmill, where square timbers were fashioned from round logs. Slabs, trimmings, bark, and sawdust were hauled to the refuse dump and burned. To help meet the growing demand for wood and wood products, it is necessary to practice even more conservation after trees are harvested and removed from the forest.

Although the U.S. wood and wood products industry is still much too wasteful of our timber resource, a definite trend toward more efficient utilization is underway. Whereas early in the timber industry wood had only two primary uses, as lumber or as fuel, through the efforts of the Forest Products Laboratory and similar research centers, a number of ingenious methods have been developed for utilizing almost every part of the tree, including the bark.

The forest industry has become much more diversified. Whereas in 1890 almost 95 percent of the forest harvest was converted into lumber, today only about 30 percent of the harvest consumed by Americans is fashioned into boards and timbers. In the last few years, techniques have been developed for making extremely useful products from scrap boards, shavings, wood chips, bark, and sawdust. For example, years ago, extremely short boards went to the scrap heap. Today, however, thanks to superior waterproof glues, such boards can be joined to form structural beams of almost unlimited length. Much wood that was once considered worthless is now converted into thousands of small chips. These chips are then compressed into sturdy and durable chipboard or hardboard.

MEETING FUTURE TIMBER DEMANDS

By 2020 Americans may be using 50 percent more timber than they do now. Because our projected annual supply of timber for the year 2020 will be only 18 billion feet, we could face an *annual deficit of 9 billion cubic feet* (Figure 12-19).

Theoretically, there are several ways in which the increasing demand for timber may be satisfied. Unfortunately, some of the solutions are fraught with economic or ecological problems. Among them are the following:

1. *Upgrading and extending forest management* in all forests, public and private, large and small. Where can the greatest gains be made? Primarily on small, privately owned woodlots. Of the 4.5 million small forests in the United States, over 50 percent are under 12 hectares (30 acres) each. Yet these small owners control over three times as much timberland as the U. S. Forest Service. Until now, few small-forest owners have cut trees on their land for commercial sale.

2. *Making more effective use of wood residues and "weed" species of trees.* In a given year, about 1.6 billion cubic feet, roughly 11 percent of the total volume of wood taken from the forest, is left as unused residue. (Of course, eventually this material will decompose and the resulting nutrients will serve to enrich the soil for the growth of future generations of trees.) Another billion cubic feet of wood is left as milling residue. It may well be, however, that the value of such residues and weed species as a source of fuel will exceed their value as wood products.

3. *Developing superior (faster-growing, better-grained, and disease-, insect-, fire-, and drought-resistant) trees through the techniques of grafting, hybridization, and genetic engineering.*

4. *Increasing the use of wood substitutes.* Plastic and aluminum foil might be substituted for wood in packaging; the fibrous waste left over after the juice has been extracted from sugar cane in the manufacture of paper. It must be emphasized, however, that the manufacture of some of these substitute materials is dependent on the intensive use of energy from oil fuels—a source that is quickly being depleted. Moreover, the extensive use of plastics is fraught with problems. Plastics do not decompose easily and therefore pose a serious waste disposal dilemma.

5. *Increasing imports.* It is estimated that by the year 2000 we will have to import 5 billion cubic feet of roundwood—108 percent more than the 2.4 billion cubic imported in 1970. Our Canadian imports have been increasing rapidly in the past few years. In 1985, for instance, Canada provided 31 percent of all the softwood used in the United States (Figure 12-20). However, the best we can expect from our Canadian source by 2000 is about 3 billion cubic feet of softwood annually. In addition, we will import Canadian newsprint and woodpulp. This will tax Canadian supplies to the limit. Current imports of hardwood plywood from Japan and the Philippines might be expanded.

6. *Recycling paper to reduce demand.*

7. *Reducing demand by building smaller houses or reducing paper packaging.*

FIGURE 12-19 In 1970 timber demand equaled supply. However, by 2020 timber demands will exceed supply by 50 percent. Several options are possible. We can cut demand by building smaller homes. We can recycle paper and cardboard. We can better manage forests to improve yield.

MEETING FUTURE TIMBER DEMANDS

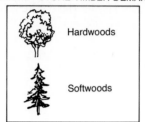

Hardwoods

Softwoods

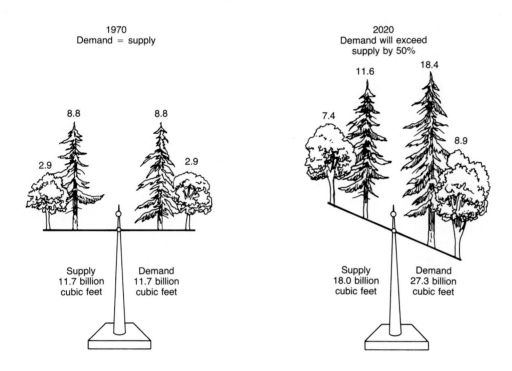

1970
Demand = supply

2020
Demand will exceed
supply by 50%

8.8   8.8

2.9   2.9

11.6   18.4

7.4   8.9

Supply
11.7 billion
cubic feet

Demand
11.7 billion
cubic feet

Supply
18.0 billion
cubic feet

Demand
27.3 billion
cubic feet

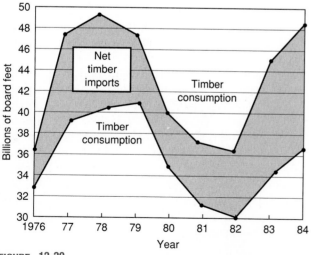

FIGURE 12-20
           U.S. timber production, consumption and imports—1976–1984.

REMOVAL OF THE TROPICAL RAIN FORESTS

Humans have already cut down 40 percent of the world's closed-canopy tropical rain forests. About 105,000 square kilometers (42,000 square miles) are destroyed annually, an area roughly the size of Tennessee. By some estimates, present rates of removal will leave only scattered remnants of tropical rain forests by the year 2025, except for parts of the Amazon basin and central Africa. Much of this destruction is promoted by the governments of poor nations who are desperately trying to pay off foreign debt and feed their exploding populations. A significant portion of the funding for these deforestation programs comes from the World Bank.

The World Bank is a United Nations agency headquartered in Washington, DC. It lends money to about 100 member nations for projects designed to upgrade their economies. Twenty percent of World Bank money, ironically, comes from U.S. taxpayers. The objective of the deforestation programs—enhancement of the quality of life in the LDCs—is certainly beyond reproach. But the means to this end—the destruction of the most biologically productive biome on the face of this planet—could create an ecological disaster.

CAUSES OF DEFORESTATION

Slash-and-Burn Agriculture

Much forest destruction can be blamed on slash-and-burn or "shifting" agriculture. Slash-and-burn farming is practiced on 1 of every 5 acres in the tropical rain forests. The farmer cuts the trees, tills the land for a few years, then abandons it—leaves it fallow—for up to 7 years. During the fallow period, the forest begins to regenerate. The deeper root systems of the trees pump up nutrients from the subsoil. If the fallow period is long enough, soil fertility is slowly restored. In theory, at least, this system appears to be ecologically sound, as long as clearcuts are kept small. On the other hand, if the clearcut areas are too large, the effects can be devastating. Because of the increasing food demands imposed by runaway population growth, the fallow period is often too short for soil fertility to be restored.

The Tropical Forests: Is Survival Possible?

You may recall that the tropical rain forest is one of the world's great biomes. It forms a broad band around the equator about 7.8 square kilometers (3 million square miles)—roughly the size of the United States (Figure 1).

Some have called it a "green hell," others a "green cathedral." Whatever its name, the world's tropical rain forests, which once covered the earth like a thick green blanket, are rapidly being reduced to shreds. And you say: "So what? After all, what is a tropical forest good for? Snakes and squawking parrots and monkeys, maybe. But what does it have to offer me?" The answer is, plenty. From the medicine you took for your last illness to the rubber tires on your car, tropical forests have a lot to do with you. And they have significance for the well-being of nations as well as individuals.

Values of Tropical Rain Forests

1. Nearly 2 billion people living in the tropics depend on food grown in soil whose development was made possible by tropical forests. The amount of food produced in this soil is equal to that grown in the United States and Canada combined.

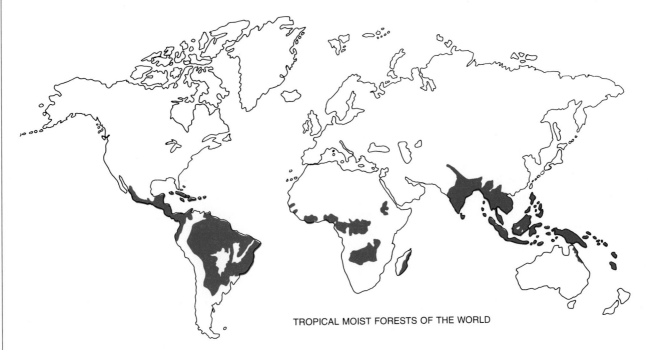

TROPICAL MOIST FORESTS OF THE WORLD

FIGURE 1 Tropical moist forests of the world.

2. Rice production and irrigation farming in the tropics depend on water supplies slowly released from tropical forests.

3. More than 1 billion cubic meters of wood are removed from the world's tropical forests for human use each year. Tropical nations receive about $5 billion annually for the export of wood from these forests. Brazil, for example, exports much of its wood to the United States.

4. Tropical forests provide habitat for an estimated 3 to 7 million species of plants and animals–the greatest variety of life occurring anywhere on this planet (Figure 2).

5. Many modern medicines, such as those that control disease (quinine) or relieve mental stress (reserpine), are derived from plants that grow in tropical forests.

6. On a global basis, the tropical forest biome has unsurpased scientific and educational value. For example, the raw material for productive studies of plant and animal ecology is almost unlimited.

7. Tropical forests influence the weather and the climate in important ways that scientists do not as yet understand. By means of transpiration in densely forested areas, such as the Amazon, large amounts of moisture are released into the air. That moisture later falls as rain.

FIGURE 2 The toucan—a colorful resident of the tropical forests of Cental and South America. Scientists believe that the enormous bill, which is multi-hued, is used during courtship display.

Fire

Fire is used as a tool in slash-and-burn farming to dispose of felled trees and to prevent the invasion of weeds and shrubs into the crop area. Millions of acres of tropical forest have been destroyed when such fires have raged out of control. Forest destruction by fire in Brazil's Amazonian rain forest is accelerating; twice as much was burned in 1988 as in 1987.

Cattle Ranching

You have seen the McDonald's sign: "Over 7 billion hamburgers served!" "But," you exclaim, "what does that have to do with the tropical forest problem?" The answer is: plenty! The beef in those hamburgers is usually imported from Central America. And in order to raise the cattle to supply the U.S. demand for hamburgers, as well as for hot dogs and luncheon meat, cattle ranchers in Central America are clearing away tropical forests and converting the newly owned areas to grazing lands at the rate of 21,500 square kilometers (8,000 square miles) per year.

In 1960 the U.S. import of beef was virtually nil. Today, however, we are importing more than 90,000 metric tons from Central America alone. Next time you bite into that Big Mac, you should momentarily reflect upon the fact that in a very small but very real way, you are contributing to one of this hemisphere's most serious environmental problems.

Gathering Fuel Wood

More than 1 billion cubic meters of wood are harvested for fuel in the tropics. This wood is either used directly for firewood or is converted to charcoal. In Haiti the production of charcoal is big business. Unfortunately, the resulting forest destruction in this country is also immense.

Industrial Logging

Commercial logging in tropical regions is frequently wasteful and inefficient. For example, during a selective logging operation in Malaysia, more than 55 percent of the trees were either severely damaged or destroyed. Until recently, commercial logging employed selective cutting. The only trees taken were mature specimens of the most valuable species, such as teak, mahogany, and rosewood. Today, however, any tree has potential value if it can be reduced to wood chips. As a result clearcutting is being more widely used. Unfortunately most clearcut areas do not become reforested by natural means. They must be replanted by people. Frequently however, forestry personnel either are not knowledge-able about effective reforestation or simply refuse to use it. Moreover, land-starved squatters move in to carve out an existence based on slash-and-burn agriculture. The impacts of tropical deforestation are covered in more detail in Chapter 13.

EFFECTS OF DEFORESTATION

Firewood Scarcity

Because of the severe firewood shortages in India, Haiti, and Nepal, hot meals are almost a thing of the past. Eric Eckholm, a former research ecologist with the Worldwatch Institute in Washington, has pinpointed the problem for the natives: "For one-third of the world's people, the energy crisis does not mean . . . high prices of petroleum. . . . It means something much more basic—the daily scramble to find the wood needed to cook dinner." As a result of increasing wood scarcity, the poor are now shifting from wood fuel to animal dung. Unfortunately, however, dung is also valuable as fertilizer. An additional 20 million tons of grain could be produced if the cow dung being burned as fuel in Africa, Asia, and the Near East were used as fertilizer instead.

Climatic Changes

When a tropical forest is removed, the radiation of heat from the denuded area is greatly increased. As a result, the local climate and even the global cli-mate may be adversely affected. The burning of wood releases carbon dioxide into the atmosphere. Trees also absorb carbon dioxide, so their loss accounts for an additional increase in global carbon dioxide levels. The result of the increased heat radiation and increased lev-els of carbon dioxide may well be a progressive warm-ing of the earth (Chapter 18). That warming, in turn, will necessitate radical shifts in agricultural and settle-ment patterns. According to some experts, increased global temperature could cause the polar icecaps to melt and the major cities on our coasts to be destroyed by floods.

Loss of Genetic "Pools"

The irreplaceable gene pools of many kinds of organ-isms are rapidly being diminished. The tropical forests contain the parental species from which many of our present agricultural crops were derived. Those species may be needed as genetic reservoirs from which new vari-eties of disease- and pest-resistant crops are developed.

Extinction of Species

The removal of the tropical rain forests also threatens the survival of many birds and mammals. Species diver-sity is greater in this biome than anywhere else on earth. The National Academy of Sciences projects that at the present rate of tropical forest destruction, more than 1 million species of organisms may be extinct by the year 2000.

WHAT CAN BE DONE TO SAVE THE TROPICAL FORESTS?

The World Bank, which has been criticized lately for providing financial support for practices resulting in tropical forest destruction, has responded constructively to suggestions from environmentalists and is now play-ing a useful role in rain forest restoration. It has recently proposed that:

1. Forest industries reseed or replant areas that they have harvested.
2. Villagers reforest areas from which they have removed trees for use as fuel. Hopefully, these fuel plantations would be harvested on a sustained-yield basis. Fast-growing trees, such as the leucana, which attains a height of 6 meters (20 feet) in 4 or 5 years, could be used.
3. Countries with rain forests provide financial grants (with United Nations financial support) to support research and education on the ecology and manage-ment of tropical forests.
4. Countries with rain forests convert 15 percent of their forests to national parks and preserves.
5. MDCs provide $5.3 billion to fund these projects.

However, in 1989, a spokesman for the govern-ment of Brazil made it plain that any pressure from the United States or the World Bank would simply turn Brazilian officials against the control of rain forest destruction. For example, Brazil was very annoyed that the World Bank held up a loan for the construction of a huge hydroelectric dam in 1989 because thousands of acres of rain forest would be flooded and many rare forms of wildlife would be killed.

The proposals of the World Bank are excellent. They should be implemented without delay. Time is running out!

RAPID REVIEW

1. Our nation's forests provide the raw materials for more than 5,000 wood products worth more than $30 billion annually.

2. Our national forests are administered and managed by four federal agencies: the Forest Service, the Soil Conservation Service, the Tennessee Valley Author-ity, and the Fish and Wildlife Service.

3. President Theodore Roosevelt appointed Gifford Pinchot to be the first chief forester of the newly created U.S. Forest Service.

4. Under the terms of the *Multiple Use–Sustained Yield Act* of 1960, natural forests must be managed for many uses in addition to timber. Among them are (a) flood and erosion control, (b) grazing land, (c) wildlife habitat, (d) biomass fuel, and (e) scientific, educational, wilderness, and recreational areas.

5. Sustained-yield management ensures that annual forest harvests are balanced by annual timber growth.

6. The Tongass is the largest of the 155 national forests in the country. Under the terms of the *Alaska Native Claims Act* of 1980, the Forest Service has tried to stimulate the forest industry in the Tongass. However, many environmental groups have branded this program a financial boondoggle.

7. *Clearcutting* is employed on even-aged stands composed of only a few species and is applicable only to species whose seedlings thrive in full sunlight, such as Douglas fir, southern pines, and aspen.

8. Opponents of clearcutting criticize it for the following reasons: (a) it accelerates surface runoff, flooding, and soil erosion, (b) wildlife-carrying capacity is sharply reduced, at least temporarily, (c) scenic beauty is destroyed, (d) fire hazard is increased, and (e) tree blow-down is facilitated.

9. Supporters of clearcutting claim that it has many advantages: (a) it is the only way to regenerate forests in some areas, (b) it can help to control certain disease and insect outbreaks, (c) it is cheaper than selective cutting, and (d) timber grows faster on clearcut areas than on areas that are selectively cut.

10. *Strip cutting* is the harvest of 80-meter-wide strips, allowing natural regrowth.

11. *Selective cutting* is the harvest of only those mature trees that are valuable as a source of saw timber or pulpwood. It is used on mixed-species stands of unevenly aged trees.

12. Selective cutting is a more costly and time-consuming method than clearcutting; however, it reduces land scarring, runoff, soil erosion, and wildlife depletion.

13. Selective cutting can be used only on species such as maple, beech, and hemlock, whose seedlings are tolerant of the shade.

14. The sustained-yield concept dictates that whenever timber is removed, the denuded area must be reforested, either by natural or by artificial means.

15. Arguments for monoculture practiced on tree farms and in national forests are that it (a) takes optimal advantage of fertilizers and pesticides, (b) is rapid and efficient, (c) makes maximal use of modern tree planting and harvesting methods, (d) is needed to satisfy America's growing demand for lumber and wood products, and (e) is appropriate for the sun-loving seedlings of timber-valuable species such as Douglas fir, lodgepole pine, and ponderosa pine.

16. Arguments against monoculture are that (a) it is an artificial system made by humans that lacks the built-in balancing mechanisms of a multispecies, multiage forest, (b) the fast-growing wood is inferior, (c) intensive fertilization causes the eutrophication of lakes and streams, (d) intensive use of pesticides may contaminate wildlife and human food chains, (e) it requires intensive inputs of costly energy derived from fossil fuels, (f) it is more susceptible to fires than the natural forest, and (g) it is highly susceptible to destructive disease and insect outbreaks.

17. A *tree farm* is a private land area that is used to grow trees for profit under sound management principles.

18. It is believed that by the year 2000 genetic engineering will develop supertrees with such desirable traits as accelerated growth, reduced need for fertilizer, and built-in chemical resistance against weeds and insects.

19. The logging plan includes (a) a map of the forest showing which the location, species, age, and volume of the species to be logged are indicated, (b) discussion of the harvesting method, (c) selection of haul roads, (d) consideration of the scientific, recreational, and wildlife functions of the forest, and (5) an estimate of gross income from the operation.

20. The logging operation includes felling trees, removing them from the forest, and transporting them to a sawmill or pulp mill. If trees are to be used as pulpwood, they are often harvested with hydraulic shears and whole tree chippers.

21. Ingenious methods have been developed to use almost every part of a tree. Useful products are being made from scrap boards, shavings, wood chips, and bark.

22. Major agents of forest destruction are diseases, insects, and fire.

23. Forest diseases such as heart rot fungus and white-

pine blister rust cause 45 percent of saw-timber destruction.

24. Insect pests, such as bark beetles, gypsy moths, and tussock moths, account for 20 percent of all saw-timber destruction. This amounts to 5 billion board feet annually—roughly 10 percent of our annual timber harvest.

25. Insect pests can be partially controlled by (a) using insecticides, (b) clearcutting the infested area, (c) using biological control agents such as viruses, parasites, and predators, and (d) replacing monotypes with heterotypes.

26. Thirty percent of the wildfires are deliberately set.

27. Fires are controlled with the use of back fires, fire lanes, fire-retardant chemicals released from planes, and water pumped from tank trucks and released from planes.

28. The idea that every forest fire is destructive has been replaced with the concept that occasional fires are a natural and beneficial feature of the forest ecosystem and are needed to maintain the forest's health.

29. Controlled fires, purposely started by highly trained personnel, serve many functions. They (a) reduce the crown-fire hazard, (b) prepare the soil as a seed bed, (c) maintain subclimax species that are valuable as timber and as a wildlife habitat, (d) control insect and disease outbreaks, (e) stimulate soil bacteria activity, and (f) increase the quality of livestock forage.

30. Projections indicate that by the year 2020 our nation's timber demand will exceed the supply by roughly 50 percent. This increased demand may be met by (a) upgrading our small private forests, (b) more effectively controlling the agents of forest destruction (diseases, insects, and harmful wildfires), (c) developing superior (faster-growing, better-grained, and insect-, disease-, and drought-resistant) trees through the techniques of grafting, hybridization, and gene splicing, (d) increasing the use of wood substitutes, and (e) increasing imports, (f) recycling paper, and (g) reducing wood use.

31. Tropical forests have multiple values: (a) erosion and flood control, (b) timber and forest products, (c) medicines, (d) wood fuel, (e) outdoor "laboratories" for scientific research, (f) the habitat of more than 3 million species of plants and animals, and (g) recreational functions.

32. Tropical forests have been greatly reduced because of (a) slash-and-burn agriculture, (b) conversion to grazing land, (c) industrial logging, and (d) fuel-wood gathering.

QUESTIONS AND TOPICS FOR DISCUSSION

1. Discuss the economic importance of our nation's forests.

2. Discuss the statement "Clearcutting is the best harvesting method for our nation's forests."

3. Describe six advantages and six disadvantages of monoculture.

4. What type of forest is most suitable for clearcutting?

5. List four factors that make reforestation by seeding difficult.

6. Describe the functions of our nation's forests in terms of: (a) flood and erosion control, (b) rangeland, (c) wildlife habitat, (d) wilderness area, and (e) source of fuel.

7. Can you think of any reason why so many of our forest pests are exotics?

8. Discuss the factors that make heterotypes resistant to violent outbreaks of insect pests.

9. Suppose a forest fire breaks out in the Rockies. Wind velocities are high. Discuss methods that might be used to bring this fire under control.

10. List eight functions of controlled burns in the longleaf pine stands of the South.

11. Describe six methods by which our nation's future timber needs might be satisfied.

12. Where are the world's major tropical forests located?

13. Suppose that tomorrow all of the tropical forests in the world were suddenly destroyed. Discuss the aftermath of such a catastrophe. What might be the long-range climatic effects? The biological effects? The social and economic effects? The effect on world peace?

KEY WORDS AND PHRASES

Bark beetle	Fire control
Board feet	Fire detection
Brown-spot needle blight	Forest compartment
Chemical bomb	records
Clearcutting	Forest conservation
Controlled burning	Forest Pest Control Act
Exotic	Genetic engineering
Federal Forest Reserve	Heart rot
Acts	Heterotype
Fire bug	Incendiary
Fire climax	Infrared system

Integrated pest manage-
  ment (IPM)
Logging plan
Longleaf Pine
Monoculture
Multiple use
Multiple Use–Sustained
  Yield Act
National Wilderness
  Preservation Act
Pest control
Gifford Pinchot
Reforestation
Theodore Roosevelt

Scientific areas
Shifting agriculture
Slash-and-burn
  agriculture
Smoke jumpers
Stripcutting
Sustained yield
Tongass National Forest
Tree farm
U.S. Forest Service
Wilderness area
Wildfire
Yield table

SUGGESTED READINGS

Bahls, J. E. "A Timber Take-Over's High Toll." *Sierra* 73(5):30, 33, 35, 1988. Highly readable discussion of how corporate raiders accelerate logging rates in the redwood forests of California.

Carey, J. "The Roads Less Traveled." *International Wildlife* 26(3):48, 50–51, 1988. A fascinating discussion that tries to explain why the U.S. Forest Service is spending millions of dollars to build logging roads and cut timber in our national forests.

Janzen, D. H. "Tropical Ecological and Biocultural Restoration." *Science* 239:243–244, 1988.

Kimmins, J. P. *Forest Ecology*. New York: Macmillan, 1987. Comprehensive, high-level material for the serious student.

Page, J. "The 'Island' Arks of Brazil." *Smithsonian* 19(1):106–119, 1988. Discusses the value of tropical forest "islands" as habitat for species threatened with extinction.

Repetto, R. *The Forest for the Trees: Government Policies and the Misuse of Forest Resources*. New York: Basic Books, 1988. Discusses the manner in which governments that are committed in principle to conservation are aggravating the losses of their forests through ill-conceived policies.

13

Wildlife Extinction

iologists estimate that 3 to 5 million species of plants, animals, and microorganisms share this planet with us. One-half of these species live in the tropics, and many of them are unknown to science. Most of the others live in areas outside of human habitation—on the outskirts of towns and cities, beyond the farms, in the wild lands fast vanishing as the human population continues to swell.

Despite the fact that your life is lived seemingly apart from the rich and varied biological world, wild plants and animals enrich your life in countless ways (Figure 13-1). If you hike, hunt, fish, bird watch, or photograph, your rewards are many: the eerie cry of a pack of coyotes, the graceful flight of the white-throated swift above a desert canyon, the cool, dark solitude of a primeval redwood forest, or the elegant landing of a pintail on a pond in the early morning sun.

Beyond the purely aesthetic benefits of wild things are the bountiful economic benefits: skin ointments, antibiotics, anticancer drugs, and a host of other medicines to combat heart disease, malaria, and numerous other diseases. Today one of every two prescription and nonprescription drugs originates from a wild plant. Worth over $20 billion a year in the United States and an estimated $40 billion in the world market, these drugs reduce human suffering and contribute significantly to our economic welfare.

The American economy also accrues benefits from the hordes of hunters, anglers, birders, and campers who annually spend billions of dollars on travel, lodging, food, and supplies. And wild species are an important reservoir of genes that aid farmers in improving food crops and livestock.

Wildlife provides food for many of the world's people, from the Chicago stockbroker who sips white wine after a shrimp dinner in an elegant lakeside restaurant to the native who, crouched by a fire in the grasslands of Africa, tears meat from the bones of the gazelle he's killed and washes it down with water from a dried gourd.

Finally, the rich and varied plants and animals form the living fabric of our ecosystem, which provides innumerable benefits—free of charge—to humankind. They control pests, recycle water, reduce flooding, and control erosion. They provide oxygen and remove carbon dioxide from the air, maintain the climate, and recycle nutrients essential to our survival.

This chapter looks at plant and wildlife extinction, what causes it and ways to prevent it. It also provides background information on plant and wildlife populations to help you better understand the natural forces at work in a population—information that is essential to understanding ways to preserve our vanishing biological resources.

EXTINCTION: REDUCING THE EARTH'S BIOLOGICAL DIVERSITY

Extinction is a biological fact of life. Biologists estimate that 500 million species have made the earth their home since life began some 3.7 billion years ago. To date, 1.4 million species have been catalogued by biologists. Just a few years ago, biologists believed that the total number of species alive today was somewhere between 3 and 5 million. Recent estimates, however, put the world total at well over 30 million species. Despite this impressive number, 95 to 99 percent of the species that once lived on this planet have vanished.

Why have so many species become extinct? Biolo-

FIGURE 13-1   Courtship dance of the whooping crane.

gists believe that many prehistoric organisms, such as the dinosaur, became extinct because they were unable to adjust to changing environmental conditions and perished, in some cases leaving only fossil remains, in other cases leaving descendants that evolved from them, and in still others leaving nothing.

What caused the environmental conditions to change? No one knows for sure, but theories abound. One popular theory to explain the disappearance of the dinosaurs some 65 million years ago says that a giant asteroid struck the earth, producing a cloud of dust that shrouded the earth and brought about a temporary but biologically devastating shift in global temperature. Alternatively, some scientists believe that worldwide, intense volcanic activity may have produced conditions hazardous to life. Gases from volcanoes may have formed harmful acids that fell on the land and waters, wiping out plants and animals. Dust from the towering volcanoes may have blocked out the sun, shading the earth and spawning periods of bitter cold.

Changing conditions today, brought about by human actions, continue to drive species to extinction (Figure 13-2). Many biologists warn that we are on the brink of a mass extinction. Today one species of vertebrate (backboned) disappears every 9 months. Add to that the plants, microorganisms, and invertebrates that disappear from the face of the earth, and the rate of extinction is an alarming one species every day! With continued population growth and economic development, especially in the biologically rich tropics, biologists fear that the rate of extinction could climb to one species every hour by the end of this decade. A million species out of

an estimated total of 5–30 million could succumb to humankind's massive global colonization between 1980 and 2000. Tearing the biological fabric into pieces, such extinctions could have widespread ecological effects.

Paul Ehrlich, ecologist and author of perhaps one of the most important books of modern times, *The Population Bomb*, argues that the human population has reached 5 billion by exploiting, degrading, and depleting the earth's fossil fuels, minerals, deep soils, water, and biological diversity. "It is the loss of biological diversity," he argues, "that may prove the most serious." The consequences of widespread loss of species are potentially far more devastating than fossil fuel depletion, economic collapse, and limited nuclear war, notes Harvard's eminent biologist, E. O. Wilson. The erosion of earth's rich biological diversity, he says, will take millions of years to repair. It is "the folly [for which] our descendants are least likely to forgive us."

Preserving biological diversity has become one of the most important environmental concerns of the 1980s, according to the Council on Environmental Quality. Before we discuss the reasons why species are vanishing from the earth and study ways to prevent extinction, we shall pause to describe some fundamental principles of wildlife populations. These supplement the ecological principles discussed in Chapter 2.

WILDLIFE POPULATIONS

Suppose that all American robins lived to be 10 years old and that each adult female annually fledged eight young. If the robin population started in 1990, a single

FIGURE 13-2 The rate of animal extinctions is increasing.

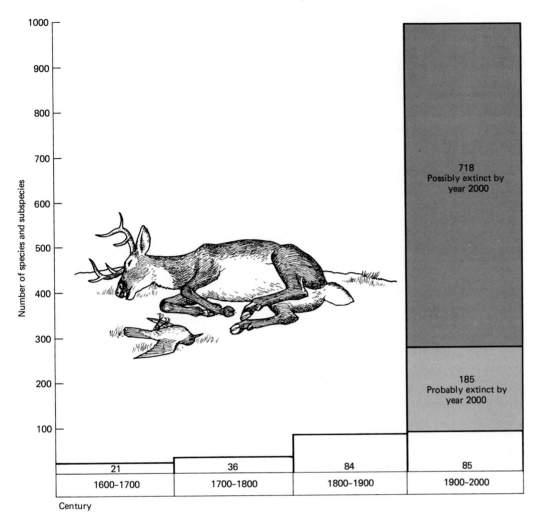

breeding pair and its offspring would produce 1,200 million robins by the year 2020. This population would require 150,000 additional planets the size of earth to accommodate it.

Biotic Potential

The theoretical maximum rate of growth for a population given unlimited resources, demonstrated previously, is called the **biotic potential**. In nature, few organisms reproduce at their full biotic potential because of environmental resistance (Chapter 9). When environmental resistance is minimized, populations may increase rapidly. For instance, a Maryland herd of white-tail deer with three bucks and three does increased to approximately 1,000 animals in only 16 years because of favorable conditions. Under optimal conditions, a herd of deer could double its population every year.

One of the greatest worries of biologists tracking the steady decline in biological diversity is that the widespread elimination of species may remove envi-

ronmental resistance that currently keeps many pest species populations under control. "Extinction's survivors," notes Edward C. Wolf of the Worldwatch Institute, "tend to be ecological opportunists." Rats, sparrows, starlings, cockroaches, and weedy plants may literally invade the world as human society destroys the intricate checks and balances of nature that reduce their biotic potential. The proliferation of these and other hardy species could also thwart the recovery of ecosystems by their prolific reproduction and intense competition for resources.

Not all species are equally vulnerable to extinction, as described later in this chapter. Those that are highly vulnerable tend to be **specialists**, organisms that live within a narrow range of tolerance. China's panda, for instance, eats the leaves of certain bamboo trees and little else. If bamboo is destroyed, the panda will inevitably follow it (Figure 13-3). **Generalists**, those organisms that occupy a variety of habitats and eat a number of different foods, generally fare better when changing environmental conditions reduce their biotic potential.

FIGURE 13-3   The panda is a specialist, feeding only on bamboo, shown here. Destruction of the bear's only food source threatens to wipe out this magnificent creature.

The study of previous extinctions caused by major climatic changes shows that tropical species are especially vulnerable to extinction. Changing environmental conditions, in other words, readily suppress the reproduction and survival of these species, resulting in massive die-offs. When periods of glaciation began, biologist believe, many tropical plants and animals retreated into tiny pockets of diversity. When the tropical weather returned, the forests were recolonized by the organisms that had taken refuge in these areas.

Many tropical ecosystems today, however, face pressures from human civilization that may erode their resilience. Forests, for instance, are indiscriminately cut down and hacked into fragments by farmers and loggers. Global changes in temperature, resulting from a buildup of atmospheric carbon dioxide, and increased ultraviolet light penetration, resulting from stratospheric ozone depletion, could further alter the remaining pockets, greatly diminishing their storehouse of plants, animals, and microorganisms.

Control of Populations

An understanding of plant and wildlife populations and their extinction requires an understanding of environmental resistance. This section looks at environmental resistance to illustrate the factors that regulate population size. Ecologists group these factors into two broad categories: density-independent factors and density-dependent factors.

DENSITY-INDEPENDENT FACTORS.   The environment often imposes limitations on the growth of plant and animal populations, irrespective of the number of organisms present in a given habitat—that is, indepen-

dent of their density. The most common of these **density-independent factors** are drought, heat waves, cold spells, tornadoes, and other storms, floods, and levels of natural contamination, such as silt.

A rare freeze in the tropics, for example, kills most members of a population of exotic butterflies, whether the population in a given area is large or small. A severe cold spell along the Texas coast in January 1940 killed 92.6 percent of the flounder population near Laguna Madre, 93.6 percent near Matagorda, and 95.4 percent near Arkansas. The percentage of flounders killed was roughly the same in all three areas, even though the flounder populations were quite different.

In the natural scheme of events, weather controls the populations of insects and annual plants (those that grow from seeds each year) in regions subject to periodic cold. In North America, for example, many insect populations are held in check by winter weather. The number of offspring produced is limited because of the limited "growing" season.

Human activities can also impose density-independent limits on the growth of the earth's organisms. For example, heated water discharged from power plants may kill all of the fish in a stream, regardless of the population density. When the range of tolerance is exceeded, all organisms perish. Likewise, many of the chemicals accidentally and intentionally released into the environment—pesticides, air and water pollutants, and toxic wastes—affect all populations, regardless of their density.

Habitat destruction also acts independently of population density. Roadways, farms, suburbs, factories, cities, and villages all obliterate vital habitats, often destroying all of the species that once lived there, regardless of their density.

Some human interventions, however, result in population increases rather than declines. In other words, they unleash biotic potential. For example, the house sparrow population has flourished in the United States because of the abundance of suitable nesting sites and food (waste grain and seeds in manure) provided by human settlements. An increase in global temperature, predicted by many experts on climate and air pollution, may shorten winters in North America, making conditions more favorable for insects. As a result, many insect populations could explode and wreak even more damage on our crops and forests.

DENSITY-DEPENDENT FACTORS. In contrast to annual plants and insects, many species have evolved mechanisms that allow them to survive winter. Birds, for instance, may migrate to warm climates when winter approaches. Some animals grow a thick coat of fur when winter approaches to protect themselves from the cold. Other animals hibernate. Perennial plants, which grow year after year from the same root structure, such as flowering trees and grasses, enter a state of dormancy. Trees like the maple, oak, and aspen, for instance, shed their leaves in the fall and greatly reduce their metabolic activity over the winter to survive the harsh conditions.

For these species, density-dependent factors tend to play a larger role than weather in controlling population growth. **Density-dependent factors** are those whose influence in controlling population size increases or decreases depending on the density of a population. Ecologists recognize at least four major factors: competition, predation, parasitism, and disease.

Take competition, for example. Suppose your yard supports 1,000 earthworms for robins to eat. If there is only one robin feeding on those worms, the limited supply is adequate. If, however, 100 robins set up residence in your yard, the competition for the limited supply of worms would be so intense that some robins would starve to death if no other food were available. Thus, competition for earthworms is a density-dependent variable.

Competition affects plants as well. For instance, if the number of oak trees in a forest increases, competition for sunlight, soil nutrients, and water increases proportionately. Individuals with shallow, less well developed root systems may die because of nutrient and water deficiencies. Stunted individuals die as they are shaded out by taller, healthier trees. Among animals when food, water, cover, nesting sites, breeding dens, and space are limited, population increases intensify competition. Inevitably this competition adversely affects the physically unfit. In their weakened condition, some may perish from disease or from injuries inflicted during fights. Some weakened individuals may be forced to colonize poorer habitats where death from starvation, disease, or predation awaits them.

A host of animals have evolved over time with remarkable adaptations that allow them to hunt and kill their prey. Known as **predators**, these animals include strictly carnivorous (meat-eating) species, such as mountain lions, coyotes, and cheetahs; herbivores (vegetation eaters), such as cows, deer, elk, and grasshoppers that "prey" on grass; and omnivores (plant and animal eaters) such as bears and human beings.

Like competition, predation is a density-dependent factor. In general, as the population density of a prey species increases, so does the percentage of organisms killed by predators. Why?

It is generally thought that as the density of a prey species increases, individuals become easier to find and attack. Furthermore, increased competition in the dense prey population may result in a larger number of weakened organisms that become easy targets for predators. Prey may also be forced into less suitable habitats and may become weakened or diseased, and again are more likely to be captured and killed by a predator. Ecologists have also found that when the density of a prey population increases, predators that eat a variety of prey tend to shift their attention to the most concentrated ones.

Parasites like tapeworms feed on the bodies of other living organisms, but generally without killing them. Most parasites have limited mobility but are easily spread from organism to organism. The higher the population density, the more readily they are transmitted. As a result, parasitism is a density- dependent factor. In Canada, for example, a species of parasitic wasp attacks webworm moths. When the moth population density is low, deaths from parasitic wasps are negligible. But when the population density increases, parasitism increases. In Colorado in the late 1970s, bighorn sheep offspring died in record numbers because of a parasite called the **lungworm**, which weakened the sheep and made them susceptible to pneumonia and other diseases. Passed from mother to fetus, the lungworm killed 97 percent of the newborn. The lungworm is a common parasite that, under normal conditions, lives in harmony with the bighorn. But because of human encroachment, the bighorn's habitat was reduced and its population density increased. Animals were forced to calve and feed on the same land. Lungworm eggs deposited in the sheep's feces increased. Browsing females picked up more and more eggs. Record numbers were found in females. The worms passed through the placenta and infected the fetuses. The newborn, too weak to withstand the parasite, perished. Fortunately, wildlife biologists found out about the problem and captured sheep, treated them, and relocated them in a suitable habitat in the Rockies.

Infectious diseases, like parasitism, increase when population density increases. When large plots are planted to a single crop species, such as wheat or corn, for instance, farmers inadvertently increase the likelihood that disease organisms will wipe out their crops. The population-reducing effects of wheat rust, corn smut, and other plant diseases are widely known. The incidence of infectious diseases in humans also increases with increasing population density. This was demonstrated by the massive death from influenza of American soldiers who were crowded shoulder to shoulder in the barracks and trenches during World War I. Because the organisms that cause infectious diseases (viruses, protozoa, and bacteria) can be transmitted by contact, through food, and by animals (insects), the greater the density, the more likely the disease will spread.

Although we have grouped the population-regulating mechanisms into two groups, density-independent and density-dependent, in reality these factors operate together on a given population. For example, disease and predation may wipe a species out during a hard winter. Heavy rains may flood land and reduce the population of a species afflicted with a disabling parasite, causing the population to plummet.

Wildlife Population Dynamics

The size of a population of any organism results from the interaction of environmental resistance and the factors that create its biotic potential. Stability is achieved in ecosystems when the two opposing sets of factors are in balance. In general, when environmental resistance climbs, a population declines. When environmental resistance falls, a population increases.

This section looks at plant and animal population dynamics—the changes that occur in populations—and explains the factors that affect it. The study of population dynamics is a key tool in wildlife management, the subject of our next chapter.

THE S-CURVE. Whenever a species is established in a new habitat with adequate resources, its population grows in a characteristic way. The growth curve that plots the population growth is called an **S-shaped**, or **sigmoidal**, **curve** (Figure 13-4A). This curve has four distinct phases, listed in chronological sequence: (1) the establishment phase, (2) the explosive (logarithmic) phase, (3) the deceleration phase, and (4) the dynamic equilibrium phase.

In the first phase, the population grows slowly as its new members explore their new habitat. Then, with unlimited resources, the population expands to fill its habitat, growing at an explosive rate. The rapid growth during the second phase eventually decreases the supply of resources and thus reduces the rate of growth, creating the third phase. Finally, once the population is well established and competition and other factors come into play, the species reaches an equilibrium. At this point, the population remains more or less constant if the ecosystem is undisturbed. True, adverse weather

may decrease the population size somewhat, but more favorable weather in subsequent years usually corrects the imbalance (Figure 13-4B). Such a system is said to be in a **dynamic equilibrium**: It changes somewhat from year to year but remains fairly constant over the long term. At this point, no further population surges are possible, for the population has attained the carrying capacity of the habitat. **Carrying capacity** is the population size of a given species that a habitat can support on a sustainable basis.

A number of species introduced into the United States from abroad—such as the English sparrow, European starling, and German carp—have experienced population growth that follows the S-shaped curve. For instance, a few pairs of house sparrows were introduced into the United States in 1899, and within 10 years the sparrow population had increased to several thousand. Although introduced with good intentions (the sparrow was brought over from Europe to control insect pests), many exotic or alien species have had a strongly adverse impact on native plants and animals. The sparrow, for instance, outcompetes songbirds for nesting and food. Other aliens have destroyed wildlife directly, disseminated diseases, or aggressively outcompeted the more valuable species for food, cover, and breeding sites.

Wildlife managers have used their understanding of the S-shaped curve and population dynamics for years to manage commercially valuable species—and will continue to do so for years to come. Wild populations of deer, cod, pine trees, or even African elephants, for example, may be periodically harvested, much like a commercial crop.

Perhaps the most important challenge facing scientists in the fields of forestry, wildlife management, agriculture, ranching, and fisheries is to find ways to secure the **maximum sustainable yield**, or **optimum yield**—that is, the best yield possible that does not harm the population's long-term survival or upset the ecological balance of an ecosystem. Optimal harvests are generally achieved at the point on the S-shaped curve between the accelerating and decelerating phases. Research has shown that in most species this point occurs when a population is at roughly 50 percent of the habitat's carrying capacity. Harvests above this level may reduce the number too severely and cause a further population decline, possibly driving the species to extinction.

IRRUPTIVE POPULATIONS. Most plant and animal populations become stable once they have reached the plateau of the S-shaped curve—that is, the carrying capacity of the ecosystem. Even so, predators, parasites, competition, climate, and other factors vary. These variations cause slight upward and downward swings in the population.

After fluctuating mildly for many years, some populations may suddenly increase sharply. This sudden

FIGURE 13-4 (A) Sigmoidal curve illustrates the growth of a population of organisms in a new environment. After an initial establishment phase, growth explodes. As environmental resistance rises, growth decelerates, then stops. (B) A dynamic equilibrium occurs at this phase. Population may rise as a result of a decrease in environmental resistance or an increase in the number of offspring (a decrease in reproductive potential). A decrease in reproductive potential or an increase in environmental resistance may cause the population to decline. Despite these shifts the population remains more or less constant over time.

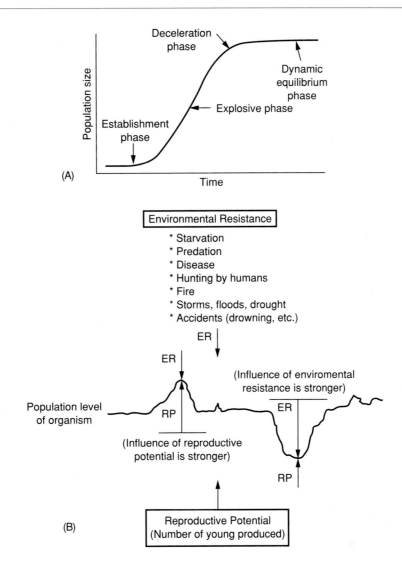

change in population size is called an *irruption* and may occur after a period of unusually favorable weather, which results in an unusually large supply of food or exceptional conditions for the survival of offspring. Expanded beyond the carrying capacity, the population typically plummets to a much lower level. Wide oscillations in the population size may continue for years if environmental conditions continue to vacillate.

In some instances, the sudden upswing in a population may cause severe damage to the ecosystem—so severe, in fact, that the population crashes. Perhaps the best-known example of this involves the mule deer in the Kaibab National Forest in the Grand Canyon of Arizona (Figure 13-5).

Approximately 4,000 to 6,000 mule deer lived in the forest for many years in a dynamic equilibrium. Wolves, coyotes, cougar, and bear helped trim the population and keep it in balance. In 1906, however, the forest took a turn for the worse when the state of Arizona placed a bounty on the wolf, cougar, and coyote. Within 15 years, the large predator populations of the forest had been severely reduced. The wolf was wiped out entirely. With environmental resistance greatly less-

ened, the deer population began to grow. By 1924, it had climbed to 100,000, a 16-fold increase in 16 years! The results were disastrous.

Well beyond the carrying capacity of the forest, the deer population devoured the shrubs, trees, and herbaceous plants. A browse line became well defined on the aspen and conifers like the high water mark of a river. Herbs were chewed to their roots. Thousands of valuable seedlings, representing the future of the forest, were destroyed. Predictably, the crash soon followed. Saved from their predators, the deer began to succumb to slow, agonizing death by starvation. Between 1924 and 1930, 80,000 deer starved. Even today, the forest has not fully recovered from the damage.

CYCLIC POPULATIONS. The brown lemming, a tiny rodent the size of a hamster, lives in the Arctic tundra of North America, a vast, treeless biome above the northern coniferous forest biome (see Chapter 2). Every 3 or 4 years, the lemming population peaks, then crashes. A study of this predictable cycle showed that the peak lemming population overgrazes the vegetation that protects it from its prey, making the lemmings highly suscepti-

FIGURE 13-5   This classic example of a deer irruption occurred in a heart of mule deer on the Kai-bab Plateau on the north edge of the Grand Canyon, Arizona. It was caused by an intensive predator-removal campaign. Note that repeated warnings of impending disaster were ignored.

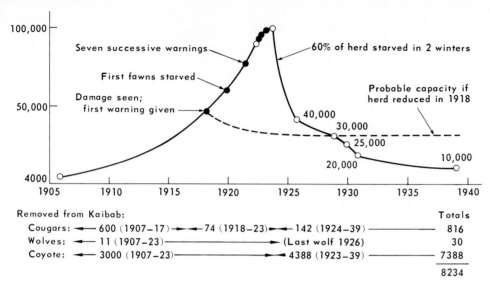

Removed from Kaibab: Totals
Cougars: ◄— 600 (1907–17) ►◄—74 (1918–23)►◄—142 (1924–39) —————— 816
Wolves: ◄— 11 (1907–23) ——————————————► (Last wolf 1926)   30
Coyote: ◄— 3000 (1907–23) ——————————►◄ 4388 (1923–39) —————— 7388
                                                                                                                 8234

ble to predators. The lemming is the principal source of food for the Arctic fox and snowy owl. Their populations vary with the lemming's, climbing in times of abundance and crashing in times of scarcity. Without alternative prey, many snowy owls starve during the winter or migrate south to the United States in times of scarcity.

Lemmings, the popular myth goes, migrate en mass to the sea when their populations top out, leaping from cliffs into the perilous waters, where they drown. While researchers have found that lemmings do indeed migrate down mountainsides from crowded breeding sites, they now know that lemmings do not migrate far, and they disperse individually, not in great masses. Furthermore, researchers note, the tiny rodents do not throw themselves into the sea, but will occasionally cross streams, where some lose their lives. But crossings are made only when they are absolutely necessary. There is no suicidal march to the sea. Such dispersals help reduce population density, whereas the mass suicides once believed to take place would have no adaptive value.

A number of other species experience regular 3- to 4-year cycles—for example, the red-tailed hawk, the meadow mouse, and the sockeye salmon. Protecting these and other cyclic species requires special attention on the part of wildlife managers. Overharvesting of commercially important species in "crash" years could readily reduce their numbers to levels that could not be sustained.

Snowshoe hare populations, found in the northern coniferous forests, undergo a 10-year boom-bust cycle (Figure 13-6). The cycle is characteristic of muskrats, grouse, and pheasant. The lynx, which preys largely on the snowshoe hare, also has a 10-year cycle that lags just behind the hare's. Both populations peak at about the same time. The original explanation given for the cycle is as follows: When hares are abundant, food for the lynx is abundant. That makes it easier for them to raise their young and increases the survival of young and adults. But the success of the lynx population leads to heavier predation on hares. This, in turn, reduces the hare population. With its food supply reduced, the lynx finds it more difficult to survive, and its numbers dwindle as well.

This simple explanation, however, may miss the boat entirely. Additional research suggests that other factors may control the hare population size. Hares living on islands with no lynx also undergo a 10-year cycle. One explanation is that the rising population of hares reduces its own food supply. Hares begin to die off, and as the hare population declines, so does the lynx population. A number of other theories have been advanced to explain the 10-year cycle, but scientists are still unable to determine which, if any, are valid. Among the causative agents in this puzzle are variations in weather, fluctuations in solar radiation, a periodic depletion of food supplies, outbreaks of disease, and changes in the nutrient levels of plants.

With this brief introduction to wildlife and plant populations, we now turn our attention to the all-important question: What causes extinction?

CAUSES OF EXTINCTION

"If a species becomes extinct," wrote David Day, author and conservationist, "its world will never come into being again. It will vanish like an exploding star. And

FIGURE 13-6   An example of a wildlife population cycle, based on pelt records of the Hudsons Bay Company. Note the approximate ten-year interval.

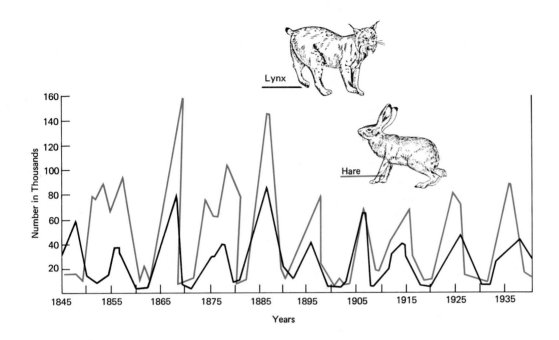

for this we hold direct responsibility." Most of the species that have become extinct since the beginning of the Industrial Revolution have done so not because they have been unable to adapt to natural changes in the conditions on earth, but rather because they have been unable to coexist with another species: *Homo sapiens.*

Plants and animals become extinct for a number of reasons. The greatest number vanish because their habitat is destroyed or altered beyond habitability. Others disappear because they are overharvested by commercial interests. Still others succumb to alien species accidentally or intentionally introduced into their habitat. An alien species may kill a native species outright or simply outcompete it. Sport hunting has contributed to the decline of some species, as have pest and predator control programs. Pollution and the pet business are also contributors to the steady decline in the number of species worldwide. This section describes the three main causes of extinction: habitat destruction and alteration, hunting (commercial and sport), and the introduction of alien species. Controlling them, especially habitat destruction, could greatly improve the chances of many of the world's vanishing species.

Habitat Destruction and Alteration

Expanding urban areas, logging, mining, and building highways, railroads, pipelines, and dams destroy valuable plant and animal habitats at an alarming rate. The destruction of habitats, or their severe alteration, has claimed innumerable species and threatened millions of others.

In many places, only tiny islands of natural habitat, called **ecological islands**, now exist amid a sea of crops, pasturelands, towns, and mines (Figure 13-7). In the eastern United States, for example, only small patches of deciduous forest exist today among the farm fields, towns, and cities. This pattern can reduce populations, making them vulnerable to extinction. Chandler Robbins of the U.S. Fish and Wildlife Service found that the fragmentation of the forests of Maryland, New York, and Pennsylvania has caused a drastic reduction in the number of birds that once bred in the forests. For reasons still unknown, the long-distance migrants, such as vireos, tanagers, and orioles, which winter in South America, have been most severely affected.

Princeton biologist Robert MacArthur studied species diversity on naturally occurring islands and found that, all other things being equal, *the smaller the island, the fewer species it supported.* Other scientists found that his conclusion was also valid for ecological islands cut off from similar habitats by human activities. Thus, a 10-hectare (25-acre) plot of deciduous forest cut from a continuous forest supports far fewer species per hectare than a 10,000-hectare (25,000-acre) plot. Why?

At least three reasons explain the reduced species diversity on ecological islands. First, small plots may not contain enough room and food for some species. The grizzly bear, for example, requires a 5,200-hectare (20-square-mile) habitat to find the food it needs. Anything

An Extinction Case History: The Passenger Pigeon

The passenger pigeon (*Ectopistes migratorius*) was once the most abundant bird on earth. Early in the nineteenth century the renowned ornithologist Alexander Wilson observed a migrating flock that streamed past him for several hours. Wilson estimated the single flock to be 1 mile wide and 240 miles long and composed of about 2 billion birds. (The population of this flock was roughly 10 times the total North American waterfowl population today.) Yet not one passenger pigeon is left.

What factors contributed to the passenger pigeon's extinction? First, many potential nest and food trees were chopped down or burned to make room for farms and settlements. The pigeon fed extensively on beechnuts and acorns; the single flock observed by Wilson could have consumed 17 million bushels per day.

Secondly, disease may have taken a severe toll. The breeding birds were suspectible to infectious-disease epidemics because they nested in dense colonies.

Third, many pigeons may have been destroyed by severe storms during the long migrations between the North American breeding grounds and the Central and South American wintering region. Cleveland Bent cites a record of an immense flock of young passenger pigeons that descended to the surface of Crooked Lake, Michigan, after becoming bewildered by a dense fog. Thousands drowned and lay a foot deep along the shore for miles.

Fourth, the low biotic potential may have been a factor in their extinction. Although many birds, such as robins, lay 4 to 6 eggs per clutch, and ducks, quail, and pheasants lay 8 to 12 eggs, the female pigeon produced only a single egg per nesting.

Fifth, the reduction of the flocks to scattered remnants possibly deprived the birds of the social stimulus requisite for mating and nesting.

Sixth, the bird's decline was hastened by persecution from market hunters. They slaughtered the birds on their nests. Every imaginable instrument of destruction was employed, including guns, dynamite, clubs, nets, fire, and traps. Over 1,300 densely massed birds were caught in one pass of the net. Pigeons were burned and smoked out of their nesting trees. Migrating flocks were riddled with shot. Over 16 tons of shot were sold to pigeon hunters in one small Wisconsin village in a single year. Pigeon flesh was considered both a delectable and fashionable dish in the plush restaurants of Chicago, Boston, and New York. Sold for two cents per bird, almost 15 million pigeons were shipped from a single nesting area at Petoskey, Michigan, in 1861. The last wild pigeon was shot in 1900. Martha, the last captive survivor, died on September 1, 1914, at the age of 29, in the Cincinnati Zoo.

smaller is simply not enough. Second, small habitats may reduce the number of organisms in a given population below the critical size needed to reproduce. For instance, the now extinct passenger pigeon once roamed in flocks that contained millions of birds (Figure 13-8). Commercial hunters eliminated the huge flocks in mass slaughters to provide food for urban dwellers. Excessive hunting accompanied by heavy deforestation spelled doom for the bird. By 1878, only 2,000 birds remained in small flocks—too small to reproduce successfully (Figure 13-9). The population had fallen below the **critical population size** and could never recover. Habitat destruction could have the same effect on other land species. Third, tiny habitats may promote extensive inbreeding—that is, mating with close relatives. Inbreeding often results in inferior offspring. (For more on the passenger pigeon, see "An Extinction Case History: The Passenger Pigeon.")

Habitat fragmentation leads to **faunal collapse**, a decrease in animal species. Edward C. Wolf of the World-watch Institute notes that the "regional and global consequences of human activities may undermine the ability of natural ecosystems to recover from this fragmentation." Chemical contaminants in the air, water, and soil may hinder reproduction or kill organisms outright. Global warming may alter the distribution of plants and eliminate the animal species dependent on them. Increased ultraviolet radiation may destroy other plants or increase cancer and mutations among animals. "The cumulative effects of such changes," notes Wolf, "can alter ecosystems in ways that increase the vulnerability of plants and animal species to extinction." Scientists call this process of change that weakens an ecosystem **biotic impoverishment**.

To protect biological diversity, human society has embarked on an ambitious program of park designation. Today 425 million hectares (1,000 million acres) of land are protected the world over. However, park protection is woefully inadequate. By some estimates, three times as much parkland is required to protect samples of each of the earth's ecological zones. Strict measures to control pollution are also needed to reduce biotic impoverishment.

Recent studies have shown that many national parks in the United States, long seen as the last hope for

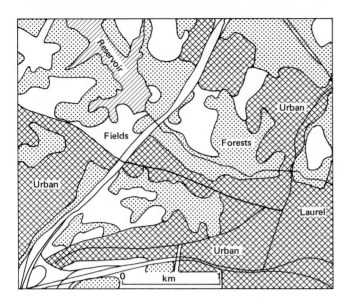

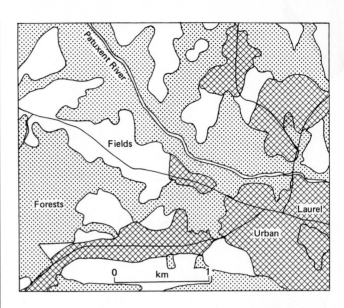

FIGURE 13-7A   Before forest fragmentation. Vicinity of Laurel, Maryland in 1951, showing forest cover (dots), fields (white), urban areas (squares), and main highways (black lines).

FIGURE 13-7B   After forest fragmentation. Same area as in Figure 13-7A. Construction activities have carved the forest habitat into small pieces. Note the Rocky Gorge Reservoir, Interstate Route 95, and Maryland Route 198 (bottom).

America's vanishing wildlife, inadequately protect species diversity. Ecologist William Newmark studied the loss of mammal species in national parks and found an alarming drop in the number of species in all but the largest parks (Table 13-1). Bryce Canyon National Park, one of the smallest, lost 36 percent of its species. Yosemite, nearly 20 times larger than Bryce, lost 23 percent. Only the mammoth parks like Yellowstone suffered minor losses.

What is the lesson from all of this? Many parks are simply too small to support their previous diverse array of species. If a park is cut off from neighboring areas, it becomes an ecological island too small to support the

diversity it once enjoyed. And what is more, researchers point out, the faunal collapse in the world's parks may be continuing today.

Nowhere is the problem of extinction as critical as in the tropical rain forests, which contain an estimated one-half to two-thirds of the world's species. The dire predictions of extinction presented at the beginning of this chapter were based on a deforestation rate of 2 percent per year. Recent work by the United Nations Food and Agricultural Organization (FAO), however, shows that deforestation may be occurring at a much slower rate than was once thought—instead of 2 percent per year, it is occurring at a rate of 0.6 percent per year

FIGURE 13-8   Shooting "wild pigeons" in Iowa. Copied from Leslie's *Illustrated Newspaper,* 21 September, 1867. Note the gunner firing point blank into the densely massed birds. Over 100 birds are resting on the bare branches of the oak in the background.

FIGURE 13-9 Extinction. When the last living passenger pigeon, Martha, died at the Cincinnati Zoo, on September 14, 1918, a unique organism was removed from the human ecosystem forever.

globally. While this rate is still significant, it suggests that extinction may not be as rapid as many ecologists once predicted.

The FAO study also shows that the two largest areas of continuous forest—the great forests of Central Africa and Amazonia—are being cut, but at very slow rates. The Central African forests of Zaire, Gabon, the Congo, and Cameroon, for instance, are in equilibrium—that is, new forests are planted at a rate nearly equal to that of deforestation. Unfortunately, these new forests are often monocultures, consisting of a single species grown for commercial use. Monocultures fail to support the biological diversity of the previous forest. In Amazonia, the rate of destruction is only 0.3 percent a year. At this rate, it would take 300 years to destroy the forest—still significant for the long-term well-being of the planet, but less pressing than some would have you think.

But global averages can be misleading, the FAO study shows. For instance, in the tropical forests of the Ivory Coast of Africa, loggers are destroying trees at a rate of 6.5 percent per year. In Nigeria, the rate is 5 percent; in Paraguay, it is 4.7 percent; in Nepal, it is 4.3 percent. It is in these and other priority areas that conservationists must begin their work—and fast.

Throughout the world, large human populations live near estuaries, bays, and other coastal wetlands. Roads, highways, cities, homes, and airports now sit where wetlands once supported an abundance of plants and animals. Inland wetlands have not fared any better. Farmers have drained swampy land and plowed it under from Florida to Wisconsin. Thus, many of the world's coastal and inland wetlands have already been destroyed. In the Philippines, for instance, 50 percent of the mangrove wetlands have been filled in or dredged. In southern California, 90 percent of the salt marsh wetlands have met a similar fate. In the United States as a whole, nearly two-thirds of the wetlands have vanished.

The benefits of wetlands are described in Chapter 10 and summarized in Table 6-1. As the benefits of wetlands are many, so are the dangers of destroying them. At least one-half of the biological production of the world's oceans occurs in coastal wetlands and estuaries. From 60 to 80 percent of the world's commercially important marine fish either spend time in estuaries or depend on them for food. And 60 percent of the fish caught in the ocean by commercial fishermen depend on the estuarine zone—the mouths of rivers and coastal wetlands.

By filling in the world's wetlands and polluting them with wastes from our homes and factories, we do a disservice both to the other species that share this plant with us and to ourselves. Sir Edmund Hillary once noted that environmental problems are really social problems. They begin with people as the cause and end with people as the victims. Deforestation and wetland

Table 13-1 Faunal Collapse in America's National Parks

Park	Area (Square Kilometers)	Share of Original Species Lost (%)
Bryce Canyon	144	36
Lassen Volcano	426	43
Zion	588	36
Crater Lake	641	31
Mount Ranier	976	32
Rocky Mountain	1,049	31
Yosemite	2,083	25
Sequoia-Kings Canyon	3,389	23
Glacier-Waterton	4,627	7
Grand Teton-Yellowstone	10,328	4
Kootenay-Banff-Jasper-Yoho	20,736	0

Source: Based on William D. Newmark, "A Land-Bridge Island Perspective on Mammalian Extinctions in Western North American Parks," *Nature*, January 29, 1987.

FIGURE 13-10 The bison, a multiple-use species. It formed an important base for the culture of the Great Plains Indians. By destroying the bison, commercial hunters reduced native Indian populations.

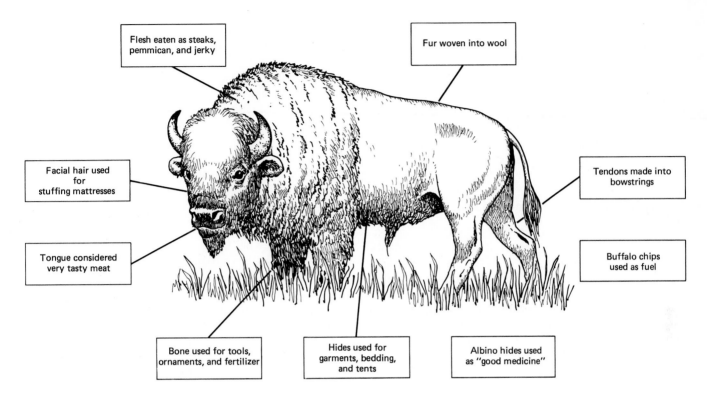

Flesh eaten as steaks, pemmican, and jerky

Fur woven into wool

Facial hair used for stuffing mattresses

Tendons made into bowstrings

Tongue considered very tasty meat

Buffalo chips used as fuel

Bone used for tools, ornaments, and fertilizer

Hides used for garments, bedding, and tents

Albino hides used as "good medicine"

destruction show this very clearly. Unfortunately, millions of species suffer along with us.

Hunting for Profit and Sport

Commercial hunting has a long history of species extinctions and near extinctions. The passenger pigeon, mentioned earlier, became extinct in the early 1900s because of widespread clubbing and shooting by commercial interests. The great auk, a large penguin-like bird that once lived along the North Atlantic coast, became extinct in 1884 as a result of overharvesting. It had been slaughtered by sailors in search of meat. The heath hen, a bird similar to the prairie chicken but living in an area that stretched from New England to Virginia, was severely depleted by commercial hunters.

At the turn of the century, women flocked to stores to buy fashionable hats adorned with the elegant plumes that came from the snowy egret. Hunters gunned the birds down mercilessly in Florida, nearly wiping out the population. Fortunately, however, when restrictive laws were passed to protect the bird early in this century, the population rebounded.

The buffalo, whose herds once blackened the prairies, remains today in tiny remnant populations. Commercial hunting and habitat destruction caused its decline (Figure 13-10). Many species of whale, like the blue whale

and the humpback, were driven to the brink of extinction by overzealous whalers. Protected today, some of them still remain in jeopardy. Many fear that the blue whale population may have been so severely depleted that it will not be able to recover. Today populations of some commercially important fish species have fallen to dangerously low levels because of overharvesting (Chapter 9).

Not all species are harvested for their food. The big cats of Africa, for instance, have been severely depleted by commercial hunters to provide furs for fashionable coats. Despite protective laws, poachers still hunt jaguars, cheetahs, tigers, and others.

Several species of African rhinoceros are in a deplorable condition. Protected by law but still poached, the rhino's horns are sold to Yemen and China. The Yeminis, wealthy beyond their wildest dreams from oil, carve the horns into dagger handles for businessmen. The Chinese grind the horns to produce an aphrodisiac (hardly needed in a country that has 1 billion people) and a fever-depressing drug that is reportedly useless.

Sport hunting may contribute to the decline of animal populations if these populations are not well managed. For the most part, however, hunting has helped wildlife populations. America's more than 400 national wildlife refuges and thousands of state wildlife areas were paid for largely by the sale of duck stamps and hunting licenses. Regulations on hunting have helped protect many species from overhunting and have become a valuable tool. And hunting helps control the population size of deer and other game species, since predators have long been eliminated from most regions.

In select instances, however, overhunting can threaten entire populations. Poor wildlife management in Canada's Spatsizi Park, for instance, threatens to eliminate mountain goats and bighorn sheep populations. And wildlife management programs aimed at improving deer and other game species, combined with animal control programs launched by state and federal governments to protect livestock, have greatly reduced the number of natural predators throughout the United States.

Introduction of Alien Species

Although with the best of intentions, humans have all too often introduced alien species of animals and plants, only to discover, too late, that their benefits never really materialized or that they became a nuisance. A classic example of this was the introduction of the water hyacinth into Florida. This South American flowering plant was brought in to adorn private ponds, but it was accidentally released into the waterways of Florida. Since that time, it has spread wildly throughout the southern states, clogging rivers and lakes, killing native plants, and making navigation impossible. Several southern states now spend millions of dollars each year to clear waterways of this fast-growing species. Another example is the mongoose imported from India to the islands of Hawaii and Puerto Rico. A fierce, quick-moving, weasel-like predator, the mongoose was introduced to control rats, which caused extensive damage to sugar cane. Unfortunately, the people in charge of this introduction had not studied the animal very carefully. Shortly after it arrived, they found that the mongoose hunts primarily during the day. The rat, on the other hand, is nocturnal. As a result, mongoose–rat encounters were rare and few rats were killed. Unfortunately, the mongoose soon began to prey on ground-nesting birds. Some, like the Newell's shearwater and the dark-rumped petrel, were eradicated from the island of Molokai. Others, such as the Hawaiian goose, were driven to the brink of extinction.

As this example shows, islands are extremely vulnerable to alien species. Why? Because native species are often ill-equipped to cope with new species and the habitat is too limited for them to escape the pressure exerted by the invaders. The Hawaiian Islands, for instance, have been particularly hard hit by alien species. Before humans settled there, the islands lacked any natural mammalian predators. Many bird species, which had lived on these volcanic islands for hundreds of years, had lost their ability to fly. What good are wings if there's plenty of food and no natural preda-

tor? Flightless birds have no other choice but to nest on the ground as well. Quite expectedly, after humans settled the islands with dogs, pigs, and goats, the flightless birds began to dwindle. The birds could easily be clubbed to death, and pigs raided their nests.

Alien species sometimes assimilate in a new ecosystem without causing a wrinkle in the ecological fabric. In other instances, they perish because their new environment lacks essential resources or because environmental conditions differ too much from those of their native habitat. Many hardy species, however, tend to thrive in new environments. Without predators, competitors, disease, or parasites, they proliferate wildly, interfering with native plants and wildlife—literally reweaving the ecological fabric, turning a rich and varied cloth into a threadless, often colorless one.

The Many Causes of Extinction

Pollution, the pet trade, pest control, and predator control—discussed in subsequent chapters—reduce wildlife populations, making them even more vulnerable. As the human population grows and more and more countries become industrialized, pollution could take a large toll on wildlife populations. Especially harmful to plants and animals will be the changes in weather and ultraviolet light penetration caused by an increase in carbon dioxide and the destruction of the ozone layer, respectively (see Chapter 18).

It should also be emphasized that many species become extinct not as the result of a single action, but of many. The California condor, with only 27 birds and all of them in captivity in southern California, once soared above much of the southern United States from California to Florida. This magnificent bird succumbed to habitat destruction, lead in its scavenged prey (pollution), and pesticides (pest control). The bald eagle, the symbol of our great nation, was pushed to the brink of extinction as a result of habitat destruction, shooting, and pesticides.

Traits of Vulnerable Species

Some species have attributes that make them more vulnerable than others. Some of the major characteristics of concern are (1) specialization, (2) low biotic potential, and (3) nonadaptive behavior.

SPECIALIZATION. As discussed earlier, specialists are more vulnerable than generalists, which occupy a variety of habitats and feed on a number of foods. In general, the more restricted the range of a species, the more vulnerable it is. Consider the Kirtland's warbler (Figure 13-11).

This tiny bird now has a population of 400 birds, so small that all of them could be held in a gunny sack. A tiny bird with a powerful song, the Kirtland's warbler has perhaps the smallest breeding range of any

Kirtland warbler at nest. Nests are located on the ground beneath the protective lower branches of a jack pine which is 5 to 20 feet in height.

North American bird—a 140-kilometer (85-mile) by 170-kilometer (100-mile) area in the north central part of Michigan's lower peninsula. The warbler lives in the jack pine habitat, where it nests in trees that are 6 to 15 years old and 2 meters (5 feet) to nearly 7 meters (20 feet) high. In the lower branches of these trees, the warbler builds its nest and rears its young. In younger trees, the lower branches do not provide adequate nesting cover; in pines older than 15 years, the bottom branches become shaded out and die and are no longer suitable for nesting.

The natural growth of the pine poses a threat to the survival of this magnificent songbird. But before humans intervened, its growth was held in check by naturally occurring forest fires. Fires wiped out sections of the forest and created new growth, which in a few years provided trees of a suitable age and size. Well-intentioned forest fire protection, however, destroyed the natural renewal and caused the forests to age, wiping out the warbler's nesting ground.

Today, the U.S. Forest Service mimics nature by periodically burning sections of the forest in **prescribed burns** (Chapter 12). These small, well-managed fires destroy the mature pines and cause the jack pine trees' cones to pop open, releasing seeds. The new seeds grow in the burned patches, ensuring a constant supply of trees of the right age for nesting.

Unfortunately, the Kirtland warbler faces another danger: the deforestation of its wintering ground in the Caribbean. Without it, the bird will invariably perish, illustrating the importance of international cooperation in protecting a species.

The restricted habitat of some species makes them targets for extinction. So do restricted diets. For in-

stance, the graceful hawk known as the Florida Everglade kite is among the rarest species of bird in the United States. There are only about 10 individuals left. (The species is well represented in Mexico and South America, however.) An important factor contributing to its falling numbers is its highly specialized diet. The bird feeds almost exclusively on snails. Because farmers, real estate developers, and government officials have drained much of the snail's marshy habitat, both snail and kite populations are in danger.

LOW BIOTIC POTENTIAL. Some animal species are extremely vulnerable to environmental stress, such as storms, drought, and disease, because of their low biotic potential. The female polar bear, for example, breeds only once every 3 years, and then gives birth to only two cubs. The female California condor lays only a single egg every other year. The problem is further complicated by the fact that condors require 6 to 7 years to reach reproductive age.

NONADAPTIVE BEHAVIOR. The Carolina parakeet, the only parrot native to the United States, became extinct in 1914 when the last survivor died in a zoo. The parakeet was hunted extensively by fruit ranchers because the birds descended on their orchards in huge flocks, ravaging the trees. However, this exquisite red, yellow, and green "paint pot" might still be with us if it were not for one peculiar trait: When one member of a flock was shot, the remaining birds would hover above it, becoming easy targets for gunners. Of more recent interest is the red-headed woodpecker, whose population has declined in the last few decades. The woodpecker has a curious tendency to fly along highways directly ahead of automobiles. Unfortunately, the latter usually win the fatal race.

METHODS OF PREVENTING EXTINCTION

Three major methods are presently used to protect wildlife and plants—not just rare and endangered species, but all species. They are (1) the zoo-botanical garden approach, (2) the species approach, and (3) the ecosystem approach.

The Zoo-Botanical Garden Approach

Wood's cycad, a tree from South America, and Cooke's kokio tree from the Hawaiian Islands cannot be found in the wild today. Were it not for botanical gardens, the species would be extinct. Nurtured in climate-controlled facilities, the trees today hang on by a thread. Many animal species face a similar future. Pere David's deer, originally from China, continues its existence in zoos throughout the world. More recently, the entire California condor population (27 animals) was trapped and caged. Now residing in southern California's zoos, the condor relies on humans, the very species that drove it to extinction, to save it.

However important they are in preserving the rich biological diversity of the world, zoos and botanical gardens have some major drawbacks. First, they are a last-ditch effort to save species before their final extinction. Second, many organisms simply do not do well in captivity. They may not breed or may succumb to disease. Animal species confined to a few square meters, when they once roamed over many square kilometers, may become bored and restless. Some refuse to care for their young. And caring for these temperamental few is costly and time-consuming.

Zoos have taken important steps to mimic a species' habitat and have provided areas that allow animals to range more widely. Their reward: healthier, more productive animals that may help save some of our endangered species.

While harboring and breeding endangered animals in zoos may help save species in the short run, this approach is of limited value—a bit like saving a few of Renoir's and Monet's paintings for the sake of art. In the long run, however, saving species requires a more permanent solution: rebuilding wild populations in protected habitats. The zoos will play a major role in this effort, and indeed have already begun to do so. The San Diego Zoo, for instance, hopes to build the condor population to a level that would sustain itself in captivity and allow biologists to release birds into a protected habitat. After years of work, at a cost of millions of dollars, the condor may once again soar above the skies of southern California. Numerous zoos throughout the world are also cooperating in a program to breed golden lion tamarins, which will be released into protected jungles of South America.

The Species Approach

Species not yet reduced to a critical level may be protected in the wild through special management programs. Scientists carefully study their niche to determine their habitat, critical food requirements, and other biological imperatives. They then design a program to enhance or expand the resources that the species needs to survive and prosper. This may require that human activities be altered. For instance, a species protection program may call for a ban on habitat destruction or controls on dangerous pollutants. In other instances, it may require measures that improve the habitat, such as fertilizers or prescribed burning and predator control. Stream improvements that protect spawning grounds and provide shelter may be needed to protect fish populations. Today the California sea otter and bison owe their survival to such actions.

One problem with this method is that it tends to overlook the needs of other species. By narrowly concentrating on one species, society may overlook species that, in the long run, are more valuable. It is quite possible, for example, that a species that might be of more value to society would be neglected in a program aimed at protecting one that happens to be visually more appealing. For example, many people who would enthusiastically support protecting the grizzly bear would balk or laugh at similar efforts in behalf of the Furbish lousewort or some insect of far greater value to society.

The Ecosystem Approach

Perhaps the most significant outcome of the science of ecology is the notion of the ecosystem—an interacting and interdependent network. It tells us that what we do to the earth we do to ourselves. It also tells us that to preserve the earth's species requires measures to preserve its ecosystems—and that this will benefit us as well.

HABITAT PROTECTION.   The ecosystem approach to preservation is perhaps the most effective and least costly means of saving plants, animals, and microorganisms. By setting aside large areas of habitat that are populated with a sufficient number of each natural species and letting nature take its course, biologists believe that we can greatly reduce species extinction. Also, by learning to live much more carefully within the environment, the human population can live alongside many wild species.

The drawbacks of such an approach, biologists are now finding, are significant. First, as described earlier in this chapter, unless the habitat is extremely large or is connected to a natural habitat that is also relatively undisturbed, faunal collapse is inevitable. A recent study of the tropical rain forests shows that 1-hectare (2.5-acres) plots lose all of their primates and other mammals and about half of their birds. Slightly larger islands, of 10 hectares, do not fare much better. Even 100-hectare plots lose nearly half of their bee species and a few of their primates. Another problem with the ecosystem approach is biotic impoverishment, described earlier.

The ecosystem approach works well, but special care must be taken to set aside a habitat sufficient to retain the biological diversity of a region. Combined with population control and reduction in pollution, the ecosystem approach remains one of the chief long-range answers to the problem of vanishing species.

HABITAT RESTORATION.   Another element of the long-range plan is restoring damaged lands. In the Amazon Basin, for instance, at least 15 to 17 million hectares of forest have been converted to cropland and pasture. Approximately one-half of this land has already been abandoned because the poor tropical forests last for only 4 to 8 years when planted in crops or grazed by livestock. Refurbishing this land and others like it throughout the world could greatly decelerate the loss of biological diversity.

But forest regeneration may be lengthy. The larger the disturbance, the slower the recovery. A large clearcut in the tropics may take 150 years to restore itself fully. A number of studies suggest that humans can accelerate forest regrowth and that careful work can reestablish a forest's full ecological diversity. But the costs could be exorbitant. Severe erosion must be stopped to prevent the soils from vanishing. Native species will have to be reintroduced to start natural succession.

In 1985, Rajiv Ghandhi, India's prime minister, established a program of tropical reforestation. Nearly 175 million hectares of land—half of India's land mass—has been deforested and lies in ruin. The government hopes to replant 5 million hectares a year, but will limit its plantings to a few species of trees that can be used as food for livestock and fuel to supply the needs of India's rural poor. This effort could help reduce soil erosion and rural despair, *will* benefit wildlife, *but will not* restore the full ecological diversity of forests long since destroyed.

Some observers point out that India could easily broaden its project to restore some land to natural forest. Research in a variety of locations indicates that native populations can restore forests to near-natural conditions and that these forests can provide food for rural populations on a sustainable basis. For example, researchers in Mexico found that descendants of the Mayans protected and cultivated forests containing a variety of fruit- and nut-bearing trees. These forests, while not identical to native forest, were in many ways similar and supported a variety of species. Similar practices have been observed in Brazil, Colombia, Java, Sumatra, Tanzania, and Venezuela.

Habitat protection and restoration are occurring throughout the world. In the United States, much of our grassland biome has been plowed under for farms. Most of the deciduous forest biome has been leveled for pastures, farmland, towns, and cities. Conservation organizations, such as The Nature Conservancy, have taken an active role in setting land aside to protect plants and animals. And efforts are being made to restore native prairie. Scientists, in fact, believe that native prairie may prove to be one of the best long-term rotation crops for farmland that has been severely compacted, eroded, and depleted of its nutrients.

THE ENDANGERED SPECIES ACT

America's first concerted effort to protect endangered species came in 1973 when Congress passed the **Endangered Species Act**. This monumental act has helped thwart the dangerous biological impoverishment here and abroad. How does it work?

The act requires the U.S. Fish and Wildlife Service to identify species that are **endangered**, that is, in imminent danger of going extinct, or **threatened**, that is, likely to become endangered in the foreseeable future. Table 13-2 lists the number of species officially listed as endangered in 1986. After a species is listed as endangered, it is afforded full legal protection under the act. Native species cannot be hunted and killed. They cannot be exported. Violators can be fined up to $20,000 and can be imprisoned for 1 year.

The act also bans the importation of endangered species or their products from outside the United States. Recognizing the importance of habitat protection, Congress also directed the Fish and Wildlife Service to identify the habitats of endangered species. Money was provided to help purchase habitats.

The Endangered Species Act also protects habitats by prohibiting federal projects or federally funded projects in these areas. Since the act was passed, thousands of projects have been modified to protect endangered species with little or no problem. The exception to the rule is the Tennessee Valley Authority's controversial Tellico Dam, whose construction was temporarily

Table 13-2 Endangered Species, 1986

Item	Mammals	Birds	Reptiles	Amphibians	Fishes	Snails	Clams	Crustaceans	Insects	Plants
Endangered species, total	279	215	74	13	52	4	25	3	8	93
U.S. only	25	60	8	5	37	3	23	3	8	87
U.S. and foreign	20	14	6	—	4	—	—	—	—	5
Foreign only†	234	141	60	8	11	1	2	—	—	1
Threatened species, total	26	5	25	3	23	5	—	1	5	28
U.S. only	4	3	8	3	20	5	—	1	5	23
U.S. and foreign	—*	2	4	—	3	—	—	—	—	3
Foreign only†	22	—	13	—	—	—	—	—	—	2

* represents zero.
† Species outside the United States and outlying areas as determined by the Fish and Wildlife Service.
Source: U.S. Fish and Wildlife Service, *Endangered Species Technical Bulletin*, 6(2), 1988.

Dam Versus Darter: A Classic Confrontation

In 1973 David Etnier, a fish expert at the University of Tennessee, discovered a new species of fish in the Little Tennessee River. The tiny fish, only 7.5 centimeters (3 inches) long, was given the name **snail darter** (*Percina tanasi*). According to Etnier, the entire world population of this species, numbering about 1,400 individuals, was confined to a 2.5 kilometers (15-mile) stretch of the Little Tennessee River. Obviously, the species qualified as endangered under the criteria of the Enangered Species Act. It was most unfortunate, however, that the fish's habitat would soon be destroyed because the Tennessee Valley Authority (TVA), a federal agency, was constructing the $116 million Tellico Dam in the Little Tennessee, a short distance from where the darter was discovered. The resulting reservoir, impounded behind the dam, would replace the shallow, fairly rapidly flowing water essential for snail darter survival with deep, quiet water—a completely different aquatic habitat.

The discovery of the tiny fish, set the stage for a confrontation between technology and a powerful federal agency (the TVA), on the one hand, and a vanishing species, supported by a few dedicated environmentalists, biologists, and nature lovers, on the other. In a letter to us, Etnier described the confrontation:

> The story is an interesting one that involves a small fish and a group of little people with virtually no resources attempting to force a governmental agency to comply with federal law. The number of participants has been immense, on both sides. Our side fought with money from the sale of snail darter T-shirts. TVA's efforts to thwart us have probably cost that agency well in excess of a million dollars in lobbying and expenses associated with their staff of lawyers, biologists, and administrators working on the case. Virtually every newspaper, press service, and TV network has devoted some time or space to the issue and magazines such as *People, The New Yorker, Time,* etc. have carried lengthy articles . . .

Eventually the case was brought to the courts. In early 1977 a federal appeals court ruled that the TVA would have to terminate construction on the Tellico Dam. But the prodam people did not give up easily. In April 1978 no less an offcial than U.S Attorney General Griffin Bell asked the U.S Supreme Court to spare the dam and scrap the darter. But to no avail. In June 1978 our nation's highest court ruled in favor of the fish.

However, legislators began pondering the question: "When we formulated and enacted the Endangered Species Act, were we really concerned about saving tiny fish, or were we thinking of eagles and moose?"

As one scientist wrote: "Congressmen are now finding themselves confronted with a Pandora's box containing infinite numbers of creeping things they never dreamed existed."

Nevertheless, in 1978, when the Tellico Dam was 90 percent finished, the Supreme Court ruled that the project had to be stopped because it violated the provisions of the Endangered Species Act. The court ruled that the act made any federal construction project illegal if it jeopardized the survival of any organism that had been formally classified as endangered under the provisions of the act.

A storm of controversy raged in Congress for many months concerning the act. Verbal battles were waged. Congressmen were heavily pressured by lobbyists. The construction industry naturally was interested in weakening the Endangered Species Act so that federal projects could be exempted. Environmentalists, on the other hand, were steadfastly opposed to any modification of the act that would lessen its influence in preserving endangered organisms.

Eventually the act was amended. Under the amendment, any requests for exemptions from the act were to be considered by a special high-level review committee. In 1979 the committee ruled to block any futher construction of the Tellico Dam on the grounds that the economic benefits resulting from its construction did not justify its costs—in addition to threatening the survival of the snail darter. However, special interest groups with a financial interest in such multi-million-dollar projects as dams, levees, reservoirs, and highways refused to concede defeat. They succeeded in convincing legislators to amend a public works bill that would permit the completion of the Tellico Dam.

The prodarter people were understandably dismayed. However, they did the best they could, under the circumstances, to preserve the fish. The entire snail darter population was removed from the Little Tennessee and introduced into the Hiwassee River nearby.

The Hiwassee River population survived the transplant and appears to be doing well in its new home. Recently, scientists have discovered snail darter populations in four additional creeks in Tennessee and Alabama.

As opponents projected, however, the TVA's Tellico Dam and reservoir have not fared as well. Built to stimulate industrial development and increase recreational fishing, the dam appears something of a failure. So far it has brought no industrial development to the region, and the projected recreation fishery is generously described as "average." Many critics think of it as a "pork barrel" project—built to please local and state politicians at a huge federal expense.

stopped when scientists discovered the tiny snail darter in the stream to be dammed (see "Dam Versus Darter: A Classic Confrontation").

Russell Peterson, former president of the national Audubon Society, argues that the Endangered Species Act has been reasonably successful in protecting endangered species in the United States, but that it lacks the funding needed to restore and set aside habitats to protect species. Furthermore, he contends, the act "fails to address the threat of extinction where it is greatest: in the undeveloped world."

That threat is now being addressed by numerous agencies and private organizations. The specter of species extinction will not go away easily, and much needs to be done here and abroad to protect the rich diversity we have come to master.

RAPID REVIEW

1. Wildlife and plants enrich our lives in many ways. Beyond the countless aesthetic benefits are purely economic ones: drugs, ointments, and foods. Sports enthusiasts and nature lovers spend billions to hunt, fish, and photograph nature's rich offering. Wild plants and animals provide food and innumerable ecological benefits, such as flood protection, erosion control, and nutrient recycling.

2. An estimated 3 to 30 million species share this planet with us, but this rich and varied biological world is fast disappearing. Currently, one vertebrate species becomes extinct every 9 months. Add to that the plants, microorganisms, and invertebrates, and the rate climbs to an alarming one species per day! If deforestation continues and the human population continues to swell, some biologists believe that a million species could become extinct by the turn of the century.

3. Preserving biological diversity has become one of the most important environmental concerns of the 1990s.

4. To understand plants and animals and the ways to protect them, one must understand ecology and especially the ways in which these populations are affected by outside forces.

5. The biotic potential of a species is the theoretical maximum rate of growth for a population given unlimited resources. In nature, few organisms reproduce at this rate for any appreciable length of time because of environmental resistance.

6. One of the greatest worries of biologists is that widespread extinction will eliminate valuable species, thus lowering environmental resistance, which promotes the survival of pest species.

7. Environmental resistance is the sum of the factors that regulate the size of a population. Ecologists recognize two types: density-dependent and density-independent factors.

8. Density-independent factors are those that operate irrespective of population density—for example, drought, cold spells, and storms. Habitat destruction by human populations is another example.

9. Density-dependent factors are those whose influence in controlling population size increases or decreases, depending on the density of a population. There are at least four major density-dependent factors: competition, predation, parasitism, and disease.

10. The size of a population of any organism results from the interaction of environmental resistance and the factors that create its biotic potential. Stability occurs when the two opposing sets of factors are in balance. In general, when environmental resistance climbs, the population declines. When it falls, the population increases.

11. Whenever a species is introduced into a new habitat with adequate resources, its population grows in a characteristic way, called the **S curve**. During the second phase, explosive growth occurs because little environmental resistance is applied. During the final phase the population stabilizes as a result of environmental resistance. At this point, the population is said to be in a dynamic equilibrium—that is, it changes somewhat from year to year but remains fairly constant over the long term. The population has reached the carrying capacity, the size a habitat can support on a sustainable basis.

12. Wildlife managers use their knowledge of population growth curves to manage wild populations and to achieve the maximum sustainable yield.

13. Not all populations remain in dynamic equilibrium. Outside forces, such as wide swings in weather, can cause populations to increase abruptly. Such irruptive growth often extends the population past the carrying capacity and may result in a crash. Human activities can easily upset the balance, resulting in irruption.

14. A number of species, such as the lemming, experience 3- to 4-year cycles. Others, like the lynx and snowshoe hare, experience 10-year cycles.

15. Most of the species that have become extinct since the beginning of the Industrial Revolution have done so not because they have been unable to adapt to natural changes in the conditions on earth, but rather because they have been unable to coexist with humans.

16. The major causes of extinction are (a) habitat alteration and destruction, (b) overhunting and overharvesting, (c) the introduction of alien species, (d) pest and predator control, (e) pollution, and (f) the pet trade. Controlling these, especially the first three, could greatly improve the chances of survival for many of the world's vanishing species.

17. In many places, only tiny islands of natural habitat, called **ecological islands**, now exist amid a sea of crops, pasturelands, towns, and mines. The smaller the island, the fewer the number of species it can support. Thus, the progressive fragmentation of the earth's biomes is gradually eroding its biological diversity. Ecologists are especially concerned with the damage now being wrought on the world's tropical rain forests.

18. Biologists once believed that tropical rain forests were falling at a rate of 2 percent per year, but recent work by the Food and Agriculture Organization of the United Nations shows that the global average is probably only about 0.6 percent. However, the average hides the rapid rate of destruction in some forests, which are now in desperate need of protection.

19. Biologists are also concerned about the impacts of destroying wetlands. Many of the world's wetlands have already been destroyed by human development. The wetlands provide many direct and indirect benefits to human society and are an important habitat in need of protection.

20. Commercial hunting has a long history of species extinctions and near extinctions. Sport hunting may contribute to the decline of animal populations if they are not well managed. For the most part, however, hunters do more good than harm.

21. Although with the best of intentions, humans have all too often introduced alien species of animals and plants, only to discover, too late, that the benefits never really materialized. In some cases, alien species proliferated and displaced native plants and animals. Islands have been particularly hard hit by alien species.

22. Many species become extinct not as a result of a single action, but of many. And some species have traits that make them more vulnerable than others, such as specialization, low biotic potential, and nonadaptive behavior.

23. Three major methods are now used to protect plants and wildlife: (a) the zoo-botanical garden approach, (b) the species approach, and (c) the ecosystem approach.

24. The zoo-botanical garden approach was once narrowly confined to raising endangered species in captivity, but has been expanded to include programs in which endangered species are bred in captivity and released in the wild.

25. The species approach involves plans developed to protect individual species by controlling human activities that threaten them and by improving their habitats.

26. The ecosystem approach is perhaps the most effective and least costly means of saving endangered species. By setting aside large areas that are populated with a sufficient number of each natural species and letting nature take its course, biologists believe that we can greatly reduce species extinction. Recent studies indicate, however, that large tracts must be set aside to preserve species diversity.

27. The ecosystem approach also entails plans to restore damaged lands and waters.

28. The Endangered Species Act of 1973 represents America's first concerted effort to protect endangered species. The act requires the U.S. Fish and Wildlife Service to identify endangered species and protect their habitat through a number of means. It has helped slow down the decline in species in the United States, but it does not address the threat of extinction where it is greatest: in the developing world.

KEY WORDS AND PHRASES

Alien species
Biotic impoverishment
Biotic potential
Carrying capacity
Competition
Critical population size
Cyclic populations
Density-dependent factors
Density-independent factors
Disease
Dynamic equilibrium
Ecosystem approach to species protection
Ecological island
Environmental resistance
Extinction
Faunal collapse
Generalists
Habitat alteration and destruction

Habitat restoration
Irruptive populations
Maximum sustainable (optimum) yield
Parasitism
Population dynamics
Predation
Predator
Prescribed burn
Shock disease
Specialists
Specialization
Species approach to species protection
S-curve (sigmoidal curve)
Wetlands
Zoo-botanical garden approach to species protection

QUESTIONS FOR DISCUSSION

1. Suppose that a classmate of yours made the statement: "I could care less about the extinction of some weed or bug in Africa." Do you consider such an attitude appropriate? Why or why not? Discuss your answer.

2. Describe the value of plants and animals to modern society.

3. Discuss why so many species have become extinct since life began on earth.

4. Describe the terms **biotic potential** and **environmental resistance**.

5. Describe and give examples of density-dependent and density-independent factors.

6. A new rodent is introduced into an island with no natural predators. Describe the likely course that its population will take. Draw a graph to show the shape of the curve and explain what happens at each stage. What factors will bring the population into a dynamic equilibrium?

7. Explain why the Kaibab deer episode demonstrates irruptive growth. What factor(s) caused this?

8. List the causes of extinction. Which ones are most important?

9. What is habitat fragmentation and why is it so harmful to species diversity?

10. Suppose that a population of 100 passenger pigeons was discovered in Illinois. Would you expect this population to survive, knowing what you do about the pigeon's reproductive requirements?

11. Give some examples in which commercial hunting has driven a species to extinction or near extinction.

12. Why are alien species such a threat to native populations?

13. Some species are vulnerable to extinction. What makes them so?

14. Suppose that fire was excluded from the Kirtland warbler's habitat. Would this promote or hinder its survival?

15. In what ways can zoos help preserve endangered plants and animals?

16. What is meant by the ecosystem approach to species protection? Describe some examples.

17. How would you respond to these questions put to you by a frustrated citizen? (a) "Who's more important, humans or alligators?" (b) "The wilderness is something I'll never be able to visit and don't care to, so why should we save it?"

SUGGESTED READINGS

Conservation Foundation. *State of the Environment: A View Toward the Nineties*. Washington, D.C.: Conservation Foundation, 1987. See Chapters 5 and 9 for a more detailed view of current trends and problems.

Council on Environmental Quality. *Environmental Quality*. Washington, D.C.: Government Printing Office, 1985. Chapter 9 contains an excellent summary of the forces resulting in biotic impoverishment of the earth and ways in which governments are fighting back.

Laycock, G. *The Alien Animals*. Garden City, N.J.: Natural History Press, 1966. Superb account of the folly of introducing alien species into the United States.

Myers, N. *A Wealth of Wild Species. Storehouse for Human Welfare*. Boulder, Colo.: Westview Press, 1983. Excellent treatise on the many benefits of wild plants and animals.

Myers, N. "The Mega-Extinctions of Animals and Plants." In *Ecology 2000: The Changing Face of Earth*, ed. Sir Edmund Hillary. New York: Beaufort Books, 1984, pp. 82–107. Excellent summary by a leader in the field.

Ola, P., and d'Aulaire, E. "Lessons from a Ravaged Jungle." *International Wildlife* 16(5):34–41, 1986. Interesting article on the ecological island in tropical rain forests.

Repetto, R., ed. *The Global Possible: Resources Development and the New Century*. New Haven, Conn.: Yale University Press, 1985. See Chapter 11 for more on preserving biological diversity.

Regenstein, L. *Politics of Extinction*. New York: Macmillan, 1975. A classic work on wildlife extinction well worth reading.

Wolf, E. C. *On the Brink of Extinction: Conserving the Diversity of Life*. Worldwatch Paper 78. Washington, D.C.: Worldwatch Institute, 1987. Exceptional review of the work needed to preserve biological diversity.

14

Wildlife Management

Wildlife management may be defined as the planned use, protection, and control of the wildlife resource by the application of ecological principles. One major function of wildlife management is to protect endangered species, as described in the previous chapter. But wildlife management has other important functions. Consider the use of wildlife in the following scenario:

> High in the Adirondacks of New York, a weary but jubilant deer hunter, clad in blazing orange, drags out a 200-pound buck, lashes it to the top of his van, 12 points and all, and speeds home to show off his trophy kill.

This episode represents the **consumptive** use of our wildlife resource. Now consider a second scenario:

> In predawn darkness, a wildlife photographer creeps into his blind on a wildlife refuge. After a few minutes of cramped suspense, the salmon flash of dawn ushers in the courtship display of prairie grouse. The camera whirs, and one of the most spectacular breeding rituals in the world of birds is captured on film.

Wildlife photography represents the **nonconsumptive** use of wildlife.

For much of this century, the management of wildlife for the hunter has been emphasized by wildlife managers. In recent years, however, management for nonconsumptive uses such as wildlife photography and bird watching has received more attention. Consider yet another episode:

> Clouds of migratory ducks and geese descend on Cy Hansen's 1300-acre wheat farm near Halleck, in the northwestern corner of Minnesota. The hungry birds trample the wheat and gorge themselves on newly ripened grain. Day after day the scene is repeated. Eventually the birds wing their way south, but not until farmer Hansen has suffered a severe financial setback.

This episode shows that under some conditions, wildlife, ordinarily a desirable resource, can be harmful to society. In such cases, the wildlife manager must develop strategies to control the destructive populations.

It is apparent that the effective management of our nation's wildlife is highly challenging and demands a great range of knowledge and skills. The involvement of well-trained professional wildlife biologists in decision making and action in many diverse arenas is essential to the wise use, protection, and control of our nation's wildlife resources.

WILDLIFE

What Is Wildlife?

The term **wildlife**, in its most comprehensive sense, includes all plants and animals on earth that have not been domesticated by humans. It therefore excludes agricultural crops and livestock. However, for most professionals in wildlife management, the term is largely restricted to birds and mammals, whether sought by the hunter, such as grouse and deer, or non-game, such as robins and eagles (Table 14-1).

Table 14-1 Classification of Wildlife

Nongame	Game
Birds	Upland game birds
Robins	Grouse
Eagles	Partridge
California condor	Pheasant
Peregrine falcon	Quail
Brown pelican	Turkey
Mammals	Waterfowl
Grizzly bear	Canada goose
Bobcat	Snow goose
Coyote	Mallard
Opossum	Wood duck
Flying squirrel	
	Big game mammals
	Deer
	Elk
	Moose
	Bighorn sheep
	Small game mammals
	Cottontail rabbits
	Gray squirrels
	Fur-bearing mammals
	Beaver
	Fox
	Mink
	Muskrat

Wildlife Habitat

The **habitat** is the general environment in which an organism lives—its natural home. It provides the essentials for survival: cover, food, water, and breeding sites (den, nest, or burrow).

COVER. Cover protects animals from adverse weather. Good examples are the dense cedar swamps that protect whitetail deer herds from winter winds and drifting snow and the leafy canopies of apple trees that shield nestling robins from the heat of the midday sun. Cover may also protect wild animals from predators (Figure 14-1). Representative of this function is the thicket into which a cottontail plunges when eluding a fox or the marsh grasses that conceal a teal from a hawk. Even water may serve as cover, as for a muskrat or beaver, providing relative security from landbound predators ranging from wolves to humans.

FOOD. Within a single species, food preference often varies widely. It also varies in individuals, depending on the health and age of the animal, season, habitat, and food availability.

Birds and mammals spend a great deal of time searching for food. An animal's access to food is influenced by many factors, including population density, weather, habitat destruction (by fire, flood, or insects), plant succession and type of habitat (Figure 14-2). Occasionally, when a food is abundant, an animal will exploit the source, even though it is not usually

FIGURE 14-1 Red fox peers out from behind a rock at Kettle Moraine State Forest, Wisconsin. In order to survive, this species requires a habitat which provides cover, food, water and adequate breeding sites.

FIGURE 14-2 Parent bluebird bringing bill full of insects to hungry young. A young bluebird can consume half its weight in insects in one day. Nesting boxes provide additional protection for the young, helping boost the survival rate of this species.

FIGURE 14-3   Wildlife habitat improvement. Chukar partridge (introduced from Asia) attracted by a "guzzler," a watering device used in desert country for wildlife.

a dietary item. Consider some examples: Even though the green-winged teal's diet is 90 percent vegetation, it avidly consumes the maggoty flesh of rotting Pacific salmon. Although the lesser scaup is not normally a scavenger, the stomachs of these ducks feeding at the mouth of a sewer have been found to be filled with slaughterhouse debris and cow hair (as well as rubber bands and paper). A house wren, normally an insect eater, fed its nestlings large quantities of newly hatched trout from an adjacent hatchery.

Animals that consume a great variety of foods are **euryphagous**. The opossum is a good example. It consumes fruits, blackberries, corn, apples, earthworms, insects, frogs, snakes, lizards, newly hatched turtles, bird eggs, young mice, and even bats. When its usual foods are scarce, the euryphagous animal is well adapted to survive.

A **stenophagous** animal, on the other hand, maintains a specialized, or limited, diet. Such species are more vulnerable to starvation when their usual foods are scarce. For example, an early freeze that kills off insects frequently causes many swifts and swallows to die of starvation. In 1932 a disease caused a 90 percent destruction of the eelgrass along the Atlantic Coast. As a result, the wintering population of brants (small geese), which depends almost exclusively on eelgrass for food, was reduced by 80 percent.

WATER.   Roughly 65 to 80 percent of wild animal weight is water. It serves many functions. It flushes wastes from the body. As a major blood constituent, it transports nutrients, hormones, enzymes, and respiratory gases.

Animals can survive for weeks without food but only a few days without water. In the nineteenth century, buffalo herds living in the arid western grasslands of the United States traveled many kilometers to find waterholes. Mourning doves may fly 50 kilometers (30 miles) from their nest site to a watering place. Dove and quail populations have been increased in the Southwest by the installation of "guzzlers"—devices that collect rainwater (Figure 14-3). Birds and mammals may get their water from dew or may drink it as it drips from foliage and tree trunks after a shower. During the northern winter, when liquid water is scarce, house sparrows and starlings will eat snow. Desert carnivores, such as the rattlesnake, fox, and bobcat, may derive water from the blood of their prey. Another desert animal, the kangaroo rat, may not need to ingest water during its entire life! It can use the water formed during cellular energy production.

The Edge Effect

The habitat essentials (cover, food, water, and breeding sites) for a given species are rarely all found in a single type of plant community. Usually an animal must rely on two or more plant communities to satisfy its needs. The region where two different ecosystems, such as marsh and oak woods, come together, is called an

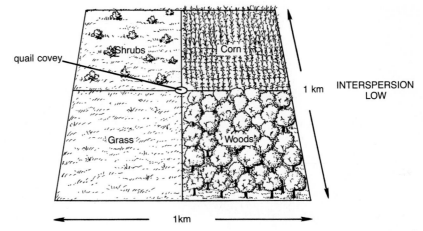

FIGURE 14-4A A square kilometer area with minimal interspersion of four habitat types. This area can support only one covey (flock) of quail.

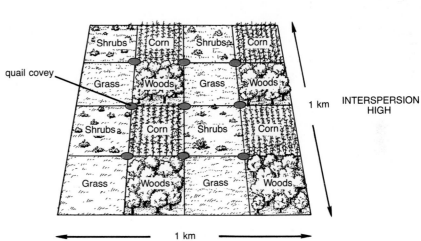

FIGURE 14-4B The same square kilometer with much greater interspersion of four habitat types. This area can support nine coveys of quail.

ecotone. Ecologists also refer to it as an **edge**. As a general rule, the greater the amount of edge, the greater the population density of any given species. For deer a clump of evergreens provides cover from storms and predators, a forest margin provides adequate food, and a dense thicket of shrubs provides a fawning site.

Let us assume that a hypothetical animal with limited mobility requires an interspersion of four types of vegetation: grassland, shrubs, cornfield, and woods. The vegetation shown in Figure 14-4A, with minimal edge, supports only one animal. On the other hand, the vegetation in Figure 14-4B, with much more edge, supports nine animals, even though the total area of each vegetational type is the same.

Home Range

Ecologists define a **home range** as the area over which an animal habitually travels while engaged in its usual activities.

The size of a home range can be determined by marking, releasing, and recapturing an animal (Figure 14-5). Animals can also be tracked with geiger counters after having been fed radioactive materials. They can be fed dyed foods that result in colored feces; the home range

can then be determined by studying the distribution of droppings. Birds can be individually marked with colored leg bands or spray paint. Small mammals can have their ears notched or toes clipped. Large animals (buffalo and elk) can be tattooed or marked with plastic collars so that visual identification is possible at a distance.

Herbivores usually have smaller home ranges than carnivores. A plant-eating moose, for example, may have a home range of only 40 hectares (100 acres) of swamp. The carnivorous grizzly bear, on the other hand, requires 52 square kilometers (20 square miles) of habitat. Timber wolves have circular runways up to 96 square kilometers (60 square miles) in diameter.

Territory

A **territory** is defined as any defended area. They are usually defended against individuals of the same species (Figure 14-6). In many kinds of birds, the threat displays (gaping, crouching, fanning the tail) and/or songs are used to defend territory rather than fighting (Figure 14-7).

Territorialism in birds may serve many functions. It can (1) provide adequate food, (2) establish and maintain the pair bond, (3) spread birds out to control infec-

FIGURE 14-5 Female mallard has been fitted with radio transmitter. After the bird is released, the radio waves generated by the transmitter will be "picked up" by the receiving set shown in the foreground. This is part of a University of Minnesota project conducted at the Cedar Creek Wildlife Area, Minnesota.

FIGURE 14-7 Ruffed grouse drumming. The sound is caused by the air rushing into a partial vacuum under the cup of the beating wing. The drumming serves not only as territorial advertisement to competitive males, but also as an attractant to prospective mates. A suitable drumming log (partially decomposed) is an essential component of the male's territory.

tious disease, (4) reduce or interfere with breeding (mating, nest building, incubation), and (5) reduce predation because the territorial birds become familiar with refuge sites.

The size of a bird's territory varies widely, from 0.3

square meters (3.3 square feet) in the black-headed gull to 9,300 hectares (23,000 acres) in the golden eagle (Figure 14-8). The majority of songbirds (like the robin) have territorial sizes of 0.1 to 0.3 hectare (0.25 to 0.75 acre).

TYPES OF ANIMAL MOVEMENTS

For the greater part of their lives, birds and mammals occupy a relatively small area represented by their home

FIGURE 14-6 Diagram of five home ranges and territories in a hypothetical animal. Note the cross-hatched areas where home ranges overlap. Territories usually do not overlap.

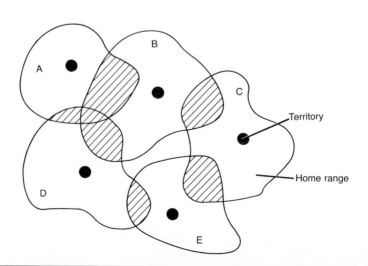

FIGURE 14-8 Territorial sizes of several species of birds, ranging from .3 square meter in the black-headed gull, to 93 million square meters in the golden eagle.

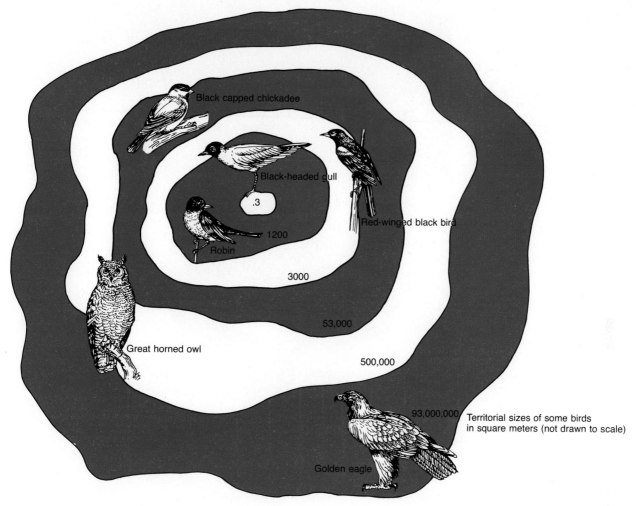

ranges and/or territories. However, under certain conditions, a given species may move considerable distances from the original home range and/or territory. Such movements promote the survival of the species. Three basic types of movements are (1) dispersal of the young, (2) mass emigration, and (3) migration.

Dispersal of the Young

The phenomenon of dispersal occurs in the young of many birds (gulls, herons, egrets, grouse, eagles, and owls) and mammals (muskrats, fox squirrels, and gray squirrels) (Figure 14-9). In a pine–oak habitat in central Pennsylvania, up to one-half of the juvenile ruffed grouse leave their nesting areas, some up to a distance of 7.5 miles (12 kilometers). Young bald eagles in Florida move north immediately after nesting, some arriving 2,400 kilometers (1,500 miles) distant in Maine and Canada by June. Up to 40 percent of a wintering muskrat population may disperse in spring. They

are primarily young animals who have been ejected by the established, more aggressive adults. Such dispersals control population densities. Many of the dispersed young move into marginal habitats, where they incur heavy mortality from predation and accidents.

Mass Emigration

Mass emigrations frequently occur when a population has peaked because of extremely favorable conditions (e.g., food or weather) and has then experienced a greatly reduced food supply. Under such conditions, the alternatives to starvation are summer dormancy, hibernation, or emigration. Snowy owl emigrations into the United States from the Canadian tundra are correlated with the population crash of their lemming prey. Ornithologists recorded 13,502 snowy owls during the 1945–1946 emigration, which extended as far south as Oregon, Illinois, and Maryland. Twenty-four were observed out over the Atlantic. Some were even seen in

FIGURE 14-9 Juvenile dispersal of young bald eagles which were leg-banded as nestlings in western Florida. Many of these birds moved up the coast, some of them as far as Labrador—1600 miles distant! The function of this dispersal is unknown. After spending their first summer in the northern states, they return south to their breeding grounds.

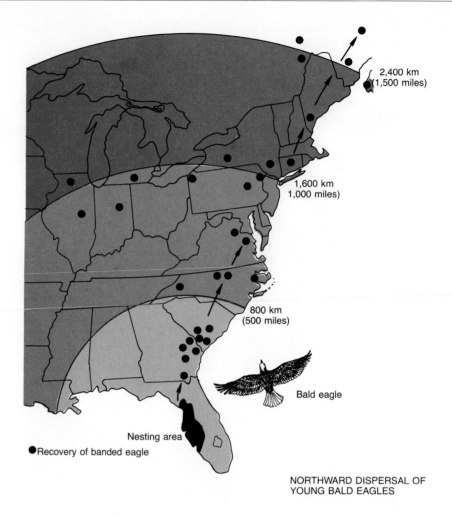

NORTHWARD DISPERSAL OF
YOUNG BALD EAGLES

Bermuda. It is believed that very few of these owls live long enough to make the return flight to the Canadian tundra the following spring. Many are shot illegally and wind up stuffed with cotton on someone's mantlepiece.

Migration

ALTITUDINAL MIGRATION. Latitudinal migrants move thousands of kilometers to find warmth and food. Altitudinal migrants achieve the same result simply by moving a few kilometers down the mountainside. The elk herds of the Rocky Mountains ascend the mountains in spring, keeping pace with the receding snow line, and spend the summer at the relatively cool upper levels. When the first snows cover their food supplies, the elk move down to the valleys for the winter. Herds of bighorn sheep make similar migrations.

LATITUDINAL MIGRATION. Winter bird densities in the southern United States are high because many birds that breed in more northern latitudes temporarily join the permanent residents. Foods such as insects, fruits, and seeds are more available in the south than in the snow-covered lands to the north. In spring,

however, the increasing day length eventually triggers hormonal secretions that stimulate migration (Figure 14-10). Presumably the northern habitats have a higher carrying capacity for the migrants and their future offspring. In far northern latitudes during the summer, there is more daylight in one 24-hour cycle for feeding the young. Biologists believe that the exploitation of two different habitats (winter and summer) may ensure a more balanced supply of vitamins and minerals.

MORTALITY FACTORS

In the ecology chapter we saw that the population level of any species at a given time is the expression of two opposing forces—the biotic potential, which tends to push the population up, and the environmental resistance or mortality factors, which tend to force it down. We shall now consider a variety of mortality factors affecting populations of deer and waterfowl.

Mortality Factors Affecting Deer

STARVATION. Winter is a critical season for deer in the northern states because available food is extremely

FIGURE 14-10 Latitudinal migration of the Arctic tern. Only the southward movement is shown. Note that many of these birds nest in the Arctic and winter in the Antarctic. During their southward migration, some of these birds will cross the Atlantic Ocean twice and will complete an annual migration of about 25,000 miles—the longest migration of any organism in the world!

LATITUDINAL MIGRATION
OF ARCTIC TERN

● Breeding areas
▲ Winter areas

limited. Food, such as herbs, mosses, fungi, seedlings, and stump sprouts, is often covered by snow. Under such conditions, the only available plant materials are buds, twigs, and foliage of conifers, such as white cedar and pine. If the deer populations grow too large, they will consume all the available browse up to the height they can reach when rearing up on their hind legs (Figure 14-11). As a result, a conspicuous browse line will form at a height of about 1.5 meters (5 feet), a definite warning to the wildlife biologist that the deer herds have overtaxed their food supplies.

Heavy snowfall in the Rocky Mountains may confine mule deer to 10 percent of their normal winter range. Under these conditions, the only available food is on the sunny south slopes, where snow melts rapidly. Of course, as deer crowd on these slopes food supplies can be depleted. One wildlife biologist counted the carcasses of 381 starved deer in only 5 square kilometers (2 square miles) of a heavily used range in the Colorado Rockies.

Emergency feeding of starving deer is not considered sound management by most wildlife biologists. They argue that it permits the survival of deer whose future progeny will exert even greater demands on the available natural browse, thus aggravating the problem. Artificial feeding also may facilitate the spread of disease by promoting concentrations of highly susceptible animals. Moreover, it is expensive.

PREDATION. A number of predators feed on deer, including wolves, cougars, bobcats, coyotes, and dogs. In the Superior National Forest (Minnesota), wolves kill 1.5 deer per 2.6 square kilometers (1 square mile) annually. One year the wolves killed 6,000 (17 percent) of the 37,000 deer in the forest. Because hunting pressure in the remote backwoods country of the Superior National Forest is extremely light, accounting for only 0.65 deer per 2.6 square kilometers, wolf predation theoretically might help control a deer herd that is often on the verge of exceeding the carrying capacity of the range. Because there are only about 1,500 wolves in the entire state of Minnesota, the impact of wolf predation on deer in that state must be negligible. Wisconsin has about 15 timber wolves; Michigan has a few.

The Human Predator

The hunter spots an elk herd edging into a clearing in the Colorado Rockies. He raises his rifle, picks out a big bull with a magnificent rack, squints down the sights, and squeezes the trigger. The crack of the rifle shot echoes through the valley. The bull staggers and slumps to the ground, blood spurting from the wound. He twitches his legs a few times and then lies still. Once again, the human predator has made a kill.

Human hunters are the most efficient predators in the animal kingdom. Hunters are similar to wild predators in many ways:

1. Both are not highly regarded by human society. Many people regard hunters as killers and place them in the same category as rattlesnakes and wolves.

2. Both are often unsuccessful in finding and killing their prey. In Isle Royal National Park in Lake Supe-

rior, for example, wolves have only a 7 percent success rate in killing moose. In Wisconsin, 7 of 10 hunters fail to get their deer even though the deer populaton is at an all-time high.

3. Both human hunters and wild predators shift their attention to alternative prey if the original prey is unavailable. Foxes, for example, will shift from rabbits to mice; wolves will shift from deer to beaver. Similarly, if human hunters are unable to obtain goose hunting permits, they may go after mallards instead.

Of course, there are also many differences between the behavior of hunters and wild predators. For instance, wolves, cougars, and other wild predators usually take prey that is weak, sick, crippled, aged, or suffering from disease. On the other hand, the human hunter prefers to bag trophy-sized animals in prime condition, which may weaken the species.

FIGURE 14-11 Starving deer rears up on hind legs for browse in a Michigan forest, a sure sign that the deer herd is over-taxing the carrying capacity of the range and that many are near the point of starvation.

Although one cougar may kill 50 or more deer annually, cougars are unimportant as regulators of deer populations because of their scarcity, except in localized areas of the Southwest.

Surprisingly, one of the more serious deer predators, other than humans, is the dog. Pregnant does and young fawns are especially vulnerable. Dogs have killed more than 1,000 deer in New York in a single month in winter.

Mortality Factors Affecting Waterfowl

We shall now discuss the following mortality factors affecting waterfowl populations: (1) wetland depletion, (2) habitat destruction by carp, (3) oil pollution, and (4) acid deposition (Figure 14-12).

DEPLETION OF WETLANDS. More than 4.4 million hectares (11 million acres) of our nation's inland wetlands were lost during the period 1955–1975. Destruction continues virtually unabated. Conversion to farmland has been responsible for about 87 percent of the losses. About 8 percent of the destruction has resulted from urban development.

Destruction of Prairie Potholes. The most productive "duck factory" on the North American continent is located in the grassland biome of Manitoba, Saskatchewan, Alberta, the Dakotas, western Minnesota, and northwestern Iowa (Figure 14-13). This region produces more than one-half of this continent's waterfowl. The ducks are raised primarily on tiny pot-

FIGURE 14-12 Survival curve for a mallard family. The population of two adults and 10 young was reduced by a variety of mortality factors to only two birds by the beginning of the next year's breeding season.

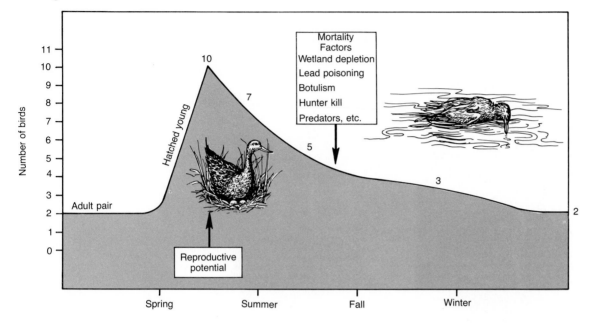

holes, 0.5 to 1 hectares (1.5 to 2.5 acres) in size, where all their requirements for food, cover, water, and nesting sites are usually met. The density of the potholes may reach 50 per square kilometer (125 per square mile). An estimated 10 million potholes once existed in the prairie provinces of Canada alone.

Unfortunately, thousands of potholes have been drained by farmers, seriously threatening waterfowl populations. Much of this drainage has been subsidized by the USDA so that more corn, wheat, and soybeans could be produced. In Iowa alone during the past 60 years, the number of potholes has been reduced by at least 94 percent. Despite the seriousness of the problem, drainage continues unabated. As a result, the number of ducks produced in the prairies of North America has dropped from 15 million to 5 million per year.

Destruction of Wetlands of the Mississippi Flood Plain. Additional wetland loss has occurred in Louisiana, Mississippi, and Arkansas. These wetlands are located in the bottomland hardwoods of the Mississippi River flood plain. More than 1.5 million hectares (3.8 million acres) have been destroyed in the past 20 years, largely because of conversion to soybean fields. Only about 20 percent of the original area, about 2 million hectares (5.2 million acres), remain.

This loss has serious adverse effects on thousands of waterfowl, like Canada geese, mallards, black ducks, wood ducks, and teal, that use wetlands as wintering grounds. Certainly this has been a factor in the 33–year decline in our nation's black duck populations.

Drought can be as destructive to wetlands as agricultural drainage. For example, about 1 million potholes

in the duck factory of Canada's prairie provinces, the Dakotas, Iowa, and Minnesota went bone dry during the drought of 1988. This was the most severe dry spell since the Dust Bowl days of the 1930s. As a result of the sharply reduced acreage of prime breeding habitat, the total North American duck population in autumn, just prior to the hunting season, was about 66 million—8 million less than in 1987 and the second lowest ever recorded.

HABITAT DESTRUCTION BY CARP. To many a barefooted youngster armed with a cane pole and worms, a carp might seem a prize, but to the educated duck hunter, it is a notorious destroyer of waterfowl habitat. Carp can eradicate dense growths of sago pondweed, water milfoil, and coontail, all favored duck foods.

Lake Koshkonong in southern Wisconsin was once almost blanketed with rafts of canvasbacks, which consumed the abundant wild celery buds and pondweed nuts. Late in the nineteenth century, however, carp were introduced to the lake. In a brief time, the fish uprooted the choice waterfowl food plants, and the thrilling panoramas of ducks quickly vanished. To make matters worse, young carp compete directly with ducklings for the protein-rich crustaceans so essential for growth and development.

Carp also stir up the bottom muds while searching for plant roots. The resulting turbidity may restrict photosynthesis sufficiently to eliminate certain plants not directly killed by the fish.

OIL POLLUTION. More than 100,000 waterfowl are killed annually by oil pollution (Figure 14-14). The tim-

FIGURE 14-13   Distribution of North American breeding and wintering ducks. More than 50 percent of North American ducks are produced in the "duck factories" of Manitoba, Saskatchewan,
Alberta, the Dakotas, western Minnesota, and north-western Iowa. The major wintering areas
are the Atlantic, Gulf and Pacific coasts, the lower Mississippi River Valley and California. Many
ducks that migrate through the United States winter in Mexico. Effective waterfowl management
obviously depends on the cooperative actions of Canada, the United States and Mexico.

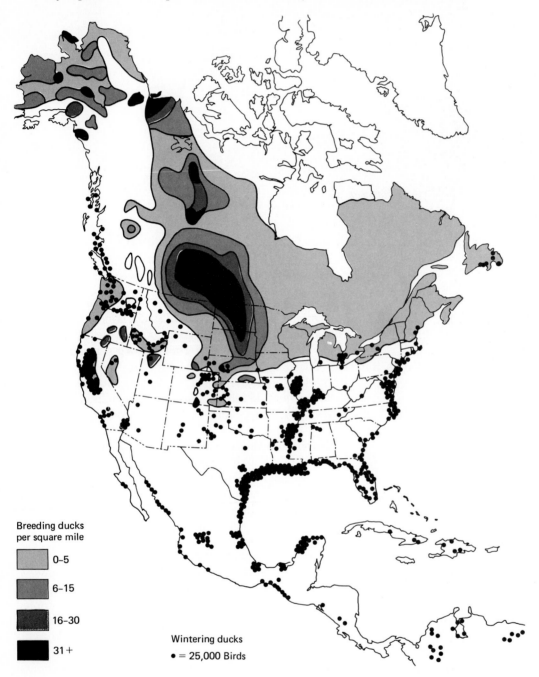

Breeding ducks
per square mile

0–5

6–15

16–30

31+

Wintering ducks
• = 25,000 Birds

ing of the spill greatly affects the mortality. On January
2, 1988, a storage tank collapsed near Pittsburgh, Pennsylvania, and released a tidal wave of diesel fuel into
the Monongahela River. The 14-mile-long slick caused
some waterfowl mortality. The death toll would have
been much higher had the spill occurred during the

spring, when thousands of ducks move up the Monongahela during their migration.
     Why does oil kill ducks? There are several reasons:
(1) Oil mats the feathers of waterfowl and reduces their
ability to keep warm in ice-cold water. Death then
results because of rapidly dropping body temperature.

FIGURE 14-14   Waterfowl mortality caused by oil spill. Oil-coated ducks pile up on the shore of the Mississippi River near Spring Lake, Minnesota. They were victims of a combined petroleum and soybean oil spill which destroyed 20,000 ducks in 1963.

So dangerous is oil that an oil-soaked area the size of a quarter is sufficient to kill some waterfowl. (2) Waterfowl with oil-matted feathers may also starve to death because they lose their ability to swim or fly in search of food. (3) The accidental swallowing of toxic oil while feeding, drinking, or preening feathers may also cause kidney and liver failure.

ACID DEPOSITION. Acid deposition, acids falling from the sky, in the United States and Canada creates another problem for waterfowl (Chapter 18). For instance, the black duck is highly prized by hunters, especially along the Atlantic Coast. It breeds in the northeastern United States and southeastern Canada, a region plagued by acid deposition (Figure 14-15). The may fly, a common aquatic insect, is a valuable food for young black ducks. Unfortunately, however, may fly populations have been sharply reduced in acidified lakes (Figure 14-16). Biologists wonder if future generations of young black ducks will be able to shift to alternative food sources. It is possible that such substitute food will be either unpalatable or too difficult to catch in sufficient quantities.

WATERFOWL SICKNESS

Lead Poisoning

Hunters deposit more than 3,000 tons of lead shot on our nation's lakes, rivers, and marshes annually. Because there are 280 pellets of No. 6 shot in one shotgun shell, and the average hunter needs six shots to kill one duck, about 1,400 pellets are deposited on waterfowl habitat for each bird taken. In one study researchers counted 150,000 pellets per hectare (60,000 per acre) in the San Joaquin River marshes of California; 300,000 per hectare (120,000 per acre) were found on the bottom of Wisconsin's Lake Puckaway.

The number of lead pellets on the bottom of the marsh depends in part on the nature of the soil. For example, many lead pellets will sink down out of sight if the bottom is composed of soft silt. On the other hand, if the bottom is hard clay, the pellets tend to accumulate and can be swallowed by waterfowl. Species that suffer the heaviest losses are the bottom feeders, such as mallards, which swallow the shot along with food and grit (Figure 14-17A).

Chemicals in the digestive tract of waterfowl cause the release of soluble lead salts, which may paralyze

FIGURE 14-15 Acid rain has been an important factor in the decline of the black duck population of eastern North America.

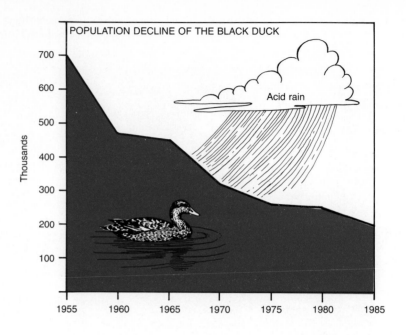

FIGURE 14-16 The breeding areas of the black duck population of eastern North America broadly overlap with regions that have acid waters. The acid conditions have caused a sharp decline in the mayfly population—an aquatic insect which is an important source of protein for young black ducks.

the gizzard and cause starvation in a month. In acute cases, poisoning of the liver, blood, and kidneys may cause death in 1 to 2 weeks.

Many hunters are not aware of the high rate of lead poisoning. One reason is that the intact lead pellets are rapidly ground up into small pieces and cannot be detected in the birds' gizzards. Furthermore, ducks suffering from lead poisoning frequently hide in the vegetation of the marsh or are often eaten by predators.

Lead poisoning from spent shot kills an estimated 2–3 percent of our waterfowl each year, an amount that nearly equals the combined duck production of North and South Dakota. (Secondary poisoning of bald eagles may occur when they eat the carcasses of lead-poisoned ducks.) The heaviest duck mortality form lead poisoning has occurred along the Mississippi Flyway, especially in Illinois, Indiana, Missouri, and Arkansas.

To reduce this problem, the U.S. Fish and Wildlife Service began phasing out lead shot and replaced it with steel shot in 1976. The mandatory use of steel shot has caused great controversy among duck hunters and waterfowl biologists. The advantage of steel shot is that it saves the lives of over 2 million ducks per year. The disadvantages of steel shot are as follows:

1. It is more expensive than lead shot.
2. Because of its light weight, steel shot will not kill at a distance of more than 40 meters (125 feet).
3. Steel shot will ruin outdated shotgun barrels made of soft steel.

Regardless of its disadvantages, steel shot is here to stay. By 1991, lead shot will be banned nationwide.

Botulism

The bodies of dead and dying ducks littered the mud flats of a western marsh. A mallard feebly fluttered its wings and excreted green droppings; a widgeon (a type of duck) struggled vainly to lift its head out of the stagnant ooze; a Canada goose was blinded by the yellowish slime that covered its eyes; a blue-winged teal gasped and died. What had happened to those birds?

They were the victims of botulism, a disease caused by the toxic metabolic wastes of the anaerobic bacterium *Clostridium botulinum*, Type C. Although most prevalent in the West, it has been recorded from Canada to Mexico and from California to New Jersey. During the summer of 1910, this microscopic organism was responsible for millions of waterfowl deaths. Even today, botulism may kill 100,000 waterfowl a year in California and Utah (Figure 14-17B).

Clostridium thrives in stagnant alkaline mudflats, where there is an abundance of trapped organic material (such as dead aquatic vegetation) and high water temperatures. These conditions are most likely

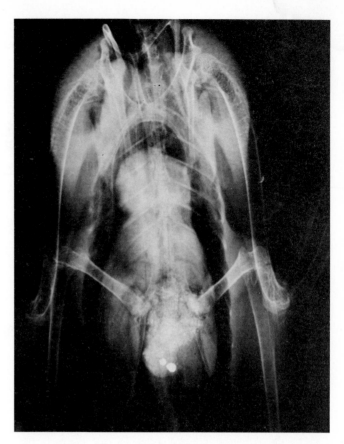

FIGURE 14-17A   X-ray photo of duck shows lead pellets in gizzard. They were accidentally swallowed while the duck was feeding.

to occur in the late summer during extended drought. Ducks become ill after eating contaminated organic material (decomposing plants and animals) or maggots and other insects that harbor the bacteria. Apparently insect larvae are a specialized microhabitats for bacteria. After being absorbed by the bloodstream of the waterfowl, the toxin produced by the bacteria eventually kills the birds by paralyzing their breathing muscles.

At the Bear River Wildlife Refuge in Utah, thousands of sick ducks have recovered after receiving antitoxin shots. Such treatment, however, would be prohibitively costly and time-consuming in the event of a major outbreak. Thus, prevention seems to be the answer. This can be done by rapidly raising the water level of the marsh or mudflat so that *Clostridium* no longer has optimal conditions for reproduction. Such flooding would also lower the water temperature and dilute the toxin.

Unfortunately, only state and federal waterfowl refuges have the facilities, such as dikes and pumps, that are needed for effective water level control. In most other waterfowl habitat, serious outbreaks of botulism may still occur.

FIGURE 14-17B   Cycle of events leading to a botulism outbreak.

CAUSE OF BOTULISM OUTBREAK

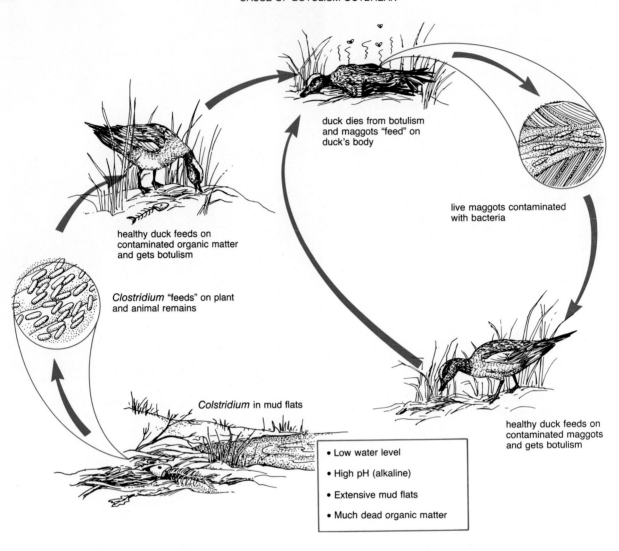

duck dies from botulism
and maggots "feed" on
duck's body

live maggots contaminated
with bacteria

healthy duck feeds on
contaminated organic matter
and gets botulism

Clostridium "feeds" on plant
and animal remains

Colstridium in mud flats

healthy duck feeds on
contaminated maggots
and gets botulism

- Low water level
- High pH (alkaline)
- Extensive mud flats
- Much dead organic matter

WILDLIFE MANAGEMENT

As you may recall, we have defined wildlife management as the planned use, protection and control of the
wildlife resource using sound ecological principles. One
basic approach to the management of wildlife is the
acquisition and development of quality wildlife habitat.

Develop Habitat for Terrestrial Wildlife

Currently, the best prospect for increasing wildlife populations is to increase the amount and quality of habitat.
Many wildlife biologists consider habitat development
to be indispensable.

The best management programs are meaningless
without habitat protection. If plenty of high-quality
wildlife habitat is available, wildlife populations will
remain relatively high, regardless of the lack of all other
management methods (Figure 14-18).

ACQUIRE WILDLIFE HABITAT.   Federal, state, and
private agencies are trying to reduce wetland loss by
habitat purchase. Federal funds for this purpose come
from an excise tax on the sale of hunting equipment.
Other monies are derived from the sale of federal duck
stamps, which must be purchased by waterfowl hunters
at the beginning of each season.

Unfortunately, federal funds have been woefully
inadequate. To help, Congress passed the Wetlands
Loan Act, which has enabled the Fish and Wildlife Service to borrow more than $300 million from federal
sources in the past two decades for wetland purchases.

Since federal and state budgets for the development of
parks and sanctuaries are tightening, private lands play
an increasingly important role in supporting wildlife.
Among the organizations that have had great success in
acquiring private land for the benefit of wildlife are the
Nature Conservancy and the National Audubon Society.

FIGURE 14-18 Wildlife biologists are developing suitable habitat for prairie chickens in Minnesota. The controlled burn will prevent plant succession and the growth of shrubs and trees. As a result, the grassland habitat, which the prairie chickens require, will be maintained.

The Nature Conservancy does not make a lot of headlines. Quietly and effectively, it goes about its business of purchasing or leasing essential habitat. It has completed more than 4,000 purchases or lease projects embracing more than 1 million hectares (2.6 million acres) in the United States, Canada, and Latin America. With the aid of a huge army of volunteers, it manages hundreds of wildlife sanctuaries in the United States. In 1989 it pursued its most ambitious project—the protection of critical wildlife habitat throughout the Florida Keys. The National Audubon Society has either leased or purchased about 100,000 hectares (250,000 acres) and has established more than 80 wildlife sanctuaries on this land.

Develop Habitat on the Farm

More than 85 percent of the hunting lands in the United States are privately owned or controlled. Private farms, ranches, and woodlots in fact produce most of the nation's grouse, quail, doves, pheasants, and rabbits. Therefore, the biggest contribution to an abundant and varied game resource (as in the case of forest development) can be made by the private citizen. Fortunately, many soil and water conservation practices, such as shelterbelting and conservation tillage, also improve the habitat for wildlife (Chapter 5).

During the Dust Bowl era of the 1930s, the USDA planted more than 30,000 kilometers (18,000 miles) of shelterbelts in the Great Plains. These narrow belts of trees on farms from the Canadian border down to Texas were planted primarily to control soil erosion. However, they also provided food, cover, and breeding sites for dozens of species of nongame birds like thrushes and warblers, as well as game such as grouse, quail, pheasants, squirrels, rabbits, and deer.

Conservation tillage has been discussed (Chapter 5) as a superb method for the control of soil erosion. The stubble and other vegetative debris from the harvested crop is left on the land. The new crop is planted the following spring directly in the stubble with special seed drills. Tillage is reduced to a minimum. The acreage of farmland that is being tilled in this way is increasing rapidly throughout the United States. Conservation tillage has benefited a great variety of wild animals, from pheasants in Nebraska to prairie chickens in Texas. Other ground-nesting species, such as quail, partridge, and early-nesting waterfowl, also benefit, since the stubble and other crop residues provide cover and breeding sites, and some food in the form of waste grain.

In 1985 Congress passed the **Food Security Act**. An extremely important provision of the act with regard to wildlife habitat improvement is the **Conservation Reserve Program** (CRP), which operates from 1986 to 1990. This provision enables the USDA to make contracts with farmers to control soil erosion. In essence, the farmers receive payments for discontinuing the farming on highly erodible land. Instead of raising crops the farmers will plant grasses or trees. The program could provide 18 million hectares (45 million acres) of marginal farmland in the United States to become high-quality wildlife habitat.

Manipulate Ecological Succession

In our discussion of succession in Chapter 2, we said that both plant and animal communities change as the physical environment changes. Thus, different organisms occupy a region as it goes through succession. Ecologist Raymond Dasmann has classified a number of species according to the successional stage: climax species (bighorn sheep, caribou, and grizzly bear); mid-

FIGURE 14-19   Forest succession and grouse habitat. Note that the carrying capacity of the forest for ruffed grouse changes as the forest succession proceeds. Note that the use of the forest as brood and breeding cover is high during the early successional stages when young aspen dominate the woods. When the aspen have attained an age of about 35 years, the grouse no longer use the forest for breeding purposes but use it primarily as a source of winter food. Grouse feed extensively on winter aspen buds. By the time the stand is 80 years old, the aspen have been completely replaced by other hardwood species which are of no value to grouse. The highest grouse densities (81 per square kilometer) occur in a forest which is about 20 years old and is dominated by aspen.

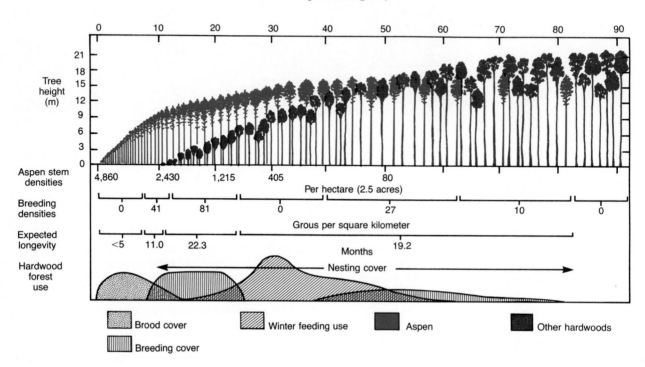

successional species (antelope, elk, moose, deer, and ruffed grouse); early-successional species (quail, dove, rabbit, and pheasant).

Wildlife biologists can regulate the abundance of these species by manipulating ecological succession. Thus, they can permit a succession to proceed on its natural course to a climax or, by employing such artificial devices as controlled (prescribed) burning, controlled flooding, plowing, and logging, can retard the succession or even return it to the pioneer stage.

The **early-successional species**, such as the rabbit, quail, and dove, depend heavily on major disturbance of the ecological succession by humans. These species prefer the weedy pioneer plants that invade an area denuded by human activity. Such vegetation may become established when farmland is abandoned and a pioneer community of invading weeds and shrubs becomes established.

Because **climax-associated** species such as caribou, bighorn sheep, and grizzly bear flourish only in relatively undisturbed climax communities, their survival depends

largely on the establishment of state and national refuges. Without such protected "islands" in the "oceans" of successional disturbance caused by humans, these climax-associated species will decline and become extinct.

DEVELOPING HABITAT FOR RUFFED GROUSE. The ruffed grouse is a highly prized game bird in the northern United States. It is named after the feathered "ruff," or collar, it displays during courtship. When flushed by the hunter, it bursts from cover with a thunderous whir. A typical mid-successional species, grouse occupy a given region only temporarily.

Gordon Gullion, the nation's leading grouse expert, has found that young aspen stands provide virtually all of the food, cover, and breeding requirements of the grouse in the Great Lakes forests. Winter aspen buds provide an abundance of high-quality nourishment during a season when other foods are scarce. Note in Figure 14-19 that the highest population density (81 birds per square kilometer) (210 per square mile) occurs in aspen forests that are 12–25 years old. However,

FIGURE 14-20 Artificial nesting islands for Canada geese. View of the Westside Pond in Canyon Ferry Lake near Townsend, Montana. Fill material was used to create about 62 artificial nesting islands. Note the Canada geese nesting on the island in the foreground.

as the succession proceeds, the aspen are gradually replaced by other hardwoods, such as oak, and the grouse population declines. Gullion found that the carrying capacity of aspen forests in northern Minnesota can be increased more than 600 percent when blocks of aspen are clearcut at 10, 20, and 30 years of age. This harvesting pattern gives grouse access to aspen stands of variable age and staves off the invasion of other tree species.

Habitat Management for Waterfowl

Waterfowl habitat can be improved by creating openings in dense marsh vegetation, constructing artificial ponds, developing artificial nests and nest sites, and establishing waterfowl refuges.

CREATING OPENINGS IN MARSHES. Although waterfowl require cover for protection from both weather and predators, they also need channels and openings through which they can paddle or waddle between nest sites and feeding areas, and between feeding and loafing areas. Channels also provide areas where the birds can feed. These essential openings result from natural causes such as hurricanes and lightning-triggered fires, or they may be made by humans.

CONSTRUCTING ARTIFICIAL PONDS. Where sloughs and potholes are scarce, waterfowl habitat can be constructed using artificial ponds. Between 1936 and 1988, the USDA assisted farmers in building 4 million farm ponds. Roughly two-thirds of those ponds are used by waterfowl, either as nesting, feeding, and

loafing areas by resident birds or as resting areas where migrating waterfowl can touch down for a brief respite before resuming their strenuous journey. Farmers can increase the carrying capacity of these ponds by erecting artificial nest boxes for mallards and wood ducks; by dumping piles of rocks or anchoring logs and bales of hay in the open water, where birds can preen and sun; and by seeding the pond with choice duck-food plants.

CONSTRUCTING ARTIFICIAL ISLANDS. In recent years, society has destroyed much valuable wildlife habitat in its attempts to promote its own welfare. As a result, wildlife populations have frequently been decimated. And for years it has been assumed, by at least a few biologists, that virtually all human-induced changes of the natural environment were detrimental to wildlife. The error of this type of thinking is shown by the effect of artificial islands in boosting waterbird populations. For example, in 1977 the Bureau of Reclamation (frequently assailed by environmentalists because of its obsession with big dam construction) used fill material to form 62 artificial nesting islands for Canada geese in Canyon Ferry Lake near Townsend, Montana (Figure 14-20). Since the construction of these artificial islands, biologist Robert Eng of Montana State University has noted a threefold increase in Canada goose production in the region.

For a number of years, the U.S. Army Corps of Engineers has constructed coastal "dredge islands" from the sand, mud, and shells it removes during dredging operations. More than 2,000 of these islands are scattered along the nation's coast from Long Island,

FIGURE 14-21   Construction of nesting boxes for wood ducks has been an important factor in the population increase of this beautiful species from a very low level earlier in this century.

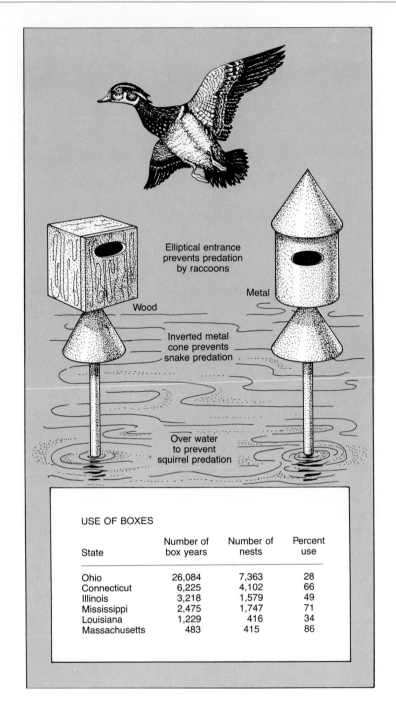

Elliptical entrance prevents predation by raccoons

Wood

Metal

Inverted metal cone prevents snake predation

Over water to prevent squirrel predation

USE OF BOXES

State	Number of box years	Number of nests	Percent use
Ohio	26,084	7,363	28
Connecticut	6,225	4,102	66
Illinois	3,218	1,579	49
Mississippi	2,475	1,747	71
Louisiana	1,229	416	34
Massachusetts	483	415	86

New York, to Brownsville, Texas. Some have also been formed in the Mississippi River, in the Great Lakes, and along the Pacific Coast. They are usually located far enough from shore to afford protection from such predators as raccoons, foxes, and free-running dogs. Moreover, because the dredge islands are frequently about 3 meters (6.6 feet) high, they are not often flooded during high tides, as are many of the low-lying natural islands near shore. Sidney Island, now administered by the National Audubon Society, was formed from spoil resulting from the dredging of the ship channel at Orange, Texas. Clouds of herons and ibises leave

their nests and circle above when visitors set foot on the island. According to Audubon Society counts, Sidney Island is home to 20,000 egrets, almost 8,000 herons, 2,000 ibises, 1,400 roseate spoonbills, and 380 cormorants. Several of these species have declined in other areas.

DEVELOPING ARTIFICIAL NESTS AND NEST SITES.   Through the process of natural selection operation for millions of years, each species of waterfowl has evolved its own unique instinct for nest-site selection and nest construction. It would appear almost impertinent, therefore, for humans to attempt to improve on nature by constructing artificial nests and sites for waterfowl. However, wildlife biologists have done precisely this, and with encouraging results (Figure 14-21). These artificial nests promote reproduction and may be even *more* effective in minimizing mortality caused by mowing machines, predators, and nest-site competitors than natural nests.

ESTABLISHING NATIONAL WILDLIFE REFUGES. America's system of national wildlife refuges was launched in 1903 by Theodore Roosevelt. He established the Pelican Island Refuge in Florida's Indian River to protect the brown pelican. From this modest beginning, the federal refuge system has grown to more than 437 refuges covering about 36 million hectares (88 million acres). Most of these were established primarily for use by waterfowl (Figure 14-22). In 1934 Congress passed the **Migratory Bird Hunting Stamp Act**, which provides funds to acquire, maintain, and develop

FIGURE 14-22 Our National Wildlife Refuge System includes more than 437 refuges covering about 32 million hectares (80 million acres).

waterfowl refuges through the sale of duck stamps. As of 1988, about $300 million had been raised nationwide.

Our national wildlife refuges provide over 1.2 billion waterfowl-use days. (One waterfowl-use day is 1 day's use by one duck, coot, swan, or goose.) Our refuges produce over 500,000 ducklings each year. The Tule Lake (California) and Agassiz (Minnesota) refuges each produce 30,000 ducks yearly, and the Malheur (Oregon) Refuge produces 40,000 annually. Huge concentrations of ducks and geese use many of the refuges during the fall migration (Figure 14-23). For example, in the Klamath Basin Refuge on the California–Oregon border, where considerable acreages of wheat and barley are grown exclusively as waterfowl food, a peak of 3.4 million ducks and geese has been recorded. Nearly 150,000 Canada geese have stopped over at the Horicon National Wildlife Refuge in southern Wisconsin—the greatest concentration of this species ever recorded in the United States. The geese fatten up or "refuel" at these stopover refuges before continuing their migration (Figure 14-24).

REGULATING POPULATIONS

In addition to habitat acquisition and development, wildlife managers use another basic approach to accomplish their objectives—the regulation of populations.

Controlling the Harvest of Game Populations

Game managers may use hunting to control the populations of well-established species. Populations of upland game birds (quail, pheasants, grouse) and small mammals (rabbits, squirrels) usually recover rapidly after being reduced by hunting. Such populations are said to be **resilient**. Such resilience is due, in part, to their high biotic potential. For example, a hen partridge may lay 20 eggs per clutch; a doe rabbit may have six young per litter and rear several litters per year. Even deer have resilient populations. Under optimal conditions, a deer herd of only 6 individuals can build up to 1,000 head in only 15 years!

In all species of animals mortality factors, or environmental resistance, counteract the biotic potential. As a consequence, the population of a species remains about the same from year to year. Wildlife biologists distinguish between two types of mortality—additive and compensatory.

Additive mortality simply adds to the deaths caused by other factors. **Compensatory mortality**, however, such as hunting, reduces the mortality caused by other factors, such as starvation, disease, and predation. Note that with or without hunting in a properly managed ecosystem, the total mortality from all causes remains the same. The number of animals taken by hunters depends upon hunting regulations. The hunting kill can

FIGURE 14-23 Sky darkened with thousands of pintail ducks at the Sacramento National Wildlife refuge in California.

be adjusted by extending or shortening the hunting season, increasing or decreasing bag limits, permitting the kill of both sexes or limiting it to males, and regulating the use of weapons (bow, rifle, shotgun, and so on).

Regulating the Deer Harvest

One of the primary objectives of deer management is to provide a **shootable surplus** for the hunter. Several decades ago, when deer were relatively scarce, state legislatures restricted hunting by closing or shortening the season, by timing the season to ensure an absence of tracking snow, by restricting firearms to shotguns, and by restricting the kill to one per hunter. The doe was afforded special status. The deer herd buildup was further promoted by winter feeding, introductions, predator control, and the establishment of refuges.

In response to these measures, as well as to the great abundance of edge and food available in the wake of extensive fires and logging, the herd increased rapidly—too rapidly. In only 13 years, the whitetail population in 45 states increased from 3.2 million (1937) to 5.1 million (1949). It soon exceeded the range's carrying capacity, browse lines appeared, winter starvation became commonplace, and the range rapidly deteriorated.

Many state game departments advised legislators to reverse the trend by liberalizing hunting regulations. After much prodding from wildlife biologists, herd reduction was implemented by opening and extending seasons, timing the seasons to coincide with the occurrence of tracking snow, legalizing the use of rifles, lifting the ban on does, establishing bow seasons, and removing bounties on predators. Roads were built to facilitate hunter access in the back country.

The overpopulation problem is far from solved. Despite liberalized laws, hunters rarely harvest more than 10 percent of herds. One reason is the deer's secretive behavior; the animals rarely emerge from protective cover during daylight hours of the hunting season. Hunters sometimes do not see a single deer even in an area with large populations. A 10 percent annual harvest is simply not enough to appreciably check herd increase (Figure 14-25). At least one-third of the autumn deer herd may be taken during the hunting season year after year without affecting deer herd size.

FIGURE 14-24 The value of "stopover" refuges in Wisconsin for the Mississippi Valley population of the Canada geese. These geese fly 450 miles non-stop to stopover refuges like Horicon Marsh in south-eastern Wisconsin. There they find an abundance of food which enables them to acquire the fat needed to fuel their 850-mile nonstop flight to their breeding ground in northern Ontario.

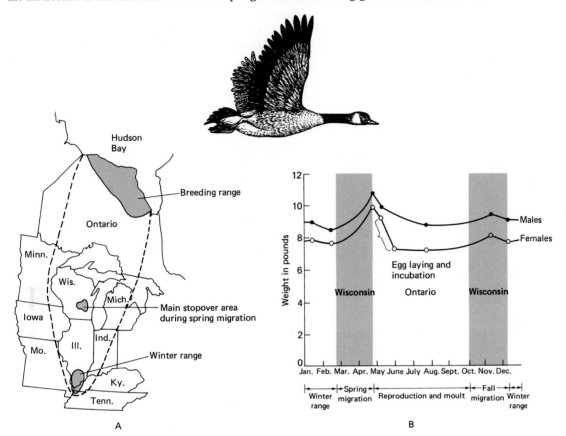

Deer populations frequently vary from region to region within a state, often being highest in semi-wooded agricultural regions and low in climax forests and urban areas. (In the late 1980s, however, it was not uncommon to see deer on the outskirts of major cities like Milwaukee and Chicago.) Therefore, a state may be divided into a number of zones, each with its own set of regulations. (One state has had 60 zones.) In zones where herds are small, the season may be closed completely or may be open to bow hunters only. In over-populated zones, the season may be opened on bucks, does, and even fawns.

In some states, wildlife managers are not permitted to practice what they preach because their technical knowledge in game management is far in advance of a receptive public or political climate. Too often the framers of our hunting laws yield to pressures exerted by hunters and resort owners, to whom the essence of game management is "more deer." Only when regulations are formulated in accordance with the advice of professionally staffed conservation departments will hunting regulations serve as an effective management tool.

Regulating the Waterfowl Harvest

The mallard is one of the most highly prized ducks sought by hunters on the North American continent. Each autumn, 12 to 18 million mallards wing their way south from their breeding grounds in southern Canada and the northern United States. And each autumn, several million duck hunters crouch in their blinds hoping to lure these swift flying birds to within shooting distance with their real-as-life decoys.

But how many mallards may the hunter take each day? One—three—five? Moreover, how many days can he or she hunt? The answers to these questions may vary from one state to another, and from year to year as well. Let's find out now how, and on what basis, such waterfowl hunting laws are made.

Much of the information on which waterfowl hunting regulations are based is derived from population censuses conducted on the breeding grounds several months before the fall migration. Regulations are also based upon population data taken in the major migratory pathways of the ducks, which are determined from studies of banded birds.

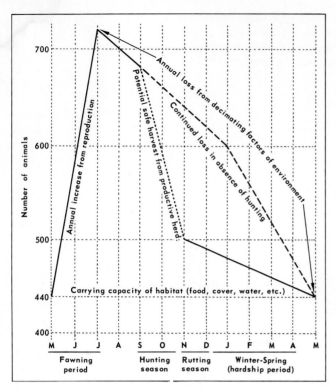

FIGURE 14-25 Annual population fluctuation in a deer herd which occupies a range with a carrying capacity for 440 head. Note that even during the closed season the various environmental resistance factors (starvation, parasites, predation, disease, and accidents) will eventually reduce the herd to the carrying capacity of the range. A considerable surplus may be safely harvested by hunters. With or without an open season, the population of the herd by the end of the winter-spring hardship period will be virtually the same.

Since 1920 more than 300,000 waterfowl have been leg-banded in the United States with serially numbered aluminum bands. These banding operations are conducted by the U.S. Fish and Wildlife Service with the aid of 100,000 volunteers. Records of the species, age, sex, weight, date, and banding locality are computerized at the Wildlife Research Center near Washington, D.C. About 32,000 waterfowl bands are recovered annually. Although most recoveries are made by hunters, a considerable number are also recovered by bird watchers and amateur naturalists who retrieve bands from birds killed by storms, pollution, predation, and disease.

Analysis of recovery data provides waterfowl biologists with information concerning growth rate, life span, and mortality, as well as the length, speed, and route of migration. For example, from such banding studies, we now know that some snow geese may travel 3,200 kilometers (2,000 miles) nonstop from James Bay, Canada, to the Texas coast in only 2 days!

From the practical standpoint of waterfowl popu-

lation management, the most significant information derived from banding studies is that waterfowl, such as mallards that breed in Canada and the northern states, migrate along four (rather poorly defined) **flyways** on their way to southern wintering grounds. Known as the **Atlantic, Mississippi, Central,** and **Pacific Flyways,** they have served as administrative units in the development of hunting regulations (Figure 14-26). These flyways have corridors that connect them (Figure 14-27). For example, a number of mallards that nest in the prairie provinces of Canada begin their fall migration by moving south along the Central Flyway into South Dakota. Eventually, however, they swerve southeastward, joining the Mississippi Flyway in Minnesota and Illinois, where they continue to their wintering grounds along the Gulf of Mexico.

Each of the four flyways is administered by a flyway council made up of directors of the various state conservation departments or their representatives. The flyway councils meet in August to frame regulations for the fall hunting season based on the size and distribution of the waterfowl population expected to be moving through their respective flyways. The councils then submit their recommendation to the U.S. Fish and Wildlife Service. The service also receives suggestions from various national conservation organizations, such as the National Audubon Society, Ducks Unlimited, and the Wildlife Management Institute. Armed with all this input, the service decides on regulations that it considers appropriate.

Let's now examine a specific example of how waterfowl hunting regulations are tailored to the population level of the target species. In 1962 the estimated mallard population on the North American continent was extremely low—about 7.6 million. Highly restrictive hunting regulations were therefore established. In the state of Washington, for example, the hunting season in 1962 was shortened to 75 days, and the daily bag limit was reduced to four. As a result, the mallard harvest in that state in 1962 was only 177,000 birds. Such restrictive laws were continued. The mallard population responded to this protection. By 1970 it reached 11.6 million.

Regulations on the mallard harvest were, therefore, liberalized. Washington extended its season to 93 days and increased the bag limit to six birds. The result was a kill of 311,000 birds.

Regulating Destructive Deer Populations

In 1988 the Wisconsin deer population stood at an all-time high of about 1 million. Since 1962 the herd has increased 162 percent for the state as a whole. However, when agricultural lands alone are considered, the increase has been a dramatic 488 percent. And these farming country deer are taking a huge $37 million annual "bite" out of Wisconsin agricultural production.

The Hunting Controversy

In 1987 about 17 million Americans hunted some form of wildlife. Ninety percent of the hunters in the United States are males. One-half of them are quite young, ranging from 16 to 34 years of age. One of every two hunters has attended college. Their occupations are highly diverse. Almost every walk of life is represented, from farmers to surgeons, from factory workers to business executives. Many are still in college. Regardless of their occupation, however, most American hunters grew up in a rural or semirural environment and received hunting instructions from their fathers when they were teenagers.

In the rural environment of the past century, hunting had much greater acceptance than it does today. Probably this was because the slaughter of livestock for food was a common farm activity. As a result, the death of animals was accepted as necessary for human survival.

Today, however, our nation is highly urbanized. Most Americans have never seen a farmer butcher a chicken, pig, or cow. Many consider the killing of wild game as unnecessary and cruel. About 50 percent of the American public today opposes hunting.

A number of citizens' groups have been organized to outlaw it. Among them are the Friends of Animals, based in New York City, and the Humane Society of the United States, with headquarters in Washington, D.C. This viewpoint is aptly expressed by Joseph Wood Krutch, a nature writer from New York City: "When a man wantonly destroys one of the works of man we call him Vandal. When he wantonly destroys one of the works of God we call him Sportsman." On the other hand, hunters have also been supported by many local sportsmen's groups as well as state and national organizations. Nationwide support for hunters is given by the National Rifle Association, the National Wildlife Federation, and the Wildlife Management Institute. Their prohunting philosophy is well represented by N. Adams in an article entitled "Hunting: An American Tradition": "You show me a person who doesn't directly or indirectly kill on a regular basis, and I'll show you a bleached, well-weathered pile of human remains. Every living creature takes life to stay alive, and if it doesn't, it quickly starves and dies a slow agonizing death."

Fields of corn and soybeans may be severely damaged if deer invade them when these crops are still in the seedling stage. The Wisconsin Department of Natural Resources has liberalized its hunting regulations in areas where deer-inflicted crop damage is high. During Wisconsin's 9-day hunting season in 1988, about 255,000 deer were taken—slightly over 25 percent of the total herd. Despite the huge annual harvests, however, deer damage to Wisconsin fields and orchards continues to rise.

The wildlife damage compensation program in Wisconsin is financed by a $1 surcharge on most hunting licenses. Farmers may be reimbursed for up to $5,000 in damages. The program also pays for the construction of deer-proof fences to keep them out of croplands and orchards. In LaCrosse, Wisconsin, one orchard alone was provided with 4 miles of fencing at a cost of nearly $40,000.

Regulating Destructive Waterfowl Populations

The most serious example of wildlife-inflicted crop damage involves grain consumption by waterfowl in Canada. Losses to Canadian grain farmers may reach 380,000 metric tons per year. Financial setbacks have approached $40 million annually, although the annual average is about $14 million.

Several strategies are being used to lessen the damage. A variety of noisemakers, including propane gas exploders, are used to scare waterfowl away from their "wheaties." In Canada, special fields are planted to "lure crops" to attract ducks and geese from privately owned wheat fields. The Canadian government offers farmers insurance programs that partially offset the financial losses caused by marauding waterfowl.

Canada geese have recently established breeding populations in some areas of northern Illinois. Unfortunately, however, huge flocks of these birds have become a serious nuisance on golf courses. Not only do they damage the greens, they cause problems at water hazards as well. In 1988 hundreds of these geese were trapped alive and transplanted to rural areas in southern Illinois, far from the golfing scene.

Regulating Rabid Animal Populations

Rabies is a disease caused by a virus that lives in the saliva of the host (carrier) animal. The virus is transmitted to humans by the bite of an infected animal. It moves along nerve cell pathways and eventually

FIGURE 14-26 Major waterfowl fly-ways. Recovery data on many thousands of waterfowl led biologists to believe, earlier in this century, that the birds migrated along four major flyways: (1) Pacific, (2) Central, (3) Mississippi and (4) Atlantic.

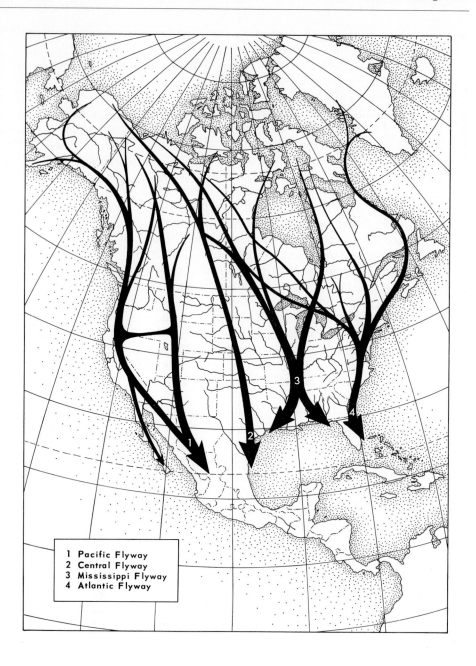

1 Pacific Flyway
2 Central Flyway
3 Mississippi Flyway
4 Atlantic Flyway

reaches the brain. Unless the infected person is vaccinated against the virus, he or she will sink into a coma and die. Rabid animals will snap and bite at animals and humans. Many different species of wild animals can harbor the rabies virus. The Centers for Disease Control in Atlanta reported the following cases of rabies in wild animals in the United States for 1979: skunks, 3,031; bats, 756; raccoons, 543; and foxes, 146. Extreme measures, such as poisoning and shooting, must sometimes be used to control rabid animals. Several years ago, strychnine-treated baits were used to control rabid foxes in Kentucky. Unfortunately, however, in addition to destroying 65 foxes, the poison killed 135 dogs. Moreover, the control measure was prohibitively expensive, costing $208 for every poisoned fox.

NONGAME MANAGEMENT

In recent years, state and federal wildlife agencies have developed a new focus of attention—nongame management. This is certainly appropriate, since Americans now spend about $7 billion annually on recreation based on nongame wildlife. Their activities range from whale watching to winter bird feeding to wildlife photography.

Population Status of Nongame Animals

The status of nongame populations, such as those of amphibians and reptiles, is not well known. On the other hand, population trends in birds have been followed very closely for a number of years through annual

FIGURE **14-27** Duck migration corridors. Wildlife biologists now know that the "flyway" concept was an oversimplification of an extremely complex migration phenomenon. The routes of many species of waterfowl may actually cross each other as shown here. Moreover, many waterfowl may fly east or west during migration rather than north or south, as suggested by the flyway concept. Frank Bellrose, of the Illinois Natural History Survey, identified migration "corridors" for southward flying ducks, and was able to estimate the approximate number of ducks using a particular corridor.

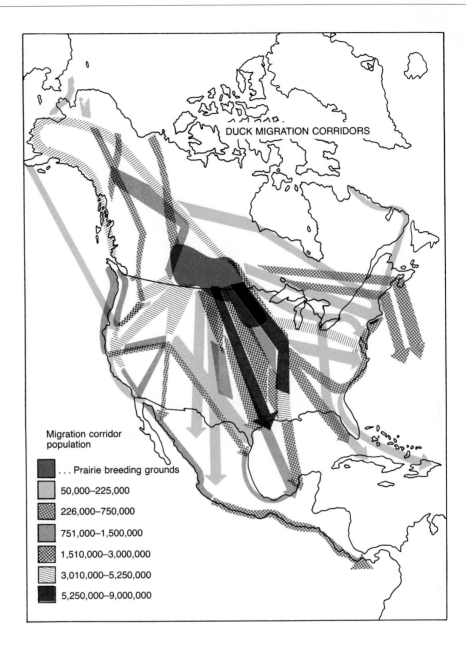

surveys conducted by the U.S. Fish and Wildlife Service and the National Audubon Society. These surveys have shown that the populations of most nongame birds are fairly stable. Indeed, the annual Christmas Bird Censuses conducted by the National Audubon Society have shown that hawk populations are on the rebound after being decimated by pesticide contamination of their food chains in the 1950s and 1960s. On the other hand, populations of many species of vireos, tanagers, and flycatchers, which winter in Central and South America, are declining. Many biologists attribute this to the destruction of tropical forest habitat on the wintering range of these species by slash-and-burn farmers and ranchers, as described in Chapter 12.

Population Decline of Great Lakes Birds

Several species of fish-eating birds of the Great Lakes have suffered dramatic population declines in the last two decades. The suspected cause is their consumption of fish contaminated with toxic chemicals such as PCBs and dioxin. Female birds transmit the poisons to their eggs. A survey conducted by John Giesy, professor of wildlife management at Michigan State University, revealed toxic chemicals in the eggs of fish-eating birds throughout the Great Lakes. Among the species most strongly affected are cormorants, terns, and gulls. Many of the poisoned eggs never hatch. Many of the chicks that do emerge from the egg cannot survive due to gross deformities. The abnormalities are crossed bills, club feet, dwarfed wings, and lack of eyes and skull. The incidence of these deformities has increased 30-fold in the last 40 years.

The restoration of the populations of these threatened species poses a formidable and ongoing challenge to state and federal wildlife managers. The eventual solution to the problem, of course, depends on the cleanup of the chemical pollution of the Great Lakes.

RAPID REVIEW

1. The *habitat* of a wild animal provides certain essentials: shelter, food, water, breeding sites, and a territory.

2. Wildlife population densities tend to be higher in areas where there is a large amount of interspersion of plant communities, or edge.

3. A *home range* is the area over which an animal habitually travels while engaged in its usual activities.

4. A *territory* is any area that is defended.

5. Bird territories may have the following functions: (a) provide a food source, (b) control infectious diseases by dispersing birds, (c) establish and maintain the pair bond, (d) reduce interference with breeding activities, and (e) reduce predation.

6. Four types of movements in wild animals are (a) dispersal of young, (b) mass emigration, (c) latitudinal migration, and (d) altitudinal migration.

7. The movements of animals promote survival by providing (a) supplies of food and water and (b) a hospitable climate.

8. The dispersal of young animals, such as muskrats and grouse, apparently is a mechanism that reduces competition for limited food supplies by reducing population density.

9. During one severe winter in Michigan, more than 115,000 deer died—one third directly from starvation and the remainder from predation and disease for which malnutrition had set the stage.

10. Emergency feeding of starving deer is not a sound management practice because it facilitates the spread of disease and is very costly.

11. Dogs are the most important predators of deer.

12. Waterfowl populations are affected by (a) wetland drainage, (b) drought, (c) oil pollution, (d) lead poisoning, (e) botulism, (f) acid precipitation, and other factors.

13. More than 50 percent of the waterfowl in North America are raised on tiny 0.5 to 1 hectare potholes (1.2 to 2.4 acres).

14. Pothole drainage has reduced North American waterfowl production from 15 million to 5 million ducks annually.

15. Lead poisoning killed 2–3 percent of our nation's waterfowl annually up to the mid-1980s.

16. Water fowl destruction by oil pollution will probably increase as more off-shore oil wells are drilled and tanker traffic increases.

17. Lead shot will be completely phased out nationwide by 1991.

18. Botulism may kill 100,000 waterfowl in California and in Utah per year.

19. Botulism may be prevented by rapidly raising the water level of a marsh so that *Clostridium* does not have good conditions for reproduction.

20. Two major wildlife management techniques are (a) habitat development and (b) regulation of wildlife populations.

21. Current hunting and trapping regulations place restrictions on the (a) species and numbers of individuals taken, (b) the season and time of day, and (c) the type of firearm or trap used.

22. The federal wildlife refuge system includes more than 350 refuges. Most of them are designed for waterfowl.

23. The best strategy for increasing wildlife populations is to increase the amount and quality of habitat.

24. Young stands of aspen supply nearly all the food, cover, and breeding requirements of ruffed grouse.

25. The carrying capacity of aspen forests for grouse is increased more than 600 percent when blocks of aspen are clearcut as 10, 20, and 30 years of age.

26. The average fur trapper catches about 112 animals yearly—most of them being raccoon, muskrat, and red fox.

KEY WORDS AND PHRASES

Acid deposition
Altitudinal migration
Artificial islands
Artificial nest sites
Artificial ponds
Biotic potential
Bird banding

Botulism
Climax species
Compensatory mortality
Conservation Reserve
 Program (CRP)
Consumptive use
Cover

Density-dependent factor
Density-independent
  factor
Dispersal of young
Duck stamps
Early successional species
Edge effect
Environmental resistance
Euryphagous species
Exotic species
Habitat development
Home range
Irruption
Latitudinal migration
Lead poisoning
Living fence
Low-succession species
Mass emigration

Mid-successional species
Migratory Bird Hunting
  Stamp Acts
Nature Conservancy
Nonconsumptive use
Nongame management
Pittman-Robertson Act
Pothole
Predator control
Rabies
Shelterbelt
Stenophagous species
Territory
Waterfowl council
Waterfowl flyway
Wildlife
Wildlife management
Wildlife refuge

QUESTIONS AND TOPICS FOR DISCUSSION

1. Compare stenophagous and euryphagous species. Give an example of each type.

2. Discuss the functions of territories.

3. Would you say that your college campus has a lot of edge? How does this edge increase survival for wildlife such as robins, squirrels, and rabbits?

4. What are the advantages of altitudinal and latitudinal migrations?

5. How can botulism be prevented or controlled?

6. What causes lead poisoning in waterfowl? How can it be prevented?

7. In what ways can acid deposition reduce waterfowl populations?

8. How can ecological succession be manipulated to improve wildlife habitat?

9. Discuss the importance of cooperation between forestry officials and wildlife managers in developing high-quality habitat for ruffed grouse.

10. Discuss the ecological and economic impacts of the American hunter.

11. Describe an example of destruction caused by waterfowl. How may such destruction be controlled?

SUGGESTED READINGS

Adam, N. "Hunting: An American Tradition." *The American Hunter* 16–17, 1982. Presents arguments supporting hunting in the United States.

Bellrose, F. C. *Ducks, Geese and Swans of North America.* Harrisburg, Pa.: Stackpole Books, 1976. The "bible" on waterfowl occurring in the United States. Excellent coverage of distribution, feeding habits, nesting behavior, migration, and mortality factors. Detailed maps of distribution and migration patterns.

Heberlein, T. A. "Stalking the Predator." *Environment* 29(7): 6–11, 30–34, 1987. A highly readable, in-depth profile of the American hunter. Discusses the ecological, economic, and social impacts of hunters in the United States.

Leopold, A. *A Sand County Almanac.* New York: Oxford University Press, 1949. A classic, written in almost poetic prose. The founder of game management provides intriguing insights into the relation between humans and wildlife.

Luoma, J. R. "Black Duck Decline: An Acid Rain Link." *Audubon* 89, 20, 22–24, 1987. Excellent nontechnical treatment of the way in which acid rain causes waterfowl population decline by disrupting protein food sources for young ducks.

Mitchell, J. G. "The Trapping Question: Soft Skins and Spring Steel." *Audubon* 84: 54–89, 1982. Interestingly written for the nonspecialist. Discusses the pros and cons of the fur-trapping controversy.

15

Pesticides: Protecting Our Crops, Our Health, and Our Environment

American industry annually produces 500,000 metric tons (1,200 million pounds) of **pesticides**, chemical substances that kill a variety of pests. Worth over $5 billion, these controversial chemicals are sprayed on crops, orchards, swamps, pastures, forests, gardens, and lawns the world over in a sometimes futile, often costly effort to control harmful insects, fungi, weeds, rodents, and other pests.

Despite their initial popularity, pesticides came under severe scrutiny in the United States in 1962 with the publication of the late Rachel Carson's *Silent Spring*. Despite increased awareness of the dangers of pesticide use and efforts to reduce our dependence on chemical pesticides, total pesticide use has nearly tripled since the early 1960s in the United States. This remarkable increase is largely due to a rise in herbicide use, which has increased sixfold in that period, while insecticide use has remained more or less constant.

As the use of these substances increases, so does the debate over several key questions: How effective are pesticides? How dangerous are they? Do alternatives exist? Are pesticides adequately regulated? This chapter examines these and a number of other important issues.

WHERE DO PESTS COME FROM?

In undisturbed ecosystems naturally occurring regulatory mechanisms keep populations in a dynamic equilibrium (Chapter 2). When humans intervene—say, by plowing up prairies and planting wheat or leveling forests and planting a single species of tree—they disrupt the complex ecological network (Figure 15-1). Lost are the density-dependent factors that keep populations in balance. The ecosystem is simplified. What is left is a greatly altered ecosystem composed of a single species, a **monoculture**, or a few species, where there once were several dozen. Vast expanses of genetically similar plants provide an enormous supply of food, tinder for an outbreak of a hungry pest species.

In simplified ecosystems, species that were once held in check by predators and restrained by a limited food supply proliferate madly. By reducing biological diversity, human civilization has inadvertently unleashed a force it now struggles to control. In the United States alone, 19,000 agricultural pests are known to exist. One thousand of these are considered major pests (Figure 15-2).

Pests may also arise from accidental or intentional introduction of insects or other organisms, as described

FIGURE 15-1   Monotype: a pest's paradise. Modern agriculture is based on the planting of mono-types—a vegetational plot made up of a single species of plant, such as the citrus trees shown in this photo of the irrigated Gila River Valley in Arizona.

in Chapter 13. In their new habitat, the aliens may find little environmental resistance. Populations explode, as illustrated by the gypsy moth (Figure 15-3).

In 1869 the pupae of the gypsy moth, a native of Europe, were shipped from France to Medford, Massachusetts, at the request of a French astronomer, Leopold Trouvelot, of Harvard University, who was interested in developing a disease-resistant silkworm moth. A few of the insects inadvertently escaped from captivity and made off into the woods, where they lived in relative obscurity. Twenty years later, however, the town of Medford was crawling with an enormous infestation of gypsy moth caterpillars. Released from their density-dependent control agents such as predators and parasites, which had kept this species in check in its native Europe, the gypsy moth population had exploded. One observer wrote, "the street was black with them . . . they were so thick on the trees that they stuck together like cold macaroni . . . the foliage was completely stripped from all the trees . . . presenting an awful picture of devastation." During the quiet of a summer's night, one could actually hear the sound of thousands of tiny mandibles shredding foliage in the trees. Pellets of waste excreted by the larvae rained down from the trees in a steady drizzle.

A single caterpillar can devour a square meter of foliage in a day. Although the larvae prefer oak leaves, they will also consume birch and ash foliage, and when fully grown they will even eat pine needles. Defoliation

sometimes kills trees outright. In other cases, it makes them more susceptible to fungus attack, winds, and drought. Several repeated seasons of defoliation will almost certainly kill them.

Since its escape from captivity, the gypsy moth has spread throughout the northeastern states and westward into Michigan, Wisconsin, Colorado, and California (Figure 15-4). Ironically, the spread of the moth to distant forests has been facilitated by recreational vehicles on which the moth frequently deposits its eggs.

In Colorado, a number of communities are now officially quarantined because of gypsy moths. Fearing further spread, California officials are now stopping Coloradans at the border to check their vehicles for eggs. California and other states that strictly enforce controls on gypsy moths require newcomers to be certified as free of them before they can enter the state. Such strict controls come in the wake of the severe outbreaks that occurred in 1980 in California and the northeastern United States. Trees were defoliated throughout a 2.5-million-hectare (5-million-acre) region from Maine to Maryland. Fruit farmers in Santa Barbara County in California feared that the caterpillars, if not controlled, would destroy their avocado and citrus trees.

Another alien species, whose impact has been strongly felt, is the fungus that causes Dutch elm disease. Accidentally introduced from Europe around 1933, the fungus thrives in the American elm, a tree

FIGURE 15-2   Insecticides are employed against the harmful species of insects shown here. Only 0.1 percent of the 800,000 species of insects in the world are considered harmful to humans.

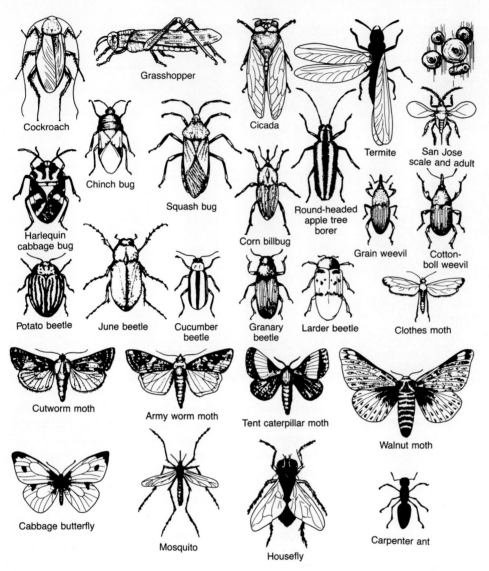

that, unlike its Dutch counterpart, is not resistant to this organism.

The American elm is a stately tree; it once graced parks, boulevards, college campuses, and suburbs throughout much of the eastern United States. Today most elms are either dead or dying of Dutch elm disease. The fungus kills trees quickly. In response to the fungus, the trees produce a number of chemicals that eventually clog the vessels carrying water from the roots to the limbs and leaves. As a result, photosynthesis stops and the tree dies. The spores of the fungus are spread by bark beetles and also from the roots of one tree to the roots of adjacent ones. Because it has been customary to plant elms in rows along residential streets, the fungus spreads rapidly from tree to tree. Attempts to stop it by killing the beetles with DDT are fruitless, and only succeed in killing many robins and other songbirds. By

1976, despite vigorous efforts to halt the disease, it had spread from Massachusetts south to Virginia and west to California. More than a million elms die each year. The lovely elms of Santa Rosa, California, once a tourist attraction, are now succumbing rapidly. In St. Paul and Minneapolis, authorities predict that all of the elms will be dead by 1989.

Alien species are a major problem in the United States. Today more than half of the weeds in the United States and many of the most destructive insect pests, such as the cotton boll weevil and the Mediterranean fruit fly, are foreigners.

HOW EFFECTIVE ARE PESTICIDES?

Each year, weeds, insects, fungi, bacteria, birds, and other pests destroy or consume 45 percent of the world's

FIGURE 15-3 Leaf-eating caterpillars of the gypsy moth damage hundreds of thousands of dollars worth of forest and shade trees in the northeastern states annually. They hatch in April from eggs laid the previous year.

food supply. Damage is much worse in the tropics, where two or three crops are grown on a field in a single year and where conditions are ripe for insect growth. But temperate countries still face enormous losses. In the United States, for example, pests annually destroy or consume 34 percent of crops and 9 percent of food at various stages after the harvest. Therefore, 43 percent of our food, worth an estimated $9 billion each year, is taken from us by pests.

How effective are the pesticides science has devised? Pest control works, to a degree, in the United States. Farmers and pesticide manufacturers argue that their toxic sprays have helped farmers produce more food on American farmland. According to the USDA, crop production per hectare in the United States has increased more than 70 percent in the past 30 years. In reality, however, only part of that increase is due to pesticide use; irrigation, fertilizers, and genetic improvements have made much larger contributions.

According to agricultural economists, each dollar invested in pesticides results in about $2 to $4 in improved yields. The Office of Technology Assessment estimates that without pesticides, we'd lose an additional 25–30 percent of our annual crop, livestock, and timber production (Figure 15-5). Without them, the

USDA estimates that food bills would be 50–75 percent higher. David Pimentel, a Cornell University expert on pest control, however, argues that these figures are exaggerated. A complete ban on pesticides, he says, would increase preharvest losses in the United States only 9 percent—from 33 to 45 percent.

Pesticides reduce damage and may have helped increase crop yields in the United States. They have also helped save millions of lives by killing insects like mosquitoes, lice, fleas, and tsetse flies, which can carry a number of fatal diseases. But in the past decade, scientists have noted that the effectiveness of these chemical weapons has steadily dwindled. In fact, despite continued pesticide use, insect damage to U.S. crops has doubled in the past 30 years. Why?

The reason is twofold. First, many insect pests have become resistant to insecticides. Each time a field is sprayed, a small percentage of the insect population survives because it is genetically resistant to the pesticide. This subset of the original population often flourishes in the absence of competition. To kill them and their offspring, farmers must spray again, using higher doses. The next application kills off much of the once genetically resistant population but again leaves behind a small number of increasingly resistant insects. In time they may flourish, creating a new and more troublesome pest. To combat it, higher doses or more frequent applications may be necessary. The net effect: New resistant strains develop and pesticide use skyrockets. This phenomenon is often called the **pesticide treadmill**. Once on this treadmill, farmers find it difficult to get off. They may switch to new pesticides, but genetic resistance invariably starts them on a new treadmill.

The rise in insect damage also results from the destruction of beneficial insects—that is, natural predators that help control the population of pests. Ladybugs, praying mantises, spiders, wasps, frogs, and birds are a few of the beneficial creatures that live among us. Free of charge, they rid our fields and lakes of potentially pesty insects. Poison them with pesticides and you destroy a helpful ally. Unleashed from their natural controls, resistant pest populations may surge. In California, the spider mite was once an innocuous insect held in check by its natural predators. Today it is the state's leading insect pest, causing over $116 million in damage each year because of pesticide use that destroyed its natural predators.

Pesticide use often results in increasing resistance and the loss of natural predators. In Nicaragua, for instance, farmers found that cotton fields in the 1960s, once sprayed 5 to 10 times a year, had to be sprayed 30 times a year to control insect pests genetically resistant to malathion and freed from predatory control. So bad had the insect problem become that cotton productivity, the mainstay of their economy, fell by 30 percent between 1960 and 1969. Rising insecticide use and falling

FIGURE 15-4   Spread of the gypsy moth, 1969–1977, shown by heavy black lines, from the general area of infestation in the Northeast. Male moths were trapped as far west as Wisconsin and as far south as Alabama. The oak forests shown on the map are potentially vulnerable to gypsy moth invasions.

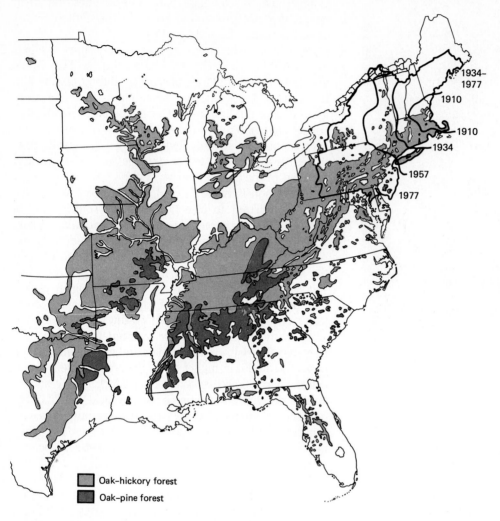

Oak–hickory forest
Oak–pine forest

productivity sent the cost of cotton production sky-ward.

Today 450–600 insect species are resistant to insecticides. Seventeen insect species are resistant to all insecticides, and that number is rapidly rising. According to David Pimentel, American farmers spend an additional $120 million a year on pesticides to battle genetically resistant insects. They spend another $150 million a year to destroy pests that have become troublesome because of the loss of natural predators. And if that's not enough, pesticides annually destroy 400,000 bee colonies in the United States. Bees pollinate many commercial crops, such as fruit trees. The destruction of these pollinators reduces crop yields, costing farmers an estimated $135 million a year.

Pesticides work in many cases, but their success is not uniform. Before we look further at the pros and cons of pesticide use, let us pause to examine the types of pesticides available today.

TYPES OF CHEMICAL PESTICIDES

A variety of chemical pesticides were used by farmers before World War II, such as arsenic mixed with ashes and hydrogen cyanide, but these substances were often highly toxic to people or ineffective against pests. In 1939, a Swiss scientist, Paul Müller, discovered that DDT, a **chlorinated hyrocarbon**, was a powerful insecticide. He started a revolution in agriculture with impacts as far-reaching as those of any technology introduced in human history.

Chlorinated Hydrocarbons

DDT was followed by a string of chlorinated hydrocarbons, such as endrin, dieldrin, mirex, heptachlor, and kepone, all of which have since been banned or severely restricted in the United States. DDT swept the market. It proved to be an extraordinary ally. It also worked well against a variety of insects, saving crops literally on the

FIGURE 15-5 Benefits derived from insecticides. Untreated cotton on the left yielded only one quarter bale per hectare. Cotton on the right, treated with insecticide, yielded 2.5 bales per hectare.

brink of destruction. The potent insecticide was used to delouse soldiers during World War II and to control the malaria-carrying mosquito in the tropics. So effective was it in malarial control that the incidence worldwide dropped to almost nothing. In India, for instance, the number of cases of malaria fell from 1 million per year in the 1950s to 50,000 in 1961. Few people questioned the wisdom of the Nobel Prize selection committee when they announced that Muller would receive the coveted award in 1944.

However, biological studies of the effects of DDT and other similar pesticides caused scientists and public policymakers to question whether the damage caused by this chemical marvel might outweigh its benefits.

Like other chlorinated hydrocarbons, DDT persists in the environment for many years because bacteria lack the enzymes needed to break it down. Some experts believe that DDT may persist for 15 to 25 years (Figure 15-6). Today, despite its banning in 1972, DDT and its breakdown product, DDE, which is equally harmful, can still be found in the mud on the bottoms of American lakes and rivers.

DDT also **bioaccumulates**—that is, builds up in body tissues, especially fat (Figures 15-7 and 15-8). Because it is fat soluble, it may remain in fat tissues for decades. And to make matters worse, DDT and other chlorinated hydrocarbons are **biomagnified**—that is, they build up in food chains, so that the highest-level consumers have

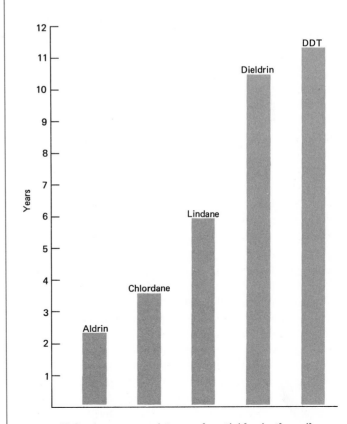

FIGURE 15-6   Average persistence of pesticides in the soil.

FIGURE 15-7 Biological magnification: the increasing concentration of toxic chemicals, such as DDT, in the food chain. A given organism takes in large amounts of contaminated food. Much of the food may not be converted into protoplasm but may be burned up as fuel during respiration, or may be excreted as waste. However, the load of pollutant, such as DDT, that was taken into the body along with the food may remain inside the cells of the organism's body. As a result, the concentration of the pollutant increases progressively from link to link in the food chain.

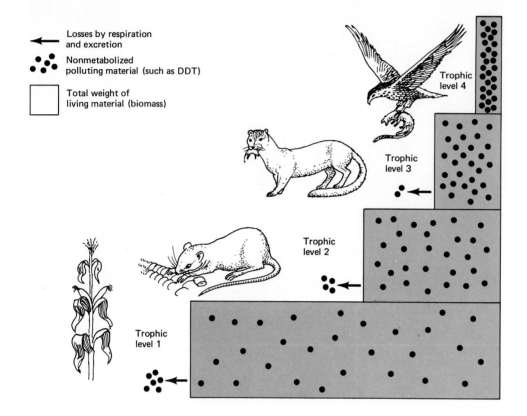

levels hundreds of thousands, sometimes millions, of times higher than that in the environment.

These problems and others described in the section on the hazards of pesticides caused a furor the world over. As the evidence grew, it became clear that the chlorinated hydrocarbons were too risky to use. Consequently, chemists introduced a new variety of pesticides, the **organic phosphates**.

Organic Phosphates

Malathion and parathion are the two best-known organic phosphates. Much more quickly degraded in the environment and unlikely to bioaccumulate and biomagnify, these substances were thought to be a safer substitute for the chlorinated hydrocarbons. However, experience soon showed that these nerve poisons, even at low levels, were too dangerous to use. Even slight exposure could lead to dizziness, vomiting, cramps, headaches, and difficulty in breathing. Higher levels led to convulsions and death. Like the chlorinated hydrocarbons, many of the organic phosphates have disappeared from the shelves or have been severely restricted in the United States.

Carbamates

Fighting increasing genetic resistance to pests and looking for a class of chemicals that biodegraded rather quickly and was safer to use, pesticide manufacturers developed a whole new line of chemicals called **carbamates**. Perhaps the best known is the commercial preparation called Sevin (carbaryl). The carbamates persist in the environment but only for a few days to 2 weeks at most, and are therefore called **nonpersistent pesticides**. They are nerve poisons like the chlorinated hydrocarbons and organic phosphates.

HOW HAZARDOUS ARE PESTICIDES?

Pests cause enormous amounts of economic damage, irritation, pain, sickness, and even death. By one estimate, rodents, weeds, and insects in the United States annually cause $2 billion, $5 billion, and $7 billion worth of damage, respectively. As already noted, in the United States, pests of various sorts consume or destroy about 43 percent of the annual food production. Ten

FIGURE 15-8 Food web of the march ecosystem off Long Island, which had been sprayed with DDT for mosquito control. Note the biological magnification of DDT as it moved up the food web. The greatest concentrations were found in the fatty tissues of fish-eating birds, such as gulls and mergansers.

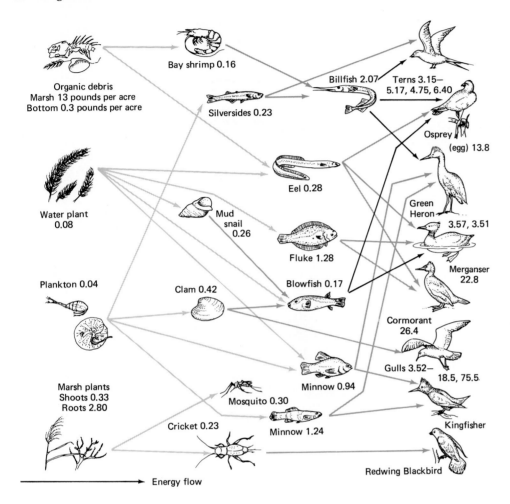

percent of the average annual cotton crop in the United States is destroyed by a single insect species, the cotton boll weevil (Figure 15-9). According to the U.S. Forest Service, pests destroy 5 billion board feet of timber annually.

It is no wonder, then, that humankind has developed its arsenal of chemical pesticides. What better way to increase crop yields and control diseases?

To assess the usefulness of pesticides adequately, however, we must look at the hazards they create and weigh the risks against the benefits.

Each year Americans apply 340 million kilograms (750 million pounds) of pesticides on their farms, forests, golf courses, roadways, rivers, lawns, and gardens (Figure 15-10). That's about 370 grams per hectare if it were evenly applied to the land area of the United States. In reality, however, not all land is treated. Fields that are treated, for instance, may receive 3 to 18 times that amount (1,100 to 6,700 grams per hectare). What is more, according to the EPA, homeowners often apply pesticides at a rate 5 to 10 times greater than farmers do.

Pesticides end up on American soils and in our water, on our food, in our wildlife, and in our people. It is this widespread contamination that worries biologists and health officials—and for just cause (see "Case History: The Kepone Story in Virginia").

Human Health Effects

Western Colorado fruit grower Dorsey Chism's health took a turn for the worse in 1984. Once a happy, optimistic man, he became irrational and depressed. His face and body became bloated, and he was constantly short of breath. Local doctors thought he had emphysema. In August, after years of spraying his fruit trees with pesticides, sometimes without a protective mask or clothing, Chism went into convulsions and was rushed to Aspen Valley hospital, where he spent 14 days in intensive care. There a doctor familiar with the

FIGURE 15-9 Cotton boll weevil attacking cotton boll. Ten percent of the average cotton crop in the United States is destroyed by this weevil. Pesticides have been employed to control its populations.

health effects of chemical toxins diagnosed his illness as chronic pesticide poisoning. In 1985 Chism died after months of lingering near death hooked up to an oxygen tank.

Chism is not alone. Lewis Regenstein, author of *America the Poisoned*, claims that at least 100,000 Americans are poisoned each year. The National Coalition Against the Misuse of Pesticides puts the number higher—300,000. Most of them are farm and factory workers exposed to high levels. The National Agricultural Chemicals Association, an industry group, claims that the figure is no higher than 20,000 a year. In fact, no precise figures on farm worker poisonings are available; the government does not keep them. There is good reason to believe that the higher estimates are accurate. In California, for instance, the only state that keeps such figures, 1,400 people are poisoned seriously enough to be reported each year. These official figures may grossly understate the real rate. For example, in a 1976 incident in Madera, California, 118 workers were poisoned but only six cases made the official list. In September 1978, pesticides sprayed on cotton fields drifted to nearby schools, causing respiratory difficulties in children. The incident was serious enough to merit closing the school for a week, but not one case made the official list. By some estimates, fewer than 1 percent of California's poisonings are reported.

All told, 200 to 1,000 Americans like Chism die each year from pesticide poisoning. Worldwide, half a million people are poisoned by pesticides. These poisonings result in 5,000 to 14,000 immediate deaths and numerous chronic and fatal illnesses.

FIGURE 15-10 Aerial spraying of sulfur, a fungicide, in order to check mildew on grapevines, twenty miles south of Fresno, California, May 1972.

Many doctors now believe that general maladies such as dizziness, insomnia, indigestion, and frequent headaches may be caused by ingesting pesticides in food. This promoted a *U.S. News and World Report* writer to write: "When an American sits down to a typical breakfast, chances are the menu includes bug spray, weed killer, an embalming agent, and arsenic."

A recent study by the National Academy of Sciences, released in May 1987, estimates that pesticides contaminating the most common American foods could cause as many as 20,000 cases of cancer a year in the United States, costing $1.1 billion in health care costs in 1980 dollars. Tomatoes, beef, potatoes, oranges, lettuce, apples, and peaches topped the list. Dr. Marshall Madell summed this situation aptly. "Future historians will say we were foolhardy. We sprayed our food with posion, then ate it."

Pesticide residues on food may be minute, but these chemicals can build up in body tissues and cause cancer, birth defects, and other problems. In 1984, for instance,

FIGURE 15-11 Avenues for the dispersal of pesticides, such as DDT, once they are released. Average values for DDT concentrations are indicated.

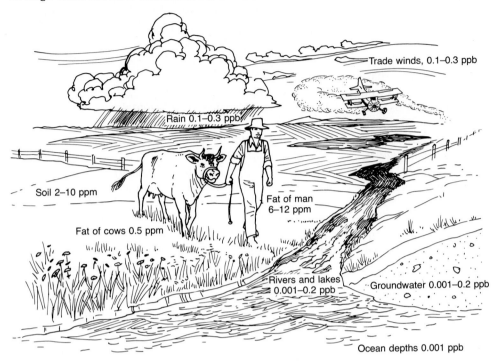

Trade winds, 0.1–0.3 ppb

Rain 0.1–0.3 ppb

Soil 2–10 ppm

Fat of man 6–12 ppm

Fat of cows 0.5 ppm

Rivers and lakes 0.001–0.2 ppb

Groundwater 0.001–0.2 ppb

Ocean depths 0.001 ppb

a University of Hawaii researcher discovered that birth defects were higher in the offspring of women who ingested milk contaminated with heptachlor, a chlorinated hydrocarbon, than in women whose milk was free of the contaminant.

In 1970, a sampling of 1,400 Americans showed that they had nearly 8 ppm of DDT in their body fat (Figure 15-11). In 1983, 11 years after DDT was banned, the level was 1.7 ppm. What the long-term effects are, no one knows. Dieldrin, chlordane, heptachlor, and others long since banned or restricted also persist in our bodies.

Herbicides, applied to fields to destroy weeds, have also been linked to a growing number of problems. For instance, two growth stimulators, 2,4-D and 2,4,5-T, which increase the metabolic activity of cells so much that the plant cannot keep up, have been linked to one form of cancer in farm workers. Shelia Hoar, a University of Kansas researcher, found that farmers and farm workers exposed to the herbicide 2,4-D for 20 days or more a year were six times more likely to develop non-Hodgkin's lymphoma than nonfarm workers. Furthermore, she found that those who were most often in contact with the chemical—for example, those who mixed it—were eight times more likely to develop this disease than nonfarm workers. In 1978 Bonnie Hixl, a young mother who lives in Alsea, Oregon, complained to the EPA that she and seven other women had aborted 10 times in 5 years. Researchers

sent to study the problem showed that spontaneous abortions occurred most frequently in these women shortly after the forests were sprayed with the herbicide 2,4,5-T to control brush growth. Although it was not certain that a cause-and-effect relationship existed, the government banned the use of this chemical for brush control.

Far better known are the multitude of health problems that resulted from the use of Agent Orange, a 50:50 mixture of 2,4-D and 2,4,5-T, during the Vietnam War. This chemical was used to defoliate trees along rivers, roadways, and around camps to reduce the chances of ambush of American soldiers and their allies. In some cases, it was sprayed on crops that could have been used to feed the enemy soldiers.

Millions of kilograms were sprayed during the war, and not long after the sprayings began, problems started to arise. Studies showed that Agent Orange was contaminated with a toxic substance called **dioxin**, believed to be largely responsible for the many health problems reported by soldiers and Vietnamese citizens. Dioxin is a potent toxic substance that causes birth defects and cancer in mice and rats.

In 1969 a Saigon newspaper reported that Vietnamese soldiers and villagers developed serious health effects and linked them to the chemical defoliants being liberally sprayed on their land. The newspaper report claimed that miscarriages and birth defects had increased in villages. Initially dismissed as propaganda, the report soon caused a furor in the United States, prompting steps to ban the use of Agent Orange in the war and some uses of 2,4,5-T in the United States.

American soldiers began complaining of numerous maladies as well—dizziness, nausea, insomnia, diarrhea, and chloracne. Soon thereafter, doctors found that the rates of certain cancers (for example, testicular cancer) were higher in Vietnam vets than in the general public and that many men who had been exposed to Agent Orange fathered children with birth defects. Health officials denied the validity of veterans' complaints, attributing many of them to stress caused by the war and fearing massive settlements in compensation for this nation's use of Agent Orange. Growing evidence, however, strongly suggests that Agent Orange was indeed the culprit. One study of 40,000 Vietnamese couples, performed by Vietnamese doctors, showed that women whose husbands had fought in areas sprayed with the defoliant were 3.5 times more likely to miscarry or give birth to babies with birth defects than women whose husbands had been lucky enough to avoid these regions.

In 1984 the Veterans Administration (VA) announced that it had reached an out-of-court settlement with veterans. The VA established a $180 million fund to compensate victims.

Pesticides are now becoming a major health concern in cities and suburbs, where they are used on gardens, trees, parks, and golf courses to control a host of insect pests. For years, pest control agents sprayed suburban areas to control mosquitoes, but they did so usually at night and raised only occasional protest. In recent years, however, a commercial lawn care industry has sprouted, skyrocketing from a smattering of small businesses in 1980 to a $1.3 billion industry in 1986, and creating a storm of protest. One Colorado woman, for instance, was sprayed by a careless applicator as she rode by on her bicycle. Her tongue went numb and her head ached for 3 days after the incident. Children are generally more sensitive and sometimes experience extreme reactions to pesticides, including difficulty in breathing. Playing on a recently treated lawn can cause severe chemical burns as well. Adults suffer from headaches, dizziness, and nausea after their lawns are sprayed with pesticides.

In 1982, Navy Lt. George Prior, an avid golfer, died after a severe reaction to a chemical pesticide (chlorothalonil) applied to a golf course. In response to this incident and to reports of bird kills and groundwater contamination, the EPA launched a study of pesticides on golf courses. The EPA's report noted that this nation's 13,000 golf courses annually apply 5,500 metric tons (12 million pounds) of 126 different pesticides to control weeds and insects.

Effects on Fish and Wildlife

Pesticides affect fish and wildlife as well. Tributyl tin (TBT), for example, is a potent biotoxin added to paint that is applied to ships to prevent the buildup of marine algae and barnacles. These organisms increase a ship's drag and therefore decrease its speed and fuel efficiency. The U.S. Navy estimates that if the entire fleet were painted with TBT-containing paints its fuel bill would fall by 15 percent, saving $150 million a year. Underwater cleanings would also be reduced, saving additional money.

Unfortunately, TBT is released from the paint and pollutes bays and harbors. In France, TBT from recreational watercraft caused massive reproductive failure in commercially important oyster beds in 1980 and 1981. Banning the use of this chemical on pleasure craft less than 25 meters in length resulted in an abrupt turnabout. Oyster reproduction resumed in 1982 and has continued ever since. In sections of San Francisco Bay, TBT levels are as high as 500 parts per trillion. Mussels, barnacles, and other marine organisms are missing from the waters.

Pesticides and other chemical pollutants are also believed to be responsible for an epidemic of fish cancers in waters of the United States. In Puget Sound, for instance, 70 percent of the English sole have liver cancer. Similar findings have been made in a number of U.S. rivers. These tumors probably result from pesticides, heavy metals, and other toxic chemicals.

Pesticides kill beneficial insects like honeybees and praying mantises, as well as birds, as described earlier. In the United States, insects pollinate about one-third of our crops. An estimated 400,000 bee colonies are destroyed or severely damaged each year.

In the 1960s and 1970s, DDT was responsible for drastic reductions in the populations of a number of flesh-eating birds. Hardest hit were peregrine falcons, ospreys, brown pelicans, and eagles (Figures 15-12 and 15-13). Biomagnified in the food chain, DDT reached high levels in fish and insectivorous birds. Predatory birds that preyed on fish and other birds, being highest on the food chain, ended up with extremely high concentrations of DDT in their tissues. DDT levels in the predatory birds were not high enough to kill adults, but they had a severe impact on reproduction. Researchers found that DDT decreases calcium deposition during eggshell formation. As a result, eggshells in DDT-contaminated peregrine falcons and other species became thin and were easily broken by the parents (Figure 15-14). The fragile eggs cracked during incubation and killed the embryos. As a result, hatching decreased. By the time scientists had discovered the problem, none of the 200 breeding pairs east of the Mississippi River was able to produce young. Peregrine populations in Europe and the western United States had fallen by 60–

FIGURE 15-12   Down and out? Pesticides are responsible for the drastic decline of the peregrine falcon in the United States. This bird is being studied at the Patuxent Wildlife Research Center, Laurel, Maryland.

FIGURE 15-13   Our nation's symbol, the bald eagle, has been placed on the official list of endangered species. Its decline has correlated closely with the volume of chlorinated hydrocarbon pesticides, such as DDT, occurring in its environment.

FIGURE 15-14   Newly hatched bald eagle in nest. One egg has not hatched. DDT-contamination of the eagle's food chain has caused an eggshell-thinning. Sometimes the embryos inside the abnormal eggs are crushed under the weight of the incubating female.

Case History: The Kepone Story in Virginia

As previously described, extensive contamination of the ecosystem with pesticides has occurred as the result of their agricultural use. Occasionally, however, gross contamination results from the ignorance, mismanagement, or irresponsibility of the pesticide producers. In July 1975, Kepone, a previously little-known insecticide, became almost a household word. Newspapers, radio, and television highlighted accounts of an environmental disaster that resulted from the discharge of Kepone waste into the James River in Virginia and ultimately into the richly productive estuarine habitat of Chesapeake Bay. The Kepone originated at Hopewell, Virginia, in a small, makeshift plant operating in a crudely converted gas station. There the Life Science Products Company, a subsidiary of Allied Chemical, produced over 1.7 million pounds of the extremely toxic chemical over a period of 16 months. Kepone was being used in ant and roach bait and to destroy pests of bananas. Most of it was exported.

Kepone is a chlorinated hydrocarbon insecticide closely related to DDT. As expected, it has many of DDT's undesirable properties, such as persistence, mobility, biological magnification, and fat solubility.

Kepone-contaminated waste was discharged from the plant into Hopewell's municipal sewage system. Sewage containing relatively high levels of Kepone was released into the James River in this manner for a period of 9 years, first by Allied Chemical and later by the Life Science Products Company. Environmental authorities first became aware of the slipshod operation of the Life Science plant shortly after a local physician discovered that one of the plant employees was suffering from a nervous disorder that caused him to tremble uncontrollably. Analysis of this worker's blood showed a high level (7.5 ppm) of Kepone. Of the 150 employees who were later examined by the Virginia State Health Department, 50 showed Kepone-related toxicity symptoms, such as blurred vision, loss of memory, and chest pains. Eventually, after investigators found Kepone dust almost everywhere in the plant, Life Science Products closed its doors forever.

The discharge of 100,000 pounds of Kepone waste into the James River contaminated a 100-mile stretch of the river downstream from Hopewell and much of the Chesapeake Bay area near the river's mouth. Because Kepone, like DDT, is not very soluble in water, it accumulated in the mud of the river bed. Kepone was gradually released from this stream-bottom reservoir, taken up by the bodies of plankton, and then moved up the food chain to contaminate commercially valuable fish, crabs, and oysters. A 2-year fish-monitoring program (1978–1980) conducted by Virginia health officials indicated that Kepone levels were gradually dropping. As a result, the 5-year ban on commercial fishing in the James River was lifted by the Virginia Board of Health. Heavy pressure from the seafood industry may have been a factor in the decision. Nevertheless, there were still some unanswered questions about the safety of eating James River fish. For example, David Stroube, Virginia's director of health protection, cautioned pregnant women against including the fish in their diet.

Many lawsuits relating to the Kepone pollution episode made their way through the courts. Allied Chemical received the stiffest federal penalty ever levied in the United States for the violation of antipollution laws: a fine of $13.2 million. The State of Virginia fined Allied Chemical $5.2 million. But that is not all. More than 10,000 fishermen, restaurant owners, resort proprietors, commercial oyster farmers, and others whose financial interests were damaged by the Kepone contamination sued Allied Chemical for $8 billion in damages in a mammoth collective-action suit. The courts, however, required Allied Chemical to pay only $500 million. The irony is that a modest expenditure of only $200,000 by the company could have prevented the incident in the first place.

90 percent. By 1970, the outlook for this regal bird was bleak. The bald eagle and brown osprey met similar fates. Today, thanks to captive breeding programs at Cornell University and Colorado State University, hundreds of peregrine falcons have been released into the wild. Free of DDT, the birds may well be able to reestablish their population. Ospreys, eagles, and brown pelicans also appear to have weathered the storm and are now making remarkable recoveries.

DDT, which was used in a vain attempt to kill the elm bark beetles thought to be responsible for the spread of Dutch elm disease, has also been linked to the death of thousands of robins and other insect-eating songbirds. Many birds died in convulsions shortly after eating insects freshly taken from sprayed trees. Others died from eating earthworms that had been contaminated by DDT. Researchers found that DDT remained on the lower sides of leaves throughout the summer despite rains. The leaves shed in the fall decomposed, contributing their DDT to the soil. DDT was taken up by earthworms, which feed on a steady diet of soil. Shortly after the summer spraying, scientists found that worms contained 4 to 400 ppm of DDT. A hungry bird returning in the spring would succumb from eating 11 worms—an hour's snack for a hungry robin. Up to 744 ppm of DDE (a breakdown product of DDT) have been found in the tissues of dead robins.

DO ALTERNATIVES EXIST?

Although chemical pesticides may substantially reduce a pest population, the success of an application is frequently only temporary. The pest population often rebounds because of the destruction of predatory insects and of genetic resistance. Such short-term successes are often costly to the ecosystem, causing widespread contamination of insects, birds, mammals, and human beings. Pesticides pose a substantial risk to the health of the world's people, especially chemical workers and farm workers. But people living in heavily sprayed rural areas may also be exposed to toxic levels because 50 to 75 percent of the spray never reaches the crop; instead, it drifts away to contaminate surrounding fields and homes. Farm workers in Third World nations, where worker protection is woefully inadequate, are at highest risk. Increasingly, urban residents are being poisoned by pesticides. But are there alternatives? And are they reliable and economical?

Fortunately, there are many alternatives to chemical pesticides. And many of them are highly effective and safer to human health and the environment. Indeed, the USDA's pest control program now spends nearly 70 percent of its money on nonpesticide approaches. Even some large chemical companies, like Monsanto, have begun to look for potentially less harmful ways to control pests.

Pest control today often takes an integrated approach to management, called **integrated pest management**, which capitalizes on four major strategies: environmental controls, genetic controls, chemical controls, and cultural control.

Environmental Controls

Environmental controls are measures that alter the biotic and abiotic environments of the pest. The most important means of environmental control are (1) crop rotation, (2) heteroculture, (3) trap crops, and (4) natural predators, parasites, and disease organisms. These measures are often simple, highly effective, inexpensive, and environmentally benign.

CROP ROTATION. Farmers use crop rotation to reduce soil erosion and increase soil fertility. As an added benefit, they find that this measure helps control pests as well. Why? Many pest species are highly specialized; they feed on one or a few species of crop plants. For example, the alfalfa weevil feeds mainly on alfalfa, the corn rootworm feeds primarily on corn, and so on. If a farmer plants corn on the same plot year after year, the corn rootworm population has little trouble satisfying its needs; a given field can support a large population. Damage would be high without pesticides. If, however, a farmer alternates corn with oats, rootworm populations can be kept low. During the "oat years," the corn rootworm's food supply is greatly diminished on that particular farm. Food becomes a limiting factor. As a result, its population greatly declines. Research has shown that alternating potatoes with alfalfa tends to reduce wireworm populations, which infest potatoes.

HETEROCULTURE. Single-crop farming simplifies the ecosystem, creating something of a "garden of Eden" for pests. Heteroculture, planting several crops on a farm instead of one large crop, is an excellent alternative that can greatly reduce pest damage. In some instances, farmers plant two different crops in alternating strips. Called **intercropping**, this method can reduce insect damage. For instance, intercropping corn and peanuts has been shown to reduce corn borers by 80 percent. Biologists do not know why it works, but they suggest that the peanuts provide habitat for predatory insects that feed on corn borers.

TRAP CROPS. Farmers can lure insects from commercially valuable crops by planting low-value trap crops nearby. For example, alfalfa may be used to lure the lygus bug from cotton, where it can cause substantial damage. In Hawaii, fields of melons and squash are bordered by rows of corn, which attract melon flies. Insecticides can then be sprayed on the trap crop to kill pests. Or, to avoid pesticide use, farmers may plow the insect-infested trap crop under or burn it. In Nicaragua, a major exporter of cotton, long stuck on the pesticide treadmill, farmers are required by law to cut and plow cotton stalks after the harvest to reduce boll weevil damage. Many also plant postharvest trap crops of cotton to attract the harmful boll weevils, which are then destroyed by insecticides. Insecticide use is greatly reduced and environmental contamination is minimized.

INTRODUCING PREDATORS, PARASITES, AND DISEASE ORGANISMS. By alternating crops, intercropping, and planting trap crops, farmers can reduce pesticide use. This may help restore the populations of predatory insects and birds that feed on harmful pests.

Farmers may also intentionally introduce these biological control agents to help reduce pest problems. The deliberate introduction of natural control agents, such as predators, parasites, and diseases, is one form of environmental control called **biological control**. This

FIGURE 15-15 Classic biological control resulting in total elimination of an insect pest as an economic problem. Biological control agents include viruses, predators, and parasites.

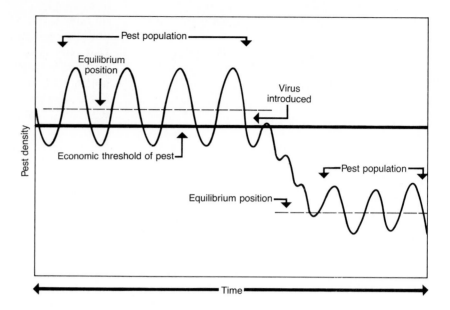

form of pest control artificially alters the biotic environment of a pest, creating additional environmental resistance to the pest population. What is more, once a natural predator or parasite is established in a farm ecosystem, it may survive and prosper from year to year, holding pest species in check without the use of costly pesticides (Figure 15-15).

Several hundred species of insects, viruses, and bacteria can be used to control pests (Figure 15-16). The first major success occurred late in the nineteenth century when agricultural scientists introduced the vedalin beetle from Australia to California to control an insect, the cottony-cushion scale, which was destroying the state's citrus crop. Since then, several hundred other parasites and predators have been successfully introduced into the United States to protect a

wide range of crops including olives, alfalfa, apples, and corn. In California, for instance, entomologists from the University of California–Davis introduced several parasitic wasps from Iran, Iraq, and Pakistan to control a pesty insect called *olive scale*, which once caused severe damage. Today these natural enemies control the olive scale completely. In Colorado, peach growers have long enjoyed the protection of a natural insect predator that is released in their orchards by state officials. The predator is grown at the state's insectary and released each year in orchards where it feeds on the oriental fruit moth, a pesty insect that bores into peaches, where it is safe from pesticides, and ruins the fruit. Colorado's insectary also releases eight species of parasites to control the alfalfa weevil. Collectively, these parasites control about 40 percent of the pest population, which, by

FIGURE 15-16 Fluctuations in population density of the cottony cushion scale on citrus trees in California. The scale pest, which was introduced accidentally in 1868, increased explosively until 1889, when species of predator ladybugs were released to control the scale insects. Unfortunately, when DDT was used on citrus trees in 1947, the scale populations again increased dramatically as a result of the destruction of ladybug populations.

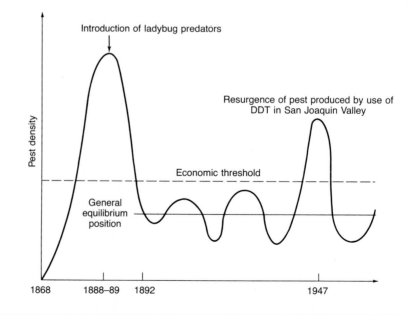

one estimate, could increase alfalfa hay production by as much as $12 million annually.

The Russian aphid, a tiny insect that sucks the juices out of wheat plants, causing considerable damage, is a serious crop pest. In 1986, Colorado farmers applied $1 million worth of insecticide to control the aphid. Scientists now are trying to control it by introducing three species of lady bugs that prey on aphids. When established, officials believe, the lady bugs could provide a permanent solution to the aphid problem.

Bacteria and other microorganisms can also be used to control harmful pests. For example, farmers, gardeners, and foresters now use a bacterium called *Bacillus thuringiensis* (BT) to control leaf-eating caterpillars. BT spores are sold as a powder that can be applied to fields and forests in large quantities. The spores are then eaten as the caterpillars devour the leaves of trees and crops. Inside the caterpillars' stomachs, however, the spores hatch and release a toxic protein that kills the hungry pests.

BT has been used successfully to control pine caterpillars and cabbage army worms in China. In the northeastern United States, it is being used to help control gypsy moths, which feed primarily on leaves from deciduous trees but, when hungry enough, devour conifers as well. California has used BT for nearly two and a half decades to control a number of caterpillars and mosquitoes, helping the state cut its insecticide use. For a discussion on the way Australia gained control of its burgeoning rabbit population, see "Controlling Rabbits with Viruses."

Biological control, while effective in many instances, has at least two important limitations. First, it is slower than conventional pesticides. When an insect population explodes, farmers may not have enough time to wait for natural predators to be introduced into their fields and to gain control. By the time they do, the field may be devastated. To compensate for this, farmers must carefully monitor pests and time the release of biological control agents to avoid outbreaks. Second, alien species introduced as biological control agents can become pests in their own right. Years of research are needed to avoid creating additional pests. Regardless, biological control agents, combined with crop rotation, heteroculture, and other techniques, can provide an important measure of protection.

Genetic Controls

Another method of control involves genetic manipulation and is called **genetic control**. At least two such methods exist: genetic resistance and the sterile-male technique.

GENETIC RESISTANCE. Chapter 6 described ways that scientists are developing high-yield crops through genetic engineering and plant breeding programs. They are also working on ways to make plants resistant to insect pests. Today, thanks to this work, much of the wheat planted in the United States is resistant to the Hessian fly, once a notoriously destructive insect causing several hundred million dollars worth of damage a year. Scientists have also developed strains of cotton, soybeans, alfalfa, and potatoes that are resistant to leafhoppers.

Combined with other control measures, genetic resistance provides an environmentally safe method of reducing pest damage while protecting the environment. Through genetic engineering, described in Chapter 6, new strains could be rapidly produced, bringing closer the day when chemical pesticide use is greatly reduced or, in some cases, eliminated entirely.

STERILE-MALE TECHNIQUE. Many female insects breed only once in their lifetime. If this mating is infertile, say because the male is sterile, the female produces no young. Knowing this, scientists devised an ingenious method of control called the *sterile-male technique*, which they have used to control several species of harmful insects. The most notable is the screwworm fly—an insect approximately three times the size of a house fly.

The screwworm fly is widely distributed in South America, Central America, and Mexico and ranges northward into Georgia, Florida, Alabama, Texas, Arizona, New Mexico, and California. During the winter, the fly is restricted to the southern portions of these states.

Shortly after mating, the adult female deposits about 100 eggs, but only in open wounds of warm-blooded animals, such as cattle or deer. The eggs soon hatch into parasitic maggots that feed ravenously on the flesh and blood of the host (Figure 15-17). As the feeding continues, the wound discharges a fluid that attracts more adult flies. Eventually, in severe infestations, more than 1,000 may feed in a single wound, killing a full-grown half-ton steer within 10 days. After 5 days of intense feeding, the larvae drop to the ground and pupate. Soon afterward, they emerge as adults. After mating with a male fly, the female lays its eggs in another open wound, thus completing its life cycle. In a single year, 10 generations of flies may be born. Livestock damage in the United States was estimated at $40 to $120 million per year until researchers started experimenting with the sterile male technique.

In the 1930s, Edward Knipling, chief of the USDA's Entomology Research Branch, conceived of controlling this highly destructive pest by sterilizing and releasing male flies. After highly successful preliminary tests on a Caribbean island, he decided to try this method in the United States. The program began in 1958. Knipling set up a sterilization "factory" in an old airplane hanger.

Controlling Rabbits with Viruses

The native Australian fauna is unique, being well represented by marsupials such as the kangaroo but being almost completely lacking in placental mammals such as the wolf, fox, coyote, cougar, squirrel, and rabbit. Sheep were introduced into Australia in the nineteenth century. Today they form the basis of a multi-million-dollar wool and mutton industry. Many of the flocks graze on semiarid ranges in the continental interior. Early in the twentieth century the European rabbit was introduced into Australia, apparently at the instigation of European immigrants who longed to indulge once again in their favorite sport of hunting the elusive brushland "bounders." Unfortunately, once they were introduced, their numbers sharply increased. Apparently there were no natural predators to serve as limiting factors in controlling their population surge.

As their numbers increased, the rabbits began to invade sheep ranges. In the semiarid grasslands of interior Australia, forage never had been lush. Now, under the combined grazing pressure of both sheep and rabbits, the rangelands rapidly deteriorated. Grasses were clipped to ground level. The denuded earth became vulnerable. Dust clouds and sand dunes were the inevitable result. Faced with impending economic ruin, Australian ranchers banded together in an all-out effort to eradicate the rabbits. They tried all the conventional control methods. They poisoned. They trapped. They staged mammoth roundups. They launched huge rabbit-hunting parties, the likes of which Europe had never seen. They even erected a fence several hundred miles long, from Queensland to North Wales, in an attempt to contain the rabbits. Their efforts were to no avail. Finally, in 1950 government biologists introduced the myxoma virus, lethal to rabbits exclusively, into the target area. It is transmitted to healthy rabbits by virus-carrying mosquitoes, which bite only live rabbits. The immediate results were spectacularly successful. Only one year later, 99.5 percent of Australia's rabbits had succumbed to the virus. Unfortunately, the rabbits gradually developed resistance to the virus, and by 1958 the mortality rate from the virus dropped to only 54 percent. Whether the rabbits will ultimately develop complete immunity to the myxoma virus and again disrupt Australia's rangeland economy remains to be seen.

FIGURE 1   The rabbit explosion in Australia. Rabbits gathering at a water hole during a period of drought. Their population was estimated at one billion in 1950 about the time this picture was taken. Although the Myxomatosis virus, introduced in 1950, has reduced their numbers by 75 percent, they still pose a problem for ranchers.

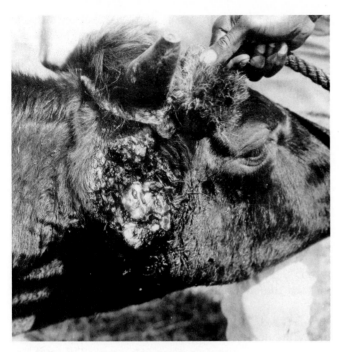

FIGURE 15-17   Screwworm infestation in the ear of a steer. An untreated, fully grown animal weighing about 1,000 pounds may be killed by several thousand maggots feeding in a single wound.

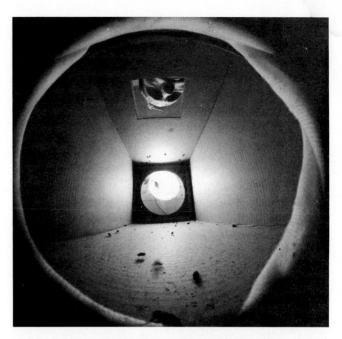

FIGURE 15-18   Sterilization of male screwworm flies. During the sterilization process, canisters containing 30,000 flies are exposed to a cobalt-60 radiation source at the "sterilization factory."

There he and other workers sterilized 50 million flies grown in captivity each week by exposing them to radioactive cobalt (Figure 15-18). Over 2 billion sterilized males were packed in boxes and dropped from airplanes over target areas in the southeastern United States. The boxes popped open when they struck the ground, releasing the flies (Figure 15-19).

The sterilized males competed with fertile wild males for mates. When the ratio of sterile to fertile males is 9:1, over 80 percent of the matings are infertile (Table 15-1). As a result, the screwworm fly population gradually declined. Eighteen months after the project was begun, the screwworm fly had been eradicated from the Southeast.

The screwworm still persists in the Southwest, where it migrates from Mexico. The continued release of sterile males in Mexico and the United States will likely keep the population of screwworms at manageable levels. The sterile-male technique has been used in California to control the Mediterranean fruit flies, or medflies, which were introduced from Hawaii. The medfly lays its eggs in over 230 fruits, nuts, and vegetables. The larvae that hatch from these eggs then consume the fruit, with potentially devastating effects. The program, when combined with other techniques, seemed to work well for a number of years, but farmers became nervous when medflies appeared outside the control area. Fearing widespread damage should the insect population become unmanageable, they pressed for spraying.

State officials bowed to federal pressure and began spraying infested areas with malathion in 1981. During that time, over 400,000 residences were sprayed as many as 24 times. The medfly was officially eradicated in September 1982. Farmers breathed a sigh of relief.

A study by Stanford University biologists, however, indicated large increases in pest populations. Whitefly and aphid populations expanded after the spraying. What caused the increases? According to the researchers, parasites and predatory insects, which are more sensitive to malathion than aphids and whiteflies, were destroyed by the sprayings, allowing the pest populations to take over.

The sterile-male technique, when it works, offers many advantages over traditional pest-control strategies. It is species specific, eliminates or greatly reduces the need for pesticides, and can work when the density of the pest population is low. Researchers note, however, that the technique has its problems. Most importantly, sterilized males may be less sexually active than fertile males, reducing the effectiveness of this approach.

Chemical Controls

Plants have evolved a number of chemical substances to ward off enemies. Biodegradable and nonpersistent, many of these chemicals are now being considered for widespread use. Rotenone, derived from the roots of certain Asiatic legumes, is used today by gardeners against

FIGURE 15-19 Release of sterilized male screwworm flies. Dr. James E. Novy breaks open a box of 2,000 sterile flies near Mission, Texas. Flies disperse in this way when the boxes strike the ground after leaving the aircraft.

an army of pests. Pyrethrum, extracted from chrysanthemums and daisy-like flowers by pesticide manufacturers, is also used in home gardens.

Aside from these chemicals, researchers are experimenting with two additional chemical groups: pheromones and insect hormones, which will now be described.

PHEROMONES. Insects and other animal species release a number of chemicals into the environment that influence other members of the same species. These chemical substances are called *pheromones*. One class of pheromones, and perhaps the most important, are the *sex attractants*, chemicals that attract males to females for mating.

Sex attractants help ensure the survival of various species and are an important adaptation. Consider the gypsy moth. Although the male moth has strong, functional wings, the female is far too heavy-bodied for effective flight. After emerging from her pupa case, the virgin female flutters about near the ground or creeps up tree trunks. Soon after emerging, she is ready to breed. To attract males, she secretes minute quantities of a sex attractant, known as **gyptol**, from glands in her abdomen (Figure 15-20). The sensitive antennal receptors of the male moth detect this scent and send him winging to find the female. Flying upwind toward the odor, he locates the female and mates with her.

Scientists at the USDA synthesized a chemically similar compound called **gyplure**, which has proven to be as effective as gyptol as a sex attractant. This and two dozen other synthetic pheromones are now used in a variety of ways to control insect pests. One of the most common uses is in **pheromone traps** (Figure 15-21). A minute amount of the pheromone is placed in a trap laced with insecticide or some sticky substance to trap the unwary male. Deluded into thinking that a willing female is waiting in the trap, the male enters and is immobilized or killed outright by the insecticide. Each year, farmers install thousands of traps to control a variety of insects.

Traps can also be used to determine when pest species emerge in the spring so that insecticide use can be carefully synchronized to do the most good. Traps can also be used to monitor population levels so that farmers know when to release predatory insects or if an outbreak is occurring.

Unsuspecting male insects can also be duped by another ingenious technique. Farmers impregnate wood chips or cardboard shards with sex attractants. Then, flying over infested fields and orchards, they drop their payload. Alerted by the sudden presence of female sex attractant, eager males fly off in search of females but find only the wood chips. Undaunted by the lack of

Table 15-1 Population Reduction of a Pest Population When a Constant Number of Sterilized Males are Released in a Pest Population of 1 Million Males and 1 Million Females

Generation	Number of Virgin Females	Number of Sterile Males Released	Ratio Sterile to Fertile Males	Number of Fertile Females in the Next Generation
1	1,000,000	2,000,000	2:1	333,333
2	333,333	2,000,000	6:1	47,619
3	47,619	2,000,000	42:1	1,107
4	1,107	2,000,000	1,807:1	Less than 1

FIGURE 15-20 Male gypsy moth attracted to a female by the sex attractant gyptol, which she emits (top). Male gypsy moth lured into a trap baited with synthetic gyplure (center). Male gypsy moth, confused by multiple sources of gyplure, is unable to find a female gypsy moth with which to mate.

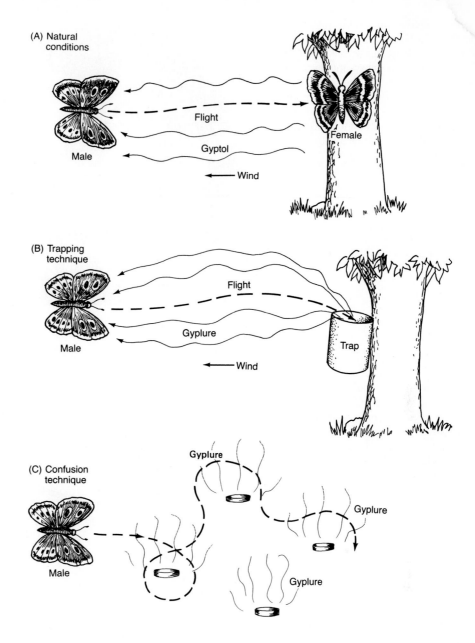

(A) Natural conditions

Flight

Gyptol

Wind

Male

Female

(B) Trapping technique

Flight

Gyplure

Wind

Male

Trap

(C) Confusion technique

Gyplure

Gyplure

Gyplure

Male

physical similarity, many males mount the wood chips and try to mate with them. Alternatively, farmers may simply spray the sex attractant over the infested area. The males spend much of their time and energy tracking down nonexistent females. In either case, pheromones decrease the likelihood that a male will find a female. This technique is appropriately called the **confusion technique** (Figure 15-20). In one experiment, researchers found that gyplure applied at a rate of only 5 grams per hectare (12 grams per acre) reduced mating by gypsy moths by 94 percent.

Sex attractants are nontoxic, species specific, and biodegradable. Moreover, it is impossible for an insect to develop resistance to them without, at the same time, developing resistance to the very act of reproduction. Since its first use on the gypsy moth, the pheromone

technique has been used successfully on many other insect pests, such as the cabbage borer, European corn borer, cotton boll weevil, Japanese beetle, tomato hornworm, and tobacco budworm.

INSECT HORMONES. Many insects hatch from eggs and pass through larval and pupal stages before maturing (Figure 15-22). Caterpillars, for instance, are larvae that develop into moths and butterflies. During the larval stage, the caterpillar produces a hormone, called **juvenile hormone**, that keeps it in its immature state. When levels fall, the insect pupates.

By spraying insects with juvenile hormone, farmers can prevent them from maturing. Although the larval forms of most insects do the greatest damage, they cannot survive long in this state. Furthermore, by prevent-

FIGURE 15-21 Cape Cod, Massachusetts. This is a typical gypsy-moth trap picked up in the field. It contains captured gypsy moths lured into the trap by gyplure, a synthetic attractant that confuses male moths into "thinking" a female is inside the trap. Once inside, the moth becomes entangled in a sticky substance and is unable to extricate itself.

FIGURE 15-22 Life cycle of insects. The role of hormones in insect metamorphosis. The juvenile hormone, secreted mainly during the larva stage, keeps the caterpillar in this immature state until it is ready to metamorphose into a pupa and adult. The hormones must be secreted in the right amounts at the right time. (Redrawn from *Fortune*, July, 1968.)

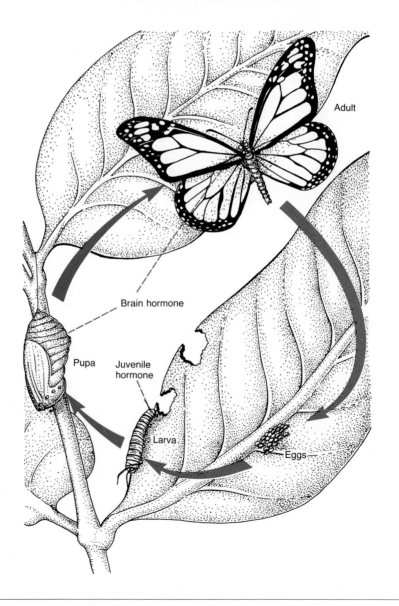

ing the larvae from maturing and, therefore, reproducing, farmers can ensure lower future populations.

Juvenile hormone has been successfully used to control mosquitoes in Central and South America and could be used on a variety of other pests. Environmentally safe because it is biodegradable, nonpersistent, and nontoxic, juvenile hormone is, unfortunately, not as species specific as pheromones. As a result, it may kill predatory insects and nonpest species, seriously upsetting the ecological balance. In addition, juvenile hormone acts more slowly than traditional chemical pesticides. A week or two may be required before hungry crop-eating larvae die, and by that time they may have devastated a crop or forest. Furthermore, juvenile hormone is relatively unstable in the environment—so much so that it often breaks down before it can act. Chemists hope to find ways to make it last longer in the environment. Finally, juvenile hormone must be applied at the precise time that endogenous levels (those in the caterpillar) of the hormone fall, for this signals maturation. Only if it is applied at that time will the larva remain immature.

To avoid these problems, scientists are now developing **hormone inhibitors**, which inhibit the secretion of juvenile hormone by larvae. If they are successful, this new line of nontoxic chemicals may cause the larva to mature early, disrupting its life cycle and killing the insect.

Cultural Control

Cultural control is a catchall term covering all of the techniques that do not fit into the other categories of pest controls—for example, scarecrows and noisemakers that frighten birds away from crops, electrocution devices that zap unsuspecting bugs, and agricultural inspection stations that monitor the flow of fruits and vegetables across state and national borders. Herbicide use can be reduced by using special wick applicators that, unlike sprays from planes and tractors, apply the chemicals only on the weeds between the rows of crops. All of these are essential elements of integrated pest management.

Changes in our attitudes about our fruit and vegetables—another cultural control—could also go a long way toward reducing the contamination of our environment with chemical pesticides. Thousands of tons of insecticide are sprayed on American orchards each year to prevent cosmetic damage to fruits. The San Jose scale, for example, is an insect that creates tiny blemishes on apples, pears, peaches, plums, and apricots and is now controlled by insecticides. Orchards are sprayed every 10 to 14 days throughout the growing season to produce picture-perfect fruit. Eliminating the spray, at least in part, would yield less aesthetically appealing fruit that tastes just as good as its blemish-free counterparts. The hidden benefit would be a cleaner, healthier environment. Society must choose. Would it rather have perfect fruit or a few more birds overhead?

Integrated Pest Management

Environmental, genetic, chemical, and cultural controls offer abundant opportunities to get off the pesticide treadmill and to clean up our environment. Which of these solutions is best?

In truth, the best strategy often involves a combination of methods, called **integrated pest management**. Farmers may plant pest-resistant crops, for example, and may rotate crops, alternate crops, use trap crops, and apply insect hormones or pheromones to reduce pests to economically acceptable levels. Integrated pest management emphasizes control, not the complete eradication of pests, which is often expensive and environmentally disastrous. The various strategies may be used singly or in combination, simultaneously or in sequence, depending on the particular pest. They call on our ingenuity and our knowledge of the life cycles of pests. No doubt insecticides will continue to be used to control insects, but, if successful, integrated pest management could greatly reduce their use. Human civilization has destroyed the ecological balance of much of its land by converting forests and grasslands into farmlands. That balance can never be fully restored, but with care and intelligence we can establish new ecological balances that we can live with.

Integrated pest management is not just a theoretical daydream. Studies show that it works. In Texas, for example, researchers applied a variety of techniques to control the cotton boll weevil once controlled by heavy doses of pesticides. By planting an early-fruiting variety of cotton that was unappealing to the weevil, and by reducing the spacing between rows, fertilizer use, and irrigation water, researchers were able to reduce pest populations and cut back on costly pesticide applications—from 12 per growing season to virtually none. Banks that once balked at lending farmers money for cotton, because of average crop losses of $4.60 per hectare ($1.88 per acre), were suddenly thrilled to dole out funds to farmers who enjoyed a $900 per hectare ($364 per acre) profit.

ARE PESTICIDES ADEQUATELY REGULATED?

Pesticides are one of the pillars of modern agriculture, but critics warn that these economically important chemicals may be threatening the health and well-being of the planet and must be properly regulated. Are they regulated properly?

Federal Regulation

Formal regulation of pesticides at the federal level began in 1947 when Congress passed the Federal Insecticide, Fungicide, and Rodenticide Act (FIFRA). This law required manufacturers to register pesticides being shipped across state borders with the USDA and to label them as well. No attempt was made to control their use or to limit potentially harmful chemicals. In actuality, the law provided little protection.

Because of an outpouring of public concern regarding the harmful effects of pesticides in the 1960s, Congress amended the FIFRA in 1972, 1975, and 1978. Broadening the scope of the act, the amendments required manufacturers to register with the EPA virtually all new pesticides, regardless of their place of origin, to be sold and used in the United States. Each registration specifies the crops and insects on which the pesticide is to be used, supported by research data. Careful analysis of the costs and benefits are made by EPA officials during this process. The EPA then approves pesticides that are deemed effective and safe. Those that aren't considered safe or worth the risk are not registered.

To gain some measure of control over the use of pesticides, the act also called on the EPA to classify pesticides as either general or restricted. The latter can be applied only by state-certified applicators. And to monitor usage, the EPA can inspect applicators' facilities to be certain that the pesticide is being used according to directions.

The registration of pesticides is the foundation of the FIFRA, but the cancellation stipulations are what attract the most attention. Under certain circumstances, the EPA can cancel its registration of pesticides that new information suggests are highly likely to threaten human health and the environment. Cancellations may require months or years of red tape. During that period, production and sales can continue. If, however, the EPA believes that a chemical being considered for cancellation is imminently hazardous, it can suspend its use to protect human health and the environment while the cancellation procedure lumbers on. In this process, the EPA weighs the economic, social, and environmental benefits against all costs.

The United States took the lead in pesticide management. On December 31, 1972, for instance, the EPA officially banned DDT for all uses except emergencies. (In early 1974 the EPA did permit the U.S. Forest Service to use DDT to control a highly destructive outbreak of the tussock moth in valuable coniferous forests in the Northwest.) In the years since the ban, the concentrations of DDT in the soil, water, and wildlife have declined substantially.

In August 1974, after 2 years of hearings, the EPA also banned the general use of two additional chlorinated hydrocarbons, aldrin and dieldrin, considered by some authorities to be even more toxic than DDT. The EPA also suspended the use of heptachlor, endrin, lindane, Kepone, and toxaphene, all chemical cousins of DDT.

Are We Adequately Protected?

Despite strict laws and regulations on U.S. pesticide manufacturing and production, these substances continue to cause problems. One of the biggest problems is the enforcement of safe use. The EPA dictates who can apply what chemicals, but enforcement is generally left to the states, and the level of enforcement varies widely from state to state. Poorly educated farm workers are especially at risk and difficult to patrol. Unable to read and understand labels, they often misuse products or are not provided with protective clothing and headgear. Farmers who ought to know better, like Dorsey Chism, mentioned earlier in the chapter, often apply chemicals excessively without using protective gear and often suffer the consequences.

Another problem comes with unanticipated effects. Invariably, new products, which were deemed safe on the basis of toxicity data provided for EPA registration, sometimes have adverse effects on human health and wildlife, which were not anticipated by EPA officials. In such instances, public outcry may be needed to get the EPA to reverse a pesticide's registration. To make matters worse, in 1976 the Food and Drug Administration (FDA) found that Industrial Bio-Test, a leading testing facility that provided toxicity data for many chemical manufacturers, had falsified its toxicity data for a decade, providing a rosy picture of harmful substances. Several health-threatening pesticides (toxaphene, paraquat, and DBCP) were registered by the EPA on the basis of these data.

Since 1945, approximately 1,500 chemical pesticides and more than 35,000 different formulations have been introduced to the pesticide market. A U.S. congressional investigation found that 60 percent of those now in use lacked adequate information on their potential to cause birth defects, 80 percent lacked adequate cancer data, and 90 percent had not been sufficiently tested for possible mutations.

Insufficient testing remains a major stumbling block in government efforts to protect human health. Another major problem is accurately monitoring pesticide levels in the 130 million metric tons (290 billion pounds) of food Americans consume every year, 15 percent of which is imported. Between 1979 and 1985, approximately 3 percent of the domestic food and 6 percent of the imported food sampled by the USDA was contaminated by unacceptably high levels of pesticides. The tests covered only two-thirds of the currently used pesticides. Furthermore, the FDA does not know all of the pesticides used on food grown abroad and, therefore, what chemicals it should be looking for.

CLOSING THE CIRCLE OF POISONS. Nine years after the EPA's ban on DDT, USDA officials turned back a shipload of beef headed for U.S. consumers from

Central America because the meat contained unacceptably high levels of DDT. This pointed out a major problem in U.S. pesticide policy: Substances banned here were being sold abroad and reimported in food products, something called the *boomerang effect* or the *circle of poisons*.

Today a dozen chemical companies supply about 90 percent of the world's pesticides. These European and American companies sell banned or restricted pesticides, such as DDT, chlordane, and dieldrin, to developing countries, which use 30 percent of the world's pesticides and are the fastest-growing market. While current estimates are not available, in 1979, 25 percent of the exported chemicals were either banned or severely restricted in the United States. When the substances started showing up both in food imported from these countries and in migratory birds that wintered in the warm equatorial countries, many people grew alarmed.

Because of public interest, Congress amended the FIFRA. Under the new amendment, the EPA is required to notify all governments and international organizations worldwide each time it cancels or suspends a pesticide's registration. The EPA also requires manufacturers and exporters of pesticides that have been banned or are not registered in the United States to notify the purchaser of the status of the pesticide. The EPA also notifies the government through the U.S. State Department. Other countries have agreed to send out similar notifications.

Notification is only a small step, however, in protecting the farmers and farm workers of the developing nations. Countries must have an intact system of internal regulation as well. However, a recent survey by the International Pesticide Industry Association found that only 51 countries have strict controls on pesticides, 43 have less stringent controls, and 41 have no controls whatsoever. Mistakes, carelessness, and ignorance resulting from lack of information or poor training injure and kill many farm workers each year. Even though container labels describe, in the language of the importing country, ways to apply the chemicals safely, farm workers often ignore the warnings or may not be able to read them.

CONTROLLING THE LAWN-CARE INDUSTRY. Throughout the nation, citizens have been pressing their representatives to regulate the lawn-care industry—and with growing success. Already, Maryland and a host of towns and counties throughout the United States have passed right-to-know laws and ordinances that require applicators to notify residents in advance of sprayings and to post warning signs after application. Rhode Island, Massachusetts, Minnesota, and Iowa have similar regulations, and Connecticut, New York, Michigan, Illinois, and Ohio are currently considering such standards. Some critics say that this is not enough. Signs are too small and are placed at ground level, making them difficult to see. The information they contain is vague and not really a warning.

The lawn-care industry may find it advantageous to switch to integrated pest management, as Jay Kolby, president of Chem-Free Lawns, Inc., of Lancaster, New York (outside Buffalo), did. His thriving business relies on naturally occurring pesticides and biological controls. "It all works a little slower," says Kolby, "but in the long run it's actually better; you get a better lawn."

Modern society has come a long way in regulating pesticides, but much more needs to be done. Stronger laws, much better enforcement, and worker education are badly needed, especially in the Third World. Many experts believe that we must reduce our use of pesticides, relying instead on integrated pest management. Natural predators and crop rotation, as well as other methods, hold promise for a pesticide-free world.

RAPID REVIEW

1. American industry produces half a million metric tons of pesticides every year for use here and abroad. Despite increased awareness of the dangers of pesticide use and efforts to reduce our dependence on these substances, total pesticide use in the United States has nearly tripled since the early 1960s. Insecticide use has remained more or less constant, while hebicide use has climbed sixfold.

2. Insects become pests when humans simplify ecosystems, destroying the complex ecological control mechanisms that hold populations in balance. Planting a single or a few species also provides insects with an enormous supply of food. Pests may also arise from the accidental or intentional introduction of insects (e.g., gypsy moths) or other organisms (e.g., rabbits) into environments in which there is little environmental resistance.

3. Each year, pests destroy or consume about 45 percent of the world's food supply. Damage is much worse in the tropics, where two or three crops are grown on a field in a single year and where conditions are ideal for insects.

4. Pesticides help control the damage caused by pests. According to agricultural economists, each dollar invested in pesticides results in about $2 to $4 in improved yields. By some estimates, abandoning pesticides would cause a 25–30 percent reduction in food production in the United States, and food bills would be 50–75 percent higher. David Pimentel of Cornell University, an authority on pests, however, argues that these figures are exaggerated. A complete ban on pesticides would, he says, increase preharvest losses in the United States by only 9 percent.

5. Pesticides also help control disease-carrying insects, such as the mosquito, which transmits malaria.

6. Scientists are finding that the effectiveness of pesticides is rapidly dwindling because hundreds of insects have become genetically resistant to insecticides. Widespread use of insecticides also destroys insects and other organisms, like birds, that help hold pest populations in check.

7. Today at least 450 insects are resistant to insecticides. Seventeen species are resistant to all insecticides, and that number is rapidly rising.

8. A variety of chemical pesticides were used by farmers before World War II, including ashes with arsenic and hydrogen cyanide. In 1939, however, a Swiss scientist, Paul Muller, discovered that DDT, a chlorinated hydrocarbon, was a powerful insecticide. He started a revolution in agricultural pest control.

9. DDT was followed by a string of chlorinated hydrocarbons. All of them have since been banned or severely restricted in the United States. Chlorinated hydrocarbons persist in the environment for many years, bioaccumulate, and biomagnify.

10. As a result of growing discontent with chlorinated hydrocarbons, chemical manufacturers created a new line of pesticides—the organic phosphates. They decompose more rapidly in the environment and are less likely to bioaccumulate and biomagnify. These substances, however, are potent nerve toxins.

11. Pesticide manufacturers produced a newer line of potentially safer insecticides, called *carbamates*, that are even more quickly degraded than the organic phosphates and chlorinated organics.

12. Pesticides end up in American soils and water, on our food, in our wildlife, and in our people. Each year approximately 100,000 to 300,000 Americans are poisoned by pesticides; most of them are chemical or farm workers. All told, 200 to 1,000 Americans die from pesticide poisoning. Worldwide, at least 500,000 people are poisoned by pesticides each year, and an estimated 5,000 to 14,000 die.

13. Some doctors believe that general maladies, such as dizziness, insomnia, indigestion, and headaches, may be caused by ingesting pesticides in food. A recent study estimates that pesticides in food cause as many as 20,000 cases of cancer a year in the United States. A University of Hawaii researcher discovered that birth defects were higher in the offspring of women who ingested milk contaminated with heptachlor, a chlorinated hydrocarbon.

14. Herbicides, applied to fields to destroy weeds, have also been linked to a growing number of problems, such as cancer, birth defects, and nervous disorders. Agent Orange, an herbicide used in the Vietnam War, was found to be contaminated with dioxin, which is believed to be largely responsible for many health problems reported by veterans and Vietnamese citizens.

15. Pesticides affect wildlife as well. Tributyl tin, a potent biotoxin added to paint to retard the buildup of algae and barnacles, is released from paint on ships' hulls and pollutes bays and harbors, killing algae and shellfish.

16. Pesticides have been implicated in the rash of fish cancers reported in American lakes and rivers. And each year, insecticides destroy an estimated 400,000 bee colonies.

17. DDT has been linked to the decline in eagle, osprey, pelican, and peregrine falcon populations in the United States. Scientists have found that it also disrupted calcium deposition in eggshells, resulting in eggshell thinning and low embryonic survival.

18. Scientific researchers have turned up numerous alternatives to pesticides. Pest control today often takes an integrated approach, called **integrated pest management**, which capitalizes on four major strategies: environmental controls, genetic controls, chemical controls, and cultural controls.

19. Environmental controls are measures that alter the biotic and abiotic environments of the pest. The most important ones are (a) crop rotation, (b) heteroculture, (c) trap crops, and (d) natural predators, parasites, and disease organisms. These measures are often simple, effective, inexpensive, and environmentally benign.

20. Genetic controls include (a) the sterile-male technique, in which sterilized males of the pest species are released into the wild in infested areas to breed with fertile females, which results in infertile mating and greatly cuts down on pest populations, and (b) genetic resistance, efforts to increase the genetic resistance of plants and animals to pests through genetic engineering and conventional animal and plant breeding programs.

21. Chemical controls include (a) natural chemical substances produced by plants to ward off insects, (b) pheromones, the sex attractants produced by females to attract males for mating, which can be synthesized and applied to infested fields to confuse males, and (c) insect hormones, which can be applied to crops to alter the life cycle of pests and, ultimately, reduce their number.

22. Cultural controls include all other techniques, such as scarecrows, noisemakers, electrocution devices, agricultural inspection stations, and changes in attitudes about blemish-free fruits and vegetables.

23. Formal regulation of pesticides at the federal level began in 1947 when Congress passed the Federal Insecticide, Fungicide, and Rodenticide Act. Since that time, the act has been substantially strengthened to improve control. The amendments require all manufacturers to register with the EPA virtually all new pesticides to be sold and used in the United States. The EPA approves only those substances in which it believes the benefits outweigh the potential risks. The EPA also classifies pesticides as either general or restricted, and can cancel or suspend the registration of pesticides that experience shows are unsafe. To protect overseas users, the EPA must now notify all governments when it cancels or suspends a pesticide registration. It also requires exporters to notify customers if they are importing a substance whose use has been banned or restricted in the United States.

24. Despite strict laws and regulations, pesticides continue to cause problems. Enforcement of proper use remains one of the largest headaches. Additionally, many products deemed safe on the basis of toxicity data provided for EPA registration are shown to cause unexpected damage when used in the field. Moreover, many chemicals in use today have not been adequately tested.

KEY WORDS AND PHRASES

Agent Orange
Beneficial insects
Bioaccumulation
Biological control
Biological diversity
Biomagnification
Cancellation of
    registration
Carbamates
Chemical control
Chlorinated hydrocarbons
Confusion technique
Crop rotation
Cultural control
Dioxin
DDT
Ecosystem simplification
Eggshell thinning
Environmental controls
Federal Insecticide,
    Fungicide, and
    Rodenticide Act

Genetic control
Genetic resistance
Gyptol
Herbicide
Heteroculture
Hormone inhibitors
Insect hormones
Integrated pest
    management
Intercropping
Juvenile hormone
Natural predators
Nonpersistent pesticides
Organic phosphates
Persistence
Pesticide
Pesticide treadmill
Pheromone
Pheromone trap
Registration of
    pesticides
Sex attractants

Sterile-male technique
Suspension of pesticides

Trap crops
Tributyl tin

QUESTIONS AND TOPICS FOR DISCUSSION

1. In what ways do ecosystem simplification and monoculture create pests?

2. Why do alien species often become pests? Give some examples.

3. Describe the pros and cons of pesticide use.

4. What is the pesticide treadmill?

5. Discuss why insect damage has doubled in the past 30 years.

6. Name the three types of chemical pesticides and give an example of each one.

7. Given what you know about the harmful effects of pesticides, describe a perfect chemical pesticide. What characteristics would it have? Can you think of any potential candidates?

8. Describe some of the health effects of pesticide use. Which sector of our population is most likely to be affected?

9. What is Agent Orange? Where was it used? Why? What are some of the consequences of its use?

10. Describe the effects of pesticides on wildlife. Give some examples.

11. Define integrated pest management. What are the major strategies of this technique?

12. "Insecticides are the only way to control insects," says one midwestern wheat farmer. Do you agree or disagree? What suggestions might you make to the farmer?

13. Describe how crop rotation and heteroculture keep pest populations in check.

14. What is a trap crop? How can it be used to reduce insecticide use?

15. Describe the pros and cons of biological control.

16. How can scientists alter the genetic resistance of crops and livestock to reduce pest damage?

17. Describe the principle behind the sterile-male technique.

18. Define the terms **pheromone** and **insect hormone**. How are they different and how are they similar?

19. Describe the major provisions of the Federal Insecticide, Fungicide, and Rodenticide Act.

20. You are a farmer. You want to grow corn, alfalfa, and potatoes without pesticides. How would you go about it?

SUGGESTED READINGS

Allen, G. E., and J. E. Bath. "The Conceptual and Institutional Aspects of Integrated Pest Management." *Bioscience*, 30 (Oct. 1980): 658–664. This article is written for a sophisticated reader. It describes the concepts of IPM and its institutionalization at the state, regional, and national levels. It also explains the role of the USDA and the EPA, and outlines future prospects.

Boraiko, A. "The Pesticide Dilemma." *National Geographic*, 157 (Feb. 1980): 145–182. This article is written for the general public. It is effectively illustrated with graphs, maps, and color photos. It considers the pros and cons of chemical control, and the advantages of biological and cultural control and IPM. It is highly readable.

Goldberg. E. D. "TBT: An Environmental Dilemma." *Environment* 28: 17–20, 42–44, 1986. Semitechnical discussion of TBT that suggests regulations for the United States.

Kriebel, D. "The Dioxins: Toxic and Still Troublesome." *Environment*, 23 (Jan./Feb. 1981): 6–12. The author is a researcher at Queens College, Flushing, New York, who has written for the nonspecialist. The article is an easily understood treatment of the source, dispersal, and effects of dioxin on humans in Vietnam and in the United States.

Marshall, E. "Man Versus Medfly: Some Tactical Blunders." *Science*, 213 (July 24, 1981): 417–418. This is a nontechnical account of the accidental release of *fertile* flies in an attempt to control the Medfly by means of the sterilization-and-release method.

Regenstein, L. *America the Poisoned*. Washington, D.C.: Acropolis, 1982. Detailed, highly readable account of the adverse effects of toxic chemicals, especially pesticides, on our health and our environment.

Shute, N. "Toxic Green." *The Amicus Journal* 9:10–17, 1987. Informative article on the fight to reduce urban pesticide use.

Strobel, G. A., and G. N. Lanier. "Dutch Elm Disease." *Scientific American*, 245 (Aug. 1981): 56–66. This is a highly readable account of the causes and symptoms of Dutch elm disease, its spread across the United States, and novel biological techniques that attack both the fungus and the beetles that spread it.

Swezey, S. L., Murray, D. L., and Daxl, R. G. "Nicaragua's Revolution in Pesticide Policy." *Environment* 28: 6–9, 29–36, 1986. Fascinating account of the evolution of Nicaragua's pesticide policy away from chemical insecticides.

U.S. Office of Technology Assessment. *Pest Management Strategies in Crop Protection*. Vol. 1. Washington, D.C.: Government Printing Office, 1979. This authoritative report evaluates the tactics presently used to control agricultural pests in the United States. It was written with the assistance of a panel of scientists, farmers, consumers, and representatives of industry and public interest groups.

Wallis, C. "Bad News for the Birds." *Time,* 118 (Oct. 5, 1981): 52. This is a nontechnical, highly readable account of how, in the spring of 1981, endrin, a highly toxic chlorinated hydrocarbon, was used to control wheat-eating cutworms in several western states. The aftermath was widespread contamination of waterfowl and a near closing of the duck-goose hunting season.

Wilcox, F. A. *Waiting for an Army to Die: The Tragedy of Agent Orange*. New York: Vintage Books, 1983. A superb book on the troubles facing Vietnam veterans.

16

Managing Wastes in the Human Environment

"America the Beautiful" is by far the world's leader in creating garbage. Each day an average Los Angeles resident, for instance, produces 3 kilograms (nearly 7 pounds) of municipal solid waste. Over a year, that's more than 1 metric ton! By one estimate, Californians annually produce enough trash to form a pile 30 meters (100 feet) wide and 10 meters (30 feet) high, extending from Oregon to Mexico.

More frugal than their California counterparts, New York City residents produce 40 percent less trash—about 1.8 kilograms (4 pounds) waste per day. But they still throw away twice as much garbage as the Japanese and Europeans and 4.5 times more than the average resident of Mexico City (Table 16-1).

America is also the world's leader in hazardous waste production. By one estimate, this country produces over 260 million metric tons of hazardous waste each year—over 1 metric ton per person. Nearly 70 percent of these wastes come from two industries, the chemical and petroleum industries, which provide hundreds of products used in and around the home: pesticides, fertilizers, rubber, medicines, paints, adhesives, and a whole host of plastic products.

This chapter looks at waste—municipal waste and hazardous wastes—and shows where they come from and how to deal with them. Its aim is to outline better disposal methods and—more important—to show ways that we can reduce our output of waste and build a sustainable society.

MUNICIPAL WASTE: TAPPING A WASTED RESOURCE

American cities and towns generate 135 million metric tons of municipal solid waste every year. Over 70 million metric tons of solid waste are produced by industries. Most of the waste from our cities—that is, **municipal waste**—is paper and yard wastes (grass clippings and leaves) with lesser amounts of metals, glass, and plastics making up the balance (Figure 16-1). Unfortunately, only 10 percent of our solid waste is recovered for reuse and recycling, and only 4 percent is burned to generate energy. The rest, some 113 million metric tons, is dumped in landfills, where it is covered with dirt and forgotten.

David Morris of the Washington-based Institute for Local Self Reliance wrote that "A city the size of San Francisco disposes of more aluminum than is produced by a small bauxite mine, more copper than a medium copper mine, and more paper than a good sized timber stand." San Francisco's trash is a gold mine of wastes, offering a wealth of resources, if only we were smart enough—or farsighted enough—to tap it and the steady stream of recoverable resources pouring out of our cities, towns, and homes each day.

Paper

Nearly two-fifths of America's municipal waste is paper—packaging, direct-mail advertising, newspapers,

Table 16-1   Per Capita Garbage Production Rates in Selected Cities

City	Kilograms per Day
Developed Countries	
Los Angeles	3.0
New York	1.8
Tokyo	1.38
Paris	1.10
Singapore	0.87
Hamburg	0.85
Rome	0.69
Developing Countries	
Lahore, Pakistan	0.60
Tunis, Tunisia	0.56
Calcutta, India	0.51
Kano, Nigeria	0.46

Source: Worldwatch Institute.

magazines, and so on (Figure 16-1). The amount of paper discarded in our garbage has grown steadily for three decades, largely as a result of an upsurge in packaging. In New York State alone, packaging doubled between 1960 and 1986.

Cynthia Pollock of the Worldwatch Institute notes that nearly $1 of every $10 Americans spend on food and beverages pays for packaging of various kinds. Americans, in fact, spent more for food packaging in 1986—$28 billion—than the nation's farmers received in net income.

In developed countries 30–50 percent of the municipal trash is discarded packaging, half of which is paper. Packaging is not the only wasteful use of paper. As any homeowner can attest, a stream of

often annoying direct-mail advertisements and—in recent years—newletters of questionable value from banks, print shops, lawn-care companies, and charitable organizations fills his or her mailbox with wasted resources, which are often discarded without a moment's hesitation. Even many well-meaning environmental groups fighting to save forests and promote better use of our resources, including recycling, barrage their members with wasteful mail. One group fighting to protect the world's forests, for instance, routinely sends its members appeals asking for emergency money that contain a two-page single-spaced letter (which few have time to read), a brochure (which summarizes what the letter says), a card to send in with the donation, and a return envelope—perhaps twice as much paper as is really needed to get the message across.

Americans recycle only one-fifth of all their paper and cardboard, despite the relative ease and the economic and environmental benefits of this practice (Table 16-2). Recycling has not always stood in such poor stead, however. During World War II, 45 percent of all the paper and cardboard used by Americans made its way to recycling plants.

Worldwide, the paper recycling rate is a paltry 26 percent. Fiber-rich nations such as Sweden and Canada recycle only small amounts of paper, while the less well endowed nations, like Mexico and Japan, recycle half of theirs.

According to many experts, worldwide paper recycling could double by 2000. This goal would meet nearly three-quarters of the projected increase in demand over the coming decade and would save 8 million hectares (20 million acres) of forest from cutting—an area the size of South Carolina.

Individuals can also help. Recycling a 4-foot-high stack of newspapers, for instance, saves a 40-foot Douglas fir tree. A ton of paper saves 17 trees. Individual efforts added to those of others can have an enormous impact. If, for instance, the United States increased paper recycling by 30 percent, an estimated 350 million trees could be saved annually. Enough electrical power would be saved to supply 10 million people.

Paper recycling also saves other resources as well. Each ton of paper recycled saves 125 kilograms (275 pounds) of sulfur, 160 kilograms (350 pounds) of lime-

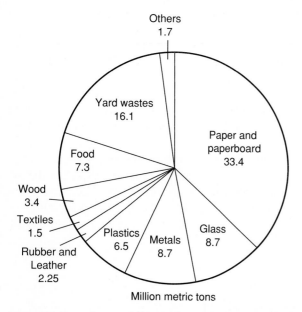

FIGURE 16-1   Composition of America's municipal waste stream.

Table 16-2   The Benefits of Recycling

Material	Energy Savings (%)	Solid Waste Reduction (%)	Air Pollution Reduction (%)
Paper	30–55	100	95
Aluminum	90–95	100	95
Iron/Steel	60–70	95	30

Source: Worldwatch Institute.

stone, 230,000 liters (60,000 gallons) of water, and 225 kilowatt-hours of electricity—enough to run your refrigerator for a year. Recycling paper produces only 5 percent of the air pollution that comes from paper manufacturing from trees and cuts water pollution as well (Table 16-2).

Aluminum

In 1963, Americans used 11.5 billion beverage cans, most of which were made of steel coated with a thin layer of tin. By 1985, however, the number of cans had skyrocketed to 70 billion, 94 percent (or 66 billion) of which were made of aluminum. That's 270 aluminum cans per person per year or 45 six-packs a year for every man, woman, and child. Over half of the aluminum cans we use each year are recycled.

As shown in Table 16-2, producing an aluminum can by recycling uses 95 percent less energy than making it from aluminum ore, or bauxite. Each recycled can saves the energy equivalent of a half a can (6 ounces) of gasoline. The 33 billion recycled aluminum cans, therefore, save the energy equivalent of nearly 6 billion liters (1.5 billion gallons) of gasoline, or enough gasoline to power 2.7 million cars for a year.

Aluminum is a lighter packaging material than glass and tin-coated steel, and saves enormous amounts of transportation energy, but aluminum has many other uses in the industrialized world. For example, when mixed with copper and zinc, it forms a lightweight alloy well suited for jet airplanes. It can also be substituted for steel in automobiles.

Because losses are inevitable and some uses tie up aluminum more or less permanently, most experts believe that 60–80 percent of the aluminum produced by society can be recycled. Most nations, however, fall well below that theoretical limit. The Netherlands and Italy, for example, recycle only 40 percent of their aluminum, and the United States and the United Kingdom recycle only 32 and 28 percent, respectively. Worldwide, the average recycling rate is about 28 percent. Doubling the worldwide rate of aluminum recycling would eliminate 1 million tons of air pollution a year and save enormous amounts of energy. In 1985, for instance, the aluminum recycled in just 10 nations eliminated the need for five large power plants.

Steel

America is a country made of steel. Skyscrapers, bridges, automobiles, tractors, trains, printing presses, tools, wood stoves, beverage and food cans, chairs, desks, and a host of appliances are among the many products made from this valuable metal.

Despite its importance in American society, only 35 percent of the steel we use is recycled. Worldwide, the average is an abysmal 25 percent. Why? For one thing,

some of the steel we use goes into bridges and buildings and is tied up more or less permanently. Another reason for the low recycling rate is the abundance of iron ore, from which steel is made. In countries that have abundant native sources, for instance, recycling is generally low. In nations that must import steel, the opposite is true.

However, using iron ore simply because it is available or abundant may not always be the most economical approach. Scrap metal costs a little more but can be converted to steel much more cheaply. The **electric arc furnace**, used in many countries, can produce steel entirely from scrap, compared to the more prevalent **oxygen furnaces** that produce 61 percent of U.S. steel with only 28 percent scrap. The electric arc furnace also uses 75 percent less energy, is half as expensive to build, and produces steel as much as $180 per ton cheaper. It is fitting that countries with electric arc furnaces like South Korea now lead the world in steel production, while the U.S. steel industry lingers near death because it persists in using less efficient open-hearth and oxygen furnaces.

Glass

Americans use enormous quantities of glass every year for a variety of purposes. Like other resources, glass can be easily recycled. Unfortunately, however, only a tiny fraction (7 percent) makes its way back into recycling bins. For that reason, nearly 10 percent of our municipal trash is glass.

Until 1975, manufacturers produced a variety of returnable bottles that consumers took back to stores for a deposit refund. The stores then shipped the bottles to factories where they were washed and refilled, saving enormous amounts of energy and raw materials and eliminating large amounts of pollution. A single bottle routinely traveled through the system 30 to 50 times. But the times changed. The bottling industry launched a major campaign to promote the convenient "no-deposit, no-return" container, and by 1985 the returnable bottle was a thing of the past.

Today only a small fraction of our beverages can be purchased in refillable glass containers. Aluminum and plastic have taken over, with nearly 70 percent of all beverage containers made from these materials. The balance is made up of steel and glass throwaway containers, and **aseptic containers**—those odd little boxes made of paper, plastic, and aluminum (Figure 16-2).

In all changes some good must occur, and this was no exception, for aluminum and plastic are much lighter than glass. Shipping requires less energy and saves producers money. On the downside, however, the shift to throwaway glass containers has resulted in a tripling of the energy consumption by the bottle industry.

Glass manufacturers routinely add 15–20 percent recycled glass, called **cullet**, to manufacture new glass.

FIGURE 16-2 Aseptic containers like this one are made of many different materials and are nonrecyclable.

Several newer systems, however, can use 100 percent recycled glass to make new bottles and jars. A 10 percent increase in the amount of cullet used decreases the energy required to make glass by 2 to 5 percent. Using cullet also cuts back on water pollution, mining wastes, and water demand.

Plastics

Plastics have invaded our lives. For better or for worse, we are inundated with a host of plastic products—from kayaks to disposable pens, from plastic bags to plastic milk cartons—worth tens of billions of dollars a year.

Nowhere has the growth of plastics consumption been as great as in the packaging industry. Plastic manufacturers have methodically sought out new markets and have successfully captured them one by one. Today, fewer and fewer glass containers can be found on store shelves.

Since 1977, plastic sales have climbed at a remarkable rate of nearly 5 percent per year. Not content with their market dominance, manufacturers are now looking at ways in which plastics can replace the tin-coated steel cans used to package everything from peaches to pie fillings.

Today plastics make up 10 percent of our municipal waste; only a tiny fraction of the millions of tons of plastic used each year in the United States is recovered, for plastic is difficult to reuse and recycle. Why? At least 46 different kinds of plastic are on the market. To make matters worse, plastic products often contain two or more of these plastics, something that the recycling processes often cannot handle. The typical plastic ketchup bottle, for instance, contains six different plastics, layered to give the bottle flexibility, strength, and impermeability. Today plastics are also being used with other materials, such as foils and paper, making many modern packages, like the aseptic container, almost impossible to recycle.

Another problem with plastics is that they resist breakdown by sunlight or bacteria. All but a few new

FIGURE 16-3 Slow strangulation? This encounter between a Canada goose and the plastic frame for a six-pack of beer is an eloquent testimonial to the ubiquitous occurrence of litter and solid waste in the ecosystems of both wildlife and humans.

varieties, which are coming into use more and more, remain intact for hundreds of years. It takes 240 years for a plastic bag to deteriorate under the influence of sunshine and weather. Plastics can be burned, but burning them releases toxic chemicals, like the corrosive hydrochloric acid and polyvinyl chloride, both injurious to humans and plant life.

Plastics discarded in oceans and lakes threaten aquatic life (Figure 16-3). And some plastic materials, such as Styrofoam, are manufactured with chlorofluorocarbons, which destroy the ozone layer (see Chapter 18). (Efforts are underway to find less-damaging substitutes for CFCs). Plastic recycling is increasing here and abroad, but efforts have only just begun.

MANAGING OUR MUNICIPAL SOLID WASTES

Many modern industrial societies have traditionally viewed municipal waste as something to be rid of—to dump in the ground or at sea as far away as possible—with little regard for the wealth of materials it contains. When one dump site was full, city planners found another. Faced with shortages of suitable dump sites and growing transportation costs to haul the mountains of trash to outlying sites, however, city planners are beginning to look skeptically at the "discard approach." As conservationists and environmentalists have long said, this approach is ecologically unwise and unsustainable. This view was recently expressed by the World Commission on Environment and Development in a 1987 report entitled *Our Common Future.*. "Many present efforts to guard and maintain human progress, to meet human needs, and to realize human ambitions," said the commissioners, "are simply unsustainable—in both the rich and poor nations. They draw too heavily, too quickly, on already overdrawn environmental resource accounts to be affordable far into the future without bankrupting those accounts." Looking at the impact of our actions on future generations, they wrote, "We borrow environmental capital from future generations with no intention or prospect of repaying. They may damn us for our spendthrift ways, but they can never collect on our debt to them."

Two approaches can be used to stretch our resource supplies, save energy, reduce pollution, and cut back on habitat destruction—in short, to reduce our destruction of environmental capital: (1) a reduction approach that calls for lower levels of material consumption in society and (2) a reuse and recycling approach that maximizes the life span of a material in the production–consumption cycle.

The Reduction Approach

By reducing their per capita consumption of natural resources, modern societies can make tremendous inroads into the solid waste problem. But this approach is often unattractive to individuals and businesses. Why cut back on our pleasures and our profits to save a few birds?

As the supply of some minerals begins to fall (see Chapter 17) and as oil prices rise (see Chapter 20), however, reduced consumption may become an economic fact of life in materialistic countries like ours. To postpone this day and the hardship that may result, why not begin now by using less? "Sustainable global development," says the World Commission on Environment and Development, "requires that those who are more affluent adopt lifestyles within the planet's ecological means."

Individuals can reduce consumption by purchasing more durable items. A car that lasts for 20 years, rather than the typical 7–10 years, for instance, can greatly reduce your consumption of steel and other materials. If you live to be 70 and buy your first car at 20, you would purchase two to three automobiles in your lifetime if each one lasted for 20 years. If, on the other hand, your vehicle falls apart every 7 years, you'd need seven

cars. Durable clothing, tools, furniture, computers, and calculators outlast their cheap counterparts and greatly reduce resource demand—energy, water, land, and so on. Buying sturdy goods casts a vote for environmental protection that will not escape the attention of business leaders.

Faced with rising energy and mineral prices in the 1970s, many manufacturers found another route to reduce material consumption: miniaturization. For more on this, see Chapter 19.

The Reuse and Recycling Approach

You've worn a pair of pants for a year and, even though they're in pretty good shape, you've grown tired of them. What do you do? If you're like many Americans, you throw them away. But why not drop your usable goods off at one of the many charitable groups, like Goodwill or Disabled American Veterans, that resells them to benefit other people?

Advocates of the reuse strategy point out that there are many products that can be reused—boxes, appliances, clothes, furniture, grocery bags, and so on. Newspapers, for instance, can be ground up and used for insulation. Boxes can be used for moving or ground up and turned into mulch, which enhances the soil structure of farmland. Glass can be crushed, mixed with asphalt, and used for paving highways (Figure 16-4). Used office paper can be donated to schools for art projects. By diverting trash-bound items to collection centers for reuse, we can greatly extend the useful life of the products. Our efforts help reduce resource consumption, pollution, and land disposal.

FIGURE 16-4A An ingredient of "glasphalt." Ground-up glass crystals that look like rock candy are the glass part of the new "glasphalt" (glass and asphalt) pavement laid at Owens-Illinois Inc.'s Technical Center in Toledo in an experiment by O-I and the University of Missouri (at Rolla) to find a new use for discarded glass containers.

Reuse closely follows the reduction approach in its ecological appeal. For materials that cannot be reused, however, the next best approach is recycling. Recycled materials can be extracted from municipal trash at central stations, which is convenient for the consumer but often costly. This is called **end-point separation**. Recyclables can also be separated at the source—at homes and factories—and picked up by recyclers or delivered to recycling centers by producers (Figure 16-5). This option is called **source separation**. It involves considerably more citizen participation than end-point separation but reduces the costs of separation facilities.

Almost any material that can be crushed and melted down can be recycled. However, the more materials involved, the more difficult and costly recycling becomes. The benefits of recycling are described in the previous section and in Table 16-2.

Currently, the United States recycles about 10 percent of its solid municipal waste, but the EPA believes that we could easily double that amount. A 60–80 percent recovery rate may eventually be achieved as energy prices rise and resource supplies begin to fall.

Model Recycling Programs

Japan, the Netherlands, Mexico, and South Korea lead the world in paper recycling. South Korea and Mexico, in fact, now import waste paper from other countries for recycling. These countries are models of wise resource use.

Japan, a leading consumer of paper, intensified its paper recycling program in the mid-1960s. Short on landfill sites and tree poor, the nation launched a major recycling program with prodding from environmentally concerned citizens. In Hiroshima, citizens separate their wastes and carry paper to local collection centers for recycling. Bottles, cans, and other items are also recycled. Thanks to widespread citizen cooperation, the city cut its municipal solid waste by 40 percent between 1976 and 1983. In Machida, Japan, an astounding 90 percent of the city's waste is recycled thanks to citizens' efforts to separate trash and a highly computerized recycling system.

The Japanese need to recycle paper and other goods because they import much of their energy, have little land for waste disposal, and lack the great forests of other nations, like the United States and Canada. But the success of their programs stems from more than necessity. The unity of the Japanese and their willingness to cooperate to solve a problem are crucial to their success. The government has also helped out in important ways. In Fuchu City, a Tokyo suburb, for instance, the government purchased the costly recycling equipment and then turned it over to a private company, which operates it with profits earned from the sale of recycled materials.

FIGURE 16-5 Garbage garbage everywhere. Workers at Ecocycle in Boulder, Colorado sort recyclable materials that will be shipped to market and used to make new products at a fraction of the energy cost of their counterparts made from virgin materials, and with much less pollution.

The Netherlands is also a leader in paper recycling. Like Japan, it is short on land and forests. To reduce waste, the government established a waste exchange, a service that matches buyers and sellers of waste. The government also established a way to stabilize prices. The cost of recyclables vacillates wildly according to supply and demand. In periods of low demand, recyclers may find few markets and prices too low to stay in business. To buffer against these destabilizing cycles, the government buys recyclables at a set price when demand or market values drop. When the prices increase, the government sells off its supplies and replenishes the funds that keep this system and the country's recyclers in business.

The Netherlands also promote source separation. But unlike Japan, where source separation is merely promoted, in the Netherlands, it's the law. The state of New Jersey and the town of Islip, New York, have similar mandatory recycling programs.

The United States is fast becoming a model aluminum recycling nation. In 1972 only 15 percent of our aluminum cans were recycled. Today 54 percent of them make their way back to furnaces where they are melted and refashioned into new cans. Because of the dramatic increase in recycling and the tremendous economic and energy savings produced, American can manufacturers used 22 percent less energy to produce a pound of aluminum in 1984 than in 1972.

The American success is due to increased public awareness, the work of private companies, and the can and bottle bills that require customers to pay a deposit on all beverage containers, which is returned to them when they return the container to a store. Nine states now have container deposit laws: Oregon, Vermont, Maine, Michigan, Iowa, Connecticut, Massachusetts, Delaware, and New York. According to Cynthia Pollock

of the Worldwatch Institute, in America the average can that comes out of a store is remelted and back on the supermarket shelf in 6 weeks.

Can and bottle bills have been the cornerstone of our recycling strategy. In Oregon, the state with the first bottle bill in 1972, 95 percent of the refillable bottles and 92 percent of the aluminum cans are returned. In Michigan, 96 percent of the beverage bottles and cans are returned. Similar rates are found in other states as well.

The benefits of these programs are enormous. In states with container deposit laws, the volume of roadside litter has been reduced by 35–40 percent. In New York State, where 400 million cases of beverages are sold each year, the Beer Wholesalers Association found that, in 2 years, the deposit law saved the state $50 million in cleanup costs, $19 million in solid waste disposal costs, and $50 to $100 million in energy. The program created 3,800 net jobs—that is, 3,800 more jobs than were lost. In Michigan, 4,600 net jobs were created. A nationwide bill would create 100,000 net jobs, according to the U.S. General Accounting Office.

Commercial interests have responded well to the need for aluminum recycling. Coors, a Colorado-based brewery, has recycling centers throughout the United States. Other private companies have installed automated aluminum recycling machines called **reverse vending machines** (Figure 16-6). Customers feed their aluminum cans into the machine, where they are weighed and crushed. The machine then pays the consumers for the recycled aluminum. In Denver, for example, 20 Canbank machines paid out over $1 million in an 18-month period. A reverse vending machine is now available for glass, and one company is working on a machine that will accept the plastic 2-liter beverage bottles.

In 1986, once again leading the nation in its efforts to

FIGURE 16-6   Reverse vending machine.

promote recycling, Oregon passed the **Recycling Opportunity Act**. This law requires all cities with over 4,000 people to start a curbside recycling program that picks up materials at least once a month. For smaller communities, the law requires city officials to establish recycling centers at landfills. The Recycling Opportunity Act also ranks the waste management options available to the state in their order of desirability. First on the list are efforts to reduce the amount of waste generated—the reduction approach. Next comes reuse. Reuse is followed by recycling. Finally, all leftovers must be buried in approved landfills—the discard approach.

Deepening Our Commitment to the Wise Use of Resources

Most conservationists applaud the remarkable gains in resource recovery throughout the world. They argue, however, that modern society has only begun to come to grips with waste and that much more must be done—and soon—to avoid widespread shortage and economic upheaval. The waste problem, they say, can be approached on at least two fronts: by promoting recovery and by stimulating demand for recycled goods.

PROMOTING RECOVERY.   Governments can play a key role in promoting reuse and recycling. For instance, state and local governments can launch reuse and recycling campaigns via television advertisements, billboards, and publicly distributed pamphlets. But governments can take a more active role. Some may choose to make recycling mandatory. Others may want to invest in the recycling equipment and turn it over to private interests to run. Still others may find it desirable to set up **waste exchanges**, clearinghouses where consumers

of reusable and recyclable materials find out what is available from various producers.

Governments can also provide tax breaks to recyclers or remove subsidies from raw materials and energy, which will make the reuse and recycling option more attractive to commercial interests. Many current policies discriminate against recycled materials. For instance, the U.S. Forest Service sells timber each year at a substantial loss, helping to hold down the price of wood. In the past 10 years, the Service has lost $2 billion in wood sales; the taxpayer, therefore, subsidizes the cost of raw wood. Charging companies more realistically would raise the price of wood and wood products but would be a shot in the arm to the recycling industry.

Cheap energy, a major factor in the production of goods from raw materials, is also heavily subsidized, and that hinders recycling efforts. In 1984, for instance, subsidies to energy producers—in the form of low-interest loans and tax breaks—cost American taxpayers $44 billion, according to the Fund for Renewable Energy and the Environment. "By underpricing energy and other natural resources," says Cynthia Pollock, "governments subsidize the continuation of a throwaway society and the disruption of ecosystems."

Attempting to offset the subsidies, California is considering legislation that would give recycled products a 22 percent tax credit, similar to special allowances made to the oil industry. Should this become law, it would eliminate an estimated 315,000 metric tons of waste from California's landfills every year. It would also expand the recycling industry and create an estimated 1,400 new jobs.

Recycling and reuse could also be stimulated by reducing the complexity of our waste stream. For example, manufacturers can eliminate containers made of several different types of plastics, which are difficult to recycle. Aluminum cans could replace the difficult-to-recycle tin-coated steel cans now used for fruits, vegetables, and other food products.

In the South Pacific Island of Fiji, soft drinks come in one type of refillable glass container. These containers can be returned to any manufacturer to be washed and refilled. In Denmark and Norway, the governments allow fewer than 20 different returnable containers for beer and soft drinks. Standardization facilitates reuse. This eliminates the cost of transporting bottles to distant manufacturers when a local one can use the same container.

INCREASING THE DEMAND FOR RECYCLED MATERIALS.   The strategies we've just described would help to increase the supply of recyclable materials by increasing recovery. But increasing the recovery rate is only half the battle. Governments must also look for ways to improve the markets for recycled goods.

To stimulate demand, governments could also require their agencies and branches to buy products made from recycled materials. At the national level, such actions could greatly stimulate the demand for recycled products, with spillover effects on the general economy. Recognizing the importance of recycling and the potential influence it could have on recycling, Congress in 1976 passed the **Resource Conservation and Recovery Act**, which, among other things, requires the federal government and its contractors to purchase recycled materials. The EPA was charged with drawing up guidelines within 2 years after the act passed. But to the dismay of Congress and many conservationists, the EPA has dragged its feet for over a decade. Thanks to pressure put on them by environmental groups, the EPA has issued guidelines for a dozen materials, such as paper, tires, and fly ash from coal-fired power plants, which can be used in concrete and cement.

Also in response to the federal government's slow pace, Maryland and 12 other states have passed similar laws. Since 1977, Maryland has purchased over 1 million reams of recycled paper products worth an estimated $17 million. Should the EPA's bid to force the federal government to comply with the law prove successful, America could become a world leader in recycled goods.

Proper Waste Disposal

Ecologists envision an ideal world—we'll call it Ectopia—in which there is no waste. In Ectopia plastics are either recycled or reused. Those that cannot be recycled are banned altogether. Waste paper, aluminum, steel, glass, and other materials are separated at their source and shipped off to recycling facilities. Yard wastes—grass clippings and leaves—are either used by homeowners to enrich soils or shipped to Ectopia's composting facilities, where they are piled in huge windrows and left to decay. Eventually, the rich organic materials are combined with wastes from municipal sewage treatment plants and sold as soil conditioners to gardeners and farmers.

Ectopia may be years, maybe decades, away. Until that time, modern industrial societies will undoubtedly continue to rely on the discard approach.

Dumps and Sanitary Landfills

In the year 500 B.C., the Greeks and Romans hauled their trash outside of the city walls and dumped it downwind, so as not to offend the residents. Flies and rats undoubtedly invaded the debris, and when the wind shifted, few people were spared the odorous onslaught.

Over 2,000 years later in America, the most technologically advanced nation on earth, many cities and towns still followed the same tradition. Open festering sores, with rotting garbage swarming with flies and rats, dotted the American landscape. To make matters worse, officials periodically burned the accumulating garbage to reduce its volume (Figure 16-7). Black smoke, filled with the toxic by-products from burning rubber and plastic, billowed out of dumps everywhere. Rain and snowmelt trickled through the garbage, carrying sometimes hazardous liquids into the underlying groundwater, threatening drinking water supplies. Threatened by their own garbage Americans called for changes.

In 1976 their demands were met. Congress passed the Resource Conservation and Recovery Act to address municipal solid waste and hazardous waste. Among its many key provisions was an end to **open dumps** by 1983. What replaced them was the **sanitary landfill**, an

FIGURE 16-7 Smoke from the Redding, California, city dump, December 13, 1965, resulting from the burning of trash.

FIGURE 16-8 Sanitary landfill operation. The bulldozer spreads and compacts solid wastes. The scraper (foreground) is used to haul the cover material at the end of the day's operations. Note the portable fence that catches any blowing debris.

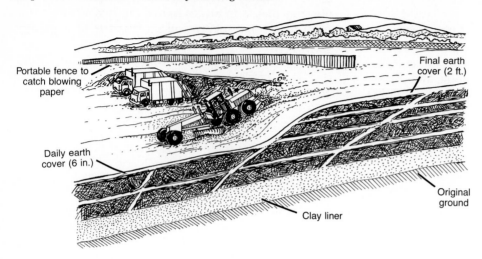

excavation or hollow in the ground in which garbage was dumped, compacted, and covered daily with a fresh layer of dirt (Figure 16-8).

Used today throughout the developed world, the sanitary landfill is far superior to the open dump. It reduces smelly air pollution caused by rotting garbage and periodic burning. Because a soil layer is placed over the trash, compacted, and generally sloped to reduce water percolation into the garbage, groundwater contamination can be greatly reduced or eliminated. The protective layer of soil also reduces insects and other pests that carry disease.

Landfills offer many other advantages as well. Besides being cleaner, they can be reclaimed—that is, returned to a previous use or given over to a new use. In Denver, Colorado, for example, the Mile-High Stadium, a shopping center, and a park are all located on former landfills. In Evanston, Illinois, city officials built a park with baseball fields, tennis courts, and toboggan runs on Mount Trashmore, a hill 30 meters (60 feet) high and underlain by garbage. In Maryland, wastes from 87 roadside dumps were hauled to abandoned coal strip mines. After the gullies were filled with waste, the site was covered with soil and replanted. Acid mine drainage was reduced because workers compacted the soil to reduce groundwater percolation, graded the land to improve drainage, and placed drainage canals to draw off rain and snowmelt.

Advantageous as they may seem, however, landfills are still a primitive method of waste management. If the soil or rock below a landfill is permeable, for instance, pollutants may drain into underlying aquifers, polluting water needed by municipalities, farms, or industry. Rotting debris also produces methane, a potentially explosive gas. Ordinarily methane production is greatest during the first 2 years of operation but is not high enough to be hazardous. However, if large concentrations build up, they can pass through the soil into buildings, where, if they reach sufficient concentration, they can explode.

More importantly, though, landfills are a waste of valuable resources that could be recycled or reused. They also require large tracts of land. A town of 10,000 people, for instance, annually produces enough trash to cover a 0.4 hectare (1-acre) site 3 meters (10 feet) deep. Landfills are also expensive and are growing more expensive by the day. According to researchers at the Institute for Local Self Reliance, by 1990 more than one-half of the cities in the United States will have used up their landfill sites. Because of the growing shortage of suitable sites, city officials are often forced to haul their trash farther and farther from the site of production. As a result, the cost has begun to skyrocket. Philadelphia, for instance, has used up all of its landfill sites and must now transport its garbage to Ohio and Virginia. Between 1980 and 1987, the cost of disposing of a ton of Philadelphia's municipal solid waste climbed from $20 to $90 per ton.

Worldwatch Institute's Cynthia Pollock notes, however, that in many areas landfill fees are held artificially low by local governments. For this reason, trash removal companies and local governments have little incentive to make better use of their wasted resources.

Composting

Many local governments reduce their solid waste disposal by **composting**, a process in which organic matter—leaves, grass clippings, paper, cardboard, and even sewage sludge—is separated from nonorganic trash and piled in vacant fields, where it is left to decay. Aerobic (oxygen-requiring) bacteria and fungi in the waste decompose the organic matter to produce a stable, humus-like material. Individuals may do the same with organic matter to create a local source of soil conditioner (Figure 16-9). Bacterial decomposition releases heat, and in a few days the internal temperature of the compost pile may reach 150°F, sufficient to destroy pathogenic (disease-causing) bacteria that might be present.

In light of the progressive deterioration of American soils and the increasing demand for food, it would seem that composting would be a popular disposal method in this country. However, because the final product is relatively low in nitrogen and phosphorus, many farmers prefer to use commercial fertilizers. Another problem is the cost of removing nonorganics from the waste stream. Source separation could greatly reduce this problem and make composting more feasible. Still another problem is that large tracts of land are needed to store compost,

FIGURE 16-9 Worker at Seattle's zoodoo composting program. Manure and bedding from zoo animals is composted and turned into soil supplements that are sold to area residents. This program cuts down on waste and reduces pollution and makes the city a healthy profit.

and these must be located far away from population centers to avoid problems with insects and odor.

Composting is much more popular in Israel and in frugal European nations—in particular, Italy, England, Holland, and Belgium. In Holland, for example, a single company produces 180,000 metric tons of compost annually from the waste generated by 1 million people.

Incineration

Another strategy now being used in the United States and abroad to reduce waste and capture part of its intrinsic value is **incineration**. Incinerators can burn unseparated trash—mixed with plastics, metals, and glass—or pellets or a confetti-like material free of glass and metal. The heat produced during combustion is used to generate steam for industrial processes, home heating, or electrical generation.

Incineration became popular during the oil crises of the 1970s, but proponents soon found that the technology was plagued with problems—most notably, toxic air pollutants. Thanks to experience gained in Europe and refinements in technology, many American cities have once again turned to this option. In 1986, for instance, there were 69 operating incinerators in the United States and an additional 61 in the planning stages or under construction. By comparison, there are 350 incinerators in Western Europe, Japan, the Soviet Union, and Brazil. Remarkably, over one-half of the municipal solid waste is burned in Japan, Sweden, Denmark, and Switzerland.

Incineration is desirable for a number of reasons. First, it captures energy that would otherwise be lost. It also fits nicely with the existing waste management practices and requires less land than landfills. No modifications of the pickup system are needed. Incinerators can be designed to scale, providing flexibility to serve towns that produce as few as 100 metric tons of garbage a day, as well as larger cities with over 3,000 metric tons.

Despite their mushrooming popularity, incinerators are still viewed skeptically by some air quality experts. Despite improvements in design and controls on air pollution, incinerators that burn plastics and other materials containing chlorine, say the critics, emit a dangerous class of compounds called **dioxins** (see Chapter 15). Dioxins have been linked to cancer, birth defects, and other problems. Recent evidence indicates that they may also weaken the immune system, making individuals more susceptible to cancer. Concerned about potential health problems, Sweden and Denmark have halted the construction of additional incinerators until their medical scientists can determine how substantial a risk they may pose.

Toxic heavy metals and acidic substances like hydrochloric acid—produced when plastics are burned—are also emitted from waste incinerators. Critics argue that if these facilities are to gain widespread acceptance, emissions standards must be developed. Better air pollution controls must also be installed. Requiring residents to separate nonburnables and plastics could help reduce toxic emissions.

Critics also note that pollution control devices generate a hazardous residue called **fly ash**—materials that are removed from the smokestack gases. The ash in the bottom of the incinerator, called **bottom ash**, is also potentially toxic. In fact, some countries now classify bottom and fly ash from incinerators as hazardous materials that must be properly disposed of to protect human health.

HAZARDOUS WASTES

Growing discontent in the 1960s brought about sweeping changes in governmental policy on waste disposal. The citizens of the developed world could no longer tolerate the flagrant and filthy habits of a wasteful society. But few people could have anticipated the shock waves that would be generated by Love Canal—an abandoned canal in Niagara Falls, New York, that had been the repository for over 20,000 metric tons of hazardous wastes, including dioxin, from 1947 to 1952 (see "The Chemical Time Bomb at Love Canal"). Trouble began in the late 1950s after city pressure forced the Hooker Chemical Corporation to turn over the land to them to build a school and a residential community. Workers broke through the clay cap covering the dump site, and trouble soon began. Toxic chemicals from the rusted steel drums oozed out of the ground. Health studies showed a significantly higher incidence of birth defects, respiratory difficulties, and other illnesses. State and federal officials evacuated hundreds of families.

But Love Canal was not an isolated case. The Netherlands, Austria, Hungary, and Sweden all witnessed similar problems. One incident after another set the world community in a state of shock (Figure 16-10). As people began to realize that highly toxic materials had long been carelessly discarded on the land and in the water, they began to call for action. Governments and international agencies struggled in vain to understand the problem, to draft rules and regulations to prevent further incidents, and to clean up the thousands of potentially harmful toxic waste dumps already in existence. Despite over a decade of work on the problem, progress has been exceedingly slow, and many countries have come to realize that hazardous waste management is something of a regulatory nightmare.

How Big Is the Problem?

Hazardous wastes are broadly defined as substances that adversely affect a wide array of organisms, causing death or debilitating illness if improperly stored, transported, disposed of, or handled. Estimating the production of hazardous wastes is nearly impossible. Third World countries, for instance, have no laws governing hazardous materials, and government officials have no idea how much is produced. One country may classify one substance as hazardous that another country does not. Even states may classify materials as hazardous that federal governments do not.

Difficulties aside, experts estimate world production of hazardous materials to be between about 600 to 700 million metric tons. The United States, one of the few countries for which good information is available, produces the lion's share of these potentially harmful materials—approximately 264 million metric tons each year. That's over 1 metric ton of hazardous waste for every man, woman, and child.

FIGURE 16-10 Workers clad in protective clothing and face masks pump toxic materials into a tank truck from barrels at an abandoned paint factory.

The Legacy of Years of Improper Disposal

For a century or more, hazardous wastes have been indiscriminately strewn about the landscape. Until quite recently, wastes were frequently dumped in large steel drums in landfills or on vacant lots, and the drums were left to rust. Over time leaks developed, sending a steady trickle of harmful chemicals into the soil that percolated into the underlying groundwater draining into lakes and streams. In other instances, hazardous wastes were merely pumped into deep wells or municipal sewage systems or directly into lakes and streams. Some companies poured their wastes into sandy pits, where they seeped into the ground. Some unsavory individuals pulled their trucks up to streams and discharged wastes under the cover of darkness. Others opened the spigots and drove along highways at night, spilling tons of toxic wastes.

Years of careless disposal have left a legacy of contaminated sites that pollute lakes, streams, and aquifers. In Europe and North America, hazardous waste dumps have caused entire communities to be uprooted. Every country in Europe, say the authors of *World Resources 1987*, is plagued with an abundance of toxic waste sites—both old and new—needing urgent attention. In the United Kingdom alone 5.5 million metric tons of hazardous wastes were discarded in 1980; three-quarters of this material was dumped in landfills without adequate liners to prevent them from leaking from the site. In the Netherlands, an estimated 8 million metric tons of hazardous materials are buried in the soil, mostly in leaky steel drums. The cleanup bill is estimated at $3 to $6 million.

"For many countries, locating and cleaning up all of the leaking landfills and waste lagoons scattered across the industrial landscape," notes Worldwatch Institute's senior researcher Sandra Postel, "will be among the highest priced items on their environmental agenda." In the United States, for instance, estimates vary on the number of sites in need of cleanup and the eventual cost. The EPA currently includes nearly 900 sites on its National Priority List requiring cleanup but thinks that the number could go higher— perhaps as high as 2,500. This, EPA officials estimate, could cost approximately $23 billion and would require 8 to 10 years to complete. But the Government Accounting Office sees it differently. They estimate that the number of sites on the National Priority List may reach 4,000, costing $40 billion and taking much longer. Even less optimistically, the Office of Technology Assessment believes that the list may eventually expand to include 10,000 sites, costing $100 billion to clean up and requiring about 50 years. Any way you look at it, cleaning up past mistakes will be costly and time-consuming.

In 1980, alarmed at the number of hazardous waste sites in need of cleanup, the U.S. Congress passed the **Comprehensive Environmental Response, Compensation, and Liability Act**, commonly called the **Superfund Act** or **CERCLA**. It called on the EPA to identify and clean up hazardous waste sites with the assistance of state governments (which chipped in 10 percent of the cost). The Superfund Act created a $1.6 billion fund from taxes levied on the petroleum refining and chemical manufacturing industries between 1981 and 1985. During that period, however, only 13 sites were cleaned up, and some of these efforts, say critics, were inadequate. Regulators soon found out that cleaning toxic waste dumps was much more difficult and costly than anticipated. In many cases, toxic residues and contaminated soil had to be excavated and transported to new landfill sites properly lined with clay and synthetic liners. Some critics believe that landfills, no matter how carefully planned and constructed, may eventually leak and therefore will create a problem for future generations.

The Superfund Act ran out in 1985 and was not reauthorized until late in 1986, after 2 years of bitter debate between the Reagan administration and Congress. The new law set up a $9 billion fund for 5 years, based on an even broader business tax. It also provided money for research on new hazardous waste treatment technologies. Critics say that the Superfund Act is an important step in cleaning up our polluted lands, but they warn us that many additional billions will have to be spent to clean up the thousands of contaminated aquifers and landfills throughout the United States.

Managing Hazardous Wastes: The Unmet Challenge

Cleaning up past mistakes is only half of the solution to our hazardous waste problem. The other half is preventing it from occurring again. "Unless the wastes currently produced are better managed," argues Sandra Postel, "new threats will simply replace the old ones, committing society to a costly and perpetual mission of toxic chemical cleanups."

To prevent the indiscriminate and illegal disposal of hazardous wastes, Congress passed the Resource Conservation and Recovery Act of 1976. This far-reaching law, already mentioned in this chapter in regard to solid waste, requires producers, transporters, and disposers of these materials to register them with the EPA. The materials can then be tracked from the site of production to the site of disposal—or from "cradle to grave" in the words of waste managers. Many other nations have formulated similar policies. But tracking hazardous wastes is just part of the solution. Needed are better ways to eliminate wastes altogether.

The Resource Conservation and Recovery Act also ordered the EPA to set standards for packaging, shipping, and disposing of wastes. To prevent further contamination, it required waste disposal companies to obtain a license. Only licensed facilities could legally accept hazardous wastes.

Like municipal wastes, hazardous wastes can be dealt with in three basic ways, which are listed in order of desirability: the reduction approach, the reuse and recycling approach, and the discard approach. Hazardous wastes, however, are amenable to a fourth approach as well, called **detoxification**.

Unfortunately, the discard approach is the most widely used method, and comparatively little recycling and reuse are practiced. In fact, the countries of the Organization for Economic Cooperation and Development (North America, Europe, and Japan) recycle or reuse only about 5 percent and incinerate only 5–10 percent of their hazardous waste. The rest of the waste still ends up in landfills, in disposal wells drilled deep into the earth, or in water bodies. In Europe, for instance, 80 percent of the hazardous material generated each year ends up in deep wells or landfills. In the Communist nations 90-95 percent has a similar fate. Reducing the outflow of wastes remains an unmet challenge.

REDUCING HAZARDOUS WASTES. Manufacturers have a number of options available to reduce hazardous wastes. The first line of attack, and often the cheapest, is **process manipulation**—or redesign. By modifying or redesigning the manufacturing processes that create hazardous wastes, companies can significantly reduce waste production. For instance, the Borden Chemical Company of California redesigned an equipment-cleaning procedure that used toxic organic solvents and produced a dangerous sludge. The redesign reduced their discharge of toxic organic solvents by 93 percent and cut sludge wastes by

about 350 cubic meters to 25 cubic meters per year. As an added benefit, the changes saved the company about $50,000 a year.

The Minnesota Mining and Manufacturing Company (3M), a leader in waste reduction since 1975, has cut its waste production in half and saved nearly $300 million in the process (Figure 16-11). A large chemical company in the Netherlands has installed a new manufacturing process that has cut its waste production by 95 percent.

Companies throughout America, like Borden Chemical and 3M, are learning that pollution prevention pays. Today, at the University of North Carolina's School of Engineering, researchers are working on ways to further source reduction, primarily through process manipulation. The program also promotes the concept in the business community. In 1985, 40 companies participated in their program and saved an astonishing $12 million for their efforts. As hazardous waste disposal costs continue to rise, more and more companies will find ways to modify their manufacturing processes.

Companies can also substitute safe materials for more harmful ones. A company based in Indianapolis, for instance, has introduced a new line of nonhazardous, biodegradable industrial cleaners called **Work-safe**. These could replace highly toxic organic cleaners. Water-based paints are another example.

Despite these gains, waste reduction has only begun to be tapped. According to a recent survey, fewer than one-quarter of the companies recently surveyed in the United States had made any reductions in waste. Conservatively, nationwide efforts to modify manufacturing processes and substitute biodegradable compounds for toxic ones could reduce our waste stream by 15–30 percent.

But waste reduction represents a new way of thinking for businesses. For it to become mainstream, more

FIGURE 16-11 The 3M corporation has been a leader in pollution prevention, finding ways to cut pollution and save money.

companies must realize that waste is a sign of inefficiency and higher costs. Top-level management must commit itself to a program of waste reduction like that of 3M and other companies. Surprisingly small efforts could produce big savings. USS Chemicals, for example, is a company whose management is committed to waste reduction. It has established a reward system for employees who suggest implementable waste-saving techniques. By 1986, the company had paid out $70,000 in rewards for projects that had saved the company $500,000.

Source reduction is far more popular outside the United States. The governments of Canada, Japan, Sweden, West Germany, Denmark, and the Netherlands for instance, actively promote nonwaste and low-waste technologies.

REUSING AND RECYCLING HAZARDOUS WASTES. Manufacturers can also make significant inroads into hazardous wastes by reusing or recyling them (Figure 16-12). After source reduction, reuse and recycling are the preferred methods of waste management. Individual companies, for instance, may be able to reuse for other manufacturing processes relatively pure but toxic materials that might otherwise have been disposed of. In some cases, the materials may have to be purified to remove contaminants, but either way, the savings can be substantial. If a company cannot reuse or recycle its own effluents, it may find another company that can. This reduces the cost of waste disposal for the seller and cuts the cost of raw materials for the buyer.

To facilitate the exchange of wastes, the Netherlands put into operation a hazardous waste clearinghouse, or **waste exchange**. Established in 1969, it keeps track of 150 different chemical substances produced by industry and helps link buyers and sellers. Numerous private and nonprofit clearinghouses now exist in many U.S. cities and throughout the rest of the developed world. The Northeast Industrial Waste Exchange in Syracuse, New York, operates a computerized network listing wastes from five different regions. Anyone with a computer and modem and the proper password can gain access to the files to find out what is available or to list wastes for sale.

Despite the many benefits of recycling, few countries pursue this option actively. In Denmark, long known for its exemplary state-run waste management program, only 5 percent of the industrial waste handled by the government's central hazardous waste facility is recycled. Even without advances in technology, Danish engineers believe that this figure could be easily raised to 20–25 percent. In the United States, only a tiny fraction of our hazardous waste—about 4 percent—is recycled.

The world may look to Japan for guidance on this issue. Today the Japanese produce about 200 million metric tons of industrial waste, both nonhazardous and hazardous. Collectively they recycle over one-half of that material. Another 30 percent is incinerated. What is left—18 percent of the industrial waste stream—is disposed of, mostly in landfills.

DETOXIFICATION. Some hazardous wastes cannot be reused or recycled but are amenable to biological, chemical, and physical detoxification. For example, organic wastes such as PCBs, DDT, and even dioxin can be burned in high-temperature incinerators. Incineration converts harmful organic substances into relatively harmless carbon dioxide (a global pollutant in its own right, but not responsible for adverse health effects) and water.

Long criticized by many in the environmental community because they do not completely eliminate toxic emissions, incinerators are growing in popularity. The EPA has a mobile incinerator that destroys 99.999 percent of the dioxin wastes in soils and liquids. It can be delivered to waste sites, avoiding transportation costs and dangers.

Another option is to burn wastes at sea. At least six European nations currently ship some of their toxic wastes to hugh ocean-going vessels equipped with high-temperature incinerators. These ships then head out to sea to burn the wastes (Figure 16-13). But before critics will accept further burning at sea, they want tighter controls on emissions. The same demand is now being made for land-based incinerators. A newly developed plasma arc incinerator, for instance, burns toxic wastes at a temperature of 45,000°F, destroying all traces of PCBs and other organic wastes; it may mark the way of the future.

FIGURE 16-12 Whether a given substance is considered a waste or a valuable resource depends on an industry's point of view. Some industries are now selling their "wastes" to other industries for use as valuable raw materials in their manufacturing processes.

FIGURE 16-13 The Dutch incinerator ship "Vulcanus" burns hazardous waste at sea. Is this a suitable way to get rid of the many hazardous organic wastes industrial societies generate or will it lead to widespread pollution of air and water with potentially dangerous chemicals?

Another promising development is the combustion of hazardous organic wastes in existing cement and lime kilns. Typically powered by oil, kilns may be an efficient and cost-effective alternative to traditional incinerators. In Sweden, for instance, kiln operators burn a mixture of oil and hazardous organic materials. Most kilns already have state-of-the-art pollution control equipment. Basic materials in the kiln also neutralize acidic emissions. Cement companies are paid to incinerate wastes and are able to cut down on their own fuel consumption in the process, saving money on operations.

On another front, genetic engineers have recently developed strains of bacteria that decompose chemical solvents, such as benzene, toluene, and xylene, converting them into carbon dioxide and water. Scientists have also found bacteria that successfully degrade oil wastes in soil and water.

Numerous chemical methods are also available. For instance, ozone can be used to destroy organic compounds. Special ion-exchange columns can efficiently separate out metals. Various bases can be used to neutralize acids.

Proper Disposal of Hazardous Waste

In an ideal world, hazardous wastes could be reduced by 60–75 percent by process manipulation, reuse, recycling, and detoxification. The remaining material could be disposed of by any one of a half dozen or so techniques, such as secured landfills, deep geologic salt beds, surface impoundments, warehouses, and deep injection wells. Secured landfills and deep injection wells will be discussed here, since they are the preferred methods.

SECURED LANDFILLS. The most popular discard approach today is the **secured landfill**—a clay-lined pit designed to hold hazardous wastes (Figure 16-14). The thick, supposedly impermeable clay liners are often supplemented by synthetic liners and detection wells, from which groundwater samples can be taken to determine if wastes are leaking out of the site. Special drain systems also pump liquid wastes from the bottom of the pit to treatment facilities where they are detoxified, thus minimizing the migration of these substances out of the site. Careful siting also minimizes the risk to ground and surface water. Grading and compaction of the soil over the site minimize the penetration of rain and snowmelt, thus reducing leaching.

Although extraordinary precautions are taken to prevent the escape of materials from landfills, critics are unconvinced that they can contain waste in the long term. Cracks in the liner and clay seal, for instance, could emit wastes that drain into groundwater and contaminate aquifers. Earthquakes could tear asunder the careful controls. Lax monitoring could unleash a local environmental catastrophe.

DEEP INJECTION WELLS. Perhaps the least talked about but most important problem in hazardous waste management is that about 85 percent of the hazardous wastes are highly diluted in water. Given off from factories in enormous amounts, this material has been exceedingly difficult to regulate. And separating out the hazardous materials is costly and expensive. For this reason, companies frequently dispose of their liquid wastes in deep wells or, illegally, into lakes and sewage systems.

Deep wells are drilled into the earth's crust to porous zones sandwiched between impermeable rock layers. In theory, the hazardous material remains in place forever. In practice, though, this is not always what happens. Liquid wastes can migrate through unexpected fissures in the "impermeable" rock strata and contaminate aquifers. Cracks in the well casing can also result in leakage. Injecting large quantities of liquids into

FIGURE 16-14 Drawing of secured landfill showing monitoring wells, clas and synthetic liner, and treatment facilities for leachate.

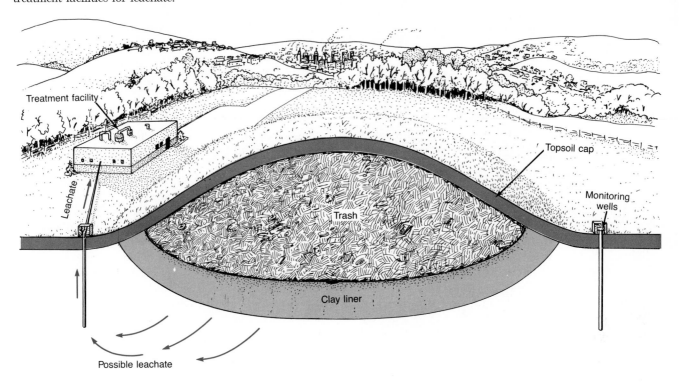

The Chemical Time Bomb at Love Canal

In the 1880s, William T. Love began constructing a canal that would provide water and electrical power to the growing city of Niagara Falls, New York. Connecting the Niagara River just above the falls to a point below the falls, the canal would be a focal point of industrial development. But because of economic troubles, the project was abandoned. Many parts were filled in as the city expanded, and by the 1900s only a 900-meter section of the ill-fated canal remained— a mute testimony to one man's dream gone sour.

In 1942, the Hooker Chemical Company entered into an agreement with the canal's owner, the Niagara Power and Development Corporation, that allowed the company to use the remaining section as a hazardous waste dump. There were no regulations for waste disposal at the time, and very little concern over the impacts of burying steel drums in the earth among politicians, citizens, and business.

In 1946 Hooker purchased the canal from Niagara Power, and for the next 6 years dumped into it thousands of steel drums containing 20,000 metric tons of hazardous materials. Then in 1952, the city of Niagara Falls, looking for land on which to build a school and a residential community, began condemnation proceedings—to literally take the land from the company. Hooker caved in to the pressure,

received a nominal $1 payment, and sealed off the site with a clay liner before turning it over to the city, allegedly with a warning not to build on the dump site itself. In turn, the city signed an agreement releasing the company from any damages that might occur.

In 1954 the city began building the 99th Street Elementary School right over the dump. Nearby, 239 homes went up, and another 700 soon skirted the chemical time bomb. A few years later, troubles began. Rusty and leaking barrels began to emerge in low spots. Chemical wastes pooled on the surface. Residents noticed harsh chemical smells so powerful that they killed grass and vegetables and took the bark off trees. Children playing near them suffered serious chemical burns; some became ill, and a few even died.

Then in 1977, 20 years later, unusually heavy rain and snow converted the site into a sea of mud. Through the years, corrosion had turned the steel drums into leaking sieves. Toxic wastes came bubbling up to the surface, pooling in people's backyards and filling basements with a black, smelly goo. Residents complained of strange odors. Pets began to die mysteriously. Many residents complained of severe headaches and rectal bleeding. Children playing in the area were seriously burned by chemicals. Concerned with the many complaints

FIGURE 1 Toxic chemicals and rusted drums have worked their way to the surface in Love Canal, forcing the State of New York to evacuate hundreds of families.

it was receiving, the New York State Health Department initiated a health study. To their surprise, they found a high incidence of liver, kidney, and respiratory disorders, as well as epilepsy and cancer. In addition, the rate of miscarriages and birth defects among residents was found to be three times higher than the national average. In July 1978 the Health Department strongly recommended that pregnant women and children under 2 years of age move out of the area.

In the fall of 1978, officials began a massive cleanup of the dump site. Some homes were bulldozed; others were left intact, their doors and windows boarded up.

In an ensuing investigation, more than 80 toxic chemicals were indentified at the site. At least 12 were known carcinogens. As the evidence grew, city and state officials closed down the school, fenced it off, and evacuated several hundred families. On May 21, 1980, President Jimmy Carter declared Love Canal a disaster area. The federal government evacuated over 780 more families, and provided housing for them at a cost of $30 million.

As the cleanup proceeded, additional studies by the EPA revealed that the immediate vicinity was badly polluted but that the toxic wastes had not migrated much past the first two rows of houses on either side of the canal. The EPA concluded, therefore, that the 1980 evacuation was unwarranted. The study also showed that the chemical wastes had not migrated to deep aquifers and were unlikely to move much further.

Love Canal and the school yard where children once played are surrounded by a chain link fence with bright yellow signs warning passersby of the hazardous wastes. Boarded-up houses give the area an eerie feeling. What will be done with it? Probably nothing. Love Canal will remain, fenced off and cleaned up as best as possible, a sort of national monument to our carelessness and, hopefully, our newfound commitment to solve the growing waste problem.

FIGURE 2   One family took their home with them, leaving only the foundation as an eerie reminder of what had happened. Abandoned houses in the background are boarded up.

the earth can destabilize rock layers, greatly increasing minor earthquakes.

Because of these problems and the general lack of appeal of this method, many people in the environmental community would like to eliminate it entirely, preferring instead ways to separate out the hazardous materials for detoxification, incineration, or some other disposal method.

THE NIMBY SYNDROME: TAKING PERSONAL RESPONSIBILITY. Perhaps no subject stirs as much controversy as the siting of a hazardous waste facility, and for good reason. Few people want a hazardous thing—a landfill or a deep injection well, for example—near their homes or farms or schools.

Public policy makers have dubbed this the **NIMBY syndrome**—*not in my backyard*. It presents a colossal public policy dilemma that boils down to this: Most people want the amenities provided by manufacturers, but they want nothing to do with the waste that comes from them. Let some other community take it.

It is time, say some proponents of responsible living, to take action individually. By cutting back on the use of hazardous materials—pesticides, herbicides, solvents, cleaners, and so on—individuals can help reduce the volume of hazardous wastes churned out by our factories. Reducing unnecessary consumption of plastics and other goods can also help. Individuals can also deliver hazardous materials from their homes (discarded paints, solvents, and so on) to special pickup points provided by many cities. Beyond that, citizens can join environmental groups such as the Worldwatch Institute, World Resources Institute, Institute for Local Self Reliance, and the National Coalition for Recyclable Waste, which are all working on this and other issues. Citizens can write letters to government officials asking for more efforts to reduce, reuse, and recycle wastes. Without greater source reduction, reuse, and recycling, the hazardous waste problem will continue to worsen, overwhelming future generations as surely as it has overwhelmed us.

RAPID REVIEW

1. American Cities and towns generate 135 million metric tons of municipal solid waste each year. Unfortunately, only about 10 percent of the solid waste is recovered for reuse and recycling, and only 4 percent is burned to generate energy.

2. Nearly two-fifths of our solid waste is paper, much of which comes from packaging and direct-mail advertising. Americans recycle only about 20 percent of their paper and cardboard despite the economic and environmental benefits of recycling. Worldwide, about 26 percent of the paper and cardboard used each day is recycled. According to many experts, however, this figure could double by 2000.

3. Americans use 66 billion aluminum cans a year; about one-half of them are recycled. Recycling aluminum is 95 percent more energy efficient than producing aluminum cans from bauxite.

4. Because losses are inevitable and some uses tie up aluminum more or less permanently, most experts believe that only 60–80 percent of the aluminum produced each year can be recycled. Most nations, however, fall well below that theoretical limit. The United States, for instance, recycles only 32 percent of its aluminum.

5. America is a country made of steel. Despite its importance, however, we recycled only 35 percent of it. Worldwide, average recycling is only 25 percent. One of the chief reasons for this is the relative abundance of iron ore, from which steel is made. But using iron ore, rather than recycling, simply because it is available or abundant may not be the most economical approach. It is certainly not the most environmentally sound approach.

6. Americans use hugh quantities of glass every year. Like other nonrenewable resources, glass can be easily recycled. Unfortunately, only a tiny fraction (7 percent) makes its way back into the system.

7. Glass manufacturers have routinely added 15–20 percent recycled glass, called *cullet,* to manufacture new glass. Several newer systems, however, can use 100 percent recycled glass to make new bottles and jars. A 10 percent increase in the amount of cullet used decreases the energy required by 2–5 percent.

8. Plastics have invaded our lives. Nowhere has the growth of plastics consumption been as great as in the packaging industry. Today, as a result, plastics make up 10 percent of our municipal waste; however, only a tiny fraction of the millions of tons used each year in the United States is recovered for reuse and recycling. Plastic is difficult to reuse and recycle because there are so many different kinds of it. And many plastic products contain two or more different plastics.

9. Most plastics resist breakdown by sunlight or bacteria. Unlike other materials, the growing use of plastics probably will not be offset by recycling. We must find other ways to reduce this growing problem.

10. Many modern industrial societies have traditionally viewed municipal waste as something to be rid of—to dump in the ground or at sea as far away as possible—with little regard for the wealth of materials it contains. This is the discard approach.

11. Two other environmentally more sound approaches exist: the reduction approach, which calls for lower levels of material consumption, and the reuse and recycling approach, which maximizes the life span of materials.

12. Reducing per capita consumption of natural resources, while unpopular, may become an economic fact of life in materialistic societies like ours as resource supplies begin to fall. Individuals can help by buying durable items and avoiding unnecessary purchases. Miniaturization has helped us reduce resource consumption and will continue to be useful in the years to come.

13. Reuse and recycling can also help reduce solid waste and conserve valuable resources. Advocates of this strategy point out that many products can be reused. For materials that cannot be reused, however, the next best approach is recycling.

14. Recycled materials can be extracted from municipal trash at central stations or separated out of the trash at the source. Currently, the United States recycles only about 10 percent of its solid municipal waste, but the EPA believes that this rate could easily double. Based on the experience of the Japanese and others, a 60–80 percent recovery could be achieved.

15. Many nations now have successful recycling programs. Japan, the Netherlands, Mexico, and South Korea lead the world in recycling paper. The United States is slowly on its way to becoming a leader in aluminum recycling. Can and bottle laws, now found in nine states, are the cornerstone of our recycling strategy. In Oregon, the state with the first bottle bill, 95 percent of all refillable bottles and 92 percent of all aluminum cans are returned each year.

16. While the gains in recycling and reuse are commendable, many conservationists argue that modern society has only just begun to tap the vast potential of its waste. Needed are ways to promote recycling and to stimulate the demand for recycled goods.

17. Governments can play a key role in promoting reuse and recycling. Television ads, billboards, and pamphlets can encourage the public to take a more active role. New recycling laws, recycling centers, waste exchanges, and tax incentives offered by governments can increase recycling as well.

18. Governments and businesses can also look for ways to improve the market for recycled goods. Governments, for instance, can require their agencies to purchase recycled materials.

19. For years, Americans discarded their wastes in open dumps that were periodically burned to reduce their volume. Then in the 1960s, they began to revolt. In 1976, Congress passed the Resource Conservation and Recovery Act, which, among other things, called for a complete end to open dumps by 1983. The sanitary landfill replaced the dump.

20. Landfills are excavations or natural depressions in which garbage is dumped, compacted, and covered daily with a layer of soil to reduce pests. Landfills offer many advantages. Besides being cleaner than dumps, they can be reclaimed—returned to a previous use or given over to a new use. But they do have their problems. Pollutants may drain into underlying aquifers, polluting groundwater. Rotting garbage also produces methane, a potentially explosive gas. In addition, landfills are a waste of valuable resources that could be recycled or reused. They also require large tracts of land.

21. Many local governments reduce their solid waste disposal by composting, in which organic matter is piled in vacant lots and left to decay. Aerobic bacteria in the waste decompose the organic matter to produce a stable, humus-like material, which can be used to condition and fertilize soil.

22. Another strategy now being used in the United States and elsewhere is incineration. Incinerators burn unseparated trash or glass- and metal-free trash to generate heat for industrial processes, home heating, or electrical generation.

23. Incineration is growing in popularity but remains a troublesome source of air pollutants and ash, a hazardous waste.

24. No sooner had various nations moved to solve their hazardous waste problems than they discovered another problem: thousands of hazardous waste sites strewn about the country, resulting from more than a century of disposal techniques now viewed as dangerous and foolish.

25. Hazardous wastes are substances that adversely affect a wide array of organisms, causing death or debilitating disease if improperly stored, transported, disposed of, or handled.

26. Although on one knows for sure, it is believed that about 600 to over 700 million metric tons of hazardous waste are produced worldwide each year. The United States alone produces about 264 million metric tons.

27. Locating and cleaning up contaminated sites will be among the highest-priced items on the environmen-

tal agenda of many industrialized nations. In 1980 the U.S. Congress passed the Comprehensive Environmental Response, Compensation, and Liability Act, or Superfund Act. This important law calls on the EPA to identify and clean up hazardous waste sites in the United States, using money largely from taxes levied on the petroleum and chemical manufacturing industries.

28. Cleaning up past mistakes is only half of the solution to our hazardous waste problem; the other half is preventing them from occurring again. The Resource Conservation and Recovery Act helps to do this by monitoring hazardous wastes from cradle to grave. It also gives the EPA the power to set up standards for packaging, shipping, and disposal of wastes and licenses hazardous waste disposal facilities.

29. Like municipal wastes, hazardous wastes can be dealt with in three basic ways, in order of desirability: reduction, reuse and recycling, and discarding. Unfortunately, the discard approach is the most widely used method.

30. To reduce hazardous wastes, manufacturers can modify or redesign their processes. They can also substitute safe materials for more harmful ones.

31. Manufacturers can also reduce the hazardous waste output of their factories by reusing and recycling wastes. Hazardous waste clearinghouses can help facilitate the exchange of wastes between businesses.

32. Some hazardous wastes that cannot be reused or recycled can be detoxified. For instance, organic wastes can be incinerated or decomposed by bacteria.

33. Some hazardous waste will inevitably be produced. This must be disposed of safely for hundreds, perhaps thousands of years. Secured landfills, the most popular approach today, are seen by few as a permanent solution. Many critics believe that they will eventually leak, creating problems for future generations. Deep injection wells are also popular for the disposal of liquid wastes but are riddled with problems.

KEY TERMS AND CONCEPTS

Aseptic containers
Bottom ash
Composting
Cullet
Deep injection wells
Detoxification
Dioxins
Electric arc furnace
End-point separation
Fly ash
Hazardous waste
Incineration
Municipal solid waste
NIMBY syndrome
Open dumps
Oxygen furnaces
Process manipulation
Recycling
Recycling Opportunity Act
Resource Conservation and Recovery Act
Reuse
Reverse vending machines
Sanitary landfill
Secured landfill
Source separation
Superfund Act
Waste exchange

QUESTIONS AND TOPICS FOR DISCUSSION

1. Debate the following statement: "By refusing to reuse and recycle municipal wastes, America is throwing away its future."

2. Describe the three main techniques for managing municipal wastes. Discuss the pros and cons of each one. Give specific examples of each.

3. Outline a plan to reduce your family's trash. What obstacles stand in the way of reducing the volume by 50 percent? How can they be overcome?

4. Why is it theoretically possible to recycle only 60–80 percent of America's aluminum?

5. Debate this statement: "In countries with large resource supplies, it is more economical to use raw ore than recyclable materials."

6. Why are plastics so hard to recycle? How could this problem be solved?

7. Outline a plan for your city or town to reduce its solid and hazardous wastes. Would you involve private citizens and, if so, how? Contact local officials and ask them whether reuse and recycling programs exist and what the obstacles are to further waste reduction.

8. Describe ways to increase the demand for recycled goods.

9. List the pros and cons of sanitary landfills, compost facilities, and incinerators.

10. What is a hazardous waste? How can such wastes best be reduced?

11. What problem does the Superfund Act address, and how does it address it?

12. What hazardous waste problem does the Resource Conservation and Recovery Act address, and how does it address it?

13. Describe ways that manufacturers can reduce hazardous wastes.

14. Discuss the following statement: "It is absurd to think that companies can recycle hazardous wastes."

15. List and describe several methods of hazardous waste detoxification.

16. Debate the following statement: "Secured landfills are the safest way to dispose of hazardous wastes."

SUGGESTED READINGS

Municipal Wastes

Conservation Foundation. *State of the Environment: A View Toward the Nineties.* Washington, D.C.: Conservation Foundation, 1987. See Chapters 3 and 7 for more information on toxic and municipal wastes.

Chandler, W. U. *Materials Recycling: The Virtue of Necessity.* Worldwatch Paper 56. Washington, D.C.: Worldwatch Institute, October 1983. Fact-filled analysis of global achievements in recycling.

Parkinson, A. "Responsible Waste Management in a Shrinking World." *Environment* 25(10): 61–67, 1983. Good overview of the problem

Pollock, C. *Mining Urban Wastes: The Potential for Recycling.* Worldwatch Paper 76. Washington, D.C.: Worldwatch Institute, April 1987. Enormously informative coverage of the vast untapped potential of recycling.

White, P., and Psihoyos, L. "The Fascinating World of Trash." *National Geographic* 163(4): 424–457, 1983. A graphic but somewhat humorous look at trash.

Hazardous Wastes

Berger, J. J. *Restoring the Earth.* New York: Knopf, 1985. See Chapter 10 for a chilling account of waste mismanagement.

Holdren, C. "Toxic Substances: A Cause for Concern?" In *The Cassandra Conference: Resources and the Human Predicament,* P. R. Ehrlich and J. P. Holdren, eds. College Station, Texas: Texas A&M University Press, 1988. An exciting, worthwhile collection of essays.

International Institute for Environment and Development and World Resources Institute. *World Resources 1987.* New York: Basic Books, 1987. Chapter 13 is a superb overview of global hazardous waste management, the problems and the challenges.

Martin, L. "The Case for Stopping Wastes at Their Source." *Environment* 28(3): 35–37, 1986. Interesting case study supporting the idea of waste reduction as the first line of attack.

Postel, S. *Defusing the Toxics Threat: Controlling Pesticides and Industrial Waste.* Worldwatch Paper 79. Washington, D.C.: Worldwatch Institute, September 1987. Excellent overview of ways to better manage hazardous wastes, especially by reducing, reusing, and recycling them (pp. 36–46).

Regenstein, L. *America the Poisoned.* Washington, D.C.: Acropolis Books, 1982. Packed full of information on toxic chemicals. Chapter 3 is an excellent overview of hazardous wastes.

17

Air Pollution

Human beings breathe in and out about once every 4 seconds, 16 times a minute, 960 times an hour—nearly 8.5 million times a year. We breathe nearly 4 million liters (1 million gallons) of oxygen-containing air every year from the earth's atmosphere (Table 17-1).

In addition to being a vital source of oxygen, the earth's atmosphere is of value to us in many other ways. Without the insulation and heat distribution provided by the atmosphere, the earth would be subjected to drastic day–night temperature changes completely incompatible with survival. Without an atmosphere, sound vibrations could not be transmitted; the earth would be silent. There would be no weather, no spring rains for crops and lawns, no snow, hail, or fog. Without its atmospheric shield, our planet would be more heavily bombarded with meteorites and would be exposed to potentially lethal radiation from the sun. Without an atmosphere, the earth would be as lifeless as the moon.

POLLUTION OF THE ATMOSPHERE

Natural Pollution

Long before the first white settlers set foot on American soil, the atmosphere was to some degree polluted, not from artificial sources but from natural causes. Smoke from lightning-triggered forest fires billowed darkly across the land.

Natural pollution is still with us. In May 1980, the massive eruption of Mount St. Helens in Washington released thousands of tons of dust and ash into the air and briefly caused breathing problems for both humans and wildlife downwind from the blast (Figures 17-1 and 17-2). A given sample of today's atmosphere may contain a host of natural contaminants, ranging from ragweed pollen to fungal spores and from disease-causing bacteria to minute particles of volcanic ash and salt.

Pollution Caused by Humans

Homo sapiens has been fouling the atmosphere ever since Stone Age people first roasted a deer over an open fire. The smoke smudged some of the magnificent cave-wall paintings in southern France—perhaps the first serious property damage caused by air pollution. In 1306 Parliament passed a law making it illegal to burn coal in a furnace in London; at least one violator was actually tortured for his offense. However, it was not until the Industrial Revolution that air pollution began to seriously affect the health of large segments of society. In 1909 over 1,000 people died in Glasgow, Scotland, as a result of polluted air. In conjunction with this incident, the word **smog** was coined as a contraction of **smoke** and **fog**. Let us examine the major pollutants that concern us today.

MAJOR ATMOSPHERIC POLLUTANTS

The major air pollutants in the United States are carbon monoxide, oxides of sulfur, particulate matter, hydrocarbons, and oxides of nitrogen (Figure 17-3, Table 17-2).

Table 17-1 Composition of Clean, Dry Air at Sea Level

Gas	Volume Percent
Nitrogen	78.08
Oxygen	20.94
Argon	0.9340
Carbon Dioxide	0.0310
Neon	0.0018
Helium	0.0005
Methane	0.0002
Krypton	0.0001
Sulfur dioxide	0.0001

Note: Gases such as carbon dioxide, methane, and sulfur dioxide are normal constituents of clean air. However, they often reach much higher concentrations in polluted air, and may have adverse effects on the environment and/or human health.

Carbon Monoxide

When the senior author was in college, carbon monoxide poisoning was usually associated with suicide; a running car and a closed garage took many a life. Since then, however, because of the rapidly mounting levels of carbon monoxide above our city streets and freeway systems, hundreds of thousands of Americans are suffering from a subtle, unwanted type of carbon monoxide poisoning, one not severe enough to cause death but causing marked effects on human health.

Rather surprisingly, roughly 93 percent of the carbon monoxide in the global atmosphere is derived from natural sources, such as the oxidation of methane (marsh gas), which in turn is formed by the decay of marshland organisms. However, this carbon monoxide does not build up to harmful concentrations because it is produced from widely dispersed sources and, because it is quickly converted into carbon dioxide.

It might reasonably be asked, then, why we are so concerned with carbon monoxide as an atmospheric pollutant? The answer is that the seemingly insignificant 7 percent of the carbon monoxide generated by human activities, largely as the result of the incomplete combustion of fossil fuels, is concentrated in a relatively small volume of air in the world's major cities. In fact, the carbon monoxide concentrations of urban areas are 50 to 100 times greater than the worldwide average.

Oxides of Sulfur

Oxides of sulfur form whenever sulfur-containing fuels, such as coal and oil, are burned. About 21 million metric tons of sulfur oxides are released into our nation's atmosphere each year. As every chemistry student knows, colorless sulfur dioxide stings the eyes and burns the throat. About 1 percent of the population will develop chronic weariness, tortured breathing, sore throat, tonsillitis, coughing, and wheezing when exposed for lengthy periods to the concentrations of sulfur dioxide normally occurring in polluted urban air. Because sulfur dioxide may slow down or even halt the cleansing mechanism of the lungs, it contributes importantly to such chronic diseases as bronchitis and emphysema.

FIGURE 17-1 Mount Saint Helens erupts. Generally, pollution from natural sources is far less harmful than pollution from human sources. That's because natural sources tend to release small quantities over huge areas, which results in low ambient levels. The eruption of Mount Saint Helens is an exception.

FIGURE 17-2 Shaded area shows approximate path of ashes emitted into the air by the eruption of Mt. St. Helens.

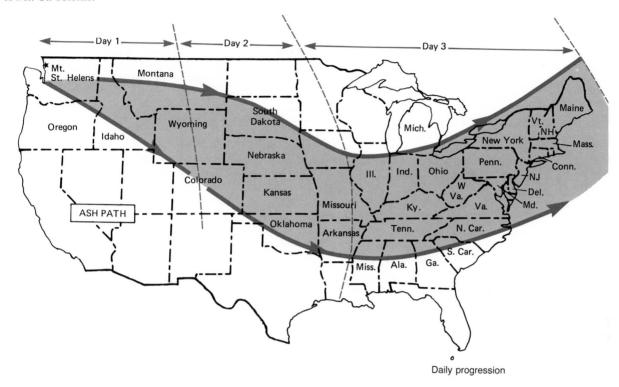

FIGURE 17-2 Shaded area shows approximate path of ashes emitted into the air by the eruption of Mt. St. Helens.

Particulate Matter

Particulate matter can be defined as small solid particles and liquid droplets suspended in the air (Figure 17-4). Depending on their size and weight, the particles may remain suspended in the air for periods ranging from a few seconds to several months. Most of the particulate matter is emitted by facilities that use coal as fuel, such as power plants, iron and steel mills, and foundries. About 7 million metric tons of particulate matter are injected into our atmosphere yearly.

For years, **lead** was added to gasoline to enhance its octane rating, that is, the efficiency with which it burns. Humans take this lead into our system when inhaling air polluted with motor exhaust. A cumulative poison, it is also ingested with food or water. It can damage the kidneys, blood, and liver. Moreover, it can damage the brains of youngsters.

On the basis of lead concentrations in snows at high elevations in the Rockies, Clare C. Patterson, a California Institute of Technology geochemist, has suggested that lead concentrations in humans are 100 times the level of two centuries ago. In 1973 the EPA began restricting lead in gasoline, imposing a 90 percent reduction by the end of 1985. The EPA proposes to eliminate lead from gasoline by 1995.

Hydrocarbons

A **hydrocarbon**, as the name suggests, is simply an organic compound that is composed of hydrogen and carbon. Good examples are methane, benzene, and ethylene. In urban areas, humans may generate more than 200 kinds of hydrocarbons. These hydrocarbons can react with nitrogen oxides in the presence of sun-

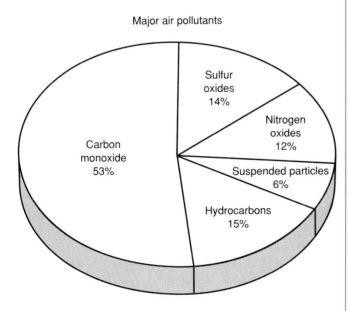

Major air pollutants

Carbon monoxide 53%

Sulfur oxides 14%

Nitrogen oxides 12%

Suspended particles 6%

Hydrocarbons 15%

FIGURE 17-3 Major pollutants released into the air over the United States.

Table 17-2 Sources and Effects of Major Air Pollutants

Pollutant	Description and Major Sources	Human and Environmental Effects
Total suspended particulates	Solid or liquid particles produced by combustion and other processes at major industrial sources (e.g., steel mills, power plants, chemical plants, cement plants, incinerators)	Respiratory irritant, aggravates asthma and other lung and heart diseases (especially in combination with sulfur dioxide); many are known carcinogens. Toxic gases and heavy metals adsorb onto these particulates and are commonly carried deep into the lungs.
Sulfur dioxide	Colorless gas produced by combustion at power plants and certain industrial sources.	Respiratory irritant, aggravates asthma and other lung and heart diseases, reduces lung function. Sulfur dioxide damages plants and is a precursor to acid rain.
Carbon monoxide	Colorless gas produced by motor vehicles and some industrial processes	Interferes with the blood's ability to absorb oxygen; can cause dizziness, drowziness; impairs motor reflexes; may bring on angina.
Nitrogen dioxide	Brownish-orange gas produced by motor vehicles and combustion at major industrial sources	Respiratory irritant, aggravates asthma and other lung and heart diseases.
Ozone	A colorless gas formed from a reaction between motor vehicle emissions and sunlight; it is the major component of smog	Respiratory irritant, aggravates asthma and other lung and heart diseases, impairs lung functions. Ozone is toxic to plants and corrodes materials.
Hydrocarbons	Small quantities of hazardous pollutants emitted from industrial processes and diesel motor vehicle exhaust	Linked to organ damage, serious chronic diseases, and various types of cancer.
Lead	Very small particles emitted from motor vehicles and smelters	Toxic to nervous and blood-forming systems; can cause brain and organ damage in high concentrations.

light to form **photochemical smog**. Much hydrocarbon pollution results from the evaporation of gasoline from carburetors, crankcases, and gas tanks of cars and trucks. In addition, unburned hydrocarbons are released from the exhaust pipes of motor vehicles.

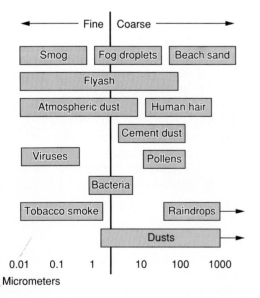

FIGURE 17-4 Size ranges of some airborne particulates. Some particles in smog, fly ash, dust, and tobacco smoke are only .01 micron in diameter, much too small even to be seen under an ordinary microscope.

Oxides of Nitrogen

Nitric oxide is formed when atmospheric nitrogen combines with oxygen at the high temperatures generated in the internal-combustion engine. It is relatively harmless at ordinary concentrations. At unusually high concentrations, nitric oxide may be lethal, causing death by asphyxiation because it combines 300,000 times more readily with hemoglobin than does oxygen.

Nitric oxide also combines with atmospheric oxygen to form **nitrogen dioxide**, a reddish-brown gas with a pungent, choking odor. Nitrogen dioxide is a major component of photochemical smog. It causes a variety of human ailments ranging from gum inflammation and internal bleeding to emphysema and increased susceptibility to pneumonia and lung cancer. Nitrogen dioxide is considered four times as toxic as nitric oxide. Major sources of the oxides of nitrogen are shown in Figure 17-5. Unlike most of our other major pollutants, the emission of nitrogen dioxide into the atmosphere has gradually been increasing.

OZONE AND PHOTOCHEMICAL SMOG. **Ozone** is a major component of photochemical smog—the brownish haze that shrouds many urban areas during the hot, sunny days of summer. Ozone is produced by chemical reactions between hydrocarbons and nitrogen oxides. These reactions are powered by sunlight—hence the term photochemical smog. The greater the intensity of sunlight and the warmer the day, the larger the amount of ozone produced. Since hydrocarbons and

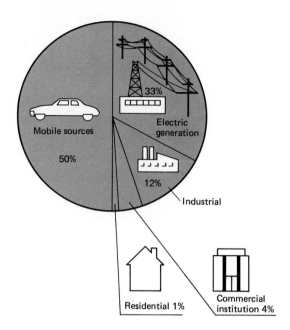

FIGURE 17-5 Major sources of nitrogen oxides in the United States.

oxides of nitrogen are mainly generated by motor vehicles, the ozone levels gradually rise in the morning and peak between noon and 4 P.M. On cloudy days, ozone production is reduced; after sunset, it stops altogether.

Photochemical smog has traditionally been associated with Los Angeles, where it was first recognized and has been a severe problem. However, during the 1970s and 1980s, it has proved to be a daunting challenge to

health officials in Denver, Salt Lake City, Milwaukee, Chicago, New York, and Boston as well. In fact, during the extremely hot summer of 1988, many East Coast towns and cities were plagued with record high ozone levels. In fact, the EPA reported that in 1988 more than 70 cities failed to comply with the federal ozone standard (Figure 17-6). Standards are discussed shortly.

As many summer visitors to Los Angeles well know, the ozone in photochemical smog irritates the eyes, nose and throat, and makes breathing difficult. Recent scientific studies, however, have shown that ozone pollution may have much more serious consequences. For example, even low-level, short-term exposure to ozone can cause both weight reduction and chromosome damage in rodents. Other animal studies conducted in 1988 showed that chronic exposure to ozone causes permanent lung damage, including stiffening of the wall of the lung, which is normally associated with the aging process. Dr. Morton Lippmann, professor of environmental medicine at New York University, reported in 1988 that jogging in an ozone-polluted urban environment may do the runner more harm than good. In fact, it can be as dangerous to one's health as smoking. The effect is cumulative. With each breath, the runner's lungs are damaged a little more. Says Lippman: "People won't fall over from exercising one or two days, but you may have breathing difficulties later on."

But this is not all. The health of farm crops is adversely affected by ozone as well. For example, the U.S. Office of Technology has reported that an ozone-induced yield reduction of only four major crops—wheat, corn, soybeans, and peanuts—results in an

FIGURE 17-6 Counties not meeting ozone standards in 1985.

FIGURE 17-7 USDA research compares two potato plants. The sickly plant on the right was grown in polluted air; the healthy plant on the left was grown in filtered air.

estimated $3.2 billion annual loss to American agriculture (Figure 17-7, Table 17-3).

The maximum concentration of ozone permitted under current EPA regulations is 0.12 ppm as an average over a 1-hour period. If the ozone in a city's air exceeds that level more than once in a given year, the city is subject to economic sanctions, such as the withdrawal of federal funds for highway construction.

However, this standard was set in 1979, some time before the medical findings reported earlier. As a result, the EPA is being pressured by public health officials, medical doctors, and environmentalists to tighten the ozone standard. It must be admitted, however, that it may be extremely difficult for some cities, like New York or Los Angeles, to comply with tougher standards unless severe restrictions on motor vehicle use are imposed (Figure 17-8 and Figure 17-9).

EFFECT OF CLIMATE ON AIR POLLUTION

Thermal Inversion

The buildup of atmospheric contaminants to high levels is facilitated by a meteorological condition known as a **thermal inversion**. Under normal daytime conditions, the air temperature *gradually decreases with altitude* from ground level to a height of several miles above the earth's surface. With this thermal pattern, it is possible for pollutants to rise. However, during a thermal inversion, such dispersion is impossible. There are two basic types of inversions: radiation and subsidence.

RADIATION INVERSION. At night, heat radiates from the earth's surface into the atmosphere. The earth is a better radiator than the atmosphere. As a result, both the ground and the air layer next to it cool off rapidly—more quickly than the air above them. Consequently, a warmer layer of air forms, perhaps 300 meters (1,000 feet) aboveground, which creates a "lid" over the cooler air beneath it. This lid prevents any vertical mixing of air and atmospheric pollutants. The result is a **radiation inversion.** If winds are present, however, pollutants may disperse horizontally. When pollutants are not blown horizontally, they may build up to dangerous levels. Such inversions are common in many areas of the United States, especially in mountainous regions. However, they are

Table 17-3 The Effect of Ozone on Plants

Plant	Ozone Concentration (ppm)	Duration of Exposure	Reduction in Weight or Height
Alfalfa	0.10	7 hr/day/70 days	51% total dry wt.
Soybeans	0.10	6 hr/day/133 days	55% seed wt.
Sweet corn	0.10	6 hr/day/64 days	45% seed wt.
Wheat	0.20	4 hr/day/7 days	30% seed wt.
Beets	0.20	2 hr/day/38 days	40% root wt.
Ponderosa pine	0.10	6 hr/day/126 days	21% stem wt.
Hybrid poplar	0.15	12 hr/day/102 days	58% height
Red maple	0.25	8 hr/day/6 weeks	37% height

FIGURE 17-8 Aerial view of smog over New York City. Cleaning up the air may be difficult because of the high volume of traffic.

usually confined to small areas. They usually dissipate by late morning when the earth's surface is warmed by the sun. The air immediately above the earth then warms up as well. As the day advances, the inversion gradually disappears.

SUBSIDENCE INVERSION. Although less common than radiation inversions, **subsidence inversions** usually last longer and may be much more extensive. Sometimes the subsidence inversion forms a canopy over several states. It is formed when a high-pressure air mass (one that is sinking and, hence, warming up) stalls over an area and sinks toward the ground, at times as low as 600 meters (2,000 feet) above the ground. This type of inversion worsens the air pollution problems of Los Angeles in the summer (Figures 17-10 and 17-11). During the summer months, a warm, high-pressure air mass is constantly present above the Pacific Ocean off the California coast. This air mass occasionally moves inland over Los Angeles, Oakland, and other coastal cities and puts a lid on the pollutant-laden air near the ground that has been cooled by ocean currents moving along the coast. Coastal California experiences this type of inversion on 9 of every 10 days in summer.

Dust Domes and Heat Islands

Any motorist speeding toward the outskirts of Chicago, St. Louis, Des Moines, or any other large city has observed the haze of smoke and dust that frequently forms an "umbrella" over the town. This shroud of pollutants, known as a **dust dome**, is caused by a unique atmospheric circulation pattern that depends on the marked temperature differences between the city proper and outlying regions. Although the average annual temperature of a city might be only 0.9°C (1.7°F) higher than that of the surrounding rural areas on a given day, occasionally a city may actually be 20°C (27°F) warmer. Meteorologists call this a **heat island** (Figure 17-12).

Contributing to the warmth of the city are such heat-generating sources as people, kitchen stoves, industrial furnaces, utility boilers, and motor vehicles, as well as the heat-radiating surfaces of streets, parking lots, and buildings. In rural areas, on the other hand, heat-generating and -radiating structures are much less numerous. Moreover, there is more evaporative cooling in rural areas.

The urban–rural temperature differential creates an atmospheric circulation pattern in which cool air from

FIGURE 17-9A Aerial view of Los Angeles on a clear day.

FIGURE 17-9B Aerial view of Los Angeles under smog. The smog in this picture is trapped about 300 feet above the ground by a temperature inversion. Inversions are present over the Los Angeles Basin about 320 days of the year!

the countryside moves into the city to replace warm air rising from the urban center. As a result, smoke dust, nitrogen dioxide, and other aerial "garbage" tend to concentrate in a dome above the city (Figure 17-13). *One thousand times as much dust* may be present immediately over an urban industrial area as in the air of the nearby countryside.

When the air is calm, the dust dome persists; however, when wind speeds rise to 12.8 kilometers (8 miles) per hour or more, the dome is pushed downward and horizontally into an elongated **dust plume**. Such plumes originating in Chicago are occasionally seen from a distance of 240 kilometers (150 miles).

EFFECTS OF AIR POLLUTION ON CLIMATE

Air pollution can reduce sunlight penetration, decrease air temperature, affect cloud formation, and alter precipitation levels. Such dramatic climatic changes may disrupt terrestrial and aquatic ecosystems.

Air Pollution and Sunlight

Particulate matter can reduce the amount of sunlight that reaches the earth because particles scatter and absorb solar radiation. Washington, D.C. and Los Angeles, for example, receive 10 percent less sunlight than they did at the beginning of this century, when the air was relatively unpolluted.

This phenomenon is not limited to urban areas because wind currents disperse particulates widely. The pollution from a city, for example, may eventually shroud an area 50 times the size of the urban source. Such a reduction of solar energy—the power base of all ecological systems—could conceivably have profound ecological effects, by reducing plant growth. It also affects our everyday lives. The darkened skies of cities force urban residents to turn on lights in homes and shops somewhat earlier in the day—resulting in an estimated $20 million increase in our nation's yearly light bills (and incidentally more pollution).

Air Pollution and Precipitation

Moisture emitted from industrial smokestacks and motorcars forms clouds above cities, especially in winter. To make matters worse, particulates (soot and dust) in urban air serve as **condensation nuclei** that

FIGURE 17-10 The effect of a radiation temperature inversion on the distribution of air pollution.

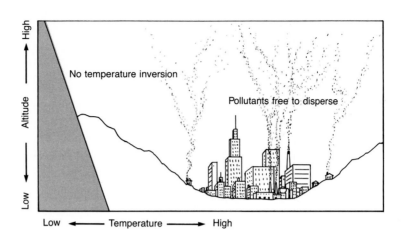

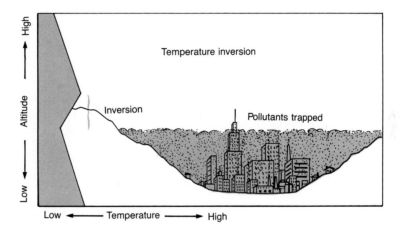

absorb tiny moisture droplets. Particulates, therefore, can promote cloud formation and increase rainfall. Now, if human-generated air pollution does indeed induce rainfall, we would expect more rainy days from Monday to Friday, when factories are operating and pollutants are generated, than on weekends, when plants are closed. This is precisely the case. For example, in Paris, France, the average daily rainfall on weekdays is 31 percent higher than on weekends. Industrial contaminants, such as particulates, generated in Chicago

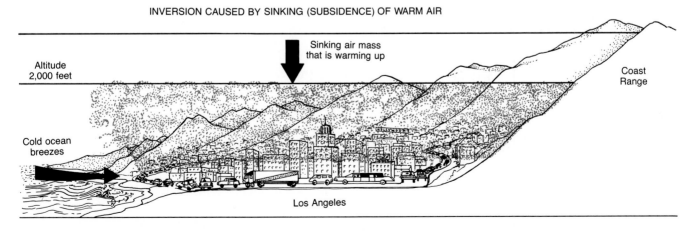

FIGURE 17-11 The nature of a subsidence inversion.

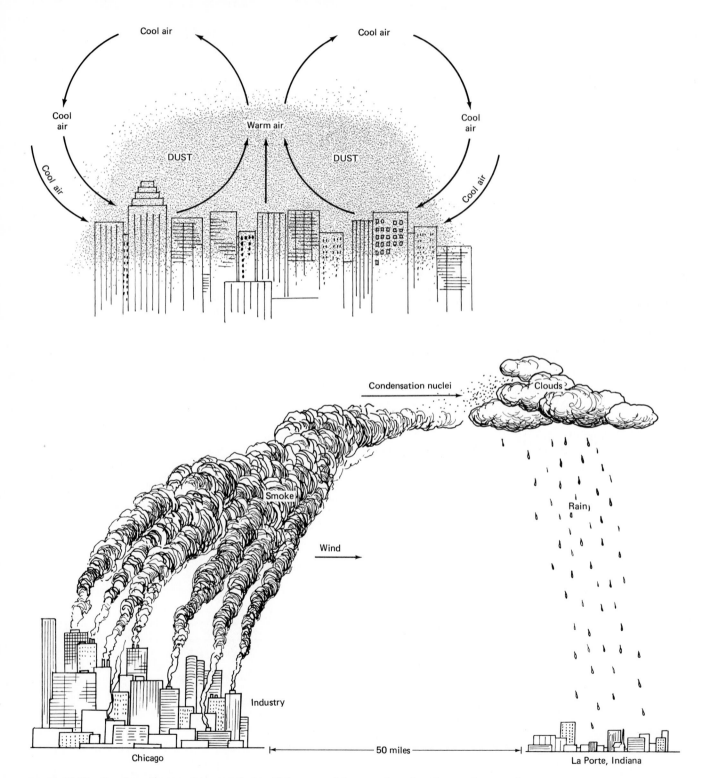

FIGURE 17-12 Heat island effect of a city. The air is warmed up in the city because of large numbers of industrial furnaces, car motors, human bodies, heat-absorbing surfaces and so on. This warm air moves upward and eventually cools. It may then sink, because of its greater density, move back into the city along with other cool air from the countryside, and be warmed again. As a result, a circular flow of air occurs. Any dust in the air will remain suspended above the city in a mushroom-like formation known as a dust dome.

FIGURE 17-13 Condensation nuclei generated in Chicago are blown eastward and cause increased levels of precipitation in La Porte, Indiana, 50 miles downwind.

are blown to the general region of LaPorte, Indiana, 48 kilometers (30 miles) to the east, where they trigger considerable amounts of rainfall.

Air Pollution and Decreased Average Temperature

The total annual load of particulates generated directly or indirectly by human activities the world over amounts to 800 million metric tons. Sources contributing to this particulate load include the combustion of fossil fuels; the razing of old buildings; agricultural activities such as plowing, cultivating, and harvesting; slash-and-burn farming in Asia, Africa, and South America; forest fires; debris burning by loggers; dust storms; and strip-mine operations.

An increase in particulate matter may have a cooling effect. Particulates may block the incoming rays of the sun, cooling the earth. The cooling effect of particulate matter was impressively demonstrated in 1883 when the island of Krakatoa in the Dutch East Indies partially disintegrated because of a gigantic volcanic eruption that injected tons of fine dust particles high into the atmosphere. Over a period of years, these particles eventually circled the globe several times. A short time after the eruption, the United States experienced a cooling trend; Bostonians, for example, had the rare privilege of throwing snowballs in June.

EFFECTS OF AIR POLLUTION ON HUMAN HEALTH

Scientists estimate that 40,000 to 50,000 Americans die each year at least partly because of pollutants. That is about the number of American soldiers who were killed in the Vietnam War.

When many people die from air pollution in a short time, the episode is called a **disaster**. When most of the air pollution disasters are studied, a common pattern is revealed: (1) they occur in densely populated areas; (2) they occur in heavily industrialized centers where pollution sources are abundant; (3) they occur in valleys, which might serve as topographical receptacles for receiving and retaining pollutants; (4) they are accompanied by fog—it appears that the minute droplets of moisture are absorbed on the surfaces of the pollutants; and (5) they are accompanied by a thermal inversion that effectively puts a meteorological lid on the air mass in the valley and contributes to its stagnation.

The Donora Disaster

Forty-eight kilometers (30 miles) south of Pittsburgh, Pennsylvania, in a horseshoe-shaped bend of the Monongahela River, nestles the industrial community of Donora, Pennsylvania, with a population of 12,000. This grimy steel town is almost encircled by hills rising to a height of 116 meters (350 feet). Factories manufacturing steel, wire, and sulfuric acid, in addition to zinc-smelting plants, are crowded along the river margin for 5 kilometers (3 miles).

On October 26, 1948, a thermal inversion occurred. Soon afterward, a fog closed in on the valley. There was hardly a breath of air stirring. The black, red, and yellow smoke fumes that belched from the Donora smokestacks merged to form a multicolored blanket over the valley town. In a short time, the pungent odor of sulfur dioxide permeated the air. In addition to sulfur dioxide, the air over Donora contained high levels of nitrogen dioxide and hydrocarbons, which resulted from burning coal to provide heat and electricity for shops and homes. A sluggishly played football game between the Donora and Monongahela high schools was canceled in midplay when several of the players complained of chest pains and tortured breathing. Streets, sidewalks, and porches were covered with a film of soot so thick that it recorded the footprints of pedestrians. Motorists had to pull off to the side of the road because they could not drive safely. People who had lived in Donora for over half a century got lost in their own hometown. The smog was so dense that it was extremely difficult to see from one side of the street to the other. The Donora fire department hauled oxygen tanks around the clock to people experiencing breathing difficulties.

Of the total population, roughly 43 percent—5,910 people—became ill, the most prevalent symptoms being nausea, vomiting, and severe headaches; nose, eye, and throat irritation; and labored breathing and constriction of the chest. Even pets and wildlife suffered. A veterinarian reported that the dense smoke caused the death of seven chickens, three canaries, two rats, two rabbits, and two dogs.

Evidence of the human loss of life resulting from the air pollution episode is etched on Donora's gravestones. As environmentalist Croswell Bowen writes:

High on the windblown rim of the hill overlooking the bowl-shaped river valley are the town's cemeteries. In St. Dominic's Catholic Cemetery, near the winding road inside the gates, the visitor can see a headstone marking the grave of Iven Ceh: (Born) May 6, 1879, (Died) October 30, 1948. Only the date of his death hints that he figured in the Donora smog tragedy.

But Ceh's death was only the first. One hour after his passing, the smog claimed another life, and by 10 A.M. nine corpses were laid out at one mortuary, and one each at two others.

The complete death toll for Donora's "Black Saturday" was 17. Two more deaths occurred on Sunday.

Then on Sunday night, climatic conditions changed. A heavy rain washed some of the pollutants from the air. A breeze drove much of the smoke away. Visibility improved and breathing became easier. The worst air pollution disaster in American history was over. Although the smog had persisted for only 5 days, it left 20 people dead in its wake.

Human Illness Caused by Air Pollution

There is substantial evidence that air pollution can kill people. But it kills slowly and quietly, making the line between cause and effect difficult to detect. Thus, instead of stating that the deceased breathed in too much carbon monoxide, sulfur dioxide, nitrogen oxides, or particulates, the death certificate simply states that death was caused by lung cancer, emphysema, or a heart attack.

CARBON MONOXIDE POISONING. Carbon monoxide combines 210 times more readily with hemoglobin than does oxygen. It therefore tends to replace oxygen in the bloodstream. Exposure to 80 ppm of carbon monoxide for 8 hours, which might be encountered in a tunnel or a toll booth, causes cellular oxygen starvation equivalent to losing 1 pint of blood.

Informed citizens are well aware that smoking is injurious to the health of the smoker. For example, at least one health expert has suggested that we call cigarettes "cancer sticks." But even more discouraging is that smoking may also be injurious to the *nonsmoker*. Researchers have shown that cigarette smoke may contain 300 ppm of carbon monoxide. Carbon monoxide levels in a room of smokers can reach high levels, sufficient to deactivate roughly *10 percent* of the victimized nonsmoker's hemoglobin. The next time a person asks automatically "Mind if I smoke?" as he or she whisks out a cigarette, you have the right to politely respond "Yes, I do."

The presence of carbon monoxide in the bloodstream of a pregnant woman has been suggested as a possible cause of stillbirths and deformed offspring. Certain conditions may render some people especially susceptible to carbon monoxide poisoning. They include heart disease, asthma, diseased lungs, high altitude, and high humidity.

Carbon monoxide may be the indirect cause of many fatal traffic accidents in the United States yearly. The effects of low-level carbon monoxide poisoning are similar to those of alcohol or fatigue; they impair the motorist's ability to control the vehicle (Figure 17-14). Because carbon monoxide is colorless and odorless, harmful levels may build up within the car without the driver being aware of them.

EMPHYSEMA. When air enters the air sacs of the lung, oxygen passes through the membranes of the sacs into the blood capillaries, while carbon dioxide passes from the capillaries to the air sacs. The total respiratory membrane surface presented by each lung's 300 million air sacs is about the size of a tennis court. In exhalation, the elastic connective tissue in the walls of the alveoli provides resilience, allowing the sacs to recoil, forcing air out of the lungs. In a person suffering from emphysema, the elastic tissue is progressively destroyed. In some cases, almost 50 percent of the lung's elastic tissue may be destroyed before the victim is aware of the problem. As a result of the decline in elasticity, the emphysemic can inhale easily, thus inflating the lungs, but finds it difficult to exhale. The air sacs retain carbon dioxide, which poisons the body. With each incoming breath, the air sac becomes overinflated. This process is repeated may times until the sac "pops" like a burst ballon, resulting in the destruction of both the respiratory membrane and blood capillaries. Eventually, therefore, the area available for the exchange of respiratory gases is greatly reduced (Figure 17-15).

In a severe case of emphysema, the cells throughout the body suffer from oxygen starvation. To counteract this, the victim's breathing accelerates in a vain attempt to aerate the blood properly. The heart speeds up to propel the blood more rapidly. The skin of some sufferers turns slightly bluish (cyanosis) as a result of the relatively high level of carbon dioxide.

Although the cause of emphysema is unknown, many researchers believe that smoking and air pollution are primarily responsible. The emphysema rate is 13 times greater in smokers than in nonsmokers. The death toll from emphysema in the United States rose dramatically from a mere 1,500 in 1950 to more than 30,000 in 1970—a 20-fold increase. This mortality increase coincided with increased levels of atmospheric pollution in the areas where the fatalities occurred.

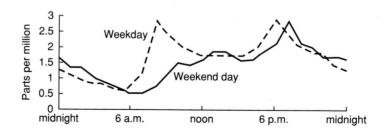

FIGURE 17-14 Carbon monoxide levels on weekdays and weekends in Washington, D.C.

Parts per million

3 — 2.5 — 2 — 1.5 — 1 — 0.5 — 0

Weekday

Weekend day

midnight   6 a.m.   noon   6 p.m.   midnight

FIGURE **17-15** Bronchioles and air sacs of healthy lung compared to lung diseased by air pollution. Note how air sacs break down in diseased lung.

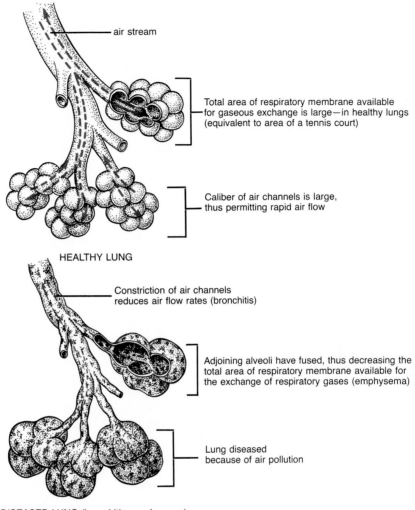

air stream

Total area of respiratory membrane available for gaseous exchange is large—in healthy lungs (equivalent to area of a tennis court)

Caliber of air channels is large, thus permitting rapid air flow

HEALTHY LUNG

Constriction of air channels reduces air flow rates (bronchitis)

Adjoining alveoli have fused, thus decreasing the total area of respiratory membrane available for the exchange of respiratory gases (emphysema)

Lung diseased because of air pollution

DISEASED LUNG (bronchitis, emphysema)

Lung Cancer. Several atmospheric contaminants have been strongly implicated as **carcinogens**—cancer-producing materials. Among them are benzopyrene, asbestos, nickel, and beryllium. For example, cancers have been induced in laboratory animals either by injecting benzopyrene or by implanting it under the skin. The hydrocarbon benzopyrene can get into the lungs from several sources: from the coal smoke issuing from industrial smokestacks or from the smoke issuing from cigarettes. The smoke generated when fat drippings from a charcoal-broiled steak sputter on the hot coals is also a little-suspected source of benzopyrene. Just one smoked steak may contain as much benzopyrene as 600 cigarettes!

Researchers have shown in laboratory experiments on rats and mice that, although two air pollutants may not induce cancer independently, cancer *is* induced when an animal is exposed to both pollutants *simultaneously*. Such an effect is called **synergistic**. For example, lung cancers resembling those in humans have been induced in laboratory animals by first exposing the animals to influenza virus and then to artificial smog. Tumors have also been generated in laboratory animals by forcing them to inhale a combination of benzopyrene and sulfur dioxide.

Researchers have found that the lung cancer rate of men over 45 living on Staten Island, New York, is 155 per 100,000 in the smoggiest area compared to only 40 per 100,000 in the less smoggy region. To research biologists, such data strongly indicate a cause-and-effect relationship between atmospheric pollution and lung cancer in humans.

Asbestos: The Dangers
of a Useful Product

Because of its flexibility, great tensile strength, and resistance to heat, friction, and acid, asbestos has found extensive industrial use, especially since World War II. Roughly 30 million metric tons were used in the United States during the period 1900–1988. It has been used in more than 5,000 products, from pipe and boiler insulation to ironing board pads, from brake linings to protective clothing for fire fighters, from hair dryers to baby talcum. In the construction industry, it is used to strengthen cement and plastics and to fireproof skyscrapers.

Dispersal Through the Environment

Wherever asbestos is mined or processed, or wherever asbestos products undergo wear, asbestos dust, composed of extremely minute fibers, is released into the atmosphere. For example, a woman sets her iron down on her ironing board pad, inadvertently sending asbestos dust into the air; a carpenter's saw cuts through plasterboard, again generating asbestos dust. What happens to the material worn from brake linings? It's still around, in pulverized form, some of it as asbestos dust, possibly floating in the air, possibly forming a thin film on roads and highways, or possibly adhering to the soft, delicate lining of human lungs. Even food, water, and beverages may contain some asbestos fibers. In Rockville, Maryland, several years ago, large areas of the city became contaminated by asbestos-containing crushed rock applied to school playgrounds and city streets. One wonders how many millions of asbestos fibers from that rock were eventually inhaled by school children during recess or by motorists driving by with their windows open.

Asbestos "time bombs" may be ticking away in thousands of schoolrooms throughout America. The reason? In the 1940s and 1950s, asbestos was mixed with paint and sprayed on ceilings and walls for fireproofing and sound insulation. (Such uses were banned by the EPA in 1974.) Dr. Lyman Condie, a toxicologist with the EPA, comments on the problem: "When sprayed surfaces are exposed to student activities—bouncing basketballs off gymnasium ceilings, or children running their hands along stairway ceilings—the asbestos can flake off into the air. Because the fibers are very small and light, they can move throughout the building, even though only a very small area was originally disturbed."

Of our nation's 87,000 school buildings, at least 30,000 contain asbestos in their walls and ceilings. As a result, roughly 15 million students face an asbestos-related threat—one that may not result in serious human illness until some of these schoolchildren have long since graduated, married, and raised children of their own.

Human Illness Caused by Asbestos

The symptoms of chronic asbestosis, which currently afflicts 65,000 Americans, include breathlessness, coughing, chest pains, barrel-shaped chest, club-shaped fingers, and bluish discoloration of the skin. A curious thing is that these symptoms may not appear until 20–30 years after the exposure to asbestos. Over 50 percent of the people suffering from asbestosis eventually die from lung cancer. It is estimated that 3,000 to 12,000 asbestos-induced cancer deaths occur in the United States annually. Cigarette smoking increases the incidence dramatically. For example, a cigarette-smoking asbestos worker has 90 times the chance of developing lung cancer as a nonsmoker who has no contact with asbestos! As might be expected, surveys have revealed a relatively high incidence of asbestos-related lung cancers among the 120,000 people (miners, asbestos product processors, and so on) in the United States who work directly with asbestos.

Another cancer, **Mesothelioma** (cancer of the chest-cavity lining), formerly quite rare, has become much more common in the U.S., especially among asbestos workers. Many of these cancer-stricken people, or their families, have sued the companies where their occupational exposure to the asbestos occurred. In Virginia alone, for example, asbestos product manufacturers were sued by 100 people for $300 million during a single year.

Control of Asbestos Emissions

In the 1970s, the EPA launched an aggressive program to remove asbestos from the walls and ceilings of schools, convention halls, theaters, and other public buildings. However, as of 1989, discouragingly little progress has been made. Part of the problem is monetary. It would cost at least $2 billion for a comprehensive, nationwide cleanup in schools alone.

Sites where old buildings are being razed are also significant sources of asbestos emissions. Moreover, they far outnumber such sources as factories. The problem is complicated by the fact that demolition contractors frequently ignore federal regulations on asbestos removal. Federal law requires that all asbestos fibers be wetted down before removal. This material then must be placed in leakproof containers, such as plastic bags, and conspicuously marked.

The asbestos industry, under regulations formulated by the EPA, has taken steps to reduce occupational exposure to the life-threatening fibers. The asbestos concentration in the air inhaled by the workers must be less than one fiber per cubic meter of air. The problem has been further diminished by the use of vacuum devices, by the mandatory use of masks, and by automating many manufacturing processes.

The EPA has recently proposed a ban on the use of asbestos in many products for which safe substitutes are available. For example, asbestos would no longer be used to make fire-retarding clothing, vinyl tile, or certain roofing materials.

According to the EPA, perhaps the most disturbing feature of the asbestos problem is that control measures have not prevented the gradual long-term development of cancer in persons who come into occasional, slight, or temporary contact with asbestos. Families of asbestos workers, for example, may inhale asbestos fiber dust inadvertently brought into the home on the workers' clothing and shoes. Such slightly exposed people also include those who live within 1.5 kilometers (0.93 mile) of an asbestos plant. Of the almost 2,000 autopsies of such people in New York City, one-half revealed asbestos fibers in the lungs.

THE POLLUTION STANDARDS INDEX

In 1976, as a result of the coordinated efforts of a number of federal agencies, a **Pollution Standards Index (PSI)** was developed. This index makes it possible to compare the air quality of different urban areas and its potential threat to human health (Table 17-4).

The EPA has established acceptable standards of air pollution—**National Ambient Air Quality Standards (NAAQS)**. If a pollutant in a city is at the standard, it is given an index rating of 100. Any index value below

Table 17-4 Atmospheric Pollutant Standards Index

	Index Value	Pollutant Levels (in Micrograms per Liter) Air Quality Level	General Health Effects	Cautionary Statements
Hazardous	500	Significant harm	Premature death of ill and elderly. Healthy people will experience adverse symptoms that affect their normal activity	All persons should remain indoors, keeping windows and doors closed. All persons should minimize physical exertion and avoid traffic.
	400	Emergency	Premature onset of certain diseases in addition to significant aggravation of symptoms and decreased exercise tolerance in healthy persons	Elderly and persons with existing diseases should stay indoors and avoid physical exertion. General population should avoid outdoor activity.
Very Unhealthful	300	Warning	Significant aggravation of symptoms and decreased exercise tolerance in persons with heart or lung disease, with widespread symptoms in the healthy population.	Elderly and persons with existing heart or lung disease should stay indoors and reduce physical activity.
Unhealthful	200	Alert	Mild aggravation of symptoms in susceptible persons, with irritation symptoms in the healthy population.	Persons with existing heart or respiratory ailments should reduce physical exertion and outdoor activity.
Moderate	100	National Ambient Air Quality Standard		
	50	50 percent of National Ambient Air Quality Standard		
Good	0			

Source: Environmental Protection Agency, *Guideline for Public Reporting of Daily Air Quality—Pollutant Standards Index (PSI)*, EPA–450/2—76-023, OAQPS 1.2-044 (Research Triangle Park, NC: Environmental Protection Agency, 1976), Table 3, p. 10.

FIGURE **17-16** Pollution Standards
Index.

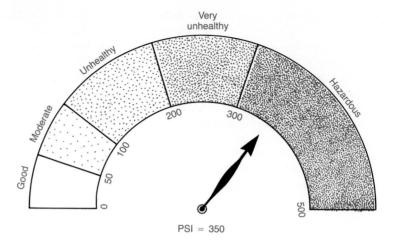

PSI = 350

100 suggests relatively clean air with minimal health effects. However, as the index value rises to about 100, the air is progressively more polluted and the health effects correspondingly severe. An index value of 400 or above suggests that air pollution is "very hazardous" (Figure 17-16). It may cause the premature death of the sick and elderly. Under those conditions, all persons are advised to remain indoors.

PSI values for various atmospheric contaminants are frequently reported on daily local newspapers in major urban areas. On the basis of PSI ratings, Los Angeles has the most badly polluted air of any city in America. During the period 1978–1980, for example, Los Angeles experienced an annual average of 113 days (or 32 percent of the year) in which PSI values indicated that the city's air was either "very unhealthful or hazardous." After Los Angeles, the cities with the most badly polluted air in the United States are San Bernardino, New York, Denver, Pittsburgh, and Houston.

AIR POLLUTION ABATEMENT AND CONTROL

Pollution Control in Factories and Power Plants

Although many of the pollution-control devices currently available are not 100 percent efficient in removing industrial contaminants, they often significantly reduce emission levels. Certainly industry cannot wait another few years for the perfect control device to be developed; that day may never come.

CONTROLLING PARTICULATES. Three standard types of equipment for controlling particulates are available. The **fabric filter bag house** operates like a giant vacuum cleaner, collecting particles from smoke stacks in huge cloth bags (Figure 17-17). A large filter bag house may consist of more than 1,000 elongated filter bags, each of which is several meters

long. Up to 99.9 percent of the dust particles may be removed from the stack gases.

The **electrostatic precipitator** removes solid particles (dust, fly ash, asbestos fibers, and lead salts) less than 1 micron in diameter from the gases in a smokestack (Figure 17-18). The pollutants pass between pairs of positively and negatively charged electrodes. The particles become negatively charged and are then attracted to a positively charged collector electrode. Although the initial cost of a large precipitator can be more than $1 million, the power and maintenance costs are small. One unfortunate feature, however, is that the precipitator is more effective when high-sulfur rather than low-sulfur coal is burned.

The **cyclone filter** removes heavy dust particles with the aid of gravity and a downward-spiraling air stream (Figure 17-19).

SULFUR OXIDES. As we have just seen, the release of sulfur oxides into the atmosphere from transportation, industrial, and residential sources, adversely affects human health, wildlife, forests, and farm crops, as well as irreplaceable paintings, monuments, stonework, and statuary.

How can the emission of sulfur oxides be controlled? There are several possible approaches. Although no method will be satisfactory by itself, if the following approaches are used in combination, the sulfur oxide problem will at least be greatly reduced.

1. *Shifting from high- to low-sulfur coal.* Much of the industrial coal consumed before 1970 had a relatively high sulfur content (up to 3 percent or more). This coal came from mines in Pennsylvania, West Virginia, and Illinois. Once health officials became aware of the problems posed by oxides of sulfur, however, municipal, state, and federal regulations were passed to limit the burning of high-sulfur coal. Fortunately, there exist vast supplies of low-sulfur coal in such western states as Colorado, Montana,

FIGURE 17-17 Filter bag house. Solid particles are removed from exhaust gases by long "vacuum-cleaner" type bags that pick up particulates as air is passed through them.

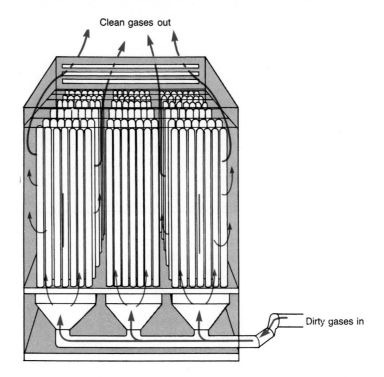

Dirty gases in

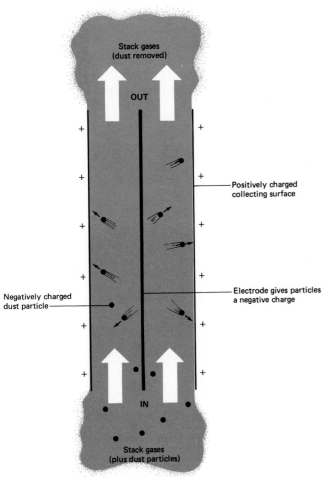

Stack gases (dust removed)

OUT

Positively charged collecting surface

Electrode gives particles a negative charge

Negatively charged dust particle

IN

Stack gases (plus dust particles)

FIGURE 17-18 Electrostatic precipitator. As the soot, dust and other particulates pass through the precipitator, they are given a negative charge. They are then attracted to the positively charged wall of the precipitator. After accumulating on this collecting surface they are periodically released to a collecting chamber when the surface is made to vibrate.

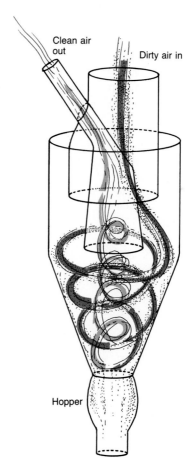

Clean air out

Dirty air in

Hopper

FIGURE 17-19 Cyclone filter. Large solid particles are removed by centrifugal force and are collected in a hopper.

and Wyoming, which can be obtained by strip mining. Strip mining can be very destructive to the environment, and thus precautions must be taken to restore the sites to their original condition.

2. *Removing sulfur from high-sulfur coal before burning it.* Transporting low-sulfur coal a distance of more than 1,600 kilometers (1,000 miles) to eastern industrial plants would add greatly to the cost of the coal. An alternative is to mine the high-sulfur coal available in the Midwest and East, where it is close to the industry that will use it, and then remove much of the sulfur before burning it. Much of the weight of high-sulfur coal is actually caused by an impurity known as **iron pyrite**. It can be removed from the coal without sacrificing its fuel value. Since pyrite is heavier than the coal, it sinks to the bottom of a tank containing a mixture of pulverized coal and water and can easily be removed (Figure 17-20).

3. *Flue gas desulfurization process.* This process, commonly known as **scrubbing**, is most widely used to remove sulfur from smokestack gases of power plants and industry (Figure 17-21). A mist consisting of ground limestone and water is sprayed into the sulfur dioxide–laden stack gases. The calcium in the lime reacts with the sulfur to form calcium sulfate. Scrubbers can remove up to 95 percent of the sulfur dioxide in stack gases. The calcium sulfate sludge

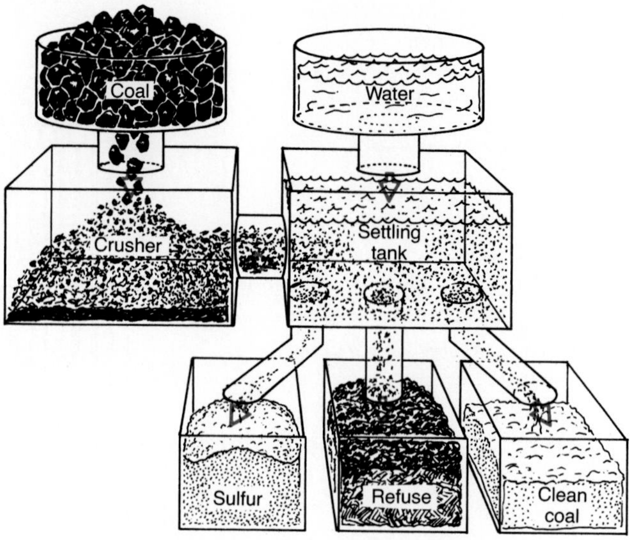

FIGURE 17-20   Method for removing sulfur from coal.

may be used in road beds or other construction projects, but is most commonly disposed of in landfills. A big advantage of scrubbers is that they can be added to existing plants, as well as being used on new ones. The process is costly, however, and solves an air pollution problem by creating a solid waste problem.

FIGURE 17-21 Flue gas desulfurization (FGD). Downward-streaming water and powdered limestone (CaCO3) "scrubs out" sulfur dioxide from stack gases. A sludge of calcium sulphate forms and must be removed.

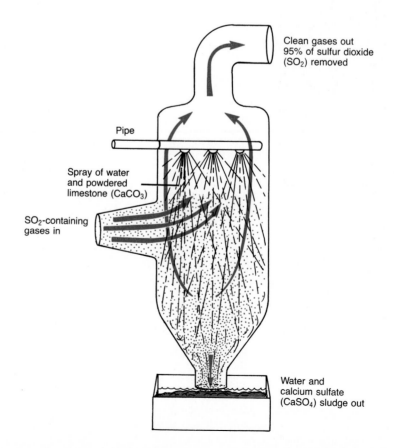

Clean gases out 95% of sulfur dioxide (SO_2) removed

Pipe

Spray of water and powdered limestone ($CaCO_3$)

SO_2-containing gases in

Water and calcium sulfate ($CaSO_4$) sludge out

The Control of Automotive Emissions

Automobile emissions can be controlled three ways: (1) by reducing traffic volume; (2) by reducing emissions from the conventional internal combustion engines; and (3) by developing alternative engine types operated by steam or electricity.

REDUCING TRAFFIC VOLUME.   The EPA has made several proposals to reduce traffic volume in large urban areas (Figure 17-22). Among them are (1) terminating free parking facilities for employees by their employers; placing an added tax on downtown parking fees; and (3) prohibiting commuters from driving to work 1 day per week, thus reducing commuter traffic by 20 percent.

The overall pollution-reducing strategy in New York City includes (1) banning all street parking in the main business section of Manhattan; (2) restricting cruising by Manhattan taxis; (3) placing several Manhattan bridges on the toll system; and (4) setting aside one lane on busy roads for the exclusive use of buses (Figure 17-23).

In 1989 the EPA exerted strong pressure on the city of Los Angeles to clean up the smog for which this city has become notorious. In response to this federal pressure, as well as to growing local anxiety concerning increasing traffic congestion, its mayor strongly encouraged the motorists of Los Angeles either to use public transporation or to share rides.

REDUCING POLLUTANT EMISSIONS FROM THE INTERNAL COMBUSTION ENGINE.   The automobile industry has fought efforts to reduce exhaust emissions. The industry may be beginning to realize that it has to make radical changes in motor design; consumers and pollution-control agencies want nothing less.

Using Catalytic Converters.   In order to reduce the pollutant emissions from automobiles, as required by the 1977 amendment to the Clean Air Act of 1970, auto manufacturers have relied heavily on a device known as a **catalytic converter** (Figure 17-24). The converter is a muffler-shaped device that is incorporated into the exhaust system of the car. One type of converter, used by the Ford Motor Company, has a honeycomb-like interior. The cells of the honeycomb are coated with the catalyst platinum or palladium. The products of

FIGURE 17-22   Traffic comes to a standstill in San Francisco. Like many cities, San Francisco faces a traffic crisis. Cars back up on the freeway during rush hour, making the commute a major ordeal and creating incredible amounts of air pollution.

FIGURE 17-23   In Manhattan and some other major urban centers special lanes on busy thoroughfares are reserved for the exclusive use of express buses. This strategy has proven effective in reducing commuter traffic volume and air pollution.

FIGURE 17-24 Cutaway illustration of a catalytic converter used by the Ford Motor Company. Resembling a small muffler, the emission-control device converts hydrocarbons and carbon monoxide into harmless carbon dioxide and water. The chemical reaction depends upon the platinum or palladium catalysts that line the internal surfaces of the converter.

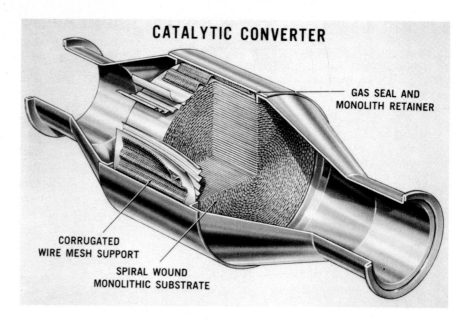

CATALYTIC CONVERTER

GAS SEAL AND MONOLITH RETAINER

CORRUGATED WIRE MESH SUPPORT

SPIRAL WOUND MONOLITHIC SUBSTRATE

incompletely burned gasoline, such as carbon monoxide and hydrocarbons, pass through the cells of the catalytic converter. The catalyst increases the rate at which these exhaust gases react with oxygen, thus forming carbon dioxide and water.

A three-way converter has recently been developed to reduce nitrogen oxides in automobile exhaust, as well as carbon monoxide and hydrocarbons. In this converter, nitric oxide oxidizes carbon monoxide to harmless carbon dioxide and hydrocarbons to carbon dioxide and water. During this process, the nitric oxide is broken down to nitrogen and oxygen.

A serious problem associated with the use of converters was that the lead in leaded gasoline, which was used to stop engine knocking, actually "knocked out" the catalyst. Lead forms a thin coating over the catalyst and thus reduces its surface area. Because the auto manufacturers would have had an extremely difficult time meeting the federal emission standards without the converter, they put pressure on the oil industry to produce **unleaded gasoline**. Unleaded gasoline became available to the motorist in about 1975 and had to be used on cars with a catalytic converter. The shift toward unleaded gasoline was acclaimed by environmentalists and health authorities generally because of the health threat posed by high lead levels in the air of our major cities.

Inspection and Maintenance Programs. Under the terms of the 1977 amendments to the Clean Air Act, **inspection-and-maintenance (IM)** programs are mandatory for vehicles in those parts of the country where air-quality standards for carbon monoxide and ozone were not met by 1982. Under the program, emissions are checked each year by state or federal inspectors (Figure 17-25). When levels of pollutants in the exhaust, such as sulfur dioxide and carbon monoxide, are too high, the owner must have the vehicle modified to meet EPA standards. This often requires only minor adjustments

of the carburetor. In Portland, Oregon, such an IM program resulted in a 40 percent reduction in emissions the very first year.

The most common repairs, such as spark plug replacements and carburetor adjustments, may reduce pollutant emissions by 25 percent. The IM program in California, known as Smog Check, has cut smog-forming nitrogen oxides and hydrocarbons by 18 and 90 metric tons per day, respectively, and emissions of carbon monoxide by 1,350 metric tons daily for the state as a whole. California tests 12 million cars and trucks every 2 years in the state's eight largest cities.

Increasing Fuel Efficiency. Increasing the fuel efficiency of vehicles reduces the emission of pollutants from the exhaust pipe. In 1975 a new federal law placed a federal excise tax on all cars of a particular model that did not attain a minimum standard of efficiency set by the EPA. The size of the tax is inversely related to the car's fuel efficiency. For example, in 1987, the biggest "gas guzzler" on the American market was an Italian import, the Lamborghini Countach, which achieved only 2.5 kilometers per liter (6 mpg) in the city—the lowest fuel efficiency ever recorded by the EPA. The tax on this car was a hefty $3,850. The most efficient model in 1987 was the Japanese-made Chevrolet Sprint, which gets 22.7 kilometers per liter (54 mpg) in city traffic and 24.3 kilometers per liter (58 mpg) on the highway.

The minimum efficiency required in 1989 models is a city-country average mileage of 11.5 kilometers per liter (27.5 mpg). Some experts believe that in the not too distant future, a fuel efficiency of 33 kilometers per liter (80 mpg) will be attained by American cars. The Japanese already have a model that seats five and gets 33 kilometers per liter (80 mpg) on the highway.

Replacing Gasoline with Less Polluting Fuels. Ethanol can be produced from fermented grains such as corn and sugar cane. It is capable of powering a vehicle

FIGURE 17-25 Examination time! An EPA emission-testing facility at Ann Arbor, Michigan, analyzes and measures the exhaust emitted from new motor vehicles. Annual checks help motorists keep cars tuned and help reduce urban air pollution.

as efficiently as gasoline. Moreover, it pollutes less than gasoline, producing less carbon monoxide, hydrocarbons, and sulfur oxides. (Ethanol produces no net carbon dioxide and could therefore help reduce global warming.) Ethanol is used widely by motorists in Brazil today. Under the terms of the Energy Security Act of 1980, our national goal is to produce 10,000 barrels of ethanol daily by 1990. Unfortunately, since it is estimated that ethanol will cost $0.82 per liter ($3.14 per gallon—almost three times the cost of gasoline at the time of this writing), the prospect of its replacing gasoline in sufficient quantities to result in a substantial reduction in exhaust pollutants does not seem very bright. (For more on ethanol, see Chapter 18.) As fossil fuels decline over the next decade or two ethanol could become more attractive.

DEVELOPING ALTERNATIVES TO THE INTERNAL COMBUSTION ENGINE. Since 1970, when the Clean Air Act was passed, emissions of hydrocarbons and carbon monoxide by the average car have been reduced by 90 percent and emissions of oxides of nitrogen by 75 percent. As of 1989, however, federal analysts were increasingly skeptical that further substantial overall reductions could be made, even with the use of the emission control strategies described earlier. The reason? The rapid increase in motor vehicles on our highways. The number of passenger cars in the United States climbed from 147 million in 1977 to 183 million in 1988—about a 25 percent increase in only 11 years! During this same period, the number of trucks increased 40 percent to 40 million. Some people think that what is really needed is a radical shift from the traditional

internal combustion engine to an engine powered by solar electricity or even steam.

Electric Cars. In Europe, Japan, and the United States 6,000 electric cars are produced each year. Several American cities, including San Francisco and New York, are making limited use of electric buses and delivery vans. Some experimental cars recently developed have a top speed of 128 kilometers (80 miles) per hour. However, although the electric car itself is relatively pollution free, the battery eventually has to be recharged—a process that utilizes electricity generated by centrally located power plants. Thus, in one sense, instead of having numerous, widely dispersed mobile sources of pollution (automobiles), the pollution problem is merely transferred to a few large stationary sources (power plants). It is true, however, that effective emission control in this case would be much easier. Another big disadvantage of the electric car is that the batteries required to power the car would be rather bulky. Solar voltaic cells, should they become economical, could also be used to create electricity for these cars. Recent improvements in their efficiency could make them economical in the near future.

Hybrid Cars. One strategy that would eliminate some of the disadvantages of the electric cars now on the road would be to develop *hybrid* cars equipped with both an electric and an internal combustion engine. The hybrid would rely on its electric batteries to power it on short trips through urban areas—for example, on a shopping trip or a visit to the theater. The motor power for a highway trip of several hundred kilometers would be provided by an alternative source: the conventional internal combustion engine. Additional generators could help charge the batteries on such trips.

Steam Cars. Another possible alternative to the internal combustion engine is the steam engine. The propulsive steam is generated by burning kerosene. The spent steam is then converted to liquid water and used over again. Because kerosene is almost totally combusted, the pollutants emitted from the engine would be minimal.

The car can be highly durable; it is not too expensive; it runs quietly; there is no need for a transmission system; and its performance, in terms of speed, safety, and reliability, is quite acceptable. Why, then, hasn't the automobile industry generated any enthusiasm about mass-producing the vehicle? The reasons are economic. Too much money has been invested by the industry on the internal combustion engine to allow a switch to steam-powered vehicles. Moreover, independent manufacturers would find it prohibitively costly to enter steam cars into competition with brands already on the market.

Mass Transit. Mass transit—busses and trains—carry passengers four to five times more efficiently than automobiles. They produce four to five times less pollution per passenger mile as well. As fossil fuel supplies (especially oil) decline, more and more mass transit will be installed to transport people to and from work in urban environments.

INDOOR AIR POLLUTION
Sources and Effects

When you think of air pollution, the sources that come to mind are belching smokestacks and the exhaust fumes of motor cars. But how about your family living room or kitchen? Recently, scientists have been finding that the air we breathe in our own homes, as well as in schools, stores, and offices, may be more dangerous to our health than the smog-ridden air outside (Figure 17-26). Concern about indoor quality is justifiable, first of all, because people spend much of their time indoors. In an attempt to reduce their home heating bills, many homeowners have insulated their homes and caulked cracks, locking pollutants *in*. Before the energy crisis, the average residence time for a given molecule of gas inside the home was about 1 hour. However, in an airtight home, the residence time is about 400 percent greater. Scientists at the Lawrence Berkeley Laboratory in California measured concentrations of pollutants inside a well-insulated house in which a gas stove and oven were used in ordinary meal preparation. What did they find? Concentrations of carbon monoxide and nitrogen dioxide in the kitchen, bedroom, and living room from the gas stove actually exceeded the levels of these gases outdoors! In fact, in some homes, the level

FIGURE 17-26 Indoor air pollution. These burning candles release a small amount of carbon dioxide and carbon monoxide. Much more significant pollution, of course, results from wood-burning in indoor fire places and from the use of gas stoves.

of nitrogen dioxide may be two to seven times higher than is considered acceptable for outside air.

FORMALDEHYDE. You probably remember formaldehyde as the fluid used to preserve frogs and fetal pigs in biology class. You may be surprised to learn that it is commonly found in foam insulation, furniture, carpets, particle board, and plywood. Formaldehyde causes a variety of human health problems including eye irritation, nausea, respiratory problems, and cancer.

The Occupational Safety and Health Administration (OSHA) has set 3 ppm as the maximum formaldehyde concentration permitted inside industrial plants. Studies in Europe and the United States have shown that formaldehyde levels inside homes are often higher. In Mission Viejo, California, for instance, formaldehyde concentrations in a research house having no furniture were relatively low. However, when furniture was added, formaldehyde levels increased almost threefold.

The cancer risk from breathing formaldehyde fumes is especially high in our nation's more than 5 million mobile homes due to (1) their relatively small air volume; (2) their poor air circulation; and (3) the relatively large amounts of formaldehyde-containing materials they contain, such as particle board and plywood.

RADON. Radium is a radioactive element that decays spontaneously to **radon gas**. Although radium is widely distributed in the rocks and soils of the United States, its abundance varies considerably from place to place. The radon gas from the decay of radium diffuses from the soil directly into the outside air. However, since the radon gas quickly disperses, its concentration in the atmosphere is negligible, only about 0.5 percent of the EPA's recommended safe level of 4 picocuries* per liter of air.

By contrast, radon levels inside homes and other buildings are much higher because most homes have a lower atmospheric pressure than the outside air. The reason is that the inside air is "pumped" outside by clothes driers, fireplaces, and furnaces, especially during cold winter weather. As a result, radon gas is sucked up through cracks in the cement foundation from the underlying soil and rocks. Residents of the home are generally unaware of the presence of radon because it is tasteless, odorless, and colorless. The radon gas eventually decays into such products as lead and polonium, which are also highly radioactive. These radioactive pollutants may then be inhaled, lodge in lung tissue, and eventually cause cancer. In fact, the EPA estimates that 20,000 of the 130,000 lung cancer deaths in the United States each year are caused by radon.

Radon accounts for 55 percent of the annual radiation dose sustained by the average American from all sources, both natural (radon, cosmic rays) and artificial (television, nuclear power plants, X-rays for medical purposes, and so on.) In fact, Anthony Nero, a nuclear scientist with the Lawrence Berkeley Laboratory believes that hundreds of thousands of Americans living in homes with high radon levels are exposed to as much health-threatening radiation as the Russians who were living in the vicinity of the Chernobyl nuclear plant in 1986—the year of the disaster.

The radon levels in some American dwellings are alarmingly high. Take a home in Boyerstown, Pennsylvania, owned by the Watras family, as an example. The Watras home may have the dubious distinction of having the highest radon level of any dwelling in the United States—about 675 times higher than is considered acceptable even in a uranium mine. The lung cancer risk to the four occupants was equal to that of smoking 220 packs of cigarettes per day! Radon levels in some Wisconsin homes exceed 100 picocuries per

*A picocurie is a unit of measurement of radioactivity.

liter—a higher level of radiation than one would get from 20,000 chest X-rays.

The EPA regulations for controlling levels of outdoor pollutants are usually set to keep the estimated risk of premature death below 1 in 100,000 (0.001 percent). In contrast, however, the estimated radon risk for most Americans in the United States is 4 in 1,000 (0.4 percent)—400 times higher.

For several years, it has been known that a region extending from Reading, Pennsylvania, into New York and New Jersey has very high levels of radon. However, a 10-state survey conducted by the EPA during the winter of 1987–1988 revealed other "hot spots" as well. For example, 63 percent of the homes surveyed in North Dakota and 46 percent of those in Minnesota had radon levels above the EPA guideline.

In late 1988, Lee Thomas, then head of the EPA, announced that residential radon pollution in the United States was both sufficiently widespread and sufficiently serious that every home should be tested. Fortunately for the home owner, this can be easily done with a radon-detection kit that can be purchased for about $15–$30 from most hardware stores. In 1988 the U.S. Senate passed a bill that would provide about $40 million to aid states in developing effective programs for controlling the residential radon problem.

Control of Indoor Air Pollution

A number of methods are available for reducing the levels of indoor air pollutants. Among them are the following:

1. *Installation of an air-to-air heat exchanger.* This device, costing $1,000 to $2,000, expels the polluted inside air to the outside and replaces it with fresh outside air. (Part of the heat from the inside air is added to the fresh air coming into the house to save energy.)

2. *The use of vegetation as living air purifiers.* Certain types of house plants, such as the spider plant, are very effective in removing harmful gases, especially the fumes of formaldehyde. The gaseous pollutants are taken into the plant via the millions of breathing pores present on the leaves.

3. *The use of a sub-basement vent system.* In homes overlying rock or soil that emit radon gas, this system is probably an absolute necessity (Figure 17-27). It consists of a network of perforated drain tiles set in a gravel bed under the basement floor. The radon diffuses from the soil and rock, passes through the perforations, and accumulates inside the tiles. The radon is then vented to the outside air.

4. *The establishment of regulations to protect lot and home buyers from high radon levels.* Laws can be passed to require the seller of any lot to inform the

FIGURE 17-27   A sub-basement system for venting cancer-causing radon gas from the home. Several options are available to the home builder. Both types require a porous gravel bed laid down before the basement is poured. (A) Radon is drawn out of the gravel passively through pipes that penetrate the floor slab. (B) porous pipes laid in the gravel collect radon, which is pumped outside by a small pump in the basement.

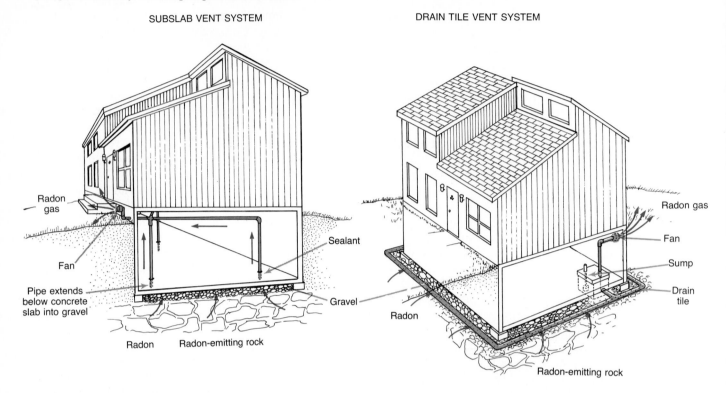

prospective buyer of the level of radon gas in the air immediately above the property. Similarly, the contractor should be required to inform the future owners of a new home about precisely what levels of radon, formaldehyde, and other pollutants might be expected inside the home during normal living on a day-to-day basis.

Our knowledge concerning the identity, source, concentrations, and health effects of indoor pollutants is still very incomplete. Much more research is needed.

COMPARATIVE EXPOSURE TO INDOOR AND OUTDOOR POLLUTANTS

In late 1988 an important article entitled "Air Pollution: Assessing Total Exposure in the United States" appeared in *Environment* magazine. It was written by Kirk R. Smith of the Environment and Policy Institute of Honolulu, Hawaii. With the publication of this article, many Americans became aware for the first time of the misdirection of our nation's efforts to control air pollution at least in trying to protect human health.

Many environmental health experts now believe that it is much more effective to control actual *exposures* of people to pollutants than to control the *tonnage* of the pollutants emitted. In other words, the pollutants that have the greatest threat to human health are those that humans are most likely to *inhale*. Most such air pollution exposure actually occurs *indoors*, where humans spend 90 percent of their time.

In his article, Kirk Smith focused on particulates (Figure 17-28). What is the most cost-effective way to control them? Particulate emissions from coal-fired power plants are 25 times greater in tonnage than those emitted from cigarette smoke. However, Harvard researchers have recently found that particulates emitted inside the home, such as from cigarettes, are 1,700 times *more likely to be inhaled* than power plant particulates. (This ignores the particulates inhaled by the smokers themselves.) The total population exposure from environmental tobacco smoke (ETS) is 40 times the exposure to particulates from power plants. Therefore, the reduction of ETS by only 3 percent would be equivalent to the total elimination of particulate exposure from all power plants. The interesting point is that this 3 percent reduction in ETS can be attained if only 1.5 percent of the cigarettes are smoked outdoors rather than inside the home or workplace. When one focuses on actual *expo-*

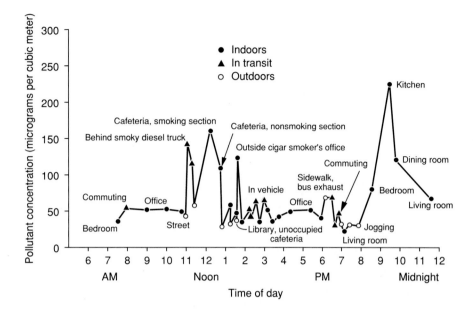

FIGURE 17-28 Continuous record of one man's exposure to particulate pollution from 7:30 A.M. to 11:30 P.M., October 16, 1979.

sure rather than on *emission tonnage*, a health-conscious society should be willing to pay 1,000 times more to reduce a gram of ETS than a gram of outside particulates generated by a power plant.

The message is clear. For many pollutants, such as particulates, oxides of nitrogen, carbon monoxide, and hydrocarbons (benzene, chloroform), indoor pollution is much more serious a health threat than outdoor pollution (outdoor pollution must be controlled to protect crops, forests, buildings and other species.)

What is the federal government doing about this problem? Not very much. After all, a big shift in funding from outdoor to indoor pollution control could threaten the professional and political careers of many people. As a result, in fiscal 1988, the federal budget for the control of indoor pollutants was a mere $2.6 million—less than 1 percent of the funding committed to the regulation of outdoor contaminants.

THE CLEAN AIR ACT

The Clean Air Act of 1970 is one of the most effective environmental laws ever enacted in the United States. Under its terms, the EPA was given the responsibility and authority to clean up the nation's dirty air. Levels of major types of atmospheric pollutants, such as sulfur dioxide, ozone, lead, particulates, nitrogen oxides, carbon monoxide, and hydrocarbons, were closely monitored, and safety standards for their concentration in the atmosphere were set to protect the health of humans and other organisms. A steady reduction in emissions from smokestacks and exhaust was mandated by the act. Violators were subject to stiff fines. With the aid of the legal "muscle" granted it by the act, the EPA has prodded the states to come to grips with their air pollution problems. Under the terms of the act, the EPA

can halt construction of new industrial plants, prevent expansion of existing industrial facilities, and cut off federal money for highway construction in states that do not develop suitable pollution control plans.

The improvement of our nation's air quality since 1970, in some respects, has been gratifying. For example, the emissions of particulates have been reduced by 64 percent, the emissions of carbon monoxide have fallen by 30 percent, and sulfur dioxide levels have been reduced by 20 percent, largely due to the Clean Air Act. The air pollution in at least 20 large urban areas of the United States has diminished. The gray-brown haze that used to shroud heavily industrialized cities like Cleveland, Pittsburgh, and Baltimore has largely dissipated. The number of cases of heart disease induced by atmospheric contaminants nationwide has also fallen. But not all the news is good. Nitrogen oxide levels have increased since 1970 and, according to a recent EPA study, over 110 million Americans now live in unhealthy air. In 1987 at least 36 urban areas, including Los Angeles, Chicago, and Milwaukee, failed to meet the federal standards for ozone, the ozone levels in Milwaukee being the highest since 1977.

During the 8 years of the Reagan administration, the EPA experienced much frustration in its attempt to clean up our nation's air. For example, the slashing of its budget made it extremely difficult to conduct research and weakened its ability to vigorously enforce the Clean Air Act.

Controlling air pollution is no easy task. Some federal departments sometimes promote policies at odds with those of the EPA. A good example involves the Department of Transportation and the EPA. On the one hand, the Transportation Department supports the construction of freeways that facilitate long-distance travel. However, this, in turn, sharply increases the consumption of gasoline, and hence the release of the atmospheric pollutants that the EPA is committed to control. Take another example. The EPA has encouraged power plants to switch from coal to nuclear power to reduce emissions of sulfur dioxide—one of the chemical precursors of acid rain. At the same time, the Department of Energy is promoting the use of coal by utilities in order to make the United States less dependent on foreign oil.

At this writing, most of the provisions of the Clean Air Act are still intact, thanks to strong public opinion and to environmentally sensitive members of Congress. Nevertheless, both industries and utilities continuously exert strong pressure on congressional representatives (by way of well-paid professional lobbyists) to relax the emission standards of the present Clean Air Act or extend emission reduction deadlines. In 1987, the deadline for cities to comply with the act was extended to 1992. Many cities have been dragging their feet, unwilling to take the necessary steps to cut pollution.

A revision of the Clean Air Act has been on the congressional agenda time and again for the past several years without ever coming to a vote. It was up for consideration again in 1989. Should the provisions of the act be tightened or relaxed? Recent studies conducted by hundreds of respected scientists on the staffs of universities, major hospitals, and state and federal environmental agencies, including the EPA itself, strongly suggest that the control of chlorofluorocarbons, carbon dioxide, oxides of nitrogen and sulfur, and hazardous pollutants, such as lead and asbestos, be tightened rather than relaxed. Time is of the essence. If there are more years of delay and inaction on the part of Congress, such formidable problems as the greenhouse effect, acid deposition, and decreased levels of stratospheric ozone, discussed in the next chapter, may eventually be beyond realistic control.

RAPID REVIEW

1. Naturally occurring contaminants of the atmosphere include (a) volcanic dust and ash, (b) ragweed pollen, (c) disease-causing bacteria, (d) fungal spores, (e) windblown soil particles, (f) salt spray, and (g) methane, carbon monoxide, and sulfur dioxide resulting from the decay of organic material.

2. It was not until the Industrial Revolution that air pollution became a severe threat to humans.

3. The term *smog* is a contraction of the words *smoke* and *fog*.

4. Only 7 percent of the carbon monoxide in the earth's atmosphere is generated by human activities. Nevertheless, it is this carbon monoxide that poses a threat to human health because it is concentrated in heavily populated areas. The concentration of carbon monoxide in urban areas may be 50 to 100 times the global average.

5. Much of the sulfur dioxide generated by humans results from the burning of sulfur-containing fossil fuels in power plants and other industries.

6. The solid and liquid particles suspended in the air are known as *particulates*. Major sources are coal-burning facilities such as power plants, steel mills, fertilizer plants, and foundries.

7. Lead is added to gasoline to improve its octane rating. It is released from auto exhaust into the air. After being inhaled, lead can eventually have harmful effects on the kidneys, blood, and liver. Furthermore, it can impair proper brain development in children. The EPA has proposed to ban leaded gasoline completely by 1995.

8. A *hydrocarbon* is an organic compound composed of hydrogen and carbon. Good examples of hydrocarbon pollutants of the atmosphere are methane and benzene. In general, the most significant effect of the hydrocarbons is their essential role in the formation of photochemical smog.

9. *Photochemical smog* is caused by the reaction between hydrocarbons, nitrogen oxides, and atmospheric oxygen in the presence of sunlight. Ozone is the principal component of photochemical smog.

10. Radiation inversions occur primarily at night when heat radiates from the earth's surface into the atmosphere. As a result, both the ground and the layer of air next to it begin to cool off rapidly. The warmer layer above then forms a lid on the cooler layer underneath, preventing pollution from dispersing vertically.

11. A subsidence inversion is formed when a high-pressure air mass sinks down and warms up. Here again, the warm air now forms a lid on the cool air nearer the ground.

12. Because of the *heat island* effect, some cities, such as Cleveland and St. Louis, may be 15°C (27°F) warmer than the surrounding rural areas.

13. The heat island effect causes pollutants to concentrate in a *dust dome* above a city.

14. Air pollution may have a number of effects on climate, such as (a) increasing the earth's average temperature, (b) decreasing sunlight penetration, (c) reducing the amount of sunlight reaching the earth, and (d) inducing precipitation.

15. The major illnesses caused by air pollution include lung cancer, emphysema, chronic bronchitis, and skin cancer.

16. The first major air pollution disaster in the United States occurred in Donora, Pennsylvania, in October 1948; it caused the death of 20 people.

17. Factors that contribute to air pollution disasters include (a) a dense population, (b) a dense concentration of industries, (c) location of cities in a topographical receptacle, (d) the presence of a thermal inversion, and (e) the presence of fog.

18. Asbestos is used in pipe and boiler insulation, brake linings, paint, plastics, and many other products and materials. People who inhale asbestos fibers may develop asbestosis, characterized by coughing, chest pains, and bluish discoloration of the skin. Over 50 percent of the people who have asbestosis eventually die from lung cancer.

19. More than 15 million students face a health threat because of asbestos fibers in the walls and ceilings of 30,000 classrooms in the United States. Occupational exposure to asbestos has been reduced by the use of vacuum devices, the mandatory use of masks, and the automation of many manufacturing processes.

20. The Pollution Standards Index (PSI) makes it possible to compare the air quality of different cities. An index value under 100 indicates relatively clean air. An index value of 400 and above suggests that the air is "very hazardous." On the basis of PSI ratings, the most badly polluted air occurs in Los Angeles, New York, Denver, and Pittsburgh.

21. An increasing number of industries are controlling air pollution by converting the original contaminants into useful products. For example, sulfur dioxide can be converted into sulfuric acid and high-carbon fly ash can be used directly as fuel or can be converted into cinder blocks, paving materials, abrasives, and cement.

22. Catalytic converters increase the rate at which carbon monoxide and hydrocarbons are oxidized to carbon dioxide and water, respectively.

23. Pollution control devices employed by utilities and industries include electrostatic precipitators, cyclone filters, fabric filter bag houses, and flue gas desulfurization systems, popularly known as *scrubbers*.

24. Flue gas desulfurization is the most widely used method for controlling sulfur dioxide emissions by industry and utilities.

25. Five general strategies for controlling auto emissions are (a) reducing traffic volume, (b) modifying the internal combustion engine, (c) replacing the internal combustion engine with electric and steam engines, and (d) developing a hybrid car (combining internal combustion and electric engines), and (e) increasing the use of mass transit.

26. Recent attempts to insulate homes have worsened indoor air pollution problems from carbon monoxide, formaldehyde, and radon gas.

27. Indoor air pollution may be controlled by (a) the use of air-to-air heat exchangers, (b) the use of house plants as living air purifiers, (c) the use of subbasement venting systems, and (d) the establishment of regulations that will protect lot and home buyers from living in a high-radon environment.

KEY WORDS AND PHRASES

Carbon monoxide poisoning
Carcinogens
Catalytic converter
Chronic bronchitis
Clean Air Act
Cyclone filter
Donora disaster
Dust domes
Dust plumes
Electric car
Electrostatic precipitator
Emphysema
Fabric filter bag house
Flue gas desulfurization
Formaldehyde
Fuel cell
Heat islands
Hybrid cars
Hydrocarbons
Indoor air pollution
Inspection and maintenance programs (IM)
Lead poisoning
Lung cancer
Mesothelioma
Natural pollution
Nitric oxide
Nitrogen dioxide
Ozone
Particulates
Photochemical smog
Pollution disaster
Pollution Standards Index (PSI)
Polonium
Radiation inversion
San Bernardino National Forest
Smog
Smog Check Program
Steam car
Subsidence inversion
Sulfur dioxide
Synergistic
Thermal inversion

QUESTIONS AND TOPICS FOR DISCUSSION

1. Briefly describe the biological significance of the major components of nonpolluted air.

2. Suppose that the percentages for carbon dioxide and oxygen in nonpolluted air were reversed. Would this reversal have any effect on the structure and function of ecosystems? How would your life be affected?

3. Briefly list three sources of natural pollution.

4. Discuss the health effects of each of the following air pollutants: (a) carbon monoxide, (b) oxides of sulfur, (c) oxides of nitrogen, (d) hydrocarbons, (e) ozone, and (f) lead.

5. List the major human-generated sources of carbon monoxide, oxides of sulfur, oxides of nitrogen, hydrocarbons, ozone, and lead.

6. Describe the formation of photochemical smog.

7. Cite an example of how severe air pollution actually caused the "death" of a town.

8. List five conditions that usually are associated with an air pollution disaster.

9. Describe three conditions that contribute to the heat island phenomenon.

10. Discuss the environmental advantages and disadvantages of "superstacks."

11. Which climatic conditions would be most conducive to the rapid dispersal of atmospheric pollutants? To their concentration in a localized area?

12. Discuss the advantages and disadvantages of the electric car and the steam car.

13. Discuss the advantages and disadvantages of replacing gasoline with ethanol.

14. Now that you have studied this material on air pollution, what changes, if any, do you plan to make with respect to the use of your automobile?

SUGGESTED READINGS

Boerner, D. A. "Sins of Emission." *American Forests* 93 (3–4): 24–27, 1987. Criticizes the use of firewood in the home because of the health-threatening pollutants that are released.

Conservation Foundation. "Air Quality." *State of the Environment: A View Toward the Nineties*. Washington, D.C.: Conservation Foundation, 1987, pp. 54–71. A comprehensive discussion of traditional atmospheric pollutants, their effects and control.

Smith, K. R. "Air Pollution: Assessing Total Exposure in the United States." *Environment* 30(8): 10–15, 33–38, 1988.

Sun, M. "Radon's Health Risks." *Science* 239 (4837): 250, 1988. A report on the latest EPA study of radon gas as an indoor pollution threat.

18

Air Pollution: Global Problems

Consider the following events: (1) In 1987 an enormous chunk of ice, twice the size of Rhode Island, broke away from the Antarctic Icefield and splashed into the sea. (2) Shortly after developing off the west coast of Africa in August 1988, hurricane Gilbert attained wind speeds of more than 200 mph. It was the most violent hurricane ever experienced in the Western Hemisphere.(3) During the summer of 1988, all-time heat records for many cities throughout the United States were shattered with dizzying frequency. On August 1, for example, Furnace Creek, California, lived up to its name with an oven-like 47°C (116°F).

At first glance, it would appear that these events have little in common. Nevertheless, these seemingly unrelated episodes may all occur in the future as the result of a global climatic phenomenon called the **greenhouse effect**.

The Greenhouse Effect

A number of gaseous pollutants released into the air because of human activity, such as carbon dioxide, water vapor, ozone, nitrous oxide, methane, and chlorofluorocarbons, are responsible for the greenhouse effect. What is it? Let's give a familiar example. You know what happens if you park your car in the campus parking lot on a hot summer day and forget to leave the windows open. When you reenter your car after class, it feels like an oven. This rapid increase in temperature is due to the greenhouse effect. The radiant energy from the sun passes through the car's windows. Some of this energy is then converted into heat (infrared waves)

energy. Since infrared radiation cannot readily escape through the windows, it is trapped inside the car.

Carbon dioxide, methane, and the other greenhouse gases act like the glass in a greenhouse. They, in fact, form a vast global "greenhouse" around the earth. These gases trap heat (infrared waves) escaping from the earth's surface (Figure 18-1). Although the concentration of all the earth-warming gases is increasing rapidly, the most significant one at the present time is **carbon dioxide**. Remember our study of the carbon cycle (Chapter 2)? We learned that carbon dioxide is continuously removed from the atmosphere by green plants (during photosynthesis) and by the ocean. On the other hand, carbon dioxide is gradually released back into the air when plants and animals respire, when organic matter decays or is oxidized, when forests, grasslands, or any organic material is burned, or when it is liberated from the ocean. For thousands of years, these processes were in balance—the amount of carbon dioxide removed from the atmosphere equalled the amount entering it. Scientists have determined the carbon dioxide concentration in the atmosphere of long ago by examining air bubbles trapped in glacial ice and by analyzing the wood of centuries-old trees. Such investigations have shown that carbon dioxide levels remained at about 270 ppm from the end of the last ice age until the nineteenth century. However, since 1860, the concentration has risen from 290 ppm to 350 ppm—an increase of more than 20 percent (Figure 18-2). This increase has largely been caused by human activities such as the consumption of fossil fuels (coal, oil, natural gas) and by the clearing and burning of tropical forests to make room for cattle

FIGURE 18-1 "Filling up!" Global warming is a problem caused by all of us. Automobiles and other forms of transportation are a major producer of carbon dioxide.

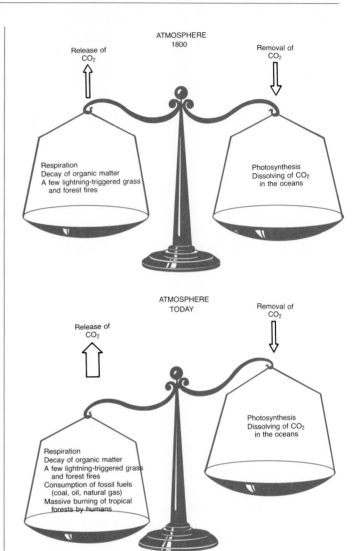

FIGURE 18-2 Release and removal of atmospheric carbon dioxide today as compared with 1800.

ranches and farms. Global fossil fuel consumption alone is responsible for the annual release of 5 billion metric tons of carbon into the air—roughly 1 ton for each person on earth. The rate of carbon release from this combustion has increased 53-fold since 1860! The clearing and burning of tropical rain forests releases about 1.6 billion tons into the air, about one-third the amount released by the consumption of fossil fuels.

Carbon dioxide levels in the atmosphere have been closely monitored by sensitive instruments atop Mauna Loa, an extinct Hawaiian volcano, since 1958. They have recorded a rise from 315 ppm in 1957 to 350 ppm in 1986—more than a 9.5 percent increase in only 30 years (Figures 18-3 and 18-4). If the carbon dioxide concentrations continue to rise at this rate, many scientists predict that the average global temperature could increase 3°C (5°F) by 2035. However, the warmup at the poles will be considerably greater, 7–10°C (13–18°F). Many scientists theorize that eventually ocean levels will rise as a result of the melting of polar ice caps and alpine glaciers. Indeed, in the past 100 years, ocean levels have already risen about 0.3 meter (1 foot). According to the EPA, they will rise another meter (3.3 feet) by 2030.

Effects of Global Warming

The predicted effects of global warming by the year 2035 are numerous; a few of them are beneficial.

BENEFICIAL EFFECTS

1. The cost of heating buildings during the winter in the high latitudes would be reduced. Fossil fuels would be conserved.
2. The far northern latitudes (tundra biome) might become more suitable for human settlement. Similarly, the ranges of many species of fish, birds, and mammals would be extended northward in North America. Such has already been the case for the mockingbird, cardinal, and opossum.
3. Because of increased rainfall and/or a longer growing season, food production should increase in

FIGURE 18-3 Concentration of atmospheric carbon dioxide recorded at Mauna Loa (Hawaii) Observatory 1957–1986. The atmospheric carbon dioxide level has increased from about 315 ppm in 1957 to about 350 ppm in 1986.

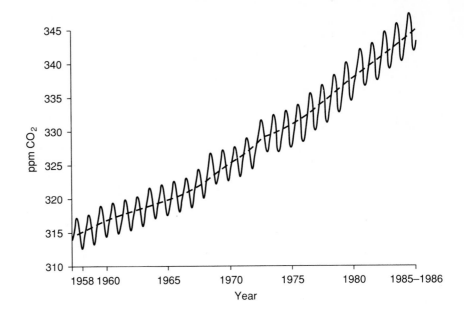

Canada, Mexico, Europe, northeast Africa, and Southeast Asia. The political and economic clout of these nations may increase substantially.

4. For every 1 percent increase in atmospheric carbon dioxide, the rate of photosynthesis will increase 0.5 percent, provided that sufficient water and nutrients are available. As a result, the yields of such crops as rice, corn, and wheat may increase.

HARMFUL EFFECTS

1. A 1-meter (3.3-foot) rise in ocean levels by 2035 would cause the seas to move 30 meters (100 feet) farther inland along many portions of our nation's coasts. Billions of dollars of coastal properties would be lost. The city of Charleston, South Carolina, alone would suffer $650 million in damage by the year 2035. Similar flood damage would probably be experienced in Boston, Philadelphia, New York City, Baltimore, Washington, Norfolk, Miami, St. Petersburg, and New Orleans.

2. Twenty percent of the most populated areas of India and Bangladesh would be inundated.

3. Large tracts of agricultural land would be destroyed because of salinization. Changing weather patterns could make huge areas infertile or uninhabitable. The result could well be more massive movements of displaced people than any in the history of this planet.

FIGURE 18-4 Global surface air temperature from 1900–1985, showing a gradual increase.

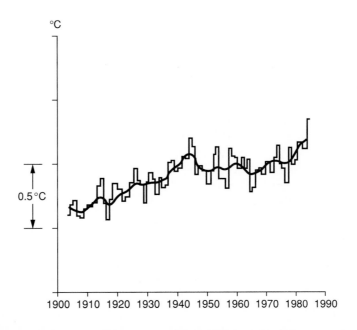

FIGURE 18-5 Reconstruction of summer rainfall patterns during the "Climatic Optimum" (1000 B.C.) as compared with today.

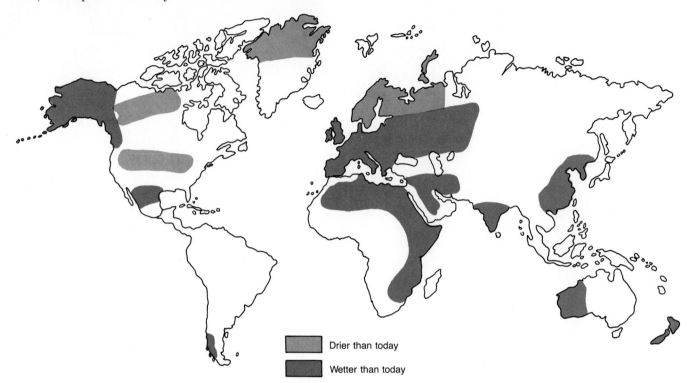

Drier than today

Wetter than today

4. Many of the world's most productive rice-growing areas would be destroyed by flood waters, including the fertile, highly populated deltas of the Indus (Pakistan), Ganges (Bangladesh), and Yang Tze (China) rivers.

5. Many aquifers along the Gulf and Atlantic coasts of the United States, which now serve as a source of drinking water for many American cities, would become contaminated by salt water from the ocean.

6. The increased salinity of many American estuaries, such as the Chesapeake Bay and Delaware River estuaries, would destroy their value as breeding and nursery grounds for many valuable species of game and commercial fish.

7. Our nation's corn-producing areas (Nebraska, Iowa, Illinois, Indiana, southern Minnesota, and southern Wisconsin) would become hotter and drier (Figure 18-5). As a result, corn production would shift northward into northern Minnesota, Wisconsin, and Canada, where soils are much less fertile. Overall corn yields, therefore, would decline. Our wheat industry would suffer a $506 million yield decline annually because of increased heat and drought.

8. Extensive drought in the Great Plains would trigger such huge dust storms that the black blizzards of the Dust Bowl days would pale by comparison.

9. By 2035, temperatures in Omaha, Nebraska, and other cities of the Great Plains would soar above 38°C (100°F) for 20 days a summer compared to only 3 days at present.

10. The carbon dioxide buildup would inflict enormous damage on the global economy. Consider, for example, just one factor—the displacement of agricultural production to the north (in the Northern Hemisphere). Such a dramatic shift would require hundreds of billions of dollars for the construction of new flood control, irrigation, drainage, and grain storage systems if a major agricultural effort were to be realized. For example, if new irrigation systems were required for just 15 percent of the existing irrigated area, the global price tag would be $200 billion—$15 billion for the United States alone. Then there would be the cost of new dikes, dams, levees, and so on to prevent the flooding of coastal areas. In fact, a doubling of the amount of carbon dioxide in the global atmosphere by 2035 would result in annual expenditures equal to 3 percent of the gross world product. Since this equals the rate of global economic growth, at that point economic growth the world over would come to a dismal halt.

11. Many plants and animals could become extinct because of the rapid change in temperature.

Controlling the Greenhouse Effect

Despite the repeated warnings of scientists that the greenhouse effect could eventually have highly adverse effects on human society, the general public, as well as policy makers, were generally unconcerned with the threat until 1988. In 1988 Americans experienced unusual drought, searing heat, floods, and hurricanes—the precise events scientists predicted would occur with increasing frequency and severity as the levels of greenhouse gases rise. The climatic disasters of 1988 may or may not have been valid signals that the greenhouse effect was finally in evidence. Nevertheless, some segments of the public, at least, have been aroused from their apathy. Even in the marbled halls of Congress, methods for controlling global warming are moving up on legislative agendas. In 1989 the EPA offered Congress specific options for mitigating global warming. Some of the EPA's proposals are described here.

REDUCING AUTOMOTIVE EMISSIONS. Carbon dioxide levels released into the atmosphere by motor vehicles could be substantially reduced by the emission-controlling strategies discussed in the previous chapter. As you recall, they include (1) reducing traffic volume; (2) instigating engine inspection and maintenance programs; (3) increasing fuel efficiency; (4) increasing the use of mass transit (buses and trains); and (5) replacing gasoline engines with those powered by electricity and/or steam.

Convert from Gasoline to Ethanol. Motor vehicle fuel could be shifted from gasoline to ethanol (grain alcohol). Ethanol could be produced from plants growing on "fuel farms." The use of ethanol has several advantages: (1) it burns cleanly; (2) although carbon dioxide is released when it is burned, the amount equals only the amount removed from the air by photosynthesis in fuel crops; (3) it will be needed sooner or later anyway to replace oil, the supplies of which are dwindling rapidly.

Impose a Tax on Fuels. The federal government could place a carbon dioxide "user fee" on all fuels that release carbon dioxide when burned. The greater the amount of carbon dioxide released from a given fuel, the higher the fee. Such a tax would encourage industries and utilities to conserve fuel or switch from oil and coal to natural gas or solar energy. Motorists would be inclined to use methane or ethanol to power their cars rather than gasoline. Revenues from the tax could be used to develop and promote energy conservation and alternative fuels (Chapter 20).

Use More Methane Fuel. Methane gas generates only about half as much carbon dioxide as coal in producing the same amount of energy. Methane can be obtained from sanitary landfills by driving a pipe into the depths of the decomposing garbage. This is already being done at many sites in the United States, including the Fresh Kills Landfill on New York City's Staten Island.

Use Genetic Engineering Methods to Develop "Gasoline Plants." With the recently developed techniques in genetic engineering, plant geneticists could develop varieties of plants that produce hydrocarbons from which energy-rich fuels might be derived (Chapter 20). Even though carbon dioxide would be released into the atmosphere when these fuels are burned, the amount would only equal that removed from the air by photosynthesis during the life of the plants. (Burning such fuels would be quite different from burning coal derived from plants that carried on photosynthesis, and hence removed carbon dioxide from the air, more than 200 million years ago.)

Halt the Deforestation in the Tropics. As described in Chapter 11, many square kilometers of tropical rain forests in Central and South America and Southeast Asia have been cut down and burned to clear areas for cattle ranches and farms. Much wood is also used as fuel. Some experts believe that 40 percent of the closed canopy (solid stands) of tropical rain forest has already been removed. At present rates of deforestation in Nepal (4 percent per year), the tropical rain forest will have been completely cleared away by the year 2012. You will recall that much of the tropical forest removal in Central America was done so that ranchers could raise beef, which would eventually wind up in the billions of hamburgers eaten by Americans at fast food chains. Removing these vast stands of tropical rain forest eliminates more than a billion tons of atmospheric carbon by photosynthesis—an obvious contributing factor to the global carbon dioxide buildup.

What can be done? Many of the deforestation projects in tropical regions have been funded with money provided by the World Bank and other international lending agencies. Roughly 20 percent of World Bank money comes from the United States. Pressure is now being exerted on the World Bank by environmental agencies to refuse to fund projects such as deforestation that would contribute to carbon dioxide buildup. New projects that encourage population control and the sustainable harvest of tropical forests could help save this vanishing resource.

Reforestation. In 1989 Frederick Bernthal, assistant secretary of state for global environmental issues, was in charge of American participation in a multinational effort to deal with global warming. In his opinion, reforestation is the least costly strategy for reducing the greenhouse effect. The American Forestry Association encourages the planting of 100 million trees yearly in the United States. Such projects will certainly help. Nevertheless, the task will be Herculean. Scientists estimate, for example, that to remove the 5 billion tons of carbon dioxide released into the air each year by human activities, the new forests would have to have an aggregate area equal to that of the continental United States!

It is encouraging to note that some major industries in the United States are cooperating vigorously in the reforestation effort. A good example is Applied Energy

Services (AES). In 1989 this giant utility forged ahead with the construction of a mammoth power plant in Uncasville, Connecticut. This plant will spew many tons of carbon dioxide into the air every day. However, to help nullify the greenhouse effect caused by these emissions, the company donated $2 million to a reforestation project in Guatemala. With this financial support, the Peace Corps, the Guatemalan Forestry Service, and 40,000 farmers will plant 92 million tree seedlings. Scientists estimate that the net carbon dioxide taken in by the trees will roughly balance that emitted from the new AES power plant during its 40-year life span. Individuals can help by planting trees, cutting back on all forms of waste, by recycling and using mass transit.

THE ACID RAIN PROBLEM

Nature of the Problem

"April showers bring May flowers." Or do they? Many scientists now believe that at least some April showers may bring death, not only to plants but also to fish, birds, and mammals and even to humans (Figure 18-6). The problem is the acid in those April showers—in other words, **acid rain**.

Where does acid rain come from? Surprisingly, a drop of acid rain may originate several hundred kilometers from where it actually falls to earth. Acid rain can be traced directly to two major atmospheric pollutants—sulfur dioxide and nitrogen dioxide. These gases combine with water and oxygen to produce sulfuric acid and nitric acid, respectively. In the eastern United States, sulfur dioxide causes most of the acidity. However, in the Rocky Mountains and along the Pacific Coast, oxides of nitrogen are the main chemical culprits.

Actually, acid rain is only one phase of the more general phenomenon of **acid deposition**, which, in fact, can be either wet or dry. Acid rain, snow, dew, fog, frost, and mist represent the *wet* form of deposition. *Dry* deposition occurs when dust particles containing sulfate or nitrate settle on earth. Later those chemicals react with water to form sulfuric and nitric acids. Dry deposition also may occur when gases like sulfur dioxide and nitric oxide come in contact with soil, trees, lakes, and streams and then react with water to form acids.

The pH scale, which ranges from 0 to 14, indicates a substance's acidity or alkalinity (Figure 18-7). A pH of 7 indicates neutrality. Numerical values above 7 indicate alkalinity. For example, lye, with a pH of 13, is extremely alkaline. Values below 7 indicate acidity. Thus, battery acid, with a pH of 1, is extremely acid. Because the scale is logarithmic, rain that has a pH of 4 is 10 times as acidic as rain with a pH of 5 and 100 times as acidic as rain with a pH of 6. Rather surprisingly, normal unpolluted rain is weakly acid, with a pH

FIGURE 18-6 "April showers bring May flowers!" However, if those showers are acidic, they may cause plants to die rather than to flower.

of 5.6. The reason is that carbon dioxide from the air reacts with the water to form carbonic acid.

In 1980 the federal government established the National Atmospheric Deposition Program. It consists of acid deposition monitoring sites scattered throughout the United States. Through this program a comprehensive assessment of acidity trends can be made and maps can be drawn. As seen in Figure 18-8, the rain in the eastern United States is quite acidic. We must remember, of course, that the pH values on the map are average values for an entire year. This trend toward increasing acidity in the northeastern United States appears to be correlated with the increasing volume of sulfur and nitrogen oxides released into the air over the Midwest. The average pH for rain in western New York, northern Pennsylvania, and lower Ontario, Canada, was 4.2, many times more acid than normal rain. In Los Angeles, a pH of 3 was recorded for a dense fog. The most acidic rain ever recorded in the United States fell at Wheeling, West Virginia. It had a pH of 1.4, making it considerably more acidic than lemon juice (pH 2.2) and almost as acidic as battery acid (pH 1).

FIGURE 18-7 The pH of acid rain as compared with fruits, vegetables and common household substances. Note the sharp decrease of the pH of New York's Adirondack lakes between 1930 and 1975.

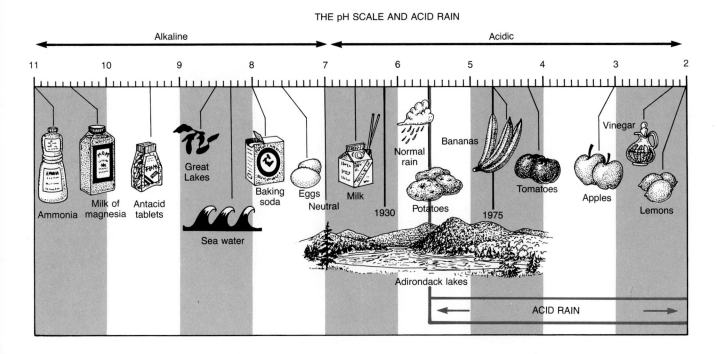

The Northeast has been the focus of many acid rain studies. Recent work shows that many other states are now experiencing acid deposition. Take California. The California Air Resources Board has documented precipitation in the state that is among the most acidic found anywhere in the world. The pH of rain in California ranges from a low of 4.4 in San Jose and Pasadena to a high of 5.4 at Big Bear. Fog in California's Central Valley had a pH of 2.6—1,000 times more acidic than nonpolluted rain. Of considerable interest is the fact that dry acid deposition is 15 times more prevalent than acid rain in parts of southern California where rainfall is scant and the nitrogen oxides emissions from motor vehicles are high.

Sulfur dioxide is released naturally from volcanoes, swamps, and the ocean. Human activity now accounts for about as much sulfur dioxide emission as does nature. Most human-generated sulfur dioxide is released from only 5 percent of the earth's surface—primarily the industrialized regions of the United States, Canada, Europe, and eastern Asia. Roughly 22 million metric tons (24 million tons) of sulfur dioxide are emitted into the atmosphere of the United States annually: 66 percent from electric power plants, 22 percent from industrial sources, and 6 percent from smelters. It is believed that about 50 percent of the acid deposition in eastern Canada has its origin in the United States. In Ohio and nearby states, high-sulfur coal is king. As a result, Ohio smokestacks alone emit more sulfur dioxide into the air than those in New York, New Jersey, and the six New

England states combined. Nitrogen oxides, on the other hand, are generated primarily by cars, trucks, buses, and power plants.

Figure 18-9 shows that some areas of the United States are much more vulnerable to acid rain than others. The most sensitive regions are the eastern United States, northern Minnesota, Wisconsin, and Michigan, certain areas in the Rockies, the Northwest, and the Pacific Coast. The vulnerability of a given region to acid deposition depends on the ability of the rocks and soils in the watershed (or the rocks on a lake bottom) to neutralize, or **buffer**, the acid. Soils derived from granite, which are low in calcium, are highly vulnerable. Soils derived from limestone, which are rich in calcium, are much more capable of buffering the acid.

Researchers at Colorado State University have found that a given molecule of sulfur dioxide may remain in the atmosphere for up to 40 hours, and a sulfate particle may remain aloft for 3 weeks. Because of their relatively long residence in the atmosphere, these molecules may be carried hundreds of kilometers from their release point. For example, sulfur dioxide molecules that originate in an Arizona copper smelter may eventually fall in acid rain on a sensitive mountain lake in Idaho. A molecule of sulfur dioxide that originated in Ohio may be transported to New York or New Jersey (Figure 18-10). Those molecules are also windblown from the United States into Canada or vice versa. It is estimated that 87 percent of the sulfate in New York and New Jersey and 92 percent of the amount in New England is

FIGURE 18-8   Acidity (pH) of North American precipitation. Note the high acidity (low pH) in the northeastern United States and southeastern Canada.

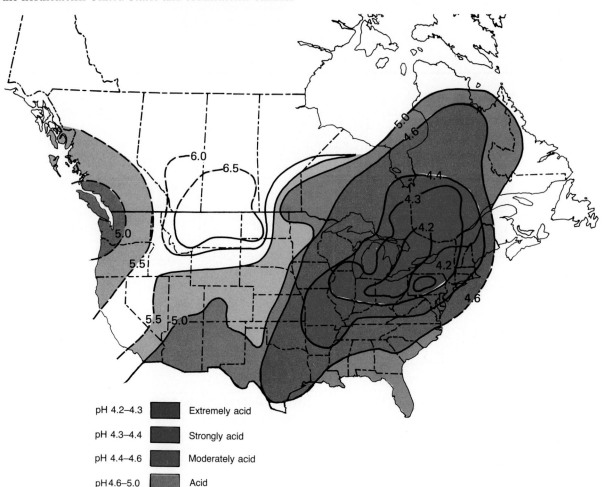

pH 4.2–4.3	Extremely acid
pH 4.3–4.4	Strongly acid
pH 4.4–4.6	Moderately acid
pH 4.6–5.0	Acid
pH 5.0–5.5	Lightly acid

delivered from outlying areas—most likely the Midwest (Figure 18-11). On the other hand, California generates all its own acid rain, receiving almost no inputs from outside its boundaries. This situation provides California legislators with a strong motive to control acid deposition, knowing that any reductions achieved in sulfur dioxide and nitrogen oxide emissions will result in a reduction in acid deposition in their state.

The superstack at the mammoth smelter at Sudbury, Ontario, which towers to a height of 380 meters (1,140 feet), releases 2,300 metric tons of sulfur dioxide into the air daily. It emits twice as much sulfur annually as did Mt. Saint Helens during its most active eruption year!. It is the largest stack in the world and serves as a symbol of the acid rain problem in North America. Incredibly, this one stack gives off 1 percent of all the sulfur dioxide released worldwide!

Many superstacks were constructed in 1970s so that emissions such as soot, sulfur dioxide, and nitrogen oxide would be diluted before they came down to the nose-and-eye levels of nearby residents. Ironically, by building those extra-tall stacks, the utility people unwittingly facilitated the *long-range* transport of gases and particulates, thus contributing to the widespread acid deposition problem facing the United States and Canada today.

In 1982 a group of environmental activists belonging to the Greenpeace organization zealously protested industry's release of acid-forming chemicals. One of their more spectacular strategies to publicize their cause was to send six climbers up the vertical face of towering smokestacks in Conesville, Ohio; Madison, Indiana; and San Manuel, Arizona. The daring young men then decorated the stacks with brightly colored banners that read: "For our children, for our land, for our future—Stop Acid Rain. Greenpeace."

Harmful Effects of Acid Deposition

EFFECTS ON BUILDINGS AND MATERIALS.   Acid rain accelerates the erosion of sandstone, limestone,

FIGURE 18-9   Each dot represents an area which emits more than 100,000 tons of sulfur dioxide annually. Arrows indicate direction of major wind movements. Shaded areas are low in natural buffers such as limestone and are therefore particularly susceptible to acidification.

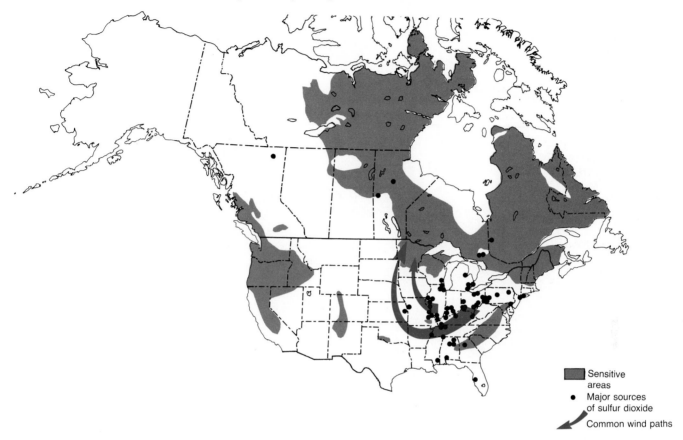

Sensitive areas

● Major sources of sulfur dioxide

Common wind paths

and marble. Priceless monuments of ancient Rome and Athens have been seriously damaged, as have the Statue of Liberty, the Washington Monument, and the Capitol in the United States. The marble statues of women in front of Field Museum in Chicago have undergone rapid deterioration in only the past 30 years. Numerous metallic structures like bridges, rails, and industrial equipment have been corroded by acid rain. The U.S. Air Force spends millions of dollars annually to repair acid rain-inflicted damage to their B-52 bombers and other planes. The overall damage to buildings and materials by acid rain has exceeded $5 billion annually in 17 eastern states alone (Figure 18-12).

EFFECTS ON SOILS.   Acid deposition, of course, adds hydrogen ions to the soil. As you learned in Chapter 5, hydrogen ions displace nutrient elements like calcium, potassium, and magnesium from the soil particles to which they are bound. Such nutrients may then be leached from the soil and carried away by runoff water. Acid deposition also inhibits the activity of nitrogen-fixing bacteria. As a result of these two effects alone, acid deposition may substantially reduce fertility in certain soils within a decade. Heavy metals

like aluminum, which normally are harmlessly bound to soil particles, are also displaced by the hydrogen ions in acid deposition. These metals then become soluble in water and can be absorbed by the roots of farm crops or trees, often with harmful results (Figure 18-13; Table 18-1).

EFFECTS ON AQUATIC ECOSYSTEM

Vulnerability of Lakes and Streams to Acidification.   Lakes and streams vary in their ability to cope with acid deposition. The most vulnerable are the soft-water lakes that contain relatively few dissolved minerals, such as calcium salts, that can neutralize acid. Many lakes in the northeastern United States and in the Rocky Mountains and Sierra Nevadas are of this type. On the other hand, in the southern and central regions of the United States, most lakes are hardwater lakes and contain acid-buffering minerals (Figure 18-14).

Acid deposition has poisoned thousands of lakes in Scandinavia, the province of Ontario, Canada, and the northeastern United States. Scientists estimate that at the present rate of acidification, at least 48,000 lakes in Ontario will be unable to support life in another 15 years. In the Adirondack Mountains of New York, 237

FIGURE 18-10   Wind transports acid to distant areas. The northeast is particularly vulnerable.

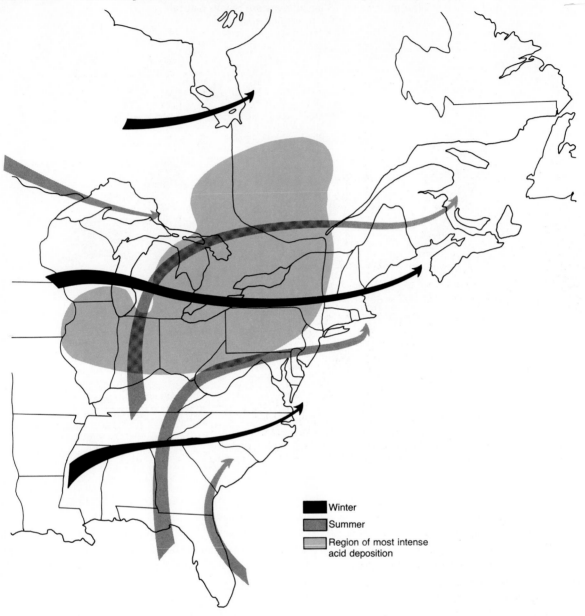

Winter

Summer

Region of most intense
acid deposition

lakes have a pH of less than 5—an acidity level lethal for many species of fish.

The Office of Technology Assessment conducted a survey of the acid rain problem in 27 eastern states. Their conclusions are as follows:

1. Eighty percent of the lakes and streams in the North-east and upper Midwest are vulnerable to acidification.

2. Seventeen percent of the lakes and 20 percent of the streams in 27 states have been damaged by acid deposition.

3. Of the 17,059 lakes studied, 2,993 have already been acidified.

4. Of the 187,876 kilometers (117,423 miles) of

streams investigated, 39,500 kilometers (24,688 miles) have already been damaged.

Harmful Effects of Acid Deposition on Lakes and Streams.   Among the adverse effects of acidification in aquatic ecosystems are the following:

1. Reproduction in many species of organisms, including fish, is either reduced or ended.

2. Acidified waters may disrupt the homing ability in sexually mature salmon. Research conducted at the University of New Hampshire has shown that when the pH of water is between 5.0 and 5.5, salmon apparently lose their ability to detect certain odors in the water. Since adult salmon depend upon chemi-

FIGURE 18-11   The acidity of the rain that falls on Adirondack lakes in New York and destroys fish and other aquatic life has its origin in sulfur dioxide emitted from industrial smokestacks in the Midwest.

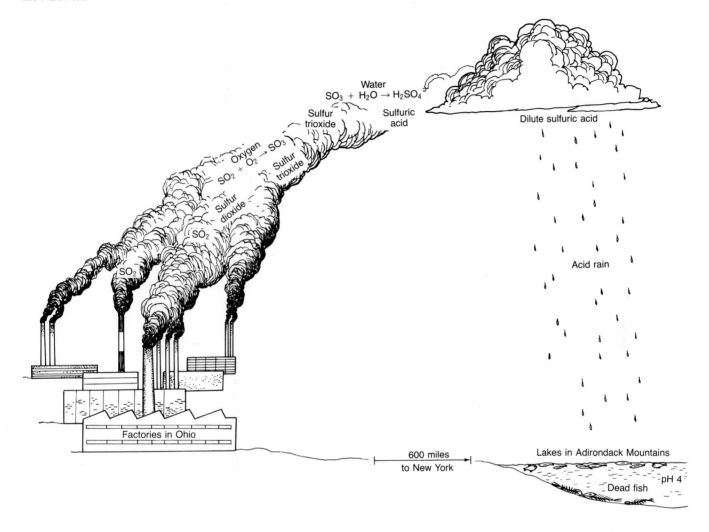

cals to guide them to their native streams so that they can spawn, the survival of the species in acidified streams is threatened.

3. Increased numbers of fish embryos and newly hatched young develop abnormally and eventually die in waters where the pH is below 5.5.

4. Populations of important fish food organisms, such as crustaceans and insect larvae, rapidly decline.

5. Game fish like bass and pike are replaced by more acid-tolerant but less desirable species such as bullheads and suckers.

6. Heavy metals, such as aluminum, mercury, copper, zinc, and nickel, are leached from soils and washed into streams and lakes. Although few studies have been undertaken, the effects of these metals on aquatic life are probably adverse. Aluminum is toxic to fish at concentrations of less than 1 ppm. At this concentration, it causes mucus buildup on gills and death by asphyxiation.

7. The mercury buildup in the body of a fish, resulting from biological accumulation in the food chain, increases in proportion to the acidification of the lake. In some acidic lakes in Wisconsin, predatory fish like salmon, lake trout, and northern pike may have mercury concentrations above 2 ppm—more than twice the level considered safe for human consumption.

8. The skeletons of fish may become weakened by decalcification. As a result, their bodies become distorted and the fish lose their ability to swim. Death from starvation, disease, or predation soon follows.

9. Bacterial decomposition is inhibited. As a result, essential nutrients like nitrogen and phosphorus stay locked up in plant and animal remains and are not available to aquatic plants—the producer base of the aquatic food webs.

EFFECTS ON HUMAN HEALTH.   Fish are not the only organisms that are adversely affected by acid

FIGURE 18-12 Acid rain is slowly causing the erosion of well-known statues in Europe and North America. Among them is this statue of Hans Christian Andersen, the celebrated author of children's books, which is located in Copenhagen, Denmark.

deposition. Humans are vulnerable as well. One of the greatest air pollution disasters the world has known occurred in London in 1952. The "killer fog" that shrouded the city for 5 days contributed to the death of more than 4,000 people from bronchitis, pneumonia, and heart disease. Although pH measurements of the fog were not recorded at the time, present-day scientists estimate that the fog was a highly diluted sulfuric acid mist with a pH ranging from 1.4 to 1.9! But that was almost four decades ago. Is acid deposition still a killer? According to the Office of Technology Assessment, more than 50,000 premature deaths are caused annually by sulfate-laden air. Acid precursors are the second largest cause of lung disease (after smoking) in the opinion of Dr. Phillip J. Landrigan of the Mount Sinai School of Medicine in New York City.

Today more than 40 million people in the United States, or about one in six, are drinking water with lead levels above 20 ppb—the level considered safe by the EPA. Where did the lead come from? It apparently was leached from galvanized water pipes and lead solder in copper pipes by the acidic drinking water. Such intake of lead by millions of Americans is cause for considerable concern because medical researchers have shown lead to be one of the factors responsible for high blood pressure and heart attacks in adults and for brain damage in children.

Some health experts believe that acid rain may also be indirectly responsible for many cases of Alzheimer's disease. This is a disease of the elderly characterized by degeneration of the brain and severe loss of memory. Chemical analyses of the brains of people who died from the disease have revealed relatively high levels of aluminum. Some researchers believe that aluminum may have caused the disease. If so, where did it come from? How did it get into the body? The involvement of acid deposition is strongly suggested.

Controlling Acid Deposition

SWITCHING FROM HIGH-SULFUR TO LOW-SULFUR COAL. The coal that is now burned in utility and industrial boilers varies greatly in sulfur content, from less than 1 percent to almost 6 percent. Wisconsin's Department of Natural Resources has estimated that coal switching in that state would cut sulfur dioxide emission levels at least 51 percent below those of 1980. Mandatory coal switching under federal law would do much to ease the acid deposition problem nationwide. The question arises: "Are our nation's supplies of low-sulfur coal sufficient for this purpose?" Apparently, the answer is "yes." A group of low-sulfur mining industries and environmentalists who have formed the Alliance for Clean Energy, has determined that more than 14.1 billion metric tons of low-sulfur coal is available—adequate to meet the needs of our utilities and industries for many years.

USING SMOKESTACK "SCRUBBERS." In 1989 Leonard Kreisle, professor of engineering at the University of Texas–Austin, announced the development of a new smokestack device for removing sulfur dioxide emissions. Known as a **synergistic reactor**, it has several advantages over the smokestack scrubbers used to date: (1) it removes 100 percent of the sulfur dioxide; (2) it is much smaller; (3) it uses only one-third as much energy; (4) it acts in seconds rather than minutes; and (5) gypsum, the only by-product, has high commercial value for use in wall-board manufacture.

It is believed that the scaled-up version of the synergistic reactor will remove 2,300 kilograms (5,000 pounds) of sulfur dioxide per minute. As the gaseous emissions pass through the reactor, they enter a chamber filled with finely ground limestone and steam. It is here that the sulfur dioxide reacts with the limestone to form gypsum. The synergistic reactor has attracted

FIGURE 18-13 Spruce die-off on Mount Mitchell, North Carolina. Note defoliated and dead trees. Scientists believe that acid deposition may have contributed to this die off.

Table 18-1 Pollution-Related Forest Declines of the Last 50 Years

Widely assumed major role
  Massive die-off of forests in Europe (*Waldsterben*)
  Decline of ponderosa and Jeffrey pines in the San Bernardino Mountains of California
  Regional decline of white pine in the eastern United States and Canada

Possible major role
  Decline of red spruce, and balsam, and Frasser firs at high elevations in the Appalachian Mountains from Georgia to New England
  Growth decline without other visible symptoms in loblolly, shortleaf, and slash pines in the Piedmont regions of Alabama, Georgia, North and South Carolina
  Growth decline without other visible symptoms in pitch and shortleaf pine in the Pine Barrens region of New Jersey
  Widespread dieback of sugar maples in northeastern United States and southeastern Canada

Declines related to biological or physical factors
  Tannensterben (white fir decline) in Europe
  Kiefersterben (Scotch pine decline) in East Germany and European Russia during early 1970s
  Oak decline in Germany and especially in France since early 1900s
  Decline of *Pinus pinaster* on the Atlantic coast of France since early 1980s
  Beech bark disease in northeastern United States and southeastern Canada
  Littleleaf disease of shortleaf pine in the southeastern United States
  Birch dieback in northeastern United States and southeastern Canada
  Poleblight of western white pine in Rocky Mountains
  Maple decline in northeastern United States and southeastern Canada
  Oak decline in Pennsylvania, Virginia, and Texas
  Ash dieback in northeastern United States and southeastern Canada
  Sweetgum blight in southeastern United States

Note: A number of the declines attributed to biological or physical factors might involve toxic air pollutants, but studies are incomplete, and evidence insufficient to make a strong connection.

considerable attention from the EPA, as well as environmental agencies from Canada, Europe, the Soviet Union, and Japan. A mini-version of the reactor could be used to remove sulfur dioxide emissions from motor vehicles.

ENERGY CONSERVATION. Writing for the highly respected Worldwatch Institute, long a leader on environmental issues, Sandra Postel argues that energy conservation is both an effective and a relatively inexpensive strategy for controlling the emissions of sulfur dioxide and nitrogen oxide, the precursors of acid deposition. Under the terms of the **National Alliance Energy Conservation Act** of 1987, higher energy efficiency standards have been established for air conditioners, refrigerators, and water heaters. According to Postel, 70,000 megawatts of electricity, equal to the output of 70 large power plants, could be saved annually this way. She estimates that about 85 million metric tons of coal would not have to be burned if we cut our electrical consumption by half. The net result: a 4 million ton (or 16 percent) annual reduction in sulfur dioxide emissions. Moreover, this would cost only 1 percent of the $5 to $10 billion expenditure on the smokestack scrubbers, which would have the same effect.

FEDERAL LEGISLATION. A number of acid deposition control bills have been considered in Congress since 1981. Unfortunately, however, all of them were locked in committee and never even came up for a vote. This hesitancy to come to grips with the problem is understandable. Any acid control bill proposed will be highly controversial. Those who prefer strong controls include environmentalists, the timber industry, fishing

FIGURE 18-14   Effect of water acidity
on aquatic organisms.

EFFECT OF WATER ACIDITY ON AQUATIC ORGANISMS

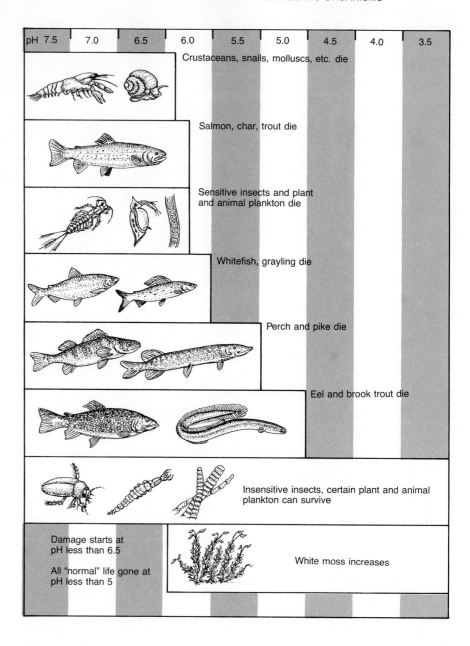

enthusiasts, owners of lake resorts, and lake recreationists, as well as many in the medical profession. Surveys have shown that the general public is aware of the seriousness of the acid problem and would support acid control legislation even if it results in an increase in their electricity bills. However, opposition to a control bill is equally strong. Included in the opposition, quite understandably, are the coal-burning utilities and industries that would have to spend substantial sums to install smokestack scrubbers. The mining companies that sell high-sulfur coal also oppose controls, since any comprehensive acid control legislation might encourage utilities and industry to switch from high-sulfur to low-sulfur coal.

Canada, with multi-billion-dollar timber and lake recreation industries at stake, has been very critical of foot dragging by the Reagan and Bush administrations and Congress as well. After all, substantial amounts of acid deposition in Canada originate in the United States. In fact, Canadian Prime Minister Brian Mulroney made a special visit to the White House in 1988 to express his concern. In an address to Congress, Mulroney warned that "acid rain is a rapidly escalating ecological tragedy in this country as well as ours." In 1989 President Bush told Mulroney that his administration would "come to grips" with the problem.

In 1986, the Canadian government had passed the

FIGURE 18-15 The ozone layer in the stratosphere shields the earth from potentially lethal ultra-violet radiation.

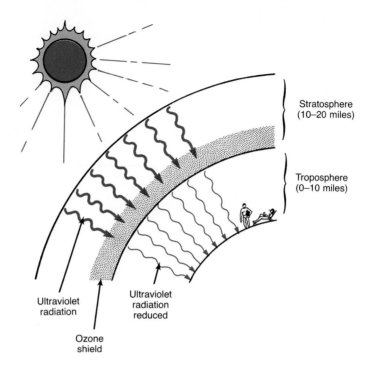

Stratosphere
(10–20 miles)

Troposphere
(0–10 miles)

Ultraviolet
radiation

Ultraviolet
radiation
reduced

Ozone
shield

toughest legislation on acid rain control on the North American continent: emissions of sulfur dioxide by smelters, utilities, and industry would be reduced 50 percent by the year 1996. The National Academy of Science, the most prestigious scientific organization in the United States, has recommended that Congress pass a similar law, one that would cut annual sulfur dioxide emissions in the United States by 10.8 million metric tons, or 50 percent by 1997. Time is of the essence. For our nation's lawmakers to delay any longer would invite grave consequences indeed, not only to forests and aquatic ecosystems, but to the health of millions of Americans.

DEPLETION OF STRATOSPHERIC OZONE

Nature of the Problem

Ozone is not *all* bad. It depends upon where it occurs. At the nose-eye-throat level, of course, it can pose a serious health hazard. Witness its effect on the citizens of Los Angeles as a component of smog. However, ozone is also found in the ozone layer of the stratosphere at a height of 25–50 kilometers (15–30 miles) above the earth's surface. And, surprisingly, human life is dependent on the presence of this ozone blanket, for this layer absorbs much of the ultraviolet (UV) light produced by the sun (Figure 18-15). Were this absorption screen of ozone not present, or were it to be thinned out, much more UV light would reach the earth's surface. The results, say the experts, would be catastrophic.

Until a few years ago, the ozone layer was in a state of dynamic equilibrium. In other words, ozone-forming

and ozone-depleting reactions proceeded at similar rates, and therefore, the amount of stratospheric ozone remained fairly constant. It is true, however, that there might be variations in abundance as high as 10 percent from year to year. And even in a given year, the amount of ozone in the stratosphere might be two or three times greater in one place than another.

In 1974, F. S. Rowland, of the University of California, startled the scientific community with this report: The chlorofluorocarbon gases (CFCs) used to propel deodorants, hair sprays, shaving creams, insecticides from spray cans, and used in refrigerators and air conditioners were accumulating in the stratosphere and causing ozone depletion. The total amount of CFCs released into the global atmosphere is considerable. In 1986, the U.S. used 320 million kilograms (700 million pounds) of CFC.

Two CFC compounds were once commonly used in the United States and abroad. In the United States, they have been manufactured primarily by the Dupont Corporation. One compound is $CFCl_3$ (spray can propellant), and the other is CF_2Cl_2 (refrigerant). Both of these compounds are extremely stable and inert under ordinary environmental conditions close to earth. Of course, it is this characteristic that makes these compounds desirable as propellants; they will not react chemically either with the contents of the spray can or with the can itself. The propellant molecules used by men to spray foamy shaving cream on the beard probably escape through the bathroom window, then float up beyond the treetops and high into the sky. Within 5 years or less, these CFC molecules may enter the stratosphere 8–30 miles above the earth. However, once in the stratosphere, these ordinarily stable compounds

Table 18-2 How CFC Impacts on the Economy

Application	Number in U.S.	Value/ $ Billions	Employ/ 1000s
Refrigeration	85 million home fridges 28 million home freezers 160,000 food stores 39,000 supermarkets 178,000 trucks 250,000 restaurants 27,000 rail cars	$11.5	524
Air conditioning	40 million homes; essentially all office, commercial, & public buildings	10.9	125
Mobile air conditioning	60–70 million	2	25
Plastic foam	Insulating foams for homes, refrigerators, food service trays and packaging, cushioning foams	2	40
Solvents	Microelectronic circuitry, high-performance air and spacecraft and computers	Valued at billions Unknown total	
Food freezants	Frozen shrimp, fish, vegetables	0.4	Less than 1000
Sterilants	Medical items, catheters, syringes, respiratory units, medical supplies, pharmaceuticals	0.1 (sterilizing equipment)	Less than 1000
TOTAL		$26.9 billion +	715 thousand

Source: Wisconsin Department of Natural Resources, "The Sky is Falling," Julian Chazin and Rick Mulhern, May–June, 1977, p. 35.

are exposed to intense radiation from UV light. As a result, the molecules decompose and release free chlorine atoms. We shall follow this process by using $CFCl_3$ as an example:

$$CFCl_3 + UV \text{ light} \rightarrow \text{free Cl atoms}$$

The free Cl atoms then catalyze the conversion of ozone (O_3) into molecular oxygen (O_2). One chlorine atom can cause the breakdown of 100,000 molecules of O_3. The reaction is as follows:

$$\underset{\text{(ozone)}}{2O_3} + Cl \rightarrow \underset{\text{(oxygen)}}{3O_2}$$

When the CFCs were first synthesized in the 1920s, they seemed too good to be true. They are inexpensive, stable, nonflammable, and nontoxic. Moreover, they vaporize at low temperatures. Furthermore, they can be produced very cheaply. As a result, they have many uses. As shown in Table 18-2, they are used in refrigeration and air-conditioning systems, solvents, and sterilants, as well as in the production of plastic foams. For many years, the McDonald's fast food chain used plastic foam containers. The CFCs produced annually worldwide have a total value of $27 billion and provide employment for 715,000 people. And, of course, some of the CFCs in the previously mentioned products

may find their way into the atmosphere. When foam plastic-burger holders crack open, or when junked refrigerators rust and deteriorate, CFCs are released into the air and eventually contribute to ozone depletion.

The atmospheric concentrations of the ozone-depleting gases are measured each day by scientists in Oregon, Ireland, Tasmania (off the coast of Australia), the Barbados (northeast of Venezuela), and Samoa (the South Pacific). Since these gases have long life spans and are broken down only by the action of sunlight, an 85 percent reduction in CFC emissions would be required simply to ensure that the CFC concentration in the atmosphere could be maintained at current levels.

In 1989, the atmospheric concentrations of CFC_{11} and CFC_{12} in the ozone layer were about 230 and 400 parts per trillion, respectively. These gases are increasing at the rate of 5 percent annually. Since the average life span of a $CFCl_3$ molecule is about 75 years and that of CF_2Cl_2 is 110 years, these gases freely move through the stratosphere all the way around the globe. As a result, they become widely dispersed over both heavily industrialized and wilderness areas.

Harmful Effects of UV Radiation

Scientists have estimated that if the release of CFCs into the atmosphere continues at the present rate, by the

FIGURE 18-16   "Getting a sun tan!" However, this "sun-worshipper" may also be getting skin cancer some time in the future because of exposure to ultraviolet radiation.

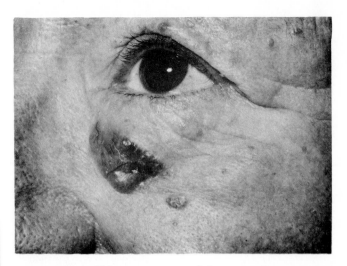

FIGURE 18-17   Skin cancer caused by excessive exposure to ultraviolet radiation in sunlight. Thinning of the ozone "shield" will cause a sharp increase in the incidence of such cancers.

year 2025 there will be 1.4 million additional cases of skin cancer worldwide (Figures 18-16 and 18-17). There will also be an increased frequency of cataracts—a clouding of the lens of the eye that results in blurred vision. Exposure of laboratory animals to increased UV radiation reduces their ability to fight off bacterial infections. It is probable that humans suffer similar effects. Scientists estimate that the increased UV levels now experienced in the United States will reduce cotton production by 3 percent and will decrease corn and wheat yields as well. The study of UV radiation on natural ecosystems such as forests, grasslands, lakes, streams, and estuaries has only recently begun. Studies of shallow-water ecosystems, however, indicate UV radiation can severely depress populations of phytoplankton, small crustaceans, and larval fish. Thus, say scientists, the depletion of the ozone layer will result in a diminished supply of animal protein for millions of hungry people in poor nations, where malnutrition is already a way of life.

THE OZONE HOLE OVER THE ANTARCTIC.   In 1979, atmospheric scientists were both surprised and mystified by the appearance of a gigantic "hole" in the ozone shield during the fall months over Antarctica. The level of ozone in this hole, which extended over the entire Antarctic continent, was 50 percent below normal. In 1988 the Ozone Trends Panel of the National Aeronautics and Space Administration (NASA) concluded: "The weight of evidence strongly indicates that man-made chlorine compounds are primarily responsible for the hole." Recent studies indicate that the ozone breakdown is accelerated in the presence of ice crystals and sunlight. The implications are disturbing. As Rowland states: "There's a distinct

worry that what's happening in Antarctica could happen here."

THE OZONE HOLE OVER THE ARCTIC.   In 1988 there were indications that a similar hole was developing each year in the stratospheric ozone over the Arctic. If this is indeed true, the Arctic hole would be of even more concern than that in the Antarctic, because the Arctic and sub-Arctic regions are much more heavily populated. An international team of American and Russian scientists conducted an intensive study of the chemistry of the stratosphere over the Arctic in 1989 from bases in Canada, Norway, and Siberia. Information was collected with the aid of ground stations, balloons, airplanes, and the Nimbus-7 research satellite. The data are being analyzed at the time of this writing.

Control of Ozone Depletion

The slowdown or, even better, the reversal of the present CFC buildup in the atmosphere (Figure 18-18) can only be accomplished by a dedicated effort on the part of governments, manufacturers, and users of CFCs *throughout the world*. In September 1987, 24 CFC-producing nations, including the United States, met in Montreal and signed an agreement to cut CFC emissions by 50 percent by 1999. Unfortunately, however, there are several problems with this agreement. First, reductions will be extremely slow—so gradual that it will be difficult for scientists to monitor them. Second, the agreement permits the Soviet Union to complete two large CFC plants. It also gives Third World nations a 10-year grace period during which they can increase their use of CFCs as much as they want. Third, many environmentalists believe that the treaty does not go far

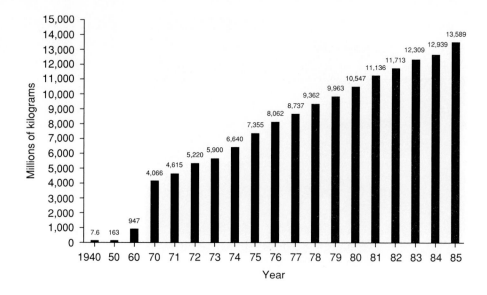

FIGURE 18-18 Cumulative release of CFC_{11} and CFC_{12} into the global atmosphere, 1940–1985.

enough. They cite a recent NASA/EPA report that says that even if we cut CFCs by 80–85 percent, the ozone levels would still be reduced by 5 percent.

The decisions made at the Montreal Conference appeared even more important when released the sobering results of its 1988 ozone-monitoring study. The study showed that the ozone over the United States had been depleted by 2.3 percent and even more over South America. This new information is indeed distressing. According to the EPA, a 2.3 percent reduction of the stratospheric ozone shield would result in a 6 percent increase in the amount of UV radiation reaching the earth's surface. This radiation, in turn, would result in a 14 percent increase in the most common types of skin cancers. As a result of the NASA report, the Dupont Chemical Company, which sells $600 million of CFCs annually, announced its decision to gradually phase out all production of these chemicals by 2000. However, some environmentalists feel that even this timetable should be stepped up. Attorney David Doniger, spokesman for the Natural Resources Defense Council, has emphasized that to delay a massive cut of CFC production and emissions for several more years could be disastrous. "After all," states Doniger, "we will then be facing an emergency that will make the Chernobyl nuclear accident look like a trash fire at the county dump."

RAPID REVIEW

1. The greenhouse effect is caused by gases such as carbon dioxide, which trap infrared waves that radiate from the earth's surface. As a result of human activity, such as the consumption of fossil fuels, the carbon dioxide level has risen more than 20 percent in the past century.

2. Fossil fuel consumption alone is responsible for the annual release of 5 billion metric tons of carbon into the air—roughly 1 metric ton for each person on earth.

3. The harmful effects of an increased global average temperature of 3°C (5°F) by 2035 include the following: (a) inundation of coastal areas; (b) billions of dollars of property damage in the United States alone; (c) saltwater contamination of aquifers; (d) drought-triggered dust storms in the Great Plains; (e) inundation of major rice-producing regions; and (f) termination of economic growth throughout the world.

4. The wet deposition of acid may be in the form of rain, snow, fog, dew, or frost. The dry deposition of acid-forming materials takes place when dust particles containing nitrates and sulfates settle on the earth, water, or vegetation. Later those materials may react with water to form sulfuric or nitric acid.

5. The pH scale ranges from 0 to 14. A pH of 7 indicates neutrality. Values above 7 indicate increasing alkalinity. Values below 7 indicate increasing acidity.

6. The pH of normal, nonpolluted rain is about 5.6. This slight acidity is the result of the small amount of carbon dioxide dissolved in the water to form carbonic acid.

7. Rainfall in much of the northeastern United States has a pH of 4.5 or lower because of the accelerated release of oxides of sulfur and nitrogen in the Midwest during the last few decades.

8. Because emissions generated in the United States may be transported by winds to Canada and vice

versa, the control of the acid rain problem requires *international* cooperation.

9. The superstack at the nickel smelter at Sudbury, Ontario, releases 1 percent of all the atmospheric sulfur dioxide emitted worldwide.

10. An estimated 237 lakes in the Adirondacks have a pH of less than 5—an acidity level considered lethal for many species of fish.

11. Eighty percent of the lakes and streams in the Northeast and the upper Midwest are vulnerable to acidification.

12. Among the adverse effects of acid deposition on aquatic ecosystems are the following: (a) reproduction in many aquatic organisms is reduced or terminated; (b) the homing ability of salmon is disrupted; (c) fish embryos develop abnormally; (d) fish food organisms decline in number; (e) desirable species of fish like bass and pike are replaced by less desirable species like carp and bullheads; (f) increased levels of aluminum interfere with normal gill function in fish; (g) mercury levels increase to the point where fish cannot be safely eaten; and (h) nutrient elements are locked up in the remains of aquatic organisms because the activity of the bacteria of decay is inhibited.

13. The ultraviolet (UV) light produced by the sun causes skin cancer in humans. However, under natural conditions, we are shielded from these UV rays by stratospheric ozone. In recent years, this ozone shield has been partially depleted by gases such as CFCs and nitrous oxides that result from human activities. If the release of CFCs continues at the present rate, there will be 1.4 million additional cases of skin cancer worldwide, an increased frequency of cataracts, and reduced ability to fight off bacterial infections. Corn, cotton, and wheat yields will drop. Aquatic ecosystems will be harmed as well. In 1987 the United States and 23 other nations signed an agreement to cut CFC emissions by 50 percent by 1999.

14. Delays in tightening the emission restrictions on CFCs, carbon dioxide, and the oxides of sulfur and nitrogen may make it extremely difficult to control such formidable environmental problems as global warming, acid deposition, and the thinning of the ozone shield in the stratosphere.

KEY WORDS AND PHRASES

Acid deposition
Acid rain
Alzheimer's disease
Buffer action
Carbon dioxide
Chlorofluorocarbons (CFCs)
Dry deposition
Freons
Greenhouse effect
Liming lakes
Methane
National Atmospheric Deposition Program
Nitric acid
Ozone
pH scale
Skin cancer
Stratosphere
Sulfur dioxide
Sulfuric acid
Synergistic reactor
Wet deposition

QUESTIONS AND TOPICS FOR DISCUSSION

1. Is there a possible cause-and-effect relationship between air pollution and the northward extension of the ranges of the armadillo, opossum, cardinal, and mockingbird in the United States during this century?

2. In what way are human beings changing the normal flow of carbon through its elemental cycle?

3. Discuss both the benefits and the adverse effects of the carbon dioxide buildup in the global atmosphere.

4. Discuss the harmful effects of acid deposition on aquatic ecosystems, soils, forests, and human health.

5. Lakes A and B are located only 80 kilometers (50 miles) apart and receive the same amount of precipitation, the average annual pH of which is 4.5. Yet, lake A is devoid of fish, whereas lake B abounds with them. Explain.

6. Many representatives of the electric power and automotive industries feel that much more research on acid rain is needed before stricter controls on the release of acid-forming chemicals are mandated by federal law. Do you support this view? Why or why not?

7. Discuss three strategies that can be used to bring the acid deposition problem under control.

8. Discuss the statement "Ozone may be both beneficial and harmful to human health."

9. Why is international cooperation needed to control the problems of global warming, acid deposition, and ozone-thinning in the stratosphere?

SUGGESTED READINGS

Ember, L. R., Layman, P. L., Lepkowski, W., and Zurer, P. S. "The Changing Atmosphere: Implications for Mankind." *Chemical and Engineering News* 64(47): 14–64, 1986. Comprehensive analysis of the major atmospheric changes caused by pollutants. Detailed presentation of global warming, acid deposition, and the depletion of stratospheric ozone.

Mooney, H. A., Vitousek, P. M., and Matson, P. A. "Exchange of Materials between Terrestrial Ecosystems and Atmospheres." *Science* 238(4829): 926–931, 1987.

Examines the interactions between the earth and the atmosphere that influence the buildup of gases such as carbon dioxide, methane, and oxides of nitrogen. Effects on humans are discussed.

Scotto, J., Cotton, G., Merbach, F., Berger, D., and Fears, T. "Biologically Effective Ultraviolet Radiation: Surface Measurements in the United States, 1974–1985." *Science* 239(4841): 762–764, 1988. Report on long-term measurement of ultraviolet radiation levels in the United States. The relation to thinning of stratospheric ozone screen is discussed.

Shell, E. R. "Probing the Ozone Hole." *Smithsonian* 18(11): 142–157, 1988. Excellent overview.

Sun, M. "Radon's Health Risks." *Science* 239(4839): 250, 1988. Good summary.

19

Minerals, Mining, and Society

The earth's mineral wealth has been tapped for thousands of years. Its surface is scarred with mines and discarded mine wastes, a telling sign of humankind's unrelenting search and all too frequent carelessness (Figure 19-1). Where once humans scratched the earth's surface with primitive tools to extract valuable minerals, today huge mining machines extract the earth's mineral resources to support a society so dependent on them that a shortage of any one of a few dozen would bring our nation to its knees. The sheer magnitude of mining and our dependence on minerals make mining and mineral production an issue of extreme importance. Truly, the near-term future of modern civilization depends on the way we manage our mineral resources.

This chapter deals primarily with two basic issues of concern to conservationists: the supply of minerals and the impacts of mineral mining and processing. It provides background information on minerals and answers four key questions crucial to modern society: (1) Are we running out of minerals? (2) Can we expand our mineral supplies? (3) What are the environmental impacts of our mineral-intensive lifestyle? (4) How can we reduce environmental damage?

SUPPLY AND DEMAND

The automobile is perhaps the most visible sign of the industrialized world's dependence on minerals. In the United States, for instance, the automobile industry uses enormous amounts of metals refined from minerals. Approximately 7 percent of all the copper, 10 percent of the aluminum, 13 percent of the nickel, 20 percent of the steel, 35 percent of the zinc, and 50 percent of the lead our nation uses each year are for automobile

manufacturing. These minerals come from widely scattered parts of the world. Copper, for instance, comes from mines in Arizona, Chile, and Canada. Aluminum ore (bauxite) comes from the tiny island of Japan and from our neighbor, Canada. Nickel, on the other hand, is shipped from Australia, Norway, and Botswana and trucked from Canada. Iron ore comes primarily from U.S. mines, but also from mines in Canada, Liberia, and Brazil. Lead comes mostly from U.S. mines as well, with smaller contributions from other countries.

Some Features of Minerals

Unlike forests, wildlife, fisheries, and even soil, minerals are **nonrenewable**. Like oil, natural gas, and coal, minerals are a finite, or limited, resource. Therefore, each aluminum can carelessly tossed away and buried in a landfill depletes the world's supply of aluminum. But unlike oil and coal, minerals and metals can be recycled over and over, thus greatly extending their lifetime. So far, however, many industrial societies, especially our own, have treated these finite resources as if they were inexhaustible and of little consequence to our future well-being.

The great majority of minerals now used by society are extracted from the earth's crust, the outer layer of the planet extending 24 kilometers (15 miles) below the earth's surface. Some valuable minerals in the earth's crust occur in elemental form, such as gold and silver. Most minerals, however, exist as chemical compounds consisting of two or more elements. For example, copper exists most commonly in the form of copper sulfide (CuS). Aluminum exists as aluminum oxide (Al_2O_3) and lead as lead carbonate ($PbCO_3$). Most of these compounds are found in rock, which contains other mate-

FIGURE 19-1 This open pit mine in the desert southwest is a blatant reminder of the damage humans create in supplying their needs.

rials as well. A rock containing important minerals is called an **ore**—for example, iron ore and aluminum ore (bauxite). To extract the metals, the ore must be crushed and treated by heat or chemicals.

Although there are over 2,000 minerals in the earth's crust, only a handful of them are abundant enough to be economically worth extracting. A deposit rich enough to be mined is called an **ore deposit**. Ores may be classified as high or low grade, depending on their mineral concentration. For instance, copper ore containing 3 percent copper is considered high-grade ore, whereas copper ore with only 0.3 percent copper is considered low-grade ore.

Mineral Production and Consumption

The United States annually mines ores worth an estimated $23 billion, which, when refined into metals, is worth $240 billion—or about 6 percent of our gross national product (the total value of all goods and services produced by the nation). The leading mining states are Texas, Louisiana, California, and West Virginia. The leading mining nations are Australia, the Soviet Union, the United States, and Canada.

Although the United States has only 5 percent of the world's population, it consumes about 20 percent of the world's nonfuel minerals each year. Enormous amounts of steel, copper, aluminum, and other metals are used to produce a variety of products that give us one of the highest standards of living in the world. In fact, to raise the rest of the world to our level of material wealth would require staggering amounts of the world's fixed supply of minerals: about 30 billion metric tons of iron, 300 million metric tons of zinc, and 50 million metric tons of tin. Even if such quantities were available, and even if all the mines and processing facilities on earth operated at full speed, this production goal could not be accomplished in fewer than 100 years!

America's prodigious use of minerals has made it a great and prosperous nation but also a vulnerable one, since many of the materials it depends on for commerce and defense are imported from politically volatile regions of Africa (Figure 19-2). These **strategic minerals** are essential to our economic health and our military security. Chromium, for instance, is used in steel alloys, which are employed to make engine parts and tools. Eighty-five percent of the chromium we use each year comes from abroad, most of it from troubled South Africa. Ninety-nine percent of our manganese, also used in high-grade steels, comes from foreign sources. Eighty-one percent of our platinum, which is used in catalytic converters for automobiles, comes from overseas.

In 1987, the United States spent nearly $40 billion to import minerals and metals. By 2000, imports could reach $60 billion a year. Many experts warn that widespread dependence on foreign sources—especially politically volatile ones—could prove disastrous. In 1978, for instance, Cuban troops invaded the African country of Zaire from nearby Angola. The U.S. supply of cobalt was temporarily halted as a result. Prices increased sixfold. To cope with such temporary cutoffs, the United States and other industrialized nations routinely stockpile strategic minerals and metals.

Stockpiling may help in the short run, but it is not a long-term solution to the problem of vanishing mineral supplies. Nor is it an adequate solution to potential cartels—groups of mineral-exporting nations that ban together to control the supplies and prices of strategic minerals. China, for instance, controls most of the world's tungsten. What would happen if it and other tungsten-exporting nations joined forces to control tungsten exports to the United States? Or what would happen if the Soviet Union, which holds most of the world's palladium, decided to do the same?

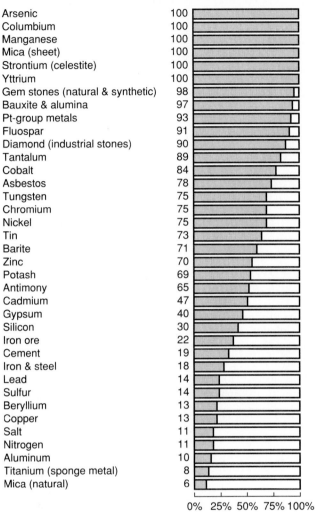

1988 NET IMPORT RELIANCE[e] [1]
OF SELECTED NONFUEL MINERAL MATERIALS
AS A PERCENT OF APPARENT CONSUMPTION [2]

Mineral	%
Arsenic	100
Columbium	100
Manganese	100
Mica (sheet)	100
Strontium (celestite)	100
Yttrium	100
Gem stones (natural & synthetic)	98
Bauxite & alumina	97
Pt-group metals	93
Fluospar	91
Diamond (industrial stones)	90
Tantalum	89
Cobalt	84
Asbestos	78
Tungsten	75
Chromium	75
Nickel	75
Tin	73
Barite	71
Zinc	70
Potash	69
Antimony	65
Cadmium	47
Gypsum	40
Silicon	30
Iron ore	22
Cement	19
Iron & steel	18
Lead	14
Sulfur	14
Beryllium	13
Copper	13
Salt	11
Nitrogen	11
Aluminum	10
Titanium (sponge metal)	8
Mica (natural)	6

0% 25% 50% 75% 100%

[e] Estimated
[1] Net import reliance = imports − exports + adjustments for
Government and industry stock changes.
[2] Apparent consumption = U.S. primary = secondary production
+ net import reliance.

FIGURE 19-2 U.S. net import reliance of selected minerals and metals as a percentage of consumption in 1988.

Many experts believe that cartels are unlikely, since the producer countries are generally dependent on steady exports of minerals for foreign exchange. Zambia's mineral exports, for instance, provide over one-half of its national income. Many industrialized nations import minerals from Third World countries, refine them, and sell the metals at 10 times the price of the minerals. Third World nations feel deprived of the economic gains of their resources and have urged the developed world to import more refined metals from them to offset this imbalance. Such actions on the part of the rich, industrialized nations could greatly reduce

the tensions that might cause mineral-exporting nations to ban together to control prices.

Mineral Supplies—Are We Running Out?

With this background information in mind, let us look at an important question raised earlier in this chapter: Are we running out of minerals?

Determining the life span of minerals is no easy task. Geologists must first determine the rate of consumption and estimate the growth in consumption, bearing in mind that even a modest growth rate can result in a rapid increase in the amount of minerals a nation consumes. For instance, a resource with a 1-billion-year life span will last only 580 years at a 3 percent growth rate.

Next, geologists must determine the economically recoverable supply or **reserve** of each mineral in the earth's crust. The reserve must not be mistaken for a similar value, the total **resources**, which is the total amount of mineral in the earth's crust (Figure 19-3). The important difference is that the reserve includes only deposits that are feasible to mine, whereas total resources include all minerals, no matter how low their concentration may be.

The total resources of a mineral are often many times greater than the reserve value. To understand why, consider copper. A copper deposit 10 miles below the surface of the earth is part of the total resources but is not part of the reserve because it would be too costly to mine. The world resources for copper are currently estimated at 1,600 million tons, whereas the reserve base is only 566 million tons.

The amount of mineral reserve is not permanently fixed; it can expand and contract, depending on a number of variables. For instance, new discoveries of economically recoverable minerals can expand the reserve base. Economic incentives from the government can make it profitable for a mining company to extract marginal or subeconomic ores. The price of energy, heavily used in mining and processing minerals, also affects the reserve base. When energy is cheap, marginal ore deposits may become economical, thus expanding the reserve base. On the other hand, when energy prices rise, ores that were once economical to mine may become too costly. The reserve base therefore shrinks. Environmental and worker protection laws can also affect the reserve base. For instance, environmental laws requiring companies to reduce pollution from mines and to reclaim mines add to the cost of mining and may make marginally profitable reserves too costly to mine. Likewise, the lax laws of many Third World nations help stimulate mining and expand the reserve base, often at a substantial cost to the environment. Labor costs can also profoundly shape the economic picture of mining and influence the reserve base. Finally, new technologies can also cause the reserve base to expand.

FIGURE 19-3   Resources may be classified as reserves and resources. Total resources includes all the deposits
in the world. Reserves may be broken
into many categories. The demonstrated reserves are ones that geologists are fairly sure exist: they have
been measured or their presence is
indicated by geological data.

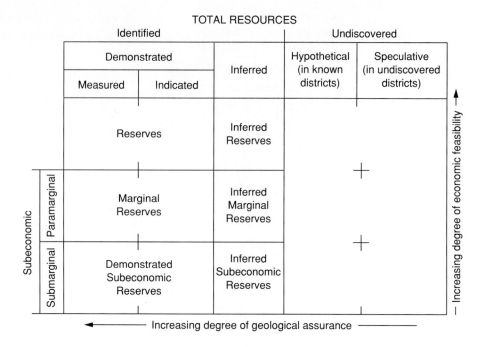

CAN WE EXPAND OUR MINERAL SUPPLIES?

Highly efficient processes to extract and refine minerals, for instance, can reduce the price of mining marginal or subeconomic ores. This, like a variety of other factors, can increase the reserve base.

Based on existing estimates of world reserves and projections of consumption, it appears that three-quarters of the 80 or so economically important minerals are abundant enough to meet our needs for many years—or, if they are not, have adequate substitutes. At least 18 economically essential minerals, however, are bound to fall into short supply—some within a decade or two—even if nations greatly step up recovery and recycling. Gold, silver, mercury, lead, sulfur, tin, tungsten, and zinc are in this endangered group. Even if new discoveries and new technologies make it possible to mine five times the currently known reserves of these materials, this group will be 80 percent depleted on or before 2040.

CAN WE EXPAND OUR MINERAL SUPPLIES?

Something must be done, and quickly, to forestall the depletion of key mineral resources. But what can we do?

Unfortunately, there is no consensus on ways to satisfy future demand and prevent the economic turmoil that could result from widespread shortages of essential minerals. Some people, in fact, flatly dismiss the possibility of future shortages. They are called **technological optimists**, largely because they count on technological answers to this and a host of other environmental problems. The optimists are opposed by another group, often called the **pessimists** but more appropriately labeled **realists** because they recognize the finite nature of our mineral resources and seek ways to cope with it.

This section looks at the views of the optimists and pessimists to answer the second question posed at the outset of this chapter: Can we expand our mineral supplies?

New Discoveries

A large portion of the earth's crust has not been intensively explored for mineral deposits, say the optimists. By using current technologies, major finds are possible in Asia, Africa, South America, and Australia. The optimists point to substantial mineral discoveries in recent years as proof that current estimates of the world's mineral reserves fall far short of the real reserves. The pessimists, on the other hand, argue that the extremely rich deposits needed to expand our reserve base substantially simply do not exist. Regardless, even a fivefold expansion of the world reserves of critical minerals will only slightly offset the rapid depletion.

Extracting Minerals from Seawater

William Page, a researcher from Great Britain, summarizes the viewpoint of optimists: "Seawater is estimated to contain 1,000 million years' supply of sodium chloride; more than one million years of molybdenum (used to harden steel), uranium, tin, and cobalt; more than 1,000 years of nickel and copper. A cubic kilometer (0.25 cubic mile) of seawater contains approximately 11 metric tons each of aluminum, iron, and zinc." The oceans contain approximately 1,300 cubic kilometers (330 million cubic miles) of water, or about 14,000 million metric tons of each of these metals.

Not bad, say the pessimists, but there's a hitch. Even though the oceans contain vast quantities of dissolved minerals, except for bromine, magnesium, and table salt, most minerals are found in very low concentrations. The energy cost of extracting them would be prohibitive. In fact, just to extract 0.003 percent of the zinc our nation uses each year would require a plant that would process a water volume equal to the combined annual flows of the Hudson and Delaware rivers! (Mining the sea bed is discussed at the end of this chapter.)

Improved Extraction Technologies

As new extraction technologies are developed, say the optimists, the mining industry will be able to obtain more and more minerals from low-grade ores. The history of copper mining in the United States provides a good example. At the start of this century, only the very high-grade ore, containing 60 pounds of copper per ton, was mined. As new advances in mining and processing came on line, progressively leaner ores, with 50, 40, 30, and 20 pounds of copper per ton, could be used. And today, a very low-grade ore containing only 0.3 percent copper (6 pounds per ton) can be mined at a profit.

Pessimists admit that new technologies do permit the use of lower-grade ores. However, they point out that the lower the concentration of mineral in an ore, the greater the energy demand for mining and processing (Figure 19-4). For example, it requires twice as much energy to produce a ton of aluminum from 10 percent bauxite as from 20 percent bauxite. Further reductions in mineral concentration result in even larger increases in energy demand. To make matters worse, the lower the concentration of the mineral, the greater the amount of rock that must be mined and processed to produce a ton of mineral. Therefore, the greater the amount of environmental damage—pollution from smelters, surface disruption at mines, and mine waste.

Tapping Abundant Low-Grade Ores

As a general rule, optimists point out that for many minerals the total amount of ore increases as the grade decreases. Thus, the deeper miners dig into the earth, the more ore they find. This principle was stated by S. G. Lasky of the U.S. Geological Survey in 1950 and appears to hold for a number of minerals, such as iron and aluminum. Optimists note, then, that as the technologies for deeper mining and for mineral extraction from lower-grade ores are developed, a literal bonanza of mineral wealth awaits the mining industry.

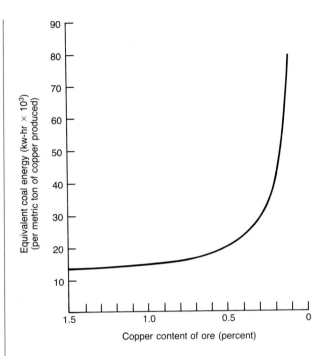

FIGURE 19-4 Graphical representation of the amount of energy needed to extract a mineral as the concentration of the ore decreases. Note that once the concentration falls to a critical level, energy consumption increases drastically.

Pessimists are quick to note, however, that this principle does not apply to all ores, such as nickel, copper, and manganese. The amount of copper ore, for instance, increases up to a point as the grade decreases. Thus, there is more 1 percent ore than 2 percent ore, but below 1 percent the rule fails. The 0.3 percent ore is one-fourth the amount of 1 percent ore.

Finding Substitutes

The substitution concept arose during World War II, when, to save copper, government mints began turning out steel pennies. Within the last three decades, numerous substitutes have been devised. Plastics have been a key alternative, and have replaced wood and steel in a wide variety of products from fishing rods and speedboats to bathtubs and motor cars. Aluminum, another popular substitute, has replaced steel in beverage cans, airplanes, and vehicles. Magnesium is being substituted for zinc in an increasing number of products, such as chemicals and pigments. Indeed, either naturally occurring or synthetic substitutes can be found for most metals used today.

Pessimists point out that not all materials have adequate substitutes. For example, there is no other metal that has the unique chemical and physical properties of mercury or the high melting point of tungsten, which makes it so valuable in high-speed tools and cutting edges. Furthermore, it may be impossible to find substitutes for the manganese in desulfurized steel, the nickel and chromium in stainless steel, the tin in solder, and the silver in photographic films.

Pessimists also note that some substitutes are clearly inferior to the materials they replace—as anyone who has used a plastic snow shovel knows. Aluminum, iron, magnesium, and titanium are among the most abundant elements in the earth's crust and have great potential for substitution. However, they do not stand up to the task in all situations.

A final problem is that some substitutes are scarce as well. This is certainly true of the molybdenum that is now being used in place of tungsten. The cadmium and lead that have replaced mercury in some types of batteries are also in short supply.

THE MINERAL CONSERVATION STRATEGY

The optimist would have us believe that our mineral future is secure and that worries over mineral supplies are needless. New discoveries, seawater, lower-grade ores, new mining technologies, and substitutions, they often assure us, will come to the rescue. The pessimist, however, knows that these avenues are limited at best. We must, the pessimist points out, look for additional ways to meet our needs. Thus, the pessimist supports a variety of efforts that conserve mineral supplies.

Reducing Demand

One of the chief ways of conserving minerals is to reduce the demand for them. This can be achieved by reducing population growth, cutting back per capita consumption, and decreasing the size of products while increasing product durability.

Population control was discussed in Chapter 3. It is, as we have pointed out before, the cornerstone of all resource conservation strategies. Beyond that, individuals can reduce per capita consumption by reducing unnecessary purchases and avoiding discardable items.

Manufacturers can contribute by reducing wasteful packaging and throwaways. But perhaps the most effective way of cutting back on mineral demand is by increasing product durability—that is, making products last longer. Today, however, many manufacturers crank out flimsy tools, toys, appliances, and automobiles for a price-conscious public—which, often blind to quality, gobbles them up and throws them out when they break or are no longer in fashion. Consider the automobile. Built to become obsolete within 7 to 10 years, the automobile, if properly manufactured, could be made to last twice as long. By doubling a car's longevity, manufacturers could cut their mineral consumption in half, greatly extending our mineral supplies, reducing energy demand, and decreasing pollution.

In addition to increasing product durability, manufacturers can make products smaller, thus further stretching mineral supplies. Consider the gas guzzlers of a decade ago. Today's compact models are 140 kilograms (300 pounds) lighter than their bulky predecessors (Figure 19-5). Manufacturers have produced a whole variety of household appliances such as clocks, toasters, refrigerators, telephones, and stoves that are smaller and lighter than those on the market a decade or so ago. Calculators, when they first arrived, were heavy and cumbersome. They would fit into a briefcase but might take up one-third of the space. Today solar-powered calculators slip into a breast pocket with room to spare.

Recycling

Ruben L. Parson, a geography professor at St. Cloud State University, Minnesota, wrote that during "World War II we reclaimed anything metallic, from abandoned streetcar tracks and worn-out machinery to horseshoes and tin cans. Reclaimed metal gave us the machines that crushed Hitler's armored legions. We became scrap-conscious as never before. But we have too read-

FIGURE 19-5A   A Cadillac of the 1960s. Long, sleek and energy wasteful.

FIGURE 19-5B   A Cadillac of the 1980s. A more compact model that requires less metal and uses gas more efficiently.

ily reverted to the reckless, wasteful discard of material that is typically American."

Three factors are bound to spur much greater interest in recycling in the United States again: (1) the inevitable rise in oil prices that will occur in the next decade or so (Chapter 20), (2) the depletion of strategic minerals, (3) and the shortage of landfill (Chapter 16). Already signs of this recycling revolution are beginning to appear. In 1987, for instance, New Jersey passed a statewide law that required all communities to recycle at least three commodities because of a shortage of landfill sites. Other states are bound to follow. (For more on recycling programs, see Chapter 16.)

Unfortunately, the federal government still provides economic incentives to the mining industry that puts the recycling industry at a grave disadvantage. First, the government provides billions of dollars in depletion allowances—tax breaks that go to mining companies as they deplete their reserves. The tax breaks were designed to help mining companies invest in exploration needed to unearth additional mineral supplies. The net effect is that this policy makes virgin minerals artificially cheap and gives them a competitive advantage over recycled materials. To make matters worse, freight costs for shipping raw materials are, by law, lower than rates for metals bound for recycling plants. Ending these two unfair practices would benefit the recycling industry enormously.

Individual Efforts

You and thousands of resource-conscious allies can play a significant role in reducing mineral consumption by using several simple measures. You can recycle all glass, aluminum cans, waste copper, and other metals (Figure 19-6). Recycling has the added benefit of saving energy and reducing environmental pollution. You can also reduce your consumption of unnecessary items. Buy durable clothes and goods. Avoid throwaways. When you have a choice between a recyclable and a nonrecyclable good—say, a beverage container—choose the recyclable one even if it costs a little more. When you have a choice between a product made from a renewable resource (such as wood) and one made from a nonrenewable material (such as aluminum), choose the renewable one.

Your actions, multiplied by hundreds of thousands, can significantly reduce our reliance on minerals. If you are inclined toward action, you could organize a recycling program on your campus, in your community, or just in your home. Armed with statistics on the benefits of recycling and enthusiasm, you could become an instrument of social change in our transition to a sustainable society.

ENVIRONMENTAL IMPACTS OF MINERAL PRODUCTION

A few miles from the scenic town of Aspen, Colorado, is an ugly scar called Climax. Climax is not a town. No one would want to live there, for it is the site of Amax's huge molybdenum mine and waste dump. Molybdenum, called Molly-B for short, is a mineral used to harden steel in automobiles.

At Climax, miners have torn down half of a mountain to extract this mineral (Figure 19-7). Found in a concentra-

FIGURE 19-6 Reverse vending machine for recycling aluminum in Colorado parking lot. Customers drop cans in receptical. Cans are then weighed and customer is paid in cash.

FIGURE 19-7 This mountain is being torn down by molybdenum miners in Climax, Colorado. The ore is then processed and waste is dumped in a nearby valley. Molybdenum is used to harden steel.

tion of only about 0.2 percent, molybdenum is separated from the ore and trucked away for sale. The remaining material is washed down the mountain to a huge valley, where, over the years, it has transformed what was once a splendid mountain valley into a huge moonscape, stark and ugly in a land otherwise breathtaking.

This is but one example of the impact of our dependence on minerals. This section takes a broad look at the many impacts of mining and mineral processing and suggests ways to minimize them.

Mining Impacts

Ninety percent of our nonfuel minerals are extracted from surface mines, excavations in the earth's surface that allow miners to reach the underlying deposits. Surface mines are particularly destructive because the overlying soil and rock, called **overburden**, must first be removed and placed elsewhere. As a result, mining can quickly transform a scenic area into an ugly landscape (see Figure 19-7). Reclamation is often difficult because many open pit mines extend deep into the earth's crust. (Coal surface mining is discussed in Chapter 20.)

Underground mines provide a smaller percentage of our minerals but create enormous waste heaps. As with surface mines, wastes must be removed from the mine and dumped elsewhere. Waste piles from both types of mines cause additional environmental problems if they are not vegetated and stabilized, for heavy rains can wash the unstable soils into streams and lakes. Sediment in streams and lakes increases water temperatures, lowers the concentration of dissolved oxygen, disrupts food chains, destroys spawning beds, kills aquatic plants and animals, and destroys scenic beauty and recreational uses. Sedimentation also increases flooding because it reduces a stream's water-carrying capacity. When heavy rains come, water flows over the banks more easily, flooding nearby towns, farms, and pastures. Wind, like water, also carries away tons of barren spoils, depositing them elsewhere.

Each year, 1.7 billion metric tons of mine waste are produced from U.S. surface mines, with 5 percent coming from mineral surface mines and the rest from coal surface mines. Mine wastes contribute toxic materials to nearby waterways. For example, zinc, arsenic, lead, and other toxic metals may be leached from the spoils of iron ore mines by rainwater. Rainwater combines with iron pyrite in gold and silver mine wastes in the West, creating sulfuric acid, which leaks from the spoils as **acid mine drainage** and drains into nearby streams, killing fish and other aquatic organisms. Unstable spoil piles can also form dangerous landslides when rainfall is heavy.

Certain minerals, such as salt and potash, which are water soluble, may be removed by **solution mining**. In this technique, water is pumped into the deposit, where it dissolves much of the mineral, then pumped back

to the surface. Although safe, this technique can pollute groundwater supplies. In Colorado, companies are proposing an offshoot of the solution mining technique that would use a solution of deadly cyanide to extract gold from rock. Many Colorado environmentalists are justifiably alarmed by the prospects for contamination. Besides creating eyesores, enhancing erosion, and polluting nearby streams, mining activities compete with other users of wild lands. Mining in our national forests and wilderness areas, for instance, disturbs wildlife and outdoor recreationists. It can destroy valuable timberland and grassland as well.

Mining also uses tremendous quantities of water. The lower the grade of the ore, the greater the volume of water required. For example, in the hydraulic mining of gold and silver, powerful blasts of water are used to wash soils from hillsides, which are then treated to extract the precious metals. In some areas, then, mining can divert water from ranches, farms, businesses, and municipalities.

Processing Minerals

Many ores are heated to high temperatures in specially built ovens that separate metals from the ore. A variety of toxic materials may be realeased into the atmosphere as a result of this process, call **smelting** (Figure 19-8). Smelters emit arsenic, mercury, zinc, and other toxic chemicals that are dangerous to bees and other animals. Especially harmful is fluoride gas, which is released from phosphate smelters and settles on vegetation around smelters. Fluoride can be ingested by cattle and other livestock. In high enough levels, fluoride causes a disease called **fluorosis**, characterized by pain in an animal's joints and softened bones and teeth, which leads to an inability to stand or move around.

Perhaps the best-known effect of smelting results from the release of sulfur dioxide, a corrosive gas that combines with atmospheric moisture and oxygen to produce sulfuric acid, described more fully in Chapter 17. Sulfuric acid and sulfur dioxide are lethal to plants and aquatic life, and are suspected of having adverse effects on human health as well.

The huge copper and nickel smelter in Sudbury, Ontario—long a major producer of sulfur dioxide—has turned the neighboring lands into a barren wasteland. Now that taller stacks are used, the pollutants are able to spread out further, polluting distant lakes and killing fish and other aquatic organisms hundreds of kilometers from the source. Similar devastation has occurred in Montana and Tennessee.

Reducing the Impact of Our Mineral Dependence

Mining and processing of minerals are two of the most environmentally damaging activities of humankind. By

FIGURE 19-8 Aerial view of a mineral smelter in New Mexico showing the tall stack that emits toxic gases into the atmosphere.

reducing demand and recycling, Americans can reduce their need for virgin materials and decrease the associated impacts. But conservation is not enough. Minerals will continue to be extracted and fashioned into useful products. Thus, society must find ways to reduce the impact created by its legitimate needs.

One important way of reducing the impact is through **reclamation**, the rehabilitation of land altered by mining (Figure 19-9). Surface mines, for instance, can be filled and the ground recontoured and planted to establish a vegetative cover that protects the soil. During mining, topsoil and wastes can be set aside and stabilized to minimize erosion, leaching, and landslides.

In 1977, Congress passed the **Surface Mining Control and Reclamation Act**, which requires coal mining com-

panies to reclaim all surface-mined land. By law, companies must restore surface-mined land to its premining condition. Unfortunately, this law pertains only to coal mining; no specific federal legislation requiring reclamation on mineral lands exists, and state laws and regulations are often weak. According to the Bureau of Mines, between 1930 and 1980 only 8 percent of the land mined for metals and only 27 percent of the land mined for minerals was reclaimed. Showing how effective surface mining laws are, however, the bureau noted that 75 percent of the land on which coal was mined has been reclaimed.

By one estimate, recontouring and planting the vast unreclaimed lands and leveling the spoil piles from all surface and underground mines would cost this nation

FIGURE 19-9 Reclaimed land that has been surface mined to remove coal.

an estimated $30 billion. Given the huge federal debt—well over $100 billion a year—and the desire to reduce federal spending, it is unlikely that America will make much progress in refurbishing the lands so recklessly mined by companies eager to make a profit and move to other undisturbed land unless citizens put the pressure on Congress. Monetary shortages have also weakened the inspection and enforcement of the Surface Mining Control and Reclamation Act. Left on their own, mining companies could return to earlier practices that left the land in a shambles.

We need strong enforcement, and we need money to reclaim abandoned lands. Concerned citizens can write their representatives to support continued funding of reclamation programs. To raise money, governments could increase taxes on minerals; these monies would be earmarked for land rehabilitation.

MINERALS FROM THE SEA

Far-reaching optimists look to outer space to provide minerals for earth, ignoring the exorbitant costs and energy requirements of these far-out plans. Another group, looking a little closer to home, sees the oceans as an important source of minerals for the future. However, they are not looking at minerals dissolved in seawater, but at mineral deposits in the continental shelf and on the floor of the sea.

Minerals of the Continental Shelf

Because the continental shelf is an extension of the continent that happens to be underwater, it is not surprising that it could yield many of the minerals now extracted from mines on dry land. By one estimate, the continental shelf contains about 15 percent of the world's minerals. Tapping the economically feasible deposits, say the optimists, could expand our reserve base, postponing the day of depletion. The United States, for instance, has rich deposits of copper and zinc off the coasts of Washington and Oregon. Attractive as these deposits may be, however, mining them could be costly and could disrupt the marine environment.

Minerals on the Sea Bottom

In 1900 an American marine expedition discovered curious nodules, called **manganese nodules**, on the floor of the Pacific Ocean (Figure 19-10). Rich in manganese, they also contain nickel, iron, copper, cobalt, molybdenum, and aluminum. Manganese nodules cover about one-fourth of the ocean's floor, mostly in international waters. Most are the size of potatoes, although they vary in size from tiny granules to cantaloupes.

The aggregate weight of these nodules in the Pacific alone is estimated at about 1,500 billion metric tons. The supply of copper is now thought to last for on-

FIGURE 19-10   Manganese nodules taken from the floor of the ocean could help provide iron, nickel, copper, cobalt, and manganese.

ly a few more decades. Tapping the copper of manganese nodules could extend our reserve for thousands of years.

Problems with Mining the Sea

Although attractive, mining seafloor mineral deposits and manganese nodules is fraught with problems. Ships would scour the oceans with huge devices much like large vacuum cleaners, sucking the nodules up from the bottom. Recovering the solid nodules, however, would be more difficult and costly than using current oil and gas wells. In addition, the impacts of such activities could be far-reaching. Dredging or scooping up the minerals from the continental shelf and the seabed would increase the turbidity of the water, possibly affecting a wide array of sea creatures. Clouding of shallow waters could increase the water temperature and make it unfit for many creatures adapted to cooler waters. Ocean-mining equipment would require enormous amounts of energy and cooling water. Heated water released back into the ocean could augment the adverse impacts caused by turbidity and heating resulting from increased sediment.

A final, and major, problem has more to do with politics than with the environment. Most nations claim ownership of waters 330 kilometers (200 miles) off their coasts. They presumably own the minerals in the continental shelf. But what of the manganese nodules on the ocean floor outside of territorial waters? Who, if anyone, owns the minerals in international waters?

Many people in the industrialized countries with the wealth and resources to mine manganese nodules believe that they are legally entitled to these riches. However, the poorer nations want to know, is this fair to them? Shouldn't they share in the wealth, since international waters are a common resource?

To settle this question of ownership—and, more importantly, of who will profit from the riches of international waters—the United Nations began extensive negotiations in 1958. But progress has been slow. In 1982, 100 nations signed the **Law of the Sea Treaty**. The treaty places deep-sea mining outside territorial waters under international regulation. It also calls for a tax on seabed minerals, the proceeds of which would go to help Third World nations improve agriculture and develop economically. Believing that the seabed minerals belong to whoever can afford to mine them, many wealthy nations have refused to sign, among them the United States, West Germany, and Great Britain. President Ronald Reagan refused to sign in 1981 because he felt that it would jeopardize the ocean-mining interest of private American firms. Unfortunately, the Reagan administration offered no alternatives. The treaty is in trouble even among signatory nations. Only nine nations that signed it have ratified it. Meanwhile, private commercial interests in the United States have begun plans to mine nodules off the coast of the Hawaiian Islands.

Seafloor minerals may someday help us meet our mineral needs. Experts warn, however, that the cost may be high—both environmentally and economically. Seabed mining will be energy intensive, and in the light of declining fossil fuel supplies, the price of energy is bound to increase (see Chapter 20). Considering the shaky future of metals and minerals, it seems imperative that we conserve what we have and find substitutes where we can. Recycling these minerals generously supplied by the earth and reducing our demand can help us continue as we have. But eventually, unless adequate substitutes can be found, many agree, we will have to change our ways—reduce the global population, develop less resource-intensive lifestyles, and shift our dependence to renewable resources, which, if managed properly, can ensure a sustainable society.

RAPID REVIEW

1. The earth's mineral wealth has been tapped for thousands of years, and all around us are the signs of our dependence on minerals and our often reckless exploitation of the earth to get them. The sheer magnitude of our dependence and the impact that mineral mining and processing have on our environment make minerals an important environmental issue.

2. The automobile is perhaps the most visible sign of the industrialized world's dependence on minerals. In the United States, automobile manufacturing requires enormous amounts of metals refined from minerals. These minerals come from widely scattered parts of the world, many of them politically unstable.

3. Unlike forests and wildlife, minerals are nonrenewable. They can be recycled, but so far, most industrial societies have treated these finite resources as if they were inexhaustible and inconsequential.

4. Minerals come from the earth's crust, and most minerals exist as chemical compounds consisting of two or more elements. A rock containing minerals is called an **ore**.

5. The United States annually mines ores worth an estimated $23 billion. When refined, they become 10 times more valuable.

6. Although the United States has only 5 percent of the world's population, it consumes about 20 percent of the world's nonfuel minerals. To raise the world to our consumption level would create an environmental disaster and would be impossible because of a lack of reserves.

7. The prodigious use of minerals by the United States has made it a great and prosperous nation but also a vulnerable one, since many of the strategic minerals needed for commerce and defense come from unstable countries. To reduce our vulnerability, the government has stockpiled many of these strategic minerals.

8. Stockpiling may help in the short run, but it does nothing to protect us from vanishing mineral supplies or the formation of cartels—groups of mineral-exporting nations that may band together to control the supplies and prices of minerals.

9. Many experts believe that cartels will not form around minerals because so many of the exporting nations need their mineral exports to produce foreign exchange.

10. To determine the life span of minerals is no easy task. First, scientists must determine the rate of consumption. Second, they must project future consumption levels, bearing in mind that increases in the consumption rate can greatly accelerate the depletion of a finite resource. Third, they must determine the economically recoverable supply, or reserve, of each mineral. The reserve must not be mistaken for the total resources, the total amount of mineral in the earth's crust.

11. The reserve capacity of the world is not permanently fixed; it can expand and contract, depending on a number of factors—for instance, new discoveries, economic incentives from governments, new technologies that allow miners to extract and process lower grades of ore more efficiently, the price of energy and labor, and the level of environmental controls.

12. Based on existing estimates, it appears that world reserves of three-quarters of 80 or so economically important minerals are abundant enough to meet our needs for many years. If they are not, adequate substitutes are available.

13. However, at least 18 economically important minerals are bound to fall into short supply—some within a decade or two.

14. Something must be done, and quickly, to forestall the depletion of key mineral resources. Unfortunately, there is no consensus. Optimists believe that new discoveries, seawater mineral extraction, improved extraction technologies, low-grade ores, and substitutes will ensure generous supplies of important minerals. Pessimists, however, find serious fault with each of these strategies and argue that if we depend on them, we will encounter deep trouble. Pessimists believe that we must actively explore these strategies and that we must tap the generous potential of conservation.

15. One of the chief ways of conserving minerals is to reduce the demand. This can be achieved by reducing population growth, cutting back on per capita consumption, recycling, decreasing the size of products, and increasing product durability.

16. Significant progress has been made in most of these areas in the past 20 years, but there is considerable room for improvement. Perhaps one of the greatest achievements would be the abolishment of the tax breaks and freight rates that make it cheaper to use raw materials than recycled ones.

17. Individual efforts can also go a long way toward reducing mineral consumption.

18. Mining and processing of minerals has numerous impacts on the environment. Ninety percent of our nonfuel minerals are extracted from surface mines, which are particularly destructive because the overlying soil and rock must be removed to get to the mineral deposits. As a result, mining can destroy scenic beauty.

19. Underground and surface mines produce enormous amounts of waste, deposited away from the mine in huge piles that, if not revegetated, create an eyesore and may be eroded by wind and rain. Sediment from waste heaps can fill streams, increase water temperature, disrupt food chains, destroy spawning beds, kill aquatic life, and increase flooding. Mine wastes also leach toxic chemicals, such as sulfuric acid, arsenic, mercury, and zinc.

20. Many ores are heated to high temperatures in specially built ovens to separate metals from the ore. A number of toxic substances may be released into the atmosphere during this process, called **smelting**. Perhaps the most significant one is sulfur dioxide, which combines with oxygen and water in the atmosphere to produce sulfuric acid.

21. By reducing demand and by recycling, Americans can reduce their need for virgin materials and decrease the associated impacts, but conservation is not enough. Society must find ways to reduce the impact created by mining and processing.

22. One important way of reducing the impact is reclamation, the restoration of mined land. In 1977, Congress passed the Surface Mining Control and Reclamation Act, which requires coal mining companies to reclaim all surface-mined land. Unfortunately, this law does not pertain to mineral mines, and state laws are often weak.

23. The need for reclamation laws for mineral mining is evidenced by the fact that only about 8 percent of the land mined for metals and only 27 percent of the land mined for minerals was reclaimed in the United States between 1950 and 1980.

24. We need strong enforcement of state laws and money to reclaim abandoned lands. Concerned citizens can write their representatives to support continued funding of reclamation. To raise money for reclamation, governments could increase taxes on minerals.

25. Some observers believe that ocean floor minerals—deposits in the continental shelf and on the floor of the ocean—could help us stretch our mineral supplies. Manganese nodules on the ocean floor, for instance, could expand our reserve thousands of years. Manganese nodules cover about one-fourth of the ocean floor and contain many important minerals, such as copper and iron.

26. Although attractive, mining seafloor mineral deposits and manganese nodules is fraught with problems. It would be energy intensive and very costly. It could increase the turbidity and temperature of ocean waters and could upset the ecological balance of the ocean. Political problems also abound. The rich nations of the world want free access to the nodules in international waters and have refused to come to an agreement with the poorer nations, which want some of the proceeds of this international resource but have neither the money nor the resources to tap it.

27. Considering the shaky future of metals and minerals, it seems imperative that we conserve what we have and find substitutes where we can. Recycling these minerals generously supplied by the earth and reducing our demand can help us continue as we have. But eventually, unless adequate sub-

stitutes can be found, many agree, we will have to change our ways—reduce the global population, develop less resource-intensive lifestyles, and shift our dependence to renewable resources.

KEY TERMS AND CONCEPTS

Continental shelf
Depletion
Finite resource
Fluorosis
Improved extraction
  technologies
Law of the Sea Treaty
Manganese nodules
Metal
Mineral
Mineral conservation
  strategy
Mineral processing
Mining
Nonrenewable resource
Ore
Ore deposit
Overburden

Product durability
Reclamation
Recycling
Reducing demand
Reserve
Reserve base
Smelter
Solution mining
Stockpiling
Strategic mineral
Substitution
Surface Mine Control and
  Reclamation Act
Surface mining
Technological optimist
Technological pessimist
Total resources
Waste piles

QUESTIONS AND TOPICS FOR DISCUSSION

1. Explain the paradoxical statement "An American car is, in a sense, really a foreign car."

2. What is an ore?

3. In what form are most minerals found?

4. What percentage of the world's population lives in the United States? What percentage of the world's minerals do we consume?

5. Do you agree with the statement "The heavy reliance of the United States on imported minerals makes it highly vulnerable"? Why or why not?

6. Define the terms *reserve* and *total resource*. How

are they different? Why is it incorrect to calculate the life span of minerals based on total resources?

7. What factors cause the reserve base to shrink? What factors cause it to expand?

8. Debate the statement "Our mineral supplies are adequate for many years to come, so we need not worry about shortages."

9. List and describe the major ways in which the reserve base may be expanded. Describe the pros and cons of each technique.

10. Describe the mineral conservation strategy. How can you implement this strategy?

11. Why is recycling at a competitive disadvantage compared to using raw minerals?

12. Describe the major impacts of surface and underground mining and describe how they can be lessened.

13. Do you agree with this statement? "The wealthy countries can afford to mine manganese nodules and should be allowed to do so without cutting the Third World nations in on the profits."

14. List and describe the impacts of manganese nodule mining.

SUGGESTED READINGS

Brown, L. R., Chandler, W. U., Flavin, C., Jacobson, J., Pollock, C., Postel, S., Starke, L., and Wolf, E. C. *State of the World, 1987*. New York: Norton, 1987. See Chapter 6 for up-to-date information on the untapped potential of recycling.

Chandler, W. U. *Materials Recyling: The Virtue of Necessity*. Worldwatch Paper 56. Washington, D.C.: Worldwatch Institute, 1983. An important work on global recycling.

U.S. Bureau of Mines. *The Domestic Supply of Critical Minerals*. Washington, D.C.: U.S. Government Printing Office, 1983. Contains criitical information on mineral supplies.

U.S. Bureau of Mines. *Mineral Commodity Summaries*. Washington, D.C.: U.S. Government Printing Office, 1987. Important source of data for all minerals. Published annually.

20

Energy

The twin oil crises of the 1970s shook the industrialized world like nothing else before them, creating a fear that awakened the developed countries to the extraordinary cost of their dependence on energy—especially imported oil. The first shock wave hit in 1973 when the Organization of Petroleum Exporting Countries (OPEC) imposed an embargo on oil, cutting back on exports and raising the price. The brainchild of a Venezuelan multimillionaire, Juan Perez Alfonzo, who rode a bicycle to work and, reportedly, read by candlelight, the oil embargo was conceived largely as a measure to reduce the waste of energy by the West and to slow down the rapid depletion of OPEC's vast but finite reserves.

Iran's 1979 oil embargo, largely for political reasons, dealt another tragic blow. In the perilous decade of the 1970s, crude oil prices shot up from $3 per barrel to $35. Inflation set in, reaching over 18 percent a year in the United States in 1978. High prices dampened consumer spending. One after another, manufacturers shut down operations, laying off workers by the thousands, until 70 percent of our industrial capacity lay idle. Some industries, like steel, never recovered.

The oil crises drove home the extent of our energy dependence and taught Americans that virtually everything we bought or did required energy—and lots of it. If it were priced too high, inflation, unemployment, and recession would emerge with devastating power.

This chapter is about energy—our supplies and our options. It begins by describing the major sources of energy worldwide—in rich nations as well as poor nations. Then it presents the startling facts on the dwindling supplies of many important sources. It concludes by describing the pros and cons of the options at our disposal, suggesting the best ones to develop a sustainable energy strategy—one that can provide the energy we need, safely and consistently, not just in the next 10 years but for hundreds of years to come.

GLOBAL ENERGY SOURCES

In the developed world, **fossil fuels** top the list of energy sources. So named because they were formed from plant and animal remains buried in the earth millions of years ago, fossil fuels provide 85–90 percent of the energy demand of the industrialized world. Three fuels predominate—oil, gas, and coal—and all are nonrenewable (Figure 20-1). A small amount of our energy also comes from nuclear fuel, which is also nonrenewable. Of all these options, oil is the major source of energy for industrialized countries, but it is fast on the decline. Most of us will live to see the end of oil.

Since the oil crises of the 1970s, many countries have turned to conservation and renewable energy sources. Conservation can save enormous amounts of energy, thus greatly extending our supplies of other fuels. John Herrington, the Secretary of Energy, calls it "our single largest resource."

Of the renewable energy sources in use today, only two have made a significant contribution to the energy needs of developed countries; they are **hydropower**, electricity from flowing rivers, and **biomass**, crop residues, wood, and the like that can be burned or converted to gas or alcohol. However, important strides have also been made in solar voltaics, solar collectors for hot water, and wind energy, discussed later in this chapter.

FIGURE 20-1 Energy consumption by the Developed and developing countries. From World Resources 1987, page 95.

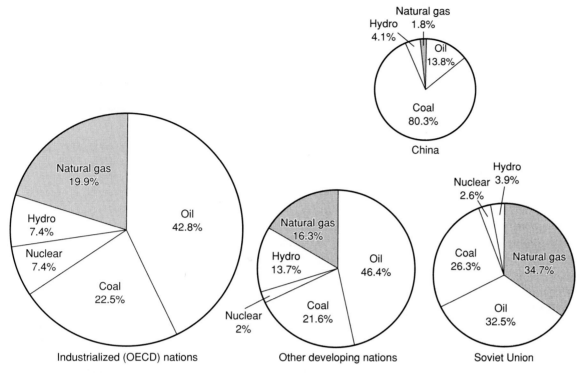

Note: The size of each circle represents the relative amount of energy consumed by that country or group of countries.

In sharp contrast, the Third World relies most heavily on renewable fuels—wood, charcoal, cattle dung, and crop residues. In fact, 2.5 billion people use wood as their primary source of energy, making it by far the major source of energy. Although wood is renewable, excessive exploitation—caused largely by overpopulation—has resulted in widespread shortages and deforestation. In many rural villages in India, Bangladesh, and Nepal, for instance, villagers must travel great distances to find a few sticks of fuel to cook the evening meal. Trees around villages are stripped bare or missing altogether, torn down by desperate peasants. Without wood, peasants have begun using dried cattle dung as a fuel, depriving farm fields of a once rich source of fertilizer.

Struggling to industrialize, the Third World has begun to use increasing amounts of oil. However, rising demand and rapidly falling supplies of oil could result in dramatic increases in prices that will cripple their efforts.

A CLOSER LOOK AT NONRENEWABLE ENERGY RESOURCES

This section looks at nonrenewable energy resources. It gives a brief history of their use, starting with coal; describes the benefits each provides; and looks at the impacts of our dependence on each of them.

Coal

Coal began to form 225 to 350 million years ago in the hot, muggy regions of the earth. Ancient plants flourished in and along the banks of lakes, streams, and coastal swamps; leaves fell into the water and accumulated on the bottom faster than they could be decomposed by bacteria. Eventually, this rich organic material was covered by mud or sediment eroded from the land and, over time, heat and pressure converted the organic material into peat and then coal.

Coal is burned today by electric utilities and in some factories and homes, where it releases the solar energy captured in the leaves of plants millions of years ago by photosynthesis. Today coal supplies about 22 percent of the energy consumed each year in the United States.

The value of coal as a fuel was first discovered in the twelfth or thirteenth century by the inhabitants of the northeast coast of England, who discovered that certain black rocks found along the shores, called **sea coals**, burned. This monumental discovery led to coal mining for domestic heating and, much later, provided the impetus for the Industrial Revolution in the 1700s in England and the 1800s in the United States.

FIGURE 20-2 The pattern of U.S. energy consumption from 1850, including a question about our future patterns of energy use. As supplies of petroleum become exhausted, what alternative sources will be exploited?

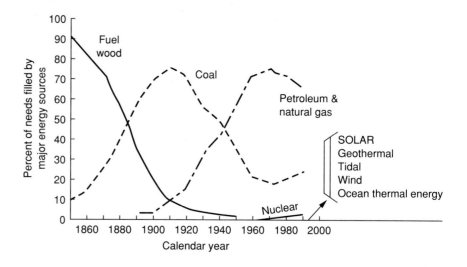

Coal mining started in the United States around 1860. Nevertheless, coal did not replace wood as a major fuel source until the early 1900s. Shortly after World War II, oil and gas replaced coal because they were much easier to transport and cheaper to extract (Figure 20-2).

TYPES OF COAL. Geologists recognize three major types of coal: **lignite** (brown coal), **bituminous** (soft coal), and **anthracite** (hard coal). These types vary in several respects, the most important being their heat value—that the amount of heat they produce when burned per unit weight—and their carbon content. Lignite has the lowest carbon content and heat value, anthracite the highest. As a general rule, the more heat and pressure applied to a bed of coal, the higher the grade. Most of America's coal is bituminous.

COAL RESERVES. Because coal deposits lie just below the surface of the earth, scientists have been able to make fairly accurate estimates of worldwide coal reserves by drilling test holes in U.S. coal seams. A map of U.S. coal deposits is shown in Figure 20-3.

These surveys show that, of all the fossil fuels, coal is by far the most abundant. The proven coal reserves worldwide are nearly 700 billion metric tons. At the current rate of consumption, the proven reserves would last for approximately 200 years. Undiscovered reserves are believed to be massive as well. Some experts believe that the world's recoverable coal supply may be close to 1,700 years at the current rate of consumption.

The United States has about 30 percent of the world's coal and is sometimes called the "Saudi Arabia of coal." At the current rate of consumption, U.S. coal would last for 200 years. But coal has limited use. It cannot be used easily or efficiently to power automobiles or jet planes like liquid fuels derived from oil, whose supplies are limited. It cannot be used easily or efficiently to heat homes or cook meals like natural gas, whose supplies are greater than oil's but still limited. (Coal can be con-

verted into synthetic gas and oil, as described later, but the process is costly and dirty.) And coal is a dirty fuel. Mining it causes enormous impacts. Unless we find much cleaner ways to burn it and strengthen our efforts to reclaim surface-mined land, much of our impressive coal deposits may lie forever buried in the earth's crust.

ENVIRONMENTAL IMPACTS OF SURFACE MINING. America consumes over 720 million metric tons of coal each year. About two-thirds of that coal comes from surface mines, of which there are two basic types (Figure 20-4). In the **contour mine**, which is found on hilly terrain in the East, coal seams are exposed by bulldozers or steam shovels that rip away the overlying rock and dirt, called **overburden**. Before 1979, miners simply pushed the overburden over the side of the hill, destroying vegetation and creating serious erosion problems that filled nearby streams with sediment. Now, thanks to tougher mining regulations, miners must first remove the topsoil and set it aside for later reuse. Then they must dig up the underlying layers, haul them away to a safe place, and hold them until they are trucked back to recontour the area when mining is completed.

The **area strip mine** is found on flat terrain in the Midwest and West (Figure 20-4B). As in contour mines, topsoil is first removed by bulldozers and set aside for later use. Then huge shovels called **draglines** dig up the overburden, placing it in piles next to the excavation. The exposed coal seam is then dynamited and loaded into trucks. After the coal has been removed, the process begins again, one strip at a time. The overburden from each new one is placed in the previous excavation. Reclamation can begin on previously mined land after two or three strips have been cut. Bulldozers first recontour the land and then spread the topsoil over the surface of the overburden, which is often replanted with native species or fast-growing cover crops that protect the soils from wind and rain.

FIGURE 20-3   Distribution of U.S. coal resources.

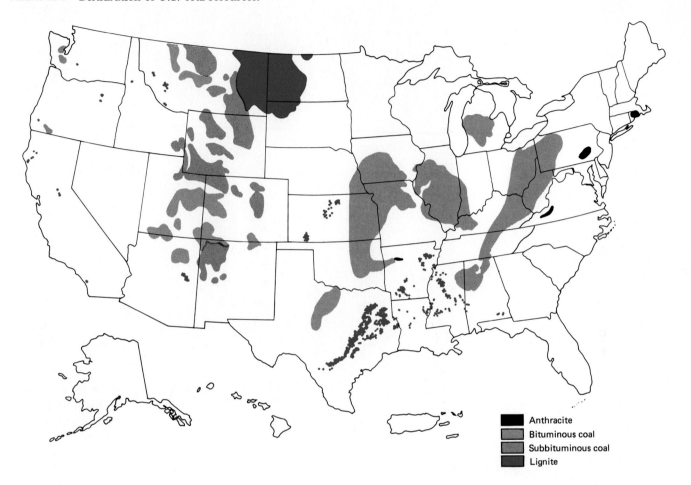

Anthracite
Bituminous coal
Subbituminous coal
Lignite

Surface mining is a fast and efficient way of removing coal, but it creates an ugly eyesore that can erode away if proper precautions are not taken, spilling sediment into streams and lakes and destroying fish habitat, recreational sites, and reservoirs that supply water for human populations. By one estimate, there are 0.6 million hectares (1.5 million acres) of unreclaimed coal-mined land in the United States in need of reclamation, but only about a third of it must be reclaimed by law. The rest had been mined before the passage of the surface mining legislation and is exempt from reclamation.

Access roads can also be eroded away by rain and snowmelt, further adding to the sediment load of nearby streams and lakes. Surface mining creates dust and noise and destroys wildlife habitat, at least temporarily. Surface mines can also cause groundwater levels to fall considerably, drying up municipal and agricultural wells in neighboring fields.

Coal is also mined in underground mines. Ironically, underground mines disturb about as much land as surface mines per ton of coal removed because the materials removed to reach coal seams must be stored outside the mine. Underground mines can also collapse, killing workers and causing **subsidence**, a sinking of the surface

above them. Over 100,000 workers have been killed and over 1 million have been permanently disabled in underground mine accidents in the United States since 1900. Subsidence is a problem because it causes buildings and roadways over mine shafts to sink and often split open. Imagine waking up one day to find your two-story house ripped in two because the ground underneath it had given way. Cracks in the earth's surface can also swallow streams, sending water into coal seams.

Water that seeps into mines, either naturally or as a result of subsidence cracks, combines with naturally occurring iron pyrite (a sulfur-bearing mineral) and oxygen to produce **sulfuric acid**. If not captured and neutralized, the acidic outflow, called **acid mine drainage**, leaks out of mines and pollutes nearby streams. Abandoned underground mines in the United States produce 2.7 million metric tons of acid each year and pollute 11,000 kilometers (7,000 miles) of stream, most of which are in Appalachia. Stopping the flow from active mines is quite feasible, but acid mine drainage from abandoned mines has proved difficult, if not impossible, to control.

The 1977 **Surface Mining Control and Reclamation Act**, which went into effect in 1979, required all mining

FIGURE 20-4A Photograph of a contour mine from the eastern United States. Soil erosion at this site during rain storms and snow melt leads to serious siltation.

FIGURE 20-4B Surface view of an area strip mine. Coal is extracted after dragline removes overburden. Spoil piles will be recontoured and reseeded after mining.

companies to reclaim their land and set up state and federal watchdog agencies to monitor reclamation. The law required companies to restore the original contour of the land, replant it, and control on-site erosion and acid contamination of nearby lakes and streams. The act also placed a federal tax on coal to finance the reclamation of land destroyed by previous strip-mining operations. The estimated $4 billion the fund will yield is well below the $8 billion needed to complete the reclamation.

THE IMPACTS OF COAL COMBUSTION. A second major concern of environmentalists is the pollution produced by the combustion of coal. Four pollutants are of particular interest: carbon dioxide, sulfur dioxide, nitrogen dioxide, and particulates.

The combustion of coal and other fossil fuels has resulted in a massive buildup of carbon dioxide in the atmosphere, which may result in a significant increase in average global temperature that could disrupt our lives profoundly (see Chapter 19 for a discussion of the greenhouse effect).

Sulfur dioxide and nitrogen dioxide, discussed in more detail in Chapter 17, are **acid precursors**; they form sulfuric and nitric acids, respectively, when they combine with oxygen and water in the atmosphere. These acids fall to the earth in rain and snow, acidifying lakes and streams, killing trees, and damaging crops, buildings, and statues. To control the emissions of sulfur dioxide, many utilities have switched to low-sulfur coal or have installed **smokestack scrubbers**, special devices that remove much of the gas from the smokestack. Unfortunately, controlling nitrogen dioxide is no easy matter. The gas is not very soluble in water and therefore is not removed by scrubbers. The only measure utilities use now is the control of combustion temperatures, but this has only a minor effect. Currently, American utilities and factories produce about 20 million metric tons of nitrogen dioxide a year. Unlike sulfur dioxide, whose emissions have been steadily falling, its levels have remained the same over the past decade and are projected to climb even higher as our coal dependence increases.

Coal combustion also produces enormous quantities of particulates. Like sulfur dioxide, they are relatively easy to control. Even with the best pollution control, however, a single power plant supplying a million people produces 1,500 to 30,000 metric tons of particulates a year.

FLUIDIZED BED COMBUSTION. What's needed, agree most experts, is a cleaner technology to burn coal, and although work on alternative technologies has been underway for some time, a cleaner technology on a commercial scale is many years away. One of the most promising of the dozen or so alternative technologies is **fluidized bed combustion**, in which crushed coal is mixed with bits of limestone and propelled into a furnace in a strong current of air (Figure 20-5). The particles mix turbulently in the combustion chamber, ensuring very efficient combustion and therefore low levels of carbon monoxide. The furnace also operates at a much lower temperature than a conventional coal boiler, thus

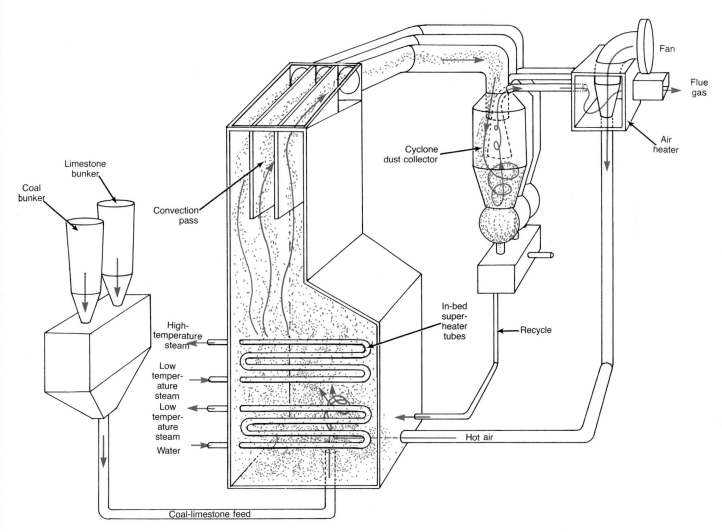

FIGURE 20-5 Fluidized bed combustion. This process burns crushed coal blown into a furnace mixed with tiny limestone particles. The air turbulence in the furnace ensures thorough combustion, thus increasing efficiency. The limestone reacts with sulfur oxide gases removing most of them from the smokestack. Steam pipes in the furnace help maximize heat efficiency.

reducing nitrogen oxide emissions. The limestone reacts with sulfur oxide gases, producing calcium sulfite or calcium sulfate, reducing sulfur oxide emissions from the stack gases.

Several large demonstration projects are operating now in Colorado and Kentucky. Should they prove successful, they could pave the way for wider use of this technology. But don't expect an overnight transition—at least 30 to 50 years would be required for this technology to make a substantial contribution to our electrical generating capacity. And should further signs of global warming become evident, modern society may find itself switching entirely away from coal to conservation, solar energy, and biofuels that do not contribute carbon dioxide to the atmosphere.

COAL GASIFICATION. Another promising technology is **coal gasification**, a process in which combustible gas is produced from coal by one of several methods. The technology could provide a supply of gas to replace declining domestic reserves of natural gas and can be designed to be cleaner than conventional coal boilers now in place throughout the country. In the example in Figure 20-6, a coal–water mixture, called a **slurry** is injected with oxygen into a heated chamber, producing three combustible gases: carbon monoxide, hydrogen, and some methane. The heated gas is then cooled a bit and purified. The resultant gas burns as cleanly as natural gas, and this particular technology, surprisingly, is as efficient as natural gas combustion.

Commonly used in the mid-1800s to produce gas from coal, coal gasification could provide gas for home heating and other uses, a need that will become acute as domestic natural gas supplies become depleted. Like fluidized bed combustion, gasification produces less nitrogen oxide than conventional coal boilers and eliminates much of the sulfur dioxide as well. Both technologies, however, produce solid wastes that must be carefully disposed of to prevent groundwater contamination.

Researchers have also been exploring the possibility of converting coal to gas underground—or *in situ*,

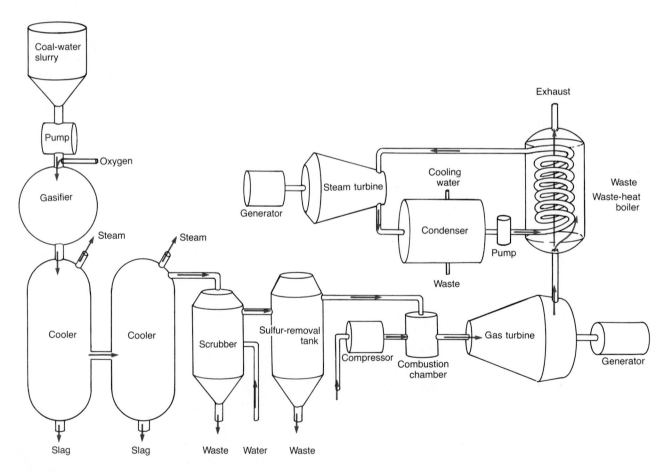

FIGURE 20-6 An efficient coal gasification process. In this process coal particles mixed with water are sprayed into a heated furnace (gasifier) where steam and combustible gases are produced. The gases are then cleaned by passing them through water. The gases are next burned and the exhaust gas is used to spin one of two electrical generators. The heat is also captured to generate steam, which operates another generator.

literally in place. To do this, oxygen is pumped into coalbeds, which are then ignited. Hydrogen, carbon monoxide, and methane gases are released from the smoldering fire and pumped back to the surface, where they can be burned to produce electricity. This process eliminates the need to surface-mine the coal for above-ground gasification, but it could result in widespread subsidence and uncontrollable underground fires that might smolder for decades.

COAL LIQUEFACTION. Coal can also be treated to produce a thick, oily substance in a process called **coal liquefaction**. At least four major processes now exist, each of which adds hydrogen to coal to produce oil. The oil can then be refined like crude oil to produce a variety of products like jet fuel, gasoline, kerosene, and many chemicals used to manufacture drugs, plastics, and a host of other products.

Coal liquefaction plants currently in operation show that this technology, while feasible, will be costly. It also generates numerous pollutants, like phenol, which are potentially harmful. And it would do nothing to reduce carbon dioxide levels. Nevertheless, coal liquefaction remains an energy option that may become more attractive as world oil supplies plummet.

Oil

The year was 1859 and the place was Titusville, Pennsylvania. When "Colonel" Edwin Drake's steel drill hit 20 meters (70 feet), a black, foul-smelling liquid came gushing from the well, signaling the dawn of a new energy era (Figure 20-7). Less than a century later, oil had become our nation's most important source of energy.

Being liquid and relatively easy to transport long distances, either by ship or by pipeline, oil is an ideal fuel, burning dirtier than natural gas but cleaner than coal. It provides about 43 percent of U.S. energy needs.

OIL RESERVES. Unlike coal, oil is in short supply. By various estimates, the known global reserves of oil—that amount known to exist and to be economically recoverable—are about 500 billion barrels. That may sound like a lot of oil, but it's only enough to last for about 25 years *at the current rate of consumption*. The undiscovered global reserves—that is, oil we think exists and can be recovered economically—amounts to 1,000 billion barrels. That's enough oil for another 50 years at the current rate of consumption.

Unfortunately, global energy use, except for two brief periods, has risen 5 percent per year since 1860. Should this continue, oil's modest 75-year life span would be sharply reduced. Many experts believe that oil prices will begin to climb in the 1990s, once again reaching $35 per barrel by 1995. They also believe that drastic shortages could occur early in the next century, creating a new oil crisis that could cripple the world economy.

The outlook for oil in the United States is even grimmer. Domestic production has been falling steadily. In 1985 domestic wells produced only 8.9 million barrels per day from 38,000 wells compared to 11 million per day in 1973 from 10,000 wells. The ultimate oil reserves—the amount believed to be recoverable—are about 200 billion barrels. Half of that oil has already been used up, leaving 100 billion barrels, enough to last for 17 years at the current rate of consumption. The United States has less than 6 percent of the world's oil reserves. This means that we will become more and more dependent on OPEC oil in the very near future

FIGURE 20-7 America's first oil well at Titusville, Pennsylvania. Photo taken in 1864.

and subject to their price controls. Unless a clean, economical substitute is found—and soon—our country will face frightening economic times.

THE IMPACTS OF OIL PRODUCTION AND CONSUMPTION. Oil comes from wells on land and at sea (Figure 20-8). The impacts of oil on the sea are discussed in Chapter 10. Land-based drilling can have many impacts as well. Roads and well sites, for instance, destroy wildlife habitat and wilderness. They also increase soil erosion. Leaks from wells or spills from pipelines can cover land with a thick, gooey residue that is difficult and costly to remove. Oil kills vegetation and seeps into the ground. Government plans to sell oil and gas leases in the 0.6-million-hectare (1.5-million-acre) coastal plain of the Arctic National Wildlife Refuge in Alaska's northeast corner have created a storm of controversy. By one estimate, 20–40 percent of the caribou population would be forced to move out of this enormous 8-million-hectare (19.5-

FIGURE 20-8 Offshore oil-drilling platform. Standing on rigid steel legs high above the water off Louisana's Gulf Coast, this barge-mounted rig drills for oil beneath the bottom of the sea.

million-acre) refuge or perish as a result of habitat loss. Huge flocks of snow geese, estimated at 300,000 birds, which use the coastal plain as a staging ground on their annual migration, would also be forced to find new territory; many would likely die. Musk oxen, only just reintroduced in 1969 and 1970 and now numbering about 500, would feel the ill effects of oil development.

No one knows how much oil, if any, lies underneath the sensitive coastal plain. The mean estimate is 3.2 billion barrels, with a 19 percent probability of occurrence. Full-scale development of the region would supply only about 4 percent of the projected oil demand by 2005 and less than 3 percent by 2010. Experience in nearby Prudhoe Bay—which lies 160 kilometers (100 miles) to the west—suggests that the risks may be too great to support development. According to a recent report on Prudhoe Bay, between 400 and 600 oil spills are reported *every year*. In 1986, 240 million liters (64 million gallons) of toxic wastewater containing a variety of heavy metals, hydrocarbons, and chemical additives were released onto the tundra. Gas vapors and combustible liquids routinely burned in oil fields created plumes of black smoke that stretched 100 miles from the oil fields. Nitrogen oxide and sulfur dioxide emissions from plants, biologists feared, would acidify the fragile tundra ecosystem. To make matters worse, the landscape around Prudhoe Bay is littered with broken-down vehicles, junked airplanes, used batteries, Styrofoam insulation, tires, scrap metals, and so on. The damage, some environmental scientists fear, may be irreparable.

Natural Gas

Natural gas is primarily methane (CH_4). Like coal and oil, it is a fossil fuel. It was given off by decomposing plant and animal remains that were buried in the earth by sedimentary deposits for millions of years. For this reason, natural gas deposits often accompany coal and oil deposits.

Today natural gas supplies about 26 percent of the energy needs of the United States. Easily transported within the country by pipeline, it is used primarily for heating buildings, home cooking, industrial processes, and generating electricity.

NATURAL GAS RESERVES. The picture for natural gas is a bit brighter than that of oil *globally*, but not as good as that of coal. Estimates on the amount of natural gas that will ultimately be recovered from the earth before supplies run out—called the **ultimate production**—vary considerably. By one fairly generous estimate, the global ultimate production is 10,000 trillion cubic feet. To date, global consumption has amounted to about 2,000 trillion cubic feet. Of the remaining 8,000 trillion cubic feet, only 2,000 are proven reserves—that is, known to exist. The rest are undiscovered reserves. The global proven reserves will last for about 40 years at the current rate of consumption; the undiscovered reserves will last for about 120 years. At best, there's a 160-year supply, but increased consumption is likely, and with that, so is a drastic reduction in global supplies.

Domestically, the outlook for natural gas is much dimmer. There are only about 200 trillion cubic feet of recoverable natural gas left in the United States—only enough for the next 11 years at the current rate of consumption. Even a modest increase in natural gas use could cut this supply in half. As with oil, something must be done—and soon—about our rapidly declining natural gas reserves.

What could replace natural gas? Conservation, improved energy efficiency, gas from coal, hydrogen, gas from crops, and gas from wastes such as garbage, sewage, sludge, and livestock manure—options discussed under alternative energy sources.

In the immediate future, the only way the United States can meet the demand for gas is by importing large quantities from abroad, especially from Canada and Mexico. Natural gas can be transported in ships in a liquid form—liquid natural gas (LNG)—from South America, Africa, Alaska, and the North Sea. However, transporting liquid natural gas is costly and dangerous. A tanker accident, for example, would produce a vapor cloud about 2 kilometers wide and 7 meters deep. The cloud could ignite if struck by lightning or if it drifted into populated regions. Were it to drift ashore and ignite, it could set a city or forest on fire.

Oil Shale

Oil shale is a grayish-brown sedimentary rock that was formed millions of years ago from the mud at the bottom of lakes. Contained within the rock is a solid organic material known as **kerogen** (Figure 20-9). When heated to high temperatures, the rock gives off its oily residue, called **shale oil**. High-grade oil shale can produce up to 120 liters (30 gallons, or about three-fourths of a barrel) of shale oil per ton of rock. Like petroleum, this oil can be refined to produce gasoline, jet fuel, kerosene, and a variety of feedstocks used by the chemical industry to produce fabrics, drugs, and plastics.

The most valuable deposit in the United States is in the Green River Formation, a 16,500-square-mile region located in Colorado, Wyoming, and Utah (Figure 20-10). Eighty percent of this land is federally owned.

Scientists estimate that, with current technologies, 80 to 300 billion barrels of oil could be extracted from these deposits. That's enough oil to satisfy domestic demands (at the current rate of consumption) for 7 to 28 years. Doing so, however, would exact enormous economic and environmental costs.

ENVIRONMENTAL IMPACTS OF OIL SHALE PRODUCTION. Oil shale can be processed in **surface retorts**, large vessels in which crushed shale is heated

FIGURE 20-9 Block of oil shale and a beaker of the oil that can be extracted from the shale. This project is located in Laramie, Wyoming.

FIGURE 20-10   Location of our nation's main oil-shale deposits in Colorado, Utah, and Wyoming.

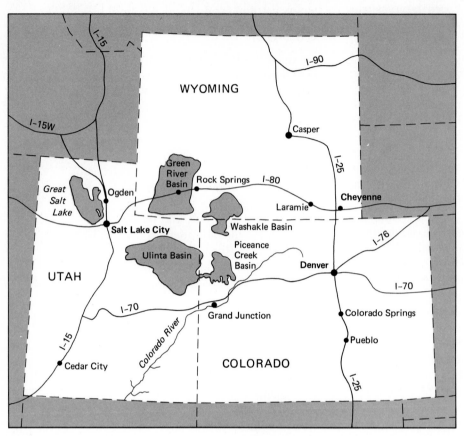

to drive off the oil. Shale to supply surface retorts may come from either underground mines or surface mines, depending on the depth of the deposit. Surface mines in the Green River Formation will tear up large tracts of land, much of which is prime habitat for hundreds of thousands of mule deer. The retorts themselves produce enormous amounts of **spent shale**—shale after it has been burned. A modest 50,000-barrel-per-day operation, for instance, would produce 53,000 metric tons of spent shale. It must be disposed of properly to avoid contaminating groundwater and surface waters. Adding to the problem, crushing the shale before it can be retorted increases the volume of the shale by about 12 percent—so not all of it can go back in the mine.

Retorts are notorious polluters. Sulfur oxides, nitrogen oxides, heavy metals, and various organic pollutants—all toxic to humans and wildlife—could foul the western skies if oil shale operations expand beyond the current pilot projects. And surface retorts require tremendous volumes of cooling water—about 2.5 barrels per barrel of shale oil produced. Water, of course, is a hotly contested commodity in the rapidly growing arid West.

Some companies have experimented with another process, called *in situ* **retorting**, to avoid the solid waste problems. In an *in situ* retort, the oil shale deposit is fractured with dynamite and set afire underground. The fire burns the shale and drives off the kerogen, which, in a vapor state, is pumped out of the deposit, condensed, and later refined. Tried in the late 1970s to avoid disturbing the land and generating solid wastes, *in situ* retorting has proved difficult to master. Fires go out easily because of incomplete fracturing. Complicating matters even more, groundwater often seeps into the oil shale bed, dousing the fire. Controlling pollution is also more difficult in the *in situ* process. Because of these difficulties, this technique has largely been abandoned.

Tar Sands

In some parts of the world, oil has migrated into neighboring layers of sandstone, creating **tar sands**. The thick, oily residue, called **bitumen**, can be extracted from the rock and refined to produce a variety of fuels and chemicals in much the same way that shale oil can be processed.

Significant deposits of bitumen are found in Alberta, Canada, and in the United States. Although six states have economically attractive deposits, Utah is the leader, with over 90 percent of the commercially feasible tar sands.

U.S. deposits are much smaller than Canadian deposits. Lying deep within the earth's crust, U.S. deposits contain an estimated 27 billion barrels of bitumen but are not readily surface-mined. To recover the oil, hot steam is generally passed down into the deposits to free the bitumen, which is pumped to the surface in recovery wells. When all is said and done, only about 1 billion barrels are likely to be recovered from our deposits, which is about one-sixth of our annual oil consumption.

The richer Canadian deposits, on the other hand, are readily surface-mined and can be processed in above-ground facilities. Containing an estimated 900 billion barrels of oil, these deposits are now actively being mined and processed to produce 175,000 barrels of oil per day. By 2000, Canada expects to acquire 40 percent of its oil from these deposits. Despite this, Canadian supplies will probably not last long. By one estimate, only about 38 billion barrels of oil will ever come from the rich tar sand deposits of our northern neighbor. In a world that uses over 20 billion barrels of oil per day, the Canadian deposits are a mere drop in the bucket.

Why are tar sands of so little value? To mine and process enough tar sand to produce a barrel of oil requires six-tenths of the energy contained in one barrel. This **low net energy efficiency**—the amount of energy invested in the system—will stifle tar sand production.

The Future of Fossil Fuels

The energy supply picture boils down to this: Oil, our most widely used fuel, is fast on the decline—here and abroad. The demand is expected to outstrip the supply sometime in the middle to late 1990s or—at the latest—in the early 2000s, causing a drastic increase in price and severe economic problems for countries that have not switched to alternative fuels.

The prospects for natural gas are better globally, but in the United States the supplies are fast on the decline. Only another 11 years of gas are available at the current rate of consumption. The only way to meet our demand is to import liquid natural gas, a costly and potentially dangerous activity. Eventually, though, natural gas supplies will run out and society will be forced to turn to other sources.

The prospects for coal are the best. The world has abundant supplies of coal, and the United States has about a third of the world's supplies. But coal combustion, no matter how efficient, will continue to add to the global warming trend. Reducing the emissions of acid-generating pollutants from coal-fired power plants

only shifts the problem. Instead of going up the smokestack, the pollutants are trapped and become a hazardous waste in need of careful disposal (see Chapter 16). It is time, say many experts, to find a substitute for oil—used to heat homes, produce liquid fuels, and produce chemicals. Oil shale and tar sands are two alternatives, but their reserves are small compared to the demand, and they are costly to develop, both environmentally and economically. Biofuels—for instance, ethanol from crops—may be the answer, as will strict energy conservation.

It is also time to look for substitutes for natural gas. Methane from trash or crop residues could help. Conservation, of course, will be invaluable. For coal, largely used to generate electricity, the immediate goal may be to find much cleaner ways to burn it, lest we poison the earth we live on. Should the predictions of global warming come true, coal will be tossed out as well, leaving society with the colossal task of finding a substitute for it.

ALTERNATIVE ENERGY SOURCES

What could replace fossil fuels? Environmentalists see a variety of alternatives on the horizon, many of which are already in place on a small scale today. These include conservation, solar energy, wind energy, biomass, hydropower, geothermal energy, and possibly others. Other people see nuclear energy—both fusion and fission power—as a significant source of energy for future generations. (Nuclear energy is discussed in the next chapter.)

Solar Energy

Our nation should hitch its "energy wagon" to a star—the sun, say many environmentalists. Why? Sunlight is the ultimate source of energy that powers the global ecosystem, and it is destined to last for several billion years. It comes to us free of charge and is a clean source of fuel. All we need to do is find ways to capture it and put it to use.

The thought of harnessing solar energy has piqued the interest of humans for ages. The Greeks used it 2,000 years ago to heat their homes—and, in fact, considered those who didn't orient their homes to the south to tap the sun's generous heat to be barbarians. The Anasazi Indians of the desert Southwest used it, building their homes in south-facing rock walls protected from the summer sun but open to the winter sun for heat.

The amount of solar energy striking the earth's surface on a cloudless day is over 100,000 times greater than the world's presently installed electrical capacity. The sunlight striking an area the size of Connecticut

FIGURE 20-11   The potential for solar energy use in different regions of the United States.

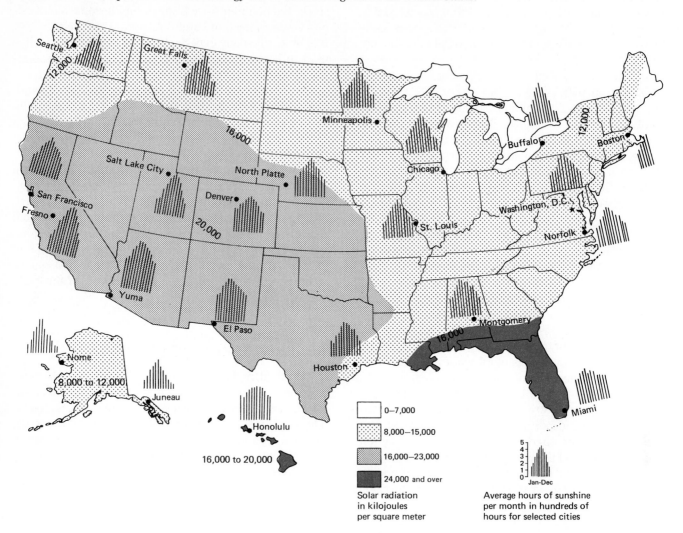

each year could provide all of the energy needed by the entire United States, and yet Americans have only tapped a tiny portion of the sun's potential (Figure 20-11).

The sun's awesome power is amply illustrated by the world's largest solar furnace in the French Pyrenees (Figure 20-12). This power plant has a 45-meter (150-foot) mirror that focuses sunlight on a boiler. Concentrated sunlight raises the temperature to 3,500°C (6,300°F)—sufficiently hot to melt a 1-foot-wide hole in a steel plate three-eighths of an inch thick in only 60 seconds. The solar potential for heating homes and buildings is enormous.

SOLAR HEATING.   Without the sun, the earth's average temperature would be a chilling –230°C (–450°F), so in many ways we already use the sun for heating—albeit unintentionally. The intentional use of sunlight for heating takes two forms—active solar heating and passive solar heating.

Active solar systems, like the one shown in Figure 20-13, are generally mounted on rooftops and gather sunlight in collectors, closed boxes with black backgrounds to absorb light. Collectors are insulated and covered with glass to prevent heat loss. The heat is removed from the collector by air or a fluid flowing in pipes within the collector itself, as illustrated in Figure 20-14. The heat can then be transferred directly to the room or transported to a storage device for later use.

Most active solar systems in use today provide hot water for domestic use—washing dishes, clothes, and people. Domestic hot water systems can provide 50–90 percent of this hot water, reducing gas and electric bills.

Passive solar systems are designed for space heating. The building itself becomes a collector and heat-storing device. In the passive solar home shown in Figure 20-15, belonging to the junior author, south-facing windows and skylights let the winter sun penetrate the interior of the house. The sunlight strikes the walls and floors and is converted into heat. Special cement or

FIGURE 20-12 French solar furnace. This solar furnace, located near Odeillo in the Pyrenees Mountains of southern France, was built to test materials under extremely high temperatures. In the foreground, an array of 63 mirrors (heliostats), each measuring 6 meters by $7\frac{1}{2}$ meters, reflects sunlight onto the curved mirror surface of the office building in the background. This in turn focuses the sunlight on an aperture in the tower at the center, where temperatures of 7,000°F can be produced—enough heat to melt any known material.

FIGURE 20-13 Mt. Rushmore goes solar, Mt. Rushmore, South Dakota, site of the famed sculpted faces of former presidents, has a new solar-energy system. Solar collectors on the roof of the Visitor's Center transform the rays of the sun into energy for heating and air conditioning. The solar panels were developed by Honeywell. The system provides energy for 53 percent of the heating and 41 percent of the cooling for the 9,250-square-foot building.

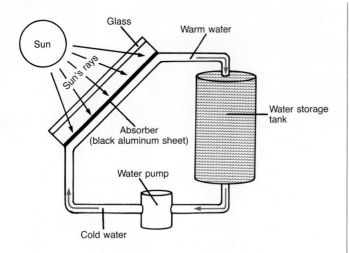

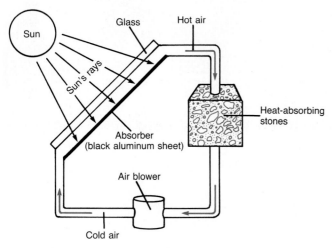

FIGURE 20-14 Two types of solar space-heating systems.

FIGURE 20-15 Photograph of passive solar home at 8,000 feet in the Foothills of the Rockies featuring south-facing windows and skylights that let the winter sun in. Superinsulation and high efficiency gas backup heat keep winter heat bills low—about $100 a year.

block walls inside store the heat and radiate it out into the room at night. An overhang on the south-facing windows prevents the summer sun from entering the house, thus keeping it comfortable all year round. Passive solar homes must be well insulated; windows generally have double or triple panes and thick curtains to prevent heat loss during the night.

Surprisingly, passive solar, well-insulated homes can function efficiently in fairly cold climates. One home built by the engineering department at the University of Saskatchewan had an annual heating bill of $40 compared to $1,400 for a conventional home of the same size. One hundred percent passive solar homes now operate in Maine, Vermont, and Wisconsin, as well as other states.

Passive solar energy can be used to heat commercial buildings as well. Ontario Hydro, a Canadian energy company, built a mammoth office building in Toronto that relies entirely on a solar energy system that captures waste heat from people, lights, and equipment and reuses it (Figure 20-16). Despite the frigid winter weather, the building stays warm and comfortable. In Soldier's Grove, Wisconsin, the entire business community moved out of the flood plain to avoid the periodic flooding that wreaked havoc on their town. The citizens decided to convert the town into a solar town. They now have a solar post office, fire station, library, gas station, wood-working shop, American Legion hall, grocery store, and others; for the first 3 years, despite harsh winters, the grocery store's heating bill was zero—thanks to passive solar energy, superb insulation, and a system that captures waste heat from compressors and pumps it back into the 7,000-square-foot store. Remarkably, the entire system paid for itself in those 3 years.

SOLAR ELECTRICITY. Solar energy can also be used to generate electricity. The French solar furnace, described earlier and shown in Figure 20-12, heats water with sunlight and creates steam that runs an electrical generator. Somewhat similar systems are now operating in Sandia, New Mexico, and Barstow, California. These prototype "power towers," completed in 1977, are small plants—producing only 1 megawatt of electricity. A conventional coal-fired power plant typically produces 500 to 1,000 megawatts. The power tower stands about 15 stories high and is located in a large field of movable mirrors. Controlled by a computer, the mirrors track the sun across the sky and focus their beam of energy on the top of the tower. The intense heat produced there boils water, which is converted to steam to run an electrical generator (Figure 20-17).

Don't get your hopes up for this technology, though. To produce a mere 50 megawatts of energy would require a field of 1.6 square kilometers, or about 1 square mile. The ideal locations for solar power towers

FIGURE 20-16 Ontario Hydro's energy efficient, solar office building in Canada.

are deserts, which are notoriously short on the water needed for cooling.

Far more promising is a technology called **photovoltaics**, thin wafers mounted singly or, more commonly, in small arrays, as shown in Figure 20-18. Photovoltaic cells convert sunlight energy directly into electricity. Each cell is a thin wafer of silicon or other material that, when struck by sunlight, emits electrons. Developed in 1954 by Bell Laboratories, photovoltaics were first used in 1958 to provide power for the Vanguard I, America's second space satellite. Since that time, photovoltaics have provided power for dozens of other satellites and are now being used on earth in remote locations where electricity is not available or is too expensive to install. River flow monitors in remote country, mountaintop radio relays, remote irrigation pumps, highway signs in unpopulated areas, lighthouses, and buoys all use them to provide energy. Photovoltaics also have some uses much closer to home, such as in calculators, watches, and other electronic devices. In 1980, photovoltaic cells powered the first flight of the *Gossamer Penguin*, a one-person solar airplane. Despite these many uses, photovoltaics contribute very little of our overall energy consumption. As prices go down, however, experts predict that they will become more widely used.

Photovoltaics are an attractive option. The fuel is free and virtually inexhaustible. It is a clean technology as well. Widespread use would eliminate acid precipita-

tion, strip mining, and all the other impacts now created by the use of coal. They would also eliminate the need for nuclear waste dumps and the other impacts of nuclear power, discussed in the next chapter. So why haven't photovoltaics made it to the rooftop of every house in America?

The answer is their cost. The silicon used to make solar cells comes from sand, one of the most abundant elements on earth, but making solar cells is costly and tedious. And the solar cells commercially available are fairly inefficient—10–15 percent at best. A 1-square-meter panel is only enough to power a single 120-watt lightbulb, and that panel costs about $500. A whole house would require a large array of solar cells costing about $50,000.

What is needed, say the supporters of photovoltaics, are more efficient solar cells and mass production, both of which would help lower their cost and make them competitive with other sources of electricity. In 1986 researchers at Stanford University announced a new design that uses a parabolic mirror to concentrate sunlight on the solar cells. This could boost the efficiency from 10–15 percent to close to 30 percent, a tremendous boon for the industry. If tests prove successful, these more efficient solar cells could be on the market soon. Photovoltaic costs have tumbled in the past 30 years, from nearly $600 a peak-watt to $5 in 1986. To be competitive, however, they must continue to fall, reaching $1.50 per peak-watt output.

FIGURE 20-17A View of solar-power tower located at the Department of Energy's test facility at Sandia Laboratories in Albuquerque, New Mexico.

Photovoltaics could provide Americans with much of their electricity needs as fossil fuel prices rise in the 1990s. In fact, all of the electrical power required by the United States could theoretically come from 12,000 square kilometers of solar cells—roughly the area occupied by all the buildings in the lower 48 states. Brown University professor Joseph Loferski estimated that photovoltaics mounted on only 20 percent of Rhode Island's rooftops would provide all of the electrical power needs of the state. The electrical power would be generated only a few feet from where it would be used, thus removing the need for costly, inefficient, and ugly transmission lines, which in 1987 were linked to at least one form of cancer—leukemia in children. By 2000, experts predict, photovoltaics will provide about 5,000 to 10,000 megawatts of power—or enough energy for 5 to 10 million people. If these systems prove economical and reliable, solar cells could become a major source of electrical energy by the year 2030.

Solar voltaics do have some drawbacks. Sunlight is inconsistent, and some kind of storage would be necessary. Backup systems, perhaps using fossil fuels, would also be needed to provide energy for long sunless periods. Solar voltaic production also generates hazardous wastes.

SATELLITE SOLAR POWER STATION. Imagine a huge array of solar cells circling the earth. Such a solar satellite would convert sunlight into electricity, which then would be converted into **microwaves**, high-frequency electromagnetic waves. The microwaves would be transmitted to earth in a 8.3-kilometer (5-mile) -wide beam. Picked up by a huge antenna, the microwaves would be reconverted into electricity on earth and transmitted to users.

The advantage of this system is that it can trap solar energy outside the earth's atmosphere, where it is eight times more intense. And the satellite could orbit in such a way that it would be immersed in constant daylight, avoiding the problem of an earth-based system. All of this sounds good until you look a little more closely. That's when the drawbacks begin to become evident.

The first problem is cost. A demonstration project could cost as much as $50 billion, money better spent on conservation and other more sensible schemes. The second problem is the size of the system. For example, just to produce 60 percent of the electricity needed by New York City, or about 5,000 megawatts, would require a solar array 13 kilometers (8 miles) long and 5 kilometers (3 miles) wide. It would weigh 20,000 to 40,000 metric tons and would need to be built in space, which would require 360 space shuttle flights to deliver parts and workers. Third, microwave beams could disrupt military and commercial radar. Fourth, microwaves would kill large numbers of migrating birds that got in the way, roasting them almost as if they were in a microwave oven. Fifth, microwaves could adversely affect human health, causing cataracts, damage to the nervous system, and genetic defects.

Our Solar Future

Researchers at the Fund for Renewable Energy and the Environment (FREE) recently reported that the federal government provided the energy industry with $44 billion in subsidies in 1984. Meanwhile, federal support of conservation, solar energy, and other renewable energy sources has been cut to the bones. Federal conservation programs alone were cut 91 percent between 1981 and 1987.

By supporting nonrenewable energy sources and neglecting conservation and renewable sources, our government may be sowing the seeds of its social and economic disruption. It is time, say supporters of solar and other renewable energy sources, to reverse this trend. "The transition to the solar future," says Professor Kurt Hohenemser of Washington University, is "a gigantic technological enterprise" that would require a century to complete. It would be much easier to accomplish if we start now, while we still have cheap fossil fuels. "The question," he continues, "should not be how to extend our growth-based industrial and economic sys-

FIGURE 20-17B The solar-power tower. The concentrated rays of the sun convert water to steam, which in turn propels the turbine.

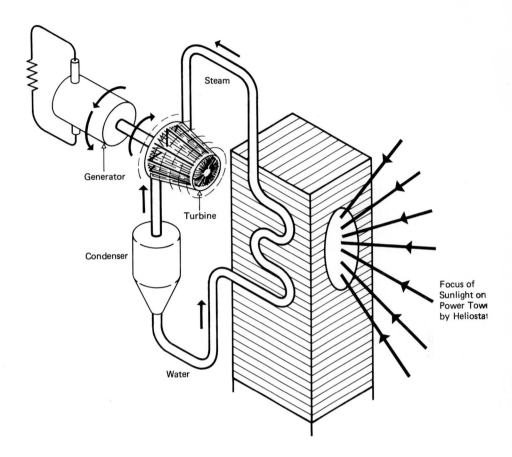

tem a little longer by still faster extraction of our finite resources, but rather how to spend some of our remaining resources wisely . . . to accomplish a smooth transition to a solar-based society."

Geothermal Energy

On New Zealand's north island, the junior author ran across an electrical power plant on the banks of

FIGURE 20-18 Photovoltaic cells. These thin wafers of silicon absorb sunlight and generate an electrical current.

the Waikato River. Surprisingly, there were no smelly plumes of smoke from coal or oil combustion. Instead, huge silver pipes transported steam from a geyser and a hot spring region nearby. At the plant, the steam was used to turn a turbine to generate electricity.

The earth stores enormous amounts of heat, or **geothermal energy**, which comes from the radioactive decay of naturally occurring radioactive substances in the earth's crust and from molten rock in its interior (Figure 20-19). In some places, groundwater heated by the earth's interior spews to the surface in remarkable displays called **geysers**. In others, the water merely bubbles up, filling pools (hot springs) or trickling into nearby streams. These regions are called **hydrothermal convection zones**. In other regions, groundwater may be trapped by impervious rock layers. These are called **geopressurized zones**. Heated by molten rock underneath, the steam and superheated water can only be tapped by drilling holes into the pockets of steam. In still other areas, magma heats overlying rock, forming **hot rock zones**. Recent studies show that water can be pumped into these zones and then pumped out where the energy is used for heating or electric generation.

Most geothermal energy today comes from hydrothermal convection zones (Figure 20-20). They are the easiest and cheapest to tap. Steam or hot water from these zones can be used to heat all sorts of buildings. For

FIGURE 20-19   Map of geothermal areas in the world. Most are located in regions of volcanic activity, past or present.

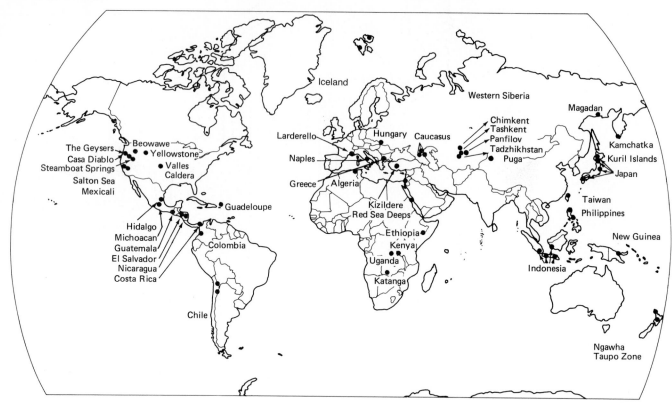

example, almost all of the houses in Reykjavik, the capital city of Iceland, are heated by geothermal steam. Icelanders grow a variety of vegetables in steam-heated greenhouses as well. In the United States, at least 300 communities use geothermal heat for one reason or another. One rancher in South Dakota uses geothermal energy to heat his home and several buildings. He also uses it to dry several thousand bushels of grain each year. All told, geothermal energy saves him over $5,000 a year in fuel bills.

Steam or hot water can be used, as mentioned earlier, to generate electricity. First used successfully in 1904 in Larderello, Italy, geothermal electricity is now found in New Zealand, Japan, Mexico, the United States, the Philippines, Italy, Iceland, and the Soviet Union. One of the world's largest projects is in northern California on the slope of an extinct volcano. Started in 1960, the project has a 900-megawatt capacity, supplying nearly a million people (Figure 20-21).

Despite these success stories, geothermal energy produces very little electricity worldwide. The total global capacity is now only about 5,000 megawatts, equivalent to that of five large nuclear power plants. By 1990 it is expected to increase to 6,400 megawatts. Further gains are predicted. By one seemingly generous esti-

mate, by the year 2000 the United States alone could produce 27,000 megawatts of electricity from geothermal sources. California, a leader in conservation and alternative energies, hopes to eventually get 25 percent of its electricity from geothermal sources.

Geothermal power is relatively inexpensive and much cleaner than coal-fired and nuclear power plants. The capital investment—the money needed to start a plant— is 40 percent lower than for a coal-fired power plant and 300 percent cheaper than a nuclear power plant. However, there are some drawbacks. First, minerals dissolved in the steam may corrode pipes and turbine blades. The plants can also be noisy. Another problem is the gaseous contaminants, such as hydrogen sulfide, carbon dioxide, ammonia, and methane, that often occur in the steam and require pollution control devices. Steam cannot be transported long distances, thus necessitating the construction of industries near sources. Finally, most of the hydrothermal convection zones in the United States are located along the Pacific Coast; the highly populated East Coast, where the demand for energy is greatest, would have to rely on hot rock zones, which are found throughout the United States but are more costly and difficult to tap.

FIGURE 20-20   Schematic view of a geothermal-power-plant operation.

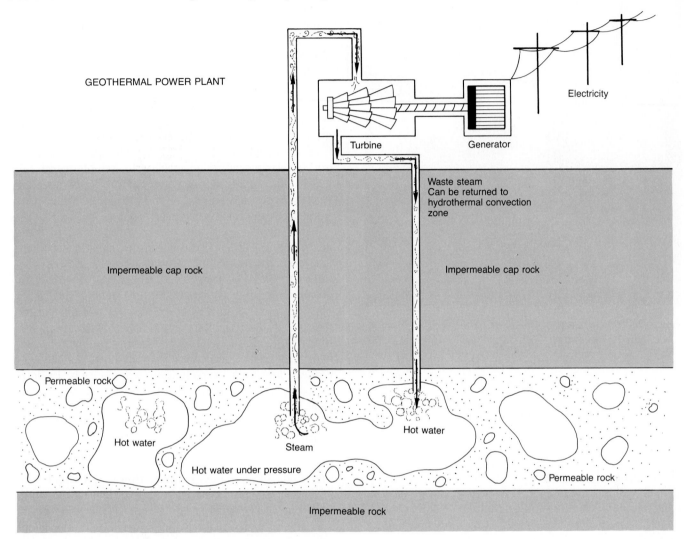

Hydropower

Humans have tapped the power of flowing rivers for thousands of years. In the United States, hydropower was used extensively in the 1800s to grind wheat and corn, saw logs, power textile mills, and water cattle. Today hydropower provides about 14 percent of America's electricity, or about 4 percent of our total energy consumption (Figure 20-22).

Hydropower offers several advantages: (1) it is relatively inexpensive, (2) it is pollution free, (3) it is a potentially renewable source, provided that reservoirs can be kept free of sediment, and (4) enormous untapped resources exist. Today only about 17 percent of the potential hydropower is now being used.

You might assume, therefore, that when the supply of fossil fuels falls so low that it becomes too expensive, the world can turn to hydropower. Unfortunately, it is not quite that simple. Several problems cloud the prospects for hydropower.

First, the greatest hydropower potential lies in the developing countries of Africa, South America, and Asia. Because many developing countries lack financial and other resources, their hydropower potential is not likely to be developed. Second, the massive and costly dams, with price tags ranging from $300 million to $2 billion, often have a short life span because of the heavy sedimentation caused by poor land management—deforestation, overgrazing, and poor farming practices. This problem threatens many projects. For example, Egypt's Aswan Dam, the world's largest, probably will have a functional life of less than 200 years. In the United States, over 2,000 reservoirs have

FIGURE 20-21 Geothermal wells at The Geysers, California. More than 100 wells have been drilled at The Geysers, in an area 2 × 8 miles in extent. The deepest of these is more than 8,000 feet. Temperatures of the underground reservoirs from which the heat is drawn are about 255°C (480°F). The basic source appears to be a mass of heated rocks at a depth of three to five miles and covering an area of about 100 to 500 square miles.

been filled with sediment; some succumbed in fewer than 20 years. Pakistan's $1.3 billion Tarbella Dam, which took 9 years to build, could be filled by sediment in 20 years. Third, dams destroy the scenic beauty of wild canyons used by anglers, kayakers, rafters, canoeists, and a variety of others. Fourth, reservoirs behind dams inundate forests, farmland, and wildlife habitat. Fifth, dams reduce the natural flow of sediment-bearing nutrients to estuaries and disrupt aquatic food chains in these ecologically and economically important zones. Sixth, dams can interfere with the migration of fish, such as salmon, and fluctuating levels can kill fish eggs laid in shallow waters near shore. Seventh, in arid regions, reservoirs accelerate evaporation. In some cases, evaporation reduces the amount of available irrigation water. Eighth, dams may collapse, flooding downstream towns and killing people.

Despite these disadvantages, hydropower is here to stay and is likely to expand in the near future. But the generous estimates of untapped potential should be viewed cautiously. For instance, the United States currently generates 70,000 megawatts of energy from hydroelectric plants and has, according to estimates, an additional 160,000 megawatts of untapped potential. However, this untapped energy lies in out-of-the-way places where dams may be economically and environmentally unfeasible. In fact, half of our untapped potential lies in Alaska, far from industrial and population centers. Much of the untapped potential in Africa, Asia, and South America is also in remote locations.

Most hydropower projections focus on large dams, with little consideration for smaller projects ranging from 1 to 10 megawatts. It is these small projects, some proponents argue, that could provide enormous amounts of energy in countries throughout the world. China, for instance, has 90,000 small dams on streams and rivers providing electricity to remote rural villages—equivalent to one-third of the country's total electrical production. France and the United States have numerous small dams as well.

Although these structures are inexpensive to build and operate, and provide energy to consumers where it is needed without huge transmission losses, they significantly alter streams, affecting fish and other aquatic organisms. Some environmentalists believe that a far better strategy would be to retrofit the 50,000 nonhydroelectric dams in the Untied States with small turbines to generate electricity. The environmental damage, they argue, has already been done, so why not make a dam built for recreation, water supply, or flood control, for instance, do double duty—that is, generate electricity as well?

Windpower

For many decades, Great Plains farmers harnessed the winds sweeping across their rolling grasslands and wheat fields with a relatively simple device: the windmill (Figure 20-23). Used to pump water, grind grain, and generate electricity to light their barns, the windmill fell out of vogue in the 1930s as rural electric lines began to spring up, connecting central power plants with remote farms. Soon thereafter, the sight of windmill silhouettes etched darkly against the blue prairie skies gradually faded. Starting in the 1970s, however, windmills began to pop up across the nation, this time on special wind farms or in the backyards of suburban homes.

Wind energy contributed little to global energy needs 10 years ago. In fact, in 1980 the global capacity was a paltry 600 megawatts. In 1986, however, 13,000 wind turbines in California provided 1,100 megawatts of power—enough electricity for a million people. Most of these turbines are on specially built wind farms located on mountain passes and connected to the existing electrical grid. By the year 2000, California officials hope to provide 8 percent of the state's electrical needs from wind energy. The World Meteorological Organization estimates that 7–19 percent of the electricity the United States needs could come from wind by the year 2000.

FIGURE 20-22 Hydroelectric power. Aerial view of Hoover Dam and Lake Mead on the Arizona-Nevada border. This world-famous dam spans the Colorado River. Built in 1935, the dam provides multiple benefits, such as flood protection, water storage for irrigation purposes, and hydroelectric power.

FIGURE 20-23 The windmill of the past. Many-bladed windmills like these were once characteristic landmarks on American farms. They were used to pump water. Farmers stopped using them following the successful rural electrification program of the 1930s. Now farmers need alternative power sources to pump irrigation water because of high prices for gas and other fuels.

FIGURE **20-24** Experimental wind generator near Bushland, Texas produces electricity from wind. This unit is 50 meters high and can produce about half the electricity consumed in the Bushland community when the winds are blowing.

Wind farms have also been erected in Denmark, India, and the Netherlands. The highly respected Worldwatch Institute predicts that wind energy could provide 20–30 percent of the electricity needed by many countries. And some experts believe that wind pumps— similar to the windmills of the past—could be used in remote rural villages of India and Africa to provide drinking and irrigation water.

Many versions of the windmill are currently under study, ranging from huge units with 20-meter blades to tiny backyard wind machines that provide electricity for individual homes (Figure 20-24). One large wind generator in Boone, North Carolina, for example, sits atop a 40-meter (140-foot) tower. Its huge blades rotate 35 times a minute in a 50-kilometer (30-mile) -per-hour wind; the wind generator supplies electricity to 500 homes.

Wind energy comes free of charge, is clean, and is renewable. It requires little land and does not preclude many other uses, such as grazing. Electricity from wind energy is currently only slightly more expensive (12 to 20 cents per kilowatt) than electricity from nuclear power (10 to 12 cents per kilowatt). What is more, costs have dropped steadily, and by 1990, the Worldwatch Institute projects, wind may be one of the cheapest sources of electricity available.

Unfortunately, wind power has been fraught with problems. Large generators are unsightly and can interfere with radio and television reception, as well as with the microwave transmission used by telephone companies. Furthermore, materials tend to wear out, necessitating replacement. To make matters worse, winds are not constant, making some means of storing electricity mandatory. However, electrical storage is not well developed on a large scale. Nevertheless, given the expected rise in the cost of electricity from conventional power plants, wind could become a major source of electricity in the not too distant future.

Biomass

Wood, manure, crop wastes, and other forms of biomass supply about 14–19 percent of the world's energy. In developing nations, where fossil fuel consumption is low, biomass may provide up to 90 percent of the total energy demand. What makes this fuel so attractive is that it is renewable, helps reduce wastes, is often inexpensive, and does not add to the global carbon dioxide problem. Furthermore, biomass can be burned directly or converted into liquid and gaseous fuels, giving it a wide range of applications. And biomass fuels are labor intensive—that is, they require many workers to produce. In the Third World, where employment is a major problem, labor-intensive fuels could provide work and income for many people.

WOOD. Wood is the most widely used form of biomass. Worldwide, its use increased 33 percent between 1970 and 1982. In developed countries, such as the United States, Norway, and Sweden, wood supplies about 10 percent of the home heating fuel. In Canada and the United States, 3–4 percent of the total energy consumed each year comes from wood. Most of this wood is burned by the wood and wood products industries, which were hard hit by the high cost of fossil fuels in the 1970s (Figure 20-25).

FIGURE 20-25 This biomas-to-fuel oil plant in Albany, Oregon, converts feedstock, such as Douglas fir wood chips in the foreground, into fuel oil. The wood chips are combined with carbon monoxide and hydrogen at high temperatures and pressures.

Unfortunately, wood is a somewhat dirty fuel. Burned in wood stoves, it becomes a major source of particulates and other pollutants in many of America's urban areas. Today many areas that do not meet National Ambient Air Quality Standards restrict wood burning on high-pollution days. Some restrict the number of wood stoves and fireplaces, and some even require catalytic converters to reduce pollution on new wood stoves.

In the developing world, where as many as 2.5 billion people depend on wood for cooking and heating, shortages are becoming widespread. A recent report by the Food and Agriculture Organization of the United Nations, for instance, noted that 1.3 billion people currently meet their need for wood by depleting existing supplies—cutting trees down faster than they can be replenished. Two-thirds of these people live in Asia, especially near the Himalayas. Many of the rest live in arid parts of Central Africa and the Andean plateau of South America. In Africa, women and children may travel 50 kilometers (30 miles) a day in search of fuel wood. By 2000, the report predicts, the number of people who have a problem collecting enough wood to meet their needs will climb to 3 billion unless something

is done—and quickly. Depletion of wood creates enormous human suffering and leads to widespread ecological damage: erosion, desertification, flooding, and habitat destruction.

What can be done? First and foremost, population growth must be controlled. Second, forests can be planted near villages and managed to produce a sustained yield (Chapter 12). In the Philippines, for instance, the government launched a program to replant marginal rural land in trees to provide wood fuel for numerous small power plants aimed at providing outlying villages with electricity. Third, new, more efficient cooking stoves can be used by villagers to cut the demand. Fourth, substitute energy sources such as wind energy, photovoltaics, and small hydroelectric plants could be developed with the assistance of the United Nations and developed nations.

OTHER BIOFUELS. Wood is only one of many forms of biomass that can be used to produce energy. Garbage, for instance, can be incinerated to produce steam heat and electricity, as discussed in Chapter 16. Manure, human wastes, and other organic wastes can be used to produce methane gas. When mixed with water and heated in a closed container, organic material is degraded by anaerobic bacteria. The methane given off can be burned to produce heat and electricity. In fact, many sewage treatment plants here and abroad now capture methane that was once vented to the atmosphere; they use it to heat offices, generate electricity needed by the plant, and often sell the excess to local utilities.

Last, but not least, plant material can be used to generate ethanol, a liquid fuel that can be mixed with gasoline in a ratio of 1:9 and burned in automobiles. Called **gasohol**, it results in more complete combustion and fewer pollutants. Alcohol can also be burned without dilution in specially designed cars and in factories. Most ethanol currently comes from corn, but virtually any crop material, when properly fermented, can produce alcohol. Brazil uses sugar cane to produce alcohol and cut its imports of foreign oil by 30 percent between 1980 and 1984 as a result. One day, Brazil hopes to fuel its entire automobile and truck fleet with pure alcohol.

Fuel farms could provide much of America's liquid fuel in the coming years. Excess wheat and other crops, for instance, could be used to produce substantial amounts of liquid fuel. As many Third World nations become self-sufficient in food production, countries like Canada, Australia, and the United States, which currently export large amounts of food, could become major producers of ethanol fuel.

As promising as it may seem, ethanol production has a major obstacle that we must overcome before it can become widely used. The net energy yield of ethanol production is about zero; in other words, you get about

FIGURE 20-26 In a tidal power plant, water flows through small openings in the dam, spinning a propellor that generates electricity.

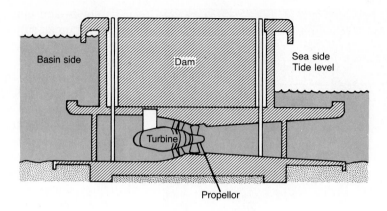

Hydrogen

Hydrogen gas is another potentially useful fuel that could someday be substituted for gasoline, jet fuel, and natural gas. Derived from water, it is one of the most abundant fuels available.

Hydrogen production is simple but costly. It is generated by passing an electric current through water in the presence of certain catalysts. Heat or sunlight can also break water down, as long as appropriate catalysts are present.

Hydrogen gas burns readily in air, for it combines rapidly with oxygen, reforming water. In its favor is that hydrogen combustion does not produce particulates, carbon dioxide, and sulfur oxides, those undesirable products of fossil fuel combustion. Instead, hydrogen combustion yields three products: energy, water, and a little nitrogen dioxide, the last produced because the heat causes oxygen and nitrogen in the air to combine.

Unfortunately, because energy is required in most hydrogen-producing processes, the net energy efficiency is negative, making production costly. Hydrogen is fairly explosive as well. And to be used in automobiles, it would have to be liquefied. One way to do this would be to cool it to very low temperatures, but this process consumes additional energy. Finding a way to store hydrogen safely, without requiring energy, is another major goal of current research on this fuel.

Tidal Power

President Franklin Roosevelt often watched the rise and fall of the tides near his summer home on the Bay of Fundy. He was impressed with the potential power of the surging waters, for the tides of Fundy are the largest on earth—up to 16 meters (50 feet). He wondered, no doubt, if the energy of those tides could somehow be captured—perhaps by finding a way to channel that energy through turbines similar to those in power plants, where spinning blades produce electrical energy (Figure 20-26).

The world's first tidal-electric installation was built in 1966 in the La Rance estuary in France. It produces about 240 megawatts of electricity today. A similar plant has been constructed in the Soviet Union. The power plant channels the tides through openings in a massive dam built at the mouth of the river. The water spins an underwater turbine, generating electricity.

Tidal power has many advantages. It is relatively inexpensive to tap, produces no toxic wastes or pollutants, and is renewable. On the down side, there are only about 24 good sites worldwide, and they would only produce about 5 percent of the current electrical demand of the Untied States. The dams also impair the movement of ships and could upset aquatic life.

Ocean Thermal Energy Conversion

The ocean is a vast storehouse of heat, which could be tapped by specially designed **ocean thermal energy conversion (OTEC)** plants (Figure 20-27); these plants exploit the temperature difference between warm surface waters and cold bottom waters in tropical areas. Each OTEC plant consists of a floating platform with enormous pipes that extend to a depth of 900 meters (3,000 feet). On the surface platform, ammonia gas, which boils at a relatively low temperature, is circulated through a series of tubes. The warm surface waters convert the ammonia into a gas that drives the blades of an electric turbine (Figure 20-28). The gas is then recondensed by cool water pumped up from the depths to start the cycle over again.

Electicity produced by OTEC plants can be transmitted to the shore for use by homes and businesses. Some plants could use it to desalinate salt water, thus providing drinking water for local populations.

FIGURE 20-27   Artist's conception of a 100-MWE ocean thermal energy conversion plant. Seawater is vaporized. The steam drives a turbine with a 125-foot diameter. The steam is then condensed, using 40°F water pumped from an ocean depth of 3,000 feet. This plant would make significant amounts of fresh water as a byproduct.

FIGURE 20-28   Schematic diagram of a closed-cycle ocean thermal power plant.

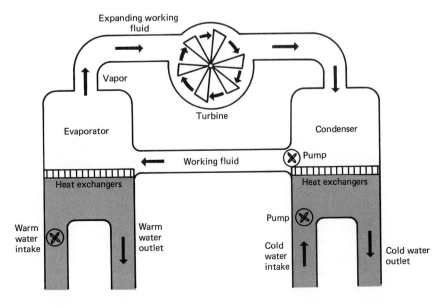

OTEC plants could theoretically operate day and night in tropical waters, providing energy for nearby cities and towns. However, like many other technologically feasible ways to generate energy, this one has some problems. The first one is its efficiency. Since large amounts of water must be used, a considerable amount of energy must be spent to pump water to the surface. An experimental plant off the coast of Hawaii, for example, used 80 percent of the electricity it generated just to pump water, giving it a low net energy yield. Second, suitable locations for OTEC plants are limited to a few places, such as the Gulf Coast and the waters off Hawaii, Guam, and Puerto Rico. These plants would also release considerable amounts of carbon dioxide into the atmosphere as cold waters in which this gas was once dissolved are heated at the surface. Cooling surface waters could affect fisheries and the local climate, increasing rainfall. Deeper waters, rich in nutrients, could also stimulate the growth of phytoplankton in surface waters, thus upsetting the ecological balance.

CONSERVATION

In America's attempt to satisfy future energy needs, most of our attention has focused on methods of producing more fossil fuels or on developing alternatives. Not enough attention has been given to ways of reducing energy consumption. In a Harvard Business School report entitled *Energy Future*, conservation is described as "no less an energy alternative than oil, gas, coal, or nuclear. Indeed in the near term," say the authors, "conservation could do more than any of the conventional sources to help the country deal with the energy problem."

Conservation's Short-Lived Triumph

Following the oil crises of the 1970s, the United States took drastic measures to slash energy waste—at home, at work, in the air, and on the highways. Consumers added insulation to their attics, bought smaller cars, and turned down their thermostats, saving enormous amounts of energy (Figure 20-29). The average gas mileage of a new car increased from a paltry 14 miles per gallon in 1974 to 26 miles per gallon in 1986, thanks to congressional action. Over the same period, factories cut their energy use; consequently, the amount of energy needed to produce a dollar of gross national product dropped 25 percent.

Conservation stemmed the tide of high oil prices and helped our ailing economy gain a foothold. In the early 1980s, however, the cutbacks in oil consumption and production by non-OPEC nations resulted in a glut of oil and stable oil prices. Stable oil prices helped stabilize the cost of consumer goods, quelling the economic turmoil that had strangled the United States and much of the rest of the world.

Because many non-OPEC nations, like Great Britain, increased exploration and oil production, OPEC's share of the world oil market fell. In 1977 OPEC nations supplied two-thirds of the world's oil. By 1985, their share had dropped to one-third. To combat their loss in market share, OPEC announced on December 1985 that they would cut prices to regain their position in the market; by April 1986, crude oil prices had been slashed in half.

Lowered energy prices, while good for many sectors of the economy, seem to have eroded our nation's resolve to conserve energy. In the past 7 years, energy conservation programs have been slashed from the federal budget. Many state and local governments now show little interest in the conservation programs they implemented in the 1970s. Alternative energy programs that promote solar and wind power, for instance, have been similarly dismantled or left to atrophy. Contributing to the rush back to our wasteful past, in 1985 at the request of Ford and General Motors, Congress rolled back the 27.5 miles-per-gallon (mpg) requirement for new automobiles to 26 mpg. The most recent retroaction came in 1987 with the passage of a popular highway law that allows states to increase the speed limit to 65 miles per hour on rural sections of their interstate highways, a measure that is bound to increase fuel consumption.

In many ways, cheap energy prices have headed us back to the wasteful pre-OPEC days. The American public and Congress appear to have forgotten the chief lesson of the 1970s: that nations dependent on oil cannot afford to waste it.

Compounding our troubles, warns Christopher Flavin, senior researcher at the Worldwatch Institute, is that current waste may be setting the stage for an even stronger OPEC. The OPEC nations have 56 percent of the world's oil reserves. Wasting our oil and the oil of non-OPEC nations, he says, only hastens the day when OPEC once again pulls the strings.

Getting Back on Track

Contrary to popular belief, the energy crisis is still with us. Today's cheap oil is a temporary market condition that has many people fooled. But we ignore the truth about oil's limited supply at our own peril. What we do about oil today—whether we waste it because it is temporarily cheap or use it wisely because it is ultimately limited—will profoundly influence our lives and the lives of our children.

We must stem the tide of the dangerous energy nonchalance now sweeping the nation and get back on track. The benefits of such action are many. Besides saving fuel, energy conservation reduces pollu-

FIGURE 20-29 Getting ready for winter. Adding insulation yourself will result in both energy and money savings. Many families in the northern states—New York, Pennsylvania, and Michigan—are investing in insulation, caulking, weather stripping, and storm windows. Their homes will be snug despite the icy blasts of winter.

tion, and by helping us stretch world oil supplies, it gives researchers additional time to develop alternatives to oil that are affordable and environmentally safe. Conservation can also help us sustain lower oil prices and retain our hard-won economic stability. Energy conservation is to our economy what preventive medicine is to health care.

The Untapped Potential

Despite what some government officials tell us, Americans have only begun to tap conservation. Enormous opportunities exist in buildings, industry, motorized vehicles, and appliances.

Consider some examples. Portland, Oregon, has adopted one of the nation's toughest building codes, requiring insulation in new as well as old homes, apartments, and office buildings. City officials predict that insulation alone will cut energy consumption in the city by 35 percent by 1995.

On another front, several auto manufacturers have test models that get 98 miles per gallon. The U.S. new car mileage (26 miles per gallon) is the lowest in the developed world. By increasing it to 40 or 50 miles per gallon, which some experts believe is easy to achieve, America could greatly stretch its oil supplies—creating more time to develop more efficient vehicles and alternative liquid fuels.

On still another front are enormous savings from lighting. The United States has 4.7 billion square meters (50 billion square feet) of commercial space, requiring roughly 100 power plants just to supply it with electricity for lighting. In Seattle, officials predict that they could cut their electrical demand for lighting by 80 percent. How? By switching to special 18-watt fluorescent screw-in bulbs that produce as much light as 75-watt bulbs, by changing to energy-efficient light switches,

and by using brighter interior surfaces and special sensors that shut off interior lights when natural light is sufficient. Nationwide, the savings of such a plan boggle the mind.

New, energy-efficient bulbs can be used in the home as well. Panasonic produces a screw-in, compact fluorescent bulb that will outlast nine standard incandescent lamps and saves enormous amounts of energy. The 15-watt bulb, for instance, replaces a 60-watt incandescent lamp and yields as much light. The $15 bulb will save $30 to $50 in electricity over its lifetime, depending on the cost of electricity. And, says the Fund for Renewable Energy and the Environment, if every home in America replaced just four of its frequently used light bulbs with these bulbs, the nation would save more electricity than is produced by six large power plants.

Finally, consider appliances. By 1992, California plans to cut the maximum allowable energy use in new refrigerators by half, saving enormous amounts of energy. This and other conservation measures have allowed California to contain its growth in energy demand at one-half the national average.

Perhaps one of the only major gains in conservation nationwide was the recent National Appliance Energy Conservation Act (1987). It calls for a mandatory 15–20 percent reduction in appliance energy use nationwide that will, in the next 20 years, eliminate the need for 22,000 megawatts of electricity—the amount of energy produced by 22 large power plants. It will save Americans well over $28 billion in electric bills.

Energy conservation makes good economic sense for the consumer and the producer. For example, improving the efficiency of machines and appliances—that is, reducing their energy demand—costs about 1 to 2 cents per kilowatt-hour of energy saved. In contrast, coal-fired power plants produce electricity for 5 to 7 cents

20 Energy

per kilowatt-hour. Nuclear power plants produce it for 10 to 12 cents per kilowatt-hour.

Resetting Our National Priorities

Americans conserved their way out of the economic maelstrom of the 1970s. Today, however, through energy nonchalance, waste, and the pure market approach to energy supply, we may well be seeding a new storm with far more devastating effects. It is time to reset our national priorities—to raise energy conservation to its full importance.

It is in the wisdom of our follies, says the French axiom, that we show our intelligence. But today wisdom is not enough. We need action. Through our colleges and universities, through our public schools, through government study and political leadership, we must raise the American consciousness about the primacy of energy and the dangers of ignoring the exponential depletion of this finite resource. The federal government and the states must take leadership roles in making energy conservation once again a national priority. Our long-term economic security depends on bringing energy conservation back into the American mainstream.

Personal Actions

There's almost no end to the things you can do to reduce energy use. This abundance of options is, in itself, both a blessing and a problem. It's a blessing because it gives you a wide assortment of areas to choose from; it's a curse because, faced with such choices, many people simply don't know which one or ones to choose, and so do nothing.

We have limited the following discussion to individual actions that do the most good—that is, those things that cost very little and yet make significant inroads into energy use. After reading this material, you may want to draw up your own plan to reduce resource consumption.

ENERGY CONSERVATION AROUND THE HOUSE. Whether you live in an apartment or a house, you can make significant contributions to resource conservation with little effort or monetary investment. You can begin by turning down the thermostat, which is one of the easiest and most cost-effective strategies available. A 4°C (6°F) drop in room temperature can reduce fuel consumption by 15–20 percent. Keeping your furnace thermostat at 15–20°C (60–68°F) can save enormous amounts of energy.

Try turning your thermostat down gradually. Drop it, on average, 1°F every few weeks until you reach the desired setting. This will give your body a chance to adjust. To help counterbalance the dropping temperature, you may want to dress more warmly. Insulated underwear, sweaters, and heavy socks can help you stay comfortable. Putting on a sweater is equivalent to raising the room temperature nearly 4°F. Wrapping up in a blanket while watching television or reading has the same effect.

You can drop the thermostat even further at night and stay perfectly warm without an electric blanket. Your body produces enormous amounts of heat (about as much as a 100-watt light bulb) and can keep you comfortable even in the coldest weather with blankets.

You can install an automatic thermostat to adjust daytime and nighttime temperatures in order to save heat. Automatic thermostats, in fact, pay for themselves in reduced energy bills in as few as 2 or 3 months to as many as 3 years, depending on who installs them and other factors.

To some people, turning down the thermostat means that they'll end up being cold and uncomfortable. There's a good reason for this: Many houses are too drafty, and lowering the thermostat setting reveals the frigid internal winds created by leaks. In the 1970s, many people who tried to conserve energy found their homes extremely uncomfortable and simply turned up the heat to fight drafts, complaining that conservation was a bad idea. This strategy is short-sighted and wasteful. It's far cheaper and a far wiser use of resources to seal the cracks through which air escapes with caulk and weather stripping.

Caulking and weather stripping have an astonishingly fast payback. In cold climates, they pay for themselves in reduced energy bills in 6 months to 1 year if you do the work yourself, or a little longer if you hire someone to do it for you. By reducing drafts, they will make your home more comfortable.

Turning down the setting on your water heater is another simple measure to reduce energy consumption. By turning the water heater to 140°F if you have a dishwasher and 120°F if you don't, you can save hundreds of kilowatts of energy a year. A study by Oak Ridge National Laboratory, for instance, showed that lowering the setting from 160°F to 140°F saves 400 kilowatts a year—as much electricity as some households use in a month or two. Lowering your water heater's thermostat is fairly easy and won't affect personal hygiene at all.

The measures just discussed achieve significant energy savings with virtually no expenditure. For homeowners willing to invest a little money to cut energy demands, four additional approaches with relatively quick paybacks are recommended. The first is ceiling insulation. Since most heat escapes through the ceiling, upgrading the insulation in your attic to R-30 (a measure of heat retention) can help cut energy consumption drastically. Depending on where you live and how warm you like your house to be, insulation can pay for itself in 3 to 7 years.

The second measure is storm windows. Self-installed,

storm windows may take 5 to 7 years to pay for themselves. If someone else does the work, the payback period is doubled.

In a society addicted to its creature comforts, however, it's important to remember that the payback for insulation and storm windows in one respect is immediate. Ceiling insulation, by far the easiest and cheapest to install in an existing home, reduces heat loss. This slows down the movement of air in the house and, like caulking and weather stripping, creates a cozier domicile— a payback few people seem to consider when debating whether to install insulation. Storm windows have the same effect. They eliminate cold spots and drafts and greatly increase the comfort level. What is more, they help reduce energy consumption, with all of its attendant environmental benefits. You save money and help reduce environmental deterioration—not a bad investment!

The third inexpensive energy conservation measure, which rapidly pays for itself, is insulation for water heaters and hot water pipes. Now available for $10 to $20, insulating blankets help hold in heat and reduce the overall energy demand. Easy to install insulation for hot water pipes has a similar effect.

The fourth measure is energy-efficient light bulbs. Now available in most grocery stores, the General Electric Miser series saves approximately 10 percent of energy. As mentioned earlier, Panasonic and Mitsubishi both sell screw-in fluorescent bulbs that use one-fourth of the energy of conventional incandescent bulbs. The Fund for Renewable Energy and the Environment sells these and other energy-saving devices through its *Renew America Catalog*.

ENERGY CONSERVATION ON THE ROAD.   Nationwide, automobiles consume approximately 280 billion liters (73 billion gallons) of gasoline each year. Much of that fuel is wasted by people driving erratically and at excessive speeds. By driving reasonably and sticking to the speed limit, you can cut personal gasoline consumption by 10 percent, saving $40 to $50 a year, and reducing pollution and the environmental impacts of oil production. Short trips that can be combined into one trip, or replaced by walking or riding a bicycle, could help further cut energy use.

Perhaps one of the biggest wastes of fuel occurs in commuting. Each year, commuters travel billions of kilometers. Often only one or two passengers ride in each car. This common practice wastes fuel and creates unnecessary pollution and crowding on our highways. Individuals can help reduce these and other problems by joining a van pool or taking a bus to work or school. Van pooling and buses are, on average, nearly five times more energy efficient than the automobile. For example, it takes 400 kilojoules (a unit of energy) to move a passenger 1 kilometer (0.6 mile) by van pool, train, or bus. Passenger cars consume 1,800 kilojoules and air-

lines, incidentally, require 3,800 kilojoules. In addition to being more efficient, van pools and mass transit pollute less per passenger kilometer traveled. If you can join a van pool or ride the bus, even occasionally, you might consider doing it. Your contribution, combined with that of other like-minded individuals, can add up quickly.

One of the wisest steps is purchasing an energy-efficient automobile. Certain models on the road, like the Chevy Sprint, get 58 mpg on the highway. If you must have a larger car, find the model that gets the best mileage.

No greater challenge exists for a democratic nation besieged with pressing problems than to identify, among the frantic rush of minor crises, the long-term problems that could potentially cripple it—and to act on them. At no time in our history has such action been so badly needed. Faced with shortages in important fossil fuels, it is time to redirect our society to build a sustainable energy system.

RAPID REVIEW

1. The twin oil crises of the 1970s awakened the developed countries to the extraordinary cost of their dependence on energy—especially imported oil. It showed us that everything we bought or did required energy, and lots of it.

2. In developed countries, fossil fuels, such as coal, oil, and natural gas, are the predominant sources of energy. Nuclear energy, conservation, and renewable energy sources have grown in importance since the oil crises.

3. In the Third World, renewable fuels form the mainstay of the energy diet.

4. Coal supplies about 23 percent of America's energy needs. It is burned today in electric utilities and in some factories and homes, where it releases the solar energy captured in the leaves of plants by photosynthesis millions of years ago.

5. Proven global coal reserves are estimated to be about 700 billion metric tons, enough to last for about 200 years. Undiscovered global reserves could last for another 1,700 years. Domestic coal supplies could last for 200 years at the current rate of consumption, making coal a likely energy source for many years to come.

6. Unfortunately, coal cannot be substituted easily or efficiently for oil and natural gas. And coal is a dirty fuel. Mining it causes enormous impacts. Unless we find much cleaner ways to burn it and strengthen our efforts to reclaim surface-mined land, many of our impressive coal deposits may lie forever buried in the earth's crust.

7. Fluidized bed combustion offers a way to burn coal cleanly and efficiently. Crushed coal is mixed with bits of limestone and propelled into a furnace in a strong current of air. The limestone reacts with the sulfur oxide gases, eliminating them from the smokestack gases. Despite the advantages of this technology, should global warming continue, modern society may switch from coal to other forms of energy that do not contribute carbon dioxide to the atmosphere.

8. Another promising technology is coal gasification, in which a combustible gas is produced from coal. New developments in this technology have greatly improved its efficiency.

9. Coal can also be treated to produce a thick, oily substance in a process called *coal liquefaction*. The oily product can be refined like crude oil to produce a variety of useful products, such as jet fuel, gasoline, kerosene, and chemicals needed to make drugs and plastics.

10. Unlike coal, oil is in short supply. By various estimates, the global proven reserves will last for only about 25 years at the current rate of consumption; the undiscovered reserves will last for only another 50 years at the current rate of consumption. With rising global consumption inevitable, these reserves could be depleted much sooner, creating enormous economic turmoil the world over unless we act— and act quickly—to find replacements.

11. U.S. oil reserves are in even worse condition. An estimated 100 billion barrels of oil now remain in the United States—enough for only 17 years at the current rate of consumption.

12. The picture for natural gas is a bit brighter than for oil globally, but not as good as for coal. Although estimates vary, proven and undiscovered reserves will last for 160 years at the current rate of consumption, but increased consumption is likely to reduce global supplies dramatically.

13. Domestically, the outlook for natural gas is much dimmer. The remaining 200 trillion cubic feet of gas will last for only 11 years. In the immediate future, the only way the United States can meet the demand for gas is by importing large quantities of liquid natural gas from abroad. However, transporting liquid natural gas is costly and dangerous.

14. Oil shale is a sedimentary rock formed millions of years ago from the mud at the bottom of lakes. It contains a solid organic material known as *kerogen*, which when heated is released from the rock.

15. The most valuable deposit of oil shale in the United States is found in Colorado, Wyoming, and Utah. With current technologies, 80 to 300 billion barrels of oil could be extracted, enough to last for 7 to 28 years.

16. Unfortunately, oil shale development is economically and environmentally costly.

17. Tar sands contain a thick, oily residue called *bitumen*, which can be extracted and refined, much like shale oil. Unfortunately, tar sand deposits are not extensive. Only about 1 billion barrels could be recovered from U.S. deposits, and only about 38 billion barrels could come from Canadian deposits.

18. It is clear that an immediate substitute for oil is needed. It is also time to start developing alternatives to natural gas and coal, especially some that do not add to global carbon dioxide levels.

19. Thankfully, numerous alternatives exist. The most likely candidates include nuclear energy, conservation, solar energy, wind energy, biomass, hydropower, and geothermal energy.

20. The sunlight striking an area the size of Connecticut each year could provide all the energy needed by the United States, and yet Americans have tapped only a tiny portion of the sun's potential.

21. Solar energy can be used to heat water for homes and industries and to heat building interiors. Two major heating systems are available: active and passive.

22. Active solar systems consist of solar collectors that absorb sunlight and convert it to heat. The heat is then carried away and used to heat building interiors or water.

23. Passive solar systems are strictly for space heating. The building itself becomes a collector and heat-storage device. South-facing windows and skylights let the winter sun penetrate the interior of the building. Sunlight strikes the walls and floors and is converted into heat. Cement or block walls store the heat and radiate it out into the room at night.

24. Solar energy can also be used to generate electricity. Sunlight may be concentrated by mirrors to boil water to run an electrical turbine. Electricity may also be formed in photovoltaic cells, thin wafers of silicon and other materials that, when struck by light, produce an electrical current. Solar cells could become a major source of energy as fossil fuels run out, but they are too highly priced now. What is needed is a more efficient solar cell and mass production to make it competitive with other forms of electricity.

25. The federal government currently provides $44 billion in subsidies to the nuclear, coal, oil, and

gas industries but almost no support to alternative sources. It is time to reverse this trend and build a sustainable energy system.

26. The earth stores enormous amounts of heat, or geothermal energy, which comes from the decay of naturally occurring radioactive substances and from molten rock in the earth's interior.

27. Most commercial geothermal energy today comes from hydrothermal convection zones, where heated underground water emerges as geysers or hot springs. Steam or hot water from these zones can be used to heat buildings and generate electricity. Despite the ease with which it can be used, the global geothermal capacity is small.

28. Hydropower makes a significant contribution to global energy and is bound to increase in the future. Unfortunately, much of the untapped hydropower is in regions far from population centers and industry. Some environmentalists believe that retrofitting existing nonhydroelectric dams with small generators could provide additional electricity without the environmental impacts created by building new dams.

29. Wind energy is contributing more and more energy to global electricity needs. The World Meteorological Organization estimates that 7–19 percent of the electricity needed by the United States could come from wind by 2000. Wind energy may also provide electricity to rural villages in the Third World, where large electric generating plants are unfeasible.

30. Wood, manure, crop wastes, and other forms of biomass supply 14–19 percent of the world's energy demands. In developing nations, where fossil fuel consumption is low, biomass may provide up to 90 percent of the total energy needed.

31. Wood is the most widely used form of biomass. In developed countries, like Norway and the United States, wood supplies about 10 percent of the home heating fuel. But most of the wood in these countries is burned by the forest products industry.

32. In developing nations, 2.5 billion people depend on wood as their primary fuel. Over half of them are depleting local wood reserves faster than they can be replenished. Should this population continue to rise and should nothing be done to replenish the forests, by 2000 the number of persons facing shortages or depleting their supplies will reach 3 billion.

33. Other forms of biomass can also be used to produce energy. Manure, human wastes, and other organic wastes, for instance, can be used to produce methane gas. Plant material can be used to generate ethanol. Fuel farms that produce crops to make ethanol could provide much of America's liquid fuel in the coming years if the net energy yield of the process can be improved.

34. Hydrogen gas, produced from water, is a renewable fuel that burns very cleanly. Unfortunately, hydrogen is costly and explosive. Using inexpensive renewable energy resources could make it more affordable in the coming years.

35. The tides can be tapped by special dams that channel the water through openings equipped with turbines. Unfortunately, the global energy capacity of tides is rather small.

36. The ocean is a vast storehouse of heat, which could be tapped by specially designed ocean thermal energy conversion (OTEC) plants. These plants use the warm surface waters to vaporize ammonia gas, which then runs an electric turbine. The gas is cooled by cold bottom waters that are pumped to the surface. Unfortunately, the energy yield of OTEC plants is poor, making the electricity uncompetitive.

37. In America's attempt to satisfy future energy needs, most of our attention has focused on methods of producing more fossil fuels or on developing alternatives. Not enough attention has been given to ways of reducing energy consumption. Nevertheless, conservation has created some enormous fuel savings. The average gas mileage of a new car, for instance, increased from 14 mpg in 1974 to 26 mpg in 1986. Over the same period, factories cut their energy use as well; the amount of energy needed to produce a dollar of gross national product dropped 25 percent. Conservation helped stem the tide of high oil prices by creating a temporary oversupply of oil, allowing consumer prices to stabilize and our economy to recover.

38. Lowered energy prices, while good for many sectors of the economy, seem to have eroded our nation's resolve to conserve energy. Federal conservation programs have been cut drastically. Many state and local governments now show little interest in the conservation programs they implemented in the 1970s.

39. The American public and Congress appear to have forgotten the chief lesson of the 1970s: that nations that depend on oil cannot afford to waste it.

40. Compounding our troubles, current waste may be setting the stage for an even stronger OPEC.

41. Despite what some government officials tell us, Americans have only begun to tap conservation. Enormous opportunities exist in buildings, industry, motorized vehicles, and appliances. Energy conservation makes good economic sense for consumers and producers. For example, improving the efficiency of machines and appliances costs about 1 to 2 cents per kilowatt-hour of energy saved, one-fifth of what it costs to produce electricity from coal and one-tenth of what it costs to produce electricity from nuclear energy.

42. We need personal actions as well. Consumers can begin by turning down their thermostats and wearing more clothes in the winter, caulking and weather stripping, turning down the setting on water heaters, insulating water heaters, driving at the speed limit, car pooling, using mass transit, and buying energy-efficient vehicles.

KEY TERMS AND CONCEPTS

Acid mine drainage
Acid precursors
Active solar systems
Anthracite
Arctic National Wildlife Refuge
Area strip mine
Biomass
Bitumen
Bituminous
Coal
Coal liquefaction
Conservation
Contour mine
Draglines
Fluidized bed combustion
Fossil fuel
Fuel Farms
Gasification
Gasohol
Geopressurized zones
Geothermal energy
Hot rock zones
Hydrogen
Hydropower
Hydrothermal convection zones
In situ retort
Kerogen
Lignite
Microwaves
Natural gas

Net energy efficiency
Ocean thermal energy conversion (OTEC)
Oil
Oil shale
Organization of Petroleum Exporting Countries (OPEC)
Overburden
Passive solar systems
Photovoltaics
Proven reserves
Satellite solar power station
Shale oil
Slurry
Smokestack scrubbers
Solar electricity
Solar energy
Spent shale
Subsidence
Sulfuric acid
Surface retorts
Surface Mining Control and Reclamation Act
Tar sands
Tidal power
Ultimate production
Wind farm
Windmill
Wind power

QUESTIONS FOR STUDY AND DISCUSSION

1. Debate the statement "America seems to have forgotten the chief lessons learned from the oil crises of the 1970s."

2. Describe the major sources of energy used by developed countries. Which ones are in short supply? Which ones do you expect to be plentiful 50 years from now?

3. Debate the statement "The Third World relies primarily on renewable energy. Since it is renewable, they have nothing to worry about."

4. Define the terms **proven reserves**, **ultimate reserves**, and **undiscovered reserves**.

5. How large is the global proven reserve of coal? How long will that last at the current rate of consumption?

6. Describe the environmental impacts of surface and underground mining of coal.

7. Describe fluidized bed combustion and draw a schematic diagram of the process. Why does it produce more energy and less airborne pollution than a conventional coal-fired power plant?

8. Debate the statement "The world has abundant coal. Consequently, coal will become our major fuel source when oil runs out."

9. Define coal gasification and coal liquefaction.

10. How much oil is left globally, and how long will it last at the current rate of consumption? How much oil does the United States have within its boundaries?

11. Discuss the pros and cons of drilling for oil in the Arctic National Wildlife Refuge.

12. What is the estimated global ultimate production of natural gas? How long will that last? What is the estimated proven reserves of natural gas for the United States?

13. Describe oil shale and tar sands. What are they? Where did they come from? How big are the deposits? What are the impacts of their production?

14. Make a list of the conventional energy sources and what they are used for; then make another list of alternative energy sources that could replace them. For instance, ethanol and coal liquefaction could replace oil.

15. What is an active solar system? What is a passive solar system? How are they similar? How are they different?

16. Describe two methods by which electricity can be generated from sunlight.

17. How realistic are plans to capture solar energy in space and beam it to earth?

18. An engineering professor has discovered a new source of energy. What would you want to know about it before promoting its widespread use?

19. What is geothermal energy? What form of geothermal energy is most readily accessible?

20. Debate the statement "The United States has vast untapped hydropower potential, which could produce enormous amounts of electricity."

21. What are the problems associated with wind energy, and how can they be overcome?

22. What is biomass energy? How important is it to our energy future?

23. Describe the pros and cons of tidal power, hydrogen, and ocean thermal energy conversion.

24. Do you agree with the following statement? "Conservation is no less an energy alternative than oil, gas, coal, and nuclear energy and is often much cheaper."

25. Make a list of ways you can cut energy consumption by 10 percent.

26. You are appointed head of your city's energy department and asked to devise a long-term energy strategy that will carry your city well into the middle of the next century. Prepare your plan and defend it.

SUGGESTED READINGS

Balzhiser, R. E. and Yeager, K. E. "Coal-fired Power Plants of the Future." *Scientific American* 257(3): 100–107, 1987. Very readable account of fluidized bed combustion and coal gasification.

Borrelli, P. "Oilscam." *The Amicus Journal* 9(4): 20–25, 1987. Good account of the proposals to drill for oil in the Arctic National Wildlife Refuge.

Chandler, W. U. *Energy Productivity: Key to Environmental Protection and Economic Progress. Worldwatch Paper 63. Washington, D.C.: Worldwatch Institute, 1985. Superb coverage of energy efficiency in transportation, industry, and the home.*

Crawford, M. "Back to the Energy Crisis." *Science* 235: 626–627, 1987. Contains shocking predictions on the future cost of oil.

Flavin, C. *Electricity's Future: The Shift to Efficiency and Small-Scale Power.* Worldwatch Paper 61. Washington, D.C.: Worldwatch Institute, 1984. Detailed analysis of electrical energy production in the United States, offering alternatives to the conventional sources of electricity.

Flavin, C. *World Oil: Coping with the Dangers of Success.* Worldwatch Paper 66. Washington, D.C.: Worldwatch Institute, 1985. Excellent analysis of world oil.

Flavin, C. *Electricity for a Developing World: New Directions.* Worldwatch Paper 70. Washington, D.C.: Worldwatch Institute, 1986. Intriguing look at ways to satisfy rural energy demands in the developing world.

Flavin, C., and Durning, A. B. *Building on Success: The Age of Energy Efficiency.* Worldwatch Paper 82. Washington, D.C.: Worldwatch Institute, 1988. Excellent coverage of energy conservation strategies.

Fri, R. W. "Rethinking Energy Security: New Directions for Oil Policy." *Environment* 29(5): 16–20, 38–42, 1987. Detailed report on oil and the directions the U.S. government should take.

Hirsch, R. L. "Impending United States Energy Crisis." *Science* 235: 1467–1472, 1987. A sobering look at our energy future.

International Institute for Environment and Development and the World Resources Institute. *World Resources 1987.* New York: Basic Books, 1987. Excellent overview of global energy trends.

Landsberg, H. H. "Rethinking Energy Security: The Case for Coal in the United States." *Environment* 29(6): 18–20, 38–43, 1987. Detailed and somewhat technical assessment of coal.

Reisner, M. "The Rise and Fall and Rise of Energy Conservation." *The Amicus Journal* 9(2): 22–31, 1987. Excellent overview of energy conservation, especially the untapped potential of this resource.

Renner, M. *Rethinking the Role of the Automobile.* Worldwatch Paper 84. Washington, D.C.: Worldwatch Institute, 1988. Detailed discussion of ways to improve mileage and reduce emissions of the world automobile fleet.

21

Nuclear Energy and Radiation

The world's first atomic bomb was dropped on Hiroshima, Japan, in 1945. From the huge explosion shot an intense flash of light that blinded many onlookers, some permanently. With it came a surge of intense heat that burned the flesh of people in its path, killing many outright and disfiguring others. The heat wave also ignited fires in buildings that set the city ablaze. The light and heat flashes were followed in quick succession by a powerful shock wave that flattened buildings in a huge circle around the blast. An enormous mushroom-shaped cloud rose from the city, carrying with it radioactive dust that spread throughout the world (Figure 21-1).

This momentous and catastrophic explosion, which many people think helped bring the long and costly Second World War to an end, also ushered in the Nuclear Age—an age of nuclear weapons and nuclear power. The power of the atom, we now find, has become a double-edged sword, bearing vast potential for destruction, on the one hand, and holding a promise for huge quantities of energy, on the other. This chapter is primarily about nuclear energy and radiation. It looks at the impacts of nuclear power as well as its benefits, starting with some background information.

UNDERSTANDING ATOMIC ENERGY AND RADIATION

Atomic Structure

All matter—whether solid, liquid, or gaseous—is composed of tiny particles called **atoms**. They are the fundamental units of all living and nonliving matter. Each atom, in turn, is composed of a dense, centrally located **nucleus** containing positively charged particles called **protons** and electrically neutral particles called **neutrons**. The nucleus contains virtually all of the mass of an atom. Surrounding the nucleus is a region called the **electron cloud**, where tiny, almost massless, negatively charged particles, called **electrons**, are found. They spin in an orbit around the nucleus, ever attracted to its positive charge and always in motion at nearly the speed of light.

Atoms combine with other atoms to form molecules, like water (H_2O), which contains two atoms of the element hydrogen and one atom of the element oxygen.

Isotopes and the Origin of Radiation

There are over 100 different elements known to science, 92 of which occur naturally in the earth's crust. Each element differs from the next in the number of protons it contains in its nucleus. Thus, the element carbon always has 12 protons and the element oxygen always has 16 protons. Scientists classify the elements by the number of protons in their nuclei; this is called the **atomic number**. The atomic number of carbon is 12, and that of oxygen is 16.

In any given element, the number of electrons in the electron cloud of its atoms is always equal to the number of protons in the nucleus. Thus, atoms are electrically neutral.

The number of protons in the atoms of any given

FIGURE 21-1 Nuclear bomb detonation in the Pacific test area on February 28, 1954. Note the characteristic mushroom-shaped cloud of highly radioactive dust.

element is always the same. The number of neutrons, however, may vary. For instance, all atoms of the element uranium have 92 protons in their nuclei. However, some uranium nuclei contain 143 neutrons and others have 146 neutrons. These different forms of the same element are called **isotopes**. The mass of an atom is equal to the sum of the number of protons and neutrons; thus, some uranium atoms have an atomic mass of 235 and others have a mass of 238. Most elements are a mixture of isotopes; some of them are stable, some are not. The unstable ones give off radiation and are therefore called **radioisotopes**.

The Nature of Radiation

In 1896 the scientist Henri Becquerel accidentally discovered that the element radium, when placed over a photographic plate in the dark, exposed the film. Pierre and Marie Curie, two French scientists, later discovered that radium was radioactive—that is, it emitted radiation, which was responsible for Becquerel's unexplained phenomenon. Three forms of radiation come from the nuclei of radium atoms: **alpha particles**, containing two protons and two neutrons; **beta particles**, negatively charged particles similar to electrons; and **gamma rays**, which are similar to X-rays. These are the major forms of radiation.

Alpha particles are relatively heavy. They can travel only 8 centimeters (3 inches) in air and can be easily stopped by material as thin as a sheet of paper or human skin (Figure 21-2). They are dangerous, however, if they are breathed into the lungs or ingested in contaminated food. In the lung or in the digestive tract, they can irradiate cells, causing mutations and cancer.

Beta particles, on the other hand, are much lighter and can travel much greater distances. They can even penetrate skin to irradiate underlying tissues. Wood or a thin layer of lead will stop them dead in their tracks.

Gamma rays are potentially the most dangerous form of radiation, for they can pass through walls and can easily penetrate the skin, reaching internal organs. A thick concrete or lead shield is needed to block them.

Radioactive Decay

Radioisotopes emit radiation—alpha particles, beta particles, gamma rays, and others of lesser importance—from their nuclei to become more stable. Thus, over time, a mass of radioactive material actually decreases. The measure of its decrease in mass is called its **half-life**. A kilogram of a radioactive compound with a half-life of 10 years, for instance, will weigh one-half of a kilogram if left to sit from 1985 to 1995. By 2005, it will weigh one-quarter of a kilogram.

The half-lives of isotopes vary from a fraction of a second to tens of thousands of years. For example, iodine-131 has a half-life of 8 days; cesium-137, 27 years; strontium-90, 28 years; carbon-14, 5,600 years; and plutonium-239, 24,000 years.

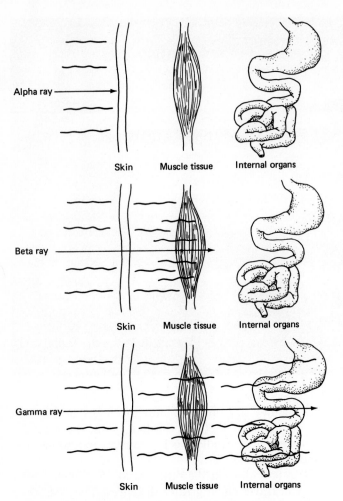

FIGURE 21-2 Relative ability of alpha, beta, gamma rays to penetrate the body.

THE HEALTH EFFECTS OF RADIATION

The extensive use of nuclear energy for electrical production, at least for the next few decades, as well as the increasing use of radiation in medicine for diagnosis and treatment, could mean that humans will be subjected to ever-increasing levels of radiation in the coming decades. It is important, therefore, to understand the impact of radiation on human life. In the following section, we discuss two broad categories of effects: nongenetic and genetic effects.

The effects of radiation, in general, vary with the age of the individual. Fetuses and newborns are, therefore, much more sensitive than adults. Sensitivity also varies according to the type of tissue or organ. Fast-growing cells, such as those lining the intestines, those that produce hairs, and those in the bone marrow, are most sensitive. Cartilage, muscle, and nervous tissues, which do not divide, are much more resistant.

The effects of radiation also vary with the intensity of exposure. The higher the dose, the more serious the effects, and the more quickly they are manifested.

Radiation doses are frequently measured in *rads*, a measure of energy absorption by the tissue (radiation absorbed dose). A rad is equal to about 100 ergs of energy per gram of tissue. An erg is an extremely small amount of energy—approximately the amount imparted by a mosquito alighting on your arm.

Nongenetic Effects

One way of looking at radiation effects is to look at three-week survival rates. Individuals exposed to 250 rads or less survive radiation exposure, but often suffer a higher incidence of cancer later on in life. However, as the dose increases to 400–500 rads, only 50 percent of the people exposed will survive for three weeks. At doses of 900 rads or greater, all people die within this period.

What are some of the symptoms displayed by persons exposed to radiation? Persons receiving less than 25 rads would not be aware of changes in their immediate health. (The likelihood of cancer, as you shall soon see, however, is increased considerably.) When the dose rises to 100 rads, they may suffer from weakness, fatigue, vomiting, and diarrhea. Eventually, however, these symptoms disappear, and the individual begins to function normally. At a radiation exposure of 400–500 rads, individuals experience extreme nausea, vomiting, hair loss, and fatigue. To make matters worse, this level of radiation impairs red blood cell production, resulting in severe anemia. White blood cell production is also severely hampered. Since white blood cells help protect the body against bacterial infection, radiation victims are susceptible to severe infections. This radiation dose also destroys blood platelets, tiny elements in the blood that promote blood clotting. The result is massive hemorrhaging and excessive blood loss. Individuals exposed to 400–500 rads, therefore, usually die from one or a combination of the following: anemia, hemorrhage, and severe bacterial infections (Table 12-1).

Much of the information on radiation's effects comes from studies of the survivors of the nuclear bomb blasts in Hiroshima and Nagasaki at the end of World War II. Thousands of people were exposed to radiation doses ranging from 100 to 150 rads. The immediate effects included burns, fever, loss of hair, fatigue, intestinal bleeding, vomiting, and diarrhea. If the radiation damaged their bone marrow, many delayed effects were observed, including anemia, leukemia (cancer of the blood), and infections due to white blood cell suppression.

The children of pregnant mothers who were within 1,200 meters of the center of the explosion were born with severe birth defects, including mental retardation

Table 21-1 The Effects of Radiation on Humans

Radiation Dosage in Rads	Percent that Will Die	Other Symptoms
Above 10,000	100	Death in two days due to brain and heart damage.
3,000	100	Permanent damage of brain, spinal cord, bone marrow and intestines; bleeding, infections.
2,000	100	Permanent destruction of bone marrow and intestines; severe dehydration, bleeding and infections.
1,000	100	Permanent destruction of bone marrow and permanent damage to intestines.
600	60	Permanent destruction of bone marrow
400–500	50	Fatigue, nausea, vomiting, loss of hair; reduced number of blood platelets and white blood cells; bleeding and infections.
100–250*	0	Fatigue, nausea, vomiting, loss of hair, diarrhea, ulcers of gut; some may suffer permanent loss of fertility.
25–100	0	No visible effects; lower number of white blood cells.
0–25	0	No measurable effects

* *Note:* All individuals exposed to 100 rads or more will experience fatigue, nausea, vomiting, diarrhea, and hair loss.

and deformities of the skull, heart, and skeleton. Many of the survivors and members of their families are shunned today by the Japanese, who are fearful of the long-term genetic effects of radiation.

Genetic Effects: Cancer, Birth Defects, and Mutations

Experiments on laboratory animals have shown that radiation causes cancer in a variety of organs, such as the lymph glands, breasts, lungs, ovaries, and skin. Years of research confirm that radiation in humans causes various forms of cancer. Consider the following examples:

1. Skin cancer was prevalent among radiologists in the early days of the profession before adequate safeguards were instituted.
2. Bone cancer appeared in many women who painted radium dials on watches in the 1940s. Apparently, the women ingested radium when drawing paint brushes to a point with their lips.
3. Uranium miners have a high incidence of lung cancer, apparently from breathing radioactive radon gas found in the air in and around mines.

4. Children irradiated in the womb (during routine maternal pelvic X-ray examinations) have a 50 percent higher cancer rate than children who were not X-rayed during gestation.
5. The rate of leukemia was substantially higher among Japanese citizens who had survived the bomb blast than in unexposed Japanese citizens from other cities. Leukemia often showed up 30 years after the bombing.

Although no one knows exactly what causes cancer, many experts believe that most tumors result from genetic changes in the cells of the body. These changes, or **mutations**, may be caused by chemical agents or by physical agents such as radiation. These mutagenic agents, scientists believe, cause cells to divide uncontrollably, thus forming a tumor. The resultant tumor grows, draining the individual's strength, and often spreads through the lymphatic vessels to other parts of the body, where secondary tumors form. Eventually drained by the rapidly growing tumors, the individual dies.

Scientists have long known that radiation can also damage the chromosomes of germ cells—the sperm and ova. These mutations can be passed to an individual's offspring, and may show up as birth defects or result in cancer early in life. Background radiation probably results in one mutation for every million sperm or ova produced. Additional radiation, say from X-rays or from an accident at a nuclear power plant, can greatly increase the rate of mutation. James F. Crow, an eminent University of Wisconsin geneticist, suggests that any amount of radiation is potentially damaging to genetic material.

New and controversial research shows that exceedingly low levels of radiation have a more significant effect than was previously thought. Studies also indicate that radiation is cumulative—that is, low levels add up over many years. A study by the National Academy of Sciences suggests that the current health standard—0.17 rad per year for the general public—may be too high. This level of exposure, the study asserts, could increase cancer rates by 2 percent and increase the incidence of genetic defects by about 1 per 2,000 newborns. Against strong opposition, the academy and other scientists have suggested reducing the allowable level of radiation to 0.017 rad per year.

NUCLEAR POWER

Atomic Fission and Chain Reactions

Nuclear reactors and the first generation of nuclear bombs (the so-called fission bombs) do not capture energy from radioactive decay, but instead draw their energy from **nuclear fission**—the splitting of certain atoms that occurs when they are struck by certain forms of radiation. Uranium atoms are highly fissionable, or fissile. When struck by neutrons, a form of radiation given off by uranium nuclei, they split into fragments, called **daughter nuclei** (Figure 21-3). Enormous amounts of energy are given off during fission. So are additional neutrons. The neutrons continue to bombard other uranium nuclei, causing still other fissions. In power plants, the rate of fission is controlled by limiting the concentration of uranium in the fuel and by other means discussed later. Exceedingly complex in design, nuclear plants use the energy given off by this carefully controlled **chain reaction** to boil water to make steam that turns electrical turbines. In atomic bombs, uranium is more highly concentrated and the chain reaction is uncontrolled or unmodulated, causing a huge explosion that releases enormous amounts of energy. Atomic explosions cannot occur in reactors because of the low concentration of fuel. As we shall see in our discussion of Chernobyl and Three Mile Island, however, nonnuclear explosions can rip apart a reactor, spewing radioactive material into the air.

Uranium contains a lot of energy. A kilogram (2.2 pounds) of uranium, for instance, produces the same explosive force as 9,000 metric tons of TNT. Half a kilogram (1.1 pound) of uranium releases as much fuel as 1,450 metric tons of coal. It is no wonder, then, that modern civilization has set its sights on this technology.

Nuclear Reactors

The uranium fuel used in all large nuclear power plants is uranium-235 (Figure 21-4). It comes from uranium ore, found largely in the western United States. Uranium ore is a mixture of uranium-235, which is fissionable, and uranium-238, which is nonfissionable. Uranium-235 forms less than 1 percent of most uranium ores; uranium-238 makes up the balance.

To create fuel for nuclear power plants, the nuclear industry must first increase the concentration of uranium-235 to about 3 percent at a fuel enrichment plant. The enriched fuel, called **yellow cake**, is then formed into pellets. These are inserted into thin, stainless-steel

FIGURE 21-3 Nuclear fission. The chain reaction starts when a uranium-235 atomis is struck by a neutron given off by other uranium-235 nuclei. Uranium is split into fission fragments or daughter nuclei. Additional neutrons are given off, thus splitting other atoms.

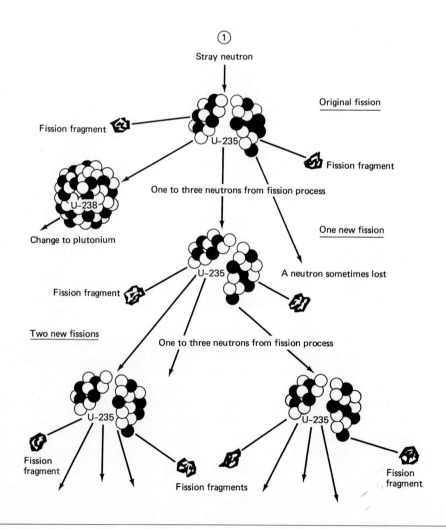

tubes, forming **fuel rods**. About 4 meters (12 feet) long and about 1.2 centimeters ($^1/_2$ inch) in diameter, fuel rods are then bundled together, 30 to 300 per bundle, and lowered into the core of the reactor (Figure 21-5).

The **reactor core** provides a site where nuclear fission can be carefully controlled. Bathed in water to draw off heat, the reactor core is contained by a **reactor vessel** with a 15-centimeter (6-inch) steel casing (Figures 21-6, 21-7, and 21-8).

In most countries, the reactor vessel is usually housed in a **containment building**, a dome-like structure with 1.2-meter (4-foot) walls of cement (Figure 21-9). Its function is to contain the radiation in case the reactor vessel or pipes rupture during an accident. Unfortunately, not all reactors have complete containment buildings; the infamous nuclear reactor at Chernobyl, discussed shortly, had only a partial containment building, which proved inadequate in the fateful accident in 1986. Twenty of the Soviet Union's 44 reactors now in operation and one U.S. reactor in the state of Washington (closed down shortly after the Chernobyl disaster) used to make plutonium for nuclear weapons have the same design.

The intensity of the chain reaction is controlled pri-

marily by neutron-absorbing **control rods**. Made of cadmium or boron steel, the control rods fit in between the fuel rods and can be raised or lowered to control the rate of fission. Raising them starts the chain reaction and lowering them back in place can shut it down almost entirely. Intermediate levels of fission occur between these two extremes.

The energy released from nuclear fission in the fuel rods heats the water bathing the reactor core, as mentioned earlier. But to avoid radioactive contamination, this heat is transferred to water contained in huge pipes in the wall of the reactor vessel. The superheated water boils and produces steam (Figure 21-10). The steam is used to spin an electrical turbine.

Besides the reactor vessel and the containment building, nuclear reactors are equipped with a host of safety devices—for example, backup power units for the controls, redundant electrical wiring in case some of it burns out, and redundant pipes in case one bursts. Perhaps the most important safety device is the *emergency cooling system*, which provides cold water to the reactor core should it become overheated. The result is a technology that exceeds most others known to modern civilization. This complex technol-

FIGURE 21-4 The largest operating nuclear power plant in New England. This is the Millstone Nuclear Power Station, Waterford, Connecticut, located on the north shore of Long Island Sound.

FIGURE 21-5 A nuclear-fuel-assembly storage rack at the Yankee Nuclear Power Station.

FIGURE 21-6 An 800-ton nuclear vessel dwarfs on-lookers as it leaves the site at Mount Vernon, Indiana, where it was fabricated. It is 72 feet long and 22 feet in diameter. Heat from the nuclear reactions contained in the vessel will produce steam sufficient to generate 809 megawatts of electrical power.

ogy can yield some unpleasant and costly surprises. The hydrogen bubble that built up in the Three Mile Island reactor, which exposed the core and threatened to blow a hole in the reactor vessel, is one of those surprises described shortly. So was the catastrophic steam explosion at the Chernobyl reactor. Both were events that nuclear engineers had simply not foreseen.

Pros and Cons of Nuclear Fission

Few technologies have been as hotly debated as nuclear power. The following discussion summarizes the major views for and against nuclear power.

VIEW IN FAVOR OF NUCLEAR POWER

1. *Provides an abundant fuel supply.* Uranium-235 is a limited resource, but proponents of nuclear power believe that a family of reactors, called **breeder reactors**, which convert uranium-238 into fissionable plutonium-239, could provide energy for hundreds of years. Spent fuel rods and wastes from uranium processing plants in the United States, predict some experts, could last for 1,000 years.

2. *Helps reduce our dependence on foreign oil.* Proponents of nuclear power believe that further reductions in our dependence on foreign oil could be made by switching to electricity from nuclear power plants.

3. *Produces low radiation exposure.* Nuclear power plants, when operating normally, release very little radiation. In fact, one study showed that coal-fired power plants released more radiation from their smokestacks. On the average, Americans receive 0.003 millirem (a measure of exposure) a year from nuclear power plants but as much as 100 to 250 millirems from X-rays, television sets, and naturally occurring radioactivity. The added risk of cancer to an individual is equivalent to smoking one cigarette per year.

4. *Is environmentally safe.* A properly functioning nuclear power plant is a much cleaner source of energy than a coal-fired power plant. In one year, a coal-fired plant producing 1,000 megawatts of electricity also produces 300,000 metric tons of ash; a nuclear plant produces only about a ton of fission waste per year. Coal plants also release sulfur dioxide, nitrogen oxides, carbon dioxide, particulates, mercury, and other air pollutants. Solid wastes from coal plants contain selenium, mercury, benzopyrene, and some radioactive materials, such as uranium and thorium.

FIGURE 21-7 Loading nuclear fuel. The first fuel bundle at the Duane Arnold Energy Center near Palo, Iowa, is being lowered into its slot in the nuclear reactor. The reactor contains a grid guide structure (visible in the reactor vessel), control rods, and water. The 600-pound fuel bundle is supported by a cable in the center. The cartridge-like posts ringing the reactor are the bolts for fastening the reactor vessel head in place. This reactor has a capacity of 550 megawatts. It would require burning 25,000 acres of redwoods or $3\frac{1}{2}$ million tons of garbage each year to furnish the energy equivalent to that from the 19 tons of nuclear fuel that will be consumed each year in this reactor.

5. *Is safe.* The probability of an accident in the United States that would release large amounts of radioactivity, said the supporters for many years, is no more than 1 in 1 million—about the probability of being struck by lightning. Other sources of electricity appear to pose far greater risks. For instance, each year 30 to 110 people lose their lives in coal mine accidents, mishaps during coal transportation, and from air pollution resulting from coal combustion.

VIEW OPPOSED TO NUCLEAR POWER

1. *Provides an abundant fuel supply.* Opponents of nuclear power remind nuclear supporters that the

FIGURE 21-8 Reactor vessel. This is the "heart" of the 500 megawatt nuclear-fueled electric generating plant near Monticello, Minnesota. The tubular structures seen in the picture contain the uranium oxide fuel. A reactor vessel such as this may receive over 100,000 pounds of uranium oxide. Cooling water keeps the heat generated by the vessel at about 1,000°F.

FIGURE 21-9 This is the Portland General Electric Nuclear Plant on the shores of the Columbia River at Rainier, Oregon. The dome-shaped containment building that shields the reactor is a characteristic feature of nuclear plants. Note the mammoth cooling tower to the left.

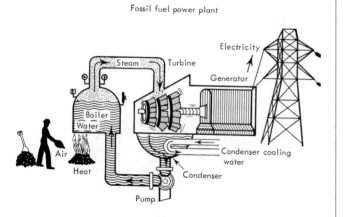

Fossil fuel power plant

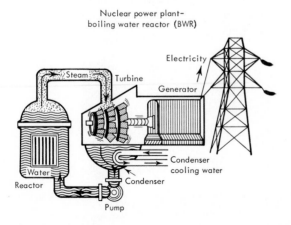

Nuclear power plant–
boiling water reactor (BWR)

FIGURE 21-10 Comparison of cooling systems for fossil-fuel power plant and nuclear power plant (boiling water reactor).

U.S. breeder program was canceled in 1983 by the U.S. Congress because of high costs and other problems. France, which now has breeder reactors in operation, has found that they are costly and not as effective as was once hoped. The average breeder reactor requires about 30 years to reach the breakeven point—that is, the point at which it produces as much plutonium fuel as it has consumed in the form of uranium-235. Since reactors have a 30-year life span at best, the breeder may never deliver on the promise of abundant fuel. Without the breeder, the nuclear industry will be forced to rely on relatively scarce uranium-235, the supply of which may last for only another 40 years or so.

2. *Helps reduce our dependence on foreign oil.* Not much oil is freed up for other uses by the use of nuclear energy to produce electricity because most power plants consume coal. Our dependence on foreign oil has actually begun to increase again in recent years because of falling domestic supplies and despite an expansion of our nuclear capacity. The truth is that oil and nuclear energy are two very different forms of energy, used for very different purposes.

3. *Produces low radiation exposure.* Although the radiation released from the routine operation of a nuclear plant is very small, some isotopes released from plants accumulate in animal tissues. For instance, cesium-137 concentrates in muscles, and iodine-131 concentrates in the milk of cattle and in the human thyroid. Thus, low background levels can result in significant exposure to internal organs. Radiation is also released from uranium mines and mills, ura-

nium mill tailings piles, processing plants, waste dumps, and transportation accidents, resulting in significant exposure.

An accident at a nuclear power plant can release enormous amounts of radiation. For instance, the major disaster at the Soviet Union's Chernobyl reactor in 1986 released 7,000 kilograms (15,400 pounds) of radioactive materials that contaminated many European countries. That accident injured 1,000 people, killed 31, caused at least a $3 to $5 billion loss to the Soviet Union, and may result in 5,000 to 1,000,000 cases of cancer in the Soviet Union and Europe. If the Chernobyl accident had taken place at one of the many nuclear power plants closer to major urban centers, the damage would have been substantially higher. If, for instance, it had taken place at the Salem 2 Nuclear Reactor in Salem, New Jersey, about 100,000 people would have died within a few months of the accident from radiation poisoning. Approximately 40,000 cases of cancer would have resulted from a similar accident, and the economic damage would have come to $150 billion (Table 21-2).

4. *Is environmentally safe.* Nuclear power plants are generally cleaner than coal-fired power plants, but they produce 40 percent more thermal pollution per kilowatt of electricity than a coal-fired power plant because fission releases more heat than coal, oil, and natural gas.

5. *Is safe.* Several minor and two major nuclear reactor accidents have already occurred in the 40-year life span of the nuclear industry. A near meltdown of the reactor resulted from a fire in 1975 at the Brown's Ferry plant in Alabama. A study by a prominent nuclear engineer and nuclear advocate, Norman Rasmussen of the Massachusetts Institute of Techno-

logy, however, determined that the probability of an accident was not more than 1 in 10,000 reactor years. What does this mean? In 1986, 374 nuclear reactors were in operation worldwide; another 157 were on order. Given the Rasmussen report estimates, when all 531 reactors are in operation, we can expect a major nuclear accident every 19 years.

The Rasmussen report is now largely discredited. It is no longer considered valid because, critics say, it greatly underestimates the probability of a nuclear accident. Interestingly, the Three Mile Island and Chernobyl accidents were only 7 years apart.

6. *Is costly.* When nuclear power was first conceived, proponents argued that it would be so cheap to produce that it wouldn't be economical to meter it. Today, 40 years later, that situation is far from reality. Nuclear power is, in fact, one of the most expensive forms of electricity now commercially available, costing 10 to 12 cents per kilowatt compared to 5 to 7 cents per kilowatt for coal (Table 21-3).

One of the chief reasons why nuclear power plants are so costly is that they are expensive to build. A large plant costs $2 to $4 billion. A comparable coal-fired power plant costs $0.5 to $1 billion. Repairs are extraordinarily costly and time-consuming as well, because of the danger of radiation exposure to workers. Thus, what would be a simple and inexpensive repair may take months and may cost millions of dollars, further adding to the cost of the electricity. Finally, after a plant's useful life span of 20 to 30 years, it must be disassembled and disposed of. The estimated costs for "decommissioning" nuclear plants is about $0.5 million to $1 million per megawatt of power generation

Table 21-2 Potential Severity of Nuclear Reactor Accidents

| Plant* | Location | Deaths (Thousands) | | Financial Losses (Billion 1980 Dollars) |
		Early	Cancer	
Salem 2	Salem, N.J.	100	40	150
Peach Bottom 2	Peach Bottom, Penn.	72	37	119
Limerick 1	Montgomery, Penn.	74	34	213
Waterford 3	St. Charles, La.	96	9	131
Susquehanna 1	Berwick, Penn	67	28	143
Shoreham	Wading River, N.Y.	40	35	157
3 Mile Island 1	Middletown, Penn.	42	26	102
Indian Point 3	Buchanan, N.Y.	50	14	314
Milestone 3	Waterford, Conn.	23	38	174
Dresden 3	Morris, Ill.	42	13	90

* Plants listed are those in densely populated areas.
Sources: Sandia National Laboratory, "Estimates of the Financial Consequences of Nuclear Power Reactor Accidents," prepared for the Nuclear Regulatory Commission, Washington, D.C., November 1982; Critical Mass Energy Project.

Table 21-3   Cost of Electricity from Different Sources

Source	1983	1990
	(Cents per Kilowatt-Hour)*	
Cogeneration	4–6	4–6
Coal	5–7	7–9
Small hydropower	8–10	10–12
Biomass	8–15	7–10
Nuclear	10–12	14–16
Wind power	12–20	6–10
Photovoltaics	50–100	10–12

* Costs expressed in 1982 dollars.
Source: Worldwatch Institute.

capacity. A 1,000-megawatt plant would cost an additional $0.5 billion to $1 billion to decommission; the costs of decommissioning have not been added to fuel bills and will invariably be included as the older plants now reaching obsolescence are disassembled, making nuclear power even more expensive.

7. *Lacks public and private support.* In 1975, well before the Chernobyl accident, 64 percent of the American population polled supported the use of nuclear power; in 1986, after this tragic and costly accident, public support had nearly vanished, dropping to a remarkable 19 percent. Similar trends have been witnessed in other countries as well.

Long before Chernobyl, however, U.S. banks and insurance companies had withdrawn their support from the nuclear power industry. It was, they said, too costly and too risky an endeavor to support. For this reason, the U.S. nuclear power industry has been on a downward spiral since 1979. Not one new nuclear plant has been ordered in the United States since then, and many more, either in the planning stages or during construction, have been canceled.

Three Mile Island: The Beginning of the End?

On March 28, 1979, disaster struck at the Three Mile Island nuclear power plant 10 miles from Harrisburg, Pennsylvania (Figure 21-11). The 3-month-old reactor ran amok when a valve failed to close. That triggered a series of events that resulted in the most costly and potentially dangerous accident in the history of the nuclear industry up to that point. Although the details of the accident are difficult to understand for all but trained nuclear engineers, the results were clear: Radioactive steam was dumped into the containment building of the reactor and into the air outside the plant. A cloud of radioactive steam drifted through the valley, sending residents scurrying for safety. Bursting pipes spilled radioactive cooling water into two buildings. In

one of them, 1 million liters of radioactive water accumulated ankle deep.

Something unusual then followed: Mysteriously, hydrogen gas began to accumulate in the reactor vessel, threatening to expose the core and cause a meltdown. The pressure, some experts feared, could result in an explosion of the reactor vessel and possibly of the containment building that would release enormous amounts of radioactive material. Fortunately, the utility was able to draw off the hydrogen and prevent an explosion. A year later, photographs taken in the core by a remote camera showed that the nuclear fuel had indeed melted down, rendering the reactor useless and adding to the cleanup costs.

The human toll—besides the agony and fear of those close to the reactor—was minimal. Eight workers inside the plant were exposed to high levels of radiation and, some say, are likely candidates for cancer. Fifty thousand people in the vicinity of the plant were evacuated, and 130,000 people in outlying regions were warned to stay indoors to avoid being exposed to radiation (Figure 21-12).

After several days of feverish efforts, nuclear engineers from the Nuclear Regulatory Commission and Metropolitan Edison, the company that owns the reactor, were able to shut the plant down, thus ending the release of radiation. And so began the long and expensive cleanup, which has already cost $1 billion and is still far from complete.

Studies of the accident showed that human error, mechanical failures, and design flaws were the cause. Inexperienced operators working late at night, for instance, turned off the emergency core cooling system at the wrong time, closed valves on an emergency cooling system when they should have left them open, and disengaged water pumps that should have been left operable.

Three Mile Island was a disaster of minor proportions, say utility officials and supporters of nuclear energy in general. No one died during the accident, and many health officials believe that the radiation released into the air and water will have little, if any, effect on local residents. Two noted and controversial radiation experts, however, believe that 300 and possibly as many as 900 cases of cancer and leukemia will result from the incident. Many residents, they say, were exposed for 100 hours or more to low levels of radiation, enough to increase noticeably the incidence of cancer in the region. Unfortunately, only time will tell if they are correct.

Fallout from the Chernobyl Accident

The accident at Three Mile Island marked the beginning of the end of the nuclear power industry, already burdened by high construction costs and growing public skepticism. The accident at Chernobyl, however,

FIGURE 21-11 Map of area within 100 miles of Three Mile Island nuclear plant.

may have sealed the fate of this troubled industry forever.

At 1:00 A.M. on April 26, 1987, the operators at the Chernobyl nuclear power plant in the Soviet Union had just completed a full day of testing on the fourth and newest reactor. In the course of the test, the operators had shut down safety systems and had violated a number of operating procedures. They could not have known what the end result would be, but each of these violations made the reactor terribly unstable.

By 1:23 A.M., the reactor's power had fallen to only 6 percent of its operating level. With the emergency cool-

ing system and other safety systems shut off and the control rods part way out of the reactor core, power began to build in the reactor. However, when the operators pushed the button to drop the control rods back in place, they found that the rods wouldn't budge. The core, experts now believe, had already begun to melt down, preventing the rods from falling into place to stop the runaway reactor. A few seconds later, shock waves like a mild earthquake tremor shook the plant. Two large explosions then shook the complex, and the operators knew that they were in deep trouble (Figure 21-13).

FIGURE 21-12   Three Mile Island nuclear accident, March 28, 1979.

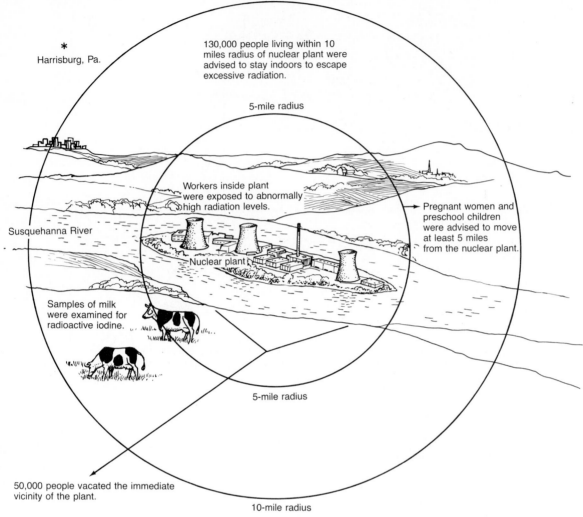

FIGURE 21-13   Aerial view of the damaged Soviet nuclear reactor building at Chernobyl after the fateful accident in 1986, which killed 31 people and may cause cancer in tens of thousands of others.

Experts believe that the explosions occurred when the fuel rods split open in the intensely hot reactor core. Enormous amounts of energy were released from the fuel rods, superheating the reactor cooling water and suddenly converting it into steam, which ripped open the partial reactor containment building. The 1,000-ton concrete slab above the reactor was thrown aside as steam, nuclear fuel, and graphite (one of the components of this nuclear reactor) were hurled skyward.

Helicopter pilots arriving soon after the explosion reported that they could see down into the glowing red core of the reactor through a gaping hole in the reactor building. To put out the fire and stop the spread of radiation, the helicopter pilots, at a substantial risk to their health, dropped 40 tons of boron carbide, 800 tons of limestone, 2,400 tons of lead, and thousands of tons of sand and clay on the damaged reactor over the next few days. The fire went out soon, but the reactor smoldered for several days, continuing to release millions of curies of radiation a day for nearly 2 weeks. On the eleventh day, liquid nitrogen was pumped under the reactor in an emergency cooling system installed after the accident. The molten fuel cooled enough to end the release of radiation.

News of the Chernobyl accident came on April 29, several days after the explosion, and only after Sweden and other countries reported high levels of radiation drifting in from the Soviet Union. The world press picked up the story that day and hastily put together the scanty facts they could uncover while the world looked on in terror. The earliest reports from diplomats in the Soviet Union suggested that 2,000 people had been killed by the accident, now the most serious accident in the history of nuclear power.

When the dust settled and Western reporters were allowed access to the facts, it became clear that the initial reports of human fatalities were grossly exaggerated. Four months after the accident, the death toll had reached 31. Most of the victims were workers who had been exposed to high levels of radiation. All told, 237 people were hospitalized with acute radiation poisoning and burns. Although most of them are alive today, doctors believe that their long-term prospects are not good. The high levels of radiation to which they were exposed will greatly increase their risk of cancer.

UCLA's Dr. Robert Gale and an assortment of international experts on bone marrow transplantation were flown to the Soviet Union to perform bone marrow transplants on many of the severely irradiated victims. But within 3 months, three-quarters of the patients had died, often from infections that their damaged immune systems could not fight.

All told, 135,000 people were evacuated from a 30-kilometer (18-mile) region, mostly north of the plant. Many of them will never be able to return home but will live in a new city built by the government. A quarter of a million school children were sent away from Kiev, a city 80 kilometers (50 miles) south of the plant, on an early summer vacation a few weeks after the explosion. By various estimates, 150 square kilometers (60 square miles) of prime farmland around the plant has been so badly contaminated with radiation that it will lie fallow for many decades. The reactor itself has been sealed in concrete to prevent further radiation leakage, and it may be several hundred years before workers can safely remove what is left of the reactor core.

The cost of this accident is difficult to estimate. Soviet officials estimate the damages to be about $3 to $5 billion. But outside experts believe that the total costs could exceed $10 billion when all the indirect effects are taken into account. Outside the Soviet Union, the costs are beginning to be known. In the United Kingdom, sheep farmers, whose livestock were contaminated by radiation and thus rendered unsuitable for food, estimate that they've lost $15 million. Swedish officials believe that their country's losses amount to $145 million, and the West German government, it says, will pay farmers $240 million for lost crops and livestock.

In all, 20 countries were dusted with radiation, the long-term health effects of which no one really knows. Although it is difficult to estimate, Soviet scientists believe that the Chernobyl accident will result in 5,000 to 100,000 additional cases of cancer in their country. Outside of the Soviet Union, estimates range from as few as 2,500 cancers to as many as 300,000. John Gofman, who predicted a higher incidence of cancer following the Three Mile Island disaster than other authorities, believes that the total number of cancer cases could range from 600,000 to 1,000,000. Half of these, he predicts, would be fatal.

Chernobyl was a disaster of epic proportions made worse by the Soviet Union's initial secrecy. Three days passed before they admitted that the accident had occurred, and then only after European nations, which had detected radiation wafting in from the Soviet Union, complained bitterly to Soviet officials, asking for the details.

To many observers, the disaster showed that the world was largely ill prepared to handle the consequences of a major nuclear accident. The officials of many nations expressed frustration; they simply had to wait and see if the winds would carry radiation across their borders and then do what they could to protect their people, their land, and their water. Confusion arose among downwind nations over what constituted acceptable levels of radiation in food. Many governments were torn between protecting the health of the people and protecting economic interests. They feared substantial economic losses from widespread food contamination and lost livestock. Some countries erred on the conservative side, downplaying the health consequences and, in some cases, even giving false information about the levels of radiation. The French government, for instance, told its people that the winds carrying the fallout had missed France altogether. Only when independent scientists began to detect radiation in their monitors and complained to the pronuclear French government did officials admit that they were wrong.

The accident at Chernobyl raised questions about the wisdom of nuclear power. While many experts believe that an accident of this magnitude could not happen here, others are not so sure. Antinuclear sentiment has skyrocketed here and abroad. About one-half of the European population favor shutting down existing nuclear power plants. In the West German state of Hesse, government officials have decided to push for a phaseout of nuclear power. In Poland the nuclear program has been slowed. In Sweden the government established a commission to consider phasing out nuclear energy. Swiss officials, long committed to nuclear power, have postponed further expansion of their nuclear power capability.

Chernobyl has intensified the fears of many Americans and Europeans over the consequences of a nuclear accident near major urban areas. Denmark, in fact, has asked Sweden to close a plant only 30 kilometers (18 miles) from Copenhagen, fearing that evacuation of the capital city of 1.5 million people in the event of an accident would be nearly impossible and that an accident at the plant would have a devastating effect on this city, which houses nearly one-third of Denmark's population. Austria has formally requested that West Germany close its nuclear fuel reprocessing plant located in Bavaria near the border of the two nations. And local government officials in West Germany have asked French officials to reconsider building the huge power station consisting of four 1,300-megawatt reactors at Cattenom, right over the border.

THE NUCLEAR WASTE ISSUE

After accidents, one of the biggest concerns of the environmental community, the public, and many government officials is radioactive waste disposal. Fission by-products begin to build up in fuel rods within a year or two of their installation. These radioactive materials absorb free neutrons, and as they build up, they slow down the rate of fission, reducing the plant's operating efficiency. Therefore, each year about one-third (40 to 60) of the old fuel rods are replaced by new ones. But what happens to the spent fuel?

In many countries, the spent rods are stored underwater and then transported to reprocessing plants that remove the highly radioactive by-products (Figure 21-14). Reprocessing plants recover uranium-235 that has not fissioned and also plutonium-239, which forms from uranium-238. At the reprocessing plant, the fuel

rods are cut into small pieces and the contents are dissolved in acid. The usable uranium-235 and plutonium are then separated from the waste. During this process, however, about 460 liters (120 gallons) of highly radioactive liquid waste are produced for each metric ton of spent fuel. Reprocessing plants also emit approximately 100 times as much radiation as a properly operating nuclear power plant.

One of the greatest problems of the U.S. nuclear power industry is that today, despite the fact that we have over 100 functioning reactors, no reprocessing plants are now operating in the United States. The plant at West Valley, New York, just south of Buffalo, was closed down in the storm of controversy in the early 1970s because of improper waste disposal practices and serious environmental contamination. Failing to meet federal licensing standards, the plant at Barnwell, South Carolina, was kept from opening, and the facility at Morris Plains, Illinois, owned by General Electric, was scheduled to start operating in 1973 but was never opened because of a faulty design. As a result, tens of thousands of metric tons of highly radioactive waste are now stored in water tanks at nuclear plants all over the country (Figure 21-15). Delays in establishing a permanent waste repository for high-level radioactive materials, writes California's Congressman George Brown, Jr., have turned our reactors into de facto long-term disposal sites. The mounting high-level waste potentially increases the severity of accidents. To make matters worse, many reactors are now reaching the end of their useful life. "To continue the temporary storage of fuel rods at these sites would be asking for trouble," writes Congressman Brown. Since almost all of these soon-to-be-closed reactors are near rivers and lakes for easy access to cooling water, a catastrophic accident at any one of them could result in widespread contamination of local waterways.

In 1976 the California legislature passed a law prohibiting the construction of any new nuclear power plants until a high-level waste disposal site is in operation. In an effort to solve America's high-level waste problem, Congress passed the **Nuclear Waste Policy Act** in 1982. It called on the Department of Energy to choose two sites for the disposal of high-level radioactive waste by 1987—one in the East and one in the West.

Despite a flurry of optimism, site selection has proved extraordinarily difficult. In 1986 the Department of Energy proposed three sites: the Hanford nuclear reservation in southeast Washington; Yucca Mountain in southwest Nevada; and Deaf Smith County on the high plains of west Texas. Each of these sites, selected from a far larger field, was then to be studied in detail, at a cost of $1 billion apiece, to determine which was best.

Long before the official notification of the three finalists, the controversy had heated up. All three states

FIGURE 21-14   Nuclear fuel-and-waste cycle. Radioactive contamination of the human environment is most likely to occur during the transport of spent fuel for reprocessing and during the transport and disposal of nuclear waste.

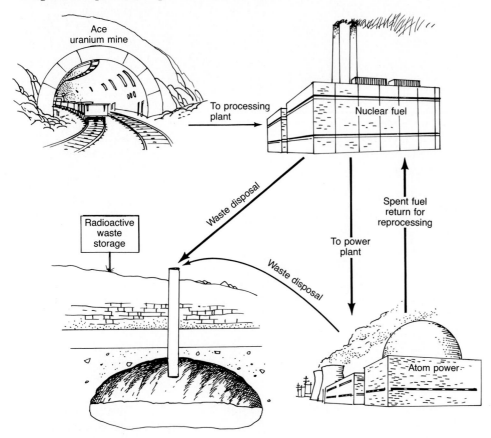

were opposed to high-level nuclear wastes for various reasons. Matters were made worse when the Department of Energy indefinitely postponed the search for an eastern repository under political pressure from a White House worried that the nuclear waste-siting controversy might contribute to a loss of Republican control of the Senate in the 1986 election. Enraged, western congressional leaders cut off money to the Department of Energy to run the tests on western sites. As a result, the deadline for site selection has been postponed to 1991 as additional wastes build up. Unfortunately, the cost of selecting and building a site has also escalated from the original estimate of $1 to $2 billion to a staggering $30 to $40 billion, further adding to the economic burden of nuclear energy.

Most experts agree that high-level wastes should be disposed of in deep caverns carved out of ancient salt beds, granite, volcanic tuff, or basalt. The experts hope that in these geologically stable sites the wastes will remain for thousands of years without leaking into groundwater and threatening human health. At Hanford, Washington, the depository would be built in basalt, but many critics warn that it is too close to the Columbia River, which is important to Washington

and Oregon. At Hanford, groundwater and geological problems could result in flooding of the repository. The Deaf Smith site in Texas lies under the Ogallala aquifer, which many farmers tap for irrigation water. At Deaf Smith, experts worry that salt will creep or flow in response to pressure and heat, creating problems of containment and making it more difficult to remove the waste should it prove necessary to transfer it to another site at some other time. In many ways, the best site is Yucca Mountain. It appears to be free from earthquakes and is dry. The repository would be constructed above the water table, which lies 700 meters (2,000 feet) below the surface. Unfortunately, Nevada's governor, Richard Bryan, and three-quarters of the people in the state oppose the site, fearing that it is not as stable as government scientists believe and wanting to avoid the stigma of being the country's "nuclear wasteland."

To save money, the federal government decided to concentrate its efforts on the Nevada site. Research is now actively underway to determine if the site at Yucca Mountain will be suitable for long-term storage of wastes. This site would store nuclear waste from utilities and defense installations—mostly factories where atomic weapons are made. It is hoped that the site will

FIGURE 21-15 Spent nuclear fuel "cooling off" under water. The spent fuel assemblies from the Savannah River Plant in Georgia illuminate a cooling basin. In the photo, spent fuel of three different "ages" is shown under 20 feet of water. The brightest assemblies (top center) were just discharged from the reactor. In front of them are assemblies that were discharged a month earlier. Barely visible on the lower extreme left are assemblies that have "cooled" by radioactive decay for $3\frac{1}{2}$ months.

be operating by 1998, but many doubt that the project will be completed on time. While many people believe that it was a mistake to build nuclear power plants in the first place, says California's Congressman Brown, the truth is that there are 109 reactors on line today and 16 under construction. By 2000, 43,000 metric tons of high-level waste will have built up from commercial reactors. Truly, we must solve the waste problem that we have created. We have no other choice.

ALTERNATIVE NUCLEAR TECHNOLOGIES

Breeder Reactors

Only 0.7 percent of the uranium found in nature is fissionable uranium-235. At the current rate of consumption, our nation's supply could run out in about 40 years. For this reason, nuclear engineers have proposed developing a new line of reactors, called **breeder reac-**

tors, mentioned earlier in this chapter. Breeder reactors would convert our abundant nonfissionable uranium-238 into a fissionable isotope, plutonium-239, thus tapping a fuel supply that could potentially last for hundreds of years.

The core of breeder reactors contains small amounts of uranium-235 surrounded by a blanket of uranium-238. Neutrons given off by uranium-235 are absorbed by uranium-238, converting it to plutonium-239. Plutonium-239 undergoes fission, producing energy. In theory, breeder reactors create more plutonium than they consume. For every 100 atoms of plutonium-239 that fission, 130 atoms are produced. This fissionable fuel could be extracted and used to generate power in other reactors.

It was once hoped that breeder reactors would replace conventional fission reactors by 2000, allowing the nuclear industry to tap the generous supply of nuclear wastes from uranium enrichment plants and spent fuel from conventional fission reactors.

Attractive as the fast breeder reactor may seem, it has some serious problems. In addition to all of the problems of any fission reactors discussed earlier, the breeder reactors now in use in France, and supposedly the prototype for future development, use liquid sodium as a coolant instead of water. Liquid sodium reacts violently with water and burns in air. Therefore, even a small leak in the cooling system could result in a disastrous accident, possibly leading to a meltdown of the reactor's core.

A second major concern is the rate at which breeders make plutonium fuel from uranium-235. Current models reach the breakeven point in about 30 years. But most reactors have a life span of 30 years. To be feasible, the breeder reactor must have a faster payback period. Breeder reactors are also more expensive to build than conventional fission reactors—about $4 to $8 billion.

Despite the potential benefits of the breeder reactor, it seems to be a technology that may become obsolete before it has even gained a foothold.

Nuclear Fusion

The brilliant sunshine that helps to brighten your day had its origin in countless nuclear fusion reactions occurring on the surface of the sun. In a sense, nuclear fusion is the opposite of fission. Fission involves the splitting apart of atomic nuclei, whereas fusion requires a union of two nuclei to form a new one. In nuclear fission, heavy nuclei, like those of uranium, are used because they tend to be unstable. In nuclear fusion, two light nuclei are brought together by overcoming the mutual repulsion resulting from the positively charged protons in each nucleus. Light nuclei are used because they repel each other much less than heavy nuclei. When two nuclei fuse, energy is released that eventually can be used to generate electricity.

Hydrogen atoms are used in experimental fusion reactors because they are the lightest elements known to science. Hydrogen atoms have one proton and no neutrons in their nuclei. The repulsive force is therefore quite small. Another advantage of hydrogen is that it is extremely abundant. Hydrogen has two isotopes, deuterium and tritium. Deuterium has a proton and a neutron in its nuclei; tritium has a proton and two neutrons. A deuterium nucleus may be fused with another deuterium nucleus or with a tritium nucleus.

To overcome the repulsive force, the nuclei must be supplied with enormous amounts of energy. This can be done by bombarding a fuel pellet containing deuterium and tritium with a laser beam. Thus energized, the fuel turns into a hot mixture of nuclei and electrons known as **plasma**. In the plasma, nuclei can speed toward each other, collide, and fuse. The fusion of two nuclei releases enormous amounts of energy, potentially much more than is needed to initiate the reaction.

The 40,000,000°C heat required to start the reaction creates some design problems. No known metal can withstand temperatures anywhere near those required by fusion reactors. Therefore, scientists have proposed two major designs. The more popular one is called **magnetic confinement**. In this technique, a magnetic field suspends the plasma long enough for fusion to occur (Figure 21-16). The heat given off is picked up by liquid lithium, transferred to liquid potassium, and then to water, which boils to generate steam and electricity.

Nuclear fusion offers several advantages over nuclear fission. First, the fuel is abundant and inexpensive. The deuterium in only 1 square kilometer of seawater could provide us with as much energy as 1,500 billion barrels of oil—three times as much oil as the world has consumed in the history of human civilization. Nuclear fusion is believed to be much safer as well. If a fusion reactor malfunctioned, the reaction would simply stop. There is, say experts, no chance of an explosion. An accident would not release the massive quantities of radiation produced by a fission reactor. Finally, because a fusion reaction is much more efficient than a fission reaction, less waste heat is released. As a result, a fusion reactor's potential for thermal pollution is considerably less. Less cooling water would also be needed.

Promising as it may seem, fusion has certain drawbacks—some so significant that they could forever keep this form of energy out of our grasp. One of the most important hazards is tritium, the radioactive isotope of hydrogen used as a fuel. At high temperatures, tritium is extremely difficult to control and can pass right through metal. A second major problem is that despite four decades of research, scientists have been unable to reach the breakeven point at which energy produced equals energy consumed. To be economical, fusion reactors must generate electricity at a price we can afford. Even though the costs cannot be predicted with great accuracy, it is quite possible that commercial fusion reactors could cost $12 to $20 billion, far in excess of the cost of breeder reactors and conventional fission reactors. Fusion reactors also produce highly energetic neutrons that bombard the containment vessel, weakening the metal and requiring frequent replacement. The containment vessel would also become radioactive. Furthermore, if a vessel burst, it would release radioactive tritium and molten lithium, the coolant, which burns spontaneously and vigorously in air.

In 1980, Congress passed the **Magnetic Fusion Energy Emergency Act** to promote fusion energy. This law authorizes the Department of Energy to spend roughly $1 billion per year from 1980 to 2000 on fusion research and development. The hard economic times of the 1980s, however, put an end to much of

FIGURE 21-16A Fusion Research Device. This diagram shows one research device that could bring the United States closer to controlling fusion, the force that powers the sun and the stars. Because it is easier to work with, this device will use hydrogen as its fusion fuel. Later-generation devices will employ deuterium and tritium as fuels. This device is known as the Princeton Large Torus (PLT).

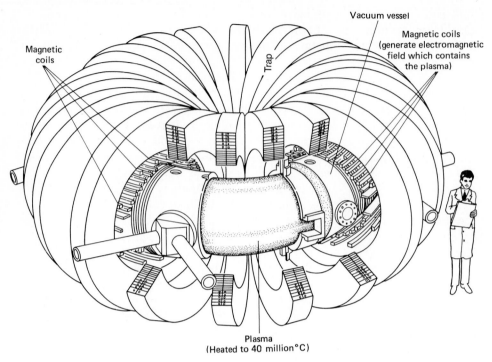

FIGURE 21-16B Nuclear-fusion research. Magnetic coils used to confine and compress fusion plasma are visible in this fusion device. Microwave power levels are increased for the early-stage testing of a technique to heat plasma to the very high temperatures needed for fusion reactions. This device, known as the Elmo Bumpy Torus, is located at the Department of Energy's Holifield National Laboratory.

this money, further dimming the prospects for fusion energy.

AMERICA'S ENERGY FUTURE

The last two chapters have shown that the world is fast running out of oil and that natural gas is also on the decline. These chapters also show, however, that we have many options to choose from. Nuclear fission is one of them, but given its high costs and poor safety record, it seems likely that fission will gradually die of its own accord. Fusion offers the promise of unlimited energy but, because of its high costs and potential dangers, fusion may never become commercially feasible.

What about coal? As you well know, enormous deposits of this fuel lie beneath the earth's surface, but serious environmental obstacles prevent much further development of this technology, global warming and acid rain being the most significant.

That leaves conservation and a whole host of renewable energy resources like solar energy, wind energy, geothermal energy, hydropower, and biomass. Although some of these sources of energy are not yet commercially available, most of you will see them become increasingly popular and less expensive as conventional fuel sources decline. Widespread government support of these technologies, akin to that now given to the fossil fuel and nuclear industries, amounting to over $40 billion a year, could greatly enhance these environmentally clean and renewable energy resources. Individual efforts can also help. By writing to your congressional leaders, by building passive-solar, well-insulated homes, and by conserving energy (see Chapter 18), you can voice your support for the sustainable energy system that is bound to be common someday soon, even in the rich, industrialized nations of the world.

RAPID REVIEW

1. All matter is composed of atoms. Each atom is composed of a dense, centrally located nucleus containing protons, positively charged particles, and neutrons, particles without a charge. Surrounding the nucleus is the electron cloud, where tiny negatively charged particles, the electrons, are found.

2. There are over 100 different elements known to science. Each element differs from the next in the number of protons in its nucleus. The number of protons in the atoms of a given element, however, is always the same. The number of electrons always equals the number of protons, so that atoms are electrically neutral. What varies in any given element is the number of neutrons. Thus, an element may have several alternative forms, or isotopes. If these forms are unstable, they are called **radioisotopes**.

3. Radiation consists of particles or electromagnetic waves given off by the nuclei of radioisotopes in an attempt to reach stability. Three forms of radiation are most common: alpha, beta, and gamma. Over time, radioactive elements decrease in mass as a result of the release of radiation. The measure of its decrease is called the **half-life**.

4. The effects of radiation vary with the age of the individual. Fetuses and newborns, for instance, are much more sensitive than adults. Fast-growing cells are much more sensitive than cells that do not divide.

5. Radiation exposure can be measured in rads, the radiation absorbed dose. Individuals receiving 400 to 500 rads of radiation suffer extreme mortality; only one-half of them will be alive after 3 weeks. Individuals receiving doses of less than 25 rads will not be aware of changes in their health. When the dose rises to 100 rads, however, they may suffer from weakness, fatigue, vomiting, and diarrhea. Eventually, these symptoms disappear. These seemingly low levels of exposure, nonetheless, often result in an increase in cancer and birth defects in offspring.

6. Numerous studies show that radiation increases the incidence of a number of cancers—including leukemia, bone cancer, lung cancer, and skin cancer. Medical scientists believe that most tumors result from genetic changes in the cells of the body that cause them to divide uncontrollably. Radiation can also damage the chromosomes of germ cells; the resulting mutations can be passed on to an individual's offspring, and may show up as birth defects or may result in cancer early in life.

7. Nuclear reactors (and the first generation of nuclear bombs) capture energy from nuclear fission, the splitting of atoms. Fission occurs when certain atoms, such as uranium, are bombarded by neutrons given off by other uranium atoms. Enormous amounts of energy are released during this process. So are additional neutrons. These neutrons continue to bombard other nuclei, causing still other fissions in a chain reaction. Nuclear power plants use the energy given off by carefully controlled chain reactions to boil water to make steam that turns electrical turbines.

8. The uranium fuel used in all large nuclear power plants is uranium-235. It comes from uranium ore, a mixture of uranium-235 (1 percent) and uranium-238 (98 percent). To create fuel, the nuclear industry must first increase the concentration of

fissionable uranium-235 to about 3 percent. The product, called yellow cake, is then packed in pellets and inserted in fuel rods. The fuel rods are then inserted into the core of the nuclear reactor. The rate of fission is moderated by the neutron-absorbing materials of the control rods. The entire assemblage of control and fuel rods is housed in a reactor vessel within a containment building.

9. Supporters of nuclear power argue that this technology offers many advantages that make it a desirable energy source: (a) should the breeder reactor become feasible, the fuel supply would be abundant; (b) nuclear power could help us reduce our dependence on foreign oil; (c) properly operating plants release little radiation—in fact, a coal-fired power plant releases more radiation than a nuclear plant; (d) nuclear plants release fewer solid wastes and air pollutants; (e) the probability of an accident, they once argued, was quite slim.

10. Opponents take exception. They note that: (a) the breeder reactor is costly, fraught with safety problems, and plagued by a slow payback period; (b) nuclear power replaces very little imported oil; (c) accidents at nuclear power plants can release enormous amounts of radiation with potentially devastating effects; (d) nuclear power plants, operating normally, release more thermal pollution than coal-fired power plants; (e) accidents at nuclear power plants occur with a rather high frequency; (f) nuclear power is an expensive form of energy, bound to increase in cost as we grapple with waste disposal and ways to decommission reactors; and (g) the nuclear industry is fast losing public and private support.

11. Disaster struck the Three Mile Island power plant in Pennsylvania in March 1979 when a valve failed to close. As a result of mechanical and operator errors, radioactive steam escaped from the plant and radioactive cooling water spilled into buildings. Hydrogen gas began to build up in the reactor core, which partially melted down. Had the hydrogen exploded, some experts fear that the reactor vessel and the containment building may not have been able to contain it.

12. Although no one died during the Three Mile Island accident, a number of workers were exposed to high levels of radiation and 50,000 people were evacuated. The cleanup has cost $1 billion and is far from complete. While some health officials believe that the accident will have little, if any, effect on the rate of cancer among the local population, others are not so sure. Two medical experts, for instance, predict that the accident could result in 300 to 900 cases of cancer.

13. The accident at Three Mile Island pales by comparison to the one at the Soviet Union's Chernobyl plant in 1986. Caused largely by operator error, this accident resulted in an explosion that spewed 50 million curies of radiation throughout the world, mostly in European nations and the Soviet Union. Experts believe that the explosions occurred when the fuel rods split open.

14. What made the Chernobyl accident even more frustrating was the lack of warning from the Soviet Union. It was not until 3 days after the accident that the Soviet Union admitted that an accident had occurred, and then only after intense pressure from outside nations.

15. Four months after the accident, 31 people had died from the Chernobyl accident. All told, 237 people were hospitalized with acute radiation poisoning. They are likely candidates for cancer. The accident caused the evacuation of 135,000 people living mostly north of the plant; many of these people will never be able to return home. The accident could cost the Soviets $3 to $5 billion, perhaps as much as $10 billion. Outside nations have suffered enormous economic losses as well, largely resulting from radioactive contamination of crops and livestock. Although scientists are uncertain how many cases of cancer will result from the accident, estimates range from 5,000 to 1,000,000.

16. The accident at Chernobyl raised questions about the wisdom of nuclear power. Antinuclear sentiment has skyrocketed here and abroad, which could well spell the end of the already troubled nuclear industry.

17. After a nuclear accident, one of the biggest concerns of many people is radioactive waste disposal. In the United States, highly radioactive reactor and military waste has been building up for over four decades. We have neither reprocessing facilities to extract usable fuel from the waste nor high-level radioactive waste disposal sites. To solve this dilemma, Congress passed the Nuclear Policy Waste Act in 1982. It calls on the Department of Energy to choose sites for disposal, but site selection has been plagued with difficulties. The biggest problem is that no one wants a high-level radioactive waste dump in their state. While many people believe that it was a mistake to build nuclear power plants in the first place, the truth is that there are 109 reactors on line today, and an additional 16 under construction. By 2000, 43,000 metric tons of high-level waste will have built up from commercial reactors. Truly, we must solve the waste problem that we have created. We have no other choice.

18. Fusion reactors are fueled by deuterium and tritium, isotopes of hydrogen, which unite to form larger nuclei. To make them fuse, however, enormous amounts of energy must be supplied. Theoretically, the fusion of smaller nuclei releases a lot more energy than is needed to overcome the repulsion of the nuclei, although experimental fusion reactors have not yet reached this point after four decades of research and development. One of the main attractions of fusion power is that the fuel supply is exceptionally abundant. And fewer wastes would be produced than with a conventional fission reactor. However, fusion reactors are likely to be prohibitively expensive and could be dangerous, since the coolant, molten lithium, burns upon contact with air. A tiny leak could destroy a reactor.

KEY TERMS AND CONCEPTS

Alpha particles	Mutations
Atomic number	Neutrons
Atoms	Nuclear fission
Breeder reactors	Nuclear fusion
Chain reaction	Nuclear reactors
Containment building	Nuclear Waste Policy Act
Control rods	Nucleus
Daughter nuclei	Protons
Electron cloud	Rad
Electrons	Radioactive decay
Emergency cooling system	Radioisotopes
Fuel rods	Reactor core
Gamma rays	Reactor vessel
Half-life	Yellow cake
Isotopes	

QUESTIONS FOR STUDY AND DISCUSSION

1. Describe the structure of an atom and define the terms **isotope**, **radioisotope**, **radiation**, and **half-life**.

2. Which cells of the body are most sensitive to radiation? How can this knowledge be used to explain the nongenetic effects of high levels of radiation—say, above 300 rads?

3. List some examples of cancers caused by radiation.

4. Describe how a nuclear power plant works, being sure to mention the following terms: **fission, neutrons, daughter nuclei, uranium-235, fuel rods, control rods, reactor core, chain reaction, containment vessel,** and **emergency cooling system**.

5. Do you agree with the following statement? "Nuclear fission is a clean, safe alternative to coal-fired power plants." Why or why not?

6. Why is nuclear power so expensive?

7. Describe the accident at Three Mile Island and its impacts.

8. Describe the accident at Chernobyl and its impacts on the environment, human health, the Soviet economy, and the nuclear power industry.

9. What are the major provisions of the Nuclear Policy Waste Act? Why has the Department of Energy had so much difficulty fulfilling the requirements of this law?

10. How does a breeder reactor differ from a conventional fission reactor? What are the pros and cons of the breeder reactor? What unique problems does it have?

11. How does a fusion reactor operate? What is its fuel? What are the pros and cons of nuclear fusion?

12. Suppose that the utility company proposed building a nuclear power plant near your campus. The construction of the plant, the utility claims, would revitalize the local economy. Critics say that although it would create a number of jobs, most of the workers would be brought in from outside. What would be your response to the proposed project?

SUGGESTED READINGS

Brown, G. E. "U.S. Nuclear Waste Policy: Flawed but Feasible." *Environment* 29(8): 6–7, 25, 1987. Overview of the nuclear waste issue.

Carter, L. J. "Siting the Nuclear Waste Repository: Last Stand at Yucca Mountain." *Environment* 29(8): 8–13, 26–31, 1987. Superb look at the controversy surrounding one of America's proposed high-level nuclear waste repositories.

Flavin, C. *Nuclear Power: The Market Test.* Worldwatch Paper 57. Washington, D.C.: Worldwatch Institute, 1983. Detailed study of the economics of nuclear power.

Flavin, C. *Reassessing Nuclear Power: The Fallout from Chernobyl.* Worldwatch Paper 75. Washington, D.C.: Worldwatch Institute, 1983. Highly readable account of the Chernobyl accident and its political, environmental, and health effects.

Jungk, R. *The New Tyranny.* New York: Warner Books, 1979. An extremely readable book on the social impacts of increasing our dependence on nuclear power.

Manning, R. "The Future of Nuclear Power." *Environment* 27(4): 12–17, 31–37, 1985. Industry's view of what must be done to revive the nuclear industry.

Pollock, C. "Decommissioning Nuclear Power Plants." *Environment* 28(2): 11–15, 33–36, 1986. Superb analysis of a largely unrecognized problem.

GLOSSARY

Abortion. The premature expulsion of the fetus from the uterus.

Abyssal Zone. The bottom zone of the ocean; characterized by darkness, close to freezing temperatures, and high water pressures.

Accelerated Erosion. A rapid type of soil erosion that is induced by human activities, in contrast to the relatively slow processes of geological erosion.

Acid Mine Drainage. Sulfuric acid produced by underground coal mines in areas with high levels of iron pyrite in the soil.

Acid Precipitation. Deposition of acids in rain, snow, mist, and fog.

Acid Rain. Rain that has a lower pH than "normal" rain—in other words, lower than pH 5.7. It is caused by the release of oxides of sulfur and nitrogen into the atmosphere.

Activated Sludge. The solid organic waste that has been intensively aerated and "seeded" with bacteria (in a secondary or tertiary sewage-treatment process) to promote rapid bacterial decomposition.

Active Solar System. System to gather energy from the sun and store it for heating water or rooms.

Adsorption. The process by which nutrient particles form a loose chemical bond with the surface of a clay particle.

Age-Structure Diagram (or Population Histogram). Graphical representation of population broken down by age and sex. Aids in forecasting population trends.

Aggregate. A grouping of soil particles. Soil aeration, moisture content, fertility, and erosion resistance are in part dependent on the aggregate patterns of soil particles.

Alfisols. An order of soils that develops under deciduous forest (elms, maples, beech, and oak) cover; aluminum and iron are characteristic components of the B horizon.

Algal Bloom. Dramatic increase in algal growth in a lake or stream resulting from high levels of nutrient pollution.

Alluvial Soil. A type of soil that develops from waterborne sediment; frequently very fertile.

Alpha Particle. A positively charged particle (proton) that is emitted from the nucleus of a radioactive atom.

Altitudinal Migration. Seasonal movement of birds (grosbeaks and finches) and mammals (elk and bighorn sheep) up and down mountain slopes.

Ammonification. The process by which the bacteria of decay convert complex nitrogenous compounds occurring in animal carcasses and the excretions of animals, as well as the dead bodies of plants, into relatively simple ammonia (NH_3) compounds.

Anadromous Fish. A fish, such as the Pacific salmon, that spawns and spends its early life in fresh water but moves into the ocean where it attains sexual maturity and spends most of its life span.

Annular Ring. A concentric ring, visible in the cross-section of a tree trunk, that is useful in determining the age of the tree.

Antimycin. A toxic substance that has been rather extensively used by fisheries biologists to eradicate carp.

Aquifer. A subterranean layer of porous water-bearing rock, gravel, or sand.

Aridisol. An order of soils that develops under desert vegetation. The thin band of topsoil contains a relatively small amount of organic matter.

Artificial Insemination. The technique employed by cattle breeders in which sperm from a bull of one breed, such as Hereford, might be refrigerated and used, over a period of time, to fertilize the eggs of the same breed or other breeds of cattle, possibly from widely separated localities.

Artificial Reef. A reef constructed of housing debris, rubble, junked automobile bodies, tires, and so on, frequently placed in relatively shallow water near the coast. A method for increasing the number of breeding sites and providing more cover for marine fish.

Bioaccumulation. Concentration of a chemical substance in an organism.

Biological Control. Means of controlling pests using natural enemies or other potentially less enviromentally harmful measures than chemical pesticides.

Biological Magnification (or Biomagnification). Process in which a chemical substance increases in concentration in a food web from lower levels to highest levels.

Biological Oxygen Demand (BOD). Measure of organic matter in water samples. Assesses oxygen used by decomposing bacteria.

Biomass. Technically refers to the dry weight of an organism, population, or community.

Biome. Region of the earth with characteristic climate and characteristic community of living organisms.

Biotic Potential (BP). The theoretical reproductive capacity of a species.

Birth Rate. Number of births per 1000 people in a population.

Black Lung Disease. An occupational disease frequently contracted by coal miners.

Blister Rust. A fungus-caused disease of the white pine; characterized by the appearance of orange "blisters" on the bark.

Botulism. A waterfowl disease caused by a bacterium and characterized by eventual respiratory paralysis and death.

Breeder Reactor. A nuclear reactor that uses a relatively small amount of uranium-235 as a "primer" to release energy from the much more abundant uranium-238. Produces plutonium-239 in the process.

Brown Lung Disease. An occupational disease frequently contracted by textile workers.

Browse Line. A line delimiting the browsed and unbrowsed portions of shrubs and trees in an area where the deer population exceeds the carrying capacity of the range.

Buckshot Urbanization. The random hit-and-miss pattern of urban development that has effectively reduced the acreage of prime agricultural land and suitable wildlife habitat in the United States within the past few decades.

Buffer Action. The action of limestone-derived soils in neutralizing the acidity of acid rain.

Carbon Absorption. A process employed by a tertiary sewage-treatment plant by which dissolved organic compounds are removed from the effluent as they pass through a tower packed with small particles of carbon.

Carbon Dioxide Fixation. The incorporation of carbon dioxide into glucose molecules during the process of photosynthesis.

Carcinogen. A cancer-causing chemical.

Carrying Capacity. The capacity of a given habitat to sustain a population of animals for an indefinite period of time.

Catadromous Fish. A type of fish, such as the American eel, that grows to sexual maturity in fresh water but migrates to the ocean for spawning purposes.

Catalytic Converter. Device attached to exhaust system of automobiles that oxidizes hydrocarbons to carbon dioxide and water and converts carbon monoxide to carbon dioxide.

Central Arizona Project. A multimillion-dollar project to alleviate water-shortage problems in Arizona by transporting water from the Colorado River.

Chain Reaction. The sequence of events that occurs when neutrons that have been emitted from a radioactive atom bombard another atom and cause it to emit neutrons that in turn bombard yet another atom, and so on.

Channelization. The process by which a natural stream is converted into a ditch for the ostensible purpose of flood control. Attendant environmental abuse is severe.

Chlorinated Hydrocarbon. A "family" of nondegradable pesticides such as DDT, dieldrin, and toxaphene. They may have a harmful effect on nontarget organisms such as fish and birds. They have long persistence in the environment and undergo biological magnification as they move through food chains.

Chlororganics. Potentially toxic organic compounds that form in water treated with chlorine. A good example is chloroform and carbon tetrachloride.

Clear Cutting. A method of harvesting timber in which *all* trees are removed from a given patch or block of forest. This is the method of choice when harvesting a stand composed of a single species in which all trees are of the same age.

Climax Community. The stable terminal stage of an ecological succession.

Closed-Cycle Cooling System. A method of cooling power plants in which the cooling water is continuously recirculated instead of being discharged into a stream and causing thermal pollution.

Coal Gasification. Production of combustible gas from coal.

Coal Liquefaction. Production of oil from coal.

Coliform Bacteria. A type of bacterium occurring in the human gut. It is used as an index of the degree to which stream or lake water has been contaminated with human sewage.

Community. All species living in a given area. For example, the community of an oak woods, an abandoned field, or a cattail marsh.

Compensation Depth. The depth in a lake at which photosynthesis balances respiration. This level delimits the upper limnetic zone from the lower profundal zone.

Compost. Partially decomposed organic matter that can be used as a soil conditioner and fertilizer.

Condensation Nuclei. Particulates in the air that absorb moisture and can facilitate cloud formation.

Conservation Tillage. Sometimes called minimal tillage, this is a method of cultivating farmland with a minimal amount of disturbance to the soil. Soil erosion is minimized.

Consumer. A term used for any animal "link" in a food chain.

Contour Farming. Plowing, cultivating, and harvesting crops along the contour of the land rather than up and down the slope. An effective technique for controlling soil erosion.

Contour Mine. Mine used for coal and other minerals in hilly terrain. Cuts made along the contour of the land.

Cooling Tower. Device used to reduce thermal pollution before releasing cooling water from power plants and factories into lakes and streams.

Critical Population Size. Population size below which recovery is impossible.

Crown Fire. The most destructive type of forest fire. A fire that consumes the entire tree, including the crown.

Cyanosis. A disease characterized by a bluish discoloration of the skin. This is caused by the impaired effectiveness of hemoglobin in carrying oxygen. An infant that drinks water carrying too high a level of nitrates may undergo chemical changes of its hemoglobin that in turn will result in cyanosis of the skin.

Cyclic Population. A population that peaks and troughs at regular intervals. Good examples are the four-year cycle of the lemming and the ten-year cycle of the ruffed grouse.

Cyclone Filter. A type of air-pollution control device that removes particulate matter (dust) with the aid of gravity and a downward spiraling air stream.

Death Rate. Number of deaths per 1000 people in a population.

Demographic Transition. A change in a population that is characterized by decreasing birth and death rates. It usually occurs when a nation becomes industrialized.

Denitrification. The decomposition of ammonia compounds, nitrites, and nitrates by bacteria that results in the eventual release of nitrogen into the atmosphere.

Density-Dependent Factor. A population-regulating factor, such as predation or infectious disease, whose effect on a population is dependent upon the population density.

Density-Independent Factor. A population-regulating factor such as storm, drought, flood, or volcanic eruption, whose effect is independent of population density.

Depletion Time. The time required until 80 percent of the available mineral supply is consumed.

Desalinization. The removal of salt from seawater in order to make it usable to humans, crops, and wildlife.

Desert Pavement. The stony surface of some deserts caused by excessive erosion of the thin topsoil resulting from occasionally heavy rainfall.

Desertification. Production of desert in semiarid climates due principally to human mismanagement and climatic shift.

Detritus. General term referring to organic matter derived from dead bodies of animals, insects, plants, and so on.

Detritus Food Chain. Sequence of organisms each feeding on the one before it, starting with dead organic material (waste or animal and plant remains).

Deuterium. An isotope of hydrogen that may serve as fuel in nuclear fusion reactions.

Dioxin. An extremely toxic chemical occurring in the herbicide 2,4,5-T. In some areas it is suspected of causing birth defects and miscarriages.

Drainage Basin. See watershed.

Dust Dome. A shroud of dust particles characteristically found over urban areas. It is caused by the unique atmospheric circulation pattern that results from the marked temperature differences between the urban area and outlying farmlands.

Dynamic Equilibrium. Describes any process or system in which change can occur, but is corrected by natural mechanisms so that the system remains more or less the same over long periods.

Ecological Island. Habitat cut off from surrounding area by natural features such as water or by farms, cities, roads, and so on. Highly vulnerable to species loss.

Ecology. The study of the interrelationships that occur between organisms and their environment.

Ecosphere. The total area in which living organisms occur.

Ecosystem. A contraction for ecological system.

Edge. The interspersion of various habitat types; densities of game animals tend to be greater in areas that have a substantial amount of edge.

Electromagnetic Spectrum. Range of energy given off by the sun. At the lower end are low-energy radio waves and at the higher end are high-energy gamma rays. Visible light falls in the middle of the spectrum.

Electron. A negatively charged particle occurring in the orbit of an atom.

Electrostatic Precipitator. Device to remove particulates from smoke stack gases.

Elemental Cycle. The "circular" movement of an element (nitrogen, carbon) from the nonliving environment (air, water, soil) into the bodies of living organisms and then back into the nonliving environment.

Emphysema. A potentially lethal disease characterized by a reduction in the number of alveoli in the lungs as well as a reduction in total respiratory membrane area.

Endangered Species. Species that is in immediate danger of extinction.

Energy. Defined by physicists as the ability to do work. Two basic forms exist: potential energy and kinetic energy.

Energy Pyramid. Graphical representation of the energy in the various trophic layers in a food chain.

Entropy. Disorder or randomness in any system.

Environmental Resistance (ER). Any factor in the environment of an organism that tends to limit its numbers.

Epilimnion. The upper stratum of a lake that is characterized by a temperature gradient of less than 1°C per meter of depth.

Euphotic Zone. The open-water zone of the ocean, characterized by sufficient sunlight penetration to support photosynthesis; located just above the bathyal zone.

Euryphagous. An organism having a highly varied diet, such as a pheasant or opossum, in contrast to an animal having a narrow or stenophagous diet, such as an ivory-billed woodpecker.

Eutrophication. The enrichment of an aquatic ecosystem with nutrients (nitrates, phosphates) that promote biological productivity (growth of algae and weeds).

Exponential Growth. Growth of any entity, such as population or resource demand, that occurs by a fixed annual percentage when the annual growth is added to the base amount.

Extended Economic Zone (EEZ). The 200-mile zone extending from the coastline, over which a nation has control over such commercial activities as fishing and mineral extraction.

Fabric Filter Baghouse. An air-pollution-control device that operates somewhat like a giant vacuum cleaner in removing solid particles from industrial smokestacks.

Fall Overturn. The thorough mixing of lake waters during autumn.

Faunal Collapse. Dramatic decrease in animal species.

Fibrous Root System. A complex root system, such as that of grass plants, in which there are several major roots and a great number of primary, secondary, and tertiary branches; useful in "binding" soil in place and preventing erosion.

Field Capacity. The amount of water that remains in the soil after the excess has drained away from soil that had been water saturated.

First Law of Energy (or Thermodynamics). Energy can be neither created nor destroyed but can be converted from one form to another.

Fish Ladder. Devices constructed to bypass dams and other obstructions on rivers to allow fish like salmon to migrate.

Flood Plain. Low-lying land along streams or rivers. Periodically floods.

Fluorocarbons. A group of chemical compounds containing the elements carbon, chlorine, and fluorine. One group of these compounds manufactured by Dupont under the trade name Freons has been used in refrigerators, air conditioners, and aerosol spray bombs.

Fluorosis. A disease in animals caused by fluoride poisoning; symptoms in livestock include thickened bones and stiff joints.

Flyway. One of the major migration pathways used by waterfowl, for example, Atlantic Flyway and Pacific Flyway.

Food Chain. The flow of nutrients and energy from one organism to another by means of a series of eating processes.

Food Web. An interconnected series of food chains.

Fossil Fuel. Organic fuels derived from ancient plant or animal matter, including coal, oil, shale oil, and natural gas.

Freons. A group of fluorocarbon compounds manufactured by Dupont for use in refrigerators, air conditioners, and aerosol spray bombs. Unfortunately, Freons have contributed to the breakdown of the shield of ozone in the upper stratosphere that protects humans from ultraviolet radiation.

Fuel Crops. Crops grown to generate ethanol or some other fuel that could replace traditional fossil fuels or other energy resources.

Fuel Rods. Rods packed with enriched uranium used for fueling nuclear power plants.

Gamma Radiation. An intense type of radiation, similar to X rays, that is easily capable of penetrating the human body.

Generalist. Species that can live anywhere and eat many different types of food.

Genetic Diversity. A term used to indicate a great variety of organisms (many different species) occupying a given area.

Geological Erosion. Erosion of soil and rock that occurs via natural geophysical processes. Generally occurs much more slowly than accelerated erosion caused by human activities.

Geothermal Energy. Heat produced by the earth from naturally occurring radioactive decay and from magma. Can be tapped to heat buildings or to produce electricity.

Glasphalt. A type of road surfacing material that employs crushed glass in its manufacture rather than sand; more durable than ordinary asphalt.

Glassification. A method of disposing of radioactive waste by concentrating it and enclosing it in solid ceramic bricks.

Grazing Food Chain. Sequence of organisms each feeding on the one before it, starting with plants or algae.

Greenhouse Effect. The warming influence caused by

the increased concentration of carbon dioxide and several other pollutants in the earth's atmosphere.

Green Manure. The bodies of green plants (alfalfa, vetch, for example) that have been plowed under to increase soil fertility.

Green Revolution. The increased food-production capability made possible in recent years because of selective breeding, increased use of fertilizer, development of seed banks, and more intensive use of herbicides and insecticides.

Gross National Product (GNP). The sum total of expenditures by governments and individuals for goods, services, and investments.

Groundwater. Water that has infiltrated the ground, in contrast to runoff water, which flows over the ground surface.

Gully Reclamation. The mending of a gully by either physical methods (check dams of boulders or cement) or vegetational means (planting of rapidly growing shrubs on the slopes).

Gyptol. The sex attractant produced by the female gypsy moth, which serves to attract the male moth from considerable distances.

Habitat. The immediate environment in which an organism lives; it includes such components as cover, food, shelter, water, and breeding sites.

Half-life. The time required for one half of the radioactivity of a given radioactive isotope (uranium, strontium) to be dissipated.

Hardwood. A species of tree, such as oak, hickory, and maple, that has relatively hard wood in contrast to the soft woods of the conifers such as spruce and pine; synonymous with deciduous.

Hazardous Wastes. Substances produced by homes and factories that pollute our air, water, and soils and can have adverse effects on the environment and human health.

Heartwood. The dark central portion of a tree trunk characterized by the presence of dead xylem cells that have become filled with gums and resins.

Heat Island. The tendency for the atmosphere of a city to be warmer than the air in the surrounding farmlands. This is partly the result of the greater number of heat-generating sources (autos, factories, human bodies) in the city.

Home Range. The total area occupied by an animal during its life cycle—that is, the area required for feeding, breeding, loafing, and securing refuge from the weather and from predators.

Horizon. One of the horizontal layers (A, B, C, and D) visible in a cross section of soil.

Humus. Dark, rich organic material produced from the decay of plants and animals and their waste products.

Hybrid. The offspring that results from a cross of two different species or strains of animals or plants; for example, the Santa Gertrudis cattle resulted from a series of crosses involving two parental types, the Brahmin cattle and the shorthorn.

Hydraulic Mining. A mining technique used to extract gold and silver in which a powerful stream of water is directed against the face of the rock containing the minerals.

Hydrologic Cycle. The circular movement of water from the ocean reservoir to the air (clouds), to the earth in the form of rain and snow, and finally back to the ocean reservoir via streams and estuaries.

Hydrolysis. A type of chemical reaction in which a compound is broken down into simpler components by the action of water.

Hydroponics. The technique of growing crops in an aqueous nutrient solution without soil.

Hydropower. Power generated by the flow of water. Usually tapped by dams.

Hydroseeder. A machine employed to disperse grass seed, water, and fertilizer on steep banks.

Hypolimnion. The bottom layer of a lake.

Industrial Fixation. The "fixing" of nitrogen (in other words, combining it with hydrogen to form ammonia) by industrial means rather than by natural methods such as bacterial action.

Infiltration. The percolation of water from snow or rainwater through the soil.

Input Control. Any strategy that seeks to reduce the production of pollutants, such as modifying processes and reducing demand for goods.

Integrated Pest Control. A method of pest control that judiciously employs chemical, biological, and other methods (cultural), depending on the specific problem; the use of chemicals is minimized to avoid environmental damage.

Intercropping. A cultural method of pest control in which the farmer intermixes a number of different crops in a small area instead of devoting the entire area to a single crop.

Introduction. The bringing in of an exotic plant or animal to a new region—for example, the introduction of the European carp into the United States and of the coho salmon from the Pacific Coast to Lake Michigan.

Invader. A term employed in rangeland management that refers to establishing a pioneer species of plant, usually a noxious weed, in an overgrazed pasture.

Irruption. A sudden increase in the population of an organism that is followed by a precipitous decline (crash); frequently the carrying capacity of the habitat is reduced for many years thereafter—for example, the Kaibab deer irruption.

Isotope. A form of an element identical to the regular element except for a difference in atomic weight. Thus, deuterium is an isotope of hydrogen.

Juvenile Dispersal. The dispersal of young animals (bald eagles, ruffed grouse, muskrats) from the general region of their hatching or birth site; the presumed function is to prevent overpopulation in the parental area.

Kepone. A highly toxic insecticide manufactured by a company in Hopewell, Virginia. As a result of carelessness the chemical was allowed to contaminate the James River and destroy much aquatic life.

Kerogen. The solid organic material that contains shale oil.

Krill. The crustaceans and other small marine organisms that are used as food by the baleen whales.

Kwashiorkor. Deficiency of protein intake.

Land Ethic. A view put forth by Aldo Leopold calling on humans to respect the land and all living things.

Landfill. A method of solid waste disposal in which the waste is dumped, compacted, and then covered with a layer of soil.

Lasky's Principle. The principle that, in many mineral deposits in which there is a gradual decrease in the richness of the ore with depth, the tonnage of the ore increases at an exponential rate.

Latitudinal Migration. The north-south migration characteristic of caribou, gray whale, and many birds.

Law of Tolerance. Says that organisms can live within a range of conditions; beyond that range, they are unable to survive.

Legume. Any of the member of plants, including peas, beans, and clover, that can fix atmospheric nitrogen.

Levee. A dike composed of earth, stone, or concrete that is erected along the margin of a river for purposes of flood control.

Limiting Factors. Any factor in the environment of an organism, such as radiation, excessive heat, floods, drought, disease, or lack of micronutrients, that tends to reduce the population of that organism.

Limnetic Zone. The region of open water in a lake, beyond the littoral zone, down to the maximal depth at which there is sufficient sunlight for photosynthesis.

Littoral Zone. The shallow, marginal region of a lake characterized by rooted vegetation.

Loam. The most desirable type of soil from an agricultural viewpoint; composed of a mixture of sand, silt, and clay.

Macronutrient. Mineral nutrient used by organisms in relatively large quantities (calcium, nitrogen, potassium, phosphorus).

Macropores. A large space that occurs between the individual soil particles.

Malnutrition. Dietary deficiency resulting from inadequate intake of nutrients.

Malthusian Overpopulation. The type of overpopulation described by Robert Malthus; it results in an overtaxing of available food supplies and eventual massive starvation.

Manganese Nodules. Mineral-rich nodular accumulations found on much of the ocean floor. Contains manganese, nickel, iron, copper, cobalt, and other minerals.

Marasmus. Deficiency of proteins and calories.

Mass Emigration. The mass movement of a given species from an area. For example, the mass movement of the snowy owl from the tundra to the United States during periods of lemming scarcity.

Mass Number. The mass number of an element is based on the total number of protons and neutrons present in the nucleus of the atom.

Maximization. The most efficient use of a resource that is possible with current technology. Waste is minimized.

Maximum Sustainable Yield (or Optimum Yield). The yield of a natural resource such as fish or trees that can be maintained without damaging the resource.

Mesotrophic Lake. Any lake characterized by a moderate level of nutrients. Contrast with oligotrophic and eutrophic lakes.

Metabolic Reserve. The lower 50 percent of a grass shoot that is required by a grazed plant for survival; contains the minimum amount of photosynthetic equipment needed for food-production purposes.

Microcephaly. A birth defect characterized by an abnormally small brain; associated with mental retardation; may be induced by radiation.

Microhabitat. The immediate, localized environment of an organism.

Micronutrient. A mineral nutrient required by organisms in only minute quantities (iodine, zinc, copper, iron).

Millirem. One thousandth of a *rem*, which is a unit for measuring the effect of radiation on the body of a living organism.

Mollisols. The order of soils developing under a prairie type of vegetation, characterized by a fertile, thick, blackish-brown topsoil.

Monoculture. Greatly altered ecosystem consisting of one or a few species. Generally more vulnerable to insects, disease, and adverse weather conditions than diverse ecosystems.

Monotype. An agricultural or forest planting composed of only one species.

Mulch. Dead plant material that accumulates on the ground surface; a reliable indicator of range condition.

Mutation. Any one of several changes in the genetic material (chromosomes) of an organism. Caused by radiation, chemicals in the environment, and other agents.

Mycelia. The branching "root system" of a fungus.

Mycorrhiza. An intimate relationship between the root systems of trees and soil fungi.

Myxomatosis Virus. The virus that was used to control the rabbit outbreak in Australia; animals become infected when they consume contaminated forage.

Natural Resource. Any component of the natural environment, such as soil, water, rangeland, forest, wildlife, and minerals, that species depend on for their welfare.

Nematode. An extremely abundant and ubiquitous type of worm (roundworm) that occurs in soil, water, and the bodies of plants and animals; some are free-living, others are parasitic.

Neritic Zone. The relatively warm, nutrient-rich, shallow water zone of the ocean that overlies the continental shelf; valuable in terms of fish production.

Net Energy Efficiency Yield. Amount of energy produced by a system when taking into account the total amount invested in the first place.

Net Production. The total energy incorporated into the body of a plant as a result of photosynthesis minus the energy required for respiration.

Neutron. The electrically neutral particle in the nucleus of an atom.

Niche. Habitat and total functional role of an organism in an ecosystem—that is, the relationship to all biotic and abiotic factors.

NIMBY Syndrome. *Not-in-my*-backyard syndrome. General and widespread resistance to siting waste dumps or other potentially dangerous or unsightly facilities near someone's place of residence or community.

Nitrate Bacteria. Bacteria that have the ability to convert nitrites into nitrates; essential bacteria in the cycling of nitrogen.

Nitrogen Dioxide. Air pollutant produced during combustion of any organic material. Combines with water to produce nitric acid.

Nitrogen Fixation. Process of converting atmospheric nitrogen into an inorganic form that can be used by plants.

Nonbiodegradable Material. Material not susceptible to decomposition by bacteria. For example, DDT and other chlorinated hydrocarbon pesticides would be relatively nonbiodegradable.

Nonrenewable Resources. Resources such as coal, oil, and minerals that cannot be replenished within a reasonable period by natural processes. Occur in a fixed amount.

North American Water and Power Alliance (NAWAPA). Scheme for transferring water from the water-rich, low population areas of northwestern Canada to the water-deficient areas of the United States and Mexico.

Nuclear Fusion. The generation of energy by causing the fusion of the nuclei of two atoms of a very light element such as hydrogen under temperatures of around 40 million °C.

Ocean Thermal Energy Conversion. A method of using the temperature differential between different levels of the ocean to alternately gasify and condense a working fluid such as ammonia and in this way propel a turbine for the purpose of electrical power production.

Oligotrophic Lake. A nutrient-poor lake occurring in the northern states and in high mountain areas, characterized by great depth, sandy or gravelly bottom, sparse amount of rooted vegetation, low production of plankton and fish; for example, Lake Superior, Finger Lakes of New York.

Organic Compounds. Any of many thousands of chemicals made principally from carbon, hydrogen, and oxygen.

Organic Phosphorus Pesticides. A group of pesticides (malathion and parathion, for example) that are lethal to insects because they reduce the supply of cholinesterase at the junction (synapse) between two nerve cells in a nerve cell chain.

Output Control. Any strategy that seeks to reduce pollution after it has been produced, such as pollution control devices or disposal methods.

Oxidation. The chemical union of oxygen with metals (iron, aluminum) or organic compounds (sugars); the former process is an important factor in soil formation; the latter process permits the release of energy from cellular fuels (sugars, fats).

Oyster Watch. A well-coordinated program employed along our coast that involves the use of oysters as biological monitors of marine pollutants.

Ozone. A gaseous component of the atmosphere; normally occurs at elevations of about 20 miles; important to humans because it shields us from the ultraviolet radiation of the sun; also represents one of the products resulting from the action of sunlight on the hydrocarbons emitted from the internal combustion engine.

Particulate Matter. Minute solid and liquid particles in the atmosphere (soot).

Passive Solar System. Building designed to capture sunlight energy and produce heat for space heating.

Pheromone. Chemical substance released by insects that affect other insects. Some of the best known examples are sex attractant pheromones released by females to attract males.

Phloem. The elongate food-conducting cells of the trunk and branches of a tree; these cells convey food from the leaves downward to the root system.

Photochemical Smog. The type of smog that has plagued Los Angeles and other California towns, as well as other areas in the United States; formed as a result of the action of sunlight on the hydrocarbon and nitrogen oxide emissions from motor cars and other sources; at nightfall the production of this type of smog ceases.

Photosynthesis. The process occurring in green plants by which solar energy is utilized in the conversion of carbon dioxide and water into sugar.

Photovoltaics. See solar cell.

Phytoplankton. Minute plants, such as algae, living in lakes, streams, and oceans, that are passively transported by water currents or wave action.

Pioneer Community. First community to become established in barren land.

Plankton. Tiny plants (algae) and animals (protozoa, small crustaceans, fish embryos, insect larvae) that live in aquatic ecosystems and are moved about by water currents and wave action.

Point Pollution. Pollution that is discharged from an extremely restricted area or "point," such as the discharge of sulfur dioxide from a smokestack or the discharge of carbon monoxide from the exhaust pipe of a motor car. This contrasts with nonpoint pollution, such as the runoff from a farm or urban area.

Polychlorinated Biphenyls (PCBs). A class of chemicals used as electrical insulators. They persist in the environment and undergo biomagnification, causing problems in the food chain.

Population. The individuals of a species occurring in a given area; for example, the population of deer in a cedar swamp, the population of black bass in a lake.

Population Growth Rate. Birth rate minus death rate plus net immigration multiplied by 100.

Prescribed Burning. A type of surface burning (used by foresters, wildlife biologists, and ranchers) to improve the quality of forest, range, or wildlife habitat.

Primary Production. The total chemical energy produced by photosynthesis; on a global basis it amounts to about 270 billion tons annually.

Primary Sewage Treatment. A rudimentary sewage treatment that removes a substantial amount of the settleable solids and about 90 percent of the biological oxygen demand (BOD).

Primary Succession. An ecological succession that develops in an area not previously occupied by a community; for example, a succession that develops on a granite outcrop or on lava.

Producer. A plant that can carry on photosynthesis and thus produce food for itself and indirectly for other organisms in the food chain of which it is a part.

Profundal Zone. The bottom zone of a lake, which extends from the lake bottom upward to the limnetic zone; characterized by insufficient sunlight for photosynthesis.

Proton. A positively charged particle in the nucleus of an atom.

Purse Seine. A seine used by commercial fishermen that closes to entrap fish somewhat as a drawstring purse closes to "trap" money.

Pyramid of Biomass. The graphic expression of the fact that there is a progressive reduction in total biomass (protoplasm) with each successive level in a food chain.

Pyramid of Energy. The graphic expression of the second law of thermodynamics as applied to the energy transfer in food chains—a certain amount of energy is lost in the form of heat as it moves through the links of a food chain, the greatest amount being present in the basal link (producer) and the least amount being present in the terminal link (carnivore).

Pyramid of Numbers. The graphic expression of the fact that the number of individuals in a given food chain is generally greatest at the producer level, less at the herbivore level, and least at the carnivore level.

Pyrolysis. The destructive distillation of solid waste.

Quadrillion. The number 1 followed by 15 zeros.

Rad. A unit devised to measure the amount of radiation absorbed by living tissue; a rad is 100 ergs (an erg is a unit of energy) absorbed by one gram of tissue; about 1 roentgen, which is about the amount of radioactivity received from a single dental X-ray.

Radiation Inversion. Temperature inversion occurring because the ground cools faster than the air above it. Results in build-up of air pollution at ground level.

Radioisotope. Radioactive form of an atom.

Radon. Naturally occurring radioactive gas. Can leak into houses and other buildings where it can cause lung cancer.

Range of Tolerance. The tolerance range of a species for certain factors in its environment such as moisture, temperature, radiation, micronutrients, and oxygen.

Rem. A unit of absorbed radiation dose taking into account the relative biological effect of various types of radiation; about 1 roentgen, which is roughly the amount of radiation received from a single dental X-ray.

Renewable Resources. Resources such as solar energy, trees, grass, and fish that replenish naturally through some biological or geophysical process.

Replacement-Level Fertility. Number of children a couple must have to replace themselves.

Resource Conservation and Recovery Act (RCRA). Under terms of this act the EPA was given full authority to control pollution by solid waste just as it had authority for controlling air and water pollution.

Respiration. The process by means of which cellular fuels are burned with the aid of oxygen to permit the release of the energy required to sustain life; during respiration oxygen is used up and carbon dioxide is given off.

Retort. Vessel used to heat crushed oil shale rock to produce shale oil.

Rhizobium. One of a genus of nitrogen-fixing bacteria that lives in the root nodules of legumes (alfalfa, clover).

Rhizome. An underground stem; occurs in grasses; permits vegetative reproduction because the tip of the rhizome may develop a bud that can develop into a new plant.

Rhizosphere. The soil in the immediate vicinity of a plant root system.

Rotenone. A poisonous substance derived from the roots of an Asiatic legume; has been extensively used to control rough fish populations.

Rough Fish. Undesirable trash fish such as garpike and carp.

Runoff Water. The water that flows over the land surface after rainfall or snowmelt and eventually forms streams, lakes, and marshes.

Salinization. An adverse aftereffect of irrigating land that has poor drainage properties; as a result, especially in the arid western states, evaporation of the salty water leaves a salt accumulation on the land, which renders the soil unsuitable for crop production.

Saltwater Intrusion. The contamination of freshwater aquifers with salt water as the result of excessive exploitation of those aquifers in coastal regions near the ocean.

Sanitary Landfill. A dump for municipal garbage. Refuse is covered daily with a layer of dirt to reduce flies, odors, and rodents.

Sapwood. The lighter, moist, more porous layer of xylem tissue immediately ensheathing the heartwood; composed of water and nutrient-transporting xylem cells.

Scrubber. Device to remove particulates and sulfur dioxide from air pollution in smoke stacks.

Secondary Sewage Treatment. An advanced type of sewage treatment that involves both mechanical and biological (bacterial action) phases; although superior to primary treatment, many of the phosphates and nitrates remain in the effluent.

Secondary Succession. An ecological succession that occurs in an area that had at one time already supported living organisms; for example, a succession developing in a burned-over forest or in an abandoned field.

Second Law of Energy (or Thermodynamics). During energy conversions entropy increases.

Secured Landfill. Clay-lined landfill designed to hold hazardous wastes.

Selective Cutting. Procedure in which only certain trees are cut from forest. Contrast to clear cutting.

Septic Tank. A part of a rudimentary type of sewage treatment system used commonly by families who are located in rural areas; the sewage flows into the subterranean septic tank and is gradually decomposed by bacterial action.

Shade-Tolerant Plants. A species of plant, such as the sugar maple, that reproduces well under conditions of reduced light intensity.

Shale Oil. Oil produced by heating (retorting) oil shale. Can be refined and made into a variety of combustible products in much the same way that crude oil is refined.

Sheet Irrigation. A type of irrigation in which water flows slowly over the land in the form of a "sheet."

Shelter Belt. Rows of trees and shrubs arranged at right angles to the prevalent wind for the purpose of diminishing the desiccating and eroding effects of the wind on crop and range land; commonly employed in the Great Plains.

Sigmoid Growth Curve. The S-shaped curve commonly followed by the population of an animal (deer, grouse, rabbit) when it has been newly introduced into a habitat with good carrying capacity.

Siltation. The filling up of a stream or reservoir with water-borne sediment.

Slash-and-Burn Agriculture. A type of agriculture maintained by natives of tropical rain-forest regions in which a patch of forest is cut and burned, crops are grown in the clearing for a few years until the fertility of the soil is exhausted, and then the area is deserted because the farmers move to another part of the forest to repeat the process.

Smelter. Device that melts ore to separate metals from the ore.

Smog. Term coined to refer to a combination of smoke and fog. Now used more broadly to include urban pollution.

Softwood. A species of tree such as spruce, pine, and fir, that has softer wood than hardwoods such as oak and hickory; usually synonymous with conifer.

Soil Fire. A slowly burning fire that consumes the organic material in the earth; characterized by little flame but considerable smoke.

Soil Profile. A cross-sectional view of a particular soil type in which the characteristic layers or horizons are well represented.

Soil Structure. The arrangement or grouping of the soil's primary particles into granules or aggregates; a soil with good structure has a spongy or crumbly quality with an abundance of pores through which water and oxygen can move.

Soil Texture. The size of the individual soil particles; the four textural categories ranging from the smallest to the largest sized particles are clay, silt, sand, and gravel.

Solar Cell. A platelike device composed of two layers of silicon that converts solar energy directly into electricity.

Solar Energy. The radiant energy generated by the sun that "powers" all energy-consuming processes on earth, whether biological or nonbiological.

Specialist. Organism that feeds on only one or a few types of food and can live only in a certain habitat.

Spodosols. An order of soils that develops under coniferous forest cover. This soil is relatively acid and infertile.

Spoil Bank. The mounds of overburden that accumulate during a strip-mining operation; unless properly limed and then vegetated, these spoil banks may be an important source of acid mine drainage and erosion.

Spring Overturn. The complete top-to-bottom mixing of water in a lake during the spring of the year when all the water is of about the same temperature and density.

Stamen. The club-shaped, pollen-producing part of a flower.

Stenophagous. Having a very specialized diet; for example, the ivory-billed woodpecker, which consumes beetle larvae secured only from recently dead trees, or the Everglade kite, which feeds almost exclusively on the snail *Pomacea caliginosa.*

Sterilization. A method of human population control involving the cutting and tying of the sperm ducts in the male and the oviducts in the female.

Strategic Minerals. Minerals that are essential to the economic well-being and/or security of a nation.

Strip-Cropping. An agricultural practice in which an open row crop (potatoes, corn, cotton) is alternated with a cover crop (alfalfa, clover) to minimize soil erosion.

Strip-Mining. The type of mining in which coal or iron, for example, is scooped from the earth by giant earth-moving machines.

Subsidence. Land collapse resulting from mining underground water reservoirs (aquifers).

Subsidence Inversion. Temperature inversion caused when a mass of high pressure air settles over an area. Causes pollutants to build up at ground level.

Succession. The replacement of one community by another in an orderly and predictable manner. The succession begins with a pioneer community and terminates with a climax community.

Superfund Act (CERCLA). The act that provided a fund to the EPA to clean up extremely hazardous waste sites.

Surface Fire. A type of forest fire that moves along the surface of the forest floor; it consumes litter, herbs, shrubs, and seedlings.

Surface Mining Control and Reclamation Act. Under terms of this act, which became effective in 1979, mining companies must restore a strip-mined area to its original condition, within the limits of available technology.

Surface Water. Any water body above the ground surface, including lakes, rivers, and ponds.

Sustainable Society. Society based on conservation, recycling, renewable resources, and population control. Respects nature and seeks to find a sustainable relationship between humans and other species.

Sustained Yield. The concept that a forest or wildlife resource can be managed in such a way that a modest crop can be harvested year after year without depletion of the resource as long as annual decrements are counterbalanced by annual growth increments.

Synergistic Effect. A condition in which the toxic effect of two or more pollutants (copper, zinc, heat) is much greater than the sum of the effects of the pollutants when operating individually.

Taiga. The northern coniferous forest biome, which is typically composed of spruce, fir, and pine.

Taproot. The type of root system characterized by one large main root; for example, that of a beet or carrot.

Technological Overpopulation. The type of overpopulation that results in massive pollution and resource exhaustion because of the high technological level maintained by the population. People die because of toxic contamination of the environment rather than because of food shortages.

Telemetry. The electronic technique involving a transmitter-receiver system in which the movements and behavior of animals (deer, elk, grizzly bear, salmon) are monitored from a distance.

Terracing. A soil-conservation technique in which steep slopes are converted into a series of broad-based "steps"; the velocity of runoff water is thus retarded and soil erosion is arrested.

Territory. An area that is defended by a member of one species against other members of that same species.

Tertiary Sewage Treatment. The most advanced type of sewage treatment, which not only removes the BOD and the solids, but also the phosphates and nitrates; the installation of such a plant at Lake Tahoe has arrested eutrophication of the lake.

Thermal Inversion. An abnormal temperature stratification of the lower atmosphere in which a layer of warm air overlies a layer of cooler air. Such an inversion frequently occurs at heights from 100 to 3,000 feet, resulting in stagnation of the air mass below the inversion; it contributes to air-pollution problems, especially in industrial areas.

Thermal Pollution. Increase (or decrease) in water temperature that adversely affects aquatic organisms.

Thermocline. The middle layer of water in a lake in summer characterized by a temperature gradient of more than 1°C per meter of depth.

Threatened Species. Species that is likely to become endangered in the near future.

Throughput. An economics term that relates to the amount of materials being produced and consumed in a given society.

Topsoil. Uppermost layer of soil. Comprised of organic and inorganic matter and pore spaces.

Total Fertility Rate. Projected number of children that women in a population will produce in their lifetime given current trends.

Toxic Substances Control Act (TOSCA). This act makes it mandatory for a company to notify the EPA 90 days in advance of its intention to manufacture a new chemical. If the EPA concludes that the chemical may be harmful to human health or may be environmentally destructive, they can deny the company permission to produce the chemical.

Transpiration. The evaporation of water from the breathing pores of a plant leaf.

Trickling Filter. Device used in secondary sewage treatment to reduce organic matter as well as nitrogen and phosphorous levels in human waste. Sewage is dripped over a bed of stones or bark coated with decomposer organisms.

Tritium. An isotope of hydrogen. A potential fuel for a nuclear fusion reactor.

Tundra. The type of biome occurring in northern Canada and Eurasia north of the timberline. It is characterized by fewer than 10 inches of annual rainfall, subzero weather in winter, a low-lying vegetation composed of grasses, dwarf willows, and lichens, and a fauna consisting of lemmings, Arctic foxes, Arctic wolves, caribou, and snowy owls, among other species. The growing season lasts only six to seven weeks.

2,4-D. A herbicide that kills a weed because it mimics the plant's growth hormones, causing more rapid growth than can be sustained by its supply of oxygen and food materials.

2,4,5-T. A herbicide that operates on the same principle as 2,4-D. It kills a weed because it mimics the plant's growth hormones, causing more rapid growth than can be sustained by its supply of food, moisture, and oxygen.

Ultimate Production. Amount of a natural resource that will probably have been removed after total supplies have been depleted.

Undernutrition. Dietary deficiency resulting from an inadequate intake of food.

Upwelling. The movement of nutrient-rich cold water from the ocean bottom to higher levels by means of vertically moving currents.

Vessel Element. The elongate xylem cell in a tree trunk or branch that has water transportation as a major function.

Waterlogging. Saturation of the root zone with water. Chokes plants and kills them. Usually caused by excess irrigation in poorly drained soils.

Watershed. The total area drained by a particular stream; may range from a few square miles in the case of a small stream to thousands of square miles in the case of the Mississippi River.

Water Table. The upper level of water-saturated ground.

Wetlands. Land that is flooded part or all of the time, including swamps, river bottoms, bays, lagoons, salt marshes, and freshwater marches.

Wildlife. Includes all plants and animals on earth that are not domesticated; as generally used, the term is restricted to birds and mammals.

Wilting Point. Occurs when soil moisture levels decline so that the only moisture left forms a thin film lining pore spaces.

Xerophytes. Specialized plants that are well adapted to survive in arid regions because of such water-conserving features as reduced leaves, recessed stomata, thick cuticles, accelerated life cycles, periodic dormancy, and the presence of water-storing (succulent) tissues.

Xylem. A type of tissue occurring in the trunks and branches of trees (and other plants) that serves to transport water and nutrients from the roots to the leaves and also provides support.

Zero Population Growth. Condition in which the growth rate of a country equals zero.

Zone of Deposition. Refers to the B horizon, or subsoil, which receives and accumulates the soluble salts and organic matter carried downward from the A horizon by percolating water.

Zone of Leaching. Refers to the A horizon, or topsoil, because many soluble salts are carried downward or leached from this horizon to the B horizon below it.

Zooplankton. Minute animals (protozoans, crustaceans, fish embryos, insect larvae) that live in a lake, stream, or ocean and are moved by water currents and wave action.

Illustration Acknowledgments

1-1 Cartoon by Ray Osrin. Reproduced with permission from the *Cleveland Plain Dealer*.

1-2 AP/Wide World Photos.

1-3 New York State Department of Health photo by M. Dixon.

1-4 Environmental Protection Agency Documerica photo by Marc St. Gill.

1-5, 1-6 After David Van Vleck, *The Crucial Generation* (Charlotte, VT: Optimum Population, Inc., 1971); Original source: Donella E. Meadows, et al., *The Limits to Growth* (New York: Universe Books, 1974, graphics by Potomac Association).

1-7, 2-4, 4-10, 5-12, 5-22, 6-10, 6-14, 7-16, 9-7, 11-14, 12-3, 12-16, 15-3, 15-5, 15-9, 15-17, 15-18, 15-21, 17-7, 20-23 U.S. Department of Agriculture.

2-2 After Amos Turk, Jonathan Turk, and Janet T. Wittes, *Ecology, Pollution, and Environment* (Philadelphia: Saunders, 1972).

2-25 U.S. Fish and Wildlife Service photo by Paul Adams.

2-26 U.S. Fish and Wildlife Service photo by J. Malcolm Greany.

2-27, 4-3, 4-21, 4-22, 5-2, 5-7, 5-8, 5-10, 5-17, 5-18 U.S. Department of Agriculture, Soil Conservation Service.

Page 35 Box Figure 1 U.S. Geological Survey.

3-4, 3-9, 10-24 U.S. Bureau of the Census.

3-6 Redrawn from Thomas W. Merrick, et al., "World Population in Transition," *Population Bulletin*, Vol. 41, No. 2 (1986): 4.

3-11 World Food Programme.

4-2, 7-3 U.S. Forest Service.

4-4, 4-5, 4-8 Redrawn from Nyle C. Brady, *The Nature of Properties of Soils*, 8th ed. (New York: Macmillan, 1974).

4-9 After Bernard J. Nebel, *Environmental Sciences* (Englewood Cliffs, NJ: Prentice-Hall, 1981).

4-12, 4-15 Adapted from Roy L. Donahue, Roy L. Follett, and Rodney W. Tulloch, *Our Soils and Their Management* (Danville, IL: Interstate, 1976).

4-16 W. B. Clapham, Jr., *Human Ecosystems* (New York: Macmillan, 1981).

4-17 U.S. Department of Agriculture and U.S. Department of Interior.

4-18 After David Greenland, *Guidelines for Modern Resource Management* (Columbus, OH: Merrill, 1983).

4-19 Adapted from Raymond F. Dasmann, *Environmental Conservation* (New York: Wiley, 1968).

5-1 From Council on Environmental Quality, "Environmental Trends," 1981.

5-5 From Rice Odell, *Environmental Awakening* (Cambridge, MA: Ballinger, 1980).

5-6 After Andrew Goudie, *The Human Impact on the Natural Environment* (Cambridge: MIT Press, 1986).

5-9, 5-14, 7-12 From U.S. Department of Agriculture, *America's Soil Water: Conditions and Trends* (Washington, D.C.: U.S. Government Printing Office, 1981).

5-13 From Allen and Leonard, *Conserving Natural Resources* (New York: McGraw-Hill, 1966. Copyright ©1966 by McGraw-Hill. Used by permission of McGraw-Hill Book Company).

5-23 Hyponex.

6-1 After Norman Myers, ed., *Gaia: Atlas of Planet Management* (Garden City, NY: Anchor Books, 1984).

6-3, 6-4 U.N. Food and Agriculture Organization photos by P. Pitter.

6-5 U.N. photo by John Isaac.

6-6 Courtesy of State of Virginia. Photo by Tim McCabe.

6-7, 6-8, 6-15 U.N. Food and Agriculture Organization.

6-9 U.N. Food and Agriculture Organization photo by D. Mason.

6-11 World Food Programme photo by Peyton Johnson.

6-12 U.S. Department of Agriculture and Colorado State University.

6-13 From U.S. Department of Agriculture.

7-1 From Ben Osborne and Phoebe Harrison, *Water . . . and the Land* (Washington, D.C.: Department of Agriculture, Soil Conservation Service, SCS-TP-147, July 1965).

7-2 After P. Walter Purdom and Stanley H. Anderson, *Environmental Science*, 2nd ed. (Columbus, OH: Merrill, 1983).

7-9 Edwin G. Gutentag and John B. Weeks, "Water Table in the High Plains Aquifer in 1978 in Parts of Colorado, Kansas, Nebraska, New Mexico, Oklahoma, South Dakota, Texas and Wyoming," *Hydrologic Investigation Atlas* HA-642 (Reston, VA: U.S. Geological Survey, 1980).

7-10, 7-23 From U.S. Department of Agriculture, *Soil Water Resources Conservation Act: 1980—Appraisal, Part One* (Washington, D.C.: U.S. Government Printing Office, 1981).

7-11 American Red Cross.

7-13, 7-18, 7-21, 7-25 Bureau of Reclamation photo by E. E. Hertzog.

7-14 U.S. Department of Agriculture, Soil Conservation Service photo by John McConnell.

7-15 Bureau of Reclamation photo by Glade Walker.

7-17 Roy L. Donahue, Roy L. Follet, and Rodney W. Tulloch, *Our Soils and Their Management* (Danville, IL: Interstate, 1976).

7-22 Arthur F. Pillsbury, "The Salinity of Rivers," *Scientific American*, July 1981.

7-26, 10-6, 10-21 California Department of Water Resources.

8-1 Hammond, Indiana, *Times*.

8-2 J. Edwin Becht and L. D. Belzung, *World Resource Management* (Englewood Cliffs, NJ: Prentice-Hall, 1975; adapted from American Geological Society).

8-6, 10-25, 20-7, 20-22 U.S. Department of Interior.

8-8 Environmental Protection Agency photo by Belinda Rain.

8-9 Bureau of Reclamation photo by H. L. Personius.

8-11 U.S. Department of Agriculture, Soil Conservation Service photo by Erwin W. Cole.

8-13 University of Wisconsin Sea Grant Institute.

8-14–8-16 Courtesy of Carolina Biological Supply Company.

8-17, 8-18 Pennsylvania Power and Light.

8-20 After James M. Moran, Michael D. Morgan, and James H. Wiersma, *An Introduction to Environmental Sciences* (Boston: Little, Brown, 1973. Copyright ©1973, Little, Brown and Co).

8-24 Bureau of Reclamation.

8-27, 8-28 Milwaukee Metropolitan Sewage District, Milwaukee, Wisconsin.

9-6 Data from G. W. Burton and E. P. Odum, "The Distribution of Stream Fish in the Vicinity of Mountain Lake, Virginia," *Ecology*, 26: 182–193.

9-8 Data source: J. H. Peters "Effects on a Trout Stream of Sediment from Agricultural Practices," *Journal of Wildlife Management*, 31 (1967): 805–812.

9-13 From *Warm Water Game Fisheries of California 1981.* Department of Fish and Game, Sacramento, CA.

9-14 From Howard E. Snow, "The Constant Northern," *Wisconsin Conservation Bulletin*, May–June 1973, Wisconsin Department of Natural Resources.

9-15 J. Michael Migel, *The Stream Conservation Handbook* (New York: Crown Publishers, 1974).

9-16 U.S. Fish and Wildlife Service.

9-18 From Agricultural Extension Service, *Proceedings of the Upper Midwest Trout Symposium*, I and II (St. Paul, MN: University of Minnesota, 1978).

9-19 Adapted from W. Bowers, B. Hosford, A. Oakley, and C. Bond, *Wildlife Habitats in Managed Rangelands—The Great Basin of Southeastern Oregon. Native Trout.* USDA Forest Service General Technical Report PNW-84, 1979.

9-21 Department of Natural Resources Bureau of Information and Education, State of Minnesota.

Page 196 Box Figure 1 California Department of Water Resources.

Page 197 Box Figure 2 Bureau of Reclamation photo by F. K. Noonan.

Page 198 Box Figures 1 and 2 Michigan Sea Grant Program.

Page 199 Box Figure 3 From *Great Lakes Communicator*, Great Lakes Basin Commission.

Page 200 Box Figure 5 Michigan Conservation Department.

10-2 From Robert Dolan and Harry Lins, "Beaches and Barrier Islands," *Scientific American*, July 1987.

10-3 Courtesy of North Carolina Public Information Program, Division of Postal Management. Photo by H. E. Rodenhizer III.

10-5 North Carolina Division of Coastal Management, Public Information Program, photo by H. E. Rodenhizer III.

10-8, 10-29 New Jersey Division of Fish, Game, and Wildlife.

10-9 From National Oceanic and Atmospheric Administration.

Page 224 Box Figure 1 From Environmental Protection Agency, "Research Summary: Chesapeake Bay" (Washington, D.C.: U.S. Government Printing Office, May 1980).

10-10 From George L. Clarke, *Elements of Ecology* (New York: Wiley, 1954).

10-13 Adapted from John D. Isaacs, "The Nature of Oceanic Life," *Scientific American*, September 1969.

10-14 Courtesy of City of New York, Department of Sanitation.

10-18 National Oceanic and Atmospheric Administration.

10-19 From Environmental Protection Agency, *Research Summary: Oil Spills* (Washington, D.C., U.S. Government Printing Office, February 1979).

10-20 AP/ Wide World Photos.

10-22 Courtesy of U.S. Department of Energy.

10-23 Data from U.N. Food and Agriculture Organization

10-27 From W. B. Clapham, Jr., *Human Ecosystems* (New York: MacMillan, 1981). Data from G. I. Murphy, "Population Biology of the Pacific Sardine (*Sardinops Caerulea*)," *Proceedings of the California Academy of Science* (4th Ser.), 34 (1): 1–84.

10-28 From S. J. Holt, "The Food Resources of the Ocean," *Scientific American*, 1969.

10-29 New Jersey Division of Fish, Game, and Wildlife.

10-30 After Bernard J. Nebel, *Environmental Sciences* (Englewood Cliffs, NJ: Prentice-Hall, 1981).

10-31 Cooper and Stevens, "An Experiment in Marine Fish Cultivation," *Nature*, 161 (1948): 631–633.

10-32 From *Time*, August 4, 1986.

11-4 Adapted from Ruben L. Parsons, *Conserving American Resources* (Englewood Cliffs, NJ: Prentice-Hall, 1956); After Albertson and Weaver, *Ecol. Mono.* 14 (January 1944): 1–29.

11-9 Environmental Protection Agency Documerica photo by Gene Daniels.

11-10 After A. W. Sampson, *Range Management* (New York: Wiley, 1952).

11-15, 15-12 Department of Interior, Bureau of Sport Fisheries and Wildlife.

11-17 U.S. Forest Service photo by Daniel O. Todd.

11-18 Harold Dregne, "Desertification of Arid Lands," *Economic Geography*, 53 (1977): 325.

11-19 After Bernard J. Nebel, *Environmental Sciences* (Englewood Clliffs, NJ: Prentice-Hall, 1981).

12-1 Adapted from Richard M. Highsmith, J. Granville Jensen, and Robert D. Rudd, *Conservation in the United States* (Chicago: Rand McNally, 1962).

12-7 U.S. Forest Service photo by P. F. Heim.

12-8 U.S. Forest Service.

12-12 Tennesse Valley Authority.

12-13 Courtesy of Morbark Industries.

12-14 Adapted from Guy-Harold Smith, *Conservation of Natural Resources* (New York: Wiley, 1965). Data from *Timber Resources Review,* U.S. Forest Service.

12-15 U.S. Department of Agriculture photo by Miller Cowlin.

12-17 U.S. Department of Agriculture photo by Robert W. Neelands.

12-18 U.S. Department of Agriculture, Soil Conservation Service photo by Al Crouch.

12-19 From *Environmental Quality,* Seventh Annual Report of the Council of Environmental Quality (Washington, D.C.: U.S. Government Printing Office, 1976).

Page 291 Box Figure 1 U.N. Food and Agriculture Organization, *Unasylva,* 28 (1976): 112–113.

13-1, 14-2, 14-22 U.S. Fish and Wildlife Service.

13-3 Photo by George B. Schaller.

13-5 Adapted from Edward J. Kormandy, *Concepts of Ecology* (Englewood Cliffs, NJ: Prentice-Hall, 1969). After A. S. Leopold, *Wisconsin Conservation Bulletin*, 321 (1943).

13-7 From Chandler S. Robbins, "Effect of Forest Fragmentation on Bird Population," in *Management of North Central and Northeastern Forests for Non-game Birds* (U.S. Forest Service General Technical Report NC-51, St. Paul, MN, 1979).

13-8, 13-9 State Historical Society of Wisconsin.

13-11, 14-11, 15-13, 15-14, 16-3 Michigan Department of Natural Resources

14-1 U.S. Department of Agriculture photo by Tom Beemers.

14-3 California Department of Fish and Game.

14-4 From Aldo Leopold, *Game Management* (New York: Scribner's, 1933).

14-5 Department of Natural Resources, Bureau of Information and Education (St. Paul, MN). Photo by Walter H. Wettschreck.

14-7 Wisconsin Department of Natural Resources.

14-13 From Joseph Linduska, ed., U.S. Fish and Wildlife Service, *Waterfowl Tomorrow* (Washington, D.C.: U.S. Government Printing Office, 1964).

14-14, 15-10, 17-5, 17-6, 17-14, 17-28, 18-8, 18-10 U.S. Environmental Protection Agency.

14-17A, 14-18 Department of Natural Resources Bureau of Information and Education (St. Paul, MN).

14-19 From Gordon W. Gullion, *Improving Your Forested Lands for Ruffed Grouse* (Coraopolis, PA: The Ruffed Grouse Society, 1972).

14-20 Bureau of Reclamation photo by Lyle C. Axthelm.

14-23 U.S. Fish and Wildlife Service photo by Peter J. Van Huizen.

14-24 Drawn from Richard A. Hunt and Harold C. Hansen, "The Spring Canada Goose Migration in Wisconsin," *Wisconsin Conservation Bulletin* (March–April 1975): 7–9.

14.25 After Raymond F. Dasmann, *Environmental Conservation* (New York: Wiley, 1968).

14-26 Adapted from Robert T. Orr, *Vertebrate Biology*, 2nd ed. (Philadelphia: Saunders, 1961).

15-1 U.S. Department of Interior, Bureau of Reclamation photo by E. E. Hertzog.

15-2 Courtesy of General Biological Supply House, Inc., Chicago, IL; from W. K. Beaver and G. B. Noland, *General Biology*, 8th ed. (St. Louis: Mosby, 1970).

15-4 From "The Gypsy Moth" (Washington, D.C.: U.S. Department of Agriculture, 1972).

15-7 From James W. Berry, David W. Osgood, and Philip A. St. John, *Chemical Villains: A Biology of Pollution* (St. Louis: Mosby, 1974).

15-11, Table 15-1 From Amos Turk, Janet T. Wittes, Jonathan Turk, and Robert E. Wittes, *Environmental Science* (Philadelphia: Saunders, 1978).

15-15 From Robert Van Den Bosch and P. S. Messenger, *Biological Control* (New York: Intext, 1973).

15-16 From Arthur S. Boughey, *Man and the Environment* (New York: Macmillan, 1975).

15-19 U.S. Department of Agriculture photo by Murray Lemmon.

15-22 Redrawn from *Fortune,* July 1968.

Page 362 Box Figure 1 Australian News and Information Bureau.

16-4 A and B Courtesy of Owens-Illinois.

16-5 Ecocycle Recycling Center.

16-6, 19-6 Courtesy of Recycle Now!, Denver, CO.

16-7 National Air Pollution Control Administration.

16-8 From Bureau of Solid Waste Management, *Sanitary Landfill Facts* (Washington, D.C.: U.S. Government Printing Office, 1970).

16-9 Woodland Park Zoological Gardens, Seattle, WA.

16-10 AP/Wide World Photos.

16-11 3M Corporation.

16-12 From Environmental Protection Agency, *Environmental Midwest* (Washington, D.C.: U.S. Government Printing Office, 1981).

16-13 UPI/Bettmann Newsphotos.

Page 390 Box Figure 1 Photo by Michael Philippot/Sygma.

Page 390 Box Figure 2 AP/Wide World Photos.

17-1, 19-1, 19-9, 20-4B U.S. Geological Survey.

17-2 From Associated Press map from *Salt Lake City Tribune*, May 1980.

17-3 From Environmental Protection Agency, *National Air Quality, Monitoring, and Emissions Trends Report, 1977* (Washington, D.C.: U.S. Government Printing Office, 1978).

17-4 From Environmental Protection Agency, *Research Outlook, 1978* (Washington, D.C.: U.S. Government Printing Office, 1978).

17-8 Fairchild Aerial Surveys.

17-9 A and B AP/Wide World Photos.

17-22 AP/Wide World Photos.

17-24 Courtesy of Ford Motor Company.

17-25 Environmental Protection Agency, Documerica photo by Joe Clark.

18-14 From "Acidification Today & Tomorrow," Report by The Swedish Ministry of Agriculture to the 1982 Stockholm Conference on Acidification of the Environment.

19-2 U.S. Department of the Interior, Bureau of Mines, in Bernard J. Nebel, *Environmental Science* (Englewood Cliffs, NJ: Prentice-Hall, 1981).

19-3 Adapted from W. B. Clapham, Jr., *Human Ecosystems* (New York: Macmillan, 1981). After J. J. Schanz, Jr., "Problems and Opportunities in Adapting U.S. Geological Survey Terminology to Energy Resources," in M. Grenon, ed., *Energy Resources*, Int. Inst. Appl. Syst. Anal. Conf. Proceedings, CP-76-4: 85–120, 1976.

19-4 From Nebel as adapted from Earl Cook, "Limits to Exploitation of Nonrenewable Resources," in P. H. Abelson and A. L. Hammond, eds., *Materials: Renewable and Nonrenewable Resources* (Washington, D.C.: American Association for the Advancement of Science, 1976).

19-5 A and B   General Motors—Cadillac Division.

19-8   Smithsonian Institution.

19-10   U.S. Bureau of Mines photo by David Barna.

20-1   From *World Resources* 1987, p. 95.

20-2   From Penelope Revelle and Charles Revelle, *The Environment: Issues and Choices for Society* (New York: Van Nostrand, 1981), as adapted from "A National Plan for Energy Research Development and Demonstration," issued by the Energy Research and Development Administration, now part of the U.S. Department of Energy.

20-3   From Revelle and Revelle. Source: Bureau of Land Management, 1974.

20-4A   Milton Rogovin, Photo Researchers, Inc.

20-8   Courtesy Humble Oil and Refining Company.

20-9, 20-10, 20-12, 20-13, 20-17A, 20-21, 20-24, 20-25, 20-27, 20-29   U.S. Department of Energy.

20-11   "Special Energy Report," *National Geographic* (February 1981): 68.

20-16   Ontario Hydro.

20-17B   From Revelle and Revelle, as adapted from D. Kash, et al., *Energy Alternatives*, Report to the President's Council on Environmental Quality (Washington, D.C.: U.S. Government Printing Office, 1975).

20-19   A. J. Ellis, "Geothermal Systems and Power Development," *American Scientist*, 63 (1975): 510–521.

20-28   Adapted from John R. Justus, "Renewable Sources of Energy from the Ocean," in *Project Interdependence*, Committee Print 95-3, U.S. Congress, November 1977.

21-3   From *Nuclear Power*, Edison Electric Institute Publication No. 78-24.

21-4   Courtesy of C-E Power Systems.

21-5   Courtesy of Westinghouse Atomic Power Division.

21-6   Babcock and Wilcox.

21-7   Courtesy of Iowa Light and Power Company.

21-8   Earl Chambers—Northern States Power Company.

21-9   Rollin R. Geppert.

21-10   From *Nuclear Power and the Environment* (Hinsdale, IL: American Nuclear Society, 1973).

21-11   U.S. Nuclear Regulatory Commission.

21-13   TASS from SOVFOTO.

21-14   From James W. Berry, David W. Osgood, and Philip A. St. John, *Chemical Villians: A Biology of Pollution* (St. Louis: Mosby, 1974).

21-15   Courtesy of E. I. Du Pont de Nemours and Company.

21-16B   Courtesy of Union Carbide.

INDEX

531